Multilingual Text Analysis

Challenges, Models, and Approaches

Multilingual Text Analysis

Challenges, Models, and Approaches

Editors

Marina Litvak • Natalia Vanetik

Shamoon College of Engineering, Israel

World Scientific

NEW JERSEY · LONDON · SINGAPORE · BEIJING · SHANGHAI · HONG KONG · TAIPEI · CHENNAI · TOKYO

Published by

World Scientific Publishing Co. Pte. Ltd.
5 Toh Tuck Link, Singapore 596224
USA office: 27 Warren Street, Suite 401-402, Hackensack, NJ 07601
UK office: 57 Shelton Street, Covent Garden, London WC2H 9HE

Library of Congress Cataloging-in-Publication Data
Names: Litvak, Marina, editor. | Vanetik, Natalia, editor.
Title: Multilingual text analysis : challenges, models, and approaches /
    editors Marina Litvak, Natalia Vanetik, Shamoon College of Engineering, Israel.
Description: New Jersey : World Scientific, [2019] | Includes bibliographical
    references and index.
Identifiers: LCCN 2018047796 | ISBN 9789813274877 (hardcover)
Subjects: LCSH: Critical discourse analysis. | Discourse analysis. | Written communication. |
    Content analysis (Communication)--Data processing. | Applied linguistics--Methodology.
Classification: LCC P302 .M828 2019 | DDC 401/.41--dc23
LC record available at https://lccn.loc.gov/2018047796

British Library Cataloguing-in-Publication Data
A catalogue record for this book is available from the British Library.

For any available supplementary material, please visit
https://www.worldscientific.com/worldscibooks/10.1142/11116#t=suppl

Desk Editor: Tay Yu Shan

Typeset by Stallion Press
Email: enquiries@stallionpress.com

Printed in Singapore

Acknowledgment

We are grateful to our spiritual mentor, Prof. Anatoly Dubinsky, for encouragement, support and guidance during the process of writing and organizing this book.

A very special gratitude goes out to Mr. Bill (Zeev) Kaplan for editing this book and for guiding us patiently toward its better design and structure.

We are also thankful to our families for being patient and supportive.

Preface

This book is planned and designed as a collection of chapters that can be united under the joint topic of multilingual text analysis or text analytics (TA). Text analytics is a very wide research area. Its overarching goal is to discover and present knowledge — facts, rules, and relationships — that is otherwise hidden in textual content and unattainable by automated processing. Prior to applying analytical methods, text needs to be turned into structured data through the application of natural language processing (NLP). Then, data mining techniques, including link and association analysis, visualization, and predictive analytics, can be applied to the structured input and used to produce a requested output. Typical TA tasks include text categorization, text clustering, concept/entity extraction, production of granular taxonomies, sentiment analysis, document summarization, question answering, slot filling, and entity relation modeling.

The chapters in this book describe a very wide range of TA tasks applied on various domains with different purposes. Each chapter concludes with findings that indicate whether the introduced method can be considered multilingual. This book introduces the reader to several specific examples of TA tasks, along with their problem statement, theoretic background, and implementation of the proposed solution. A reader can see which text preprocessing techniques were applied, which text representation models were used, how the evaluation process was designed and implemented, and, most important, how the authors applied their approach to specific multiple languages or how they propose to extend it to a multilingual domain.

All chapters of this volume can be categorized under the following topics: summarization (chapters 2, 3, 4, 5, 6); headline generation (chapter 7); evaluation of summarization systems (chapters 8, 9), study of summarization impact on text complexity and readability (chapter 10); social media and collaborative online encyclopedias analysis (chapters 11 and 12); and extraction and analysis of qualitative information from texts (chapter 13). The first chapter introduces the main directions and challenges in TA, both in general and with respect to multilingual domain as well as summarizes all topics represented by the book's chapters.

Contents

Acknowledgment   v

Preface   vii

1. Multilingual Text Analysis: History, Tasks,
   and Challenges   1
   Natalia Vanetik and Marina Litvak

2. Using a Polytope Model for Unsupervised Document
   Summarization   31
   Natalia Vanetik and Marina Litvak

3. MDL Approach for Unsupervised Multilingual
   Document Summarization   81
   Natalia Vanetik and Marina Litvak

4. Rich Feature Spaces and Regression Models in
   Single-Document Extractive Summarization   119
   Alexander Dlikman, Marina Litvak, and Mark Last

5. Hierarchical Topic Model and Summarization   155
   Lei Li and Yazhao Zhang

6. A Survey of Neural Models for Abstractive Summarization   175
   Tal Baumel and Michael Elhadad

ix

7. Headline Generation as a Sequence Prediction
    with Conditional Random Fields   201

    Carlos A. Colmenares, Marina Litvak, Amin Mantrach,
    Fabrizio Silvestri, and Horacio Rodríguez

8. Crowdsourcing in Single-document Summary
    Evaluation: The Argo Way   245

    Nikiforos Pittaras, Stefano Montanelli,
    George Giannakopoulos, Alfio Ferrara,
    and Vangelis Karkaletsis

9. Multilingual Summarization and Evaluation Using
    Wikipedia Featured Articles   281

    John M. Conroy, Jeff Kubina, Peter A. Rankel,
    and Julia S. Yang

10. Are Better Summaries Also Easier to Understand?
    Analyzing Text Complexity in Automatic Summarization   337

    Elena Lloret, Tatiana Vodolazova, Paloma Moreda,
    Rafael Muñoz, and Manuel Palomar

11. Twitter Event Detection, Analysis, and Summarization   371

    Natalia Vanetik, Marina Litvak, Efi Levi,
    and Andrey Vashchenko

12. Linguistic Bias in Crowdsourced Biographies:
    A Cross-lingual Examination   411

    Jahna Otterbacher, Ioannis Katakis,
    and Pantelis Agathangelou

13. Multilingual Financial Narrative Processing: Analyzing
    Annual Reports in English, Spanish, and Portuguese   441

    Mahmoud El-Haj, Paul Rayson, Paulo Alves,
    Carlos Herrero-Zorita, and Steven Young

List of Abbreviations   465

List of Contributors   471

Index   487

Chapter 1

Multilingual Text Analysis: History, Tasks, and Challenges

Natalia Vanetik* and Marina Litvak†

Shamoon College of Engineering,
Software Engineering Department,
Byalik 56, Beer Sheva 84100
* nataliav@sce.ac.il
† marinal@sce.ac.il

Text analytics (TA) is a very broad research area that deals with knowledge discovery in written text. Almost all techniques of machine learning, data mining and information retrieval are applied to TA tasks which include text categorization, summarization, question answering and many more. Among a very large variety of TA methods, multilingual techniques hold a special place. In order to be deemed as multilingual, a system or an algorithm must be able to handle texts in several languages equally well; a very good method should be able to produce good results for languages from different language families. Multilingual techniques and algorithms need to apply analysis that is not related to a linguistic structure of text in one specific language but rather relies on general statistical and mathematical properties common to many languages.

In this chapter we provide an overview of the field of multilingual text analysis, starting with description of various TA tasks and the history of TA. We then survey TA challenges related to the multilingual domain.

1. Introduction

Text analytics is a very wide research area. Its overarching goal is to discover and present knowledge — facts, rules, and relationships — that is otherwise hidden in textual content and unattainable by automated processing. Prior to applying analytical methods, text needs to be turned into structured data through the application of natural language processing (NLP). Then, data mining techniques, including link and association analysis, visualization, and predictive analytics, can be applied to the structured input

1

and used to produce a requested output. Typical TA tasks include text categorization, text clustering, concept/entity extraction, production of granular taxonomies, sentiment analysis, document summarization, question answering, slot filling, and entity relation modeling.

A list of possible subtasks composing the TA process includes but is not limited to:

- Information retrieval (IR) as a preparatory step: collecting or identifying a set of textual materials for analysis; the set may be comprised of material found in any number of places, including the Web or a file system, database, or content corpus manager;
- Advanced statistical methods, like computing word frequency distributions;
- Extensive NLP, such as part of speech (POS) tagging, syntactic parsing, and other types of linguistic analysis;
- Named entity recognition (NER) using gazetteers or statistical techniques to identify named text features such as people, organizations, places, or certain abbreviations;
- Disambiguation, which involves the use of contextual clues, may be required to decide where, for instance, "apple" can refer to a fruit, a software company, a multimedia corporation, a movie, or some other entity;
- Recognition of pattern-identified entities: features such as telephone numbers, email addresses, or quantities (with units), can be discerned through regular expression or other pattern matches;
- Coreference resolution involves finding all expressions that refer to the same entity in a text;
- Relationship, fact, concept, and event extraction involve the identification of associations among entities and other information in text;
- Sentiment analysis involves discerning subjective material and extracting various forms of attitudinal information, such as sentiment, opinion, mood, and emotion;
- Topic modeling enables the discovery of the abstract "topics" that occur in a collection of documents;
- Quantitative TA is the process of extracting semantic or grammatical relationships between words.

This chapter introduces the main directions and challenges in TA, both in general and with respect to multilingual domain. The next section summarizes the history of the TA area. Section 3 describes primary TA subareas and tasks. Section 4 provides an overview of challenges to the use of TA in the multilingual domain. Section 5 provides a brief overview of the remaining chapters in the book.

2. TA evolution

The ability to understand the key content of a text has become extremely important recently, when more and more sources in different languages are available on the net. New ideas for interesting, and even crucial, applications arise every day. Extracting the most critical facts and reducing information overload, mining opinions from social media and other domains, predicting important events, detecting fraud and security threats — these are just a small sample of current "hot topics" in the TA area. Globalization dictates its own rules — more text sources are published in original language; language that is different from English as an international standard. Therefore, all proposed methodologies must deal with an additional requirement — they must be able to process multiple languages.

The idea of using computers to analyze text and search for relevant pieces of information was raised for the first time in an article by Vannevar Bush in 1945.[1] In the 1950s, this idea was followed by several works. One of the most influential was the 1957 work of Luhn,[2] where he proposed to use words as indexing units for documents, and measure word overlap as a criterion for retrieval. A year later, Luhn published the first work on automated summarization,[3] where he proposed a statistical method for ranking sentences. Several key developments in the field happened in the 1960s. Most notable were the development of the SMART system by Gerard Salton and his students, first at Harvard University and later at Cornell University.[4] The 1970s and 1980s showed many developments built on the advances of the 1960s. An example is the famous Vector Space Model that was proposed by Salton,[5] which is still very powerful in multiple and diverse tasks of TA. However, due to lack of available large text collections, the question whether proposed models and techniques would scale to large corpora remained open. This changed in 1992 with the inception of the Text Retrieval Conference (TREC),[a] followed by the Document Understanding Conference (DUC)[b] in 2001, which was later transformed into the Text Analysis Conference (TAC)[c] in 2008. Each of these is part of a series of evaluation conferences sponsored by various US government agencies under the auspices of the National Institute of Standards and

---

[a]http://trec.nist.gov/.
[b]http://duc.nist.gov/.
[c]https://tac.nist.gov/.

Technology (NIST), which aims at encouraging research in different areas of information retrieval (IR) from large text collections. These conferences have branched IR into related and important fields like retrieval of spoken information, multilingual and cross-language retrieval, information filtering, summarization, information extraction, and automatic evaluation. This book describes multiple approaches to different TA tasks. The main focus is the multilinguality of those approaches, specifically, their ability to be applied to multiple languages.

One of the most representative examples of joint international effort in the field of multilingual TA is a series of MultiLing conferences.[6] The first MultiLing was organized in 2011, as a summarization track of DUC 2011.[7] It gathered several scientists from different countries with a joint purpose — to create the first big collection of documents in multiple languages, a collection that will permit scientists around the world to evaluate their summarization systems based on different languages. The secondary goal was to encourage people to work on summarization systems that can be applied to multiple languages. For example, in order to participate in the MultiLing contest, a team was required to apply its system to at least two languages.

3. TA overview

In this section, we describe the main areas of TA, text preprocessing methods, and a process of evaluation of TA tasks. A good overview of the main tasks in the field of TA is given in Ref. 8.

3.1. *TA areas*

Text analysis is roughly divided into several broad areas, as follows.

Text mining (TM) (first mentioned in Ref. 9) is the process of seeking or extracting useful information from the textual data. It is an exciting research area as it tries to discover knowledge from unstructured texts.[10] The scope of TM is its treatment of textual data through an application or adaptation of general knowledge discovery in databases[11,12] techniques. In order to apply these techniques, a suitable procedure among knowledge discovery methods is selected, modified to fit and handle the text data, and applied to large amounts of text. In general, text data is assumed to be available as character-based data in a standard encoding, although in many cases source documents in XML or PDF format must be cleaned and transformed into a character stream.

Information retrieval (IR) in the broader sense deals with the entire range of information processing, from data retrieval to knowledge retrieval.[13] In the world of text data, however, IR is defined as the task of finding documents that contain answers to questions.[14] In order to achieve this goal, statistical measures and methods are used for the automatic processing of text data and comparison to the given question. Information retrieval as a research area has been known for years, with the first attempts for automatic indexing made in 1975;[15] it has gained increased attention with the rise of Web search engines. The definition of IR is based on the idea of questions and answers, and designed for use with systems that retrieve documents based on keywords.

Natural Language Processing (NLP) is an area of computer science whose purpose is to achieve a better understanding of natural language by use of computers.[16] NLP methods employ simple and durable techniques for the fast processing of text.[17] These techniques range from simple methods such as string manipulation, to complex algorithms such as the automatic processing of natural language inquiries. In addition, linguistic analysis techniques are used for the processing of text.

Information extraction (IE)[18,19] is a research area whose purpose is to extract specific (i.e., pre-defined and known-in-advance) information from text documents. Natural language text contains much information that is not directly suitable for automatic analysis; however, computers can be used to process large amounts of text and extract useful information from single words, multiword expressions, phrases, or paragraphs. Therefore, IE can be viewed as a restricted form of full natural language understanding, where the information to look for is known in advance, and relevant parts of text documents must be extracted.

3.2. *Text preprocessing methods*

We give here a brief overview of widely used concepts and methods for text preprocessing.[20] It is assumed here that text data is given as a character stream. The salient preprocessing steps employed by (almost) all TA methods are described below.

Sentence boundaries detection

As a first step of text processing, the text character data needs to be broken into smaller, meaningful chunks. Usually, the basic preprocessing unit is a sentence, which is defined as "*a set of words that is complete in itself, typically containing a subject and predicate, conveying a statement, question, exclamation, or command, and consisting of a main clause and sometimes one or more subordinate clauses.*"[d] This task is called sentence boundaries detection (SBD) (also sentence splitting, sentence tokenization, or sentence segmentation). Figure 1 shows an example of English SBD.

Word tokenization

Word tokenization (often simply called tokenization or word segmentation) is the process of breaking a character stream into strings, or tokens, that represent words. In most cases, it is applied to a single sentence, after the SBD process has been completed. Figure 2 shows an example of tokenization of English text.

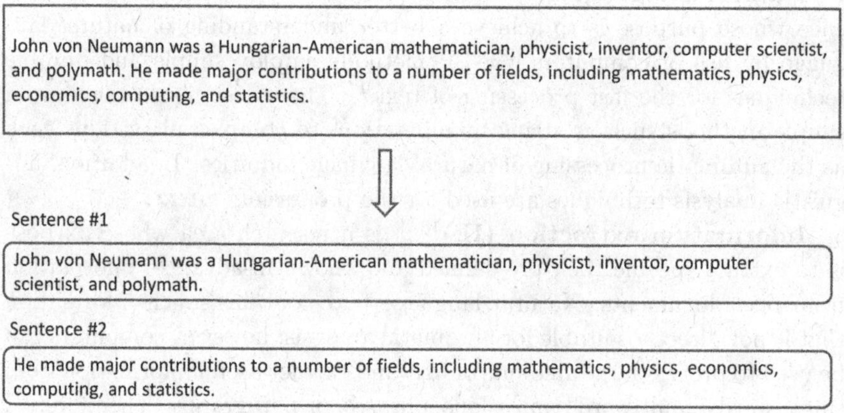

John von Neumann was a Hungarian-American mathematician, physicist, inventor, computer scientist, and polymath. He made major contributions to a number of fields, including mathematics, physics, economics, computing, and statistics.
Sentence #1
John von Neumann was a Hungarian-American mathematician, physicist, inventor, computer scientist, and polymath.
Sentence #2
He made major contributions to a number of fields, including mathematics, physics, economics, computing, and statistics.

Fig. 1. An example of English sentence splitting.

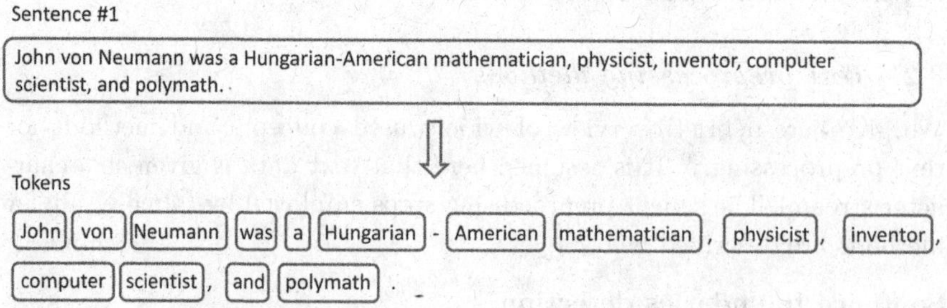

Sentence #1
John von Neumann was a Hungarian-American mathematician, physicist, inventor, computer scientist, and polymath.
Tokens
John von Neumann was a Hungarian - American mathematician , physicist , inventor ,
computer scientist , and polymath .

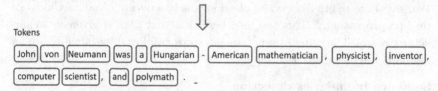

Fig. 2. An example of English tokenization.

[d]https://en.oxforddictionaries.com/definition/sentence.

Stemming and lemmatization

Stemming is the process of reducing inflected words to their word stem, base, or root form. The basic function of both stemming and lemmatization is similar. Both of them reduce a word variant to its "stem" in stemming and to its "lemma" in lemmatization.[21] Stemming usually refers to a crude heuristic process that chops off the ends of words in the hope of achieving this goal correctly most of the time, and often includes the removal of derivational affixes. Lemmatization refers to doing things properly with the use of a vocabulary and morphological analysis of words; it normally aims to remove only the inflectional endings and to return the base or dictionary form of a word, which is known as the lemma. If presented with the token *saw*, stemming might return just *s*, whereas lemmatization would attempt to return either *see* or *saw* depending on whether the use of the token was as a verb or a noun.[22] Based on described above, one may conclude that using lemmatizer is preferable than using stemmer. However, stemmers are still much more popular in NLP systems, because they require less knowledge than lemmatizers, which need a complete vocabulary and morphological analysis to correctly lemmatize words. Particular languages and domains may also require special stemming rules. Nevertheless, the exact stemmed forms do not matter, only the equivalence classes they form. Figure 3 gives an example of stemming performed by Python NLTK[23] using the Porter stemming algorithm.[24]

Synonymization

People have a variety of ways to refer to the same real-world entity, forming different synonyms for the entity.[25] Formally, a synonym is a word or phrase that means exactly or nearly the same as another word or phrase in the same language. Much research has been carried out on the search for similar words in *corpora*, mostly for applications in IR tasks. A large number of these approaches are based on the simple assumption that similar words are used in the same contexts.[26] Methods for synonym discovery range from automatic to list-based. The automatic method relies on the expectation that similar words are expected to have a similar context. The list-based method can be illustrated by Fig. 4, which is an example of some synonyms contained in the list found at http://www.englisch-hilfen.de/en/words/synonyms.htm.

Word-sense disambiguation

Word-sense disambiguation (WSD) is the process of identifying the meanings of words in context.[27] Word-sense ambiguity is prevalent in all

Fig. 3.   An example of stemming.

Word	Synonym
about	approximately
abstract	summary
to accomplish	to achieve
to accumulate	to build up

Fig. 4.   Some English synonyms.

natural languages, with a large number of the words in any given language carrying more than one meaning. The correct sense of an ambiguous word can be selected based on its context, and the problem of WSD is defined as the task of automatically assigning the most appropriate meaning to a polysemous word within a given context.[28] The English word *bass* can mean a type of fish or tones of low frequency, and its correct sense has to be determined from the context. WordNet[e] is a large lexical database of English. Nouns, verbs, adjectives, and adverbs are grouped into sets of cognitive

---

[e]https://wordnet.princeton.edu.

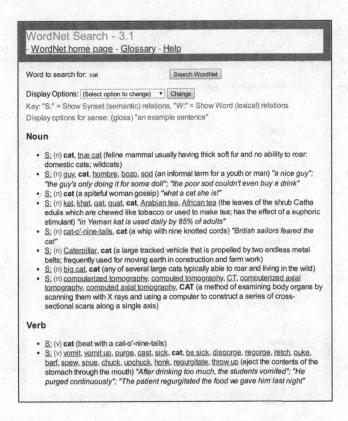

Fig. 5. An example different word senses for the word *cat*.

synonyms (synsets), each expressing a distinct concept. Synsets are inter-linked by means of conceptual-semantic and lexical relations. The resulting network of meaningfully related words and concepts can be navigated with the browser. An example of different word senses discovered with WordNet is shown in Fig. 5.

Stop-word removal

Words that are overly common have little or no value in TA tasks, as such words do not provide much help identifying important document parts; these words are called *stop words*. The general strategy for determining a stop list is to sort the terms by collection frequency, and then select the most frequent terms, often hand-filtered for their semantic content relative to the domain of the documents being indexed.[22] Lists of stop-words, stemmed or not, are used in order to identify them during automatic text preprocessing.

Default English stopwords list

This list is used in our Page Analyzer (/page-analyzer) and Article Analyzer (/article-analyzer) for English text,
when you let it use the default stopwords list.

a	ourselves
about	out
above	over
after	own
again	same
against	shan't
all	she
am	she'd
an	she'll
and	she's
any	should
are	shouldn't
aren't	so
as	some
at	such
be	than
because	that
been	that's
before	the
being	their
below	theirs
between	them
both	themselves
but	then
by	there
can't	there's
cannot	these
could	they

Fig. 6.   Partial list of English stop-words.

These lists are relatively small in comparison to text size, and the cost of stop-word removal is not high. Figure 6 shows an example of an English stop-word list from http://www.ranks.nl/stopwords, where these lists are available for over 40 languages.

Named entity recognition

Named entity recognition, also known as entity identification, entity chunking, and entity extraction, seeks to locate and classify named entities in text into pre-defined categories such as the names of persons, organizations, locations, expressions of times, quantities, monetary values, or percentages. In defining the task, people noticed that it is essential to recognize information units like names, including person, organization, and location names, as well as numeric expressions that include time, date, money, and percent expressions.[29] The task of recognizing previously unknown entities was usually based on handcrafted rules in the beginning, but the majority of currently used algorithms employ supervised learning. Figure 7 shows the output of NER performed by the Stanford NLP online toolkit (http://corenlp.run/) for English and Chinese sentences.

POS tagging

The use of POS tagging is the annotation of words with the appropriate POS tags based on the context in which they appear.[20] Tags for POS divide words into categories based on the role they play in the sentence in which they appear. These POS tags provide information about the semantic content of a word. Most POS tag sets make use of the same basic categories. The most common set of tags contains seven different tags (article, noun, verb, adjective, preposition, number, and pronoun). Figure 8 shows the output of POS tagging performed by Stanford NLP online toolkit for English and Chinese sentences.

Syntactical parsing

Syntactical parsing performs a full syntactical analysis of sentences according to a certain grammar theory of a given language. Two main grammars — *constituency* and *dependency* — are recognized.

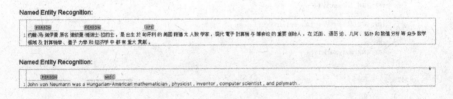

Fig. 7.   Two examples of NER.

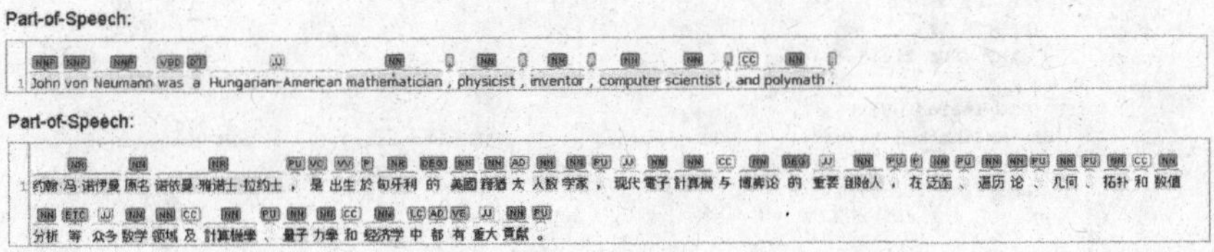

Fig. 8.   Two examples of POS tagging.

In constituency grammars, a sentence is assumed to have an hierarchical structure build of phrases. A constituent is defined as a word (or several words) that functions as a single unit within that structure, and its analysis requires the use of phrase structure grammars.[30] In these grammars, sentences are built recursively from phrases, which are sequences of syntactically grouped elements. Most common are noun, verb, prepositional, and adjective phrases. Constituency structure of a sentence forms a tree with leaves representing words. Figure 9 shows the constituency structure of an English sentence produced by Stanford NLP online toolkit.

Dependency grammars are based on dependency relations, implying that words are interconnected by directed links. In this structure, the verb is a root and all other words are either directly or indirectly connected to the verb by directed links, called *dependencies*. This structure can be either a directed tree or an acyclic directed graph, with words as its nodes and labels on its edges; these labels describe specific relations between words. For example, a subject and direct object nouns of a typical sentence depend

```
Parse
  (ROOT
    (S
      (NP (NNP John) (NNP von) (NNP Neumann))
      (VP (VBD was)
        (NP
          (NP (DT a) (JJ Hungarian-American) (NN mathematician))
          (, ,)
          (NP (NN physicist))
          (, ,)
          (NP (NN inventor))
          (, ,)
          (NP (NN computer) (NN scientist))
          (, ,)
          (CC and)
          (NP (NN polymath))))
      (. .)))

  (ROOT
    (S
      (NP (PRP He))
      (VP (VBD made)
        (NP (JJ major) (NNS contributions))
        (PP (TO to)
          (NP
            (NP (DT a) (NN number))
            (PP (IN of)
              (NP (NNS fields)))))
        (, ,)
        (PP (VBG including)
          (NP (NNS mathematics) (, ,) (NNS physics) (, ,) (NNS economics) (, ,) (NNS computing) (, ,)
          (CC and)
          (NNS statistics))))
      (. .)))
```

Fig. 9.   Result of constituency-based parsing of a sentence in English.

Basic Dependencies:
1 John von Neumann was a Hungarian-American mathematician, physicist, inventor, computer
scientist, and polymath.
NNP NNP NNP VBD DT JJ NN NN NN NN NN CC NN
compound
nsubj
cop
det
amod
conj
cc

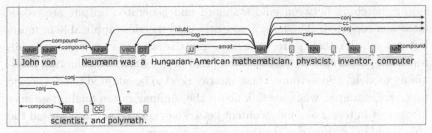

Fig. 10. Result of dependency-based parsing of a sentence in English.

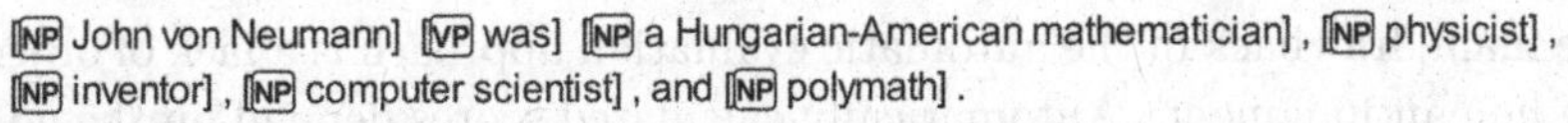

[NP John von Neumann] [VP was] [NP a Hungarian-American mathematician] , [NP physicist] ,
[NP inventor] , [NP computer scientist] , and [NP polymath] .

Fig. 11. A result of shallow parsing.

on the main verb, while an adjective depends on the noun it modifies. Figure 10 shows the dependency structure of an English sentence produced by the Stanford NLP online toolkit. Because full parsing of sentences for large *corpora* is computationally expensive (even though the problem is solved by polynomial-time algorithms), shallow parsing is often used instead for tasks that do not require full knowledge of sentence structure. Shallow parsing first identifies constituent parts of sentences and then links them to higher order units that have discrete grammatical meanings. Typically, small and simple noun and verb phrases are generated, whereas more complex clauses are not formed. Figure 11 shows the result of shallow parsing performed by the CCG tool.[31]

3.3. *Evaluation of TA tasks*

Evaluation of the performance of a TA system can be divided to *intrinsic* and *extrinsic*. Intrinsic evaluation is the direct comparison of the generated results against gold standard (human-generated with purpose of training and/or evaluation) data. Extrinsic evaluation is the indirect examination from the perspective of system's effects on the performance of another task. Both can be performed *automatically* — by calculating quality metrics — or *manually* by using human judgments. Each approach has its own advantages and drawbacks. The cheapest method in terms of time and resources is automatic intrinsic evaluation, where scores for standard metrics measuring matching between gold standard and generated output are calculated and reported. The most frequently used metrics (applicable in most, but not all, TA tasks) are: true/false positive/negative, precision, recall, f-measure, accuracy, area under curve, and perplexity (for evaluating probability models). Sometimes, those metrics need to be adapted to the specific task. For example, when we talk about the summarization quality, we may measure it in terms of a joint content between generated summaries and the gold standard summaries. In this case, recall, precision, and f-measure can be calculated in the level of single words, phrases, and word sequences both with and without gaps. This is exactly what ROUGE[32] does. ROUGE is a well-known evaluation tool that is widely used in the summarization area. The main drawback of the automatic evaluation approach is a lack of objective human judgment. Automatically calculated scores depend on the gold standard data quality and are not always objective. Also, some evaluation tools are applicable to specific languages and need to be adapted to multilingual domain. For example, ROUGE was initially designed for English, defining tokens as regular expressions above English alphabet, and requires adaptation to different languages.

Sometimes, the lack of gold standard data does not permit researchers to perform intrinsic evaluations. For example, intrinsic evaluation of an event detection algorithm is in need of annotated data — manually detected and verified events that can be compared to the generated ones. If no such data exists, extrinsic evaluations can be performed instead and show how the detected events improve the user experience or performance of other tasks. For example, using automatically detected events may improve the experience of data analysts or increase the prediction accuracy of the alert system. The former can be tested using human judgments, while the latter is directed toward running automatic experiments measuring and comparing accuracy scores, with and without the event detection.

In general, while human evaluation is considered more objective, it is also much more expensive. It requires budget, time, and human resources, and must be accurately designed to avoid repeated experiments. Unlike the automatic evaluations, which can be re-run anytime with practically no cost, each re-run of an experiment using human judgments multiplies its cost. Another frequently occurring problem with this kind of evaluation is a lack of consistent agreement between human judges. In consideration of this problem, multiple efforts have recently been made to establish systems for crowd-sourcing evaluations, which consider a judge's "quality" and the level of agreement between experts. Using a system like this helps researchers obtain more objective evaluation scores. The huge advantage of human evaluations is that it can be performed without gold standard data, saving annotators time and effort.

4. Multilingual TA: general challenges

Various TA tasks must be capable of dealing with multiple languages without a labor-consuming adaptation, meaning that they need to be *language-independent* or *multilingual*. An approach, an algorithm, or a mathematical model solving one of the TA tasks is considered to be language-independent if it requires little or no insight into a certain language, and as a result it can be adapted to different languages. However, it is nearly impossible to design an approach that uses no language-specific knowledge, because any automatic approach relies on text preprocessing, while even the most basic methods of text preprocessing depend on the language they are applied to. For example, SBD is highly nontrivial in English, word tokenization is easy in English but difficult in Chinese, while stemming is easy in Chinese and difficult in English. Therefore, a language-independent approach cannot be totally unaware of the language, although it should use appropriate tools for text preprocessing. Later, a model or algorithm is applied to processed text. Note that automatic detection of language from written text is not an easy problem, especially for different dialects.[33] Below, we elaborate on challenges of each preprocessing stage with respect to multilingual domains.

4.1. *Text preprocessing methods and multilinguality*

SBD

The task of SBD can be less or more challenging, depending on language. In English, for example, it is not easy to distinguish between a period that is a part of a previous token, such as Mrs. or Prof., and one that indicates the end of a sentence. Therefore, language-dependent heuristic rules,[34] as well as a supervised approach[35] that, together, define language-specific boundary detection models, can be applied on this task. However, in some languages, such as those in the Semitic family (such as Arabic or Hebrew), estimating the boundary of sentence is a relatively simple task, and the boundaries of the sentences and phrases can be estimated according to punctuation marks only.[36] Some approaches for a limited number of languages were proposed and evaluated. For example, the learning framework in Ref. 37 is adaptable to text of different topics and Roman-alphabet languages, and the unsupervised multilingual approach from Ref. 38 was evaluated on 11 languages above different alphabets. However, sometimes an extensive effort is needed to expand these approaches for new languages.

Tokenization

For languages using Roman script, tokenization usually involves punctuation identification and splitting, and separation of some affixes (such as *Hungarian-American* in Fig. 2). In other cases, such as Chinese, Japanese, and German, tokenization is a non-trivial step because words are not separated by spaces and the same sentence can be tokenized in many different ways. In these cases tools that are based on dictionaries and/or machine learning algorithms[39,40] are used. Tools for tokenization of various languages by explicit specification of the processed language are available.[41] Although approaches for trainable tokenizers for multilingual domains have been introduced in literature,[42–44] they are much less accurate than monolingual approaches and, therefore, are not very useful.

Stemming and lemmatization

Most existing and available algorithms for stemming and lemmatization are strictly language-dependent tasks. This is because they are based on language-specific heuristic rules (stemming) or vocabulary and morphological analysis (lemmatization) they use in order to reduce inflectional forms and derivationally related forms of a word to a common base form. Stemming algorithms for various European languages can be found in http://snowball.tartarus.org/texts/stemmersoverview.html. While language-independent stemming techniques[45,46] were introduced in the past, researchers still prefer to use language-specific algorithms because they are more accurate. Methods for automatic application of the correct language-specific stemming approach, as well as for removing the correct stop-words, based on both the language and topics of the documents, have also been proposed.[47]

Synonym resolution

If the list-based method for synonym discovery is used, then a list of synonyms must be provided for each language in a multilingual domain. The multilingual version of WordNet,[48] which covers over 150 languages, can be quite useful in this case. If the automatic method[49,50] based on the detection of words appearing in a similar context is used, then it must be applied to texts in every supported language. The data must be properly tokenized and segmented preliminarily.

WSD

Multilingual WSD can benefit from the multilingual version of WordNet,[48] BabelNet,[51] and Wikipedia sense inventory.[52–54] Different approaches for multilingual WSD were introduced in SemEval task[55] and cited in the COLING 2014 tutorial.[56]

Stopword removal

A list of stop-words must be provided or automatically built based on a frequency analysis for each language in the case of a multilingual domain. Multilingual stop-word lists for dozens of languages are available on-line.[57,58]

NER

The availability of open multilingual data, such as Wikipedia, allowed researchers to train NER models for multiple languages. For example, a Wikipedia entity type mapping is utilized in Ref. 59 to create dictionary features for training an NER system, while 7200 manually-labeled Wikipedia articles across nine languages were used for training a system in Ref. 60. Reference 61 introduces a multilingual NER approach based on a robust and general set of features across languages and datasets. The authors demonstrate that combining various data sources such as Reuters, Wikipedia, or Gigaword, enables covering different and more varied types of named entities without manual feature tuning.

POS tagging

Extensive research that has been done on multilingual POS tagging[59,62,63] has shown that it is quite feasible to apply a POS tagger on multiple languages with sufficient accuracy. For example, experiments in Ref. 59 demonstrate extremely high accuracy for the supervised tagger based on the long short-term memory (LSTM) model, for more than 20 languages from six different families.

Because we are focusing on supervised approaches, annotated data must be provided for training the tagger (NER or POS) for a new language. Recently we have seen a significant increase in available annotated data. Also, platforms assisting the annotation process exist. For example, Ref. 64 describes a system that builds NER annotators for 40 major languages using Wikipedia and Freebase.

Syntactic parsing

Most of syntactic parsers are language-specific because they employ grammar rules of a particular language. Following Chomsky's theory of universal grammar,[65,66] an extensive effort was made recently on constructing universal dependencies[67] that are multilingual. A collection of treebanks with homogeneous syntactic dependency annotation, which are applicable for crosslingual transfer parsing for several languages,[68] and multilingual parsers that are evaluated on multiple diverse languages,[69] are presented in works conducted during the last decade. However, there still remains a need to cover the many languages that demand the collaboration of linguists from multiple countries. Also, a doubt in the legitimacy of universal grammar has been raised, as the entire theory of transitional grammar was criticized.[70-72]

We must consider that all advanced preprocessing stages must be performed after the primary ones: sentence splitting and tokenization, which sometimes must be adapted to a given language.

4.2. *TA tasks and multilinguality*

Presume that we overcame the challenge of multilingual preprocessing and want to apply a method for TA on the preprocessed texts. Which challenges should we fight now?

Generally speaking, all TA tasks can be characterized as *supervised* or *unsupervised*. Supervised (a/k/a learning) tasks require training data for learning a model that is used later for decision making. Training data (a/k/a annotated or labeled data) must be created manually (or semi-manually, with non-human assistance) and contain ⟨data, solution⟩ pairs for a particular task.

For example, supervised approaches for summarization require ⟨document, summary⟩ pairs. The advantage of supervised methods is that they are able to provide a solution for any new input after sufficient training. The disadvantage is that creating training data is usually a very time- and labor-consuming process. In a multilingual domain, supervised approaches must be trained on each language, and, therefore, training data for each language must be provided. In very rare cases, it is possible for the training part of a supervised learning algorithm to be done in one language, and the algorithm application to be done in another language, usually from the same language family. In this case, an approach is called *cross-lingual*. Decision trees, neural networks, and Bayesian networks are examples of supervised models. For example, applying a decision tree model to a question answering (QA) task can classify each sentence as an "answer" or "not answer" for a given query, while a Naive Bayes model can rank sentences by their relativeness to a query. Both models need to be trained on ⟨query, answer⟩ pairs.

Unsupervised tasks do not employ training data, which is a great advantage. However, they are known as less accurate models. Moreover, unsupervised approaches utilize pre-specified heuristic rules for distinguishing between bad and good solutions, which in the TA area usually rely on language knowledge. The classic example of the unsupervised method is clustering. Clustering requires definition of a similarity measure for observed instances. For example, applying clustering for the QA task can define a group of similar sentences as answers, and even rank those sentences according to their closeness to the cluster's centroid. However, a similarity measure can employ language structure and a text representation model requires text preprocessing that is language-dependent. Other examples of unsupervised approaches are Principal Component Analysis, Singular Value Decomposition, and Eigenvalue Analysis.

In most TM tasks the process of transforming unstructured text into database transactions may include text preprocessing that, even if very basic, sometimes is based on language-specific knowledge. Standard encoding of input text can help to generalize some processes such as tokenization, but still not enough for ignoring language characteristics. Therefore, many TM tasks are adjustable to new languages, but cannot be declared as totally multilingual. Major IR tasks get text that is represented as vectors, indexes, or graphs. Building such representations also includes text preprocessing that cannot be entirely language-independent. IE tasks are often based on predefined heuristic rules that incorporate linguistic knowledge. For example, many slot filling[73,74] tasks define templates of extracted parts that include POS tags and syntactic relations.

4.3. *Evaluation in multilingual domain*

The next question is whether a model developed for a group of languages performs equally well for all the languages, and how well it works when applied to a new language. Even if a model is intended to be multilingual, it can contain intrinsic assumptions about language structure and its statistic properties. Therefore, an approach that works well on several languages from different language families is usually thought of as "truly multilingual." In order to make conclusions about multilingual abilities of an approach, evaluation of its performance on multiple languages must be performed. As we mentioned in Section 3.3, automatic evaluations need gold standard data, and in multilingual experiment it must be provided on each language. Also, tools for automatic evaluations must be adapted to various languages. Human evaluations do not require annotated data or tools, but human experts with language skills are in demand. Both scenarios create a big challenge for the *low resource languages.*

4.4. *Low resource languages*

Language resources are important for those working on computational methods to analyze and study languages. These resources are required to advance NLP research and TA.[75]

A need exists for a wide range of NLP tools that are able to analyze, parse, and annotate different languages automatically, and these include the text preprocessing tools described in previous sections. A great part of existing language resources for NLP are documented by efforts such as the Language Resources and Evaluation Map.[76]

The term *under-resourced languages* was introduced in Refs. 77 and 78; it refers to a language with at least one of the following aspects: (1) lack of a unique writing system or stable orthography, (2) limited presence on the web, (3) lack of linguistic expertise, (4) lack of electronic resources for speech and language processing. In order to objectively define the status of a language, the concept of the Basic LAnguage Resource Kit (BLARK, at http://www.elsnet.org/dox/blark.html) was defined.[77] An under-resourced language is defined as a language that has a score below 10/20. The key results show that even some European languages are still considered as under-resourced (for example, Croatian, Icelandic, Latvian, Lithuanian, Maltese, and Romanian).

An important aspect of the multilingual approach is availability of text preprocessing tools and methods for languages on which it is used. For under-resourced languages the absence of preprocessing tools and corpora is a major obstacle. For example, a syntactic parser may be unavailable for some low-source language. To develop it, necessary assumptions must be made about the language's structure and/or the supervised learning methods employed, which requires significant effort. A large high-quality annotated *corpora* is required for training to achieve good results.

A cross-lingual training can be helpful in some cases, but usually it suffers from poor performance, due to inter-language differences.

To summarize all of the above aspects, we can say that a multilingual approach/algorithm has the following qualities. First, it does not rely heavily on preprocessing tools and methods that use deep linguistic insight into a certain language, but rather on methods that are simple and available for many different languages. Second, it can be moved from one language to another if tools used by it are available for the new language. Third, it must be tested and evaluated on more than one language.

5. Overview of the chapters

All chapters of this volume can be categorized under the following topics: summarization (chapters 2, 3, 4, 5, 6); headline generation (chapter 7); evaluation of summarization systems (chapters 8, 9), study of summarization impact on different aspects, like text complexity and readability (chapter 10); social media analysis (chapter 11); study of linguistic biases on Wikipedia (chapter 12); and multilingual extraction and analysis of qualitative information from financial reports (chapter 13).

Text summarization has become an important research area due to the proliferation of large digital text collections, such as blogs or news, that produce a demand for quick automatic summarizations. Moreover, the increasing trend of cross-border globalization and acculturation requires text summarization techniques to work equally well for multiple languages. However, only some of the automated summarization methods can be defined as "language-independent," i.e., not based on any language-specific knowledge. Such methods can be used for multilingual summarization, defined in Ref. 79 as "processing several languages, with a summary in the same language as input," but, their performance is usually unsatisfactory due to the exclusion of language-specific knowledge. This book captures different approaches for the summarization that can be applied on multiple languages. Chapter 2 describes the unsupervised method that reduces the task of sentence extraction to the optimization problem and solves it by linear programming. The chapter introduces a polytope representation model for text and describes its mathematical background, geometrical meaning, and advantages over classic models. It describes multiple objective functions and reports their evaluation results on different languages and *corpora*. Chapter 3 describes another unsupervised method for extractive summarization, but it is based on the minimum description length (MDL) principle. The method uses frequent itemsets for describing and encoding the document, represented as a transactional database. The extracted sentences must cover the itemsets that best encode the document. The evaluation results on different languages demonstrate the method's effectiveness in a multilingual domain. Chapter 4 surveys the supervised approach for extractive summarization, where a final sentence score is calculated as a linear combination of multiple sentence features, with coefficients learned by a regression model. The chapter explores the contribution of various features and regression algorithms for the sentence ranking task. Chapter 5 depicts the unsupervised method that ranks and extracts sentences for a summary, using topics distribution knowledge. The authors use a hierarchical topic model for identifying important words and sentences. Chapter 6 surveys recent developments in abstractive summarization with the use of neural networks. The authors cover essential neural network concepts for abstractive summarization models, overview datasets used to train such models, and compare between four recent systems which, when combined, have resulted in dramatic improvements in single-document generic abstractive summarization in the past couple of years. Chapter 7 depicts an approach for headline generation, which is considered as a private case of the summarization task. The authors develop a supervised sequence-prediction technique for learning how editors title their news stories, which models the problem as a discrete optimization task in a feature-rich space, using conditional random fields.

The evaluation of summarization systems is a very important and challenging task. Because human evaluation is a very labor- and time-consuming process, crowdsourcing systems and automatic tools are in very high demand. Both directions are equally important, due to the subjectivity of human judgments and the limitations of automatic metrics. Two works on evaluation of summaries are presented in this volume. Chapter 8 presents the Argo crowdsourcing system for a summary evaluation. The authors evaluate the pros and cons of different approaches to single-document multilingual summary evaluation — traditional and crowdsourcing. The evaluation is performed over two languages of the MultiLing-2015 Single Document Summarization Dataset and the results are reported. Chapter 9 describes the MultiLing contest from the perspective of the organizers, including description of the participating systems, and the systems' extended evaluation. Because all systems were required to be objectively evaluated in terms of different quality aspects, the evaluation process had a crucial role for the organizers. All systems were evaluated with use of multiple automatic metrics and human grades.

Chapter 10 presents an in-depth analysis of the impact that different types of semantic information, integrated into a summarization process, affect the quality and the text complexity of generated summaries, measured with different readability metrics. According to the experimental results, the authors conclude that in terms of content and complexity, simple techniques that do not involve semantic information provide good summaries. In contrast, the addition of semantic information such as anaphora resolution, does not improve readability of the generated summaries. This highlights the importance of integrating readability issues into the summarization process.

Currently, a significant amount of textual materials are provided by social media; these materials can be analyzed with respect to different aspects. Among most prominent analytical tasks are predicting future events,[80] fraud detection,[81] brand monitoring and predicting consuming behavior,[82] opinion mining and sentiment analysis.[83] This volume contains two chapters describing approaches for analyzing social media. Chapter 11 represents a system for event detection and analysis in Twitter. Chapter 12 describes a study of linguistic biases in biographies on Wikipedia.

Besides such widely used domains for TA as news, social media, and scientific literature, there are many specific domains that can be analyzed with very specific purposes. For example, medical documents can be analyzed[84] with the purpose of disease detection or treatment assignment, web server log files can help to extract general usage patterns,[85] and analyzing car accident reports can help to predict car failures. Chapter 13 introduces an approach for multilingual extraction and analysis of qualitative information from financial reports.

Figure 12 shows the language cloud, with all languages mentioned through this book, where more frequently mentioned languages are visualized with bigger fonts.

Fig. 12.   Language cloud — visualization of languages mentioned in the book's chapters.

References

1. A. Singhal, Modern information retrieval: A brief overview, *Bulletin of the IEEE Computer Society Technical Committee on Data Engineering*, **24**(4), 35–43 (2001).

2. H. P. Luhn, A statistical approach to mechanized encoding and searching of literary information, *IBM Journal of Research and Development*, **1**(4), 309–317 (1957).

3. H. P. Luhn, The automatic creation of literature abstracts, *IBM Journal of Research and Development*, **2**, 159–165 (1958).

4. G. Salton, *The SMART Retrieval System — Experiments in Automatic Document Retrieval.* Prentice Hall Inc., Englewood Cliffs, NJ (1971).

5. G. Salton, A. Wong, and C. S. Yang, A vector space model for automatic indexing, *Communications of the ACM*, **18**(11), 613–620 (1975).

6. G. Giannakopoulos, J. M. Conroy, J. Kubina, P. A. Rankel, E. Lloret, J. Steinberger, M. Litvak, and B. Favre, Multiling 2017 overview. In *Proceedings of the MultiLing 2017 Workshop on Summarization and Summary Evaluation Across Source Types and Genres*, Valencia, Spain, pp. 1–6, ACL (2017).

7. DUC. Document Understanding Conference (2002–2011). Available at: http://duc.nist.gov.

8. A. Hotho, A. Nürnberger, and G. Paaß, A brief survey of text mining. In *Ldv Forum*, vol. 20(1), pp. 19–62, Association for Computational Linguistics (ACL) (2005).

9. R. Feldman and I. Dagan, Knowledge discovery in textual databases (KDT). In eds. U. M. Fayyad and R. Uthurusamy, *KDD*, Montreal, Canada, vol. 95, pp. 112–117, AAAI Press (1995).

10. S. Vijayarani, M. J. Ilamathi, and M. Nithya, Preprocessing techniques for text mining-an overview, *International Journal of Computer Science & Communication Networks*, **5**(1), 7–16 (2015).

11. U. M. Fayyad, G. Piatetsky-Shapiro, P. Smyth, and R. Uthurusamy, *Advances in Knowledge Discovery and Data Mining*, vol. 21, AAAI Press, Menlo Park (1996).

12. G. Piateski and W. Frawley, *Knowledge Discovery in Databases.* Springer Verlag, Heidelberg, Germany (1991).

13. K. S. Jones, *Readings in Information Retrieval.* Morgan Kaufmann, Burlington, MA (1997).

14. M. A. Hearst, Untangling text data mining. In eds. K-Y. Su, J. Su, J. Wiebe and H. Li, *Proceedings of the 37th Annual Meeting of the Association for Computational Linguistics on Computational Linguistics*, Singapore, pp. 3–10, Association for Computational Linguistics (1999).

15. G. Salton, A. Wong, and C.-S. Yang, A vector space model for automatic indexing, *Communications of the ACM*, **18**(11), 613–620 (1975).

16. Y. Kodratoff, Knowledge discovery in texts: a definition, and applications, *Foundations of Intelligent Systems*, pp. 16–29, Springer Science & Business Media, Berlin, Germany (1999).

17. R. C. Berwick, S. P. Abney, and C. Tenny, *Principle-based Parsing: Computation and Psycholinguistics*, vol. 44, Springer Science & Business Media, Berlin, Germany (1991).

18. J. Cowie and W. Lehnert, Information extraction, *Communications of the ACM*, **39**(1), 80–91 (1996).

19. M. Banko, M. J. Cafarella, S. Soderland, M. Broadhead, and O. Etzioni, Open information extraction from the web. In ed. Jérôme Lang, *Proceedings of the 20th International Joint Conference on Artificial Intelligence (IJCAI)*, Hyderabad, India vol. 7, pp. 2670–2676, Morgan Kaufmann Publishers Inc. (2007).

20. R. Feldman and J. Sanger, *The Text Mining Handbook: Advanced Approaches in Analyzing Unstructured Data*. Cambridge University Press (2007).

21. A. G. Jivani, A comparative study of stemming algorithms, *International Journal of Computer Technology and Applications*, **2**(6), 1930–1938 (2011).

22. D. Manning, Introduction. In *Introduction to Industrial Minerals*, pp. 1–16. Springer Heidelberg, Germany (1995).

23. S. Bird, NLTK: the natural language toolkit. In eds. N. Calzolari, C. Cardie, and P. Isabelle, *Proceedings of the COLING/ACL on Interactive Presentation Sessions*, Sydney, Australia, pp. 69–72, ACL (2006).

24. M. F. Porter, An algorithm for suffix stripping, *Program*, **14**(3), 130–137 (1980).

25. M. Qu, X. Ren, and J. Han, Automatic synonym discovery with knowledge bases. In *Proceedings of the 23rd ACM SIGKDD International Conference on Knowledge Discovery and Data Mining*, Halifax, Canada, pp. 997–1005, Association for Computing Machinery (ACM) (2017).

26. P. Senellart and V. D. Blondel, Automatic discovery of similar words, *Survey of Text Mining II*, **1**, 25–44 (2008).

27. M. Stevenson and Y. Wilks, Word sense disambiguation, *The Oxford Handbook of Comp. Linguistics*, pp. 249–265, Oxford University Press (2003).

28. R. Mihalcea, Word sense disambiguation. In eds. S. Claude and G. I. Webb, *Encyclopedia of Machine Learning*, pp. 1027–1030, Springer, Heidelberg, Germany (2017).

29. D. Nadeau and S. Sekine, A survey of named entity recognition and classification, *Lingvisticae Investigationes*, **30**(1), 3–26 (2007).

30. G. Gazdar, Phrase structure grammar. In eds. P. Jacobson and G. K. Pullum, *The Nature of Syntactic Representation*, pp. 131–186, D. Reidel Publishing Company, Dordrecht, Holland (1982).

31. V. Punyakanok and D. Roth, The use of classifiers in sequential inference. In eds. T. G. Dietterich, S. Becker, and Z. Ghahramani, *Neural Information Processing Systems (NIPS)*, Vancouver, Canada, pp. 995–1001, MIT Press (2001). Available at: http://cogcomp.org/papers/nips01.pdf.

32. C.-Y. Lin, Rouge: A package for automatic evaluation of summaries. In *Text Summarization Branches Out: Proceedings of the ACL-04 Workshop*, vol. 8, ACL (2004).

33. A. Ali, N. Dehak, P. Cardinal, S. Khurana, S. H. Yella, J. Glass, P. Bell, and S. Renals, Automatic dialect detection in arabic broadcast speech, *arXiv preprint arXiv:1509.06928* (2015).

34. C. D. Manning, M. Surdeanu, J. Bauer, J. Finkel, S. J. Bethard, and D. McClosky, The Stanford CoreNLP natural language processing toolkit. In eds. K. Toutanova and H. Wu, *Association for Computational Linguistics (ACL) System Demonstrations*, Baltimore, MD, USA, pp. 55–60, ACL (2014). Available at: https://aclanthology.coli.uni-saarland.de/papers/P14-5010/p14-5010.

35. B. Jurish and K.-M. Würzner, Word and sentence tokenization with hidden markov models, *Journal for Language Technology and Computational Linguistics*, **28**(2), 61–83 (2013).

36. A. H. Aliwy, Tokenization as preprocessing for arabic tagging system, *International Journal of Information and Education Technology*, **2**(4), 348 (2012).

37. D. F. Wong, L. S. Chao, and X. Zeng, iSentenizer-μ: Multilingual sentence boundary detection model, *The Scientific World Journal*, **2014**, Article ID 196574 (2014).

38. T. Kiss and J. Strunk, Unsupervised multilingual sentence boundary detection, *Computational Linguistics*, **32**(4), 485–525 (2006).

39. N. Xue, Chinese word segmentation as character tagging, *Computational Linguistics and Chinese Language Processing*, **8**(1), 29–48 (2003).

40. X. D. Zeng, F. Wong, S. Chao, and I. Trancoso, Graph-based semi-supervised model for joint chinese word segmentation and part-of-speech tagging. In ed. P. Fung, *The 51st Annual Meeting of the Association for Computational Linguistics*, Sofia, Bulgaria, pp. 770–779, ACL (2013).

41. I. K. C. M., support for Text Analytics. Tokenization. Available at: https://www.ibm.com/support/knowledgecenter/en/SSPT3X_4.0.0/com.ibm.swg.im.infosphere.biginsights.text.doc/doc/ana_txtan_tokenization.html.

42. O. Frunza, A trainable tokenizer, solution for multilingual texts and compound expression tokenization. In *The 6th International Conference on Language Resources and Evaluation (LREC 2008)*, Marrakech, Morocco, European Language Resources Association (2008).

43. E. Giguet, The stakes of multilinguality: Multilingual text tokenization in natural language diagnosis. In *Proceedings of the PRICAI Workshop on Future Issues for Multilingual Text Processing*, Cairns, Australia, PRICAI (1996).

44. B. Bigi, A multilingual text normalization approach. In eds. Z. Vetulani and J. Mariani, *Language and Technology Conference*, Poznań, Poland, pp. 515–526, Springer (2011).

45. D. W. Oard, G.-A. Levow, and C. I. Cabezas, Clef experiments at Maryland: Statistical stemming and backoff translation. In eds. C. Peters and N. Ferro, *Workshop of the Cross-Language Evaluation Forum for European Languages*, Lisbon, Portugal, pp. 176–187, Springer (2000).

46. J. A. Goldsmith, D. Higgins, and S. Soglasnova, Automatic language-specific stemming in information retrieval. In eds. C. Peters and N. Ferro, *Workshop of the Cross-Language Evaluation Forum for European Languages*, Lisbon, Portugal, pp. 273–283, Springer (2000).

47. C. Macdonald, V. Plachouras, B. He, C. Lioma, and I. Ounis, University of Glasgow at webclef 2005: Experiments in per-field normalisation and language specific stemming. In eds. C. Peters and N. Ferro, *Workshop of the Cross-Language Evaluation Forum (CLEF)*, Vienna, Austria, Springer (2005).
48. F. Bond and R. Foster, Linking and extending an open multilingual wordnet. In ed. P. Fung, *Proceedings of the 51st Annual Meeting of the Association for Computational Linguistics*, Sofia, Bulgaria, ACL (2013).
49. L. Van der Plas and J. Tiedemann, Finding synonyms using automatic word alignment and measures of distributional similarity. In *Proceedings of the COLING/ACL on Main Conference Poster Sessions*, Sydney, Australia, pp. 866–873, ACL (2006).
50. P. Turney, Mining the web for synonyms: PMI-IR Versus LSA on TOEFL. *Machine Learning: European Conference on Machine Learning 2001*, pp. 491–502 (2001).
51. R. Navigli and S. P. Ponzetto, Babelnet: The automatic construction, evaluation and application of a wide-coverage multilingual semantic network, *Artificial Intelligence*, **193**, 217–250 (2012).
52. R. Mihalcea and A. Csomai, Wikify!: Linking documents to encyclopedic knowledge. In eds. M. J. Silva, A. H. F. Laender, R. A. Baeza-Yates, D. L. McGuinness, B. Olstad, and Ø. H. Ols, *Proceedings of the Sixteenth ACM Conference on Information and Knowledge Management*, Lisbon, Portugal, pp. 233–242, ACM (2007).
53. E. Niemann and I. Gurevych, The people's web meets linguistic knowledge: Automatic sense alignment of wikipedia and wordnet. In eds. J. Bos and S. Pulman, *Proceedings of the Ninth International Conference on Computational Semantics*, Oxford, United Kingdom, pp. 205–214, ACL (2011).
54. X. Cheng and D. Roth, Relational inference for wikification, *Urbana*. **51**(61801), 16–58 (2013).
55. R. Navigli, D. Jurgens, and D. Vannella, SemEval-2013 task 12: Multilingual word sense disambiguation. In eds. M. T. Diab, T. Baldwin, and M. Baroni, *SemEval at NAACL-HLT*, pp. 222–231, ACL (2013).
56. R. Navigli and A. Moro, Multilingual word sense disambiguation and entity linking. In eds. Q. Liu and F. Xia, *Coling (Tutorials)*, Dublin, Ireland, pp. 5–7, ACL (2014).
57. C. Prokopp, Free stop word lists in 23 languages. Available at: http://www.semantikoz.com/blog/free-stop-word-lists-in-23-languages/ (2008).
58. P. Graham, Stopwords for 50 languages in JSON format. Available at: https://github.com/6/stopwords-json (2017).
59. B. Plank, A. Søgaard, and Y. Goldberg, Multilingual part-of-speech tagging with bidirectional long short-term memory models and auxiliary loss. In eds. K. Erk and N. A. Smith, *Proceedings of the 54th Annual Meeting of the Association for Computational Linguistics*, Berlin, Germany, p. 412–418, ACL (2016).
60. J. Nothman, N. Ringland, W. Radford, T. Murphy, and J. R. Curran, Learning multilingual named entity recognition from wikipedia, *Artificial Intelligence*, **194**, 151–175 (2013).

61. R. Agerri and G. Rigau, Robust multilingual named entity recognition with shallow semi-supervised features, *Artificial Intelligence*, **238**, 63–82 (2016).

62. D. Yarowsky, G. Ngai, and R. Wicentowski, Inducing multilingual text analysis tools via robust projection across aligned corpora. In *Proceedings of the First International Conference on Human Language Technology Research*, Toulouse, France, pp. 1–8, ACL (2001).

63. S. Petrov, D. Das, and R. McDonald, A universal part-of-speech tagset, *arXiv preprint arXiv:1104.2086* (2011).

64. R. Al-Rfou, V. Kulkarni, B. Perozzi, and S. Skiena, Polyglot-ner: Massive multilingual named entity recognition. In eds. S. Venkatasubramanian and J. Ye, *Proceedings of the 2015 SIAM International Conference on Data Mining*, Vancouver, Canada, pp. 586–594, SIAM (2015).

65. V. Cook and M. Newson, *Chomsky's Universal Grammar*. John Wiley & Sons (2014).

66. W. Hinzen, The philosophical significance of universal grammar, *Language Sciences*, **34**(5), 635–649 (2012).

67. J. Nivre, M.-C. de Marneffe, F. Ginter, Y. Goldberg, J. Hajic, C. D. Manning, R. McDonald, S. Petrov, S. Pyysalo, N. Silveira, R. Tsarfaty, and D. Zeman, Universal dependencies v1: A multilingual treebank collection. In eds. N. C. C. (Chair), K. Choukri, T. Declerck, M. Grobelnik, B. Maegaard, J. Mariani, A. Moreno, J. Odijk, and S. Piperidis, *International Conference on Language Resources and Evaluation (LREC 2016)*, European Language Resources Association (ELRA), Paris, France (May, 2016). Available at: https://nlp.stanford.edu/pubs/nivre2016ud.pdf.

68. R. T. McDonald, J. Nivre, Y. Quirmbach-Brundage, Y. Goldberg, D. Das, K. Ganchev, K. B. Hall, S. Petrov, H. Zhang, O. Täckström, C. Bedini, N. B. Castelló, and J. Lee, Universal dependency annotation for multilingual parsing. In *Proceedings of the 51st Annual Meeting of the Association for Computational Linguistics*, Sofia, Bulgaria, pp. 92–97, ACL (2013).

69. R. McDonald, K. Lerman, and F. Pereira, Multilingual dependency analysis with a two-stage discriminative parser. In eds. N. Calzolari, C. Cardie, and P. Isabelle, *Proceedings of the Tenth Conference on Computational Natural Language Learning*, Sydney, Australia, pp. 216–220, ACL (2006).

70. M. H. Christiansen and N. Chater, Language as shaped by the brain, *Behavioral and Brain Sciences*, **31**(5), 489–509 (2008).

71. G. Sampson, *The 'Language Instinct' Debate: Revised Edition*. A&C Black (2005).

72. P. Ibbotson and M. Tomasello, Evidence rebuts Chomsky's theory of language learning, *Scientific American*, **315**(5) (2016).

73. M. Surdeanu, D. McClosky, J. Tibshirani, J. Bauer, A. X. Chang, V. I. Spitkovsky, and C. D. Manning, A simple distant supervision approach for the tac-kbp slot filling task. In *Text Analysis Conference (TAC)*, Gaithersburg, Maryland, USA, NIST (2010).

74. G. Mesnil, Y. Dauphin, K. Yao, Y. Bengio, L. Deng, D. Hakkani-Tur, X. He, L. Heck, G. Tur, D. Yu, and G. Zweig, Using recurrent neural networks for

slot filling in spoken language understanding, *IEEE/ACM Transactions on Audio, Speech and Language Processing (TASLP)*, **23**(3), 530–539 (2015).

75. M. El-Haj, U. Kruschwitz, and C. Fox, Creating language resources for under-resourced languages: methodologies, and experiments with arabic, *Language Resources and Evaluation*, **49**(3), 549–580 (2015).

76. N. Calzolari, C. Soria, R. Del Gratta, S. Goggi, V. Quochi, I. Russo, K. Choukri, J. Mariani, and S. Piperidis, The lREC 2010 resource map. In eds. N. Calzolari, K. Choukri, B. Maegaard, J. Mariani, J. Odijk, S. Piperidis, M. Rosner, and D. Tapias, *Proceedings of the Seventh Conference on International Language Resources and Evaluation*, Valletta, Malta, ELRA (2010).

77. S. Krauwer, The basic language resource kit (blark) as the first milestone for the language resources roadmap. In *Proceedings of SPECOM 2003*, Moscow, Russia, pp. 8–15, Moscow State Linguistic University (MSLU) (2003).

78. V. Berment, *Méthodes pour informatiser les langues et les groupes de langues peu dotées*. PhD thesis, Université Joseph-Fourier-Grenoble I (2004).

79. I. Mani, *Automatic Summarization*. Natural Language Processing, John Benjamins Publishing Company (2001).

80. T. Sakaki, M. Okazaki, and Y. Matsuo, Earthquake shakes twitter users: real-time event detection by social sensors. In eds. M. Rappa, P. Jones, J. Freire, and S. Chakrabarti, *Proceedings of the 19th International Conference on World Wide Web*, Raleigh, NC, USA, pp. 851–860, ACM (2010).

81. L. Akoglu, R. Chandy, and C. Faloutsos, Opinion fraud detection in online reviews by network effects., In *Proceedings of the Seventh International AAAI Conference on Weblogs and Social Media (ICWSM)*, Cambridge, MA, USA, pp. 2–11, AAAI (2013).

82. K.-Y. Goh, C.-S. Heng, and Z. Lin, Social media brand community and consumer behavior: Quantifying the relative impact of user-and marketer-generated content, *Information Systems Research*, **24**(1), 88–107 (2013).

83. B. Pang and L. Lee, Opinion mining and sentiment analysis, *Foundations and Trends® in Information Retrieval*, **2**(1–2), 1–135 (2008).

84. G. K. Savova, J. J. Masanz, P. V. Ogren, J. Zheng, S. Sohn, K. C. Kipper-Schuler, and C. G. Chute, Mayo clinical text analysis and knowledge extraction system (ctakes): architecture, component evaluation and applications, *Journal of the American Medical Informatics Association*, **17**(5), 507–513 (2010).

85. S. Asunka, H. S. Chae, B. Hughes, and G. Natriello, Understanding academic information seeking habits through analysis of web server log files: The case of the teachers college library website, *The Journal of Academic Librarianship*, **35**(1), 33–45 (2009).

Chapter 2

Using a Polytope Model for Unsupervised Document Summarization

Natalia Vanetik[*] and Marina Litvak[†]

Shamoon College of Engineering,
Software Engineering Department,
Byalik 56, Beer Sheva 84100
[*]natalyav@sce.ac.il
[†]marinal@sce.ac.il

The problem of extractive text summarization for a collection of documents is defined as the problem of selecting a small subset of sentences so that the contents and meaning of the original document set are preserved in the best possible way. As such, summarization can be expressed as an optimization problem, where the information coverage of the original document set must be maximized in a summary. This approach is unsupervised and can be solved by linear programming (LP). The open question that remains here is how to mathematically express information coverage as an objective function. In this chapter we present a summarization technique that produces extractive summaries with the best objective value obtained by LP. We describe the polytope model, which provides real weights to term occurrences, representing their importance for a summary.

1. Introduction

In this chapter[a] we deal with the problem of extractive summarization. Our method can be generalized for both single-document and multi-document summarization. Because the method includes only very basic linguistic analysis (see Section 3.2), it can be applied to cross-lingual/multilingual summarization.

---

[a]This work was partially funded by the United States Department of Navy, Office of Naval Research.

Formally speaking, this chapter describes the following:

- A text representation model expanding a classic vector space model (VSM)[1] to hyperplane and half-spaces, named polytope model (PM);
- A re-formulated extractive summarization problem as an optimization task, with its solution using LP;
- Various objective functions, measuring information coverage we want to preserve, for ranking and extracting sentences.

The main advantage of our approach is the possibility of representing an exponential number of extracts (sentence subsets) without computing them explicitly. Given a polynomial objective function, the optimal extract can then be computed by a simple optimization of this function in polynomial time.

This chapter is organized as follows. Section 2 depicts related work. Section 3 describes problem setting and definitions. Section 4 introduces the PM text representation model. Section 5 describes the summarization task as an optimization problem and introduces multiple objective functions. It also shows how the PM can be upgraded with an additional input, such as a topical knowledge using topic modeling (TM) or frequent items of terms. Section 6 describes how we use the obtained solution of the PM model with a specified objective function for ranking and extracting sentences or their parts. Section 7 explains our approach for compressive summarization using the PM. Section 8 describes our experiments, including evaluation on multiple languages. The last section contains our future work and conclusions.

2. Related work

Extractive summarization can be considered as an optimization problem in a very natural way. We need to extract a maximum amount of information using a minimal number of words. This problem is known as NP-hard, and, unfortunately, there is no known polynomial algorithm that can tell, given a solution, whether it is optimal. Many researchers have worked in this direction during the last couple of decades, formulating the summarization as optimization problem and solving it using approximation techniques like a standard hill-climbing algorithm,[2] A* search algorithm,[3] regression models,[4] and evolutionary algorithms.[5–7]

Some authors measure information by text units such as terms and N-grams, and reduce summarization to the maximum coverage problem.[8]

The maximum coverage model extracts sentences to a summary to cover as many terms or N-grams as possible. Despite a great performance[8,9] in the summarization field, the maximum coverage problem, as a private case of a general optimization task, is also known as NP-hard.[10] Some works attempted to find a near-optimum solution by using a greedy approach.[8,11,12] Linear programming helps to find a more accurate approximated solution to the maximum coverage problem; it has become very popular in the summarization field in recent years.[9,13–16] However, most mentioned works use integer linear programming (ILP) and an exponential number of constraints. The difference with our approach lies in time complexity (because ILP is NP-hard), and the form and number of constraints. For example, in Ref. 13 constraints are hard-coded and express only the relevance and redundancy between text units, while sentence structure and other term properties are not taken into account. Trying to solve a trade-off between summary quality and time complexity, we propose a summarization model solving the approximated maximum coverage problem by fractional (not integer) linear programming in polynomial time. We measure information coverage by terms[b] and strive to obtain a summary that preserves the optimal (minimal or maximal) value of the chosen objective function (for example, total term frequency) as much as possible, in comparison to the original document. We also address the matter of redundancy, in order to avoid extracting sentences or their parts that do not contribute any new information. Formal definition of redundancy is tricky and may vary from model to model. We propose objective functions expressing our own mathematical interpretation of the redundant information. In general, various objective functions combining different parameters, such as a term's position and its frequency, are introduced and evaluated. We also address several options for possible extension and enrichment of the proposed model with advanced techniques of knowledge extraction, such as TM and frequent itemset mining, and propose relevant objective functions.

3. Definitions

3.1. *Problem setting*

We are given a set of sentences, $S_1, \ldots, S_n$, that are derived from a document or a cluster of related documents speaking on some subject. Meaningful words in these sentences are entirely described by terms

---

[b]Normalized meaningful words.

$T_1, \ldots, T_m$. Our goal is to find a subset $S_{i_1}, \ldots, S_{i_k}$ consisting of sentences such that

(1) there are at most N terms in these sentences;
(2) information coverage, which is expressed by a corresponding objective function, is preserved as much as possible with regard to the original sentence set;
(3) redundant information (also expressed mathematically as a part of an objective) among k selected sentences is minimized.

3.2. *Text preprocessing*

In order to build the matrix and then the PM, one must perform basic text preprocessing, which includes sentence splitting and tokenization. Additional steps like stopwords removal, stemming, and synonym resolution may be performed for resource-rich languages. Because the main purpose of these methods is to reduce the dimensionality of the matrix, the resultant model will be more efficient. More elaborated text preprocessing is demanded in some cases where the extended PM is applied; this is discussed in the corresponding sections.

3.3. *The matrix model*

In this section we present the matrix model that we use to represent text data — the sentence-term matrix, containing term count values per sentence. Because most of the proposed objective functions consider information coverage through frequency statistics, all necessary calculations are based on the term count. A *sentence-term matrix* is a real matrix $A = (a_{ij})$ of size $m \times n$, where

$$a_{ij} = k \text{ if term } T_i \text{ appears in sentence } S_j \text{ precisely } k \text{ times.}$$

Here, columns of A describe sentences and rows describe terms. Because we are not interested in redundant sentences, in the case of multi-document summarization, we can initially select meaningful sentences by clustering all the columns as vectors in $\mathbb{R}^n$ and choose a single representative from each cluster. In this case columns of A describe representatives of sentence clusters.

The total number of words (term appearances) in the document, denoted by S, can be computed from matrix A as

$$S = \sum_i \sum_j a_{ij}. \tag{1}$$

Here and further, we refer to A as the **sentence-term** matrix corresponding to the given document/s.

Example 1. Given the following text of $n = 3$ sentences and $m = 5$ (normalized) terms:

$$S_1 = \text{A fat cat is a cat that eats fat meat.}$$
$$S_2 = \text{My cat eats fish but he is a fat cat.}$$
$$S_3 = \text{All fat cats eat fish and meat.}$$

Matrix A, corresponding to the text above, has the following shape:

$$
\begin{array}{c}
\\
T_1 = \text{"fat"} \\
T_2 = \text{"cat"} \\
T_3 = \text{"eat"} \\
T_4 = \text{"fish"} \\
T_5 = \text{"meat"}
\end{array}
\begin{array}{ccc}
S_1 & S_2 & S_3 \\
\left[\begin{array}{ccc}
a_{11} = 2 & a_{12} = 1 & a_{13} = 1 \\
a_{21} = 2 & a_{22} = 2 & a_{23} = 1 \\
a_{31} = 1 & a_{32} = 1 & a_{33} = 1 \\
a_{41} = 0 & a_{42} = 1 & a_{43} = 1 \\
a_{51} = 1 & a_{52} = 0 & a_{53} = 1
\end{array}\right]
\end{array}
$$

where a_{ij} are term counts.

The total count of terms in this matrix is

$$S = \sum_{i=1}^{5} \sum_{j=1}^{3} a_{ij} = 16.$$

3.4. *The goal*

In this setting, our goal can be reformulated as the problem of finding subset $i_1, \ldots, i_k$ of matrix columns from A, so that the chosen submatrix represents the best possible summary under some constraints. Constraints may be defined as upper and/or lower bounds on the total number of terms or words in the summary. Because it is hard to determine what is the best summary mathematically (this task is usually left to human experts), we want to express summary quality as a polynomial (or, hopefully, even linear) function of the underlying matrix. We strive to find a summary that gives an optimal value once the function in question has been determined.

4. From matrix model to polytope

4.1. *Hyperplanes and half-spaces*

Extractive summarization aims at extracting a subset of sentences that covers as much non-redundant information as possible with regard to the source documents. Here we introduce a new and efficient text representation model with the purpose of representing all possible extracts without computing them explicitly. Because the number of potential extracts is exponential, based on the number of sentences, we would be saving a great amount of computation time. Finding an optimal extract of text units is a general problem for various information retrieval tasks like question answering or literature search; our model can be efficiently applied on all these tasks.

In our representation model, each sentence is represented by a hyperplane, and all sentences derived from a document form hyperplane intersections (polytope). Therefore, all possible extracts can be represented by subplanes of our hyperplane intersections and as such, are not located far from the boundary of the polytope. Intuitively, the boundary of the resulting polytope is a good approximation for extracts that can be generated from the given document.

4.2. *The approach*

Let A be the sentence-term matrix of given documents. We view every column of matrix A as a *linear constraint* representing a hyperplane in $\mathbb{R}^{mn}$. An occurrence of term t_i in sentence S_j is represented by variable x_{ij}. Note that the maximality constraint on the number of terms in the summary can be easily expressed as a constraint on the sum of these variables.

Together, all the columns of A define a system of linear inequalities, and we also express constraints on the number of terms or words (words is an appearance of a term in a sentence; the same word can appear in a sentence more than once) in the extract we seek. Every sentence in our document is a hyperplane in $\mathbb{R}^{mn}$, expressed with the help of columns

$$A[][j] = [a_{1j}, \ldots, a_{mj}]$$

of A and variables

$$\mathbf{x}_j = [x_{1j}, \ldots, x_{mj}] \ \forall j = 1 \ldots n$$

that represent appearances of terms in sentences. We define a system of linear inequalities where, for all $j = 1 \ldots n$, holds the following:

$$A[][j] \cdot \mathbf{x}_j^T = \sum_{i=1}^{m} a_{ij} x_{ij} \leq A[][j] \cdot \mathbf{1}^T = \sum_{i=1}^{m} a_{ij}. \tag{2}$$

Every inequality of this form defines a hyperplane H_i and its lower half-space, specified by Eq. (2):

$$A[][j] \cdot \mathbf{x}_j^T = A[][j] \cdot \mathbf{1}^T$$

and with normal vector $\mathbf{n} = (\mathbf{n}_{xy})$

$$\mathbf{n}_{xy} = \begin{cases} a_{xy}, & x = 1 \ldots m \wedge y = j \\ 0, & \text{otherwise.} \end{cases} \tag{3}$$

To express the fact that every term is either present or absent from the chosen extract, we add constraints

$$0 \leq x_{ij} \leq 1. \tag{4}$$

Intuitively, the entire hyperplane H_i and therefore, every point $p \in H_i$, represents sentence S_i. Because each extractive summary is a subset of sentences of the original documents, we observe intersections of hyperplanes as objects that represent these summaries. Define the intersection of two hyperplanes, say H_i and H_j, as a representation of a two-sentence summary containing sentences S_i and S_j. Then a subset of r sentences is represented by the intersection of r hyperplanes.

4.3. *Summary constraints*

We express summarization constraints in the form of linear inequalities in $\mathbb{R}^{mn}$, using the columns of the sentence-term matrix A as linear constraints. The maximality constraint on the number of terms in the summary can be easily expressed as a constraint on the sum of term variables x_{ij}. Because we are looking for summaries that consist of at least $T_{\min}$ and at most $T_{\max}$ terms, we introduce the following linear constraint:

$$T_{\min} \leq \sum_{i=1}^{m} \sum_{j=1}^{n} x_{ij} \leq T_{\max}. \tag{5}$$

Indeed, every variable x_{ij} stands for an appearance of term i in sentence j, and we intend for their sum to express the number of terms in selected sentences.

Additionally, we may have constraints on the minimal $W_{\min}$ and maximal $W_{\max}$ number of words in the summary. We take into account only words that remain in the text after stop-word removal and stemming. The difference between the number of terms and the number of words in a summary is that a single term can appear more than once in a sentence. Consequently, the total number of words in the text is expressed by summing up the elements of its term-count matrix. Therefore, minimality and maximality constraints for words are expressed by the following linear inequality:

$$W_{\min} \leq \sum_{i=1}^{m} \sum_{j=1}^{n} a_{ij} x_{ij} \leq W_{\max}. \tag{6}$$

Example 2. This example demonstrates variables corresponding to the 5×3 matrix A of Example 1.

$$
\begin{array}{c c c c}
 & S_1 & S_2 & S_3 \\
T_1 & \begin{bmatrix} x_{11} & x_{12} & x_{13} \\ \end{array}
$$

$$
\begin{array}{c}
T_1 \\ T_2 \\ T_3 \\ T_4 \\ T_5
\end{array}
\begin{bmatrix}
x_{11} & x_{12} & x_{13} \\
x_{21} & x_{22} & x_{23} \\
x_{31} & x_{32} & x_{33} \\
x_{41} & x_{42} & x_{43} \\
x_{51} & x_{52} & x_{53}
\end{bmatrix}
$$

Sentence-term matrix A defines the following hyperplane equations.

$$H_1 : \ 2x_{11} + 2x_{21} + x_{31} + x_{51} = 2 + 2 + 1 + 1 = 6$$
$$H_2 : \ x_{12} + 2x_{22} + x_{32} + x_{42} = 5$$
$$H_3 : \ x_{13} + x_{23} + x_{33} + x_{43} + x_{53} = 5$$

Here, a summary consisting of the first and second sentences is expressed by the intersection of hyperplanes H_1 and H_2. Figure 1 shows what a

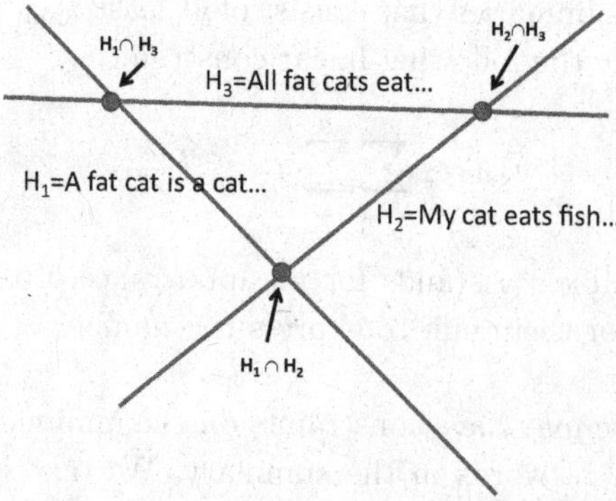

Fig. 1. Two-dimensional projection of hyperplane intersection.

two-dimensional projection of hyperplanes H_1, H_2, H_3, and their intersections looks like.

Equation (5), $T_{min} = 6$ and $T_{max} = 11$, has the form

$$0 \leq x_{ij} \leq 1, \forall i, j$$

$$6 \leq \sum_{i=1}^{5} \sum_{j=1}^{3} x_{ij} \leq 11$$

Equation (6) for the given sentence-term matrix, $W_{min} = 6$ and $W_{max} = 11$ has the form

$$6 \leq 2x_{11} + 2x_{21} + x_{31} + x_{51} + x_{12} + x_{22} + 2x_{32}$$

$$+ x_{42} + x_{52} + x_{13} + x_{23} + x_{33} + x_{43} + x_{53} \leq 11$$

If we set $T_{min} = 5$ and $T_{max} = 10$, the corresponding constraint of Eq. (5) has the form

$$5 \leq x_{11} + x_{21} + x_{31} + x_{51} + x_{12} + x_{22} + 2x_{32}$$

$$+ x_{42} + x_{52} + x_{13} + x_{23} + x_{33} + x_{43} + x_{53} \leq 10.$$

4.4. *The polytope model*

Having defined both the linear inequalities that describe each sentence in a document separately, as well as the total number of terms in the sentence subset, we can now look at them together as a system:

$$
\begin{cases}
\sum_{i=1}^{m} a_{ij} x_{ij} \leq \sum_{i=1}^{m} a_{ij}, & \forall j = 1 \ldots n \\
T_{min} \leq \sum_{i=1}^{m} \sum_{j=1}^{n} x_{ij} \leq T_{max} \\
W_{min} \leq \sum_{i=1}^{m} \sum_{j=1}^{n} a_{ij} x_{ij} \leq W_{max} \\
0 \leq x_{ij} \leq 1, & \forall i = 1 \ldots m, \ j = 1 \ldots n
\end{cases}
\tag{7}
$$

The first n inequalities describe sentences $S_1, \ldots, S_n$; the next two inequalities describe constraints on the total number of terms and words in a summary; the final constraint determines upper and lower boundaries for all sentence-term variables.

Because every inequality in the system described in Eq. (7) is linear, the entire system describes a convex polyhedron in $\mathbb{R}^{mn}$, which we denote by $\mathbf{P}$. Faces of $\mathbf{P}$ are determined by intersections of hyperplanes, defined by the equations obtained by turning all inequalities of Eq. (7) into equalities:

$$H_j = \sum_{i=1}^{m} a_{ij} x_{ij}, \quad \forall j = 1 \ldots n. \tag{8}$$

$$T_{\min} = \sum_{i=1}^{m} \sum_{j=1}^{n} x_{ij}, \quad T_{\max} = \sum_{i=1}^{m} \sum_{j=1}^{n} x_{ij}. \tag{9}$$

$$W_{\min} = \sum_{i=1}^{m} \sum_{j=1}^{n} a_{ij} x_{ij}, \quad W_{\max} = \sum_{i=1}^{m} \sum_{j=1}^{n} a_{ij} x_{ij}. \tag{10}$$

$$x_{ij} = 0, \quad x_{ij} = 1, \quad \forall i = 1 \ldots m, \ j = 1 \ldots n. \tag{11}$$

Intersections of H_js represent subsets of sentences, as the following property shows.

Property 1. Equation of the intersection $H_{1\ldots k} = H_1 \cap \cdots \cap H_k$ (which is a hyperplane by itself), satisfies

$$\sum_{i=1}^{m} \sum_{j=1}^{k} a_{ij} x_{ij} = \sum_{i=1}^{m} \sum_{j=1}^{k} a_{ij}.$$

Proof. The intersection $H_{1\ldots k}$ must satisfy all the equations of $H_1, \ldots, H_k$. Therefore, summing up the left and right sides of Eq. (2), we get for $H_1, \ldots, H_k$, we have

$$\sum_{i=1}^{m} \sum_{j=1}^{k} a_{ij} x_{ij} = \sum_{i=1}^{m} \sum_{j=1}^{k} a_{ij}.$$

Note that the choice of indexes $1, \ldots, k$ was arbitrary and the property holds for any subset of indexes. □

Therefore, the hypersurfaces representing the sentence sets we seek are in fact hyperplane intersections that form the boundaries of the polytope $\mathbf{P}$.

Figure 2 depicts the general pipeline of polytope summarization model.

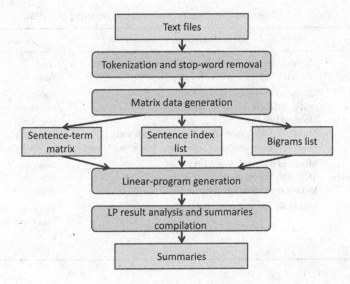

Fig. 2.   Data flow of our summarization system.

5. Objective functions for summarization

We assume here that the surface of the polyhedron **P** is a suitable representation of all the possible sentence subsets (its size, of course, is not polynomial in m and n, because the number of vertices of **P** can reach $O(2^n)$). Fortunately, we do not need to scan the whole set of **P**'s surfaces, but rather, we should try to find the point on **P** that optimizes (minimizes or maximizes) the chosen objective function. Principally, we can divide all functions that we propose in this chapter into four categories:

(1) **Minimal Distance**. Functions from this category measure and minimize a distance between a document and a generated summary. Intuitively, distance simulates a difference between the two, and its minimizing aims at obtaining a summary with a similar content.

(2) **Maximal Relevance**. All functions from this category mainly focus on maximizing information coverage, which may be expressed in various ways.

(3) **Minimal Redundancy**. This category deals with measuring and minimizing redundant information in a generated summary. The purpose of this optimization is to generate a summary that is compiled from sentences that are not only the most informative (relevant), but are also diverse.

Table 1.   Objective functions for summarization using the PM.

Category	Functions	Input
Minimal Distance	Minimal Distance to Maximal Terms Coverage, Minimal Distance to Term Frequency	Basic Basic
Maximal Relevance	Maximal Weighted Term Sum (with different types of weights), Maximal Bigram Sum, Maximal Relevance with Frequent Itemsets, Maximal Information (Topic and Lexicon) Coverage	Basic, Location, Bigrams, Frequent itemsets, Basic, Topics
Minimal Redundancy	Minimal Jaccard Similarity Minimal Overlap Minimal Cosine Similarity	Basic Basic Basic
Maximal Relevance Minimal Redundancy	Maximal (Relevance - Redundancy)	Depends on functions used

(4) **Maximal Relevance Minimal Redundancy**. This category combines the ideas of the former two, aimimg at obtaining an informative summary by maximizing the difference between relevance and redundancy.

Table 1 enumerates different objective functions that we used for summarization. Each function is assigned to one of four categories. Some functions require additional information, beyond the sentence-term matrix, as follows:

(1) **Location** — information about relative location of sentences in a summarized document must be provided;
(2) **Bigrams** — an additional step of preprocessing must be performed where the bigrams of terms are identified;
(3) **Frequent itemsets** — frequent itemsets must be calculated and provided as an input;
(4) **Topics** — here a distribution of topics must be provided.

The table also contains the input information that is required for each of these functions. The last category (Maximal Relevance Minimal Redundancy) combines ideas of the former two and, therefore, uses the same input. We denote sentence-term matrix as a **Basic** input. We elaborate more on each category and its objective functions in subsections below.

5.1. *Minimal distance functions*

This section describes objective functions for summary optimization that have the form of the distance function, i.e., they optimize the distance from the generated summary to some point that represents the "ideal" summary. We describe here two such functions. For these functions we aim to find a point on the polytope $\mathbf{P}$ that is the closest to the chosen vector $p = (p_1, \ldots, p_m)$. The vector expresses document properties we want to preserve, for each term, for all the terms $T_1, \ldots, T_m$. We use term variables $t_1, \ldots, t_m$ defined in Eq. (22) and seek to minimize the distance between $t = (t_1, \ldots, t_m)$ and the "ideal" vector $p = (p_1, \ldots, p_m)$.

5.1.1. *Minimal distance to maximal terms coverage*

Here, our best point contains all the terms precisely once, thus minimizing repetition but increasing coverage:

$$p = (1, \ldots, 1). \tag{12}$$

The distance between a point on $\mathbf{P}$ and the target point p is expressed via variables $t_1, \ldots, t_m$ as

$$\sqrt{\sum_{i=1}^{m}(t_i - 1)^2}.$$

In order to find the minimum of this function, it is sufficient to minimize the expression under the root sign. Therefore we define the objective function as

$$\min \sum_{i=1}^{m}(t_i - 1)^2. \tag{13}$$

This is a quadratic programming (QP) problem. QP can be solved efficiently both theoretically and practically.[17-19] If QP is not supported by a particular LP solving software, then we seek to minimize the Manhattan distance between the polytope and the target point, as follows:

$$\min \sum_{i=1}^{m}|t_i - 1|. \tag{14}$$

In order to express absolute values in a system of linear inequalities, we use the well-known scheme of defining auxiliary variables t_i^+, t_i^- and adding to the system equalities

$$t_i - 1 = t_i^+ - t_i^-, \quad i = 1 \ldots m.$$

Then the objective function has the following form:

$$\min \sum_{i=1}^{m}(t_i^+ + t_i^-). \tag{15}$$

Example 3. For Example 1 the Euclidean distance minimization function has the form

$$\min \sum_{i=1}^{5}(t_i - 1)^2.$$

In order to minimize the Manhattan distance, we define auxiliary variables

$$t_1 - 1 = t_1^+ - t_1^-$$
$$t_2 - 1 = t_2^+ - t_2^-$$
$$t_3 - 1 = t_3^+ - t_3^-$$
$$t_4 - 1 = t_4^+ - t_4^-$$
$$t_5 - 1 = t_5^+ - t_5^-$$

and get an objective function

$$\min \sum_{i=1}^{5}(t_i^+ + t_i^-).$$

5.1.2. *Minimal distance to term frequency*

Here we use document frequencies as the target (best) point

$$p = (\mathrm{tf}_1, \ldots, \mathrm{tf}_m), \tag{16}$$

where tf_i is the normalized term frequency of term T_i, computed as

$$\mathrm{tf}_i = \frac{\sum_{j=1}^{n} a_{ij}}{\sum_{i=1}^{m}\sum_{j=1}^{n} a_{ij}}.$$

The generated summary is described by the point

$$t = \left(\frac{t_1}{\sum_{i=1}^{m} t_i}, \ldots, \frac{t_m}{\sum_{i=1}^{m} t_i}\right)$$

where

$$\forall j = 1 \ldots m \quad \frac{t_j}{\sum_{i=1}^{m} t_i} = \frac{\sum_{i}^{m} x_{ij}}{\sum_{i}^{m}\sum_{j=1}^{n} x_{ij}}$$

is the term frequency of term T_j in generated summary. In order to find the point on **P** that is the closest to p, we need to compute term frequencies in the chosen summary. Thus, we need to address rational function optimization in a system of linear inequalities. To do so, we introduce an additional variable

$$r = \frac{1}{\sum_{i=1}^{m} t_i} \tag{17}$$

and replace all variables x_{ij} with variables r_{ij}, representing $r * x_{ij}$, and variables r_i, representing $r * t_i$.

Introducing new variables gives us the system

$$
\begin{cases}
\sum_{i=1}^{m} a_{ij} r_{ij} \leq r \sum_{i=1}^{m} a_{ij}, \quad j = 1 \ldots n \\[2mm]
r T_{\min} \leq \sum_{i=1}^{m} \sum_{j=1}^{n} r_{ij} \leq r T_{\max} \\[2mm]
r W_{\min} \leq \sum_{i=1}^{m} \sum_{j=1}^{n} a_{ij} r_{ij} \leq r W_{\max} \\[2mm]
0 \leq r_{ij} \leq r \\[2mm]
r_i = \sum_{j=1}^{n} r_{ji}, \quad i = 1 \ldots m \\[2mm]
\sum_{i=1}^{m} \sum_{j=1}^{n} r_{ij} = 1
\end{cases}
\tag{18}
$$

of linear inequalities that expresses the fact that we are looking for new rational variables. The minimal-distance objective function is

$$\min \sqrt{\sum_{i=1}^{m} (r_i - \mathrm{tf}_i)^2}, \tag{19}$$

which is equivalent to the quadratic objective function

$$\min \sum_{i=1}^{m} (r_i - \mathrm{tf}_i)^2. \tag{20}$$

In the case of the Manhattan distance, the following linear function must be used:

$$\min \sum_{i=1}^{m} |r_i - \mathrm{tf}_i|. \tag{21}$$

Example 4. For Example 1 and constraint $W_{\max} = 12$, we represent the "ideal" summary by the term frequency vector of the document:

$$p = (0.25, 0.3125, 0.1875, 0.125, 0.125).$$

Introduction of rational variables gives us the following system of inequalities:

$$\begin{cases} 2r_{11} + 2r_{21} + r_{31} + r_{51} \leq 6r \\ r_{12} + 2r_{22} + r_{32} + r_{42} \leq 5r \\ r_{13} + r_{23} + r_{33} + r_{43} + r_{53} \leq 5r, \end{cases}$$

where r is defined according to Eq. (17). The system is completed with equations

$$0 \leq r_{ij} \leq r, \quad \forall i = 1 \dots f, \; j = 1 \dots 3$$

$$\sum_{i=1}^{5} \sum_{j=1}^{3} a_{ij} r_{ij} \leq 12r$$

$$r_i = \sum_{j=1}^{3} r_{ji}, \quad i = 1 \dots 5$$

$$\sum_{i=1}^{5} \sum_{j=1}^{3} r_{ij} = 1.$$

The objective function for Euclidean distance has the form

$$\min \; \sum_{i=1}^{5} (r_i - p_i)^2$$

and for the Manhattan distance the function is

$$\min \; \sum_{i=1}^{5} (r_i^+ + r_i^-),$$

where

$$\begin{aligned} r_1 - 0.25 \;\; &= r_1^+ - r_1^- \\ r_2 - 0.3125 &= r_2^+ - r_2^- \\ r_3 - 0.1875 &= r_3^+ - r_3^- \\ r_4 - 0.125 \;\; &= r_4^+ - r_4^- \\ r_5 - 0.125 \;\; &= r_5^+ - r_5^-. \end{aligned}$$

5.2. *Maximal relevance*

5.2.1. *Maximal weighted term sum functions*

This objective function requires polytope **P** be constructed with the sentence-term matrix A.

Every term T_i, $i = 1 \ldots m$, may participate in sentences $S_1, \ldots, S_n$ and is therefore expressed by variables $x_{1i}, \ldots, x_{ni}$ in inequalities of **P** that define those sentences. We therefore define term variables $t_1, \ldots, t_m$ as sums of their appearances in all the sentences.

$$t_i = \sum_{j=1}^{n} x_{ji}, \quad i = 1 \ldots m \tag{22}$$

The weighted sum of terms then becomes the weighted sum of term variables that we want to maximize. We define the corresponding objective function as

$$\max \sum_{i=1}^{m} w_i t_i, \tag{23}$$

where w_i denotes term weight in the objective function. We explore several options for term weights:

(1) **POS_EQ**: unweighted sum where all terms are equally important

$$w_i = 1.$$

(2) **POS_F**: closeness to the beginning of the document — the term is more important if it first appears in the beginning of a document:

$$w_i = \frac{1}{app(i)}$$

where $app(i)$ is the index of a sentence in the document where the term T_i first appeared;

(3) **POS_L**: closeness to the end of the document — the term is more important if it first appears closer to the end of a document

$$w_i = app(i).$$

(4) **POS_B**: closeness to borders of the document — the term is more important if it first appears close to the beginning or the end of a document

$$w_i = \max \left\{ app(i), \frac{1}{app(i)} \right\}.$$

(5) **TF**: normalized term frequency

$$w_i = \text{tf}(i),$$

where $\text{tf}(i)$ is the normalized term frequency of T_i computed as the number of times the term appears in the document divided by the total number of term appearances of all the terms;

(6) **TF-ISF**: term frequency multiplied by the inverse sentence frequency

$$w_i = \text{tf}(i) * \text{isf}(i),$$

where $\text{tf}(i)$ is the normalized term frequency of T_i and $\text{isf}(i)$ is the inverse sentence frequency of T_i defined as

$$\log \frac{n}{|\{S_j | T_i \in S_j\}|}.$$

Example 5. In Example 1 we have term variables t_i

$$t_1 = x_{11} + x_{12} + x_{13}$$
$$t_2 = x_{21} + x_{22} + x_{23}$$
$$t_3 = x_{31} + x_{32} + x_{33}$$
$$t_4 = x_{41} + x_{42} + x_{43}$$
$$t_5 = x_{51} + x_{52} + x_{53}.$$

The weighted term objective function then has the form

$$\max \ w_1 t_1 + w_2 t_2 + w_3 t_3 + w_4 t_4 + w_5 t_5.$$

For the metric POS_EQ we have objective function:

$$\max \ t_1 + t_2 + t_3 + t_4 + t_5.$$

5.2.2. *Maximal bigram sum*

In the fields of computational linguistics and probability, an n-gram is a contiguous sequence of n items from a given sequence of text or speech. An n-gram could be any combination of text units, letters, or terms/words. An n-gram of size 1 is referred to as a "unigram"; size 2 is called a "bigram". Note that we consider a bigram to be any continuous pair of words or words separated by stopwords appearing in the same sentence.

The objective function, introduced here, maximizes the weighted sum of bigrams, where the weight of a bigram denotes its importance, which, in our version of this function, is computed as the normalized number of its appearances in the document.

In order to represent bigrams, we introduce new bigram variables bg_{ij} for $i, j = 1 \ldots m$, covering all possible term pairs. An appearance of a bigram in sentence S_k is modeled by a $0 - 1$ bounded variable bg_{ij}^k, with c_{ij}^k denoting the number of times this bigram appears in sentence S_k. A bigram is represented by a *normalized sum of its appearances* in various sentences as follows:

$$\begin{cases} 0 \le bg_{ij}^k \le 1, \quad \forall i, j, k \\ bg_{ij} = \sum_{k=1}^{n} c_{ij}^k bg_{ij}^k \Big/ \sum_{k=1}^{n} c_{ij}^k. \end{cases} \tag{24}$$

Additionally, the appearance bg_{ij}^k of a bigram in sentence S_k is tied to terms T_i and T_j composing it, with the help of variables x_{ki} and x_{kj} denoting appearances of these terms in S_k:

$$\begin{cases} bg_{ij}^k \le x_{ki} \\ bg_{ij}^k \le x_{kj} \\ x_{ki} + x_{kj} - bg_{ij}^k \le 1. \end{cases} \tag{25}$$

The constraints in Eq. (25) express the fact that a bigram cannot appear without the terms composing it, and appearance of both terms causes, in turn, the appearance of a bigram. Our objective function is:

$$\max \sum_{i=1}^{m} \sum_{j=1}^{m} count_{ij} bg_{ij}. \tag{26}$$

Example 6. In Example 1 we have 2-grams "fat,cat", "cat,eat", "eat,fat", "fat,meat", "eat,fish", "fish,meat", each appearing at most once in a sentence. Bigram variables are $bi_{12}, bi_{23}, bi_{31}, bi_{15}, bi_{34}, bi_{45}$, and new sentence equalities then have the form

$$S_1 = bi_{12} + bi_{23} + bi_{31} + bi_{15}$$
$$S_2 = bi_{23} + bi_{34} + bi_{12}$$
$$S_3 = bi_{12} + bi_{23} + bi_{34} + bi_{45}.$$

The objective function is defined as

$$\max bi_{12} + bi_{23} + bi_{31} + bi_{15} + bi_{34} + bi_{45}.$$

5.2.3. *Maximal relevance with frequent itemsets*

The objective function proposed here modifies the model so that only the most important terms are taken into account.

Let us view each sentence S_i as a sequence $(T_{i1}, \ldots, T_{in})$ of terms, where the order of terms preserves the original word order of a sentence. Source documents are viewed as a database of sentences. Database size is n. Let $s = (T_{i1}, \ldots, T_{ik})$ be a sequence of terms of size k. *Support* of s in the database is the ratio of sentences containing this sequence, to the database size n.

Given a user-defined support bound $S \in [0, 1]$, a term sequence s is *frequent* if $support(s) \geq S$. Frequent term sequences can be computed by a multitude of existing algorithms, such as Apriori,[20] FreeSpan,[21] or GSP.[22]

In order to modify the general PM described in Section 4.4, we first find all frequent sequences in the documents and store them in set F. Then we sort F first by decreasing sequence size, then by decreasing support, and finally, we keep only top B sequences for a user-defined boundary B.

We modify the general model by representing sentences as sums of their frequent sequences from F. Let $F = \{f_1, \ldots, f_k\}$, sorted by decreasing size and then by decreasing support. A sentence S_i is said to *contain* f_j if it contains it as a term sequence and no part of f_j in S_i is covered by sequences $f_1, \ldots, f_{j-1}$.

Let $count_{ij}$ denote the number of times sentence S_i contains frequent term sequence f_j. Variables f_{ij} denote the appearance of sequence f_j in sentence S_i. We replace the polytope shown in Eq. (7) by:

$$\begin{cases} \sum_{j=1}^{k} count_{ij} f_{ij} \leq \sum_{j=1}^{k} count_{ij}, \quad \forall i = 1 \ldots n \\ 0 \leq f_{ij} \leq 1, \quad \forall i = 1 \ldots n, \ j = 1 \ldots k. \end{cases} \tag{27}$$

We add variables describing the relevance of each sentence by introducing sentence variables:

$$s_i = \frac{\sum_{j=1}^{k} count_{ij} f_{ij}}{\sum_{j=1}^{k} count_{ij}}. \tag{28}$$

Defining a boundary on the length of a summary now requires an additional constraint because frequent sequences do not contain all the terms in the sentences. Summary size is bounded as follows:

$$\sum_{i=1}^{n} length_i s_i \leq MaxWords. \tag{29}$$

Here, $length_i$ is the exact word count of sentence S_i.

Relevance $freqrel_i$ of a sentence S_i is defined as a *cosine similarity* between the vector of terms in S_i covered by members of F, and the entire document. The difference between this approach and the one described in Section 5.2.4 is that only frequent terms are taken into account when computing sentence-document similarity. The resulting objective function maximizes the relevance of chosen sentences while minimizing the redundancy defined in Eq. (42):

$$\max \sum_{i=1}^{n} freqrel_i s_i - \sum_{i=1}^{n} \sum_{j=1}^{n} cosred_{ij} red_{ij}. \tag{30}$$

5.2.4. *Maximal document similarity*

This function defines relevance (rel_i) of a sentence S_i as a *cosine similarity* between the sentence, viewed as a weighted vector of its terms, and the document. Relevance values are completely determined by the text and are not affected by choice of a summary. Every sentence S_i is represented by a sentence variable:

$$s_i = \frac{\sum_{j=1}^{m} a_{ij} x_{ij}}{\sum_{j=1}^{m} a_{ij}}. \tag{31}$$

Formally, variable s_i represents the hyperplane bounding the lower halfspace of $\mathbb{R}^{mn}$ related to sentence S_i and bounding the polytope. Clearly, s_i assumes values in the $[0, 1]$ range, where 0 means that the sentence is completely omitted from the summary and 1 means that the sentence is definitely chosen for the summary. Relevance of all sentences in the summary is described by the expression

$$\sum_{i=1}^{n} rel_i s_i. \tag{32}$$

5.2.5. *Maximal information coverage*

Human readers identify good summaries intuitively, by locating main topics in a document. However, specifying summary quality as a formal function is a difficult task. Here, we propose to use a powerful methodology — TM — for discovering distribution of topics. Given the advantage of knowing the topics of a document, we strive to increase the information coverage, in terms of both *topics* and *lexicon*, in a summary. The maximal relevance is then expressed as a sum of

- maximal coverage of all topics describing a document by selected sentences and
- maximal coverage of all words in a document's lexicon by selected sentences.

In order to express these goals as a linear function, we need to introduce additional constraints to our model.

We propose to combine TM with a maximal coverage principle, enabling us to measure *information* in terms of central non-overlapping *topics* that are extracted from the input documents. At present, there is a multitude of works where topic models have been applied for better summarization of text documents in different domains. The detailed survey of such works can be seen in Section 3 of Chapter 5. We use latent Dirichlet allocation[23] (LDA) as a TM model. The detailed description of the LDA can be found in Chapter 5. A novel graph-based method for ranking and selecting the most salient topics was proposed and utilized for better performance of the optimization process. To the best of our knowledge, our method is the first that uses TM output as input for the summarization model, without requiring internal changes in the topic model itself. Also, LDA application was applied at the sentence level.

Because we are interested in summarizing a single document (a meta-document in a case of multi-document summarization), by selecting sentences covering as many of its topics as possible, we want to explore a topic distribution over sentences in each document.

We assume that documents in the same corpus "talk" about different, and possibly disjointed, topics. Therefore, we applied LDA in a non-standard way, where each document **w** was considered as a corpus and every sentence S was considered as a document. The output of such an application of LDA provides us with an importance score for a sentence in a document.[c] In our experiments, for each document, the average number of sentences is about 50, and the average number of tokens is more than 800, after removing punctuations and stopwords. The LDA model

---

[c]Normally, sentences do not have any particular importance in a standard LDA.

has been quite successful when applied to long documents. In addition, it has recently shown great potential in studying short documents. For example, the LDA model has been applied in studying social media data such as Tweets.[24] We set the number of topics as $K = 5$. This is based on our judgment and experience in studying TM in a variety of *corpora*. In our experiments, we vary the number of topics between 3 and 10. Considering the nature of short documents and results evaluation, setting the number of topics to be 5 for the following studies is a good compromise.

Four different outputs of the LDA algorithm, normalized and treated as probabilities, are relevant to our studies:

(1) Topic versus word dictionary, which gives the word w distributions for each topic P_i
(2) Inferred topic distributions for each document in the studied corpus, namely the probability (θ_i parameter of the LDA model) that a certain sentence S belongs to a topic P_i
(3) Eventual assignment of a sentence S to a topic to which it belongs, with the highest probability, which allows us to separate all sentences of a document into K sets of sentences that describe K topics
(4) Importance of every topic in a document, given as a real non-negative number.

Figure 3 shows sentences of the most significant topic found in the AP880217-100 file from the DUC 2002 corpus.

> Weighing 8 pounds and standing 13 inches tall, Oscar was created by Metro-Goldwyn-Mayer studios art director Cedric Gibbons, who went on to win 11 of the trophies. From 1942 to 1944, the trophy was made of plaster, but winners were later presented with the real thing. It got 14 nominations.

Fig. 3.   Example of a topic.

Topic coverage constraints

In our model, we have k topics denoted as $P_1, \ldots, P_k$. A topic P_i contains sentence S_j with a topic-sentence probability of $prob_{ij}$. Every sentence is eventually assigned to a topic for which the topic-sentence probability is the highest. Therefore, we also view a topic as a set of its sentences. We use two parameters: a probability with which a sentence belongs to a topic, and coverage of a topic, which is represented by a set of sentences, by a sentence. The latter is computed as a cosine similarity between a sentence S_j (treated as a vector of terms) and all sentences assigned to a topic P_i; this similarity is denoted by $tcos_{ij}$.[d] Topic-sentence assignment is expressed with *topic variables* p_i, as follows:

$$p_i = \sum_{j=1}^{n} prob_{ij} tcos_{ij} s_j. \tag{33}$$

To maximize the coverage of topics, we use a weighted sum of topic variables, where the weights are derived from normalized topic importance:

$$topCov = \sum_{i=1}^{k} importance_i p_i. \tag{34}$$

Lexicon coverage constraints

To express coverage of the entire document by every sentence separately, we first define a sentence variable s_i for every sentence S_i, as in Eq. (31). These variables represent hyperplanes bounding the polytope; their values have a range of $[0, 1]$; the higher the value the more likely the sentence is to be chosen for a summary.

We measure coverage of a document by a sentence as a cosine similarity between a vector of terms of a sentence (counting term appearances) and the document vector of terms. Cosine similarity between sentence S_i and the document is denoted by cos_i. These values are computed once from the text, during the preprocessing stage. Therefore, combined coverage of the document by a summary is computed from the following equation:

$$lexCov = \sum_{i=1}^{n} cos_i s_i. \tag{35}$$

Keeping best topics only

Optimization results for quality of sentence coverage, as described above, depend on the number of sentences in the search space, especially for large documents. We tested our approach on smaller search spaces by limiting the number of topics taken into account. However, better summaries could

---

[d]We tested several options for sentence weights in topics and this one provided better results.

not be produced simply by taking into account K best topics based on their importance $\mathbf{w}$ in a document $P(\mathbf{w}|P_i)$ that was produced by the LDA model. We employ a different approach that utilizes the order in which topics are covered by document sentences.

The approach represents a document as a *topic graph* and estimates the importance of the topic as a weighted degree of the topic node in that graph, as follows:

(1) Sentences $S_1, \ldots, S_n$ of a document are assigned to one topic each (for every sentence, a topic is selected, being that topic to which, with the highest probability, the sentence belongs).

(2) Having done that we can view a document as a sequence of topic discussions, $P_{i_1}, \ldots, P_{i_n}$, where each preceding topic P_{i_j} is different from its subsequent $P_{i_{j+1}}$. It is possible that several consecutive sentences $S_i, \ldots, S_j$ belong to the same topic P. In this case, we write the topic P just once in topic sequence $\mathcal{P}$ of a document. The topic sequence of a document is then shown as

$$\mathcal{P} = P_{i_1}, \ldots, P_{i_k}, \quad i_j \neq i_{j+1} \quad \text{for all } j.$$

For example, a document may discuss topic P_{i_1} for several sentences, then switch to a different topic P_{i_2}, and thereafter it may go back to discussing topic P_{i_1}.

(3) In order to measure the importance of each topic, we construct an undirected *topic graph* with edge weights, where topics $P_1, \ldots, P_k$ are represented by the nodes. Initially, it is a clique (there is an edge between each pair of nodes), with weight 0 on the edges. We can then scan the sequence $\mathcal{P}$ and update the edge weights so that whenever discussion in the document changes from P_i to P_j, we add 1 to the weight of the edge (P_i, P_j). We measure the importance of a topic P_i by its weighted degree in the topic graph, which is a sum of the weights of all its edges. Intuitively, if discussion in a document keeps returning to topic P_i, then this topic is important. If, however, topic P_j is spoken of just once, it is less important.

(4) Given importance scores for topics, we update our model by keeping only the best topics. Typically, we concentrate on the three most important (highest scored) topics only. If texts are short, we may choose to keep more topics in order to avoid summaries that are too short. The *topic coverage* constraints are upgraded by assigning 0 to the LP variable p_i if a topic P_i is not selected among the best topics.

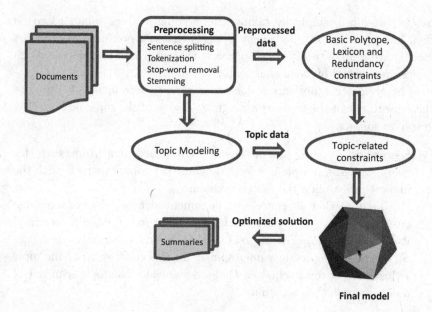

Fig. 4.   Flowchart of our approach, using polytope and topic models.

Formally, Eq. (33) is updated as follows:

$$p_i = \begin{cases} \sum_{j=1}^{n} prob_{ij} tcos_{ij} s_j, & \text{if } P_i \text{ selected} \\ 0, & \text{otherwise.} \end{cases} \tag{36}$$

Figure 4 depicts the adapted pipeline of our approach, using TM.

Relevance Objective Function

Given equations for both topic coverage Eq. (34) and lexicon coverage Eq. (35), the final relevance can be estimated as follows:

$$Rel = topCov + lexCov. \tag{37}$$

5.3. *Minimal redundancy*

For objective functions of this type we use sentence-term matrix A as a basis for polytope construction. For each pair of sentences $S_j, S_k, j < k$, we define auxiliary variables ovl_{jk} that express the similarity between S_j and S_k. Precise similarity computation depends on the measure chosen.

For every term T_i that appears in both sentences the weight $w(a_{ij}, a_{ik})$ of sentence overlap for the term T_i is defined as one of the following:

- it equals $\min(a_{ij}, a_{ik})$,
- it is 1 if the term T_i is present in both sentences S_j and S_k and is 0 otherwise.

5.3.1. *Minimal Jaccard similarity*

Overlap variable ovl_{jk} for the pair of sentences S_j, S_k is defined as sentence intersection divided by sentence union:

$$ovl_{jk} = \frac{S_j \cap S_k}{|S_j \cup S_k|} = \frac{\sum_{i=1}^{m} w(a_{ij}, a_{ik})(x_{ij} + x_{ik})}{\sum_{i=1}^{m} (a_{ij} + a_{ik})} \tag{38}$$

As a result, the overlap of two sentences S_j and S_k is represented by a variable ovl_{jk}, which is a weighted sum of variables x_{ij}:

$$ovl_{jk} = \sum_{i=1}^{m} \omega_i (x_{ij} + x_{ik}), \tag{39}$$

where

$$\omega_i = \frac{\sum_{i=1}^{m} w(a_{ij}, a_{ik})}{\sum_{i=1}^{m} (a_{ij} + a_{ik})}$$

according to Eq. (39). To minimize all pairwise sentence overlaps in the final summary, we define the objective function

$$Red = \sum_{j=1}^{n} \sum_{k=j+1}^{n} ovl_{jk}. \tag{40}$$

Example 7. In Example 1 for overlap weights $\min(a_{ij}, a_{ik})$ sentence overlaps are defined as

$$ovl_{12} = \frac{1}{11}((x_{11} + x_{12}) + 2(x_{21} + x_{22}) + (x_{31} + x_{32}))$$

$$ovl_{23} = \frac{1}{10}((x_{12} + x_{13}) + (x_{22} + x_{23}) + (x_{32} + x_{33}) + (x_{42} + x_{43}))$$

$$ovl_{13} = \frac{1}{11}((x_{11} + x_{13}) + (x_{21} + x_{23}) + (x_{31} + x_{33}) + (x_{51} + x_{53})).$$

5.3.2. *Minimal overlap*

Here, overlap variable ovl_{jk} for the pair of sentences S_j, S_k is defined as sentence intersection normalized by minimal sentence length and substituted to Eq. (40):

$$ovl_{jk} = \frac{S_j \cap S_k}{\min\{|S_j, S_k|\}} = \frac{\sum_{i=1}^{m} w(a_{ij}, a_{ik})(x_{ij} + x_{ik})}{\min\left\{\sum_{i=1}^{m} a_{ij}, \sum_{i=1}^{m} a_{ik}\right\}} \tag{41}$$

Example 8. In Example 1 for overlap weights $\min(a_{ij}, a_{ik})$, sentence overlaps are defined as

$$ovl_{12} = \frac{1}{6}((x_{11} + x_{12}) + 2(x_{21} + x_{22}) + (x_{31} + x_{32}))$$

$$ovl_{23} = \frac{1}{5}((x_{12} + x_{13}) + (x_{22} + x_{23}) + (x_{32} + x_{33}) + (x_{42} + x_{43}))$$

$$ovl_{13} = \frac{1}{6}((x_{11} + x_{13}) + (x_{21} + x_{23}) + (x_{31} + x_{33}) + (x_{51} + x_{53})).$$

5.3.3. *Minimal cosine similarity*

Here we use additional sentence pairwise redundancy variables red_{ij} for every unique pair S_i, S_j of sentences. This type of constraint was first introduced by McDonald in 13. Every one of these variables is $0 - 1$ bounded and achieves a value of 1 only if both sentences are chosen for the summary as follows:

$$\begin{cases} 0 \le red_{ij} \le 1, \, 0 \le i < j \le n \\ red_{ij} \le s_i, \, red_{ij} \le s_j \\ s_i + s_j - red_{ij} \le 1 \end{cases} \tag{42}$$

The numerical redundancy coefficient for sentences S_i and S_j is their cosine similarity as term vectors, computed during preprocessing and denoted by cos_{ij}. Therefore, combined redundancy of all sentence pairs in a summary is computed from equation:

$$Red = \sum_{i=1}^{n} \sum_{j=i+1}^{n} cos_{ij} red_{ij}. \tag{43}$$

5.4. *Maximal relevance minimal redundancy*

We combine two constraints — Maximal Relevance and Minimal Redundancy — and express all requirements for the objective function by optimizing the following expression:

$$\text{max}: Rel - Red \tag{44}$$

where *Rel* and *Red* can be any of the functions from Section 5.2 and Section 5.3, respectively.

6. Extracting the summary

Because the LP method not only finds the minimal distance but also presents evidence of that minimality in the form of a point $x = (x_{ij})$, we use the point's data to find what sentences belong to the chosen summary. For every H_i, we check if point x satisfies it as equality. If an equality holds, x lies on H_i and therefore sentence S_i is contained in the summary. Otherwise, S_i does not belong to the chosen summary. This test is straightforward and takes $O(mn)$ time. In a case of insufficient summary length, the sentences nearest to point x are extracted to a summary in a greedy manner.

Let $x = (x_{ij})$ be the point that optimizes a chosen objective function. To determine which sentence subset it describes, we perform the following:

(1) Determine normalized distance from x to every sentence hyperplane:

$$dist_j = \sum_{i=1}^{m}(a_{ij} - x_{ij}) \bigg/ \sum_{i=1}^{m} a_{ij}$$

Note that x lies in the lower half-spaces of sentence hyperplanes and thus

$$\sum_{i=1}^{m} x_{ij} \le \sum_{i=1}^{m} a_{ij}.$$

The above expression is in fact L_1 distance from x to H_j, and other types of distances can be used.

(2) Sort distances d_j in increasing order and obtain sorted list $d_{j_1}, \ldots, d_{j_m}$.

(3) Add sentences $S_{j_1}, \ldots, S_{j_k}$ for maximal k that satisfies the word count constraint.

The intuition behind our approach is as follows. Because we use fractional linear programming, the point x is an approximation of the best summary and as such it does not describe the sentences exactly. Therefore, we need to compute the distance data in order to find the sentences that are closest (L_1-wise, in our example) to the point x.

7. Compressive approach for summarization

A summary can be generated from any language unit, and not necessarily sentences. For example, it can be compiled from parts of sentences that are most informative and do not contain redundant information. We call such a summary a *compressive summary*, and an approach for generating such summaries a *compressive summarization*. We applied the PM for generating shortened versions of sentences, before their selection to a summary. We shorten sentences by iteratively removing elementary discourse units (EDUs), which were defined as grammatically independent parts of a sentence in Ref. 25. We preserve the important content by optimizing the weighting function that measures cumulative importance and preserve a valid syntax by following the syntactic structure of a sentence. The implemented approach consists of the following steps:

Term weight assignment

We apply the PM (using one of the introduced objective functions) that assigns a non-negative weight to each occurrence of every term in all sentences of the document. We denote it by a *weighting model* of the compressive approach.

EDU selection and ranking

At this stage, we prepare a list of candidate EDUs for removal. First, we generate the list of EDUs from constituency-based syntax trees[26] of sentences. Then, we omit from the list those EDUs that may create a grammatically incorrect sentence if they were to be removed. Finally, we compute weights for all remaining EDU candidates from term weights obtained in the first stage and sort them by increasing weight.

Budgeted sentence compression and selection

We define a summary cost as its length measured in words or characters.[e] We are given a budget for the summary cost, for example, the maximal number of words in a summary. The compressive part of this approach is

---

[e]This depends on user's choice of a summary maximal length.

responsible for selecting EDUs in all sentences such that

(1) the weight-to-cost ratio of the summary is maximal; and
(2) the summary length does not exceed a given budget.

The compressed sentences are expected to be more succinct than the originals, to contain the important content from the originals, and to be grammatically correct. The compressed sentences are selected to a summary by the greedy manner. The overall complexity of this approach is bound by $Nlog(N)$, where N is a number of terms in all sentences.

8. Experiments

8.1. *Experiment setup*

In order to evaluate the quality of our approach, we measured its efficiency in terms of time complexity and accuracy on various datasets, and compared our approach to multiple summarizers. Table 2 enumerates all datasets that were used for our evaluations.

We evaluated our approach, using all introduced objective functions (implemented in Java using lpsolve),[19] for generic extractive summarization on three English corpora from the Document Understanding Conference (DUC) of 2002, 2004, and 2007.[27] DUC 2002 and 2007 each contain a set of single documents, and DUC 2004 contains 50 sets of 10 related documents. In order to demonstrate the multilinguality of our approach, we applied it on three languages — English, Hebrew, and Arabic — using MultiLing datasets.[28] *Corpora* parameters appear in Table 2. Table 3 enumerates all datasets with types of experiments that were performed on them.

8.1.1. *Metrics*

The well-known automatic summarization evaluation package, ROUGE,[29] was used to evaluate the effectiveness of our approach versus multiple summarizers that participated in the generic summarization tasks.

Table 2. *Corpora* statistics.

Corpus	Type	Language	# documents	Doc size (KB)	# summaries	Summary size
DUC'02	SD	English	533	1–20	2–3	100 words
DUC'04	MD (50 × 10)	English	500	20–89	4	100 words
DUC'07	SD	English	23	28–131	4	250 words
MultiLing'13	MD (15 × 10)	multi	150	14–52	3	250 words
MultiLing'15	MD (15 × 10)	multi	150	14–52	3	250 words

Table 3.   *Corpora* assignments.

Corpus	Experiment
DUC'02	Extractive, monolingual, compressive
DUC'04	Extractive, monolingual, compressive
DUC'07	Extractive, monolingual, compressive
MultiLing'13	Extractive, multilingual
MultiLing'15	Extractive, multilingual

Table 4.   Evaluated functions.

Function	Notation	Formula	Section	Misc.
Maximal weighted term sum function	$OBJ_1^{weight\_type}$	(23)	5.2.1	$weight\_type$ is one of $POS\_*, TF, TFISF$
Minimal distance to maximal terms coverage	OBJ_2	(15)	5.1.1	
Minimal distance to term frequency	OBJ_3	(21)	5.1.2	
Maximal bigram sum	OBJ_4	(26)	5.2.2	

8.1.2. *Evaluation of relevance and distance functions*

We conduct the experiments on the datasets from the Document Understanding Conference,[30] overseen and run in the United States by the National Institute of Science and Technology, in 2002 and 2004, and the MultiLing 2013 dataset. The dataset of DUC 2002 contains 59 document collections, each having about 10 documents and two manually created abstracts for lengths of 50, 100, and 200 words. We generated summaries of 200 words and compared their quality to the Gold Standard summaries of the same size. The DUC 2004 contains 45 sets of related documents, 10 in every set. Each set is summarized by 3–4 human experts on average; in total 8 experts participated. The MultiLing dataset is composed of 15 document sets, each of 10 related documents, and three manually created abstracts of 250 words. The same length constraint was applied to the generated summaries. The dataset contains parallel *corpora* in several languages. As shown in Table 4, we used the following objective functions in our experiments:

The recall scores of ROUGE-N for $N \in 1, 2$, ROUGE-L, ROUGE-W-1.2, and ROUGE-$SU4$ are reported. The reported metrics are based on N-gram, longest common subsequence, weighted longest common subsequence, and skip-bigram plus unigram, with a maximum skip-distance of 4, matching between system summaries and reference summaries, respectively. Table 5 shows the results for DUC 2002.

As can be seen from the results, our approach, given the best objective functions, outperforms four systems that participated in the DUC 2002 competition, in terms of most metrics.

Table 6 contains ROUGE scores for DUC 2004. Due to space limitation, we omit 6 rows of scores for human annotators (top rows) and 12 rows of results for participated systems (6 rows from the mid and 6 rows from the bottom part of the table).

As related to the results on the DUC 2004 dataset, our model, given all objective functions, outperforms all 35 systems in terms of three metrics. Position-based weights behave as expected on both *corpora*: closeness to the beginning of a document is the best indication of relevance, while closeness to the end of a document, conversely, is the worst such indicator. It is worth noting that all objective functions performed poorly in terms of ROUGE-2. This performance makes logical sense because all introduced objective functions except the maximal bigram sum function are defined on single terms. Optimizing a simple, non-weighted unigram and bigram coverage proved to be insufficient for describing the optimal summary.

The same metrics are reported in Tables 7–9 for MultiLing 2013 and three languages — English, Hebrew, and Arabic.

As can be seen from the evaluation results on the MultiLing 2013 English, Hebrew, and Arabic data, only 2 to 3 out of 8 systems are outperformed by our system in English, 4 to 5 out of 7 systems in Hebrew, and 5 to 6 out of 8 systems in Arabic. It is worth noting that ID6 and ID61 are baseline systems, where ID61 is a baseline generating summaries from Gold Standard sentences while improving coverage of Gold Standard summaries.

In order to determine the reasons for such inaccurate performance, we performed an additional experiment measuring the coverage of gold standard terms by the terms selected by our model. Results confirm that all selected terms appear in gold standard summaries, and both precision and recall are high. However, because we are performing sentence extraction without preceding compression, our summaries contain "garbage" terms not selected by our algorithm as well, thus decreasing precision and recall. Better performance of our approach for longer summaries can be considered as an additional proof of this inference. An interesting outcome has been observed; our generated summaries cover document terms (in terms of recall) better than do the gold standard summaries. The most simple

Table 5. Evaluation of relevance and distance functions. DUC 2002.

System	Rouge-1	System	Rouge-2	System	Rouge-L	System	Rouge-W-1.2	System	Rouge-SU4
I	0.844	A	0.761	I	0.834	A	0.285	A	0.762
A	0.843	I	0.760	A	0.834	I	0.284	I	0.759
B	0.843	B	0.754	B	0.831	B	0.282	B	0.753
G	0.827	G	0.744	E	0.816	G	0.280	G	0.745
H	0.826	E	0.744	G	0.812	E	0.280	E	0.745
E	0.821	H	0.726	J	0.810	J	0.274	J	0.728
J	0.818	J	0.724	H	0.807	H	0.271	H	0.727
F	0.801	F	0.713	F	0.789	F	0.270	F	0.716
C	0.799	C	0.700	C	0.786	C	0.267	C	0.704
19	0.642	19	0.460	19	0.620	19	0.192	19	0.463
24	0.621	24	0.436	24	0.596	24	0.185	24	0.439
21	0.619	20	0.430	21	0.596	21	0.183	21	0.434
20	0.618	29	0.426	20	0.595	20	0.180	20	0.429
28	0.612	21	0.425	29	0.589	29	0.180	29	0.426
29	0.578	28	0.423	28	0.559	28	0.175	28	0.422
OBJ_1^{TF}	0.572	OBJ_1^{TF}	0.373	$OBJ_1^{POS\_F}$	0.548	25	0.163	25	0.374
OBJ_3	0.570	OBJ_3	0.367	OBJ_1^{TF}	0.546	$OBJ_1^{POS\_F}$	0.162	$OBJ_1^{POS\_F}$	0.368
OBJ_4	0.569	OBJ_4	0.367	OBJ_4	0.543	OBJ_3	0.162	OBJ_3	0.365
$OBJ_1^{POS\_F}$	0.566	$OBJ_1^{POS\_F}$	0.365	OBJ_3	0.542	OBJ_1^{TF}	0.162	OBJ_1^{TF}	0.365
25	0.566	$OBJ_1^{POS\_EQ}$	0.363	25	0.539	OBJ_4	0.161	OBJ_4	0.361
$OBJ_1^{POS\_EQ}$	0.565	25	0.362	$OBJ_1^{POS\_EQ}$	0.539	$OBJ_1^{POS\_EQ}$	0.160	$OBJ_1^{POS\_EQ}$	0.359
OBJ_1^{TF-ISF}	0.561	OBJ_1^{TF-ISF}	0.362	OBJ_1^{TF-ISF}	0.536	$OBJ_1^{POS\_B}$	0.159	$OBJ_1^{POS\_B}$	0.358
OBJ_2	0.559	OBJ_2	0.358	$OBJ_1^{POS\_B}$	0.533	OBJ_1^{TF-ISF}	0.158	OBJ_1^{TF-ISF}	0.357
$OBJ_1^{POS\_B}$	0.552	$OBJ_1^{POS\_B}$	0.354	OBJ_2	0.529	OBJ_2	0.157	OBJ_2	0.353
$OBJ_1^{POS\_L}$	0.549	$OBJ_1^{POS\_L}$	0.353	$OBJ_1^{POS\_L}$	0.526	$OBJ_1^{POS\_L}$	0.156	$OBJ_1^{POS\_L}$	0.351
31	0.549	31	0.339	31	0.519	31	0.153	31	0.349
16	0.517	16	0.313	16	0.488	16	0.145	16	0.328
22	0.449	22	0.271	22	0.427	22	0.128	22	0.282

Table 6. Evaluation of relevance and distance functions. DUC 2004.

System	Rouge-1	System	Rouge-2	System	Rouge-L	System	Rouge-W-1.2	System	Rouge-SU4
H	0.5635	D	0.3292	B	0.5302	H	0.2093	H	0.3634
...		...		...		...		...	
C	0.5379	G	0.3130	C	0.5063	C	0.2002	G	0.3461
$OBJ_1^{TF\text{-}ISF}$	0.4082	65	0.0920	$OBJ_1^{POS\text{-}F}$	0.3483	$OBJ_1^{TF\text{-}ISF}$	0.1177	65	0.1331
$OBJ_1^{POS\text{-}F}$	0.4074	67	0.0906	$OBJ_1^{TF\text{-}ISF}$	0.3476	$OBJ_1^{POS\text{-}F}$	0.1177	67	0.1311
OBJ_1^{TF}	0.4072	66	0.0887	OBJ_1^{TF}	0.3476	OBJ_1^{TF}	0.1173	104	0.1289
OBJ_3	0.4067	104	0.0854	OBJ_3	0.3466	OBJ_3	0.1172	35	0.1282
OBJ_2	0.4062	102	0.0846	OBJ_4	0.3462	$OBJ_1^{POS\text{-}B}$	0.1172	66	0.1281
OBJ_4	0.4058	35	0.0832	$OBJ_1^{POS\text{-}B}$	0.3455	$OBJ_1^{POS\text{-}L}$	0.1172	OBJ_2	0.1276
$OBJ_1^{POS\text{-}B}$	0.4052	124	0.0829	$OBJ_1^{POS\text{-}L}$	0.3455	OBJ_2	0.1171	$OBJ_1^{TF\text{-}ISF}$	0.1275
$OBJ_1^{POS\text{-}L}$	0.4052	81	0.0805	OBJ_2	0.3454	OBJ_4	0.1170	124	0.1273
$OBJ_1^{POS\text{-}EQ}$	0.4042	19	0.0801	$OBJ_1^{POS\text{-}EQ}$	0.3440	$OBJ_1^{POS\text{-}EQ}$	0.1152	$OBJ_1^{POS\text{-}F}$	0.1272
65	0.3822	103	0.0763	35	0.3318	65	0.1152	OBJ_3	0.1271
104	0.3742	120	0.0761	65	0.3306	35	0.1130	$OBJ_1^{POS\text{-}B}$	0.1269
35	0.3738	34	0.0756	34	0.3270	104	0.1127	$OBJ_1^{POS\text{-}L}$	0.1269
19	0.3736	44	0.0756	45	0.3270	34	0.1127	102	0.1269
124	0.3709	93	0.0747	104	0.3254	45	0.1123	OBJ_4	0.1267
67	0.3698	45	0.0738	19	0.3232	67	0.1123	OBJ_1^{TF}	0.1260
102	0.3697	138	0.0734	81	0.3229	81	0.1123	81	0.1250

(Continued)

Table 6. (Continued)

System	Rouge-1	System	Rouge-2	System	Rouge-L	System	Rouge-W-1.2	System	Rouge-SU4
34	0.3695	139	0.0722	124	0.3223	124	0.1121	$OBJ_1^{POS\_EQ}$	0.1244
81	0.3685	121	0.0715	67	0.3217	66	0.1115	19	0.1243
...		57		...		...		...	...
138	0.3462	57	0.0642	118	0.3022	57	0.1044	56	0.1129
57	0.3458	OBJ_1^{TF-ISF}	0.0636	119	0.3009	118	0.1038	103	0.1128
118	0.3440	$OBJ_1^{POS\_B}$	0.0628	57	0.3006	119	0.1036	139	0.1122
117	0.3432	$OBJ_1^{POS\_L}$	0.0628	95	0.2909	95	0.1013	57	0.1110
139	0.3418	OBJ_2	0.0626	2	0.2875	93	0.1002	117	0.1102
119	0.3407	$OBJ_1^{POS\_F}$	0.0623	36	0.2866	103	0.0994	118	0.1098
95	0.3316	OBJ_3	0.0622	93	0.2854	2	0.0993	93	0.1086
103	0.3300	OBJ_4	0.0617	103	0.2829	36	0.0987	121	0.1076
93	0.3291	OBJ_1^{TF}	0.0605	121	0.2760	121	0.0968	95	0.1065
2	0.3242	117	0.0592	138	0.2741	138	0.0965	119	0.1064
36	0.3227	118	0.0581	140	0.2734	140	0.0962	120	0.1063
121	0.3204	$OBJ_1^{POS\_EQ}$	0.0581	139	0.2703	139	0.0951	11	0.1033
120	0.3048	119	0.0580	27	0.2621	120	0.0931	2	0.1031
...		...		...		...		...	...
111	0.2410	111	0.0187	111	0.2205	111	0.0760	111	0.0625

Table 7. Evaluation of relevance and distance functions. Multiling 2013. English.

System	Rouge-1	System	Rouge-2	System	Rouge-L	System	Rouge-W-1.2	System	Rouge-SU4
C	0.767	C	0.630	C	0.755	A	0.236	C	0.628
A	0.765	A	0.626	A	0.752	C	0.236	A	0.624
B	0.755	B	0.610	B	0.742	B	0.233	B	0.610
D	0.732	D	0.592	D	0.721	D	0.226	D	0.586
ID1	0.633	ID21	0.432	ID1	0.615	ID1	0.176	ID1	0.423
ID21	0.632	ID1	0.428	ID21	0.615	ID21	0.176	ID21	0.421
ID11	0.624	ID11	0.421	ID11	0.605	ID11	0.174	ID11	0.413
ID4	0.620	ID4	0.416	ID4	0.601	ID4	0.173	ID4	0.410
ID2	0.617	ID2	0.413	ID2	0.599	ID2	0.172	ID2	0.409
ID61	0.578	OBJ_5	0.369	OBJ_5	0.557	ID61	0.159	ID61	0.371
OBJ_4	0.576	ID61	0.368	ID61	0.554	OBJ_5	0.158	OBJ_5	0.366
$OBJ_1^{POS\text{-}L}$	0.558	ID6	0.364	$OBJ_1^{POS\text{-}B}$	0.542	OBJ_4	0.154	OBJ_4	0.362
$OBJ_1^{POS\text{-}B}$	0.558	OBJ_1^{TF}	0.358	$OBJ_1^{POS\text{-}L}$	0.541	$OBJ_1^{POS\text{-}B}$	0.154	$OBJ_1^{POS\text{-}L}$	0.354
OBJ_1^{TF}	0.557	$OBJ_1^{POS\text{-}L}$	0.357	ID6	0.540	ID6	0.154	OBJ_1^{TF}	0.354
ID6	0.557	$OBJ_1^{POS\text{-}B}$	0.356	OBJ_1^{TF}	0.538	OBJ_1^{TF}	0.153	OBJ_2	0.352
OBJ_2	0.556	OBJ_2	0.354	OBJ_2	0.538	OBJ_2	0.153	$OBJ_1^{POS\text{-}B}$	0.352
$OBJ_1^{POS\text{-}F}$	0.553	$OBJ_1^{POS\text{-}F}$	0.351	$OBJ_1^{POS\text{-}F}$	0.532	$OBJ_1^{POS\text{-}F}$	0.152	$OBJ_1^{POS\text{-}F}$	0.347
$OBJ_1^{POS\text{-}EQ}$	0.545	$OBJ_1^{POS\text{-}EQ}$	0.350	$OBJ_1^{POS\text{-}EQ}$	0.531	$OBJ_1^{POS\text{-}EQ}$	0.152	$OBJ_1^{POS\text{-}EQ}$	0.346
OBJ_1^{TF-ISF}	0.545	OBJ_1^{TF-ISF}	0.349	OBJ_1^{TF-ISF}	0.529	OBJ_1^{TF-ISF}	0.151	OBJ_1^{TF-ISF}	0.345
OBJ_3	0.525	OBJ_3	0.322	OBJ_3	0.504	OBJ_3	0.144	OBJ_3	0.322
ID3	0.503	ID3	0.310	ID3	0.481	ID3	0.138	ID3	0.313

Table 8. Evaluation of relevance and distance functions. Multiling 2013. Hebrew.

System	Rouge-1	System	Rouge-2	System	Rouge-L	System	Rouge-W-1.2	System	Rouge-SU4
A	0.689	A	0.598	A	0.682	A	0.218	A	0.579
C	0.672	C	0.585	C	0.666	C	0.216	C	0.565
B	0.647	B	0.562	B	0.642	B	0.210	B	0.544
ID61	0.520	ID2	0.393	ID61	0.511	ID61	0.151	ID61	0.361
ID2	0.519	ID61	0.388	ID2	0.511	ID2	0.150	ID2	0.357
OBJ_4	0.505	ID4	0.380	ID4	0.495	ID4	0.147	ID4	0.343
ID4	0.493	OBJ_5	0.376	OBJ_5	0.488	OBJ_5	0.145	OBJ_5	0.342
OBJ_1^{TF-ISF}	0.481	OBJ_1^{TF-ISF}	0.372	OBJ_1^{TF-ISF}	0.475	OBJ_1^{TF-ISF}	0.142	OBJ_1^{TF-ISF}	0.334
$OBJ_1^{POS\_EQ}$	0.479	$OBJ_1^{POS\_EQ}$	0.369	$OBJ_1^{POS\_EQ}$	0.474	$OBJ_1^{POS\_EQ}$	0.142	$OBJ_1^{POS\_EQ}$	0.332
OBJ_1^{TF}	0.479	OBJ_1^{TF}	0.358	OBJ_1^{TF}	0.471	ID6	0.140	ID6	0.327
ID6	0.475	ID6	0.357	ID6	0.468	OBJ_1^{TF}	0.139	OBJ_1^{TF}	0.323
$OBJ_1^{POS\_L}$	0.470	$OBJ_1^{POS\_L}$	0.350	$OBJ_1^{POS\_L}$	0.462	$OBJ_1^{POS\_L}$	0.138	$OBJ_1^{POS\_L}$	0.315
$OBJ_1^{POS\_B}$	0.461	$OBJ_1^{POS\_B}$	0.338	$OBJ_1^{POS\_B}$	0.454	$OBJ_1^{POS\_B}$	0.134	$OBJ_1^{POS\_B}$	0.306
$OBJ_1^{POS\_F}$	0.457	$OBJ_1^{POS\_F}$	0.338	$OBJ_1^{POS\_F}$	0.450	$OBJ_1^{POS\_F}$	0.133	$OBJ_1^{POS\_F}$	0.304
OBJ_3	0.447	OBJ_3	0.329	OBJ_3	0.439	OBJ_2	0.131	OBJ_2	0.296
OBJ_2	0.442	OBJ_2	0.324	OBJ_2	0.436	OBJ_3	0.130	OBJ_3	0.294
ID11	0.396	ID11	0.269	ID11	0.381	ID11	0.112	ID11	0.246
ID1	0.370	ID21	0.244	ID1	0.354	ID21	0.103	ID21	0.225
ID21	0.369	ID1	0.243	ID21	0.351	ID1	0.103	ID1	0.224

Table 9. Evaluation of relevance and distance functions. Multiling 2013. Arabic.

System	Rouge-1	System	Rouge-2	System	Rouge-L	System	Rouge-W-1.2	System	Rouge-SU4
A	0.830	A	0.689	A	0.800	A	0.202	A	0.716
B	0.820	B	0.665	B	0.786	B	0.198	B	0.698
ID61	0.774	ID61	0.558	ID61	0.729	ID61	0.161	ID61	0.601
ID4	0.772	ID4	0.550	ID4	0.726	ID4	0.161	ID4	0.596
ID2	0.743	$OBJ_1^{POS\text{-}F}$	0.512	ID2	0.696	ID2	0.150	ID2	0.557
$OBJ_1^{POS\text{-}F}$	0.740	ID2	0.499	$OBJ_1^{POS\text{-}F}$	0.694	$OBJ_1^{POS\text{-}F}$	0.149	$OBJ_1^{POS\text{-}F}$	0.551
OBJ_4	0.736	OBJ_4	0.496	OBJ_4	0.694	OBJ_4	0.148	OBJ_4	0.549
$OBJ_1^{TF\text{-}ISF}$	0.736	$OBJ_1^{POS\text{-}EQ}$	0.494	$OBJ_1^{POS\text{-}EQ}$	0.692	ID6	0.146	ID6	0.549
$OBJ_1^{POS\text{-}EQ}$	0.732	$OBJ_1^{TF\text{-}ISF}$	0.486	$OBJ_1^{TF\text{-}ISF}$	0.691	$OBJ_1^{POS\text{-}EQ}$	0.145	$OBJ_1^{POS\text{-}EQ}$	0.541
ID6	0.730	ID6	0.485	ID6	0.690	$OBJ_1^{TF\text{-}ISF}$	0.145	$OBJ_1^{TF\text{-}ISF}$	0.540
$OBJ_1^{POS\text{-}L}$	0.730	$OBJ_1^{POS\text{-}L}$	0.484	$OBJ_1^{POS\text{-}L}$	0.684	$OBJ_1^{POS\text{-}L}$	0.144	$OBJ_1^{POS\text{-}L}$	0.539
OBJ_2	0.729	OBJ_2	0.483	OBJ_2	0.683	ID11	0.144	ID11	0.536
$OBJ_1^{POS\text{-}B}$	0.727	$OBJ_1^{POS\text{-}B}$	0.483	$OBJ_1^{POS\text{-}B}$	0.682	OBJ_2	0.142	OBJ_2	0.535
ID11	0.714	OBJ_1^{TF}	0.480	OBJ_1^{TF}	0.659	$OBJ_1^{POS\text{-}B}$	0.136	$OBJ_1^{POS\text{-}B}$	0.534
ID1	0.710	ID11	0.479	ID11	0.658	ID1	0.134	ID1	0.533
OBJ_1^{TF}	0.704	ID1	0.467	ID1	0.654	ID21	0.133	ID21	0.520
OBJ_3	0.704	OBJ_3	0.460	OBJ_3	0.649	OBJ_3	0.133	OBJ_3	0.517
ID21	0.700	ID21	0.454	ID21	0.643	OBJ_1^{TF}	0.130	OBJ_1^{TF}	0.511
ID3	0.691	ID3	0.449	ID3	0.638	ID3	0.127	ID3	0.504

and intuitive explanation for that is the difference between abstracts (gold standard) and extracts (generated).

8.1.3. *Taking redundancy into consideration*

Here we present the evaluation results for the maximal-relevance-minimum-redundancy function, as a result of taking part in a MultiLing 2015 competition. We report here the result for the two best combinations of introduced relevance and redundancy functions, where relevance is the maximal relevance with frequent itemsets (see Section 5.2.3) and the maximal document similarity (using cosine similarity, see Section 5.2.4); and redundancy is the minimal cosine similarity between selected sentences (see Section 5.3.3). An additional goal of this evaluation was to test the summarizer's multilingual capabilities. Therefore, we evaluated it on three languages — English, Hebrew, and Arabic.

Tables 10–12 summarize the comparative results for our summarizers (denoted in the following tables by **PolyMRFI** and **PolyMDS** for maximal relevance with frequent itemsets and maximal document similarity as relevance functions, respectively) and other participated systems in MSS (single-document summarization) task of MultiLing 2015 competition,[31] in terms of ROUGE-1. We show the results of our best objective function for each language. The results are sorted by f-measure. Also, our tables contain systems' ranks, according to their precision (P-rank), recall (R-rank), and f-measure (F-rank).

As can be seen, coverage of frequent sequences performed best for English, and maximal document similarity using meaningful words performed best for Hebrew and Arabic.

Table 10.   Evaluation of maximal relevance minimum redundancy function. MSS task. ROUGE-1. English.

System	Precision	Recall	F-measure	P-rank	R-rank	F-rank
Oracles	0.601	0.619	0.610	1	1	1
MUSE	0.488	0.500	0.494	3	2	2
CCS	0.477	0.495	0.485	6	3	4
PolyMRFI	**0.475**	**0.494**	**0.484**	**8**	**5**	**5**
EXB	0.467	0.495	0.480	13	4	9
NTNU	0.470	0.456	0.462	12	17	13
LCS-IESI	0.461	0.456	0.458	15	18	15
UA-DLSI	0.457	0.456	0.456	18	16	17
Lead	0.425	0.434	0.429	24	20	20

Table 11. Evaluation of maximal relevance minimum redundancy function. MSS task. ROUGE-1. Hebrew.

System	Precision	Recall	F-measure	P-rank	R-rank	F-rank
CCS	0.202	0.213	0.207	1	1	1
MUSE	0.196	0.210	0.203	2	2	2
PolyMDS	**0.189**	**0.203**	**0.196**	**4**	**6**	**4**
EXB	0.186	0.205	0.195	5	4	5
Oracles	0.182	0.204	0.192	6	5	6
Lead	0.168	0.178	0.173	13	12	12
LCS-IESI	0.181	0.170	0.172	7	14	13

Table 12. Evaluation of maximal relevance minimum redundancy function. MSS task. ROUGE-1. Arabic.

System	Precision	Recall	F-measure	P-rank	R-rank	F-rank
Oracles	0.630	0.658	0.644	1	1	1
MUSE	0.562	0.569	0.565	2	4	2
CCS	0.554	0.571	0.562	4	3	3
EXB	0.546	0.571	0.558	8	2	7
PolyMDS	**0.545**	**0.560**	**0.552**	**10**	**9**	**9**
LCS-IESI	0.540	0.527	0.531	11	13	12
Lead	0.524	0.535	0.529	13	12	13

The results for the MMS (multi-document summarization) task are summarized as follows. **English:** 4th place out of 9 participants. **Hebrew:** 3rd place out of 9 participants; and the highest recall score. **Arabic:** 4th place out of 9 participants and the highest recall score. As can be seen, the best performance for our summarizer has been achieved on the dataset of Hebrew documents. For example, only the top-line Oracles and the supervised MUSE summarizers outperformed our system in MSS task. Both our summarizers also outperformed the Gillick[9] model using ILP.

8.1.4. *Taking topic knowledge into consideration*

Here we present the results of our summarizer using the objective function based on TM. We evaluated our model under different settings, namely:

(1) **Lexicon Coverage** (denoted by *LexCov*): Original model, as described in Section 4.4, with only *lexicon coverage* Eq. (35) and *redundancy* (Eq. (42)) components in the objective function (Eq. (44)), (without the *topic coverage* (Eq. (34)) component). The resultant model can be considered as an approximation of McDonald's[13] model,

because it contains exactly the same constraints as in Ref. 13, except those required by ILP.[f]

(2) **Topic Coverage** (denoted by $TopCov$): Original model, as described in Section 4.4, with only the *topic coverage* (Eq. (34)) component in the objective function (Eq. (44)).

(3) **Information Coverage with Unigrams** (denoted by $InfCov$): Original model, optimizing the objective function (Eq. (44)), using *single terms* in *lexicon coverage* constraints, and considering all sentences with positive assignment probability for each topic in topic coverage constraints.

(4) **Information Coverage with Unigrams and Bigrams** (denoted by $InfCovB$): As in (3), enhanced by using *bigrams* in addition to single terms in *lexicon coverage* constraints.

(5) **Bounded Topic Coverage** (denoted by $BTopCov$): As in (2), but considering only the 10 *most salient sentences* for each topic in *topic coverage* constraints, according to their eventual assignment to a topic (see Section 5.2.5).

(6) **Bounded Information Coverage with Unigrams** (denoted by $BInfCov$): As in (3), but considering only the 10 *most salient sentences* for each topic in *topic coverage* constraints.

(7) **Bounded Information Coverage with Unigrams and Bigrams** (denoted by $BInfCovB$): As in (6), enhanced by using *bigrams* in addition to single terms in *lexicon* constraints.

Only the three best topics were considered in the experiment, according to the ranking method described in Section 5.2.5. We consider three topics because intuitively it is difficult for humans to follow more than three themes. Table 13 contains the comparative results.

As can be seen, our approach, combining both topic and lexicon knowledge, outperforms both the McDonald's ($LexCov$) and the $TopCov$ summarizers with pure lexicon and topic coverage, respectively. Namely, Bounded Information Coverage outperforms other methods in the DUC 2002 *corpus*, and Information Coverage with Bigrams has the best performance in the DUC 2004 and DUC 2007 *corpora*. Because DUC 2004 and DUC 2007 are comprised of much longer documents than DUC 2002, their coverage by bigrams improves performance of the coverage with unigrams. The

---

[f]McDonald[13] solves the maximal coverage model by ILP. Because we solve the optimization problem in LP over rationals, our model contains fewer constraints than the ILP solution requires.

Table 13.   Evaluation of TM-based objective functions. ROUGE-1.

System	DUC-2002			DUC-2004			DUC-2007		
	R	P	F	R	P	F	R	P	F
LexCov	0.4488	0.4455	0.4471	0.3206	0.3197	0.3201	0.3435	0.3387	0.3411
TopCov	0.4282	0.4251	0.4266	0.3034	0.3025	0.3029	0.3613	0.3561	0.3586
InfCov	0.4565	0.4531	0.4548	0.3258	0.3249	0.3253	0.3533	0.3483	0.3507
InfCovB	0.4468	0.4435	0.4451	**0.3361**	**0.3351**	**0.3356**	**0.3775**	**0.3718**	**0.3745**
BTopCov	0.4565	0.4532	0.4548	0.2928	0.2919	0.2924	0.3439	0.3389	0.3413
BInfCov	**0.4575**	**0.4542**	**0.4559**	0.3086	0.3079	0.3083	0.3501	0.3451	0.3475
BInfCovB	0.4566	0.4533	0.4549	0.3268	0.3260	0.3264	0.3559	0.3507	0.3532

superiority of our best approach over the *LexCov* summarizer is statistically significant in all *corpora*. As a conclusion, our hypothesis can be accepted for the unsupevised approach as well. It is worth noting that the pure topic coverage approach of *TopCov* does not perform well when compared to *LexCov*, because the issue of sentence redundancy is not handled at all (two sentences from different topics may still be very similar sentences).

8.1.5. *Evaluation of compressive summarization*

The primary objective of this part of experiments was to see whether compression improves performance of extractive summarization. Therefore, three state-of-the-art unsupervised extractive approaches were taken as baselines and used as weighting models for our approach (see the first step of the approach described in Section 7). Table 14 gives the list of evaluated approaches and their notations. The first three rows present baseline extractive approaches. All extractive approaches are assigned odd System ID numbers. The last three rows present compressive summarization approaches, where the same compression procedure, described in Section 7, was applied to generated weights. All these approaches are assigned even System ID numbers.

We used the DUC 2002 corpus, the DUC 2004 corpus, and the DUC 2007 corpus[30] for evaluations. For multi-document corpora, we merged document sets into single meta-documents by appending texts one to another.

All summarizers were evaluated by ROUGE-1 and ROUGE-2 metrics,[g] namely recall (R), precision (P), and F-measure (F).[32] The goal of this

Table 14. Evaluated extractive and compressive summarization methods.

Notation	Description	System ID
$E_{Gillick\_Favre}$	ILP concept-based extraction method of Gillick and Favre[9]	ID1
$E_{McDonald}$	ILP extraction method of McDonald[13]	ID3
E_{Poly}	Polytope extraction method with POS_F objective function	ID5
$WC_{Gillick\_Favre}$	Weighted Compression with weights generated by $E_{Gillick\_Favre}$	ID2
$WC_{McDonald}$	Weighted Compression with weights generated by $E_{McDonald}$	ID4
WC_{Poly}	Weighted Compression with weights generated by E_{Poly}	ID6

---

[g]The following command line has been used: −a −l <word count> −n 1 −2 4 −u.

Table 15. Evaluation of compressive summarization. ROUGE-1 and ROUGE-2. DUC 2002.

System	R-1 R	R-1 P	R-1 F	R-2 R	R-2 P	R-2 F
ID1	0.401	0.407	0.401	0.160	0.162	0.160
ID2	**0.410***	0.413	0.409	0.166	0.166	0.165
ID3	0.393	0.407	0.396	0.156	0.159	0.156
ID4	**0.401***	0.403	0.399	0.158	0.158	0.157
ID5	0.448	0.453	0.447	0.213	0.214	0.212
ID6	0.450	0.450	0.447	0.211	0.210	0.210

Table 16. Evaluation of compressive summarization. ROUGE-1 and ROUGE-2. DUC 2004.

System	R-1 R	R-1 P	R-1 F	R-2 R	R-2 P	R-2 F
ID1	0.291	0.292	0.292	0.051	0.051	0.051
ID2	0.296	0.297	0.296	0.051	0.051	0.051
ID3	0.285	0.285	0.285	0.045	0.045	0.045
ID4	0.285	0.286	0.285	0.047	0.047	0.047
ID5	0.282	0.281	0.282	0.046	0.046	0.046
ID6	0.283	0.283	0.283	0.047	0.047	0.047

Table 17. Evaluation of compressive summarization. ROUGE-1 and ROUGE-2. DUC 2007.

System	R-1 R	R-1 P	R-1 F	R-2 R	R-2 P	R-2 F
ID1	0.339	0.363	0.347	0.067	0.074	0.070
ID2	0.342	0.362	0.349	0.068	0.074	0.070
ID3	0.267	0.367	0.300	0.052	0.070	0.058
ID4	**0.282***	0.359	0.309	0.054	0.068	0.059
ID5	0.321	0.355	0.331	0.063	0.069	0.064
ID6	0.319	0.354	0.329	0.062	0.069	0.064

evaluation was to measure the quality of summaries in terms of content. ROUGE does this by measuring similarity between the generated summaries and the gold standard provided by human experts.

Tables 15, 16, and 17 contain results for all summarizers on DUC 2002, DUC 2004, and DUC 2007 datasets, respectively. Statistical testing (using a paired T-test) showed that there is a significant improvement in ROUGE-1 recall in ID1 versus ID2, and ID3 versus ID4 in the DUC 2002 *corpus*, and ID3 versus ID4 in the DUC 2007 *corpus* (denoted by bold font and *). There were also slight improvements in most cases when compression was applied but they are not significant. In general, we can conclude that compression improves summarization performance in terms of coverage.

9. Conclusion and future work

In this chapter we present an LP model for the problem of extractive summarization. We introduce the PM as a text representation model. The PM represents a document as a sentence-term matrix whose entries contain term count values, and then views this matrix as a set of intersecting hyperplanes. Every possible summary of a document is represented as an intersection of two or more hyperplanes, and one additional constraint is used to limit the number of terms used in a summary. We consider the summary to be the best if the optimal (maximal or minimal) value of the objective function is preserved during summarization; we also introduce multiple objective functions.

The LP problem can be solved in polynomial time.[17,18,33] Numerous packages and applications are available, such as Refs. 19 and 34. The theoretical time complexity of our approach is polynomial (quadratic, being more precise). Practically speaking, the running time for summarizing a single document set takes but a few seconds.

The results of experiments conducted on multiple datasets show that:

- our method performs quite well in terms of coverage (measured by ROUGE metrics);
- our method has polynomial time complexity, is unsupervised and therefore, provides an excellent platform for efficient summarization;
- our method is language-independent and applicable to different languages;
- additional input information, such as topic distributions, improves the performance of our method;
- the method is applicable to parts of sentences and therefore, can be extended to compressive summarization;

The general problem of automated summarization is the lack of a single objective function (so far) that can describe the best summary. Many authors have tried to express the optimum by combining multiple objectives into a single weighted function.[35-38] In the future, we intend to find an optimal linear combination of the proposed objective functions. We intend to develop more objective functions, using additional external sources such as word vectors and parsing features. In addition, we plan to extend our model to query-based summarization and apply our text representation model to such text mining tasks as text clustering and text categorization.

References

1. G. Salton, C. Yang, and A. Wong, A vector-space model for information retrieval, *Communications of the ACM*, **18**(11), 613–620 (1975).
2. M. Hassel and J. Sjobergh, Towards holistic summarization: Selecting summaries, not sentences. In eds. N. Calzolari, K. Choukri, A. Gangemi, B. Maegaard, J. Mariani, J. Odijk, and D. Tapias, In *Proceedings of LREC — International Conference on Language Resources and Evaluation*, Genoa, Italy, LREC (2006).
3. A. Aker, T. Cohn, and R. Gaizauskas, Multi-document summarization using A* search and discriminative training. In eds. H. Li and L. Marquez, *Proceedings of the 2010 Conference on Empirical Methods in Natural Language Processing (EMNLP 2010)*, Massachusetts, USA, pp. 482–491, ACL (2010).
4. Y. Ouyang, W. Li, S. Li, and Q. Lu, Applying regression models to query-focused multi-document summarization, *Information Processing and Management*. **47**, 227–237 (March 2011).
5. E. Alfonseca and P. Rodriguez, Generating extracts with genetic algorithms. In ed. F. Sebastiani, *Proceedings of the 2003 European Conference on Information Retrieval (ECIR 2003)*, Pisa, Italy, pp. 511–519, Springer (2003).
6. F. J. Kallel, M. Jaoua, L. B. Hadrich, and A. B. Hamadou, Summarization at LARIS Laboratory. In *Proceedings of the Document Understanding Conference*, Gaithersburg, Maryland, USA, ACL (2004).
7. D. Liu, Y. Wang, C. Liu, and Z. Wang, Multiple Documents Summarization Based on Genetic Algorithm. In *Fuzzy Systems and Knowledge Discovery*, vol. 4223, *Lecture Notes in Computer Science*, pp. 355–364. Springer (2006).
8. H. Takamura and M. Okumura, Text summarization model based on maximum coverage problem and its variant. In eds. A. Lascarides, C. Gardent, and J. Nivre, *Proceedings of the 12th Conference of the European Chapter of the Association for Computational Linguistics (EACL 2009)*, Athens, Greece, pp. 781–789, ACL (2009).
9. D. Gillick and B. Favre, A Scalable Global Model for Summarization. In eds. J. Clarke and S. Riedel, *Proceedings of the NAACL HLT Workshop on Integer Linear Programming for Natural Language Processing*, Singapore, pp. 10–18, ACL (2009).
10. S. Khuller, A. Moss, and J. S. Naor, The budgeted maximum coverage problem, *Information Precessing Letters*, **70**(1), 39–45 (1999).
11. E. Filatova, Event-based extractive summarization. In eds. M-F. Moens and S. Szpakowicz, *Proceedings of ACL Workshop on Summarization*, Boulder, Colorado, USA, pp. 104–111, ACL (2004).

12. X. Wan, Using only cross-document relationships for both generic and topic-focused multi-document summarizations, *Information Retrieval*, **11**, 25–49 (2008).
13. R. McDonald, A study of global inference algorithms in multi-document summarization. In eds. G. Amati, C. Carpineto, and G. Romano, *Proceedings of the 29th European Conference on IR Research (ECIR 2007)*, Rome, Italy, pp. 557–564, Springer-Verlag (2007).
14. K. Woodsend and M. Lapata, Automatic Generation of Story Highlights. In eds. J. Hajič, S. Carberry, S. Clark, and J. Nivre, *Proceedings of the 48th Annual Meeting of the Association for Computational Linguistics (ACL 2010)*, Uppsala, Sweden, pp. 565–574, ACL (2010).
15. Y. M. Hitoshi Nishikawa, Takaaki Hasegawa, and G. Kikui, Opinion Summarization with Integer Linear Programming Formulation for Sentence Extraction and Ordering. In eds. C-R. Huang and D. Jurafsky, *Coling 2010: Poster Volume*, Beijing, China, pp. 910–918, ACL (2010).
16. T. Makino, H. Takamura, and M. Okumura, Balanced coverage of aspects for text summarization. In *Proceedings of Text Analysis Conference (TAC 2011)*, Gaithersburg, Maryland, USA, NIST (2011).
17. N. Karmarkar, New polynomial-time algorithm for linear programming, *Combinatorica*, **4**, 373–395 (1984).
18. L. G. Khachiyan, Rounding of polytopes in the real number model of computation, *Mathematics of Operations Research*, **21**, 307–320 (1996).
19. M. Berkelaar, lp-solve free software (1999). Available at: http://lpsolve.sourceforge.net/5.5/.
20. R. Agrawal and R. Srikant, Fast algorithms for mining association rules. In eds. J. Bocca, M. Jarke, and C. Zaniolo, *Proceedings of the 20th International Conference on Very Large Data Bases (VLDB)*, Santiago, Chile, vol. 1215, pp. 487–499, VLDB (1994).
21. J. Han, J. Pei, B. Mortazavi-Asl, Q. Chen, U. Dayal, and M.-C. Hsu, Freespan: frequent pattern-projected sequential pattern mining. In eds. R. Ramakrishnan, S. J. Stolfo, R. J. Bayardo, and I. Parsa, *Proceedings of the 6th ACM Special Interest Group on Knowledge Discovery and Data Mining (SIGKDD) International Conference on Knowledge Discovery and Data Mining*, Boston, MA, USA, pp. 355–359, ACM (2000).
22. M. J. Zaki, Spade: An efficient algorithm for mining frequent sequences, *Machine Learning*, **42**(1–2), 31–60 (2001).
23. D. M. Blei, A. Y. Ng, and M. I. Jordan, Latent dirichlet allocation, *Journal of Machine Learning Research*, **3**, 993–1022 (2003).
24. Liangjie Hong and Brain D. Davison, Empirical study of topic modeling in twitter. In eds. B. Rao, B. Krishnapuram, A. Tomkins, and Q. Yang, *Proceedings of 1st Workshop on Social Media Analytics (SOMA 2010)*, Washington, DC, USA, pp. 80–88, KDD (2010).
25. D. Marcu, From discourse structures to text summaries. In eds. P. R. Cohen and W. Wahlster, *Proceedings of the Association for Computational Linguistics*, Madrid, Spain, vol. 97, p. 82–88, ACL (1997).

26. C. D. Manning and H. Schütze, *Foundations of Statistical Natural Language Processing*, vol. 999. MIT Press, Cambridge, MA (1999).
27. DUC. Document Understanding Conference (2002–2007). Available at: http://duc.nist.gov.
28. G. Giannakopoulos, Datasets for MultiLing 2015 tasks (2015). Available at: http://multiling.iit.demokritos.gr/pages/view/1571/datasets.
29. C.-Y. Lin, Rouge: A package for automatic evaluation of summaries. In eds. D. Scott, W. Daelemans, and M. A. Walker, *Proceedings of the Workshop on Text Summarization Branches Out (WAS 2004)*, Barcelona, Spain, pp. 25–26, ACL (2004).
30. NIST. Document understanding conferences (2001–2007). Available at: http://duc.nist.gov.
31. G. Giannakopoulos, J. Kubina, J. M. Conroy, J. Steinberger, B. Favre, M. Kabadjov, U. Kruschwitz, and M. Poesio, Multiling 2015: Multilingual summarization of single and multi-documents, on-line fora, and call-center conversations. In *Proceedings of the Special Interest Group on Discourse and Dialogue (SIGDIAL) 2015 Conference*, Prague, Czech Republic, pp. 270–274, ACL (2015).
32. C.-Y. Lin, Rouge: A package for automatic evaluation of summaries. In eds. D. Scott, W. Daelemans, and M. A. Walker. In *Proceedings of the Workshop on Text Summarization Branches Out (WAS 2004)*, Barcelona, Spain, pp. 25–26, ACL (2004).
33. L. G. Khachiyan and M. J. Todd, On the complexity of approximating the maximal inscribed ellipsoid for a polytope, *Mathematical Programming*, **61**, 137–159 (1993).
34. A. O. Makhorin, GNU Linear Programming Kit (2000). Available at: http://www.gnu.org/software/glpk/.
35. H. P. Edmundson, New methods in automatic extracting, *Journal of the Association for Computing Machinery*, **16**(2), 264–285 (1969).
36. D. Radev, S. Blair-Goldensohn, and Z. Zhang, Experiments in single and multidocument summarization using MEAD. In *First Document Understanding Conference*, Gaithersburg, MD, USA, NIST (2001).
37. H. Saggion, K. Bontcheva, and H. Cunningham. Robust generic and query-based summarisation. In *EACL '03: Proceedings of the 10th Conference on European Chapter of the Association for Computational Linguistics*, pp. 235–238, ACL (2003).
38. M. Litvak, M. Last, and M. Friedman, A new approach to improving multilingual summarization using a Genetic Algorithm. In eds. Jan Hajič, S. Carberry, S. Clark, and J. Nivre, *Proceedings of the 48th Annual Meeting of the Association for Computational Linguistics (ACL 2010)*, Uppsala, Sweden, pp. 927–936, ACL (2010).

Chapter 3

MDL Approach for Unsupervised Multilingual Document Summarization

Natalia Vanetik* and Marina Litvak†

*Shamoon College of Engineering,
Software Engineering Department,
Byalik 56, Beer Sheva 84100*
*natalyav@sce.ac.il
†marinal@sce.ac.il

In this chapter, we describe an approach for extractive summarization based on the minimum description length (MDL) principle and relying on the Krimp dataset compression algorithm.[1] We represent text as a transactional dataset, with sentences as transactions and normalized words as items; then describing the dataset by frequent itemsets of different types that provide the best compressed representation. The summary is compiled from sentences that best describe the document. The problem of extractive summarization is therefore reduced to the maximal coverage problem, following the assumption that a summary that best describes the original text should cover most of the itemsets describing the document. We test this approach on generic summarization tasks in English and Chinese, and on a query-based summarization (QS) task for English.

1. Introduction

Many unsupervised approaches for extractive text summarization follow the maximal coverage principle,[2,3] where the extract that maximally covers the information contained in the source text is selected. Because the exhaustive solution demands an exponential number of tests, approximation techniques are utilized. These techniques include a greedy approach or a global optimization of a target function. The target function that defines information coverage must be specified and maximized. The simplest one is a greedy approach, where sentences are ranked by some heuristic

81

property and then selected one by one, starting from the sentence with the highest rank, until the maximal length is reached. A global optimization takes into account all possible selections and does not rank sentences explicitly. In both approaches, it is quite common to measure text informativeness by the frequency of its components — words, phrases, concepts, and so on. In addition to term frequency, some works reduced the well-known data mining technique for calculating frequent itemsets, redirecting its focus from transactional data to the text summarization task. For example, ItemSum[4] represents sentences in a transactional data format and measures their relevancy by coverage of frequent items. SciSumm[5] uses frequent-term-based clustering for summarization of scientific papers. Opinion summarizer[6] extracts a frequent opinion feature set that was taken from review texts using the multiword approach, essentially an ordered sequence of words. The algorithm introduced in Ref. 7 extracts fuzzy association rules between weighted key phrases in collections of text documents. None of these works follow the MDL principle.

A different approach, which received much less attention, is based on the MDL principle, which defines the best summary as the one that leads to the *best compression* of the text by providing its *shortest and most concise description.*

The MDL principle is widely useful in compression techniques of non-textual data, such as the summarization of query results for online analytical processing applications.[8,9] However, only a few works that address text summarization using MDL can be found in the literature. The authors of Ref. 10 used K-means clustering extended by the MDL principle for finding diverse topics in summarized text. Nomoto, in Ref. 11, also extended the C4.5 classifier with MDL for learning rhetorical relations. In Ref. 12 the problem of micro-review summarization is formulated within the MDL framework; there the authors view the tips as being encoded by snippets, and seek to find a collection of snippets that produce the encoding with the minimum number of bits.

Nevertheless, as recent research shows, frequency analysis of a document vocabulary is not enough to express its informativeness. Extracting central topics of a document or a document set by topic modeling (TM) can guide sentence selection from the perspective of document-level knowledge, instead of analyzing isolated sentences. Most works in TM use latent Dirichlet allocation (LDA) to generate topic words. Hierarchical LDA (hLDA)[13] is an extension of LDA that can model a tree of topics, instead of a flat topic structure. hLDA is an unsupervised method in which topic numbers could grow automatically with the data set. At present, there are many works where topic models have been applied for better summarization of text documents.[14–16]

Query-based summarization is directed toward generating a summary that is most relevant to a given query. It can relate to a single document or to a multi-document input. Multiple works about query-based summarization have been published in recent years. Reference 17 presented BayeSum, a model for sentence extraction in QS. BayeSum is based on the concepts of three models: a language model, a Bayesian statistical model, and a graphical model. Reference 18 proposed an approach for QS that is based on document graphs, which are directed graphs of concepts or entity nodes and relations between them. The work of Ref. 19 introduced a graph search algorithm that looks for relevant sentences in the discourse structure represented as a graph. The author used rhetorical structure theory for creating a graph representation of a text document — a weighted graph with nodes standing for sentences and weighted edges representing a distance between sentences. Reference 20 presented the CLASSY summarizer; it uses a hidden Markov model based on signature terms and query terms for sentence selection within a document, and a pivoted question-answering algorithm for redundancy removal. Reference 21 proposed QS method with multi-document input that uses unsupervised deep learning. Reference 22 presented FastSum — a fast query-based multi-document summarizer based solely on word-frequency features of clusters, documents, and topics, where summary sentences are ranked by a regression support vector machine. Reference 23 proposed two strategies to incorporate query information into a probabilistic model. Reference 24 introduced a method that uses non-negative matrix factorization to extract query-relevant sentences. Some works deal with domain-specific data[25] and use domain-specific terms when measuring the distance between sentences and a query. Reference 26 describes a query-based multi-document summarizer based on basic elements, a head-modifier-relation triple representation of document content. Recently, many works integrate TM into their summarization models. For example, Ref. 27 extends the standard graph ranking algorithm by proposing a two-layer (sentence layer and topic layer) graph-based semi-supervised learning approach based on TM techniques. Reference 28 presents a submodular function-based framework for query-focused opinion summarization. Within framework of Reference 28, relevance ordering is produced by a statistical ranker, and information coverage with respect to topic distribution and diverse viewpoints are both encoded as submodular functions. Reference 29 uses external resources with the goal of better representing the importance of a text unit and its semantic similarity with the given query.

Reference 30 presents the Biased LexRank method, which represents a text as a graph of passages that are linked based on their pairwise lexical similarity. The method identifies passages that are likely to be relevant to a user's natural language question, and then performs a random walk on the lexical similarity graph in order to recursively retrieve additional, and similarly relevant, passages. Reference 31 provides a task-based evaluation of multiple query-based summarization methods for cross-language information retrieval. In this chapter we introduce:

- A text representation as a transactional dataset;
- The notion of frequent itemsets and different itemset types in text data;
- Specific setups for generic and query-based summarization tasks;
- MDL-based summarization algorithms applicable to generic and query-based summarization tasks.

These algorithms are introduced separately in Refs. 32–34.

This chapter is organized as follows: Section 2 describes problem setting and definitions. Section 3 describes the MDL principle and Krimp dataset compression algorithm.[1] Sections 4–6 describe adaptations of the MDL approach to generic and query-based summarization. Section 7 contains experiment setup and results. Section 8 contains conclusions and suggestions for future work.

2. Definitions

2.1. *Text preprocessing*

In order to explain the MDL model, one needs to perform basic text preprocessing first, including sentence splitting and tokenization. Additional steps like stopwords removal, stemming, and synonym resolution may be performed for resource-rich languages. Because the main purpose of these methods is to reduce the dataset size, the resultant model will be more efficient.

2.2. *Text document as transactional dataset*

We are given a single text or a collection of texts about the same subject, composed of a set of sentences $S_1, \ldots, S_n$ over terms $t_1, \ldots, t_m$. The word limit W is defined for a final summary.

We represent a text as a *transactional dataset*. Such a dataset consists of *transactions* (sentences), denoted by $T_1, \ldots, T_n$, and *items* (normalized words following tokenization, stemming, and stop-word removal) $I_1, \ldots, I_m$. Items are unique across all the dataset. The number n of transactions is called the *size* of a dataset.

2.3. *Frequent itemsets and their types*

Transaction T_i is a sequence of items from $I_1, \ldots, I_m$, denoted by $T_i = (I_{i_1}, \ldots, I_{i_k})$; the same item may appear in different places within the same transaction. *Support* of an itemset s in the dataset is the ratio of transactions containing it, to dataset size n

$$supp(s) = \frac{|\{T \in D | s \subseteq T\}|}{n}.$$

Given a support bound *Supp* $\in [0,1]$, a sequence s is called *frequent* if $supp(s) \geq Supp$. An itemset is called a *k-itemset* if it contains k items.

There are many types of frequent itemsets that can be defined in this setup, such as sets, multisets, sequences, or boolean formulas. For our summarization task, we use the following itemset types:

- *Frequent word sets*
  Itemset I is a set and it appears in transaction T if T contains every item in I, in arbitrary order. In this case, the order of item appearance and the number of times every item appears in T bears no importance.
  For instance, set $I = \{a, b, c\}$ appears in $T_1 = \{\mathbf{b}, d, \mathbf{c}, \mathbf{a}\}$ and in $T_2 = \{\mathbf{a}, \mathbf{b}, d, \mathbf{c}\}$.

- *Frequent word sequences*
  Itemset I and transaction T are sequences of terms and $I = (i_1, \ldots, i_k)$ is said to appear in transaction T if T contains it as a continuous subsequence, namely $T = (\ldots i_1, \ldots, i_k \ldots)$. An item may appear in I more than once.
  For instance, sequence $I = (a, b, b)$ appears in $T_1 = (d, \mathbf{a}, \mathbf{b}, \mathbf{b}, c)$ and $T_2 = (\mathbf{a}, \mathbf{b}, \mathbf{b}, c, b)$.

- *Frequent word sequences with gaps*
  Itemset I and transaction T are sequences of terms; $I = (i_1, \ldots, i_k)$ is said to appear in T if there exist indexes $j_1 < \cdots < j_k$ of items in T such that $t_{j_1} = i_1, \ldots, t_{j_k} = i_k$. A *gap ratio* is measured as a $k / j_k - j_1 + 1$.
  For instance, sequence $I = (a, b)$ appears in $T = (d, \mathbf{a}, c, \mathbf{b})$ with a 2/3 gap ratio.

Reference 35 has proposed Apriori and Apriori-TID, two algorithms that are used for mining frequent itemsets in large databases in efficient time.

The Apriori algorithm makes multiple passes over the database. In the first pass frequent individual items are determined. Then, for each pass where $k > 1$, the frequent itemsets from the previous pass, $k - 1$, are grouped in sets of k items to form candidate itemsets. The support for each candidate is then counted by performing passes over the database, and those with lower than minimum support are filtered out. This process continues until the set of frequent itemsets in a particular pass is an empty set.

Unlike the Apriori algorithm, the Apriori-TID algorithm uses the database only once, in the first pass. In each consecutive pass where $k > 1$ it uses a storage set C^{k-1} of pairs $< TID, X_i >$, where X_i is a candidate itemset of $k - 1$ items in transaction TID. C^1 is built during the first pass. If C^k fits in memory (as happens in processing our textual data), Apriori-TID is much faster than Apriori. In all the algorithms presented in this chapter, we use the Apriori-TID algorithm adapted for frequent set and sequence mining.

3. The Minimum Description Length principle

3.1. *Definition and rationale*

The MDL principle[36] is defined formally as follows: that the best set describing the database is a set that compresses the dataset best. Given a set of models $\mathcal{M}$, a model $M \in \mathcal{M}$ is considered the *best* if it minimizes $L(M) + L(D|M)$, where $L(M)$ is the bit length of description of M, and $L(D|M)$ is the bit length of the dataset D encoded with M.

3.2. *The idea behind the KRIMP algorithm*

The purpose of the Krimp algorithm[1] is to use frequent itemsets to compress a transactional database in order to find an MDL representation for that database. The algorithm was created to tackle the problem of explosion in the number of frequent itemsets. This problem arises when there are too few frequent itemsets for high values of support, but lowering support value results in an extremely large and unwieldy number of frequent itemsets, making it impossible to make sense of what is happening in a database. Previous attempts to fix this problem relied on pruning frequent itemsets based on their support values, such as generating only closed itemsets (where support decreases for all supersets of the given set) or only maximal itemsets (where all supersets of the given set are infrequent). However, these and similar limitations do not solve the itemset explosion problem.[37,38]

The Krimp algorithm takes a different approach to the above issue by stating that frequent itemset is considered important only if it contributes to the MDL description of the dataset. Then two goals are achieved — the number of important frequent itemsets decreases drastically, and an optimal compact description of the dataset is obtained.

The algorithm iteratively constructs a collection of frequent itemsets for the transactional dataset D, called the Coding Table (CT), so that the bit size $L(CT) + L(D|CT)$ of the dataset that is compressed with that coding table is minimal. This approach is called a *two-part MDL*, meaning that the model CT and the dataset D are encoded separately. The main idea of Krimp algorithm is shown in Fig. 1.

Coding Table CT is the main data structure of Krimp algorithm and it has the following structure:

- CT is an ordered list of pairs (*itemset, code*);
- *itemset* is a frequent itemset;

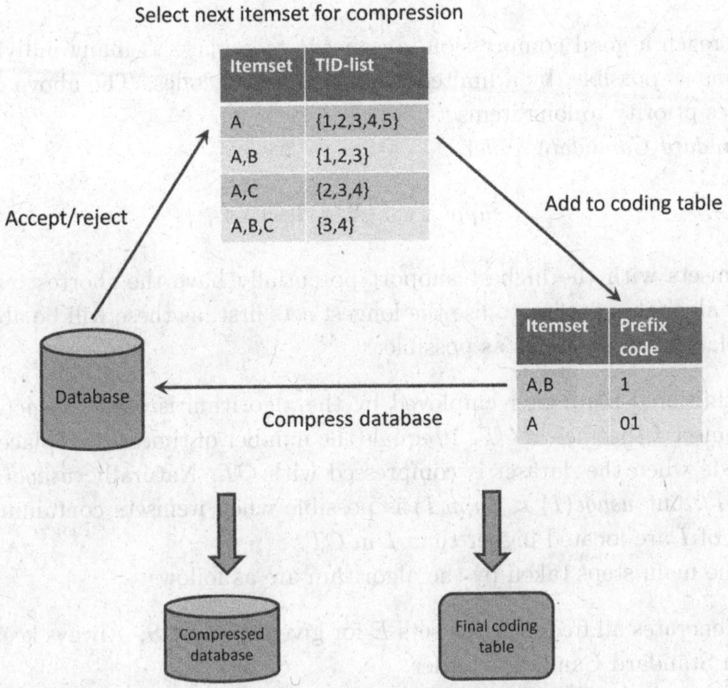

Fig. 1.   Main cycle of the Krimp algorithm.

- *code* is a prefix binary code, i.e., Huffman codes;[39]
- Codes are generated in accordance with the indices of CT entries, meaning they grow logarithmically as index increases;
- Encoding of the dataset with CT consists of replacing each itemset appearing in CT with its code. Because MDL representation does not require the knowledge of actual codes but only their length, codes are never computed explicitly.

Computing optimal MDL representation is an NP-hard problem;[40] Krimp algorithm uses a heuristic approach to solve it. The approach is based on notion of orders on frequent itemsets used in the CT construction. Denote by $|X|$ the size of itemset X (the number of items in it), by $supp(X)$ its support in D, and by $lex(X)$, its lexicographical representation. The two orders used by the algorithm are:

- *Standard Cover Order*

$$|X| \downarrow \; supp(X) \downarrow \; lex(X) \uparrow$$

To reach a good compression, one needs to replace as many individual items as possible, by a limited number of short codes. The above order gives priority to long itemsets.
- *Standard Candidate Order*

$$supp(X) \downarrow \; |X| \downarrow \; lex(X) \uparrow$$

Itemsets with the highest support potentially have the shortest codes; the algorithm prefers to use the longest sets first, as these will be able to replace as many items as possible.

An additional parameter employed by the algorithm is usage $usage(I)$ of an itemset I that lies in CT. It equals the number of times I is replaced by its code when the dataset is compressed with CT. Naturally, $usage(I) \leq supp(I)$, but $usage(I) < supp(I)$ is possible when itemsets containing all items of I are located higher than I in CT.

The main steps taken by the algorithm are as follows:

(1) Generates all frequent itemsets F for given support S. Always keeps F in Standard Candidate Order.
(2) Starts with CT that includes all 1-itemsets. Always keeps CT in Standard Cover Order.

(3) Adds the candidate itemsets from F to CT one by one.

    (a) Covers the database D with CT to compute $L(D|CT)$. Cover is computed by replacing all itemsets in CT by their codes, in the order they appear in CT.

    (b) If the resulting encoding provides a smaller dataset representation size $L(CT) + L(D|CT)$, adds it to CT. Otherwise, discards it permanently.

(4) Prunes CT.

    (a) Selects all itemsets in CT whose usage has decreased following the latest CT modification and orders them by their usage.

    (b) For every such itemset, removes it from CT permanently if its removal from CT decreases $L(CT) + L(D|CT)$.

In next sections, we show how ideas introduced in Krimp were adapted for summarization tasks. The key approach of finding MDL for a dataset remains the same, but additional measures are taken in order to produce valid summaries.

4. Generic summarization with MDL

4.1. *The goal*

In this setting, our goal can be reformulated as the problem of finding a limited-size subset of sentences in a given document or document set, which covers as much information contained in compressing itemsets as possible.

We are interested in both continuous and noncontinuous word sequences, allowing a sequence to have gaps inside it as long as the gap ratio of frequent word sequence length to sequence length with gaps does not exceed a pre-set parameter. Sequences with gaps make sense in text data, as phrasing of the same fact or entity in different sentences may differ. The name of the algorithm is GAMP, standing for GApped kriMP, and it was introduced in Ref. 32. The main idea of GAMP is shown in Fig. 2.

4.2. *Data*

Input data consists of a single text or a collection of texts about the same subject, composed of a set of sentences $\mathcal{S} = \{S_1, \ldots, S_n\}$. Every sentence is a sequence of terms from $\mathcal{T} = \{t_1, \ldots, t_m\}$, where terms are processed words after tokenization, stemming, and stop-word removal. Given a basic

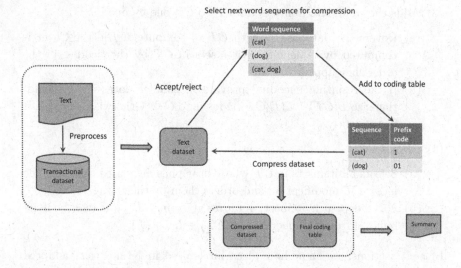

Fig. 2.   Main cycle of GAMP.

pre-processing tool, this algorithm is applicable to any language, as it does
not depend on any linguistic parameter.

4.3. *Parameters*

The GAMP algorithm accepts following parameters:

(1) A summary word limit W that defines maximal number of words in a
    summary.
(2) A support limit $Supp \in (0, 1]$ that defines minimal fraction of sentences
    containing a given frequent sequence.
(3) The maximal coding table size, where $C \in \mathbb{N}$.
(4) The maximal allowed gap ratio Gap for a frequent sequence, as defined
    in Section 2.3.

Note that the limit C can be used in Krimp,[1] resulting in a suboptimal
size of the compressed dataset. In our case, due to summary size limit W,
we do not need the optimal compression, although we seek to compress a
part of the document so that it will be included in summary. Therefore,
while this parameter can be set to an arbitrary value, we use the $C = W$
constraint in our experiments.

4.4. *Orders*

We use these orders of the Krimp method in our optimization process:

- *Standard Cover Order*

$$|X| \downarrow supp(X) \downarrow lex(X) \uparrow$$

for the coding table CT;
- *Standard Candidate Order*

$$supp(X) \downarrow |X| \downarrow lex(X) \uparrow$$

for the set F of all frequent sequences.

However, because we are interested in generating a short summary, we need to define an additional order on sentences. This order allows us to rank and select sentences from a document when compressed document representation is already found.

- *Summary Order* is defined for a set of S sentences and a set T of terms. Sentences $S \in S$ are ordered by

$$|S \cap T| \downarrow id(S) \uparrow,$$

where $|S \cap T|$ is the number of terms in T contained in sentence S, and $id(S)$ is the sentence ID, namely its serial number within a document or a document set. Here, preference is given to sentences that cover more terms, and if term coverage is identical, then sentences that are closer to the document beginning are preferred.

4.5. *GAMP algorithm*

The GAMP algorithm consists of the following steps:

(1) We find all frequent term sequences in the document using the Apriori-TID algorithm[35] for the given *Supp* and *Gap* and store them in set F. This set is kept in Standard Candidate Order.
(2) The coding table CT is initialized to contain all single normalized terms and their frequencies. CT is always kept in Standard Cover Order (lines 1–6 in Algorithm 1).
(3) We repeatedly choose frequent sequences from F so that the size of the encoded dataset is minimal, with every selected sequence replaced by its code. Selection is done by computing the decrease in size of the encoding when each one of the sequences is considered to be a candidate to be added to CT (lines 7–21 in Algorithm 1).

Algorithm 1 MDL extractive generic summarization with GAMP
Input:

      (1) document D, containing pre-processed sentences $S_1, \ldots, S_n$;
      (2) normalized terms $T_1, \ldots, T_m$;
      (3) summary size W
      (4) limit C on the number of codes to use;
      (5) minimal bound for constraint $Supp$;
      (6) maximal gap ratio gap.

Output: Extractive summary $Summary$

1: $\mathcal{F} \leftarrow$ all sequences of terms I with $supp(I) \geq Supp$ and $gap(I) \leq gap$
2: Sort $\mathcal{F}$ according to Standard Candidate Order
3: $CT \leftarrow$ all 1-itemsets from $\mathcal{F}$
4: Keep CT sorted according to Standard Cover Order
5: Initialize prefix codes according to the order of sequences in CT
6: $CodeCount \leftarrow 0$;
7: **while** $CodeCount < C$ and $\mathcal{F} \neq \emptyset$ **do**
8:     $BestCode \leftarrow c \in \mathcal{F}$ such that $L(CT \cup \{c\}) + L(D|CT \cup \{c\})$ is minimal
9:     **if** $L(CT \cup \{c\}) + L(D|CT \cup \{c\}) < L(CT) + L(D|CT)$ **then**
10:       $CT \leftarrow CT \cup \{BestCode\}$
11:       $\mathcal{F} \leftarrow \mathcal{F} \setminus \{BestCode\}$
12:     **else**
13:       $\mathcal{F} \leftarrow \mathcal{F} \setminus \{BestCode\}$
14:     **end if**
15:     $PruneCandidates \leftarrow$ all codes $c \in CT$ whose usage decreased
16:     order $PruneCandidates$ by increasing usage
17:     **for all** codes $c \in PruneCandidates$ **do**
18:       **if** $L(CT \setminus \{c\}) + L(D|CT \setminus \{c\}) < L(CT) + L(D|CT)$ **then**
19:         $CT \leftarrow CT \setminus \{c\}$
20:       **end if**
21:     **end for**
22: **end while**
23: $Summary \leftarrow \emptyset$
24: $\mathcal{T} \leftarrow$ all terms in codes of CT
25: $Sentences \leftarrow \{S_1, \ldots, S_n\}$
26: **while** $\#words(Summary) < W$ **do**
27:     sort $Sentences$ in Summary Order w.r.t. $\mathcal{T}$
28:     $S \leftarrow$ top sentence or $Sentences$ w.r.t. Summary Order
29:     $Summary \leftarrow Summary \cup \{S\}$
30:     $Sentences \leftarrow Sentences \setminus \{S\}$
31:     $\mathcal{T} \leftarrow \mathcal{T} \setminus$ terms of S
32: **end while**
33: **return** $Summary$

---

(4) The summary is constructed by incrementally adding sentences with the highest coverage of encoded term sequences that are still uncovered by previously selected sentences (lines 23–32 in Algorithm 1), according to the Summary Order. The sentences are selected in the greedy manner as long as the word limit W is not exceeded.

5. Generic summarization with MDL and topic modeling

In this section we describe an approach to unsupervised text summarization. The approach combines hierarchical TM and the MDL principle; it is tested on texts in Chinese Hanzi script, from which short Weibo[41] texts are produced. The intuition behind this approach suggests that a summary that best describes the original text should cover its main topics in the form of word sequences with the most important topic words. As such, the problem of summarization is very naturally reduced to the maximal coverage problem,[2,3] where the extract must maximally cover the information contained in the source text. We apply the greedy approximation method that ranks sentences by their coverage of best compressing topic-related word sequences and then selects the top-ranked sentences to a summary. The algorithm, which was introduced in Ref. 34, is TOpic modeling kriMP (TOMP).

5.1. *Data*

The task addressed by this algorithm is the generation of short summaries containing, at most, 140 Hanzi characters for news articles. Some of the articles are short and no sensible topic information can be extracted from them. In the case of short articles, we use the basic Krimp approach, which is not much different from the one described in Section 4. For long documents, sensible topic information can be computed and then incorporated into the algorithm. This modification is shown to improve summarization results.

5.2. *Text preprocessing for Hanzi*

Standard text preprocessing steps are performed: sentence splitting, word segmentation (or tokenization), and stop-word removal based on a stop list that contains punctuation marks and some functional words. Word segmentation is a non-trivial step in Chinese because Hanzi words are not separated by spaces. We used the ICTCLAS tool[42], which is based on a dictionary and a machine learning algorithm.

5.3. *Topic modeling for documents*

The hLDA method of Ref. 13 implements a TM that finds a hierarchy of topics forming a tree. The structure of the tree is determined by the input data. A node in this tree structure indicates a topic, with words of the document being probabilistically assigned to this topic. An algorithm of collapsed Gibbs sampling is used for approximating the posterior distribution for hLDA. A topic is defined as a probability distribution across vocabulary words. Given an input document consisting of a sequence of words, hierarchical TM finds useful sets of topics and learns to organize the topics according to a hierarchy. There are no limitations such as a maximum depth or maximum branching factor. Multiple parameters can change the structure of the resulting topics. Their adjustment can be found in Ref. 16.

In classic hLDA modeling, every document is allocated to a path from the root to a leaf in the tree. Each node is associated with a topic, which is a distribution across words. Documents sharing the same path should be similar to each other. All documents share the topic distribution associated with the root node. Because we are interested in detecting important sentences for a single-document summarization, we strive to attain a topic distribution over sentences in a document, instead of a distribution over documents in a corpus. Therefore, we applied the TM on single documents as corpora, where the model treats each sentence as a document. Despite the fact that a single sentence contains much fewer words than a document, TM provided us a considerable discrimination among sentences, which helped us to make a better sentence selection. We set the depth of the tree as 3. There are several parameters in hLDA, including ETA, GAM, GEM_MEAN, GEM_SCALE, SCALING_SHAPE, SCALING_SCALE. Different parameters lead to different trees, while the efficacy of a tree can be evaluated by human checking. The parameter settings in our system are as defined in Table 1, and explained and justified in Ref. 43.

Figure 3 shows an example hLDA hierarchy built from the M004 Chinese corpus of MultiLing 2015.

Table 1. hLDA parameters.

Parameter	Setting
ETA	1.2, 0.5, 0.05
GAM	1.0,1.0
GEM_MEAN	0.5
GEM_SCALE	100
SCALING_SHAPE	1
SCALING_SCALE	0.5

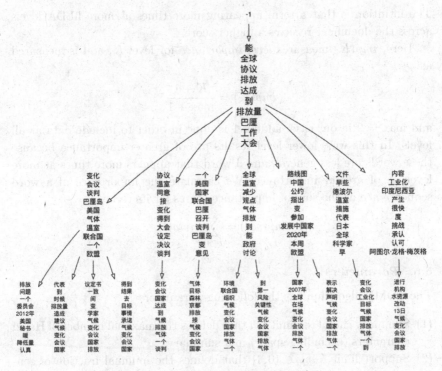

Fig. 3. An example of hLDA hierarchy.

5.4. *Topical importance*

We adapt the MDL approach to TM knowledge by using the following output of hLDA TM:

(1) Word vocabulary, i.e., words sorted by the number of times they appear in a document;

(2) Word hLDA level data for every appearance of a word in a sentence. We collected, for every word, the number of times it was classified by hLDA to be at each level K $(K = 0, 1, 2)$. Intuitively (according to our observations), words appearing at different levels many times have greater importance than words appearing at only one level, notwithstanding their having a high frequency count in the text.

We define *topical term importance* for term t as the sum of importance scores of each appearance of t in the text:

$$imp(t) = \sum_K \sum_{t \in K} imp(K).$$

The intuition is that a term appearing more times at more hLDA levels across the document receives a higher score.

Here, $imp(K)$ measures *level importance* for level K, and is measured as:

$$imp(K) = \frac{K+1}{\max+1}$$

and $\max = 2$ in our case; adding 1 is done in order to include data at all levels. In this way, lower level results are of greater importance because these words are less general, and a word that appears more times at more levels is of greater importance. We calculate the importance of a word sequence *seq* as the sum of importance scores for its terms:

$$imp(seq) = \sum_{t \in seq} imp(t).$$

5.5. *Parameters*

The TOMP algorithm has the following parameters:

(1) Summary character limit Ch that defines the maximal number of Hanzi characters (excluding space) in a summary.
(2) Support limit $Supp \in (0,1]$ that defines the minimal fraction of sentences containing a given frequent sequence.
(3) The maximal coding table size $C \in \mathbb{N}$.
(4) Frequent itemsets are sequences, as defined in Section 2.3.

Although C is a user-defined parameter, we always set it to the expected summary size Ch, following the intuition that the best codes of the coding table represent the most important information in a document, which we desire to store in a summary.

5.6. *Orders*

We use the following Krimp orders in our algorithm:

• If no topic information is available because the document is too short, we rely on standard orders as follows:

– *Standard Cover Order*

$$|X| \downarrow \; supp(X) \downarrow \; lex(X) \uparrow$$

for the coding table CT;

– *Standard Candidate Order*

$$supp(X) \downarrow |X| \downarrow lex(X) \uparrow$$

- If topic information is available for a document, TM-dependent orders are used for both the coding table CT and the candidate set $\mathcal{F}$ of frequent sequences.
  – *TM Cover Order*

$$imp(X) \downarrow |X| \downarrow supp(X) \downarrow lex(X) \uparrow$$

  for the coding table CT; preference is given to itemsets with higher topical importance. Length of an itemset still affects the order, but in a less direct way.
  – *TM Candidate Order*

$$imp(X) \downarrow supp(X) \downarrow |X| \downarrow lex(X) \uparrow$$

  for the set $\mathcal{F}$ of all frequent sequences. Unlike the case of generic non-topic dependent summarization, preference is given to sequences of higher topical importance.

The order for selecting sentences for the summary is defined as follows:

- *Updated Summary Order* is defined for a set of $\mathcal{S}$ sentences and coding table CT.

  We define $idx(x)$ to be a normalized distance of S from document's beginning. Namely, for j-th sentence S_j in a document consisting of n sentences

$$idx(S_j) = \frac{n - j + 1}{n}.$$

Sentences $S \in \mathcal{S}$ are ordered by

$$\frac{|CT \cap S|}{|CT|} * idx(S) \downarrow$$

where $CT \cap S$ denotes terms of sentence S that are contained in some itemset of CT.

Note that our algorithm very rarely selects just the leading sentences; thus coverage of terms in itemsets of CT proved to be more important than sentence index.

5.7. *Algorithm outline*

We use TM results in two stages of our algorithm, initial candidate ordering and final sentence ranking, as described in Section 5.6. Details of the TOMP algorithm appear in Algorithm 2. In lines 1–8 we find all frequent sequences of terms in the document using the Apriori-TID algorithm,[35] and store them in set $\mathcal{F}$, which is kept in TM Candidate Order (if topic data exists). The coding table CT is initialized in lines 9–11 to contain all single normalized terms and it is always kept in TM Cover Order. The MDL optimization process of search for the best set of frequent sequences compressing the document appears in lines 13–29. The summary is constructed according to Updated Summary Order in lines 30–36.

6. Query-Based summarization with MDL

6.1. *The goal*

Query-based summarization is directed toward generating a summary most relevant to a given query. It can relate to a single document or to a multi-document input. Our approach for QS is based on the MDL principle, defining the best summary as the one that leads to the best compression of the text with query-related information by providing its shortest and most concise description. The name of the algorithm is QUMP, which was introduced in Ref. 33, stands for QUery kriMP (QUMP). The main idea behind QUMP is shown in Fig. 4.

6.2. *Data*

Input data consists of a single text or a collection of texts about the same subject, composed of a set of sentences $S_1, \ldots, S_n$, and a query Q composed of sentences $Q_1, \ldots, Q_m$ (m is usually small). Both sentences and queries are sequences of terms $t_1, \ldots, t_m$. Terms are processed words after tokenization, stemming, and stop-word removal.

6.3. *MDL and queries*

In generic MDL, a model $M \in \mathcal{M}$ in a set of models $\mathcal{M}$ is considered the *best* if it minimizes $L(M) + L(D|M)$, where $L(M)$ is the bit length of description of M and $L(D|M)$ is the bit length of the dataset D encoded with M. As such, the frequency and the length of the codes that replace

---

Algorithm 2 MDL&TM summarization with TOMP

Input:

      (1) document D, containing pre-processed sentences $S_1, \ldots, S_n$;

      (2) normalized terms $T_1, \ldots, T_m$;

      (3) summary character Ch;

      (3) limit C on the number of codes to use;

      (4) minimal support bound S;

      (5) topical importance function $topImp()$.

Output: Extractive summary *Summary*

1: $\mathcal{F} \leftarrow$ all sequences I of terms with $supp(I) \geq S$
2: **if** topical knowledge available **then**
3:     CandidateOrder $\leftarrow$ TM Candidate Order
4:     CoverOrder $\leftarrow$ TM Cover Order
5: **else**
6:     CandidateOrder $\leftarrow$ Standard Candidate Order
7:     CoverOrder $\leftarrow$ Standard Cover Order
8: **end if**
9: Always keep $\mathcal{F}$ in the chosen Candidate Order
10: $CT \leftarrow$ all 1-itemsets from F
11: Always keep CT in the chosen Cover Order
12: Initialize prefix codes according to the order of sequences in CT
13: $CodeCount \leftarrow 0$;
14: **while** $CodeCount < C$ and $\mathcal{F} \neq \emptyset$ **do**
15:     $BestCode \leftarrow c \in \mathcal{F}$ such that $L(CT \cup \{c\}) + L(D|CT \cup \{c\})$ is minimal
16:     **if** $L(CT \cup \{c\}) + L(D|CT \cup \{c\}) < L(CT) + L(D|CT)$ **then**
17:         $CT \leftarrow CT \cup \{BestCode\}$
18:         $\mathcal{F} \leftarrow \mathcal{F} \setminus \{BestCode\}$
19:     **else**
20:         $\mathcal{F} \leftarrow \mathcal{F} \setminus \{BestCode\}$
21:     **end if**
22:     $PruneCandidates \leftarrow$ all codes $c \in CT$ whose usage decreased
23:     order $PruneCandidates$ by increasing usage
24:     **for all** codes $c \in PruneCandidates$ **do**
25:         **if** $L(CT \setminus \{c\}) + L(D|CT \setminus \{c\}) < L(CT) + L(D|CT)$ **then**
26:            $CT \leftarrow CT \setminus \{c\}$
27:         **end if**
28:     **end for**
29: **end while**
30: **while** $\#characters(Summary) < Ch$ **do**
31:     sort *Sentences* in Updated Summary Order w.r.t. CT
32:     $S \leftarrow$ top sentence or *Sentences* w.r.t. Summary Order
33:     $Summary \leftarrow Summary \cup \{S\}$
34:     $Sentences \leftarrow Sentences \setminus \{S\}$
35:     $CT \leftarrow CT \setminus$ codes c contained in S
36: **end while**
37: **return** *Summary*

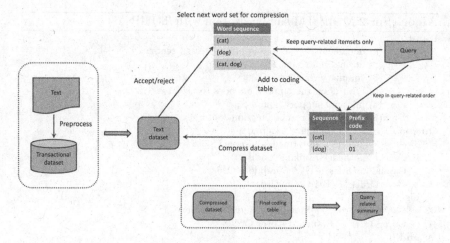

Fig. 4.   Main cycle of QUMP.

data subsets are the most important features of the MDL model. Because we aim at QS, in our approach we seek a query-dependent model M_Q that minimizes $L(M_Q) + L(D|M_Q)$; it may not be the best model overall but it has to be the best among models for the query Q.

6.4. *Parameters*

The QUMP algorithm accepts the following parameters:

(1) Summary word limit W that defines the maximal number of words in a summary.
(2) Support limit $S \in (0,1]$ that defines the minimal fraction of sentences containing a given frequent itemset.
(3) The maximal coding table size $C \in \mathbb{N}$.
(4) Frequent itemsets are proper sets, as defined in Section 2.3.
(5) *Intersection type* between frequent itemsets and query items.

   - The *ALL* intersection type, where all items of an itemset are query items.
   - The *SOME* intersection type, where at least one item is a query item.

Intersection types were chosen in order to compare between exact and partial compliance of itemsets and query.

6.5. *Orders*

We use three orders in our optimization algorithm that depend on an intersection type chosen for the algorithm. Let Q be a set of term items. The orders then are defined as follows:

- Orders for the ALL intersection type are:

  - *ALL Query Cover Order*

  $$|X| \downarrow supp(X) \downarrow lex(X) \uparrow$$

  for the coding table CT.

  Here $|X \cap Q| = |X|$ is precisely the number of query terms contained in a frequent itemset X, and itemsets containing more query terms get higher priority.

  - *Standard Candidate Order*

  $$supp(X) \downarrow |X| \downarrow lex(X) \uparrow$$

  for the set F of all frequent sequences.

- Orders for the SOME intersection type are:

  - *SOME Query Cover Order*

  $$|X \cap Q| \downarrow |X| \downarrow supp(X) \downarrow lex(X) \uparrow$$

  for the coding table CT.

  Here, a precedence is given to itemsets that have more in common with the query than do others.

  - *SOME Query Candidate Order*

  $$supp(X) \downarrow |X \cap Q| \downarrow |X| \downarrow lex(X) \uparrow$$

  for the set F of all frequent sequences.

  For itemsets with equal support, their similarity to the query (the number of common terms) is considered first in order to give precedence to query-related candidates.

The Summary Order, as shown in the following, ranks sentences in a document when used for computed query-related compressed document representation.

- *Summary Order* defined for a set of S sentences and coding table CT.

  Importance for every code $c \in CT$ is its normalized serial number in the table, i.e.,

$$importance(c) = \frac{index(c)}{|CT|}$$

For every sentence $S \in \mathcal{S}$, its rank is the sum of importance for all the codes of CT contained in S, i.e.,

$$rank(S) = \sum_{c \in CT, c \subseteq S} importance(c)$$

This type of sentence rank gives preference to sentences that cover more codes. Because codes are related to queries, sentences with better code coverage are preferred. The Summary Order is then

$$rank(S) \downarrow id(S) \downarrow$$

6.6. *Algorithm outline*

We are interested in the dataset $D|CT_Q$ after it is compressed in the best possible way with the best compressing query-related set CT_Q. The dataset $D|CT_Q$ is obtained by replacing in D every itemset in CT_Q by its code, with shorter codes selected first.

We use an upper bound C on the size of CT_Q, in order to limit document compression, and select it to be equal to the target summary size W. The ideal compression in this case will compress only words most relevant to the summary and will ignore everything else; additionally, this limitation speeds up computation. The summary is constructed by iteratively selecting the sentences from a document in Summary Order.

A detailed description appears in Algorithm 3. In lines 1–10 of Algorithm 3, frequent itemsets relevant to the query are computed and ordered according to the chosen intersection type; lines 11–31 generate best compressing itemsets as coding table CT, and lines 32–28 select sentences for a summary according to the Summary Order.

Algorithm 3 MDL extractive query-based summarization with QUMP

Input:

      (1) document D, containing pre-processed sentences $S_1, \ldots, S_n$;

      (2) normalized terms $T_1, \ldots, T_m$;

      (3) query Q, containing normalized terms $Q_1, \ldots, Q_k$;

      (4) summary size W;

      (5) limit C on the number of codes to use;

      (6) minimal support bound S;

      (7) intersection type $Int \in \{ALL, SOME\}$.

Output: Extractive query-related summary *Summary*

1: $\mathcal{F} \leftarrow$ all sets I of terms with $supp(I) \geq S$
2: **if** $Int = ALL$ **then**
3:     $\mathcal{F} \leftarrow$ all sets $I \subseteq Q$ of terms with $supp(I) \geq S$
4:     CandidateOrder $\leftarrow$ Standard Candidate Order
5:     CoverOrder $\leftarrow$ ALL Query Cover Order
6: **else**
7:     $\mathcal{F} \leftarrow$ all sets I of terms with $supp(I) \geq S$ and $I \cap Q \neq \emptyset$
8:     CandidateOrder $\leftarrow$ SOME Query Candidate Order
9:     CoverOrder $\leftarrow$ SOME Query Cover Order
10: **end if**
11: Always keep $\mathcal{F}$ in the chosen Candidate Order
12: $CT \leftarrow$ all 1-itemsets from F
13: Always keep CT in the chosen Cover Order
14: Initialize prefix codes according to the order of sequences in CT
15: $CodeCount \leftarrow 0$;
16: **while** $CodeCount < C$ and $\mathcal{F} \neq \emptyset$ **do**
17:     $BestCode \leftarrow c \in \mathcal{F}$ such that $L(CT \cup \{c\}) + L(D|CT \cup \{c\})$ is minimal
18:     **if** $L(CT \cup \{c\}) + L(D|CT \cup \{c\}) < L(CT) + L(D|CT)$ **then**
19:         $CT \leftarrow CT \cup \{BestCode\}$
20:         $\mathcal{F} \leftarrow \mathcal{F} \setminus \{BestCode\}$
21:     **else**
22:         $\mathcal{F} \leftarrow \mathcal{F} \setminus \{BestCode\}$
23:     **end if**
24:     $PruneCandidates \leftarrow$ all codes $c \in CT$ whose usage decreased
25:     order $PruneCandidates$ by increasing usage
26:     **for all** codes $c \in PruneCandidates$ **do**
27:         **if** $L(CT \setminus \{c\}) + L(D|CT \setminus \{c\}) < L(CT) + L(D|CT)$ **then**
28:             $CT \leftarrow CT \setminus \{c\}$
29:         **end if**
30:     **end for**
31: **end while**
32: **while** $\#words(Summary) < W$ **do**
33:     sort $Sentences$ in Summary Order w.r.t. CT
34:     $S \leftarrow$ top sentence or $Sentences$ w.r.t. Summary Order
35:     $Summary \leftarrow Summary \cup \{S\}$
36:     $Sentences \leftarrow Sentences \setminus \{S\}$
37:     $CT \leftarrow CT \setminus$ codes c contained in S
38: **end while**
39: **return** *Summary*

---

7. Experiments

7.1. *Experiment setup*

For generic extractive summarization, we used three English corpora from the Document Understanding Conference (DUC): 2002, 2004, and 2007,[44] summarized in Tables 2 and 3. DUC 2002 and 2007 each contain a set of single documents, and DUC 2004 contains 50 sets of 10 related documents. For generic extractive summarization, we used three English corpora from the Document Understanding Conference (DUC): 2002, 2004, and 2007,[44] summarized in Tables 2 and 3. DUC 2002 and 2007 each contain a set of single documents, and DUC 2004 contains 50 sets of 10 related documents.

For generic extractive summarization enhanced by topic modeling, we performed our experiments on Weibo-Oriented Chinese News Summarization test set data from Natural Language Processing and Chinese Computing (NLPCC) 2015 competition[45]. This corpus was constructed in an automatic way by collecting messages from a few news accounts on Sina Weibo, such as *Renminwang, Beijingdaily, SouthernMetropolisWeekly*, and *Breakingnews*. According to NLPCC 2015 competition organizers, all messages with a URL link to the full Chinese news article were kept, and the news URLs that corresponded to two different Weibo[34] messages were stored. The web pages were downloaded via the URL links and the news articles were extracted from the web pages. Each Weibo message was written and posted by a human editor; it was therefore considered to be a human-written model summary for the associated news article. As a result, two human gold standard summaries are associated with every such document.

For query-based summarization, we used two English corpora of the DUC: DUC 2006 and DUC 2005,[44] which are standard datasets used for evaluation of query-based summarization methods. The DUC 2005 dataset contains 50 document sets of 25 to 50 related documents each. The average number of words in a document set is 20,185. For every document set a short (one to three sentences) query is supplied. From 4 to 9 gold standard summaries are supplied for every document set, and the target summary size is 250 words. The DUC 2006 dataset contains 50 document sets, each with 25 related documents. The average number of words in a document set is 15,293. For every document set a short (one to three sentences) query is supplied. Four gold standard summaries are supplied for every document set, and the target summary size is 250 words. Corpora parameters appear in Tables 2 and 3.

Table 2.   Corpora statistics (1).

Corpus	Language	# documents	# summaries	Summary size
DUC'02	English	533	2–3	100 words
DUC'04	English	50	4	100 words
DUC'07	English	23	4	250 words
DUC'05	English	23	4	250 words
DUC'06	English	23	4	250 words
NLPCC'15	Chinese	250	2	140 chars

Table 3.   Corpora statistics (2).

Corpus	Doc size (KB)	Type	QB	TM
DUC'02	1–20	SD	no	no
DUC'04	20–89	MD (50x10)	no	no
DUC'07	28–131	SD	yes	no
DUC'05	28–131	SD	yes	no
DUC'06	28–131	SD	yes	no
NLPCC'15	1–19	SD	no	yes

7.2. *Evaluation setup*

We used ROUGE[46] to evaluate the effectiveness of our approach. The recall scores of ROUGE-N for $N \in 1, 2$, ROUGE-L, ROUGE-W-1.2, and ROUGE-$SU4$ which are based on N-gram, Longest Common Subsequence (LCS), Weighted Longest Common Subsequence (WLCS), and Skip-bigram plus unigram, with maximum skip-distance of 4. During the evaluation the matching between system summaries and reference summaries was computed. ROUGE parameters and text processing depends on language as follows:

- For evaluation of English summaries, we used Rouge-1.5.5 toolkit with the following command line:

  -a -l <summary size> -n 1 -2 4 -u

- For Chinese summaries, we used the ROUGE-1.5.5 toolkit adapted to Chinese, with its command line adopted from the NLPCC 2015 competition

  -c 95 -2 4 -U -r 1000 -n 4 -w 1.2 -a -l 140

Because the NLPCC 2015 competition[45] used a character-based approach to Chinese, no Chinese word segmentation needed to be performed when running the ROUGE toolkit. Instead, all Chinese characters were separated with blank spaces. We used the same approach in our experiments and separated Chinese characters in both gold standard summaries and system summaries in'order to measure ROUGE scores correctly. ROUGE scores for participating systems showed slight differences from those reported at the competition, and are due to the fact that we implemented simple Chinese character splitting ourselves. Because our system did not participate in the NLPCC competition, we re-ran all experiments.

We have tested QUMP and TOMP algorithms, and also two variations of the QUMP algorithm, QUMP-ALL and QUMP-SOME. QUMP-ALL utilizes intersection type ALL between itemsets and query terms, while QUMP-SOME uses intersection type SOME (intersection types are defined in Section 6.4). Table 4 describes what parameters were used for every one of our MDL-based algorithms and on what dataset(s) we performed experiments; support here denotes support count and not support ratio.

7.3. *Evaluation results*

7.3.1. *GAMP evaluation*

We compared the GAMP algorithm with the two known unsupervised state-of-the-art summarizers denoted by Gillick[3] and McDonald.[47] As a baseline, we used a very simple approach that takes first sentences to a summary (denoted by TopK). Table 5 contains the results of comparative evaluations. The best scores are shown in bold. GAMP outperformed the other methods on all datasets (using ROUGE-1 score). The difference between

Table 4. Algorithms' parameters (1)

Algorithm	Corpus	Summary	Support	CT size	Itemsets	Gap ratio
GAMP	DUC'02	100 words	4	100	seq w/gaps	0.8
GAMP	DUC'04	100 words	4	100	seq w/gaps	0.8
GAMP	DUC'07	250 words	4	250	seq w/gaps	0.8
TOMP	NLPCC'15	140 chars	2	50	seq	–
QUMP-ALL	DUC'05	250 words	2	250	seq	–
QUMP-ALL	DUC'06	250 words	2	250	seq	–
QUMP-SOME	DUC'05	250 words	2	250	seq	–
QUMP-SOME	DUC'06	250 words	2	250	seq	–

Table 5. GAMP algorithm evaluation.

	ROUGE-1 Recall			ROUGE-2 Recall		
Algorithm	DUC'02	DUC'04	DUC'07	DUC'02	DUC'04	DUC'07
GAMP	**0.4421**	**0.3440**	**0.3959**	0.1941	**0.0829**	**0.0942**
Gillick	0.4207	0.3314	0.3518	0.1773	0.0753	0.0650
McDonald	0.4391	0.2955	0.3500	**0.1981**	0.0556	0.0672
TopK	0.4322	0.2973	0.3525	0.1867	0.0606	0.0706

the scores of GAMP and Gillick (the second best system) on DUC 2007 is highly significant according to the Wilcoxon matched pairs test. Based on the same test, the difference of scores obtained on the DUC 2004 is considered not statistically significant, with $P = 0.0831$. On the DUC 2002, GAMP is ranked first, with no significant difference between it and the second best (McDonald's) scores. Based on this outcome, we can conclude that MDL-based summarization using frequent sequences works better on long documents or multi-document domain. Intuitively, it is a very logical conclusion, because single short documents do not contain a sufficient number of frequent sequences. It is noteworthy that, in addition to the greedy approach, we also evaluated the global optimization with maximizing coverage and minimizing redundancy using linear programming (LP). However, experimental results did not provide any improvement over the greedy approach, which is also more computationally efficient. Therefore, we report only the results of the greedy solution.

7.3.2. *TOMP evaluation*

We compared performance of the TOMP algorithm with:

- Two runs of the top system (ranked first by Rouge, F-measure) from the NLPCC 2015 competition, denoted by WUST-1 and WUST-2;
- A TM-based system without MDL, denoted by TM, to see what difference MDL makes;
- An MDL-based system without TM, denoted by MDL, to see what difference TM makes;
- A TopK system that just takes 140 top characters, as a baseline; and
- FWCov, which selects sentences ranked by coverage of singular frequent words, to see the difference between the MDL principle and simply covering frequent words.

It is worth noting that the length of summaries generated by WUST-1 and WUST-2 is not consistent; sometimes the summaries are very short (minimal length is about 20 characters).

Tables 6 and 7 contain the comparative results in terms of Rouge-1, 2, 3, and 4, recall, precision, and F-measure, with confidence intervals (95%). WUST-1 and WUST-2 denote two runs of the same system, supplied by Wuhan University of Science and Technology and denoted in[45] by NLP@WUST. It is not a purely extractive system as it sometimes selects parts of sentences instead of whole sentences.

Experimental results show that MDL with topical knowledge provides an excellent basis for extracting valuable information for generating short messages. TOMP has the best results in terms of most Rouge metrics. It is also a very interesting (however, not surprising) fact that the TopK approach performs extremely well, and even best, in some cases. According to the Wilcoxon statistical test, FWCov and TOMP significantly outperform WUST-2 (P values are 0.0237, 0.0221, and 0.0160 respectively) in terms of Rouge-1, Recall. Also, TOMP is significantly better than

Table 6.   TOMP algorithm evaluation (1).

System	R1-R	R1-P	R1-F	R2-R	R2-P	R2-F
WUST-1	0.586	0.378	0.449	0.395	0.258	0.304
WUST-2	0.599	0.378	0.455	0.409	0.261	0.312
TopK	0.558	**0.430**	**0.484**	0.414	**0.319**	0.359
FWCov	0.559	0.347	0.425	0.382	0.238	0.291
TOMP	**0.615**	0.389	0.473	**0.472**	0.298	**0.363**
TM	0.562	0.413	0.474	0.408	0.299	0.344
MDL	0.563	0.352	0.430	0.392	0.246	0.299

Table 7.   TOMP algorithm evaluation (2).

System	R3-R	R3-P	R3-F	R4-R	R4-P	R4-F
WUST-1	0.275	0.182	0.213	0.206	0.136	0.160
WUST-2	0.290	0.187	0.222	0.218	0.142	0.168
TopK	0.334	**0.257**	0.290	0.288	**0.222**	0.250
FWCov	0.291	0.182	0.222	0.246	0.154	0.188
TOMP	**0.396**	0.250	**0.304**	**0.353**	0.222	**0.270**
TM	0.326	0.238	0.274	0.283	0.206	0.238
MDL	0.303	0.190	0.231	0.256	0.160	0.195

TopK, with its P value <0.0001. Confidence intervals (95%) for FWCov, WUST-2, TopK, and TOMP are: 0.559 ± 0.023, 0.564 ± 0.023, 0.599 ± 0.027, 0.558 ± 0.022, and 0.615 ± 0.025 respectively.

7.3.3. *QUMP evaluation*

Table 8 shows the ROUGE-1 scores of our algorithm with the scores of 32 systems that participated in the DUC 2005 competition. We show the top 20 systems compared to our systems QUMP-ALL and QUMP-SOME. QUMP-SOME places third on the ROUGE-1 recall and F-measure, and the difference between the top systems (ID = 15 and ID = 4) and our algorithm is statistically insignificant.

System 15 in Table 8 stands for the NUS summarizer from the National University of Singapore. This summarizer is based on the concept link approach.[48] NUS method uses two features: sentence semantic similarity and redundancy minimization based on Maximal Marginal Relevance (MMR). System 4 in that table represents the Columbia summarizer from the Columbia University.[49] This is an adaptation of the DefScriber question answering (QA) system.[50] DefScriber (1) identifies relevant sentences that contain information pertinent to the target individual or term (i.e., the X in the "Who/What is X?" question); (2) incrementally clusters extracted sentences using a cosine distance metric; then (3) selects sentences for output summary using a fitness function that maximizes inclusion of core definitional predicates, coverage of the highest ranking clusters, and answer cohesion; and finally (4) applies reference rewriting techniques to extracted sentences to improve summary readability, using an auxiliary system.[51]

In comparison to the two top systems, QUMP does not require any pre-computed data from the external resources (as does NUS), and has a very simple pipeline with a few stages (unlike the Columbia summarizer) that do not involve external tools and have a low computational cost. The difference between QUMP-SOME and the system with ID = 17 was statistically insignificant, while the difference between QUMP-SOME and the system with ID = 11 was statistically significant.

Table 9 shows how the ROUGE-1 scores of our algorithm compare to the scores of 35 systems that participated in the DUC 2006 competition. Two options of our algorithm, QUMP-ALL and QUMP-SOME, appear in the table. QUMP-SOME places second on the ROUGE-1 recall and f-measure, and the difference between the top system (with ID = 24) and our algorithm is statistically insignificant.

Table 8.   QUMP algorithm evaluation on DUC'05.

System ID	R1-R	R1-P	R1-F
15	0.3446	0.3436	0.3440
4	0.3424	0.3355	0.3388
QUMP-SOME	0.3416	0.3334	0.3374
17	0.3400	0.3329	0.3363
11	0.3336	0.3134	0.3231
6	0.3310	0.3256	0.3282
19	0.3305	0.3249	0.3276
10	0.3304	0.3225	0.3263
7	0.3300	0.3211	0.3254
8	0.3292	0.3314	0.3301
5	0.3281	0.3406	0.3339
QUMP-ALL	0.3276	0.3194	0.3233
25	0.3264	0.3197	0.3229
24	0.3223	0.3253	0.3237
9	0.3222	0.3138	0.3179
16	0.3209	0.3203	0.3205
3	0.3177	0.3179	0.3177
14	0.3172	0.3325	0.3235
12	0.3115	0.3043	0.3078
21	0.3107	0.3095	0.3100
29	0.3107	0.3159	0.3131
27	0.3069	0.2976	0.3021
28	0.3047	0.3074	0.3059
13	0.3039	0.3186	0.3109
18	0.3003	0.3350	0.3161
32	0.2977	0.3056	0.3014
30	0.2931	0.2900	0.2914
26	0.2824	0.3088	0.2949
2	0.2801	0.3052	0.2914
22	0.2795	0.3160	0.2878
31	0.2719	0.3062	0.2797
20	0.2552	0.3554	0.2930
1	0.2532	0.3104	0.2644
23	0.1647	0.3708	0.2196

ID 24 represents the IIITH-Sum system from the International Institute of Information Technology.[52] IIITH-Sum used two features to score the sentences, and then picked the top-scored ones to a summary in the greedy manner. The first feature is a query-dependent adaptation of the Hyperspace Analogue to Language (HAL)[53] feature, where additional importance is given to a word/phrase of a query. The second feature calculates query-independent sentence importance, using external resources in the web. First, the Yahoo search engine was used to get a ranked list of retrieved

Table 9.   QUMP algorithm evaluation on DUC'06.

System ID	R1-R	R1-P	R1-F
24	0.3797	0.3781	0.3789
QUMP-SOME	0.3745	0.3732	0.3745
12	0.3736	0.3734	0.3734
31	0.3675	0.3730	0.3702
10	0.3720	0.3680	0.3699
33	0.3700	0.3698	0.3699
15	0.3717	0.3675	0.3696
23	0.3726	0.3661	0.3692
28	0.3677	0.3707	0.3691
8	0.3702	0.3665	0.3683
27	0.3574	0.3707	0.3637
5	0.3665	0.3607	0.3635
QUMP-ALL	0.3647	0.3623	0.3635
13	0.3553	0.3713	0.3629
3	0.3539	0.3650	0.3593
2	0.3587	0.3580	0.3583
6	0.3543	0.3567	0.3555
19	0.3552	0.3534	0.3542
4	0.3518	0.3567	0.3542
22	0.3518	0.3554	0.3536
29	0.3432	0.3598	0.3512
9	0.3373	0.3641	0.3492
32	0.3519	0.3466	0.3492
14	0.3501	0.3481	0.3490
30	0.3317	0.3575	0.3439
25	0.3374	0.3478	0.3425
20	0.3413	0.3412	0.3412
7	0.3417	0.3368	0.3392
16	0.3384	0.3377	0.3380
18	0.3335	0.3423	0.3377
17	0.3105	0.3647	0.3351
21	0.3244	0.3541	0.3344
34	0.3320	0.3300	0.3310
35	0.3058	0.3488	0.3242
26	0.3023	0.3399	0.3199
1	0.2789	0.3231	0.2962
11	0.1965	0.3014	0.2366

documents, and a unigram language model was learned on a text content extracted from them. Then, Information Measure (IM), using entropy to compute the information content of a sentence based on the learned unigram model, was used for scoring a sentence. The final sentence ranks were computed as a weighted linear combination of the modified HAL feature and IM.

In contrast to the IIIHT-Sum system, our approach does not require any external resources and is strictly based on the internal content of the analyzed corpus. As a result, it also consumes less run-time.

The difference between QUMP-SOME and the system with ID = 12 was statistically insignificant, and the difference between QUMP-SOME and the system with ID = 31 was statistically significant. It is not surprising that QUMP-SOME performed better than QUMP-ALL, as limiting frequent word sets to words appearing in a query only decreases the overall number of frequent word sets. In this case, many repetitive word sets that are related to the query are missed. The actual running time of QUMP was around 1–3 seconds per document set. We also learned that long sentences do not affect computation cost of our approach.

8. Conclusion

In this chapter, we described a new approach for summarizing text documents based on their MDL. We described documents using frequent itemsets composed of their words. The sentences with the highest coverage of the best compressing set are selected to a summary. Our method is completely unsupervised and language-independent, in the sense that only basic preprocessing tools such as a sentence splitter, tokenizer, and stemmer are required. It is possible to enhance our approach with synonym resolution and word embedding data, but this is left for future work. This approach was tested on two different languages, English and Chinese (Hanzi script).

We introduced three algorithms, identified as GAMP, TOMP, and QUMP. The first two algorithms perform generic summarization; GAMP uses a pure MDL approach while TOMP embeds topic modeling knowledge into the optimization procedure. The QUMP algorithm performs query-based summarization.

The experimental results of GAMP applied to DUC 2002, 2004, and 2007 datasets show that this approach outperforms other unsupervised state-of-the-art methods when summarizing long documents or sets of related documents. We would not recommend using our approach for summarizing single short documents that do not contain enough content for providing a high-quality description. The results of experiments performed on the NLPCC 2015 dataset, using the TOMP algorithm, show superiority of the proposed approach when compared to other systems that participated in the NLPCC 2015 competition. Evaluation results show that QUMP, too, has a good performance. In absolute ranking, it outperforms all but two of the participating systems in the DUC 2005 competition and all but one of the competing systems in the DUC 2006 contest.

All algorithms described in this chapter have polynomial time complexity. Runtime of algorithms is limited by Apriori, which is known as a PSPACE-complete problem. However, because it is a rare occasion to have a set of words repeated in more than 4–5 different sentences in the entire document or document set, we have $O(n^5)$ frequent itemsets at most, where n is the number of terms. The encoding process is bound by a number of frequent sets times a number of sentences (m) times a number of words (k). Therefore, the runtime of all algorithms is polynomial in the number of unique terms in a document, and is bound by $O(m \times k \times n^5)$.

In conclusion, the presented technique has the following advantages over other techniques: (1) it is unsupervised and does not require any external resources; (2) it has efficient time complexity (polynomial in the number of terms); (3) it is language-independent and can be applied on any language; to the extent that we have a tokenizer for this language; and (4) despite its robustness (independence on annotated data and language, and its efficiency), its performance is better than or comparable to one of the top systems.

References

1. J. Vreeken, M. Leeuwen, and A. Siebes, Krimp: Mining itemsets that compress, *Data Mining and Knowledge Discovery*, **23**(1), 169–214 (2011).
2. H. Takamura and M. Okumura, Text summarization model based on maximum coverage problem and its variant. In eds. A. Lascarides, C. Gardent and J. Nivre, *Proceedings of the 12th Conference of the European Chapter of the Association for Computational Linguistics*, Athens, Greece, pp. 781–789, Association for Computational Linguistics (ACL) (2009).
3. D. Gillick and B. Favre, A scalable global model for summarization. In eds. J. Clarke and S. Riedel, *Proceedings of the NAACL HLT Workshop on Integer Linear Programming for Natural Language Processing*, Singapore, pp. 10–18, Association for Computational Linguistics (2009).
4. E. Baralis, L. Cagliero, S. Jabeen, and A. Fiori, Multi-document summarization exploiting frequent itemsets. In eds. S. Ossowski and P. Lecca, *Proceedings of the 27th Annual ACM Symposium on Applied Computing*, Riva (Trento), Italy, pp. 782–786, ACM (2012).
5. N. Agarwal, K. Gvr, R. S. Reddy, and C. P. Rosé, SciSumm: A multi-document summarization system for scientific articles. In ed. S. Kurohashi, *Proceedings of the ACL-HLT 2011 System Demonstrations*, Portland, OR, USA, pp. 115–120, Association for Computational Linguistics (2011).
6. M. K. Dalal and M. A. Zaveri, Semisupervised learning based opinion summarization and classification for online product reviews, *Applied Computational Intelligence and Soft Computing*, **2013** (January), Article ID 910706 (2013).

7. G. Danon, M. Schneider, M. Last, M. Litvak, and A. Kandel, An apriori-like algorithm for extracting fuzzy association rules between keyphrases in text documents. In eds. J. P. Carvalho, M-J. Lesot, U. Kaymak, S. Vieira, B. Bouchon-Meunier, and R. R. Yager, *Proceedings of the 11th International Conference on Information Processing and Management of Uncertainty in Knowledge-Based Systems (IPMU 2006), Special Session on Fuzzy Sets in Probability and Statistics*, Paris, France, pp. 731–738, Springer (2006).

8. L. V. S. Lakshmanan, R. T. Ng, C. X. Wang, X. Zhou, and T. J. Johnson, The generalized MDL approach for summarization. In *Proceedings of the 28th International Conference on Very Large Data Bases*, Hong Kong, pp. 766–777, ACM (2002).

9. S. Bu, L. V. S. Lakshmanan, and R. T. Ng, MDL summarization with holes. In eds. K. Böhm, C. S. Jensen, L. M. Haas, M. L. Kersten, P-A. Larson, B. C. Ooi, *Proceedings of the 31st International Conference on Very Large Data Bases*, Trondheim, Norway, pp. 433–444, ACM (2005).

10. T. Nomoto and Y. Matsumoto, A new approach to unsupervised text summarization. In eds. W. B. Croft, D. J. Harper, D. H. Kraft, J. Zobel, *Proceedings of the 24th Annual International ACM SIGIR Conference on Research and Development in Information Retrieval*, New Orleans, LA, USA, pp. 26–34, ACM (2001).

11. T. Nomoto, *Machine learning approaches to rhetorical parsing and open-domain text summarization*. PhD thesis, Nara Institute of Science and Technology (2004).

12. T.-S. Nguyen, H. W. Lauw, and P. Tsaparas. Review synthesis for micro-review summarization. In eds. X. Cheng, H. Li, E. Gabrilovich, and J. Tang, *Proceedings of the Eighth ACM International Conference on Web Search and Data Mining*, Shanghai, China, pp. 169–178, ACM (2015).

13. D. M. Blei, A. Y. Ng, and M. I. Jordan, Latent dirichlet allocation, *Journal of Machine Learning Research*, **3**, 993–1022 (2003).

14. D. Wang, S. Zhu, T. Li, and Y. Gong, Multi-document summarization using sentence-based topic models. In eds. K-Y. Su, J. Su, and J. Wiebe, *Proceedings of the ACL-IJCNLP 2009 Conference Short Papers*, Singapore, pp. 297–300, Association for Computational Linguistics (2009).

15. S. Lee, S. Belkasim, and Y. Zhang, Multi-document text summarization using topic model and fuzzy logic. In *Machine Learning and Data Mining in Pattern Recognition*, pp. 159–168. Springer (2013).

16. L. Li, W. Heng, J. Yu, Y. Liu, and S. Wan, CIST system report for ACL Multiling 2013 — Track 1: Multilingual multi-document summarization, In *Proceedings of the MultiLing 2013 Workshop on Multilingual Multi-document Summarization*, pp. 39–44, Sofia, Bulgaria, ACL (2013).

17. H. Daumé III and D. Marcu, Bayesian query-focused summarization. In eds. N. Calzolari, C. Cardie, and P. Isabelle, *Proceedings of the 21st International Conference on Computational Linguistics and 44th Annual Meeting of the Association for Computational Linguistics*, Sydney, Australia, pp. 305–312, ACL (2006). doi: 10.3115/1220175.1220214. Available at: http://www.aclweb.org/anthology/P06-1039.

18. A. A. Mohamed and S. Rajasekaran, Query-based summarization based on document graphs. In *Proceedings of IEEE International Symposium on Signal Processing and Information Technology*, Vancouver, Canada, pp. 408–410, IEEE (2006).

19. W. Bosma, Query-based summarization using rhetorical structure theory, In eds. T. v. d. Wouden, M. Poss, H. Reckman, and C. Cremers, *15th Meeting of CLIN*, Amsterdam, The Netherlands, pp. 29–44, LOT (2005).

20. J. M. Conroy, J. D. Schlesinger, and J. G. Stewart, CLASSY: Query-based multi-document summarization. In *DUC 05 Conference Proceedings*, Gaithersburg, MA, USA, NIST (2005).

21. Y. Liu, S. H. Zhong, and W. Li, Query-oriented multi-document summarization via unsupervised deep learning. In eds. J. Hoffmann and B. Selman, *Proceedings of the 26th AAAI Conference on Artificial Intelligence*, Toronto, Canada, pp. 1699–1705, AAAI Press (2012).

22. F. Schilder and R. Kondadadi, Fastsum: Fast and accurate query-based multi-document summarization. In eds. J. D. Moore, S. Teufel, J. Allan, and S. Furui, *Proceedings of ACL-08: HLT, Short Papers*, Columbus, OH, USA, pp. 205–208, ACL (2008). Available at: http://www.aclweb.org/anthology/P08-2052.

23. J. Tang, L. Yao, and D. Chen, Multi-topic based query-oriented summarization. In eds. W. Wang, H. Kargupta, S. Ranka, P. S. Yu, and X. Wu, *SIAM International Conference Data Mining*, Miami, FL, USA, SIAM (2009).

24. S. Park, J.-H. Lee, C.-M. Ahn, J. S. Hong, and S.-J. Chun, Query based summarization using non-negative matrix factorization, In eds. B. Gabrys, R. Howlett, and L. Jain, *Knowledge-Based Intelligent Information and Engineering Systems*, vol. 4253, *Lecture Notes in Computer Science*, pp. 84–89. Springer (2006).

25. P. Chen and R. Verma, A query-based medical information summarization system using ontology knowledge. In *Proceedings of the 19th IEEE Symposium on Computer-Based Medical Systems (CBMS'06)*, Salt Lake City, UT, USA, pp. 37–42, IEEE (2006).

26. L. Zhou, Chin-Yew, and E. Hovy, Summarizing answers for complicated questions. In eds. N. Calzolari, K. Choukri, A. Gangemi, B. Maegaard, J. Mariani, J. Odijk, and D. Tapias, *Proceedings of the 5th International Conference on Language Resources and Evaluation (LREC-2006)*, Genoa, Italy, European Language Resources Association (2006).

27. Y. Li and S. Li, Query-focused multi-document summarization: Combining a topic model with graph-based semi-supervised learning. In eds. J. Tsujii and J. Hajic, *Proceedings of COLING 2014, the 25th International Conference on Computational Linguistics: Technical Papers*, Dublin, Ireland, pp. 1197–1207, Dublin City University and Association for Computational Linguistics (2014). Available at: http://www.aclweb.org/anthology/C14-1113.

28. L. Wang, H. Raghavan, C. Cardie, and V. Castelli, Query-focused opinion summarization for user-generated content. In eds. J. Tsujii and J. Hajic, *Proceedings of COLING 2014, the 25th International Conference on Computational Linguistics: Technical Papers*, Dublin, Ireland, pp. 1660–1669, Dublin

City University and Association for Computational Linguistics (2014). Available at: http://www.aclweb.org/anthology/C14-1157.

29. C. Li, Y. Liu, and L. Zhao, Using external resources and joint learning for bigram weighting in ilp-based multi-document summarization. In eds. R. Mihalcea, J. Chai, and A. Sarkar, *Proceedings of the 2015 Conference of the North American Chapter of the Association for Computational Linguistics: Human Language Technologies*, Denver, CO, USA, pp. 778–787, Association for Computational Linguistics (2015). Available at: http://www.aclweb.org/anthology/N15-1079.

30. J. Otterbacher, G. Erkan, and D. R. Radev, Biased lexrank: Passage retrieval using random walks with question-based priors, *Information Processing & Management*, **45**(1), 42–54 (2009).

31. J. Williams, S. Tam, and W. Shen, Finding good enough: A task-based evaluation of query biased summarization for cross-language information retrieval. In eds. A. Moschitti, B. Pang, and W. Daelemans, *Proceedings of the 2014 Conference on Empirical Methods in Natural Language Processing (EMNLP)*, Doha, Qatar, pp. 657–669, Association for Computational Linguistics (2014). Available at: http://www.aclweb.org/anthology/D14-1073.

32. M. Litvak, M. Last, and N. Vanetik, Krimping texts for better summarization. In L. Marquez, C. Callison-Burch, J. Su, D. Pighin, and Y. Marton, *Proceedings of the 2015 Conference on Empirical Methods in Natural Language Processing*, Lisbon, Portugal, pp. 1931–1935, Association for Computational Linguistics (2015). Available at: http://aclweb.org/anthology/D15-1223.

33. N. Vanetik and M. Litvak, Query-based summarization using MDL principle, In *Proceedings of the MultiLing 2017 Workshop on Summarization and Summary Evaluation Across Source Types and Genres*, pp. 22–31, Valencia, Spain, ACL (2017).

34. N. Vanetik, M. Litvak, and L. Li, Summarizing weibo with topics compression. In ed. A. Gelbukh, *18th International Conference on Computational Linguistics and Intelligent Text Processing*, Budapest, Hungary, Revised Selected Papers, Part II, Association for Computational Linguistics (2017).

35. A. R and S. R. Fast algorithms for mining association rules. In eds. J. B. Bocca, M. Jarke, and C. Zaniolo, *20th International Conference on Very Large Databases*, Santiago de Chile, Chile, pp. 487–499, VLDB (1994).

36. T. M. Mitchell, *Machine Learning*, 1st Edition. McGraw-Hill, Inc., New York (1997).

37. N. Pasquier, Y. Bastide, R. Taouil, and L. Lakhal, Discovering frequent closed itemsets for association rules. In eds. C. Beeri and P. Buneman, *International Conference on Database Theory*, Jerusalem, Israel, pp. 398–416, Springer (1999).

38. B. Goethals, Survey on frequent pattern mining, *Univ. of Helsinki*, **19**, 840–852 (2003).

39. D. A. Huffman, A method for the construction of minimum-redundancy codes, *Proceedings of the IRE*, **40**(9), 1098–1101 (1952).

40. H. Fernau, Extracting minimum length document type definitions is np-hard. In eds. G. Paliouras and Y. Sakakibara, *International Colloquium on Grammatical Inference*, Athens, Greece, pp. 277–278, Springer (2004).

41. C. Sina, Sina weibo. www.weibo.com. Available at: https://en.wikipedia.org/wiki/Sina_Weibo (2009).

42. H.-P. Zhang, H.-K. Yu, D.-Y. Xiong, and Q. Liu, HHMM-based chinese lexical analyzer ICTCLAS. In *Proceedings of the 2nd SIGHAN Workshop on Chinese Language Processing — Volume 17*, Sapporo, Japan, pp. 184–187, Association for Computational Linguistics (2003).

43. H. Wei, Y. Jia, L. Lei, and L. Yongbin, Research on key factors in multi-document topic modeling application with HLDA, *Journal of Chinese Information Processing*, **27**(6), 117–127 (2013).

44. DUC. Document Understanding Conference (2002–2007). Available at: http://duc.nist.gov.

45. X. Wan, J. Zhang, S. Wen, and J. Tan, Overview of the NLPCC 2015 shared task: Weibo-oriented chinese news summarization. In *Natural Language Processing and Chinese Computing*, vol. 9362, *Lecture Notes in Computer Science*, pp. 557–561, Springer (2015).

46. C.-Y. Lin, Rouge: A package for automatic evaluation of summaries. In *Proceedings of the Workshop on Text Summarization Branches Out (WAS 2004)*, Barcelona, Spain, pp. 25–26, Association for Computational Linguistics (2004).

47. R. McDonald, A study of global inference algorithms in multi-document summarization. In *Advances in Information Retrieval*, pp. 557—564, Springer (2007).

48. S. Ye, L. Qiu, T.-S. Chua, and M.-Y. Kan, NUS at DUC 2005: Understanding documents via concept links. In *Document Understanding Conference*, Gaithersburg, MD, USA, NIST (2005).

49. S. Blair-Goldensohn, From definitions to complex topics: Columbia university at DUC 2005. In *Document Understanding Conference*, Gaithersburg, MD, USA, NIST (2005).

50. S. Blair-Goldensohn, K. McKeown, and A. H. Schlaikjer, Answering definitional questions: A hybrid approach. In ed. M. Maybury, *New Directions In Question Answering*, chapter 4. AAAI Press (2004).

51. A. Nenkova and K. McKeown, References to named entities: a corpus study. In *NAACL-HLT 2003*, Association for Computational Linguistics (2003).

52. J. Jagarlamudi, P. Pingali, and V. Varma, Query independent sentence scoring approach to DUC 2006 (2006).

53. J. Jagadeesh, P. Pingali, and V. Varma, A relevance-based language modeling approach to DUC 2005. In *Document Understanding Conferences (along with HLT-EMNLP 2005)*, Gaithersburg, MD, USA, Association for Computational Linguistics (2005).

Chapter 4

Rich Feature Spaces and Regression Models in Single-Document Extractive Summarization

Alexander Dlikman*,‡, Marina Litvak†,§, and Mark Last*,¶

*Ben Gurion University of the Negev, Department of Software
and Information Systems Engineering,
Beer Sheva, 84105, Israel
†Shamoon College of Engineering,
Department of Software Engineering,
Beer Sheva, 84100, Israel
‡dlikman@post.bgu.ac.il
§marinal@ac.sce.ac.il
¶mlast@post.bgu.ac.il

Multiple methods of extractive text summarization have been proposed in recent years. The most common approach involves ranking sentences by various sentence scoring metrics (features) and calculating the final sentence score as a linear combination of selected features. Most currently used features are statistical and require only basic natural language processing (NLP), such as tokenization. In this chapter, we present and evaluate a set of novel — statistical and linguistic — features for sentence ranking and extraction in single documents. Statistical features are based on Topic modeling (TM). Linguistic features utilize an advanced NLP and include multi-word expressions based, named entities based, and parts of speech (POS) based. We show that the use of linguistic, POS based and topic based features improve the automated summaries compared to state-of-the-art statistical metrics. In addition, we explore the contribution of various regression algorithms for the sentence ranking task. These algorithms include: a genetic algorithm (GA), classification and regression trees, Cubist, and a linear regression model (LM). For this purpose, we introduce a sentence ranking methodology based on the similarity score between a candidate sentence and gold standard summaries. Our experiments are performed on four textual corpora accompanied by human-generated gold standard summaries: Document Understanding Conference(DUC) 2002, 2004 and 2007, and MultiLing-2013. The popular linear regression model achieved the best results in all evaluated datasets. Additionally, the linear regression model, which included POS based features, outperformed the models with statistical features only.

1. Introduction

In this chapter, we seek to improve the performance and summary quality of existing extractive summarization techniques by using novel — statistical and linguistic — features and advanced regression techniques. Our research focuses on extractive, single-document, monolingual summarization. We propose a supervised learning algorithm that is trained on a corpus of summarized documents in a given language. The induced model can be domain-specific or cross-domain, depending on the composition of the training corpus.

Based on our literature survey, there have been very few attempts to use TM or a deep linguistic analysis with an advanced NLP techniques for selecting key sentences. Also, there have been no attempts yet to employ general tree-based models for extractive summarization tasks. In this chapter, we study the contribution of these approaches to extractive summarization. We explore the effect of 8 topic features and multiple linguistic features (a total of 56) on sentence ranking and on the extraction stages of the MUSE summarization algorithm. The evaluated linguistic features include 15 novel named entities based features and 17 novel POS based features. Additionally, we extend 24 existing word-based features by using multi-word expressions.

To the best of our knowledge, this is the first time that classification and regression trees (CART) and the Cubist model are used for extractive summarization. In addition, the popular linear regression model and a genetic algorithm are evaluated and compared to state-of-the-art extractive summarization tools. All supervised models are compared across the same feature sets. The proposed supervised methodology for sentence extraction is based on a continuous similarity score between candidate sentences and human-generated gold standard summaries. For this purpose, a novel penalized precision metric is introduced.

2. Related work

2.1. *Regression and classification methods*
for sentence extraction

Several machine learning (ML) approaches are used in sentence extraction. The ML approaches require calculating various sentence scoring features (predictors) and a set of human-produced, reference summaries (also known as a gold standard or benchmark). In other words, these are supervised learning methods.

Two main schemes are used when ML techniques are applied: regression and binary classification. In the regression approach, the score of each candidate sentence s is evaluated as in Eq. (1).[1]

$$Score(s) = \sum_{i\in(set\ of\ features)}^{all\ features} w_i \cdot f_i \qquad (1)$$

where w_i is an importance weight of a feature f_i. The most common method for calculating the feature weights is a mathematical regression,[2] additional possible solution is a genetic algorithm.[3] Ouyang *et al.* (2011)[4] apply a support vector regression (SVR) model to the task of query-based, multi-document extractive summarization. In their SVR framework, they suggest a typical feature-based extractive schema and extract sentences according to a set of seven sentence features of which only four features are query independent. Their study presents several important conclusions. First, their results show that the regression approach outperforms sentence classification and ranking approaches. Second, when sentence importance score is based on similarity between candidate sentences and human-generated summaries, unigrams are more effective than bigrams.

Galanis *et al.* (2012)[5] present an integer linear programming (ILP) based approach for extractive, query-based multi-document summarization. The proposed method simultaneously maximizes both the importance of the sentences that are included in a summary as well as their diversity. In order to find a sentence's importance score, the authors use an SVR model. The "true" importance (dependent variable of the regression model) is obtained as a ROUGE score between candidate sentences and human-generated summaries. There are five various sentence features employed as SVR predictors (only three of them are query independent).

Machine learning schemes may be applied as binary classification tasks, where sentences are labeled as summary or non-summary sentences based on their features. A widerange of supervised classification models are used in this setting, including Naive Bayes,[6] artificial neural networks,[7] support vector machines,[8] maximum entropy classifiers,[9] and hidden Markov models (HMM).[10] Certain attempts have been made to employ semi-supervised learning for extractive summarization tasks.[11] In this paradigm, humans tag only a small number of examples of summary and non-summary sentences in order to reduce the amount of reference summaries.

Nenkova and McKeown (2012)[1] note that ML approaches have been shown to be more effective in single documents or domain or genre specific summarizations, where classifiers can be trained to categorize specific types of information.

Like other supervised learning approaches, summarization classifiers also require a large labeled corpus for training in order to obtain accurate results.[12] It is obvious that preparing gold standard summaries is difficult, expensive, and time consuming. In addition, most classification approaches do not have a way to limit the summary length due to the essence of binary classification.

Some cutting-edge extractive summarization approaches use genetic algorithms in the training stage.[2,3] The limitations of this optimization technique are transferred to the summarizer itself. One limitation is that the genetic algorithm approach is heuristic and does not ensure an optimal solution. Furthermore, since GA do not scale well with increasing complexity, growth in feature numbers often causes an exponential increase in the search space.

2.2. *Topic modeling for sentence extraction*

Topic model is a type of statistical model for discovering the abstract "topics" that occur in a collection of documents. Since the late 1990s, where early topic models were described by Papadimitriou *et al.* (1998)[13] and then by Hofmann,[14] topic modeling became very popular and useful as a content representation and information measurement of documents in many domains of information retrieval.

At present, there is a multitude of works where topic models have been applied for better summarization of text documents in different domains. Lee *et al.*[15] proposed a multi-document summarization method that combines topic and fuzzy logic models. The relevant topic words, extracted from source documents, are used as elements of fuzzy sets. Then, the importance of a sentence is measured by a fuzzy relevance rule generated from it. Haghighi and Vanderwende (2009)[16] introduced the HierSum summarization system, which utilizes a hierarchical LDA-style model to represent content specificity as a hierarchy of topic vocabulary distributions. Hennig and Albayrak (2010)[17] described a query-based summarizer. They represented sentences and queries in the latent topic space of the probabilistic latent semantic indexing (PLSI) model combined with a language model, and calculated a sentence importance score as a linear combination of several sentence-level features based on the similarity of sentence and query distributions over latent topics. Sentences were then selected in a greedy manner to create a summary. Gao *et al.* (2012)[18] proposed a topic modeling-based approach for summarizing trending subjects by jointly discovering the representative and complementary information from news and tweets. They combined cross-collection LDA and topic-aspect mixture models for precisely estimating sentence-level complementarity for the relevant information across different media. Delort and Alfonseca (2012)[19] presented an unsupervised probabilistic approach to model novelty in a document collection and applied it to the generation of update summaries. They proposed a non-parametric Bayesian approach — a variation of LDA — to distinguish between common and novel information. Wang and Cardie (2012)[20] presented a token-level decision summarization framework that utilizes the latent topic structures of utterances to identify "summary-worthy" words. They explored a series of unsupervised topic models and showed that fine-grained topic models, which discover topics at the utterance-level rather than the document-level, can better identify the gist of the decision making process. Wang *et al.* (2009)[21] proposed a Bayesian sentence-based topic model for summarization by making use of both term-document and term-sentence associations. In this work, the summarization task is incorporated into the Bayesian topic model.

2.3. *Topic modeling with Latent Dirichlet allocation*

Latent Dirichlet allocation (LDA), perhaps the most common topic model currently in use, is a generalization of PLSI, which was developed by Blei *et al.* (2003, 2012),[22,23] and which allowed documents to have a mixture of topics. Latent Dirichlet allocation uses a generative probabilistic approach for discovering the abstract topics, (i.e., clusters of semantically coherent documents that occur in a large collection of documents). In particular, we define a *word* as the basic discrete unit of any arbitrary text, which can be represented as an item w indexed by a vocabulary

$$\{1, 2, \ldots, |V|\}.$$

A *document* is then a sequence of N words denoted by,

$$\mathbf{w} = (w_1, w_2, \ldots, w_N),$$

where w_n is the nth word in the sequence. In fact, each document i has N_i words but the dependency on i is generally dropped. Finally, we define a *corpus* of M documents as $\mathbf{D} = \{\mathbf{w}_1, \mathbf{w}_2, \ldots, \mathbf{w}_M\}$, that is, a collection of documents. LDA finds a probabilistic model of a corpus that not only assigns high probability to members of the corpus, but also assigns high probability to other similar documents.[22]

We are particularly interested in finding K topics using the *latent* variables $\boldsymbol{\theta} = \{\theta_1, \theta_2, \ldots, \theta_M\}$, $\mathbf{z} = \bigcup z_{ij}$, and $\boldsymbol{\phi} = \{\phi_1, \phi_2, \ldots, \phi_K\}$. θ_i is the topic distribution for document i, z_{ij} is the topic for the jth word in document i, and ϕ_k is the word distribution for topic k. A graphical representation of LDA is given in Fig. 1 and a summary of parameters is given Table 1. The fundamental idea is that documents are represented as random mixtures over latent topics, where each topic is characterized by a distribution over words. While there are many variants, LDA

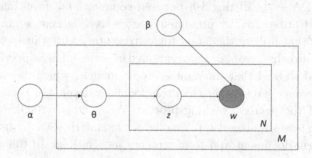

Fig. 1.   Graphical model representation of LDA.[22]

Table 1.   Parameters of the LDA algorithm.

Parameter	Notes
$\mathbf{D}$	the document collection
M	the number of documents in the document collection
N_i	the number of words in document i
α	Dirichlet prior on the per-document topic distribution
β	Dirichlet prior on the per-topic word distribution
θ_i	topic distribution of document i
ϕ_k	word distribution of topic k
z_{ij}	topic for the jth word in document i
w_{ij}	j^{th} word in document i

roughly assumes the following generative process for each document $\mathbf{w}$ in corpus $\mathbf{D}$.

- Choose $\theta_i \sim Dir(\alpha)$.
- Choose $\phi_i \sim Dir(\beta)$.
- For each $i \in \{1, 2, \ldots, M\}$ and $j \in \{1, 2, \ldots, N_i\}$ choose
  (i) a topic $z_{ij} \sim MulNom(\theta_i)$, and
  (ii) a word $w_{ij} \sim MulNom(\phi_{z_{ij}})$.

Above, $Dir(\cdot)$ is the Dirichlet and $MulNom(\cdot)$ is the multinomial distribution.

2.4. *Natural language processing operations*

In this section, we describe three popular NLP operations that are used in our work for calculating linguistic sentence features. These operations include multi-word expression (MWE) identification, named entity recognition (NER), and part of speech (POS) tagging.

Multi-word expression (MWE) identification. Multi-word expression (also referred to as a *phraseological unit* and a *collocation*) is a sequence of two or more lexemes that "has characteristics of a syntactic and semantic unit whose exact and unambiguous meaning or connotation cannot be derived directly from the meaning or connotation of its components."[24] Most collocation identification techniques are based on lexical association measures — mathematical formulas determining the strength of the connection between two or more words based on their occurrences and co-occurrences in a text corpus. The task is frequently limited to a particular subtype or subset of collocations defined, for example, by grammatical constraints (like multi-word verbs or compound nouns) or by n-gram size (usually applied only to bigrams).[25]

Pesina (2010)[25] has studied the supervised approach to collocation identification. He has mapped 82 various association measures into a vector to describe each collocation candidate. A label, indicating whether the bigram is considered to be a collocation or not, was assigned. Several machine learning methods (linear logistic regression, linear discriminant analysis, support vector machine and neural networks, which gained the best result) were applied to these measures. One of the author's conclusions was that all evaluated supervised methods significantly outperformed individual association measures.

Named entity recognition (NER). Named entities include persons, organizations and locations as well as numeric expressions such as time, date, currency, and percentage expressions. Most NER methods concentrate on narrow domains and textual genres (such as news articles, medical field, or tweets); a particular target language (most approaches primarily deal with English); or specific entity types (e.g., proper names, biological species, companies, films, scientists, email addresses for specific needs, etc.). Early approaches were typically based on handcrafted rules, but most current ones use ML schemes or combine handcrafted rules with automatic ML techniques (hybrid methods).[26]

Supervised learning is currently the leading approach for addressing NER problems. With this approach, it is necessary to train a ML algorithm on a large corpus of documents with tagged occurrences of named entities (NEs). Each NE example is characterized by a vector of various features. Typical features include, for example, whether a word is capitalized or not; if a word is in uppercase; word length in characters; if a word ends with a punctuation mark; the presence of an internal apostrophe; POS; position in sentence (in paragraph, in document); word frequency, etc. Various ML schemes are applied in order to determine whether a word is NE or not. Among the schemes implemented are hidden Markov models, decision trees, conditional random fields, and support vector machines (SVM). In addition, many algorithms involve external knowledge bases such as dictionaries that contain lists of popular names, organizations, cities, and so on. Annotating a training corpus is time-consuming and expensive. In order to overcome these difficulties, semi-supervised and even unsupervised techniques have emerged (e.g. see Ref. 27).

Part of speech (POS) tagging. Part of speech tagging is an important and basic form of syntactic analysis that has numerous uses in NLP. The aim of POS tagging is to assign a part of speech tag to each word in the input text. Common POS categories in English include nouns, verbs, articles, adjectives, prepositions, pronouns, adverbs, and conjunctions. There are other less common categories and sub-categories as well. In POS tagging it is common to identify 50 to 200 distinct POS tags for English (depending on the corpus). For instance, the Brown Corpus, one of the best-known corpora in POS tagging, contains 179 tags.[28]

The use of taggers based on Markov models is probably the most popular and conventional approach in POS tagging. The purpose of Markov models is to find the sequence of POS tags that maximize the probability that specific words will occur. According to the assumption of the hidden Markov model (HMM), the probability that a single word w_i will occur is a product of the probability of the word given POS tag $P(w_i/t_i)$ and the probability of the next tag given the current tag $P(t_{i+1}/t_i)$. The HMMs can learn the probabilities of bigrams, trigrams, and even larger sequences. All required probabilities $P(w_i/t_i)$ and $P(t_{i+1}/t_i)$ are evaluated from the training hand-tagged corpus that is necessary in this kind of models. The direct calculation is simple but can be expensive in running time, because the time complexity of the algorithm is exponential in the number of words. Various algorithms, such as Viterbi algorithm, are used to make these calculations less complex and therefore more time-efficient.[29]

One state-of-the-art POS tagger developed by Toutanova *et al.*[30] is known as the Stanford Log-linear POS Tagger. In contrast to most previous approaches, the model takes into account both past and future POS tags identities. In this novel approach, the authors are assuming that the probability of the current word tag t_0 depends not only on previous word tag t_{-1}, but also on the next word tag t_{+1}. This approach has achieved an accuracy of 97.24% in POS tagging of *Wall Street Journal* data from Penn Treebank.

2.5. *Regression models*

A regression model describes the relationship between a continuous dependent variable Y (also response, outcome) as a function of independent variables X_i (predictors, regressors, features) and unknown coefficients β_i (also weights). Various techniques are employed to estimate coefficient values.

Linear Regression Model with Ordinary Least Squares. The objective of using linear regression with ordinary least squares (OLS) is to find the vector of coefficients that minimize the sum of the squared errors (SSE):

$$SSE = \sum_{i=1}^{n}(y_i - \hat{y}_i)^2 \tag{2}$$

where y_i is an observed outcome and $\hat{y}_i$ is a predicted outcome. The value of $\hat{\beta}$, which minimizes SSE, is called the OLS estimator for β and can be found by the explicit formula (in matrix form):

$$\hat{\beta} = (X^T X)^{-1} X^T y. \tag{3}$$

The main advantages of linear regression are its simplicity, interpretability, and widespread availability in statistical software packages. On the other hand, there are several drawbacks to this method. The model's quality suffers when some predictors are highly correlated (multicollinearity phenomenon). Another limitation of OLS regression is the assumption of linearity. This means that if the data has a nonlinear structure, the linear regression will not be able to recognize it. One more disadvantage of OLS is its sensitivity to outlying observations.[31]

CART for Regression. Classification and regression trees (CART) is a tree-based method that partitions the feature space into a set of rectangles and fits a simple model, for example a constant, into each one.[32] The CART algorithm was introduced by Leo Breiman *et al.* in 1984.[33] The regression tree algorithm begins with the full dataset (S) and checks each distinct value of every predictor to find the optimal split that divides the data into two groups $(S_1$ and $S_2)$. The selected split minimizes the sum of squares error:

$$SSE = \sum_{i \in S_1} (y_i - \bar{y}_1)^2 + \sum_{i \in S_2} (y_i - \bar{y}_2)^2. \tag{4}$$

The procedure is repeated in a recursive manner for each data subset. The splitting stops when CART detects no further improvement in terms of SSE or when some stopping rules are applied. Alternatively, the data is split as much as possible and then the tree is pruned. Each branch of the tree ends in a terminal node. The predicted value is the same for all future observations at a given node and it equals to the average value of response for all training data points that fall into that node.[31,33]

Cubist. Cubist is a tree-based method for regression that is based on several publications by Ross Quinlan.[34,35] Previously, Cubist was available as a commercial software tool only, but recently the source code was released under an open source license.[31] There are several differences between Cubist and the previously described CART model: the splitting criterion is different (see the following), terminal nodes predict the response using a linear model, the specific pruning technique is different, and boosting procedure is optional. The criterion used for splitting the full data set S to p subsets is error reduction:

$$\Delta error = sd(S) - \sum_{i=1}^{P} \frac{n_i}{n} * sd(S_i) \tag{5}$$

where sd is a standard deviation. The model chooses a split with the maximum error reduction. The linear regression model is fitted into each partition using the split variable and all other variables that preceded it.

The linear models are combined using the following combination of two models, in order to determine the predictions:

$$\hat{y} = a * \hat{y}_{(k)} + (1 - a) * \hat{y}_{(p)}. \tag{6}$$

Here $\hat{y}_{(k)}$ is the prediction from the current model and $\hat{y}_{(p)}$ is the prediction from the parent node model.

The boosting approach in Cubist is optional and it is implemented as follows. The training set response is fitted based on a prior model and then the algorithm builds a new dataset using a pseudo-response. The n-th boosting model uses the following pseudo-response:[31]

$$y_{(n)}^{*} = y - (\hat{y}_{(n-1)} - y). \tag{7}$$

Genetic Algorithm. Genetic algorithms are a class of evolutionary heuristic search and optimization algorithms made popular by John Holland during the 1970s.[36] The algorithms are based on evolutionary principles of population biology and include such genetic stages as selection, crossover, and mutation. In the regression domain, GAs can be seen as a minimization problem of mean square error) (MSE) fitness function. The genetic representation in this case is a vector of β coefficients.[37]

3. Methodology

3.1. *Topic features*

We use LDA for topic modeling. Because we are interested in summarizing a single document (a meta-document in a case of multi-document summarization) by selecting sentences covering as many of its topics as possible, we want to explore a topic distribution over sentences in each document. We assume that documents in the same corpus "talk" about different, and possibly disjoint, topics. Therefore, we applied LDA in a non-standard way, where each document **w** was considered as a corpus and every sentence S was considered as a document. The output of such an application of LDA provides us with an importance score for a sentence in a document (normally, sentences do not have any particular importance in a standard LDA). In our studied corpus in the following experiments, for each document, the average number of sentences is about 50, and the average number of tokens is more than 800 after removing punctuations and stopwords. The LDA model has been quite successful when applied to long documents. Recently, it has also shown a great potential for analyzing short documents. For example, the LDA model has been applied to analyzing social media data such as Tweets.[38] We set the number of topics as $K = 5$. This is based on our judgment and experience in studying TM on a variety of corpora. In our experiments, we vary the number of topics between 3 and 10. Considering the nature of short documents and the evaluation results, setting the number of topics to 5 for the following studies is a reasonable compromise.

Four different outputs of the LDA algorithm, normalized and treated as probabilities, are relevant to our studies:

(1) Topic versus word dictionary, which gives the word w distributions $P(w|P_i)$ for each topic P_i
(2) Inferred topic distributions for each document in the studied corpus, namely the probability $P(P_i|S)$ (θ_i parameter of the LDA model) that a certain sentence S belongs to a topic P_i
(3) Eventual assignment of a sentence S to a topic to which it belongs, with the highest probability $\arg\max_i P(P_i|S)$, which allows us to separate all sentences of a document into K sets of sentences that describe K topics
(4) Importance of every topic in a document $\mathbf{w}$, $P(\mathbf{w}|P_i)$

Figure 2 shows sentences of the most significant topic found in the AP880217-100 file from the Document Understanding Conference (DUC) 2002 corpus.

We define eight sentence-level features that measure topic coverage by a sentence. Table 2 contains the topic-based features we use in this work. Because each feature expresses differently the coverage meaning, we use them all in a linear combination for computing the final importance score for a sentence. The important remark is that topic model can be applied to any language (given tokenization tool) and, therefore, MUSE with topic features is also language-independent.

> Weighing 8 pounds and standing 13 inches tall, Oscar was created by Metro-Goldwyn-Mayer studios art director Cedric Gibbons, who went on to win 11 of the trophies. From 1942 to 1944, the trophy was made of plaster, but winners were later presented with the real thing. It got 14 nominations.

Fig. 2.   Example of a topic.

Table 2.   Topic-based sentence features.

Name	Description
Topic coverage	The ratio of high-scored topics in a sentence made out of all topics, given a pre-defined threshold for $P(D|P_i)$
Topic words coverage	The ratio of high-scored topic words in a sentence out of all its words, given a pre-defined threshold for $P(w|P_i)$
Topic-based Luhn	The Luhn[39] score, where high-scored topic words are used as keywords
Central topic score	The actual score $P(P_i|S)$ of the top-ranked topic P_i for a sentence S
Topic average score	The average score $\sum_i^k P(P_i|S)/k$ of all topics assigned to a sentence
Cosine similarity to a title	The cosine similarity between vectors of a sentence S and a title (also treated as a sentence), where vectors are built from $\sum_{i=1}^k P(w|P_i) \times P(P_i|S)$ for each topic word w in S
Jaccard similarity to a title	The ratio of the number of joint title's and sentence's high-ranked topics to their union
Topic words average score	The average score $\sum_i^k \sum_j^n P(w_j|P_i)/n$ of all n topic words appearing in a sentence

3.2. *Linguistic features*

In the current subsection, we introduce various linguistic features, some of which are extensions of the original MUSE metrics presented in Ref. 3.

3.2.1. *Multi-Word Expression (MWE) based features*

We assume that using multi-words in addition to single terms will enhance existing statistical features that are based on the bag-of-words assumption (e.g., sentence to sentence similarity features). In Table 3, we present 24 original MUSE features (out of total of 31) that are extended by adding multi-word expressions. For vector-based features, we add MWEs to the existing vector representation and use the original MUSE formulas for our calculations. In this way, the MWEs appear twice, once in the usual way, separated into single words and the second time as a connected unit. MWE extended vector representation is demonstrated in the example below:

- Original sentence: Jon goes to zoological garden.
- Detected MWE: zoological_garden

Table 3. List of original MUSE
features extended by MWE.

Vector-based	Graph-based
LUHN	LUHN_DEG
KEY	KEY_DEG
COV	COV_DEG
TF	DEG
TFISF	TITLE_E_O
SVD	TITLE_E_J
TITLE_O	D_COV_E_O
TITLE_J	D_COV_E_J
TITLE_C	PR
D_COV_O	COV_PR
D_COV_J	KEY_PR
D_COV_C	LUHN_PR

- Regular vector representation: jon, go, zoological, garden
- MWE extended vector representation: jon, go, zoological, garden, zoological_garden

This representation affects both keywords and title-words, which are vector-based features. In the first case, the candidate sentence obtains the highest score when a MWE is detected as a keyword. In the second situation, the similarity between the title and candidate sentence is strongest when the same MWE occurs in both of them. For graph-based features, we build a new graph with single words and add MWE vertexes and then used original MUSE formulas for graph-based metrics for calculation. The effect on the values of the extended features is similar to the vector-based case.

3.2.2. Named entity based features

We assume that implementing existing state-of-the-art techniques for named entity recognition (rather than capturing only capitalized words as in previous approaches) and categorizing named entities by different types may enhance summarization performance. In Table 4, we introduce 15 new linguistic features based on named entities. These features take into account four different types of NEs: *location* (geographical names like countries, cities, rivers, etc.), *persons* (names), *date-time* (mention of date

Table 4. NE-based features.

Feature	Description
NE_LOC	Number of Location NEs in the sentence
NE_PER	Number of Person NEs in the sentence
NE_DATE	Number of Date-Time NEs in the sentence
NE_QU	Number of Quantitative NEs in the sentence
NE	Total number of NEs in the sentence: $|Named\_Ent(S)|$
NE_LOC_RAT	Ratio of Location NEs to all words in the sentence
NE_PER_RAT	Ratio of Person NEs to all words in the sentence
NE_DATE_RAT	Ratio of Date-Time NEs to all words in the sentence
NE_QU_RAT	Ratio of Quantitative NEs to all words in the sentence
NE_RAT	Ratio of total number of NEs to all words in the sentence: $\frac{|Named\_Ent(S)|}{N}$
NE_COV	Ratio of NEs in the sentence to NEs in document: $\frac{|Named\_Ent(S)|}{|Named\_Ent(D)|}$
NE_TFISF	$\sum_{NE\in S} tf(NE) * isf(NE);$ $isf(NE) = 1 - \frac{ln(n(NE))}{ln(n)},$ $n(NE)$ is the number of sentences containing NE
NE_FRQ_SUM	Sum of the NE frequencies: $\sum_{NE\in S} tf(NE)$
NE_TITLE	Number of NEs mentioned in the title per each sentence
NE_DEG_SUM	Sum of NE degrees: $\sum_{NE\in S} Deg(NE)$

or time including days of week, months, etc.) and *quantitative* NE (any numeric information: numbers, percentage, amounts of money, etc.). In addition, some features are related to distribution of NEs in the candidate sentence compared to the whole document and compared to the total number of words in the sentence.

3.2.3. *Part of speech based features*

We also assume that part of speech grammatical data can indicate to a certain extent the presence or absence of information content in text. Here we present a list of 17 POS features (Table 5). Some of them are novel and others are derived from our interpretation of certain metrics used by Litvak and Last (2013) in the MUSE summarizer.[40]

All proposed POS features take into account only nouns, verbs, adjectives, and adverbs due to the semantic importance of these parts of speech.[41] These features can be divided into POS ratio-based (defined as a ratio between the number of certain parts of speech in a sentence and sentence length); POS filtering (employing the original MUSE features after

Table 5. Part of speech based features.

Features	Description
POS_NN_RATIO	Ratio of nouns to all words in the sentence: $\frac{|Noun(S)|}{N}$
POS_VB_RATIO	Ratio of verbs to all words in the sentence: $\frac{|Verb(S)|}{N}$
POS_JJ_RATIO	Ratio of adjectives to all words in the sentence: $\frac{|Adj(S)|}{N}$
POS_RB_RATIO	Ratio of adverbs to all words in the sentence: $\frac{|Adv(S)|}{N}$
POS_V_TITLE_O POS_V_TITLE_J POS_V_TITLE_C POS_V_TF POS_V_COV POS_V_TFISF POS_V_KEY POS_V_D_COV_O POS_V_D_COV_J POS_V_D_COV_C	POS filtering features. MUSE, vector based features[3] calculated after keeping particular POS.
POS_N2 POS_N3 POS_N4	POS patterns features. Sum of POS 2-, 3- or 4-grams relevance measures in a sentence normalized by the total amount of n-grams (with the same n) in the sentence.

keeping particular POSs and discarding the rest of the words); and POS patterns (these features take into account n-gram parts of speech, which are frequent in human-generated summaries and, at the same time, relatively rare in the original texts).

While the first two methods do not need further explanation, the POS pattern metrics are defined as follows. We assume that the presence of a specific POS pattern in a candidate sentence may indicate sentence relevance in the summary.[42] Our method requires a preprocessing stage where the relevance of the candidate POS patterns is calculated. We define POS pattern relevance as a ratio between normalized pattern frequency in human-generated summaries and normalized pattern frequency in the corpus. The measure is greater than one when the POS n-gram is relatively more frequent in summaries than in the original texts. In the last stage, we sum up all POS n-gram relevance measures, which are greater than one, and normalize this value by the total amount of n-grams in a sentence. In the current work, we calculate the above metrics separately for 2-, 3- and 4-gram parts of speech.

3.3. *Sentence ranking*

Our methodology for the sentence ranking task includes the following steps:

(1) Feature extraction
(2) Definition and calculation of sentence similarity to a gold standard summary
(3) Data normalization
(4) Summary generation

3.3.1. *Feature extraction*

In the feature extraction stage, we generate a sentence-feature matrix for each corpus. Each row of the matrix refers to sentence i; each column refers to feature j; and an entry of the matrix ($m_i j$) indicates the score of feature j for sentence i. Obviously, each sentence should be associated with a $sentence_{ID}$ and a $document_{ID}$. For this preprocessing task, we use the existing MUSE framework and extract the values of the original MUSE features as well as our novel linguistic features.

3.3.2. *Sentence to summary similarity score*

The most complex stage is determining the similarity between each document's sentence and the gold standard summary (designated by y). Similarity measures such as ROUGE and other recall-based measures, which normalize the overlapping terms between the sentence and the gold standard summaries by a summary length, prefer longer sentences by assigning them a higher score. On the other hand, precision-based measures, which normalize overlapping terms by sentence length, prefer shorter sentences. To address those issues, we have examined the *F-score* (a.k.a. *F-measure* or *F1-score*) and our interpretation of *Bilingual Evaluation Understudy (BLEU)* measure, which was originally introduced for evaluating the quality of machine translation.[43]

The *F-measure* is a weighted average of precision and recall, which is defined as follows:

$$F = (1 + \beta^2) \frac{P * R}{(\beta^2 * P) + R}$$

$$P = \frac{|sentenceterms \cap goldstandardterms|}{|sentenceterms|}$$

$$R = \frac{|sentenceterms \cap goldstandardterms|}{|goldstandardterms|} \qquad (8)$$

Our implementation of the BLEU score is precision penalized when a sentence is "too short":

$$PenPr = P * penpen = \begin{cases} 1 & if \ length(s) > min.length \\ e^{1 - \frac{min.length}{length(s)}} & if \ length(s) \leq min.length) \end{cases} \quad (9)$$

where $min.length$ is a minimum sentence length in a gold standard summary.

When several benchmark summaries exist per each document, we calculate the $PenPr$ value for each summary separately and then provide the average value, exactly as in the ROUGE method. In order to compare both measures ($F\text{-}measure$ and $Penalizedprecision$) we performed the following experiments. $F\text{-}score$ (with $\beta = 1$) and $PenPr$-score were calculated for each sentence in a corpus. After this, two different peer summaries (for each document in the corpus) were created by extracting top n ranking sentences. One summary was created by $F\text{-}score$ rankings and the other one by the $PenPr$-score. These peer summaries were evaluated using ROUGE-1, 2, and 4 scores vs. existing gold standard summaries. The penalized precision score was found preferable to the $F\text{-}score$ in all datasets in terms of ROUGE-1 and ROUGE-2 metrics. Accordingly, in the experiments below we used the penalized precision score to determine the similarity between a sentence and a gold standard summary.

3.3.3. Data normalization

The max-min rescaling method is used to normalize feature values to the $[0, 1]$ range in the following way:

$$m_{ij}^{scaled} = \frac{m_{ij} - \min(m_j)}{\max(m_j) - \min(m_j)} \quad (10)$$

In order to normalize the values of sentence similarity to the gold standard (y), we use a different strategy. The minimum and the maximum values were calculated separately for each document:

$$y_{i;y \in doc_k}^{scaled} = \frac{y_i - \min_{doc_k}(y)}{\max_{doc_k}(y) - \min_{doc_k}(y)} \quad (11)$$

This approach makes it possible to deal with the fact that gold standard summaries in the corpus can be both extractive and abstractive (for extractive summaries, the y values intend to be higher than those for abstractive ones).

3.3.4. *Summary generation*

By using the sentence-feature matrix and sentence similarity to the gold standard as a continuous target (dependent) variable, any regression model can be trained. To summarize a new document with the induced model, we first calculate the predicted value of the similarity score ($\hat{y}$) for each document sentence. After this, n top ranked sentences (by $\hat{y}$) are extracted to a peer summary, subject to the summary length constraint.

4. Empirical evaluation

4.1. *Design of experiments*

In our experiments, we have explored the effect of linguistic features on existing extractive summarization algorithms. In the following subsections, we discuss the main components of these experiments.

4.1.1. *Datasets*

For training and testing, we used four different English corpora containing summarized documents. *DUC-2002*, which was created for the summarization competition task at the Document Understanding Conference in 2002, is a gold-standard dataset that contains 531 news articles from the *Wall Street Journal* (1987–1992) and the *Financial Times* (1991–1994). Each textual document contains at least 10 sentences and appears with two to three human-generated abstractive summaries of around 100 words.

The second experimental corpus is *DUC-2004*. The dataset contains 50 folders (topics) of 10 related documents (news items) each. Each folder is accompanied with four human-generated summaries of around 100 words each. In order to allow single-document summarization, all documents from a particular topic have been merged into one text.

The third experimental corpus is *DUC-2007*. The main task of DUC-2007 was, given a topic and a set of 25 relevant documents, to synthesize a fluent, well-organized 250-word summary of the documents that would answer the question in the topic statement (i.e., a multi-document query-based summarization). Each topic is accompanied with up to four human-generated abstractive summaries of around 250 words. In order to allow single-document training, all documents from a particular topic have been merged into one text.

Additionally, an English corpus from the MultiLing 2013 single-document summarization task was used (*MultiLing-2013*). The dataset includes 30 Wikipedia articles with one gold standard (human-generated) summary of around 270 words per article. Due to a relatively small amount of documents, MultiLing-2013 has been used only as testing data in the cross-corpus evaluation experiments.

4.1.2. *Software tools*

In our study, we have used Java-based implementation of the MUSE extractive summarization framework that was introduced by Litvak and Last (2010, 2013)[3,40] and currently is a part of the MUSEEC system.[44]

For Topic Modeling, we applied MALLET open source[a] software,[45] which implements a standard version of LDA.

We have also used jMWE, an open Java library for detecting multiword expressions in texts.[46] For the purpose of preprocessing (sentence splitting, tokenization, stop words removal, and lemmatization), NER, and POS tagging, we have used the Stanford CoreNLP toolkit,[47] an extensible pipeline that provides core natural language analysis.

For building regression models, we have used several R packages: GA[37] for genetic algorithm, $rpart$[48] for CART algorithm, and $cubist$[49] for Cubist algorithm. The $Caret$[50] R package was used for parameter optimization of those algorithms and for the cross-validation experiments described in the following.

4.2. *Topic features evaluation using MUSE algorithm*

The MUSE summarization approach can be enriched with additional knowledge and extended to a higher number of sentence features. We performed an experiment to determine whether the model extended by a topical knowledge gains larger accuracy. We performed experiments on three *corpora* from the DUC: 2002, 2004, and 2007,[51] which are described in Section 4.1.1. Because the extended models were evaluated only on English, MultiLing dataset was not utilized.

This evaluation was aimed to test the following hypothesis:

> $\mathcal{H}$: *integrating the topic knowledge into a*
> *lexicon-based model improves*
> *the summarization quality.*

---

[a]We set the initial values of the hyperparameters $\beta = 0.01$ and $\alpha_k = 0.2$, and hyperparameter optimization is enabled to allow the model to better fit the data by allowing some topics to be more prominent than others. In our experiment, besides the standard English stop-word list included in MALLET, we add additional stop-words based on studying the corpus to further improve the quality. Some of the examples include "it's," "don't," "can't," "year," "years," and "told."

In order to test our hypothesis, we evaluated and compared between the following variations of our supervised approach:

(1) **Lexicon Coverage** (denoted by *LexCov*): Only lexicon-based features, as discussed in 3, were used for sentence ranking.
(2) **Topic Coverage** (denoted by *TopCov*): Only topic features were used for sentence ranking.
(3) **Information Coverage** (denoted by *InfCov*): Both topic features and lexicon features were used for sentence ranking.

Table 6 contains the comparative evaluation results, measured by the Rouge-1 Precision, Recall, and F-measure scores. As can be seen, *InfCov*, integrating topic knowledge into a lexicon-based model, outperforms lexicon-based *LexCov* and, as such, our research hypothesis can be accepted. Another interesting point can be noticed from the results: Using only topic-based features does not improve the summarization quality significantly; despite visual improvement in score values, the difference is not statistically distinguishable. From this experiment, we can conclude that both types of features — lexical and topic-based — contribute to summarization quality, and using both types provides the best solution.

Table 6.   Comparative results of supervised approach.

DUC-2002			
System	R	P	F
LexCov	0.4443	0.4494	0.4468
TopCov	0.4499	0.4549	0.4524
InfCov	**0.4588**	**0.4568**	**0.4578**

DUC-2004			
System	R	P	F
LexCov	0.3543	0.3463	0.3502
TopCov	0.3615	**0.3555**	0.3585
InfCov	**0.3676**	0.3544	**0.3609**

DUC-2007			
System	R	P	F
LexCov	0.3768	0.3638	0.3702
TopCov	0.3886	0.3695	0.3788
InfCov	**0.3929**	**0.3711**	**0.3817**

4.3. *Linguistic features evaluation using MUSE algorithm*

4.3.1. *Multi-word expressions and named entities based features*

In the current section, we describe the experiments with MWE and NE based features and present the results. We evaluate these features in terms of ROUGE-1 and ROUGE-2 recall metrics, described in Ref. 52. Our rationale for this approach is that ROUGE-1 showed the largest variation across the methods and ROUGE-2 fits well for single-document summarization tasks. In addition, ROUGE has become the standard method of summarization evaluation.[1]

We performed nine experiments, each with a different set of features, in order to evaluate the influence of linguistic features introduced into the task of extractive summarization. We used the following groups of features: MUSE (all 30 original MUSE features; see Ref. 3); MWE (24 MUSE features extended by multi-word expressions; see 3); NE (15 new linguistic features based on named entities; see Table 4); and Structure (a subset of MUSE features, including only location and length–based sentence features). The sign "+" between group names means that several feature groups were used together.

Each experiment was evaluated using 10-fold cross validation on the DUC-2002 dataset. The MUSE feature set was chosen as a baseline since it is the state-of-the-art method that we wish to improve. The results of 10-fold cross validation are shown in Table 7 (ROUGE-1) and Table 8 (ROUGE-2), sorted in the descending order of the test scores.

In Figs. 3 and 4, we show ROUGE-1 and ROUGE-2 bar charts that compare the feature sets. The error bars in the charts represent the standard

Table 7. Results of DUC-2002 MWE + NE features 10-fold CV (ROUGE-1).

Features set	Test	Test max	Test SD	Train	Number of features
MWE+NE+Structure	0.455	0.469	0.011	0.459	45
MUSE+NE	0.453	0.486	0.018	0.459	45
MUSE+MWE+NE	0.452	0.464	0.009	0.457	69
MUSE	0.451	0.481	0.017	0.456	30
MUSE+MWE	0.450	0.466	0.014	0.455	54
MWE+ Structure	0.448	0.472	0.013	0.456	30
MWE+NE	0.438	0.458	0.014	0.443	39
MWE	0.434	0.450	0.011	0.440	24
NE	0.429	0.446	0.013	0.436	15

Table 8. Results of DUC-2002 MWE + NE features 10-fold CV (ROUGE-2).

Features set	Test	Test max	Test SD	Train	Number of features
MWE+NE+Structure	0.216	0.230	0.013	0.222	45
MUSE+NE	0.215	0.240	0.013	0.222	45
MWE+Structure	0.215	0.230	0.009	0.220	30
MUSE	0.214	0.239	0.011	0.220	30
MUSE+MWE+NE	0.212	0.238	0.013	0.221	69
MUSE+MWE	0.212	0.233	0.013	0.218	54
MWE+NE	0.200	0.219	0.014	0.206	34
MWE	0.196	0.211	0.010	0.200	24
NE	0.194	0.228	0.014	0.200	15

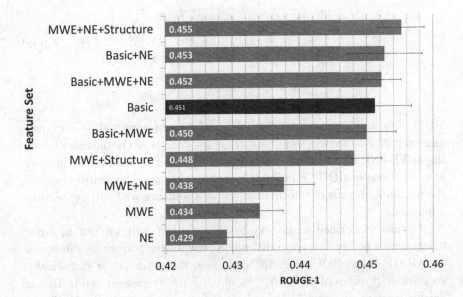

Fig. 3. ROUGE-1 bar chart.

error of the mean (the mean of 10 runs of 10-fold CV); the baseline values are marked in a different color.

We claim that the MWE set alone and, to a greater degree, NE alone are not expected to show high performance because they only represent very specific information. The NE set represents information about the presence of named entities in a sentence and the MWE set extends the keyword and the title-similarity features only. Furthermore, since the MWE and the

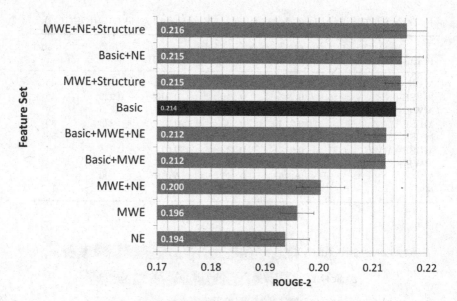

Fig. 4.   ROUGE-2 bar chart.

MUSE sets have very similar features, we have not expected an improvement in performance when applying these sets together. On the other hand, the MWE+NE+Structure combination is expected to achieve the highest score in terms of ROUGE evaluation metrics, because this feature set has the maximal amount of information about a sentence without any feature duplication.

We have performed a one way between-subject ANOVA test in order to examine whether there is a difference between the feature sets in terms of ROUGE-1 and ROUGE-2. In both cases, the difference is statistically significant (p-values of $4.3 \times 10^{(-4)}$ and $6.0 \times 10^{(-5)}$, respectively). To our disappointment, the post-hoc tests have not shown a statistically significant difference between the baselines and the proposed feature sets.

There are several possible reasons for the absence of improvement in our evaluation results. One possible explanation is the difficulty of the genetic algorithm to deal with numerous features simultaneously rather than adjusting the weight of each feature separately as is commonly the case. In comparison to the 30 features in the baseline configuration, we used 45 and even more features in our solution. Another reason for the lack of improvement may be the use of ROUGE metrics in the evaluation stage. Perhaps a certain improvement in summary quality might occur (such as general readability or coherence) but it is not covered by the recall-based evaluation methods. Furthermore, we evaluate an extractive summarization approach with abstractive reference summaries.

4.3.2. *Part of speech features*

Part of speech-based features were evaluated by five experiments performed in the same way as the one described earlier. In addition, the p-values of paired t-tests were provided (pairwise comparison of the baseline, the MUSE feature set, to each other feature combination). As shown by the results (Tables 9 and 10), POS features significantly improve the similarity of the extractive summaries to the gold standard. In both datasets, (DUC 2002 and MultiLing 2013), the top feature set containing POS-based features outperformed the baseline with p-values of 0.009 and 0.044, respectively.

It is noteworthy that the top-ranking feature set (POS + Struct) contains less features than the baseline. Additionally, this set requires a smaller computational effort compared to the baseline, as it excludes singular value decomposition (SVD), PageRank, and other features which require time-consuming graph representation of documents.

Table 9.   Results of DUC-2002 POS features 10-fold CV (ROUGE-1).

Feature set	Test	Test SD	No. of features	P-value
POS+Struct	0.459	0.012	22	0.009
MUSE+POS+10NER	0.457	0.016	57	0.032
MUSE+POS	0.456	0.018	47	0.072
MUSE	0.450	0.017	30	–
POS.only	0.448	0.014	17	–

Table 10.   Results of MultiLing-2013 POS features testing (ROUGE-1).

Feature set	Test	Test SD	No. of features	P-value
POS_STRUCT	0.352	0.046	22	0.044
POS_MUSE_NER	0.347	0.038	57	0.061
POS.only	0.344	0.034	17	0.120
POS_MUSE	0.337	0.053	47	0.137
MUSE	0.329	0.047	30	–

4.4. *Sentence ranking using regression methods*

Below we describe a series of further experiments where we introduce the sentence ranking and extraction task as a regression problem for predicting sentence similarity to a gold-standard summary (as described in Section 3.3). We assume that sentence ranking by a continuous similarity score is more suitable for sentence extraction than binary classification ("1" if a sentence belongs to the reference summary and "0" otherwise).

In the following experiments, all datasets described in Section 4.1.1 are employed. DUC-2002 and DUC-2007 are used in the 10-fold cross-validation framework, whereas MultiLing-2013 is used only as testing data for models induced from DUC-2002. Penalized precision, presented in Section 3.3.2, is used to demonstrate the "true" similarity between a sentence and the gold standard summary.

We compare four regression approaches to the sentence ranking task: CART, LM (linear regression model), GA (genetic algorithm), and Cubist. In addition, we present the results of state-of-the-art extractive summarization methods: MUSE and Gillick. Each method is evaluated with four different feature sets: MUSE (30 original MUSE features); POS (17 POS-based features, introduced in Section 3.2.3, along with sentence position and sentence length features; MUSE&POS (both MUSE and POS-based features), and POS.only (17 POS-based features only).

ROUGE-1, 2, and 4 metrics (recall, precision, and F-measure) are used for summary evaluation. In the following three sections, the results are ordered by ROUGE-1 F-measure values. The best model and the best feature set are determined using the paired t-test.

4.4.1. *DUC-2002 (ten-fold cross-validation)*

As shown in Table 11, Cubist and LM, both with the most complete features set (MUSE&POS), are the top ranking approaches. However there is a small difference between them. Since the paired t-test shows that this difference is not statistically significant (p-value of 0.205), we prefer the simpler LM approach. In further statistical tests, we compare LM models using different feature sets (Table 12). As can be seen from the results, the MUSE&POS feature combination is significantly better than the other feature sets.

Finally, in Table 13, we compare the best (LM) model using MUSE&POS features to all other models using the same features. The results are statistically significant and show that LM outperforms all other models except Cubist.

Table 11. Results of DUC-2002 sentence ranking.

Model and features	ROUGE-1			ROUGE-2		
	F	R	P	F	R	P
Cubist MUSE&POS	0.465	0.467	0.464	0.219	0.219	0.218
LM MUSE&POS	0.464	0.466	0.463	0.219	0.219	0.217
Cubist POS	0.462	0.463	0.460	0.217	0.218	0.217
Cubist MUSE	0.461	0.462	0.459	0.215	0.216	0.214
LM POS	0.460	0.462	0.459	0.217	0.218	0.216
MUSE model POS	0.460	0.460	0.464	0.219	0.220	0.221
LM MUSE	0.457	0.459	0.456	0.212	0.212	0.211
MUSE model MUSE&POS	0.457	0.457	0.461	0.216	0.216	0.217
GA POS	0.457	0.458	0.455	0.214	0.215	0.213
MUSE model	0.456	0.456	0.460	0.215	0.215	0.217
CART POS	0.455	0.456	0.453	0.211	0.212	0.210
Cubist POS.only	0.454	0.456	0.453	0.207	0.208	0.207
LM POS.only	0.454	0.456	0.453	0.208	0.209	0.208
GA MUSE	0.453	0.455	0.452	0.207	0.208	0.207
MUSE model POS.only	0.453	0.453	0.457	0.211	0.212	0.213
GA MUSE&POS	0.452	0.454	0.451	0.208	0.209	0.208
CART MUSE	0.445	0.447	0.444	0.201	0.202	0.200
GA POS.only	0.445	0.446	0.443	0.201	0.202	0.201
CART MUSE POS	0.444	0.446	0.443	0.200	0.200	0.199
CART POS.only	0.444	0.445	0.443	0.199	0.200	0.198
Gillick	0.401	0.399	0.408	0.160	0.160	0.162

Table 12. DUC-2002 LM with different feature sets.

Model	ROUGE-1 F	p-value
LM MUSE&POS	0.464	–
LM POS	0.460	0.031
LM MUSE	0.457	0.000
LM POS	0.454	0.001

Table 13. DUC-2002 best model.

Model	ROUGE-1 F	p-value
LM	0.464	–
MUSE model	0.457	0.003
GA	0.452	0.000
CART	0.444	0.000
Gillick	0.401	0.000

4.4.2. *DUC-2007 (ten-fold cross-validation)*

The DUC-2007 results (see Table 14) clearly show the advantages of the LM approach. In Table 15, we explore the influence of different features on LM performance. The results are inconclusive, MUSE&POS set's advantage is not statistically significant, hence we prefer the MUSE feature set (the baseline).

Finally, in Table 16, we compare the best (LM) model using MUSE features to all other models using the same feature set. The results are statistically significant and show that LM outperforms all the other models.

Table 14. Results of DUC-2007 sentence ranking.

Model and features	ROUGE-1			ROUGE-2		
	F	R	P	F	R	P
LM MUSE&POS	0.377	0.380	0.375	0.091	0.092	0.091
LM MUSE	0.375	0.378	0.373	0.090	0.091	0.089
LM POS	0.372	0.374	0.370	0.089	0.090	0.089
CART MUSE	0.369	0.371	0.366	0.079	0.080	0.079
GA MUSE	0.365	0.367	0.362	0.083	0.083	0.082
MUSE model	0.364	0.367	0.361	0.078	0.078	0.077
MUSE model MUSE&POS	0.363	0.366	0.361	0.080	0.080	0.079
MUSE model POS	0.363	0.365	0.361	0.080	0.081	0.080
Cubist MUSE	0.362	0.365	0.360	0.078	0.078	0.077
Cubist POS.only	0.362	0.364	0.360	0.074	0.075	0.074
LM POS.only	0.360	0.363	0.358	0.080	0.081	0.080
Cubist MUSE&POS	0.360	0.362	0.358	0.083	0.084	0.083
GA MUSE&POS	0.358	0.361	0.356	0.078	0.079	0.078
Cubist POS	0.356	0.359	0.354	0.073	0.073	0.072
MUSE model POS.only	0.356	0.359	0.353	0.075	0.076	0.074
CART MUSE&POS	0.354	0.356	0.352	0.074	0.075	0.074
GA POS.only	0.354	0.356	0.351	0.076	0.077	0.076
GA POS	0.351	0.354	0.349	0.068	0.068	0.068
Gillick	0.344	0.344	0.341	0.064	0.064	0.063
CART POS.only	0.343	0.346	0.341	0.066	0.066	0.065
CART POS	0.343	0.345	0.341	0.065	0.066	0.065

Table 15. DUC-2007 LM with different feature sets.

Model	ROUGE-1 F	p-value
LM MUSE&POS	0.377	–
LM MUSE	0.375	0.316
LM POS&Struct	0.372	0.095
LM POS.only	0.360	0.016

Table 16. DUC-2007 best model.

Model	ROUGE-1 F	p-value
LM	0.375	–
CART	0.369	0.036
GA	0.365	0.024
MUSE model	0.364	0.040
Cubist	0.362	0.011
Gillick	0.344	0.000

4.4.3. *MultiLing-2013 (training on DUC-2002)*

In the MultiLing-2013 corpus (see Table 17), both Cubist and LM with the MUSE&POS feature set are the top-ranking models. However, the paired t-test shows that the difference between them is not statistically significant (p-value of 0.134). Consequently we prefer the simpler LM approach, which provided results that were similar to those of DUC-2002. Now we can compare the linear models using different features (Table 18). The MUSE&POS feature set outperforms the baseline (MUSE feature set) with a p-value of 5%.

In the next series of paired t-tests (Table 19), we compare LM with the best features (MUSE&POS) to all other models with the same features. The results are statistically significant and show that LM outperforms all other models (except Cubist).

4.4.4. *Feature selection*

A model with less features is more interpretable and less costly.[31] In this section, we provide the results of two methods for feature selection: stepwise selection (with Akaike Information Criterion (AIC) statistics as the threshold) and genetic algorithm as described in Scrucca *et al.* (2013) and Kuhn and Johnson (2013).

In the case of GA, the genetic representation is a binary vector that has the same length as the number of features in the dataset. Each entry of this vector represents the presence or absence of a feature in the model. For the fitness function, we employ AIC:[53]

$$AIC = n * log \left(\sum_{i=1}^{n} (y_i - \hat{y}_i)^2 \right) + 2P \qquad (12)$$

where P is the number of model parameters.

Table 17.   MultiLing-2013 sentence ranking results.

Model and features	ROUGE-1			ROUGE-2		
	F	R	P	F	R	P
Cubist MUSE&POS	0.435	0.435	0.435	0.126	0.126	0.126
LM MUSE&POS	0.429	0.429	0.429	0.127	0.127	0.127
LM POS	0.427	0.427	0.427	0.122	0.122	0.122
LM MUSE	0.425	0.425	0.425	0.120	0.120	0.120
Cubist MUSE	0.421	0.421	0.421	0.120	0.120	0.120
LM POS.only	0.421	0.421	0.421	0.115	0.115	0.115
GA MUSE	0.420	0.420	0.420	0.117	0.117	0.117
Cubist POS.only	0.415	0.415	0.415	0.116	0.116	0.116
GA POS.only	0.411	0.411	0.411	0.104	0.104	0.104
Cubist POS	0.407	0.407	0.407	0.109	0.109	0.109
GA POS	0.406	0.406	0.406	0.101	0.101	0.101
GA MUSE&POS	0.406	0.406	0.406	0.096	0.096	0.096
MUSE model	0.403	0.403	0.410	0.109	0.109	0.111
MUSE model MUSE&POS	0.401	0.401	0.410	0.110	0.110	0.113
CART MUSE&POS	0.390	0.390	0.390	0.096	0.096	0.096
CART POS	0.390	0.390	0.390	0.096	0.096	0.096
CART POS.only	0.389	0.389	0.389	0.098	0.098	0.098
MUSE model POS	0.383	0.383	0.392	0.098	0.098	0.100
CART MUSE	0.382	0.382	0.382	0.091	0.091	0.091
MUSE model POS.only	0.378	0.378	0.386	0.090	0.090	0.092
Gillick	0.353	0.353	0.358	0.069	0.069	0.070

Table 18.   MultiLing-2013 LM with different feature sets.

Model	ROUGE-1 F	p-value
LM MUSE&POS	0.429	–
LM POS	0.427	0.081
LM MUSE	0.425	0.050
LM POS.only	0.421	0.026

Table 19.   MultiLing-2013 best model.

Model	ROUGE-1 F	p-value
LM	0.429	–
MUSE model	0.403	0.003
GA	0.406	0.013
CART	0.390	0.001
Gillick	0.353	0.000

Table 20. Number of selected features in each configuration.

Model and features	# MUSE features	# POS features	# Total
LM GA.selection	22	14	36
LM MUSE&POS	30	17	47
LM Stepwise	24	14	38
LM POS	5	17	22
LM MUSE	30	0	30
LM POS.only	0	17	17

Table 21. Linear models with feature selection.

Model and features	ROUGE-1			ROUGE-2		
	F	R	P	F	R	P
LM GA.select	0.430	0.430	0.430	0.125	0.125	0.125
LM MUSE&POS	0.429	0.429	0.429	0.127	0.127	0.127
LM Stepwise	0.429	0.429	0.429	0.124	0.124	0.124
LM POS	0.427	0.427	0.427	0.122	0.122	0.122
LM MUSE	0.425	0.425	0.425	0.120	0.120	0.120
LM POS.only	0.421	0.421	0.421	0.115	0.115	0.115

For both methods, we used a linear model as the main model for feature weights evaluation. The DUC-2002 corpus was used as a training dataset while for evaluation purposes we used the MultiLing-2013 corpus. The full model included MUSE features and POS-based features (a total of 47 predictors).

In Table 20, we present the results of the two approaches for feature selection (LM Stepwise and LM GA.selection) and compare them to different feature sets presented in Section 3.

As shown in Table 21, both feature selection approaches provide very similar results that are not statistically different from each other. However, the LM GA.selection model has a slight advantage due to a smaller number of features it requires (see Table 20).

5. Conclusion

In the first part of this work, we presented and evaluated topic features, derived from DLA, for sentence ranking and extraction in single-document summarization. The evaluation of the features was performed with the MUSE extractive summarization framework. Experiments showed that topic knowledge improves MUSE's performance.

Second part of our work introduced multi-word expressions (MWE), named entities (NE), and parts of speech (POS) based features (total of 56 features) for sentence ranking and extraction in single-document summarization. The evaluation of the features was also performed with the MUSE extractive summarization framework.

The proposed MWE and NE based features obtained ROUGE scores higher than the baseline MUSE features. However the difference was not statistically significant and apparently, the employment of these sentence metrics for sentence extraction is useless. One of possible reasons for the failure of NE based features could be a limitation of the genetic algorithm, which is integrated with the MUSE summarizer and which does not scale well with a growth in the number of features. A possible solution for this issue is employing NE features with other machine learning algorithms as described in Section 3.3. Another way is to perform feature selection and reduce the number of evaluated NE features.

Using POS-based features combined with straightforward structure-based features or with MUSE features improves the automatic summaries (in terms of ROUGE evaluation metrics) compared to MUSE state-of-the-art statistical features alone. The results are statistically significant with a p-value less than 5% in all tested datasets.

In the third part of our work, we explored the contribution of various machine learning algorithms to sentence ranking tasks. We also performed additional evaluation of POS features. These experiments were done outside the MUSE framework. We introduced a methodology for sentence extraction based on a continuous similarity score between a candidate sentence and human-generated benchmark summaries. For this purpose, a novel penalized precision metric is employed.

The results of our experiments show that in all evaluated textual corpora, the popular linear model outperforms the more sophisticated CART and Cubist regression models, heuristic optimization with genetic algorithm, as well as state-of-the-art summarization approaches (MUSE and Gillick). Additionally, the linear models which included POS features outperformed those with statistical features only. To achieve the best results, we suggest using the linear model with the full set of features (MUSE features and POS-based features together) or using the linear model with the features remaining after feature selection.

Future work may concentrate on extending our suggested POS-based features and sentence ranking techniques to other languages such as German, Hebrew, and Arabic. The methodology extension to any new language will rely on the NLP tools for sentence splitting, tokenization, stop words removal, lemmatization, POS tagging, NE recognition, and MWE identification that are available for that language.

In our experiments, the Cubist tree-based model for sentence ranking achieved a top ROUGE score for DUC-2002 and MultiLing corpora. We suggest that using text-based features (such as the number of sentences, percentage of named entities in a text, text genre or topic, etc.) for node splitting in the training stage and the use of sentence-based features in terminal nodes can improve the summary quality and create a model that is suitable for all kinds of texts.

Also, the sentence extraction technique can be enhanced by using both sentence-to-summary similarity scores (F-measure and Penalized Precision (PenPr)). As we show in Section 3.3.2, PenPr outperforms F-measure (ROUGE-1 F at 0.553 and 0.540, respectively). The use of the maximum of these two measures reaches the ROUGE-1 F score of 0.591. A multivariate regression algorithm that estimates a single regression model with more than one outcome variable can be used for this purpose.

References

1. A. Nenkova and K. McKeown, A survey of text summarization techniques. In *Mining Text Data*, pp. 43–76. Springer Verlag, Heidelberg, Germany (2012).
2. M. A. Fattah and F. Ren, Ga, mr, ffnn, pnn and gmm based models for automatic text summarization, *Computer Speech & Language*, **23**(1), 126–144 (2009).
3. M. Litvak, M. Last, and M. Friedman, A new approach to improving multilingual summarization using a Genetic Algorithm. In eds. J. Hajic, S. Carberry, and S. Clark, *ACL '10: Proceedings of the 48th Annual Meeting of the Association for Computational Linguistics*, Uppsala, Sweden, pp. 927–936, Association for Computational Linguistics (2010).
4. Y. Ouyang, W. Li, S. Li, and Q. Lu, Applying regression models to query-focused multi-document summarization, *Information Processing & Management*, **47**(2), 227–237 (2011).
5. D. Galanis, G. Lampouras, and I. Androutsopoulos, Extractive multi-document summarization with integer linear programming and support vector regression. In eds. C-R. Huang and D. Jurafsky, *COLING*, Beijing, China, pp. 911–926, ACL (2012).
6. K.-F. Wong, M. Wu, and W. Li, Extractive summarization using supervised and semi-supervised learning. In eds. D. Scott and H. Uszkoreit, *Proceedings of the 22nd International Conference on Computational Linguistics-Volume 1*, Manchester, UK, pp. 985–992, ACL (2008).
7. K. Kaikhah, Automatic text summarization with neural networks. In eds. V. Jotsov, *Intelligent Systems, 2004. Proceedings. 2004 2nd International IEEE Conference*, Varna, Bulgaria, vol. 1, pp. 40–44, IEEE (2004).

8. M. Fuentes, E. Alfonseca, and H. Rodríguez, Support vector machines for query-focused summarization trained and evaluated on pyramid data. In eds. A. Zaenen and A. v. d. Bosch, *Proceedings of the 45th Annual Meeting of the ACL on Interactive Poster and Demonstration Sessions*, Prague, Czech Republic, pp. 57–60, ACL (2007).

9. M. Osborne, Using maximum entropy for sentence extraction. In eds. U. Hahn and D. Harman, *Proceedings of the ACL-02 Workshop on Automatic Summarization-Volume 4*, Philadelphia, PA, USA, pp. 1–8, ACL (2002).

10. P. Fung, G. Ngai, and C.-S. Cheung, Combining optimal clustering and hidden markov models for extractive summarization. In *Proceedings of the ACL 2003 Workshop on Multilingual Summarization and Question Answering-Volume 12*, Sapporo, Japan, pp. 21–28, ACL (2003).

11. S. Xie, H. Lin, and Y. Liu, Semi-supervised extractive speech summarization via co-training algorithm. In eds. T. Kobayashi, K. Hirose, and S. Nakamura, *Eleventh Annual Conference of the International Speech Communication Association*, Makuhari, Japan, pp. 2522–2525, ISCA (2010).

12. E. Lloret and M. Palomar, Text summarisation in progress: a literature review, *Artificial Intelligence Review*, **37**(1), 1–41 (2012).

13. C. H. Papadimitriou, P. Raghavan, H. Tamaki, and S. Vempala, Latent semantic indexing: A probabilistic analysis. In eds. A. O. Mendelzon and J. Paredaens, *Proceedings of ACM PODS*, Seattle, WA, pp. 159–168, ACM (1998).

14. T. Hofmann, Probabilistic latent semantic indexing. In eds. F. C. Gey, M. A. Hearst, and R. M. Tong, *Proceedings of the Twenty-Second Annual International SIGIR Conference on Research and Development in Information Retrieval*, Berkeley, CA, USA, pp. 50–57, ACM (1999).

15. S. Lee, S. Belkasim, and Y. Zhang, Multi-document text summarization using topic model and fuzzy logic. In ed. P. Perner, *Machine Learning and Data Mining in Pattern Recognition*, New York, NY, USA, vol. 7988, *Lecture Notes in Computer Science*, pp. 159–168, ACL (2013).

16. A. Haghighi and L. Vanderwende, Exploring content models for multi-document summarization. In eds. M. Ostendorf, M. Collins, S. Narayanan, D. W. Oard, and L. Vanderwende, *Human Language Technologies: The 2009 Annual Conference of the North American Chapter of the ACL*, Boulder, Colorado, pp. 362–370 (2009).

17. L. Hennig and S. Albayrak, Personalized multi-document summarization using n-gram topic model fusion. In *International Conference on Language Resources and Evaluation (LREC 2010), 1st Workshop on Semantic Personalized Information Management (SPIM 2010)*, Valletta, Malta, pp. 24–30, LREC (2010).

18. W. Gao, P. Li, and K. Darwish, Joint topic modeling for event summarization across news and social media streams. In eds. X-W. Chen, G. Lebanon, H. Wang, and M. J. Zaki, *Proceedings of the 21st ACM International Conference on Information and Knowledge Management (CIKM 2012)*, Maui, HI, USA, pp. 1173–1182, ACM (2012).

19. J.-Y. Delort and E. Alfonseca, Dualsum: A topic-model based approach for update summarization. In ed. W. Daelemans, *Proceedings of the*

13th Conference of the European Chapter of the Association for Computational Linguistics, Avignon, France, p. 214–223, ACL (2012).

20. L. Wang and C. Cardie, Unsupervised topic modeling approaches to decision summarization in spoken meetings. In *Proceedings of the 13th Annual Meeting of the Special Interest Group on Discourse and Dialogue (SIGDIAL)*, pp. 40–49 (2012).

21. D. Wang, S. Zhu, T. Li, and Y. Gong, Multi-document summarization using sentence-based topic models. In *Proceedings of the ACL-IJCNLP 2009 Conference Short Papers*, pp. 297–300 (2009).

22. D. M. Blei, A. Y. Ng, and M. I. Jordan, Latent dirichlet allocation, *Journal of Machine Learning Research*, **3**, 993–1022 (2003).

23. D. M. Blei, Probabilistic topic models, *Communications of the ACM*, **55**(4), 77–84 (2012).

24. Y. Choueka, Looking for needles in a haystack or locating interesting collocational expressions in large textual databases. In *RIAO 88:(Recherche d'Information Assistée par Ordinateur) Conference*, pp. 609–623 (1988).

25. P. Pecina, Lexical association measures and collocation extraction, *Language resources and evaluation*, **44**(1–2), 137–158 (2010).

26. D. Nadeau and S. Sekine, A survey of named entity recognition and classification, *Lingvisticae Investigationes*, **30**(1), 3–26 (2007).

27. X. Liu, S. Zhang, F. Wei, and M. Zhou, Recognizing named entities in tweets. In *Proceedings of the 49th Annual Meeting of the Association for Computational Linguistics: Human Language Technologies — Volume 1*, pp. 359–367 (2011).

28. C. D. Manning and H. Schütze, *Foundations of Statistical Natural Language Processing*. MIT Press (1999).

29. A. R. Martinez, Part-of-speech tagging, *Wiley Interdisciplinary Reviews: Computational Statistics*, **4**(1), 107–113 (2012).

30. K. Toutanova, D. Klein, C. D. Manning, and Y. Singer, Feature-rich part-of-speech tagging with a cyclic dependency network. In *Proceedings of the 2003 Conference of the North American Chapter of the Association for Computational Linguistics on Human Language Technology — Volume 1*, pp. 173–180 (2003).

31. M. Kuhn and K. Johnson, *Applied Predictive Modeling*, vol. 810, Springer (2013).

32. J. Friedman, T. Hastie, and R. Tibshirani, *The Elements of Statistical Learning*, vol. 1, Springer Series in Statistics, New York (2001).

33. L. Breiman, J. Friedman, C. J. Stone, and R. A. Olshen, *Classification and Regression Trees*. CRC Press (1984).

34. J. R. Quinlan *et al.*, Learning with continuous classes. In *5th Australian Joint Conference on Artificial Intelligence*, vol. 92, pp. 343–348 (1992).

35. J. R. Quinlan, Combining instance-based and model-based learning. In *Proceedings of the Tenth International Conference on Machine Learning*, pp. 236–243 (1993).

36. J. H. Holland, *Adaptation in Natural and Artificial Systems: An Introductory Analysis with Applications to Biology, Control, and Artificial Intelligence*. MIT Press (1992).

37. L. Scrucca *et al.*, Ga: A package for genetic algorithms in R, *Journal of Statistical Software*, **53**(4), 1–37 (2013).

38. Liangjie Hong and Brain D. Davison, Empirical study of topic modeling in Twitter. In *Proceedings of 1st Workshop on Social Media Analytics (SOMA 2010)*, pp. 80–88 (2010).

39. H. P. Luhn, The automatic creation of literature abstracts, *IBM Journal of Research and Development*, **2**, 159–165 (1958).

40. M. Litvak and M. Last, Cross-lingual training of summarization systems using annotated corpora in a foreign language, *Information Retrieval*, **16**(5), 629–656 (2013).

41. C. Lioma and R. Blanco, Part of speech based term weighting for information retrieval. In *European Conference on Information Retrieval*, vol. 5478, pp. 412–423 (2009).

42. R. Al-Hashemi, Text summarization extraction system (tses) using extracted keywords, *International Arab Journal of Information Technology*, **1**(4), 164–168 (2010).

43. K. Papineni, S. Roukos, T. Ward, and W.-J. Zhu, Bleu: A method for automatic evaluation of machine translation. In *Proceedings of the 40th Annual Meeting on Association for Computational Linguistics*, pp. 311–318 (2002).

44. M. Litvak, N. Vanetik, M. Last, and E. Churkin, Museec: A multilingual text summarization tool. In *Proceedings of ACL-2016 System Demonstrations*, pp. 73–78 (2016).

45. A. K. McCallum, Mallet: A machine learning for language toolkit (2002). Available at: http://mallet.cs.umass.edu.

46. M. A. Finlayson and N. Kulkarni, Detecting multi-word expressions improves word sense disambiguation. In *Proceedings of the Workshop on Multiword Expressions: from Parsing and Generation to the Real World*, pp. 20–24 (2011).

47. C. D. Manning, M. Surdeanu, J. Bauer, J. R. Finkel, S. Bethard, and D. McClosky, The Stanford CoreNLP natural language processing toolkit. In *ACL (System Demonstrations)*, pp. 55–60 (2014).

48. T. Therneau, B. Atkinson, and B. Ripley, Rpart: Recursive partitioning and regression trees, R package version 4.1–10 (2015).

49. J. R. Quinlan, An overview of Cubist, Rulequest Research (2005). Available at: http://www.rulequest.com/cubist-info.html.

50. M. Kuhn, Caret: Classification and regression training, *Astrophysics Source Code Library* (2015).

51. National Institute of Standards and Technology, (NIST), Document understanding conferences (2001–2007). Available at: http://duc.nist.gov.

52. C.-Y. Lin, Rouge: A package for automatic evaluation of summaries. In *Proceedings of the Workshop on Text Summarization Branches Out (WAS 2004)*, pp. 25–26 (2004).

53. H. Akaike, A new look at the statistical model identification, *IEEE Transactions on Automatic Control*, **19**(6), 716–723 (1974). doi: 10.1109/tac.1974.1100705.

Chapter 5

Hierarchical Topic Model and Summarization

Lei Li* and Yazhao Zhang†

*School of Computer, Beijing University of Posts and Telecommunications,
10 Xitucheng Road, Haidian District, Beijing, China 100876*
*leili@bupt.edu.cn
†yazhao@bupt.edu.cn

This chapter describes the hierarchical topic model named hierarchical latent Dirichlet allocation (hLDA), together with its applications in summarization. hLDA is a representative generative probabilistic model, which can not only mine latent topics from a large amount of discrete data, but also organize these topics into a hierarchy to achieve a deeper semantic analysis. hLDA has been applied with various summarization tasks, such as single-document summarization, multi-document summarization, legal document clustering and summarization, contrastive theme summarization, and multilingual multi-document summarization.

1. Introduction

Manual summarization is a process where a person (summarizer) usually reads and understands the contents of an original document to be summarized. Then the meaning of a document is re-organized into some latent structure in which concepts and their relations are represented clearly. As a result, the main and minor contents are separated. Finally, the brief and concise summary is presented. This summary should contain the most relevant information in the original document, or documents, while complying with a predefined length limitation.

As to the latent structure of meaning, people usually prefer to see and use hierarchical structures to represent knowledge. A good instance is WordNet[1] which has become a powerful tool for various kinds of natural language processing (NLP) tasks. If we can also create a hierarchical structure to represent the meaning of original documents, then such structure should be quite useful for obtaining good summaries.

This chapter is organized as follows: Section 2 defines the approach to topic modeling of text documents with hLDA. Section 3 discusses notable prior work. Section 4 presents the theoretical model. Section 5 describes the evaluation setup and results for our approach to multilingual multi-document summarization. Section 6 contains conclusions and future work directions.

2. Topic modeling with hLDA

In recent years, following the latent semantic indexing (LSI) and probabilistic latent semantic indexing (PLSI) models, complex probabilistic models became increasingly prevalent in the field of automatic summarization. The latent Dirichlet allocation (LDA) model was proposed in Ref. 2 as a method for topic modeling capable of revealing the underlying topic information hidden in documents. LDA has been widely applied in many research fields.[3,4] There also exist some works on its improvement and generalization.[5-7]

If an assumption that the number of topics in a document set is known and fixed is waived, then the Bayesian non-parametric model provides an elegant solution for the problem. For example, Ref. 8 uses the hLDA approach[9] to exploit the hierarchical tree structure of document topics. hLDA is an unsupervised method in which topic numbers can grow with the dataset, automatically. Unlike LDA, hLDA can organize topics into a hierarchy, in which higher level topics are more abstract. This can provide a deeper semantic model similarity, which is especially helpful for summarization.

2.1. *Example*

Learning a topic hierarchy from data is an important challenge. The hLDA model is an efficient statistical method for constructing such an hierarchy, which is capable of growth and change as the data accumulates. Figure 1 gives an example of the hierarchical structure of a document whose subject is the natural resource base for renewables in Scotland, which is chosen from the corpus of the multilingual single-document summarization (MSS) shared task in the MultiLing 2015 workshop,[10] which was obtained with hLDA.

An hLDA hierarchy, as shown in Fig. 1, has form of a directed rooted tree. Each node in the hierarchy is associated with a latent topic, where a topic is a distribution over words. Note that there are many words related

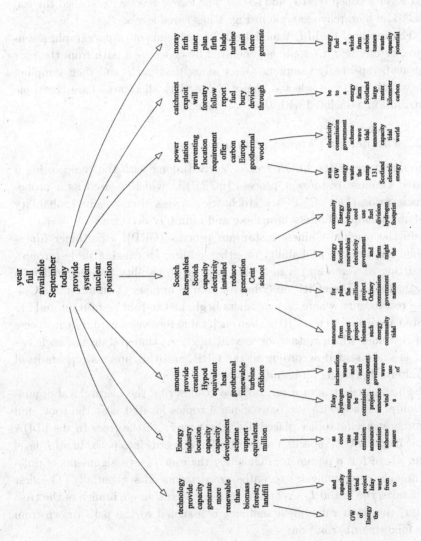

Fig. 1. An example of hierarchical structure.

to each topic with different probabilities, and we show only the most representative ones due to limited page space. All nodes are located at different levels in the tree. The highest level is called the *root level* or level 0, the next level is called *level 1*, and so on. The lowest level is also called the *leaf level*. The hierarchy example in Fig. 1 has three levels.

The input of an hLDA model can be a document, a paragraph, a sentence, or any text. A topic is generated by choosing a path from the root to a leaf, repeatedly sampling topics along that path, and then sampling the words from the selected topics. Note that all topics share the topic distribution associated with the root node.

2.2. *The nested Chinese restaurant process*

The structure of the hLDA tree is learned along with the topics using a nested Chinese restaurant process (nCRP),[11] which is used as a probabilistic prior. The nCRP is a stochastic process that assigns probability distributions to infinitely branching and infinitely deep trees.

In the original Chinese restaurant process (CRP), a customer (datapoint) has a finite probability of either joining an existing table (group), or sitting at (creating) a new one, with a probability proportional to a parameter γ. The nCRP describes an infinite number of infinite-table Chinese restaurants, where all customers begin at the root restaurant and are seated according to the CRP. Then each table receives a card that instructs the customer which restaurant to visit next. At that restaurant, each visitor is again seated according to the CRP, and this process repeats itself infinitely, describing an infinite tree.

This nested structure can be used to describe the hierarchical organization of topics, with the more general topics located near the root, and the more specific topics placed near the bottom of the tree. In the hLDA topic model, nCRP specifies a distribution of words into paths in an L-level tree, where L is a parameter defined by the user. The assignments of units (sentences or documents) to paths are determined sequentially. The first unit takes the initial L-level path, starting with a single branch of the tree. Later, the m-th subsequent sentence is assigned to the path drawn from the following distribution:

$$p(path_{old}, c|m, m_c) = \frac{m_c}{\gamma + m - 1}$$

$$p(path_{new}, c|m, m_c) = \frac{\gamma}{\gamma + m - 1},$$

(1)

Algorithm 4 hLDA topic modeling

1: For each topic $k \in T$, sample a distribution $\beta_k \sim Dirichlet(\eta)$
2: For each unit $d \in O$
3:    (a) Draw a path $c_d \sim nCRP(\gamma)$
4:    (b) Sample L-vector θ_d mixing weights, $\theta_d | \{m, \pi\} \sim GEM(m, \pi)$
5:    (c) For each word n, choose:
6:        (i) level $z_{d,n} | \theta_d$
7:        (ii) word $w_{d,n} | \{z_{d,n}, c_d, \beta\}$

In Eq. (1), $path_{old}$ and $path_{new}$ represent the existing and new paths, respectively. Parameter m_c denotes the number of previous units assigned to path c, and m is the total number of units seen so far. A hyper-parameter γ controls the probability of creating new paths. Small values of γ decrease the number of branches.

The generative process for hLDA is described in Algorithm 4.

2.3. *The Gibbs sampling algorithm*

The Gibbs sampling algorithm is designed for sampling from the posterior nested CRP and corresponding topic distributions in the hLDA model. The Gibbs sampler is a clean method that simultaneously explores both the parameter space and the model space.

The variables needed by the sampling algorithm are: $w_{m,n}$, which is the n-th word in the m-th unit; $c_{m,l}$, which is the restaurant corresponding to the l-th topic distribution in the m-th unit; and $z_{m,n}$, which is the assignment of the n-th word in the m-th unit to one of the L available topics. All other variables in the model, such as θ and β, are integrated out. The Gibbs sampler thus assesses the values of $z_{m,n}$ and $c_{m,l}$.

The conditional distribution for c_m, the L topics associated with the m-th unit, is:

$$p(c_m | w, c_{-m}, z) \propto p(w_m | c, w_{-m}, z) p(c_m | c_{-m}), \qquad (2)$$

where w_{-m} and c_{-m} denote the w and c variables for all units other than the m-th unit. This expression is an instance of Bayes' rule with $p(w_m | c, w_{-m}, z)$ as the likelihood of the data, given a particular choice of c_m and $p(c_m | c_{-m})$ as the prior on c_m implied by the nested CRP. The likelihood is obtained by integrating over the parameters β, which gives:

$$p(w_m|c, w_{-m}, z) = \prod_{l=1}^{L} \left(\frac{\Gamma(n_{c_{m,l},-m}^{(\cdot)} + W\eta)}{\prod_w \Gamma(n_{c_{m,l},-m}^{(w)} + \eta)} \right)$$
$$\times \frac{\prod_w \Gamma(n_{c_{m,l},-m}^{(w)} + n_{c_{m,l},m}^{(w)} + \eta)}{\Gamma(n_{c_{m,l},-m}^{(\cdot)} + n_{c_{m,l},m}^{(\cdot)} + W\eta)}, \qquad (3)$$

where $n_{c_{m,l},-m}^{(w)}$ is the number of instances of word w that have been assigned to the topic indexed by $c_{m,l}$, not including those in the current unit, W is the total vocabulary size, and $\Gamma(\cdot)$ denotes the standard gamma function. When c contains a previously unvisited restaurant, $n_{c_{m,l},-m}^{(w)}$ is zero. Note that the c_m must be drawn as a block. A detailed description of this process can be found in Refs. 2 and 9.

3. Prior work on summarization with hLDA

The hLDA approach has been successfully utilized for various summarization tasks.[11-16] In this section we give a brief overview of the most popular methods in this field.

3.1. *The sumHLDA algorithm*

In Ref. 12, Celikyilmaz and Hakkani-Tur propose a method, based on supervised hLDA, which performs extractive summarization in the multi-document setting. They present a novel approach that formulates multi-document summarization (MDS) as a prediction problem based on a two-step hybrid model — a generative model for hierarchical topic discovery and a regression model for inference. They investigate how a hierarchical model can be adopted to discovery of salient sentence characteristics by dividing them into hierarchies with the help of sentence-level hLDA.

In this work, Celikyilmaz and Hakkani-Tur (2010) introduce the sumHLDA algorithm (see Algorithm 5) that discovers hidden topic distributions of sentences in a given document cluster, along with providing summary sentences based on hLDA. A summary-focused hierarchical probabilistic topic model is then constructed for each document cluster at the sentence level, because it enables capturing expected topic distributions in given sentences directly from the model. A method for scoring candidate sentences from this hierarchical structure is presented as well. The sumHLDA algorithm constructs a hierarchical tree structure of candidate

---

Algorithm 5 sumHLDA algorithm

1: For each topic $k \in T$, sample a distribution $\beta_k \sim Dirichlet(\eta)$
2: For each sentence $d \in \{O \cup S\}$
3:   (a) If $d \in O$, draw a path $c_d \sim nCRP(\gamma_o)$,
  else if $d \in S$, draw a path $c_d \sim nCRP(\gamma_s)$.
4:   (b) Sample L-vector θ_d mixing weights from Dirichlet distribution,
    $\theta_d \sim Dir(\alpha)$.
5:   (c) For each word n, choose:
6:   (i) level $z_{d,n}|\theta_d$
7:   (ii) word $w_{d,n}|\{z_{d,n}, c_d, \beta\}$

---

sentences (per document cluster) by positioning summary sentences on the tree. Each sentence is represented by a path in the tree. The assumption is that sentences sharing the same path should be more similar to each other because they share the same topics. Moreover, if a path includes a summary sentence, then candidate sentences on that path are more likely to be selected for summary text.

The efficiency of their similarity measure in identifying the best matching summary sentence, is tied to the degree of expressiveness of the extracted topics of the sumHLDA models.

3.2. *PathSum: A summarization framework based on hierarchical topics*

In Ref. 11, Darling and Song (2011) present PathSum, a hierarchical topic based single- and multi-document automatic text summarization framework, as depicted in Fig. 2. This approach leverages Bayesian nonparametric methods to model sentences as paths through a tree and creates a hierarchy of topics from the input in an unsupervised setting. They argue that hLDA can generate a highly structured statistical model where content words are modeled as being generated from a hierarchical topic structure. Utilizing posterior inference, the authors of Ref. 11 use the most traveled paths through the topical tree structure to select salient sentences that both represent the document set and at the same time avoid redundancy. More formally, sentences in PathSum adhere to the generative process given in Algorithm 6.

The PathSum framework can also be used for query-focused summarization in the following way: after building the hierarchical topic structure from the input sentences, a query would then be situated along one of

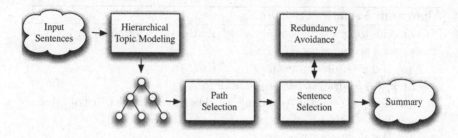

Fig. 2.   The PathSum summarization framework.

Algorithm 6 PathSum algorithm

1: For each node (topic) $t \in \mathcal{T}$, choose a topic $\phi_t \sim Dirichlet(\eta)$
2: For each sentence $s \in S$
3:      (a) draw $\rho_s \sim nCRP(\gamma)$
4:      (b) draw $\theta_s \sim Dirichlet(\alpha)$
5:      (c) For each word $w \in s$,
6:          (i) choose level $l \sim Discrete(\theta_s)$
7:          (ii) choose word $w \sim Discrete(\phi_{[\rho_s, l]})$

---

the paths in the topic tree. As in the extractive summarization approach described above, sentences would then be chosen for extraction, but only from this path.

3.3. *Legal judgement summarization with hLDA*

In Ref. 15, Venkatesh (2013) propose an approach to cluster legal judgments based on the topics obtained from hLDA using similarity measures between topics and documents, and finding the summary of each document using the same topics. In this case, the number of clusters need not be known in advance. The architecture of the proposed approach to clustering legal judgments and generating judgment summaries with hLDA topic modeling is given in Fig. 3. The process consists of following steps:

(1) Preprocessing of legal judgments to remove stop words and to find legal terms.
(2) Generation of the topics tree, for the given legal judgment corpus, using hLDA topic model.
(3) Legal judgments clustering using the topics tree, obtained from the hLDA topic model for the given corpus.

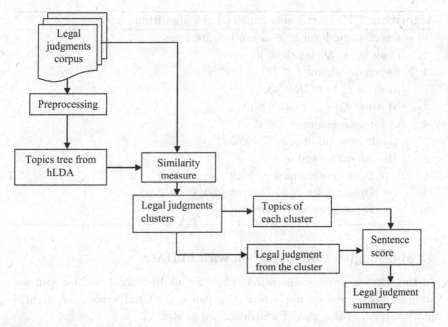

Fig. 3.   Architecture for legal judgment clustering and summarization using the hLDA topic model.

(4) Finding the sentence score, for each sentence in the judgment, using the topics of that cluster.
(5) Generation of extractive judgment summary for each judgment.

3.4.   *Contrastive theme summarization*

In Ref. 16, Ren and De Rijke (2015) put forward a contrastive theme summarization based on hLDA and structured determinantal point processes (SDPPs), which are sensitive to negative correlation. Given a set of opinionated documents, they define a *viewpoint* to be a topic with a specific sentiment label. A *theme* is a set of viewpoints around a specific set of topics and an explicit sentiment opinion. Given a set of specific topics, two themes are *contrastive* if they are related to the topics, but are opposite in terms of sentiment. The task on which this work focuses is *contrastive summarization of multiple themes*, where the output consists of sets of contrastive sentences for every detected theme. The generation process of the proposed model is shown in Algorithm 7.

Algorithm 7 Hierarchical-sentiment LDA algorithm

1: For each topic level $z^x \in \mathcal{Z}^x$ in infinite tree:
2:   Draw $\phi^x \sim Dirichlet(\beta^x)$;
3: For each document $d \in \mathcal{D}$:
4:   (a) draw $c_d^x \sim nCRP(p)$;
5:   (b) draw $\theta_d \sim Dirichlet(m)$;
6:   (c) for each sentence $s \in d$:
7:     (i) draw opinion $o_s \sim Dirichlet(\gamma)$;
8:     (ii) for each word $w \in N$:
9:         Draw sentiment $x \sim Multinomial(O_s)$;
10:        Draw topics $z_x \sim Discrete(\theta_d)$;
11:        Draw word $w \sim Discrete(\phi_{x^x, c_d^x})$;

---

4. Multilingual summarization with hLDA

In this section we describe our method for multi-lingual multi-document summarization and its implementation called the CIST system. A preliminary version of this model was described in Ref. 17.

4.1. *Problem statement*

The MultiLing 2013 Workshop at ACL 2013 posed a multi-lingual, multi-document summarization task to the summarization community, aiming to quantify and measure the performance of multi-lingual, multi-document summarization systems across languages. The task was to create a 240–250 word summary from 10 news articles, describing a given topic. The texts of each topic were provided in 10 languages (Arabic, Chinese, Czech, English, French, Greek, Hebrew, Hindi, Romanian, Spanish) and each participant generated summaries for at least 2 languages. The evaluation of the summaries was performed using automatic and manual processes. Please refer to Ref. 18 for more details about ACL MultiLing 2013. The CIST system has participated in Track 1: Multilingual Multi-document Summarization in ACL MultiLing 2013 workshop.

4.2. *Text preprocessing*

The CIST system uses unified preprocessing steps for all languages and a special step of word segmentation for Chinese. A document set is merged together by combining multiple documents into one big text (in the case of Chinese, empty lines are deleted).

In Chinese, ending punctuation marks are used to detect sentence boundaries, while other languages require sentence splitting. After sentence splitting is done, every sentence is treated as a processing unit for the topic modeling task. In the corpus there are two special lines of title and date ending with no punctuation marks, which should be identified and separated from the rest of the document. The SPLITTA machine learning method of Ref. 19 was used for this purpose and after the initial evaluation Support Vector Machine model was chosen for English and French, while the Naive Bayes model was chosen for the other seven languages. The ICTCLAS package[20] was used for word segmentation in Chinese.

Stop word removal was performed for all languages. For English and Chinese, the stop words list contains both punctuation marks and some functional words. For other languages, stop word lists contain punctuation marks only, although generally, people do not treat punctuation marks as words. Afterward, all capitalized characters are changed to lower case.

4.3. *Word dictionary construction*

After preprocessing is completed, we construct a dictionary for the remaining words, where words are sorted according to their decreasing frequency in documents. Once words are mapped to their serial number in the dictionary, the later hLDA modeling process becomes language-independent. An input file for hLDA modeling is generated, and in that file each line represents a sentence where for each word's unique index, its frequency is specified.

4.4. *Topic modeling implementation*

4.4.1. *Hierarchy construction*

Given a collection of sentences in the input file, we seek to discover common usage patterns or topics and organize them into a hierarchy. Each node is associated with a topic, which is a distribution over words. A sentence is generated by choosing a path from the root to a leaf, repeatedly sampling topics along that path, and sampling the words from the selected topics. Sentences sharing the same path should be similar to each other because they share the same sub-topics. All sentences share the topic distribution associated with the root node. In the CIST system, the hierarchy depth is set to 3.

After hLDA modeling is done, in order to make sure that a generated hierarchy is good, we evaluate the performance of the hLDA hierarchy.

This is a very difficult task when dealing with multiple languages. The best method should be human evaluation, Such a solution is impractical, especially when one considers the need to find an individual who speaks all 10 languages in question, and, after finding such a person, require him to browse all topics and all languages. Instead, a simpler and faster automatic evaluation method is used. According to this empirical analysis, if a hierarchy has more than 4 paths and the sentence numbers for all paths appear in balanced order from bigger to smaller, and the sentences in bigger paths occupy 70–85% in all sentences, a hierarchy can be considered satisfactory.

4.4.2. *Parameter tuning*

Generally speaking, when facing a new corpus, it is very difficult to set good parameters of hLDA automatically or through direct human action. We performed sampling for all languages with 100,000 iterations. However, results were poor, and tuning parameters was eventually performed by us.

We started with Chinese because it seems to be the most difficult case. We initially chose two topics at random and set parameters according to former experience. Then we evaluated the generated hLDA hierarchy using the automatic evaluation method previously mentioned. This cycle was repeated until satisfactory results were obtained. The final settings were used for the entire corpus. Table 1 shows the final settings.

After running hLDA on the entire corpus, we evaluated the results again. In most cases, the resulting hierarchy was good, except for the cases depicted in Table 2. Therefore, one set of parameter settings could not deal with all languages and topics successfully. The reason is that topics in different languages have different inherent structures.

Table 1.   Original parameter settings.

Parameter	Setting
ETA	1.2 0.5 0.05
GAM	1.0 1.0
GEM_MEAN	0.5
GEM_SCALE	100
SCALING_SHAPE	1.0
SCALING_SCALING	0.5
SAMPLE_ETA	0
SAMPLE_GAM	0

Table 2. Documents with bad topic models.

Language	Document
English	M006
Hebrew	M001 M006
Romanian	M002
Spanish	M003
Chinese	M004 M006

Table 3. Adjusted parameter settings.

Parameter	Setting
ETA	5.2 0.005 0.0005
GAM	1.0 1.0
GEM_MEAN	0.35
GEM_SCALE	100
SCALING_SHAPE	2.0
SCALING_SCALING	1.0
SAMPLE_ETA	0
SAMPLE_GAM	0

Analysis of bad results led to settings adjustments for these languages. For instance, in English document M006, there are only two paths indicating that the tree is too clustered. In this case, the ETA parameter should be lower in order to separate more sub-topics. However, if the value of ETA is too small, it may lead to hLDA failure without level assignment, resulting in limited iterations. Therefore, we adjusted the GEM parameter in order to get closer to the earlier explanation of corpus. In some cases, the values were too large for the former paths, and we adjusted the SCALING parameters in order to separate these paths to smaller ones. For the bad cases in Table 2, we used the settings shown in Table 3.

4.5. *Computing sentence importance from hLDA*

In the resulting hLDA model, sentences are clustered into sub-topics in a hierarchical tree. A sub-topic is considered to be more important than others if it contains more sentences than other sub-topics. Trivial sub-topics containing only one or two sentences can be neglected. The final summary should consist of the most representative sentences belonging to the most important sub-topics. Sentence importance in a sub-topic is computed from the three features described as follows.

4.5.1. *Sentence coverage*

This feature measures how a sentence covers words contained in a sub-topic. The sentence weight is calculated as follows:

$$S_{tf} = \frac{\sum_{i=1}^{|s|} \frac{num_s(w_i)}{n}}{|s|},$$ (4)

where w_i is the i-th word in sentence s, $num_s(w_i)$ is the number of sentences containing w_i, $|s|$ is the number of words in the sentence, and n is the total number of all sentences.

4.5.2. *Abstractive level of a word*

hLDA constructs a hierarchy by positioning all sentences on a three-level tree. Level 0 is the most abstractive one, level 2 is the most specific one, and level 1 is between them. The abstractive level of a sentence is computed as:

$$S_l = a \times \frac{num(w_0)}{|s|} + b \times \frac{num(w_1)}{|s|} + c \times \frac{num(w_2)}{|s|},$$ (5)

where $num(w_0)$, $num(w_1)$, and $num(w_2)$ represent the number of words in levels 0-2 respectively in sentence s, and a, b, and c correspond to user-defined weights for levels 0-2, respectively. Parameter $|s|$ denotes the number of words in the sentence. Although we hope the summary is abstractive, specific information is also important. For instance, earthquake news needs specific information about death toll and monetary loss.

4.5.3. *Named entities*

We also consider the number of named entities in a sentence. We use the Stanford University named entity recognition toolkit,[a] which can identify person, address, and institutional names in English. If a sentence contains more entities, it has a priority as a candidate summary sentence.

Let S_n be the number of named entity categories in a sentence. For example, if a sentence has only person names, then S_n is 1; if it also has

---

[a]http://nlp.stanford.edu/software/CRF-NER.shtml.

address information, then S_n is 2; if it contains all three categories, then S_n is 3.

4.5.4. *Combined sentence score*

At last, we calculate sentence score S using Eq. (6) for English and Eq. (7) for other languages, with d, e, and f being feature weights.

$$S = d \times S_{tf} + e \times S_l + f \times S_n. \tag{6}$$

$$S = d \times S_{tf} + e \times S_l. \tag{7}$$

Empirically, we set $\{a, b, c, d, e, f\}$ to $\{0.3, 1, 0.3, 2, 1, 0.05\}$ for English, $\{a, b, c, d, e\}$ to $\{1, 0.75, 0.25, 2, 1\}$ for Chinese without M004 and M006, and $\{0.3, 1, 0.3, 2, 1\}$ for other languages.

5. Experiments

5.1. *Setup*

The CIST system processes all 10 languages in the MultiLing 2013 summarization track. It performs multi-document summarization on document sets and generates a summary in plain text, UTF-8 encoding. At the MultiLing 2013 summarization track, each document set contained 10 documents, and the required summary size was 250 words or less. Figures 4 and 5 show the CIST framework performance for 10 languages. Because in Chinese Hanzi words are not separated by white spaces or any other separators, this required a special approach to word segmentation; therefore this module is different for Chinese, while other modules are the same. The kernel module constructs a hLDA model and it is language-independent.

5.2. *Results*

For every document set, we extracted 30 candidate sentences ordered by the final sentence rank S, and added them to the final summary until the summary length limit was exceeded.

Automatic evaluation results of the MultiLing 2013 Workshop indicated that CIST obtained the best performance in several languages, such as Hindi (according to ROUGE scores), and for some document sets, such as Arabic M104, English and Romanian M005, Czech M007, and Spanish M103.

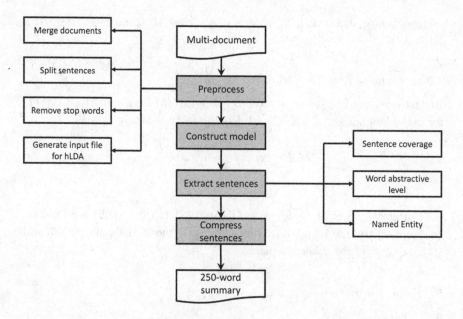

Fig. 4.   Framework for nine languages (no Chinese).

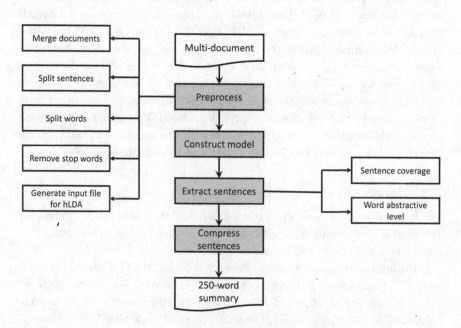

Fig. 5.   Framework for Chinese.

6. Conclusion and future work

We see that hLDA is a language-independent model that is applicable to multi-document summarization. Sometimes it performs well, but it lacks stability in the general case. Our future work in this direction will focus on parameter adjustment, modeling results evaluation, sentence evaluation, and good summary generation.

Recently, some progress has been achieved.[21] It has become apparent that combined analysis of word distribution across topics and levels of the hLDA hierarchy for Chinese texts has improved summarization quality. For instance, the root level of hLDA contains either highly frequent words or stop words with low frequency. Therefore, increasing the frequency threshold when analyzing hLDA results should help ignore stopwords or unimportant words automatically. Higher preference should also be given to words that are more specific and appear at lower levels of the hLDA hierarchy. However, non-frequent words appearing only at the lower level usually do not appear in human summaries, and can therefore be ignored. Most of the frequent words in human gold-standard summaries appear in multiple levels of hLDA hierarchy. We also discovered that applying hLDA to texts without removing stopwords results in their high appearance at all levels of hierarchy, especially in the root level. Therefore, if we do not want them to influence sentence scores, the stopwords must be removed from the text before hLDA modeling.

Because hLDA topic modeling is language-independent, the proposed summarization method is applicable to multiple languages. For adaptation, it requires basic text preprocessing tools, such as sentence splitting, tokenization and stop-word removal. Parameter tuning for this approach depends on word frequencies and on levels of topic hierarchy at which word appears. Although these parameters may differ for various languages, their computation does not require the language knowledge and is therefore language independent.

References

1. G. A. Miller, Wordnet: A lexical database for english, *Communications of the ACM*, **38**(11), 39–41 (1995).
2. D. M. Blei, A. Y. Ng, and M. I. Jordan, Latent dirichlet allocation, *Journal of Machine Learning Research*, **3**(Jan), 993–1022 (2003).
3. R. Arora and B. Ravindran, Latent dirichlet allocation based multi-document summarization. In *Proceedings of the Second Workshop on Analytics for Noisy Unstructured Text Data*, pp. 91–97, ACM (2008).

4. R. Krestel, P. Fankhauser, and W. Nejdl, Latent dirichlet allocation for tag recommendation. In *Proceedings of the Third ACM Conference on Recommender Systems*, pp. 61–68, ACM (2009).
5. T. L. Griffiths, M. Steyvers, D. M. Blei, and J. B. Tenenbaum, Integrating topics and syntax. In *Advances in Neural Information Processing Systems*, pp. 537–544, Neural Information Processing Systems Foundation, Inc. (2005).
6. D. M. Blei and J. D. Lafferty, Dynamic topic models. In *Proceedings of the 23rd International Conference on Machine Learning*, pp. 113–120, ACM (2006).
7. C. Wang and D. M. Blei, Decoupling sparsity and smoothness in the discrete hierarchical dirichlet process. In *Advances in Neural Information Processing Systems*, pp. 1982–1989, Neural Information Processing Systems Foundation, Inc. (2009).
8. Y. W. Teh, M. I. Jordan, M. J. Beal, and D. M. Blei, Sharing clusters among related groups: Hierarchical dirichlet processes. In *Advances in Neural Information Processing Systems*, pp. 1385–1392, Neural Information Processing Systems Foundation, Inc. (2005).
9. D. M. Blei, T. L. Griffiths, and M. I. Jordan, The nested chinese restaurant process and bayesian nonparametric inference of topic hierarchies, *Journal of the ACM (JACM)*, **57**(2), 7 (2010).
10. G. Giannakopoulos, J. Kubina, J. M. Conroy, J. Steinberger, B. Favre, M. A. Kabadjov, U. Kruschwitz, and M. Poesio, Multiling 2015: Multilingual summarization of single and multi-documents, on-line fora, and call-center conversations. In *SIGDIAL Conference*, pp. 270–274, ACL (2015).
11. W. M. Darling and F. Song, Pathsum: A summarization framework based on hierarchical topics. In *Proceedings of the Workshop on Automatic Text Summarization 2011*, p. 5 (2011).
12. A. Celikyilmaz and D. Hakkani-Tur, A hybrid hierarchical model for multi-document summarization. In *Proceedings of the 48th Annual Meeting of the Association for Computational Linguistics*, pp. 815–824, ACL (2010).
13. H. Liu, W. H. Ping'an Liu, W. Heng, and L. Li, The CIST summarization system at TAC 2011. In *Text Analysis Conference (TAC)*, NIST (2011).
14. H. Liu and L. Li, Multi-document summarization based on hierarchical topic model. In *2011 7th International Conference on Natural Language Processing and Knowledge Engineering (NLP-KE)*, pp. 88–91, IEEE (2011).
15. R. K. Venkatesh, Legal documents clustering and summarization using hierarchical latent dirichlet allocation, *International Journal of Artificial Intelligence*, **2**(1) (2013).
16. Z. Ren and M. de Rijke, Summarizing contrastive themes via hierarchical non-parametric processes. In *Proceedings of the 38th International ACM SIGIR Conference on Research and Development in Information Retrieval*, pp. 93–102, ACM (2015).
17. L. Li, W. Heng, J. Yu, Y. Liu, and S. Wan, CIST system report for ACL Multiling 2013 — Track 1: Multilingual multi-document summarization. In *Proceedings of the MultiLing 2013 Workshop on Multilingual Multi-document Summarization*, pp. 39–44, Sofia, Bulgaria, ACL (2013).

18. G. Giannakopoulos, Multi-document multilingual summarization and evaluation tracks in ACL 2013 Multiling workshop. In *Proceedings of the MultiLing 2013 Workshop on Multilingual Multidocument Summarization*, pp. 20–28, Sofia, Bulgaria, ACL (2013).

19. D. Gillick, Sentence boundary detection and the problem with the us. In *Proceedings of Human Language Technologies: The 2009 Annual Conference of the North American Chapter of the Association for Computational Linguistics, Companion Volume: Short Papers*, pp. 241–244, ACL (2009).

20. H.-P. Zhang, H.-K. Yu, D.-Y. Xiong, and Q. Liu, Hhmm-based chinese lexical analyzer ICTCLAS. In *Proceedings of the Second SIGHAN Workshop on Chinese Language Processing-Volume 17*, pp. 184–187, ACL (2003).

21. M. Litvak, N. Vanetik, and L. Lei, Summarizing weibo with topics compression. In *Proceedings of CICLING 2017: 18th International Conference on Intelligent Text Processing and Computational Linguistics*, Cicling (2017).

Chapter 6

A Survey of Neural Models for Abstractive Summarization

Tal Baumel* and Michael Elhadad†

*Ben-Gurion University, Computer-Science Department,
P.O.B. 653, Beer-Sheva 8410501 Israel*
*talbau@cs.bgu.ac.il
†elhadad@cs.bgu.ac.il

In this chapter, we survey recent developments in abstractive summarization which use neural networks. Those methods achieve state-of-the-art ROUGE results for summarization tasks, especially when using short text as a source, such as single sentences or short paragraphs. We cover essential neural network concepts for abstractive summarization models. Because such models require massive training data, we also overview datasets used to train such models. We first describe the basic methodological concepts (word embeddings, sequence to sequence recurrent networks and attention mechanism). We provide didactic source code in Python to explain these basic concepts. We then survey four recent systems which, when combined, have resulted in dramatic improvements in single-document generic abstractive summarization in the past couple of years. These systems introduce re-usable techniques which address each aspect of the summarization challenge: dealing with large vocabulary while exploiting the high similarity between source and target documents; dealing with rare named-entities by detecting and copying them from the source to the target; avoiding repetition and redundancy by introducing a distractor mechanism; introducing sentence level assessment with the use of reinforcement learning.

1. Introduction

Neural network models achieve state-of-the-art results in various tasks that were considered impossible less than a decade ago. Notable examples of such cases can be seen in the field of computer-vision, in which automatic object recognition is currently on par with human ability,[1,2] as well as

175

in natural language processing (NLP), where voice-to-text systems[3] and machine-translation models[4] also achieve state-of-the-art results using neural network models.

These models have been proven capable of learning complex tasks involving rich types of inputs and outputs, and for the first time, the hope of achieving truly abstractive automatic summarization systems appears reachable. In this chapter, we review key concepts in neural-networks for NLP, specifically, word embeddings and sequence-to-sequence architectures. We explore the challenges of developing abstractive summarization models, namely acquiring large scale training data needed for summarization and various problems with predicting output of very high dimensions (computing a vector of the entire vocabulary size). Finally, we survey state-of-the-art techniques addressing the task of abstractive automatic summarization.

2. Neural-network concepts for NLP

The concept of artificial neural networks was first introduced back in 1954[5] and since then has been applied and specialized to a wide range of domains. The success of neural networks achieved in the last decade is due to improvements in hardware with the introduction of general-purpose computing on graphics processing units (GPU), the wide availability of training data, advanced training methods, and better optimization methods. In this section, we review components and architectures specialized for NLP tasks.

We assume the reader is familiar with generic neural-networks techniques, including perceptrons,[6] various nonlinear activation functions (sigmoid, hyperbolic tangent, rectified linear unit, soft-max), back propagation,[7] and optimization methods (SGD, ADAM, etc.). We refer to Goldberg's survey[8] for a concise and up to date presentation of applications of neural networks to NLP.

2.1. *Word-embeddings*

Word-embeddings refer to a set of methods for representing words as dense high-dimension vectors. An example of word representation commonly used is written English, words are represented as sequences of characters. Sometimes similar sequences of letters have similar meanings (*e.g.*, "dog" vs. "dogs"). In other cases, however, slight difference in the sequence mean a great difference in meaning (*e.g.*, "cat" vs. "cut"). Another way of representing words (less common in day-to-day uses but very common for

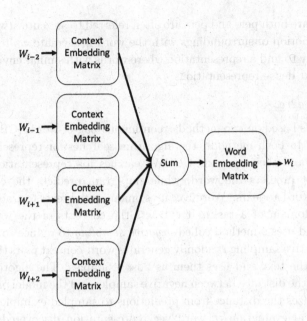

Fig. 1.   Word2Vec CBOW model illustration.

computational use) is one-hot-encoding: each word is represented by a vector and all the values of the vector are zeros except one value which is set to one. Each dimension of this sparse vector represents a different word. When using one-hot-encoding, all words are represented as orthogonal vectors hence they are equally dissimilar to each other ("dog", "dogs", "cat", "cut" are all different in the same way as far as one-hot-encoding predicts).

Word-embeddings aim to bridge the gap between representing words as sequences of characters and sparse high-dimensional vectors by representing words as dense vectors. These dense vectors are selected so that they model semantic similarity, *i.e.*, semantically similar words should be represented as similar vectors while words with no semantic similarity should have different vectors under a vector metric. Typically, vectors are compared using a metric such as cosine similarity, euclidean distance, or the earth movers distance.[9]

Notable methods to acquire such dense vector representations are word2vec[10] and GloVe.[11] Both methods are based on the concept of distributional semantics, which exploits the assumption that similar words should occur in similar surroundings. For example, the words "cat" and "dog" should appear close to the word "cute" more than the word "brick" since they are both pets and pets are often referred to as "cute" (we approximate the notion of surroundings with the word immediate *context*). Both methods try to find a representation where words with similar environments have similar dense representations.

2.1.1. *Word2vec*

Word2vec is based on two methods: continuous-bag-of-words (CBOW) and skip-gram. In both methods, the algorithm searches for representation of the words and their context. CBOW searches for representations where the context predicts the word, while skip-gram predicts the context in which the word appears. Word2vec uses unannotated texts to train (usually from the domain of a task). It extracts the contexts of the words from the text and uses a method called *negative sampling* to reduce convergence time. Negative sampling randomly generates word-context pairs that didn't appear in the text and uses them as false examples. The algorithm thus maximizes the distance between negative samples and the model predictions and minimizes the distance from predictions to sampled examples.

Empirical evaluation of word2vec representation discovered that the model not only learns word similarity, it can also be used to compute word analogies. For example the model can predict that the word "*France*" is to the word "*Paris*" as the word "*Spain*" is to the word "*Madrid*". Analogies are achieved using vector arithmetics. The word vector closest to $Vector('Paris') - Vector('France') + Vector('Spain')$ was found to be the representation of "*Madrid*". The model was tested[10] on a word analogy task and achieved 50.4% accuracy.

In various language-based tasks such as classification with low amount of training data, word2vec can be pre-trained on a larger corpus related to the task.[12]

A document can be represented as the sum of its word embeddings and be fed into a classifier such as a support vector machine (SVM) or a multi-layer perceptron (MLP). Such representations of documents are called "bag of embeddings."[13] Alternatively, a document can be encoded by feeding an ordered sequence of the word embeddings representations into a recurrent neural network (RNN). This document representation has been the basis of a wide range of successful applications called *sequence-to-sequence models*.

2.1.2. *GloVe*

The global vector model (GloVe) is aimed to achieve faster training time and more scalable model then word2vec. Like word2vec the idea behind

GloVe is to achieve word representation with the idea that similar words have similar context.

First the GloVe model constructs a co-occurrence matrix P of dimensions $|Vocab| \times |Vocab|$ where the P_{ij} entry in matrix should represent the number of times the word i appeared near word j in a given corpus. After P is constructed we can optimize the following objective functions $\frac{1}{2} \sum_{i,j=0}^{W} f(P_{i,j})(u_i^T v_j - \log(P_{i,j}))^2$ where f is a weighting function that is designed to avoid rare co-occurring words from being overweighted, u is the word representation matrix and v is the context-word representation matrix. The GloVe model training time is only dependent on vocabulary size unlike word2vec that is dependent on the corpus size.

2.2. *Sequence-to-sequence architectures*

Recurrent neural networks are useful for modeling and solving tasks where the length of the input texts vary; they allow us to avoid learning different features for each position while considering word contexts (order). RNNs refer to a family of architectures (simple RNNs, gated recurrent units (GRUs),[14] long short term memory networks (LSTMs[15]) that all implement similar interfaces: an input, input state, output state, and output (Fig. 2). All are represented as dense vectors: input and output are the same size, and input state and output state are the same size. The state vector should capture task-relevant context information needed to process the next word.

RNNs proved successful for tagging tasks such as part of speech (POS) tagging[16] since their state vector can model relevant context information for each word automatically. While previous models used Markovian assumption where only the previous n-words are relevant to the current tag, RNNs

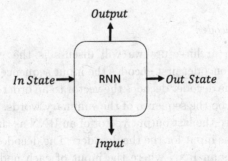

Fig. 2.   RNN interface illustration.

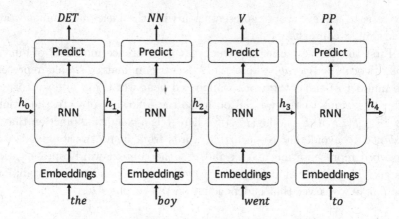

Fig. 3.   RNN network for POS tagging illustration.

enable us to capture contexts of unknown length since we can chain any number of RNN cells we wish (Fig. 3).

To capture global context information instead of just context information from the left of the current word we can use a bidirectional RNN (BiRNN).[17] BiRNNs use two RNN layers, one layer scans the input from left-to-right and the other scans the input from right-to-left. The output vector of the BiRNN for each word is the concatenation of the two RNNs output vectors for the corresponding word.

RNNs and BiRNNs can handle tasks where the input has variable length and the size of the output is constant or is the same as the input. In the task of summarization, the desired output is shorter than the input. In the next paragraphs, we discuss architectures that can handle variable length outputs and inputs, those architectures are globally known as sequence-to-sequence (seq2seq).[18]

2.2.1. Encoder-decoder

The first seq2seq architecture we will discuss is the *encoder-decoder*[19] model, where the encoder first encodes the input sequence to a fixed-length vector and then the decoder decodes the vector to an ordered list of outputs, in our case it will be the sequence of the summary words. For the encoder, it is common to use the last output vector of an RNN as the encoded vector that will be used as input for the the decoder. The decoder is also an RNN.

The decoder is an RNN where the input of each node is the encoded vector concatenated with the embedding of the last output. The decoder

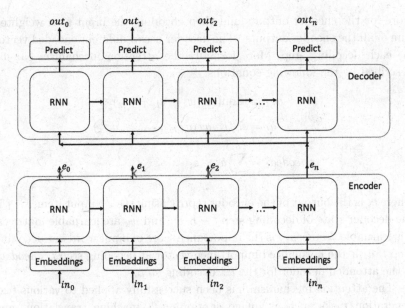

Fig. 4. Encoder-decoder model for input and output of size n.

should continue generating outputs until it generates an end-of-sequence token or reaches a predetermined maximal length. There are many ways to "wire" an encoder-decoder model but the model always uses a fixed size representation of the input sequence obtained by an RNN/BiRNN and a 2nd RNN that uses this representation to generate the output sequence (Fig. 4).

Encoder-decoder models have achieved impressive results in machine translation tasks[19] but proven less effective when translating longer sentences. The reason for the lower performance is that regardless of the input length, the model will always encode it to a same length vector. Intuitively, the longer a sentence is the more information it may contain, thus a longer vector is needed to represent it. This effect is called the *transduction bottleneck*.

2.2.2. *Attention mechanism*

One of the models created in order to solve the problem of trying to decode various length input sequences to fixed-length vector in encoder-decoder models is the attention mechanism.[4] The attention mechanism enables the decoder RNN to select which parts of the input are important at each decoding step. This is achieved by computing a normalized importance score for the encoder outputs and then encoding the input as a weighted sum of all the encoder outputs. The decoder uses a different encoded vector for each decoding step. More formally the attention mechanism can be described by the following equations:

$$a_{i,t} = \tanh(e_i \cdot w_1 + s_{t-1} \cdot w_2) \cdot v$$

$$\hat{a}_t = softmax(a_{1,t}, a_{2,t}, \ldots, a_{n,t})$$

$$encoded_t = \sum_{i=0}^{n} \hat{a}_{t,i} \cdot e_i$$

where e_i is the output of the encoder representing the ith input item, s_{t-1} is the decoder state of decoding step $t-1$, w_1 and w_2 are learnable matrices, v is learnable vector, $a_{i,t}$ is the importance score of input word i at decoding step t, $\hat{a}_t$ is the normalized importance vector at decoding step t, $encoded_t$ is the attended decoder for the tth decoding step.

The attention mechanism has been successfully applied to various text generation tasks such as image captioning,[20] machine translation, and abstractive summarization.[21]

We provide Python code implementing all the seq2seq models described above.[a]

In general, the combination of the seq2seq architecture with an attention mechanism has been demonstrated to work as a very general learnable transducer model, which can be trained in an end-to-end manner (where all components are trained simultaneously) when sufficient amounts of training pairs (input sequence, output sequence) are available. When applied to the task of summarization, specific aspects of the linguistic task make the application of this general architecture challenging.

3. Challenges of neural-networks for automatic summarization

We now discuss the challenges of applying seq2seq models for automatic abstractive summarization. These include: how to obtain training data; how to deal with very large vocabulary and a large number of proper nouns which is typical of many news-oriented summarization datasets; how to deal with the large discrepancy in length between the source and target sequences; how to improve training and generation computation time which

---

[a]https://talbaumel.github.io/attention/.

can be very slow when generating texts with a long input and very large vocabulary.

3.1. *Large-scale summarization dataset*

The de-facto datasets for automatic single document summarization are the Document Understanding Conferences (DUC) 2001–2007[22] and the Text Analysis Conferences (TAC) 2008–2016[23] all constructed under the auspices of the National Institute of Standards and Technology (NIST). The DUC and TAC datasets included various summarization variants (single-document summarization, multi-document summarization, update summarization, query focused summarization, summarization evaluation). The DUC and TAC datasets usually contain no more than 50 document clusters, each containing about 10 articles and 3–4 manually created summaries. This data is used for evaluation and is certainly insufficient (when compared to datasets discussed later) to train supervised abstractive summarization models.

In the papers we review in this chapter, training data was obtained from various dataset not originally constructed for summarization: the Gigaword corpus,[24] CNN/Daily Mail Corpus[25] and Wikipedia dataset PWKP,[26] that were adapted to simulate summarization contexts.

The Gigaword corpus was produced by the Linguistic Data Consortium (LDC) and it is an ensemble of various *corpora*: The North American News text *corpora*, DT *corpora*, the AQUAINT text corpus, and data released for the first time — all in the news domain. The data used from the Gigaword corpus include pairs of articles headline and first sentence where both share a fixed amount of words and the headline is shorter than the 1st sentence. There are 3.8 million training examples and 400,000 validation and test examples. Since the data was obtained automatically there is no guarantee that the headline is a good summarization of the 1st sentence but it is an affordable way to achieve large enough training data. The Gigaword corpus is not available for free.

The CNN/Daily Mail corpus was automatically curated by matching articles to their summary from the CNN and Daily Mail websites. The dataset includes 90,000 documents from CNN and 196,000 documents from the Daily Mail. The CNN/Daily Mail dataset is available.[b]

---

[b]https://github.com/danqi/rc-cnn-dailymail.

The PWKP dataset contains Wikipedia edit history, a subset of the edits can be considered as sentence simplification. The dataset was automatically aligned to find original sentence and simplified pairs. Again, this is not a proper summarization dataset, but it includes pairs of long sentence / short sentences which is useful to learn how to shorten and paraphrase sentences in an abstractive manner.

These datasets are good sources of knowledge to learn how to rephrase information in a compact manner. But they are weak proxies of the real summarization task: they do not cover the challenges of content selection, relevance assessment and redundancy avoidance which have been the key characteristics of the traditional DUC/TAC summarization datasets in the past. This is an important point, as it highlights that what is addressed in the group of abstractive summarization methods we survey here is a task different in nature from what was studied a decade ago. Still, the same evaluation metrics (mainly ROUGE) is applied uniformly across the two variant tasks.

3.2. *Predicting high-dimension output*

When using encoder-decoder based models, the network is required to predict the next word at each decoding step. In the Gigaword corpus, there are 69,000 unique words. To predict a word using the decoder output, it is common to apply the softmax method: formally the probability of outputting a word given the decoder output (context) is defined as:

$$P(w|c) = \frac{\exp(c^T V'_w)}{\sum_{w' \in V} \exp(c^T V'_{w'})}$$

where V' is a learnable weight matrix with a column assigned to each vocabulary word ($|C| \times |V|$). When predicting extremely large vocabulary such as in the Gigaword case, this computation is time-consuming (time complexity of $O(|V|)$) and requires maintaining many parameters (space complexity of $O(|V|)$).

3.2.1. *Sampled softmax*

One of the methods to speed up the softmax function while training is to use a variation called sampled softmax.[27] The sampled softmax method speeds up computation by approximating the denominator of the softmax function instead of computing a sum of $|V|$ vector multiplications only a

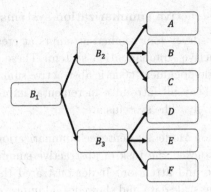

Fig. 5.   Hierarchal vocabulary tree.

subset of the vocabulary is sampled. Empirical results show low effect on accuracy while achieving a constant speedup.[c]

3.2.2. *Hierarchal softmax*

Another method to speed up the computation of softmax is the hierarchal softmax.[28] The method splits the assignment of probability to each word from the vocabulary to selecting a route in a predetermined tree where the leaves are the words from the vocabulary (Fig. 5).

Given a vocabulary arranged in a tree as seen in Fig. 1, the hierarchal softmax requires creating a softmax layer for each node of the tree. The probability of a tree node will be the multiplication of the probabilities in the path from the root to the leaf.

We provide Python code implementing hierarchal softmax.[d]

For example the probability of selecting the token "A" equals to the probability to select the path from B_1 to B_2 times the probability of selecting the path from node B_2 to "A".

$$P(w =' A'|c) = P_{B_1}(w =' B_2'|c) * P_{B_2}(w =' A'|c).$$

$$P_{B_1}(w =' B_2'|c) = \frac{\exp(c^T V'_{B_2})}{\sum_{w' \in \{B_2, B_3\}} \exp(c^T V'_{w'})}.$$

---

[c]A comprehensive list of different sampling methods to improve softmax computation is reviewed in http://sebastianruder.com/word-embeddings-softmax/index.html#samplingbasedapproaches.

[d]https://talbaumel.github.io/softmax/.

4. Survey of abstractive summarization systems

In this section, we survey four seminal attempts at creating a neural network based abstractive summarization system. These models implement full end to end single-document generic abstractive summarizers using neural architectures. They all introduce incremental improvements that can be analyzed separately. The systems are:

- A Neural Attention Model for Sentence Summarization:[21] this is the first system which attacked the task of abstractive summarization with the model of seq2seq and attention. It demonstrated the feasibility of the approach on large-scale data and showed solid improvement over existing phrase statistics based techniques.
- Abstractive Text Summarization using Sequence-to-sequence RNNs and Beyond:[29] this paper improved upon the paper by Rush *et al.* (2015) by introducing explicit mechanism to deal with large vocabulary and unknown words.
- Get To The Point: Summarization with Pointer-Generator Networks[30]
- Sentence Simplification with Deep Reinforcement Learning.[31]

4.1. *A neural attention model for sentence summarization*

In this work[21] the summarization task is described as a conditional language model, where the model should generate the most likely abstractive summarization given a document. This work explores three different methods of encoding a document, where the encoding is then used to condition the language model of the decoder. For all the encoders described, the same LSTM decoder was used to generate the output summary from the encoded input document. Beam-search was applied to avoid greedy predictions while generating output.

4.1.1. *Bag-of-words encoder*

The bag-of words encoder ignores the document word order and represents a document as the averaged sum of its word embeddings. The only learned parameter in this model is the word embeddings matrix.

The model uses the following equations, where D_i denotes the word i in the document D:

$$enc_{bow}(D) = sum(p^T \tilde{D})$$

$$\tilde{D} = [emb(D_1), emb(D_2), \ldots, emb(D_n)]$$

$$p = [1/n, 1/n, \ldots, 1/n].$$

4.1.2. *Convolutional encoder*

One of the major problems of bag-of-words based methods is the inability to understand multi-words expressions, for example if the input document contains two different full names the bag-of-words encoder cannot encode the four words representing names as two distinctive entities since it ignores all word order. The solution to this problem is the convolutional encoder (CE).[32,33] The CE applies a series of one-dimensional convolutions and max pooling operations over the embedded document in order to represent it as a fixed size vector. The convolution operation can be considered as an n-gram feature extractor.

$$enc_{conv}(D) = conv^l(\tilde{D})$$

$$\tilde{D} = [emb(D_1), emb(D_2), \ldots, emb(D_n)]$$

$$conv(V) = maxpool(conv1d(V)).$$

The parameters of this model include the embedding matrix (1 row for each word in the vocabulary times the number of dimensions used for the word embeddings), and the convolution filters.

4.1.3. *Attention-based encoder*

The last encoder described in the paper is an attention-based encoder (ATB) similar to the one described in the previous section — a combination of an RNN encoder, attention mechanism and RNN decoder. This ATB encoder produces the best results on the task.

4.1.4. *Experiments*

The model was trained on the Gigaword dataset and tested on DUC 2004 single sentence summaries and a subset of held out sentences from Gigaword (Table 1). For evaluation ROUGE[34] was used. For baseline scores, the MOSES statistical phrase translation method[35] was used: that is, abstractive summarization was cast as a problem of translating from "long source language" to "short target language." They also compare with the Topiary[36] system which was the winning system in the DUC 2004 shared task.

4.1.5. *Example of ATB encoder summaries*

INPUT: *"a detained iranian-american academic accused of acting against national security has been released from a tehran prison after a hefty bail was posted, a top judiciary official said tuesday."*

Table 1. Experimental results for "A Neural Attention Model for Sentence Summarization". ABS refers to the attention-based encoder model, BOW to the same model with bag-of-words encoder.

MODEL	DUC 2004		
	ROUGE-1	ROUGE-2	ROUGE-L
Topiary	25.12	6.46	20.12
MOSES	26.50	8.13	22.85
BOW	22.15	4.60	18.23
ABS	28.18	8.49	23.81

MODEL	GIGAWORD		
	ROUGE-1	ROUGE-2	ROUGE-L
MOSES	28.77	12.10	26.44
ABS	31.00	12.65	28.34

GOLD: *"iranian-american academic held in tehran released on bail"*
OUTPUT: *"detained iranian-american academic released from prison after hefty bail"*.

The attention-based mechanism produces much better results than the bag-of-words encoder on the task. As a language model, it also produces dramatically lower perplexity (27) than an n-gram model (perplexity of 183), the bag-of-words model (43) or the convolution model (37).

Another advantage of the attention-based model is that it produces alignment data between source and target sequences which can be visualized (see Fig. 6) and interpreted.

Training of the ABS system on the Gigaword dataset takes about four days and relies critically on GPU hardware to converge fast enough. The code of the method is available.[e]

4.2. *Abstractive text summarization using sequence-to-sequence RNNs and beyond*

The paper "Abstractive text summarization using sequence-to-sequence RNNs and beyond"[29] introduces two novel concepts to neural encoder-decoder architecture for summarization: the large vocabulary trick (LVT)[37] and Switching Generator-Pointer. The paper is also the first to use the CNN/Daily Mail corpus for training, so it is able to generate summaries longer than one sentence.

---

[e]https://github.com/facebookarchive/NAMAS.

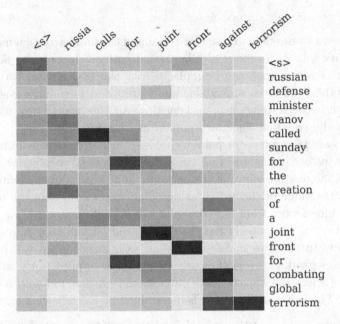

Fig. 6. Example of attention-based encoder attention weights values for different generation steps.

4.2.1. *Large vocabulary trick*

The LVT is a method to speed up neural networks that generates words from a large vocabulary by exploiting domain knowledge. As discussed earlier, in seq2seq architectures words are generated by sampling the output of a softmax distribution. The computation of this softmax function on very large vocabularies (50,000 and more distinct words) is a computational bottleneck. It is also unlikely to provide robust predictions when sampling rare words. The LVT comes to improve on this situation.

For summarization, we can assume that summaries will not introduce concepts that did not appear in the original text. In more practical terms, the output vocabulary of the network can be restricted to the vocabulary of the current input document (together with a set of stop-words/very common words). Restricting the vocabulary can be achieved by using only the relevant vectors from the matrix used to transform the decoder output to the vocabulary-size output vector. The LVT both reduces computation time (since we multiply a smaller matrix) and effectively automatically assigns zero probability to irrelevant terms, thus improving the perplexity of the model.

4.2.2. *Switching generator-pointer*

In the news stories domain used for training most summarization methods, each story introduces story specific named entities. In order to adapt to such rare entities, they can be replaced with the UNK (unknown) token. This method produces unreadable summaries and introduces systematic confusion between different named entities. Another way to deal with rare words is the switching generator-pointer mechanism.

The switching generator-pointer enables the network to copy words from its input instead of just selecting words from the general vocabulary. It does this by changing the ouput of the network: first it introduces a switch gate S_t — if the value of the switch at decoding step t is 0, then the network will produce a word from the vocabulary (using softmax over a vocabulary size vector); if the value of the switch is 1, then it will copy a word from the input. In order to make sure the attention mechanism will point to the correct word, categorical cross-entropy loss is applied to the attention weights (where the copied word value should be one and zero for other words). The value of the switch is determined by the following equation:

$$P(S_t = 1) = sigmoid(V_s \cdot (W_{s1} \cdot enc_t + W_{s2} \cdot E(O_{t-1}) + W_{s3} \cdot h_t + B_s))$$

where $V_s, W_{s1}, W_{s2}, W_{s3}, B_s$ are learned parameters, enc_t is the attended encoder output at step t, $E(O_{t-1})$ is the embedded value of the previously generated word and h_t is the decoder state.

In order to determine the word the network should copy when $S_t = 1$, the network uses the attention weights, the word with the highest attention value at decoding step t is copied.

$$Loss_t = G_t \log \hat{a}_{t_i} P(S_t) + (1 - G_t) \log (P(W_j))(1 - P(S_t)).$$

The loss at decoding step t is $Loss_t$, where G_t is the grounded switch value at step t and $P(S_t)$ is the predicted switch value, $\hat{a}_{t_i}$ is the normalized attention value of the word at index i where i is the index designated to be copied, and $P(W_i)$ is the probability of generating the word W_i (and W_i is the ground truth).

4.2.3. *Experiments*

When compared to the best model presented in the ABS system ("A neural attention model for sentence summarization") training on Gigaword and testing with DUC 2004, the addition of LVT and switching generator-pointer improves all ROUGE scores (Table 2).

Table 2. Comparison of ABS to ABS with LVT and switching generator-pointer mechanism.

| | | DUC 2004 | |
MODEL	ROUGE-1	ROUGE-2	ROUGE-L
ABS	28.18	8.49	23.81
LVT+switch	28.35	9.46	24.59

Since the paper was presented after the introduction of the CNN/Daily Mail dataset it was possible to test it on tasks longer than a single sentences. The paper tested the presented model on other DUC single document tasks but did not compare it to other abstractive models.

4.3. Get to the point: Summarization with pointer-generator networks

This paper improves the architecture to attend to another problem in existing abstractive summarization methods: repetition when generating multi-sentence text as observed in Fig. 7.

4.3.1. Coverage mechanism

The coverage mechanism contains a coverage vector C_v that contains the sum of all attention weights (a) from previous decoding steps.

$$C_t = \sum_{i=1}^{t-1} a_i.$$

Once C_v is obtained it can be used to force the attention mechanism to attend to words it did not previously attend to by using it as an input to the attention function

$$e_i^t = v^T \tanh(W_1 h_i + W_2 s_t + W_3 C_t + b_{attn})$$

and adding a special loss term to force the attention mechanism to attend to new words:

$$CovLoss = \sum_i \min(a_{t,i}, c_{t,i})$$

$$Loss_t = LogLoss + \lambda CovLoss.$$

Original Text (truncated): lagos, nigeria (cnn) a day after winning nigeria's presidency, *muhammadu buhari* told cnn's christiane amanpour that
he plans to aggressively fight corruption that has long plagued nigeria
and go after the root of the nation's unrest. *buhari* said he'll "rapidly give
attention" to curbing violence in the northeast part of nigeria, where the terrorist group boko haram operates. by cooperating with neighboring nations
chad, cameroon and niger, **he said his administration is confident it will
be able to thwart criminals** and others contributing to nigeria's instability.
for the first time in nigeria's history, the opposition defeated the ruling party
in democratic elections. *buhari* defeated incumbent goodluck jonathan by
about 2 million votes, according to nigeria's independent national electoral
commission. **the win comes after a long history of military rule, coups
and botched attempts at democracy in africa's most populous nation.**

Baseline Seq2Seq + Attention: UNK UNK says his administration is confident it will be able to **destabilize nigeria's economy.** UNK says his administration is confident it will be able to thwart criminals and other **nigerians.**
he says the country has long nigeria and nigeria's economy.

Pointer-Gen: *muhammadu buhari* says he plans to aggressively fight corruption **in the northeast part of nigeria.** he says he'll "rapidly give attention" to curbing violence **in the northeast part of nigeria.** he says his
administration is confident it will be able to thwart criminals.

Pointer-Gen + Coverage: *muhammadu buhari* says he plans to aggressively
fight corruption that has long plagued nigeria. he says his administration is
confident it will be able to thwart criminals. the win comes after a long history of military rule, coups and botched attempts at democracy in africa's
most populous nation.

Fig. 7.   Comparison of different abstractive summarization with repetition highlighted.
Repetition avoidance is achieved with a coverage mechanism.

Table 3.   Comparison of ABS to ABS with LVT and switching
generator-pointer mechanism and switching generator-pointer
mechanism and coverage mechanism.

MODEL	CNN/Daily Mail		
	ROUGE-1	ROUGE-2	ROUGE-L
ABS+	30.49	11.17	28.08
LVT+switch	35.46	13.30	32.65
switch+coverage	39.53	17.28	36.38

4.3.2. *Experiments*

A model with the coverage mechanism and switching generator-pointer was
trained and tested on the CNN/Daily Mail dataset (Table 3).

The combination of the improvements addressing large vocabulary, rare
words and named entities and coverage provides dramatic improvements

to all ROUGE measures. It also enabled the models to work in a reliable manner on longer input documents.[f]

The code of the system is available.[g]

4.4. *Sentence simplification with deep reinforcement learning*

The last improvement we will discuss is the introduction of reinforcement learning (RL) to sequence-to-sequence neural architectures. RL enables the network to be trained on sequence level loss instead of per-word loss (aka imitation learning), that enables us to train the model to achieve more abstract features such as text coherence instead of just copying the correct answer. Another important advantage to RL is "exposure bias",[38,39] the notion that while training, the model will only encounter scenarios in which all previous prediction were ground truth. This scenario is not realistic at prediction time — as soon as one prediction is "off", later predictions are performed in uncharted territory.

4.4.1. *Reinforcement learning algorithm*

The RL algorithm[40] is usually used to solve sequential-decision problems. Such problems are modeled as an agent that can take actions that affect an environment. After a sequence of actions has been executed, the agent receives a reward which enables the agent to adjust his action taking policy to maximize the reward, as Algorithm 8 and Fig. 8 show.[h]

For example in order to apply the algorithm to the game of chess, the agent will be the player, the environment will be the chessboard and position of pieces, actions are the player's moves and reward will be the eventual outcome of the game: 1 if the player won and −1 if the player lost. At each turn, the player will choose what move to make, the move will change the environment (the move of the other player will be considered as part of the change in the environment), the player will make the next move according to the changed environment. Once the game is over, we reward the player according to the score. Essentially in this scenario we are training an agent that decides on the next move to make given the state of the board.

---

[f]Training time when using the CNN/Daily Mail dataset and ge-force 1080 GPU is one week.

[g]https://github.com/abisee/pointer-generator.

[h]For further reading about reinforcement learning, we recommend this blog-post http://karpathy.github.io/2016/05/31/rl/.

Algorithm 8 Reinforcement Learning

$player \Leftarrow init\_player()$
while training **do**
  $env \Leftarrow init\_env()$
  $decisions \Leftarrow empty\_list()$
  while $env.game\_not\_ended()$ **do**
    $move \Leftarrow player.choose\_move(env)$
    $decisions.append(move, env.copy())$
    $env \Leftarrow env.update\_env(move)$
  end while
  reward = env.get_reward()
  for $move, env \Leftarrow decisions$ **do**
    $player.update\_weights(move, env)$
  end for
end while

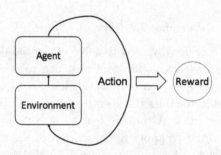

Fig. 8.   Reinforcement learning settings.

4.4.2. *Reinforcement learning for sequence-to-sequence models*

In order to adopt the RL algorithm to the context of seq2seq models, the agent will be the model, the environment will be the generated output and the reward will be a predefined score function for the complete sentence (after the model generated the end-of-sentence token). In order to speed up the learning process, instead of training the model from scratch, the model is first trained using regular per-word training and we use the RL algorithm to fine-tune the network.

Table 4. Comparison of ABS to ABS with switching generator-pointer mechanism trained using reinforcement learning algorithm.

MODEL	PWKP BLEU	SARI
ABS+	88.85	35.66
RL+switch	80.12	37.27

In order to use RL for automatic summarization, the paper[31] suggests using the following reward function.

$$Reward(sent) = \lambda_s s(sent) + \lambda_r r(sent) + \lambda_f f(sent)$$

$$s(sent) = SARI(sent)$$

$$r(sent) = cos(sent, gold)$$

$$f(sent) = LM(sent).$$

The s term represents the sentence simplicity score, it is calculated using the SARI function defined to measure text simplicity in Xu *et al.* (2016).[41] The r term represents the relevance of the output to the source sentence: it is the cosine similarity function on the generated sentence and the ground truth vectors. The f term is the fluency score (how fluent is the text) measured using an LSTM-trained language model.

4.4.3. *Experiments*

The model was trained and tested on the PWKP dataset and compared using the attention-encoder-decoder model (Table 4). The output of the model was scored using BLEU[42] and the SARI function (also used for reinforcement).

While the RL algorithm did not improve the network term coverage, it generated simpler text according to the SARI evaluation.

5. Conclusion

In this chapter, we covered recent developments in abstractive summarization using neural networks. We first covered the available datasets for the task. We then introduced the basic building blocks used by all the recent models: RNNs, sequence to sequence models, attention mechanism.

We then surveyed incremental advancements of abstractive summarization starting from the first neural encoder-decoder model with attention mechanism. The following techniques bring significant improvements to abstractive summarizers:

- Deal with large vocabularies using the large-vocabulary-trick which exploits the shared vocabulary of the input and output
- Deal with rare words by adding the ability of switching between generating words and copying pointers to the source sequence
- Avoid repetitions by adding a distraction mechanism to improve attention coverage
- Finally, we covered attempts at using reinforcement learning to fine-tune our summarization models at the sentence level.

All the methods covered have brought dramatic improvements to the field of single document generic abstractive summarization in the last couple of years. These early steps indicate that fully abstractive summarization addressing longer documents and more advanced tasks such as query-focused and multi-document summarization can be achieved by combining the re-usable building blocks we have described with higher-level models that address rhetorical and information flow aspects of the challenging summarization task.

Regarding the multilinguality, a very significant advantage of the neural networks is that they are fully data-driven and, therefore, can be considered language-independent. Theoretically, the only adaptation needed for another language, is getting more training data on that language. However, it can be observed in the literature, that not all languages achieve the same gain from new neural network architectures.

References

1. R. Wu, S. Yan, Y. Shan, Q. Dang, and G. Sun, Deep image: Scaling up image recognition, *arXiv preprint arXiv:1501.02876* (2015).
2. A. Krizhevsky, I. Sutskever, and G. E. Hinton, Imagenet classification with deep convolutional neural networks. In eds. F. Pereira, C. J. C. Burges, L. Bottou, and K. Q. Weinberger, *Advances in Neural Information Processing Systems 25*, pp. 1097–1105. Curran Associates, Inc. (2012). Available at: http://papers.nips.cc/paper/4824-imagenet-classification-with-deep-convolutional-neural-networks.pdf.
3. G. Hinton, L. Deng, D. Yu, G. E. Dahl, A.-r. Mohamed, N. Jaitly, A. Senior, V. Vanhoucke, P. Nguyen, T. N. Sainath, and B. Kingsbury, Deep neural

networks for acoustic modeling in speech recognition: The shared views of four research groups, *IEEE Signal Processing Magazine*, **29**(6), 82–97 (2012).

4. D. Bahdanau, K. Cho, and Y. Bengio, Neural machine translation by jointly learning to align and translate, *arXiv preprint arXiv:1409.0473* (2014).

5. B. Farley and W. Clark, Simulation of self-organizing systems by digital computer, *Transactions of the IRE Professional Group on Information Theory*, **4**(4), 76–84 (1954).

6. M. Minsky and S. Papert, *Perceptrons*, MIT Press (1969).

7. D. E. Rumelhart, G. E. Hinton, and R. J. Williams, Learning representations by back-propagating errors, *Cognitive Modeling*, **5**(3), 1 (1988).

8. Y. Goldberg, Neural network methods for natural language processing, *Synthesis Lectures on Human Language Technologies*, **10**(1), 1–309 (2017).

9. M. J. Kusner, Y. Sun, N. I. Kolkin, and K. Q. Weinberger, From word embeddings to document distances. In *International Conference on Machine Learning (ICML)*, ICML (2015).

10. T. Mikolov, K. Chen, G. Corrado, and J. Dean, Efficient estimation of word representations in vector space, *arXiv preprint arXiv:1301.3781* (2013).

11. J. Pennington, R. Socher, and C. D. Manning, Glove: Global vectors for word representation. In *Empirical Methods in Natural Language Processing (EMNLP)*, vol. 14, pp. 1532–1543, ACL (2014).

12. Y. Kim, Convolutional neural networks for sentence classification, *arXiv preprint arXiv:1408.5882* (2014).

13. X. C. Peng Jin, Y. Zhang and Y. Xia, Bag-of-embeddings for text classification. In *Proceedings of the 25th International Joint Conference on Artificial Intelligence (IJCAI-16)*, AAAI Press (2016).

14. J. Chung, C. Gulcehre, K. Cho, and Y. Bengio, Empirical evaluation of gated recurrent neural networks on sequence modeling, *arXiv preprint arXiv:1412.3555* (2014).

15. S. Hochreiter and J. Schmidhuber, Long short-term memory, *Neural Computation*, **9**(8), 1735–1780 (1997).

16. C. D. Santos and B. Zadrozny, Learning character-level representations for part-of-speech tagging. In *Proceedings of the 31st International Conference on Machine Learning (ICML-14)*, pp. 1818–1826, ICML (2014).

17. T. Thireou and M. Reczko, Bidirectional long short-term memory networks for predicting the subcellular localization of eukaryotic proteins, *IEEE/ACM Transactions on Computational Biology and Bioinformatics*, **4**(3) (2007).

18. I. Sutskever, O. Vinyals, and Q. V. Le, Sequence to sequence learning with neural networks. In *Advances in neural information processing systems*, pp. 3104–3112, Neural Information Processing Systems Foundation, Inc. (2014).

19. K. Cho, B. Van Merriënboer, C. Gulcehre, D. Bahdanau, F. Bougares, H. Schwenk, and Y. Bengio, Learning phrase representations using rnn encoder-decoder for statistical machine translation, *arXiv preprint arXiv:1406.1078* (2014).

20. K. Xu, J. Ba, R. Kiros, K. Cho, A. Courville, R. Salakhudinov, R. Zemel, and Y. Bengio, Show, attend and tell: Neural image caption generation

with visual attention. In *International Conference on Machine Learning*, pp. 2048–2057, ICML (2015).

21. A. M. Rush, S. Chopra, and J. Weston, A neural attention model for abstractive sentence summarization, *arXiv preprint arXiv:1509.00685* (2015).

22. A. Nenkova, Automatic text summarization of newswire: Lessons learned from the document understanding conference. In *AAAI*, vol. 5, pp. 1436–1441, AAAI (2005).

23. H. T. Dang and K. Owczarzak, Overview of the TAC 2008 update summarization task. In *Text Analysis Conference (TAC)*, NIST (2008).

24. L. D. Consortium *et al.*, English gigaword, Catalog number LDC2003T05. Available from LDC at http://www.ldc.upenn.edu (2003).

25. K. M. Hermann, T. Kocisky, E. Grefenstette, L. Espeholt, W. Kay, M. Suleyman, and P. Blunsom, Teaching machines to read and comprehend. In *Advances in Neural Information Processing Systems*, pp. 1693–1701, Neural Information Processing Systems Foundation, Inc. (2015).

26. D. Bernhard and I. Gurevych, A monolingual tree-based translation model for sentence simplification. In eds. C.-R. Huang and D. Jurafsky, *Proceedings of the 23rd International Conference on Computational Linguistics (Volume 2)*, pp. 1353–1361, ACL (2010).

27. M.-T. Luong, I. Sutskever, Q. V. Le, O. Vinyals, and W. Zaremba, Addressing the rare word problem in neural machine translation, *arXiv preprint arXiv:1410.8206* (2014).

28. F. Morin and Y. Bengio, Hierarchical probabilistic neural network language model. In eds. R. Cowell and Z. Ghahramani, *Proceedings of the 10th International Workshop on Artificial Intelligence and Statistics (AISTATS)*, vol. 5, pp. 246–252, Citeseer (2005).

29. R. Nallapati, B. Zhou, C. Gulcehre, and B. Xiang, Abstractive text summarization using sequence-to-sequence RNNS and beyond, *arXiv preprint arXiv:1602.06023* (2016).

30. A. See, P. J. Liu, and C. D. Manning, Get to the point: Summarization with pointer-generator networks, *arXiv preprint arXiv:1704.04368* (2017).

31. X. Zhang and M. Lapata, Sentence simplification with deep reinforcement learning. In *Proceedings of the 2017 Conference on Empirical Methods in Natural Language Processing*, Copenhagen, Denmark, pp. 584–594, ACL (2017).

32. N. Kalchbrenner, E. Grefenstette, and P. Blunsom, A convolutional neural network for modelling sentences, *arXiv preprint arXiv:1404.2188* (2014).

33. K. J. Lang, A. H. Waibel, and G. E. Hinton, A time-delay neural network architecture for isolated word recognition, *Neural Networks*, **3**(1), 23–43 (1990).

34. C.-Y. Lin, Rouge: A package for automatic evaluation of summaries. In *Text Summarization Branches Out: Proceedings of the ACL-04 Workshop*, vol. 8, ACL (2004).

35. P. Koehn, H. Hoang, A. Birch, C. Callison-Burch, M. Federico, N. Bertoldi, B. Cowan, W. Shen, C. Moran, R. Zens, *et al.*, Moses: Open source toolkit for statistical machine translation. In *Proceedings of the 45th Annual Meeting*

of the ACL on Interactive Poster and Demonstration Sessions, pp. 177–180, ACL (2007).

36. B. D. David Zajic and R. Schwartz, Bbn/umd at duc-2004: Topiary. In *Proceedings of the HLT-NAACL 2004 Document Understanding Workshop, Boston*, p. 112–119, NAACL (2004).

37. S. Jean, K. Cho, R. Memisevic, and Y. Bengio, On using very large target vocabulary for neural machine translation. In *Proceedings of the 53rd Annual Meeting of the Association for Computational Linguistics and the 7th International Joint Conference on Natural Language Processing*, Beijing, China, pp. 1–10, ACL (2014).

38. R. Paulus, C. Xiong, and R. Socher, A deep reinforced model for abstractive summarization, *arXiv preprint arXiv: 1705.04304* (2017).

39. A. Venkatraman, M. Hebert, and J. A. Bagnell, Improving multi-step prediction of learned time series models. In *Association for the Advancement of Artificial Intelligence (AAAI)*, pp. 3024–3030, AAAI (2015).

40. R. J. Williams, Simple statistical gradient-following algorithms for connectionist reinforcement learning, *Machine Learning*, **8**(3–4), 229–256 (1992).

41. W. Xu, C. Napoles, E. Pavlick, Q. Chen, and C. Callison-Burch, Optimizing statistical machine translation for text simplification, *Transactions of the Association for Computational Linguistics*, **4**, 401–415 (2016).

42. K. Papineni, S. Roukos, T. Ward, and W.-J. Zhu, BLEU: a method for automatic evaluation of machine translation. In *Proceedings of the 40th Annual Meeting on Association for Computational Linguistics*, pp. 311–318, ACL (2002).

Chapter 7

Headline Generation as a Sequence Prediction with Conditional Random Fields

Carlos A. Colmenares[*,||], Marina Litvak[†,**], Amin Mantrach[‡,††],
Fabrizio Silvestri[§,‡‡], and Horacio Rodríguez[¶,§§]

[*] *Google Inc., Zurich, Switzerland*
[†] *Shamoon College of Engineering, Beer Sheva, Israel*
[‡] *Criteo Labs, Palo Alto, California, USA*
[§] *Facebook, London, UK*
[¶] *TALP-UPC, Barcelona, Spain*
[||] *crcarlos@super.org*
[**] *marinal@ac.sce.ac.il*
[††] *a.mantrach@criteo.com*
[‡‡] *f.silvestri@isti.cnr.it*
[§§] *horacio@lsi.upc.es*

Automatic headline generation, or automatic one-line summarization, is a sub-task of document summarization with many reported applications in several domains. In this chapter we present a sequence-prediction technique for learning how editors title their news stories. The introduced technique models the problem as a discrete optimization task in a feature-rich space, where the global optimum can be found in polynomial time by means of dynamic programming. We train and test our model with an extensive corpus of financial news, and compare it against a number of baselines by using standard metrics from the document summarization domain, as well as some new metrics proposed in this work. The obtained results are very appealing and substantiate the soundness of the approach.

1. Introduction

Automatic document summarization, also known as automatic text summarization and hereafter referred to simply as document summarization or text summarization, is the process of automatically abridging text documents. This task has a wide range of useful applications and has been studied for decades, which has led to the development of many techniques for approaching the problem, including, by way of very limited examples, the work of Refs. 1 and 2.

Although traditionally the final objective of text summarization is to produce a paragraph, or abstract, that summarizes a rather large collection of text,[3] the task of producing a very short summary comprised of 10–15 words — sometimes called sentence compression or headline generation — has also been broadly studied. There have been many reported practical applications for this endeavor, most notably efficient web browsing on hand-held devices,[4] generation of TV captions,[5] digitization of newspaper articles that have uninformative headlines,[6] and headline generation in one language, but based on news stories written in another.[7,8]

In general terms, a headline of a news article can be defined as a short sentence that gives a reader a general idea about the main contents of the story it entitles.

The final practical objective of our study was to develop a novel technique for generating informative headlines based on news articles. The purpose of the research is two-fold: first, to offer the news editor a sketch of a headline as an alternative to one that was manually produced, and second, to be used as a short and concise summary of the story's content for indexing purposes or as a preview in contexts with very limited display capabilities.

In this work we make a number of contributions concerning statistical models for headline generation, training of the models, and their evaluation. Specifically:

(1) We describe a model that tries to learn how an editor generates headlines based on news articles. This method significantly differs from others in the way it represents possible headlines in a feature-rich space, and tries to learn how humans select what candidate compressions are more relevant. Furthermore, our model can be trained with any corpus consisting of titled articles because it does not request special conditions on the structure or provenance of the headlines.

(2) We suggest a slight, yet relevant, change of a traditional training algorithm for fitting our model.

(3) We present a simple and elegant algorithm that runs in polynomial time and finds the global optimum of our objective function. This represents an important advantage of our proposal because many former

techniques resort to heuristic-driven search algorithms that are not guaranteed to find the global optimum.

(4) Through the results of our model, and some other implemented baselines, we provide statistical evidence that traditional evaluation metrics — from the field of document summarization — are not very well suited for model selection in headline generation contexts, and in exchange we propose some new metrics for coping with the problems (but raising some others).

The rest of this chapter is organized as follows: in Section 2 we mention the related work and highlight the differences with our proposal. Section 3 introduces the background on sequence prediction models that supports our study, while Section 4 contains a broad theoretical explanation of our proposed model. In Section 5 we make a point about the engineering details that were necessary for implementing our method. In Section 6 we describe how we evaluated our system. Lastly, Section 7 presents the conclusions of our study, together with some analysis and proposals for its extension.

2. Related work

Many of the techniques used for headline generation have been inspired or derived from similar work in traditional document summarization, where the common trend consisted of performing multiple or combined steps of sentence selection and compression.[9,10] Nevertheless, several studies have reported that because classical approaches try to generate paragraph-long summaries by considering sentences as the smallest text-spans, they do not manage to scale properly when it comes to generating sentence-long summarizations. The shortcoming in these approaches lies in the inability to distill the main idea of a story, which is usually scattered between sentences.[7] As a consequence, modern techniques for headline generation opt for generating completely new sentences by recycling and reordering words present in the article. This approach, however, raises the risk of losing or changing the contextual meaning of the reused words.[11]

There has been a significant amount of research about headline generation, and therefore it is difficult to classify all the known approaches into a limited number of categories. It is possible, however, to identify three main trends of the techniques that are broadly employed in different studies:

Rule-based approaches

These methods make use of handcrafted linguistically-based rules for detecting or compressing important phrases in the text. These methods tend to be simple and lightweight, but obviously suffer from their simplicity due to their inability to explore complex relationships in the text. The most representative system for this group is the Hedge Trimmer,[12] which creates a headline by iteratively pruning constituents from the parse tree of a story's lead sentence until a desired length is reached; the pruning rules are fixed and no prior training or modelling is needed. Many modern techniques still employ tailored rule-based techniques, but as supplementary features of a larger system. For instance, Gattani[13] makes use of predefined cue-phrases for helping his algorithm detect potential important words in the text.

Statistics-based approaches

These methods make use of statistical models for learning correlations between words in headlines and those in articles. The models are fit under supervised learning environments and therefore need large amounts of labeled data. One of the most influential works in this category is the Naïve Bayes approach that is presented in Ref. 7, where a translation model is built in which the probability of a word appearing in a headline, provided it also appears in the article, is estimated. Many other proposals have been built on top of this idea, such as the machine translation model in Ref. 14 and the hidden Markov model (HMM) in Ref. 8. The use of statistical models for learning pruning rules for parse trees has also been studied, the most notable work in this area having been presented in Ref. 15, where probabilistic context-free grammars are used for scoring candidate compressions. Some other works, like Ref. 16, augment and improve that idea by enabling the model to exploit features extracted from the candidates. The method proposed in this paper is statistically based and uses several characteristics of related works, such as language models for part of speech (POS) tags, as well as word bigrams.

Summarization-based approaches

As previously stated, headlines can be regarded as very short summaries; traditional summarization methods could therefore be adapted for generating one-line compressions. The primary difficulty with these approaches is that they make use of techniques that were not initially devised for generating compressions of more than 10% of the original content, which directly affects the quality of the resulting summary.[7] Many different strategies have been explored in this category, such as surface-level approaches that detect salient phrases in the document by identifying keywords in its content,[17] as well as entity-level approaches that perform discourse analysis for spotting important concepts in Ref. 18. Most of these methods have been mixed with others that are more statistics-based, and the use generating more complex and competitive approaches. An example of such a mixture is the "Topiary System" described in Ref. 19 which combines sentence compression with unsupervised topic discovery. Our proposed method makes use of some features of these classic techniques, such as keyword detection and entity recognition.

Headline generation is sometimes confused or combined with sentence compression, which might not always refer to the same task. In its purest definition, sentence compression consists in *reducing* a long sentence to a shorter version, without altering its meaning. On the other hand, headline generation deals with *creating* a short sentence that summarizes several paragraphs. The gray area between both practices occurs when the techniques used for sentence compression are used for compacting a set of different sentences — which is sometimes called multi-sentence compression — because the result could be interpreted as a headline for the compressed text.

There has been considerable research in sentence compression, but it is particularly important to highlight the works reported in Refs. 20 and 21 which perform single-sentence compression by a method of sequence prediction very similar to the one proposed in this work. However, their objective is to compress one sentence while our goal is to summarize a whole news story into a single line, which makes our system substantially different.

Finally, it is relevant to mention that the task of headline generation gained some attention when it was included as an evaluation task of the Document Understanding Conferences (DUC) of 2003 (DUC'03) and 2004 (DUC'04).[22] Several interesting proposals arose from the challenge, where the aforementioned "Topiary System"[19] was the best-scoring proposal.

3. Sequence prediction models

Sequence models are formalizations of relationships between observed sequences of variables and predicted categories for each variable. Mathematically, let $\mathcal{X} = \{x_1, x_2, \ldots, x_N\}$ be a finite set of possible atomic observations, and let $\mathcal{Y} = \{y_1, y_2, \ldots, y_M\}$ be a finite set of possible categories that each atomic observation could belong to. Statistical sequence models try to approximate a probability distribution P with parameters ϕ capable of predicting for any sequence of n observations $\boldsymbol{x} \in \mathcal{X}^n$, and any sequence of assigned categories per observation $\boldsymbol{y} \in \mathcal{Y}^n$, the probability $P(\boldsymbol{y}|\boldsymbol{x}; \phi)$.

The final objective of these models is to predict the most likely sequence of categories $\hat{\boldsymbol{y}} \in \mathcal{Y}^n$ for any arbitrary observation sequence, which can be expressed as:

$$\hat{\boldsymbol{y}} = \arg\max_{\boldsymbol{y} \in \mathcal{Y}^n} P(\boldsymbol{y}|\boldsymbol{x}; \phi).$$

There have been many proposals for modeling the probability distribution P; the most popular of these are described in the following subsections.

3.1. *Hidden Markov model*

Hidden Markov models (HMMs) assume independence between all observed and assigned variables, except for two cases: an observation only depends on its assigned category, and an assigned category only depends on the one assigned immediately before. Mathematically:

$$P(\boldsymbol{y}|\boldsymbol{x}; \phi) = \prod_{i=1}^{n} P(y_i|x_i, y_{i-1}; \phi),$$

where $y_0 = $ init, a fixed initial category. Furthermore, HMMs give the following special form to a local probability:

$$P(y_i|x_i, y_{i-1}; \phi) = T(y_{i-1}, y_i) \times O(y_i, x_i),$$

where $\phi = \{T, O\}$, and $T : \mathcal{Y} \cup \{\text{init}\} \times \mathcal{Y} \to [0, 1]$ models the "transmission" probability $P(y_i|y_{i-1})$, and $O : \mathcal{Y} \times \mathcal{X} \to [0, 1]$ models the "observation" probability $P(x_i|y_i)$.

Finally the most likely sequence of categories is the solution of:

$$\hat{\boldsymbol{y}} = \arg\max_{\boldsymbol{y} \in \mathcal{Y}^n} \prod_{i=1}^{n} T(y_{i-1}, y_i) \times O(y_i, x_i),$$

which can be found in polynomial time using the Viterbi algorithm, as exposed in Ref. 23.

3.2. *Local log-linear classifiers*

Local log-linear classifiers assume independence between the assigned categories for each observation, and therefore model the global sequence probability as the product of local assignment probabilities. In contrast to

HMMs, independence between the observations is not assumed. Mathematically:

$$P(\boldsymbol{y}|\boldsymbol{x};\phi) = \prod_{i=1}^{n} P(y_i|\boldsymbol{x}, i; \phi),$$

where $P(y_i|\boldsymbol{x}, i; \phi)$ models the probability, given all observations, of assigning class y_i to observation x_i. Once again, there have been many proposals for modelling this local probability, where one of the most common practices is to shape it as a log-linear model:

$$P(y_i|\boldsymbol{x}, i; \phi) = \frac{exp\{\boldsymbol{w} \cdot \boldsymbol{f}(\boldsymbol{x}, i, y_i)\}}{Z(\boldsymbol{x}, i)},$$

where $\phi = \{\boldsymbol{w}\}$ and $\boldsymbol{w} \in \mathbb{R}^m$ is an m-dimensional weight vector, $\boldsymbol{f} : \mathcal{X}^* \times \mathbb{N}^+ \times \mathcal{Y} \to \mathbb{R}^m$ is a function that extracts m features that describe a category assignment, and $Z(\boldsymbol{x}, i)$ is a normalization function defined as:

$$Z(\boldsymbol{x}, i) = \sum_{y \in \mathcal{Y}} exp\{\boldsymbol{w} \cdot \boldsymbol{f}(\boldsymbol{x}, i, y)\}.$$

By choosing this model, the problem of assigning the most probable class to an observation is reduced to solving a simple linear classification:

$$\hat{y}_i = \underset{y \in \mathcal{Y}}{\arg\max} \frac{exp\{\boldsymbol{w} \cdot \boldsymbol{f}(\boldsymbol{x}, i, y)\}}{Z(\boldsymbol{x}, i)} = \underset{y \in \mathcal{Y}}{\arg\max} \ exp\{\boldsymbol{w} \cdot \boldsymbol{f}(\boldsymbol{x}, i, y)\}$$

$$= \underset{y \in \mathcal{Y}}{\arg\max} \ \boldsymbol{w} \cdot \boldsymbol{f}(\boldsymbol{x}, i, y)$$

which can be found by exhaustive search. Models of this type depend heavily on the chosen feature function $\boldsymbol{f}$, which works as a mapper between an abstract observation space and a well-defined euclidean space. This mapping allows the classification problem to be solved as a hyperplane separation task. See Section 4.3 for more details about this characteristic.

3.3. *Maximum Entropy Markov Models*

Presented by McCallum *et al.* (2000) in Ref. 24, Maximum Entropy Markov Models (MEMMs) are a mixture of local log-linear classifiers and HMMs, because they assume independence between an assigned category and all of the others, except the immediately preceding one. Formally:

$$P(\boldsymbol{y}|\boldsymbol{x};\phi) = \prod_{i=1}^{n} P(y_i|\boldsymbol{x}, i, y_{i-1}; \phi).$$

Similarly to HMMs, it is assumed that $y_0 = $ init, which is a fixed initial category. The local transition probabilities are shaped with a log-linear model:

$$P(y_i|\boldsymbol{x}, i, y_{i-1}; \phi) = \frac{exp\{\boldsymbol{w} \cdot \boldsymbol{f}(\boldsymbol{x}, i, y_{i-1}, y_i)\}}{Z(\boldsymbol{x}, i)},$$

where $\phi = \{\boldsymbol{w}\}$ and $\boldsymbol{w} \in \mathbb{R}^m$ is a weight vector, $\boldsymbol{f} : \mathcal{X}^* \times \mathbb{N}^+ \times \mathcal{Y} \times \mathcal{Y} \to \mathbb{R}^m$ is a local feature function, and $Z(\boldsymbol{x}, i)$ is a normalization function defined as:

$$Z(\boldsymbol{x}, i) = \sum_{a,b \in \mathcal{Y}} exp\{\boldsymbol{w} \cdot \boldsymbol{f}(\boldsymbol{x}, i, a, b)\}.$$

The final sequence prediction to an observation is then the solution to:

$$\hat{\boldsymbol{y}} = \arg\max_{\boldsymbol{y} \in \mathcal{Y}^n} \prod_{i=1}^{n} P(y_i|\boldsymbol{x}, i, y_{i-1}; \phi) = \arg\max_{\boldsymbol{y} \in \mathcal{Y}^n} \prod_{i=1}^{n} \frac{exp\{\boldsymbol{w} \cdot \boldsymbol{f}(\boldsymbol{x}, i, y_{i-1}, y_i)\}}{Z(\boldsymbol{x}, i)}$$

$$= \arg\max_{\boldsymbol{y} \in \mathcal{Y}^n} \prod_{i=1}^{n} exp\{\boldsymbol{w} \cdot \boldsymbol{f}(\boldsymbol{x}, i, y_{i-1}, y_i)\} = \arg\max_{\boldsymbol{y} \in \mathcal{Y}^n} \sum_{i=1}^{n} \boldsymbol{w} \cdot \boldsymbol{f}(\boldsymbol{x}, i, y_{i-1}, y_i)$$

$$= \arg\max_{\boldsymbol{y} \in \mathcal{Y}^n} \boldsymbol{w} \cdot \left[\sum_{i=1}^{n} \boldsymbol{f}(\boldsymbol{x}, i, y_{i-1}, y_i) \right]$$

which can be solved in polynomial time with a slight variant of the Viterbi algorithm. Furthermore, when defining the factored feature function $\boldsymbol{F} : \mathcal{X}^n \times \mathcal{Y}^n \to \mathbb{R}^m$ as:

$$\boldsymbol{F}(\boldsymbol{x}, \boldsymbol{y}) = \sum_{i=1}^{n} \boldsymbol{f}(\boldsymbol{x}, i, y_{i-1}, y_i).$$

We obtain that the decoding of MEMM is equivalent to solving:

$$\hat{\boldsymbol{y}} = \arg\max_{\boldsymbol{y} \in \mathcal{Y}^n} \boldsymbol{w} \cdot \boldsymbol{F}(\boldsymbol{x}, \boldsymbol{y})$$

which is a linear classification in a feature space. This important property will be very relevant for our proposed model for headline generation. See Section 4.3 for more details.

3.4. *Conditional Random Fields*

Presented by Lafferty *et al.* (2001) in Ref. 25, Conditional Random Fields (CRF) are a slight variation of MEMM, in which no independence between the assigned categories is assumed and a global feature function is used instead. However, this function is the same factored version of the local function used in MEMM. Formally, CRFs model the probability of a sequence in the following way:

$$P(\boldsymbol{y}|\boldsymbol{x};\phi) = \frac{exp\{\boldsymbol{w}\cdot\boldsymbol{F}(\boldsymbol{x},\boldsymbol{y})\}}{Z(\boldsymbol{x})}$$

where $\phi = \{\boldsymbol{w}\}$ and $\boldsymbol{w} \in \mathbb{R}^m$ is a weight vector, $\boldsymbol{F} : \mathcal{X}^n \times \mathcal{Y}^n \to \mathbb{R}^m$ is a global feature function, and $Z(\boldsymbol{x})$ is a normalization function defined as:

$$Z(\boldsymbol{x}) = \sum_{\boldsymbol{y}\in\mathcal{Y}^n} exp\{\boldsymbol{w}\cdot\boldsymbol{F}(\boldsymbol{x},\boldsymbol{y})\}.$$

Moreover, the global feature function is defined in a factored way equivalent to the one mentioned for MEMM, which is:

$$\boldsymbol{F}(\boldsymbol{x},\boldsymbol{y}) = \sum_{i=1}^{n} \boldsymbol{f}(\boldsymbol{x},i,y_{i-1},y_i)$$

and where $y_0 = $ init, which is once again a fixed initial category. Due to this definition, the decoding of CRF is equivalent to the decoding of MEMM:

$$\hat{\boldsymbol{y}} = \arg\max_{\boldsymbol{y}\in\mathcal{Y}^n} \frac{exp\{\boldsymbol{w}\cdot\boldsymbol{F}(\boldsymbol{x},\boldsymbol{y})\}}{Z(\boldsymbol{x})} = \arg\max_{\boldsymbol{y}\in\mathcal{Y}^n} exp\{\boldsymbol{w}\cdot\boldsymbol{F}(\boldsymbol{x},\boldsymbol{y})\}$$

$$= \arg\max_{\boldsymbol{y}\in\mathcal{Y}^n} \boldsymbol{w}\cdot\boldsymbol{F}(\boldsymbol{x},\boldsymbol{y}) = \arg\max_{\boldsymbol{y}\in\mathcal{Y}^n} \boldsymbol{w}\cdot\left[\sum_{i=1}^{n} \boldsymbol{f}(\boldsymbol{x},i,y_{i-1},y_i)\right].$$

The main difference between MEMM and CRF is that the former gives more probability to sequences that maximize local assignments, while the latter favors solutions that maximize global assignments. Although the decoding is the same, the training of both models will yield different solutions. The works presented in Refs. 24 and 25 contain more in-depth details of these models.

3.5. *CRF with state sequences*

In the particular case of CRF, where no independence between the assigned categories is assumed, it is possible to extend the local feature function.

Such an extension will enable it to keep more information about more previously assigned categories and not just the last one. These models are derived from the work on weighted automata and transducers presented in studies such as that of Ref. 26.

Let $\mathcal{S}$ be a state space, and s_0 be a fixed initial empty state. Let function $g : \mathcal{S} \times \mathcal{X} \times \mathbb{N}^+ \times \mathcal{Y} \to \mathcal{S}$ model state transitions. Then the global feature function can be redefined in the following way:

$$F(x, y) = \sum_{i=1}^{n} f(x, i, s_{i-1}, y_i), \quad s_i = g(s_{i-1}, x, i, y_i).$$

Note that if the state space, init state, and state transition function are defined as $\mathcal{S} = \mathcal{Y} \cup \{init\}$, $s_0 = init$, and $g(s, x, i, y) = y$, then $s_i = y_i$ and the resulting model is the standard CRF.

This slight change adds considerable power to the CRF, but depending on the way the state space $\mathcal{S}$ is defined, the decoding of the algorithm could be intractable.

4. Headline generation as sequence prediction

This chapter explains the theoretical foundations of our proposed model for headline generation. It is divided in three parts: Section 4.1 explains our proposed model based on sequence prediction, Section 4.2 details the decoding algorithm for finding the optimizer of our model, and Section 4.3 reports how the model is trained.

4.1. *Model description: headlines as bitmaps*

Sequence models[a] have been broadly used for many natural language processing (NLP) tasks, such as identification of sentence boundaries,[27] named entity (NE) recognition,[28] part of speech (POS) tagging,[29] dependency tree parsing,[30] document summarization,[31] and single-sentence compression.[30] In this section we shall incrementally propose a CRF model with state sequences for performing headline generation, which, to the best of our knowledge, has not been previously reported.

4.1.1. *Standard CRF model*

We decided to model headline generation as a sequence prediction task. In this manner a news article is seen as a series of observations, where

---

[a]Sometimes also referred to as structured predictors.

each observation is a possible token[b] in the document. Furthermore, each observation can be assigned to one of two categories: in-headline, or not-in-headline. Formally, we choose $\mathcal{X} = T$, where T represents the set of tokens in the text, and $\mathcal{Y} = \{0, 1\}$, with $y_0 = \text{init} = 0$.

Through this definition, each token in the text can (but need not) be selected to be part of the headline, hence the final headline is built by picking the chosen tokens and placing them together in the same order as they appear in the text. As an illustrative example, suppose the following news article is observed; if the words in bold case are chosen, the obtained result is a good candidate for a headline:

> *Your dentist knows how well you've been taking care of your teeth – and* **soon your toothbrush** *will, too. This summer, Oral-B* **will** *release a "connected toothbrush" that keeps* **track** *of* **your oral hygiene** *and tells your smartphone how well you're brushing.*
>
> Headline: **Soon your toothbrush will track your oral hygiene.**

Arguably, a more grammatical headline would be "Soon your toothbrush will *keep* track *of* your oral hygiene," which is not possible to generate from the text because the verb "to keep" is only present under its conjugated form "keeps."

By performing this approach, the headline of a story can be interpreted as a bitmap over its tokens, for which there is a finite amount. As discussed in Chapter 1, this technique of "recycling" the words of a text for placing them in a headline has already been explored and has proven itself to be a sound approach. Some other approaches like the one exposed in Ref. 13 allow making inflections or changes in reused words under certain conditions. We decided not to allow our system to perform this task because it would add an extra layer of complexity and sparseness to our model, which we wanted to keep lightweight.

This set-up already sets the ground for a CRF model. Nonetheless, the standard local feature function $f(\boldsymbol{x}, i, y_{i-1}, y_i)$ would only be able to know if a previous token was taken, which would not provide much information because there can be long gaps between selected tokens for the headline. For this reason, a state sequence will be integrated to the model to give it more power.

---

[b] A token is an English word or a symbol, as defined in the Penn Treebank tokenization. Available at: https://catalog.ldc.upenn.edu/LDC99T42.

4.1.2. *CRF model with state sequences*

A state $s \in S$ is defined as a triplet $(t, p, l) \in T \times PoS \times \mathbb{N}^+$, where T is the set of tokens in the document, and PoS is the set of all possible POS tags.[c] We define the initial state as $s_0 = (nil, nil, 0)$, and the state transition function as:

$$g(s, \boldsymbol{x}, i, y_i) = \begin{cases} \text{undefined} & \text{if } j \geq i \\ s & \text{if } y_i = 0 \\ (x_i, f_{PoS}(t), l+1) & \text{if } y_i = 1 \end{cases}$$

$$\text{where} \quad s = (x_j, p, l).$$

Here, function $f_{PoS} : T \to PoS$ returns the POS tag of a token from the document. In practical terms, a state holds three pieces of information:

(1) The last token that was chosen as part of the headline, or "nil" if no token has been chosen yet.
(2) The POS tag of the second-to-last word that was selected as part of the headline, or "nil" if no more than one word has been chosen for the headline.
(3) The number of words chosen to be part of the headline, which could be zero.

With this definition, the local feature function $\boldsymbol{f}(\boldsymbol{x}, i, s_{i-1}, y_i)$ will have knowledge not only of the whole text and the current token that is to be assigned to the headline, but also·the last word assigned to the headline, the POS tag of the second-to-last word assigned, and the length of the headline so far. It is important to highlight that the sole information the local feature function will know about the headline built so far, is the one provided to it by the state parameter.

4.1.3. *The local feature function*

In order to complete our model definition we devised a local feature function. The function call has the form $\boldsymbol{f}(\boldsymbol{x}, i, s_{i-1}, y_i)$ and its objective is to return a feature vector that will describe in an abstract euclidean space

---

[c]We used the set of 45 tags defined in the Penn Treebank Tag-Set. Available at: http://www.comp.leeds.ac.uk/amalgam/tagsets/upenn.html.

the outcome of placing token x_i in the headline,[d] provided that the words chosen before form the state s_{i-1}.

This section will describe all the features extracted when making one call to the feature function. For the rest of the section the token x_i, extracted from the function's parameters, will be referred as "the token under analysis" or "the token to be assigned to the headline."

We decided to make the features fire only if the token under analysis is chosen to be part of the headline. In other words, if parameter y_i is equal to 0 then $f(x, i, s_{i-1}, y_i) = 0$. The rationale of this decision will be explained in Section 4.3. Otherwise, the function extracts a total of 23 features, grouped in the following five sets:

- **Language-model features**
  This group consists of two features that are in charge of assessing the grammaticality of the headline being built, and are the only real-valued features in our model.

  Let t_i be the token under analysis (i.e., x_i), and let p_i be its POS tag. Let t_{i-1} be the last chosen token (which can be obtained from s_i), and let p_{i-1} be its POS tag. Also let p_{i-2} be the POS tag of the second-to-last token chosen to be part of the headline (again, obtained from s_i).

  One feature will be the natural logarithm of the bigram probability $P(t_i|t_{i-1})$, and another feature will be the natural logarithm of the trigram probability $P(p_i|p_{i-2}, p_{i-1})$.

  Section 5.3 describes how this word-bigram and POS-trigram models are built and smoothed.

- **Keyword features**
  This group contains five binary features that help the model detect if the token under analysis is a salient word in the text.

  As a preprocessing step the term frequency-inverse document frequency (TF-IDF) ranking of all the unigrams (i.e., tokens) in the document are calculated, then the rank of the token to be assigned to the headline is computed. After that takes place, the following five conditions are checked and mapped, each to a binary feature: (1) if the token's rank is in the document's top 5, (2) if the token's rank is below the document's top 50%, (3) if the token under analysis is next to a word ranked as top 5, (4) if the token is a stopword and is next to a word ranked as top 5, (5)

---

[d]x_i is the i-th element of the observation vector x, both being parameters of the local feature function.

if the token has no rank (i.e., it is a stopword, a symbol, or a bad-token as described in Section 5.2).

- **Dependency-tree features**
  This set of features is in charge of informing the model about syntactical dependencies[30] among the tokens placed on the headline, and assumes that the dependency tree of all the sentences in the news article are precomputed. The set can be further divided into two sub-groups:

  The first group consists of three binary features that indicate the relevance of the token under analysis for its sentence by reporting its depth in the dependency tree. The intuition is that the deeper the node the less important it is to its sentence. The features are: (1) if the token under analysis does not belong to a parse tree (because it is a symbol), (2) if the token under analysis is in the first two layers of its sentence's dependency tree, (3) if it is below the second layer.

  The second group compares the token under analysis to the last token in the headline (extracted from s_i), and consists of seven binary features: (1) if both tokens are part of the same dependency tree, (2) if one token is the father of the other, (3) if the last assigned token is the father of the token under analysis and also a verb, or (4) an adjective,[e] (5) if one token is the grandfather of the other, (6) if the tokens are siblings in the dependency tree, (7) if neither of the last conditions hold.

- **Named-entity features**
  This set helps the system discriminate named entities in the text, and also helps it detect those that are composed of several tokens; for instance "Ernst & Young" is a multi-token NE.

  The set is comprised of three binary features that correspond to the following conditions: (1) if the token under analysis is a NE, (2) if the last assigned token and the token under analysis belong to the same multi-token NE, (3) if the last assigned token and the one under analysis are NEs but do not belong to the same multi-word NE.

- **Headline-length features**
  This is a very important group because it helps the model discriminate when the headline built thus far in the process is either too short or too long. As many previous studies report, an ideal headline must have from 8 to 10 tokens.[6,7,13] Therefore we decided to include three binary

---

[e]The objective of these features is to encourage the model to favor adjective-to-noun or verb-to-predicate relations. This tries to prevent major changes in the contextual meaning of the words being extracted.

features that correspond to the following conditions: (1) if the headline length so far is less or equal to seven, (2) if the headline length so far is greater than or equal to 11, (3) if the token under analysis is assigned to the headline, which can be interpreted as a bias feature.

It is very important to highlight that none of these features take into account spacial positions of the selected words for the headline, nor gaps between them. This was made intentionally, to be able to extract features from headlines that are non-producible in the text. This will be further explained in Section 4.3.

4.2. *Decoding the model: finding the best candidate*

Our defined model is a CRF with state sequences, thus, as defined in Section 3.5, the best headline of an observed sequence is obtained by solving the following statement:

$$\hat{y} = \arg\max_{y \in \mathcal{Y}^n} \; \boldsymbol{w} \cdot \boldsymbol{F}(\boldsymbol{x}, \boldsymbol{y}) = \arg\max_{y \in \mathcal{Y}^n} \; \boldsymbol{w} \cdot \left[\sum_{i=1}^{n} \boldsymbol{f}(\boldsymbol{x}, i, s_{i-1}, y_i) \right]$$

$$= \arg\max_{y \in \mathcal{Y}^n} \sum_{i=1}^{n} \boldsymbol{w} \cdot \boldsymbol{f}(\boldsymbol{x}, i, s_{i-1}, y_i)$$

where $s_0 = \text{init}$, and $s_i = g(s_{i-1}, \boldsymbol{x}, i, y_i)$.

It is important to mention that the weight vector $\boldsymbol{w}$ is the key for discriminating which headlines are better than others, but the decoding algorithm will stay the same no matter what particular value the vector takes. In consequence, for the rest of this section it will be assumed that the vector has a fixed arbitrary value. Section 4.3 describes how our model is trained for finding the weight vector that produces headlines that are closely related to those that are generated by humans.

In order to design an algorithm that finds the optimizer of the aforementioned formula, because $\mathcal{Y} = \{0, 1\}$, the final solution $\hat{y}$ is a bitmap over the document's tokens $\boldsymbol{x}$, and n is the number of tokens in the text (recall that $\boldsymbol{x} \in \mathcal{X}^n$, and $\hat{y} \in \mathcal{Y}^n$). A naive way of solving the problem would require generating all possible bitmaps (for which there are 2^n), evaluating the score of each, and picking the one that was top-scoring. This *modus operandi* would lead to an intractable algorithm. However, there exists a more feasible method, the key to which is adapting the original algorithm to a polynomial one, which is accomplished by analyzing how a solution (i.e., a bitmap) is scored. Let $\boldsymbol{y} = \{y_1, y_2, \ldots, y_n\}$ be an arbitrary solution, then its score is computed as:

$$\sum_{i=1}^{n} \boldsymbol{w} \cdot \boldsymbol{f}(\boldsymbol{x}, i, s_{i-1}, y_i)$$

which is a sum over all the bits in the solution. Now let us focus on what is computed for an arbitrary bit y_i. The local feature function extracts features that describe the subjective value of the decision of taking or not taking token x_i, provided that the decisions taken before that point generated state s_i. This can lead us to four important observations:

(1) If the bit is off (i.e., $y_i = 0$), then due to the way our model was designed the local feature function is going to be equal to zero. Additionally, the sequence state will not change for the following call of the local feature function (i.e., $y_i = 0 \Rightarrow s_i = s_{i-1}$). This implies that both the scoring and state sequence functions only need to take into account tokens that are placed on the headline.

(2) The number of different states s_{i-1} that can be reached when analyzing the i-th bit in the solution depends solely on the tokens taken before, for which there are 2^{i-1} different combinations. Nevertheless, because a state only holds three pieces of information: the last token taken, a carried POS tag, and the total number of tokens taken before; consequently a better upper-bound to the number of possible reachable states up to the i-th bit is equal to $i \times |PoS| \times i = i^2 \times |PoS|$.

(3) When applying the local feature function to a particular token x_i (only if it is going to be placed on the headline), the value it generates will vary depending only on the state s_{i-1} it receives as a parameter. Also, this evaluation will generate a new state s_i and pass it to the next function call, where this new state includes token x_i. This implies that the whole evaluation of a solution can be completely modeled as a sequence of state transitions; i.e., it is possible to recover a solution's bitmap from its sequence of state transitions.

(4) The total amount of producible states in the whole text is equal to $\sum_{i=1}^{n} i^2 \times |PoS|$, which has the asymptotic bound $O(n^3 \times |PoS|)$. Furthermore, if the token-length of explored candidate headlines is restricted to be at most a fixed number H (i.e., the model is not allowed to produce headlines containing more than H tokens), the asymptotic bound drops to $O(H \times n^2 \times |PoS|)$.

Because any solution can be modelled as a chain of state sequences, and because the number of producible states is proportional to the square of the number of tokens in the text, the best solution can be found by generating all possible states and selecting the one that, when reached from the initial state, yields the maximum score. This task is achievable with a number of operations linearly proportional to the number of reachable states. To better explain it we will first define some auxiliary functions.

- **Set of producible states**
  This function calculates all the different sequence states that can be produced in document x, and takes an implicit parameter H, which refers to the maximum number of tokens allowed in a candidate headline. It is defined as:

$$\Pi_H : \mathcal{X}^* \to \mathcal{S}^*$$

$$\Pi_H(x) = \bigcup_{l=1}^{H} \bigcup_{i=l}^{n} \pi_x(i, l).$$

The sub-auxiliary recursive function π_x, which takes the document as an implicit parameter, calculates all the producible states that correspond to headlines having token-length l and finishing with token x_i. It is defined as:

$$\pi_x : \mathbb{N}^+ \times \mathbb{N}^+ \to \mathcal{S}^*$$

$$\pi_x(i, 0) = \{\text{init}\}$$

$$\pi_x(i, l) = \bigcup_{j=l-1}^{i-1} \{g(z, x, i, 1) | z \in \pi_x(j, l-1)\}.$$

It is important to highlight that a call to function $\pi_x(i, l)$ will result in a set of states similar to $\{(x_i, p_1, l), (x_i, p_2, l), \ldots, (x_i, p_k, l)\}$, where:

$$\{p_1, p_2, \ldots, p_k\} = \bigcup_{j=l-1}^{i-1} f_{PoS}(x_j)$$

and therefore $|\pi_x(i, l)| \leq |PoS|$.

- **Best achievable score for a state**
  This function receives a state producible in x, and returns the maximum score — induced by the weight vector w — that can be obtained by following a chain of state sequences, which must start from the init state,

and must end with the received state. Formally, the function can be expressed as:

$$\alpha_{\boldsymbol{x},\boldsymbol{w}} : \Pi_H(\boldsymbol{x}) \to \mathbb{R}$$

$$\alpha_{\boldsymbol{x},\boldsymbol{w}}(\text{init}) = 0$$

$$\alpha_{\boldsymbol{x},\boldsymbol{w}}(s) = \max_{z \in g^{-1}(s,\boldsymbol{x})} \alpha_{\boldsymbol{x},\boldsymbol{w}}(z) + \boldsymbol{w} \cdot \boldsymbol{f}(\boldsymbol{x}, i, z, 1), \quad \text{where } s = (x_i, p, l).$$

Here g^{-1} is the inverse of the state transition function; it returns all the states that can lead to a provided one by a single application of the state transition function. Mathematically:

$$\forall s \in \Pi_H(\boldsymbol{x}), \text{ where } s = (x_i, p, l), \text{ it is true that:}$$

$$\forall z \in \Pi_H(\boldsymbol{x}), \text{ if } g(z, \boldsymbol{x}, i, 1) = s, \text{ then } z \in g^{-1}(s, \boldsymbol{x}).$$

Due to the observation that any solution can be regarded as a sequence of state transitions, finding the best-scoring headline in the document is equivalent to finding the best-scoring state s^*, which is the solution to:

$$s^* = \arg\max_{s \in \Pi_H(\boldsymbol{x})} \alpha_{\boldsymbol{x},\boldsymbol{w}}(s).$$

Because both functions $\pi_{\boldsymbol{x}}$ and $\alpha_{\boldsymbol{x},\boldsymbol{w}}$ follow simple linear recursions, it is possible to write bottom-up or top-down algorithms that manage to calculate all producible states together with their best achievable score, and to trace the sequence of states that leads to the top-scoring one so as to obtain the optimal solution. The pseudo-code in Fig. 1 gives a sketch of a $O(H \times n^2 \times |PoS|)$ bottom-up implementation.

4.3. *Training the model: learning what human-generated headlines look like*

This section describes the way we train our model to learn the best value for the weight vector $\boldsymbol{w}$ that produces headlines that are closely related to human-generated ones. We further divide this section into two parts; Section 4.3.1 explains the behavior of the global feature function, and Section 4.3.2 explains the online learning method we used.

4.3.1. *Interpretation of the global feature function*

The global feature function $\boldsymbol{F}$ is responsible for taking a document and a bitmap and producing a vector that describes the candidate headline in an

```
//Constants
H <- Max number of allowed tokens in headlines
n <- number of tokens in the document
x <- array of n tokens (document)
w <- weight vector of m dimensions
g <- state transition function
f <- local feature function
s0 <- initial state

//Variables
pi <- (n * H) matrix of set of states, each initialized as {}
alpha <- (n * |PoS| * H) matrix of float, each initialized as -Inf
s_star <- nil
s_star_score <- -Inf

//Base cases
alpha[s0] = 0
for i in {0,...,n}:
    pi[i,0] <- s0

//bottom-up fill of pi and alpha
for l in {1,...,H}:
    for i in {1,...,n}:
        for j in {l-1,...,i-1}:
            for z in pi[j,l-1]:
                s <- g(z,x,i,l)
                s_score <- alpha[z] + w*f(x,i,z,l)
                pi[i,l] <- pi[i,l] + {s}
                alpha[s] = max(alpha[s],s_score)
                if s_score > s_star_score:
                    s_star, s_star_score <- s, s_score
```

Fig. 1. Sketch of a bottom-up algorithm for computing functions π_x, $\alpha_{x,w}$ and finding the top-scoring state s^* that leads to the global optimizer of our model's objective function. The code contains four for-loops; the first of these performs H iterations, the second and third execute at most n iterations each, and the last makes approximately $|PoS|$ iterations (because $\pi_x(j,l) \leq |PoS|$). This bulks down to a total number of operations asymptotically bounded by $O(H \times n^2 \times |PoS|)$, which is linearly proportional to the total number of producible states in x.

abstract feature space. As stated in Section 3.5, the decoding of the CRF model with state transitions consists in solving the formula:

$$\hat{y} = \arg\max_{y \in \mathcal{Y}^n} w \cdot F(x,y).$$

Furthermore, the global feature function is a factored version of a local feature function f, which was designed to only take into account tokens that are chosen to be part of the proposed headline.[f] This leads us to the following important remark:

The global feature function works like an accumulator of features for a proposed headline, where none of these features take into account tokens in the document that are not chosen to be part of the candidate headline, nor spatial relations or gaps between selected tokens. This means that the function only focuses on evaluating how a series of tokens that comprise a headline relate to each other and to the document.

This implies that it is possible to add any proposed headline at the beginning of the document and, by choosing the corresponding bitmap accordingly, call the feature function to obtain a description of how this — otherwise not producible — headline relates to the text. Mathematically, let $h \in \mathcal{X}^k$ be the tokenized form of any arbitrary headline consisting of k tokens, where $h = \{h_1, h_2, \ldots, h_k\}$. Then let vectors $a \in \mathcal{X}^{k+n}$ and $b \in \mathcal{Y}^{k+n}$ be defined as:

$$a = \{h_1, h_2, \ldots, h_k, x_1, x_2, \ldots, x_n\}$$
$$b = \{1_1, 1_2, \ldots, 1_k, 0_1, 0_2, \ldots, 0_n\}.$$

Then the feature vector that results from calling the global feature function as $F(a, b)$ is equivalent to a description of how headline h relates to document x. This observation is the core of our learning algorithm, because it implies that it is possible to "insert" a human-generated headline in the text and produce its description in the abstract feature space induced by F. The objective of the learning process will consist in molding a weight vector w, such that it makes the decoding algorithm favor headlines whose descriptions in the feature space resemble the characteristics of human-generated titles.

4.3.2. *Online learning of the weight vector*

Under traditional supervised learning contexts, a CRF model is trained by means of stochastic gradient descent (SGD) and requires a training corpus — referred to as the "ground truth" — consisting of several

---

[f] $F(x, y) = \sum_{i=1}^{n} f(x, i, s_{i-1}, y_i)$, where $s_i = g(s_{i-1}, x, i, y_i)$, and $s_0 = \text{init}$.

observation sequences and their corresponding correct assignment of category sequences. This generates two problems with our proposed model:

(1) To the best of our knowledge, there does not exist a publicly available dataset with news articles and related headlines generated in the same way our model operates; i.e., by picking words from the text and aligning them while preserving their order of appearance in the document. In the work presented in Ref. 19 the authors build a small corpus with our desired characteristics; however they express that many times the annotators generated headlines that looked unwieldy to their model.
(2) Our model is not a standard CRF model, but a custom-purposed one that uses very specific state transitions; this introduces several complications for being able to calculate the model's derivatives in polynomial time.

We solved the first problem by carefully designing the local feature function so that the properties explained in Section 4.3.1 hold. Our model is capable of taking any human-generated headline and producing a vector in feature space that describes its characteristics. This allowed our model to use as a training set any corpus of news articles, but added some problems for evaluating its performance that will be discussed in Chapter 6.

For solving the second problem, we resort to the same solution used by studies that deal with CRF models with state sequences, such as the dependency parsing model presented in Ref. 30. These learning schemes are based on the research presented in Ref. 32, where some variants of the perceptron algorithm are made for training CRF models. The learning framework we decided to use is an averaged perceptron with some variations. In order to explain how it works, we will first fix our attention to our model's decoding function:

$$\hat{y} = \arg\max_{y \in \mathcal{Y}^n} \ w \cdot F(x, y).$$

As previously argued, the global feature function F will work as a mapping function between candidate headlines and an abstract feature space. Let us suppose that the set $V_x = \{v_1, v_2, \ldots, v_{2^n}\}$, where $v_i \in \mathbb{R}^m$ for all i, contains the feature vectors of all the possible headlines that can be generated with our model from a document x; finding the top-scoring headline is equivalent to maximizing a dot product with a weight vector, which is related to finding the closest vector in V_x to the weight vector if all the vectors have similar norms. In precise terms:

$$\text{Provided } \boldsymbol{v_y} = \boldsymbol{F(x, y)}, \text{ then}$$

$$\hat{\boldsymbol{y}} = \underset{y \in \mathcal{Y}^n}{\arg\max} \; cos(\boldsymbol{w}, \boldsymbol{v_y}) \times ||\boldsymbol{w}|| \times ||\boldsymbol{v_y}||.$$

Furthermore, for the reasons exposed in Section 4.3.1, our model is capable of "inserting" a human generated headline in the text for later extracting its feature vector, which we will refer to as $\boldsymbol{u}$ for the rest of this chapter.[g] If the feature function succeeds in correctly describing correlations between a headline and its document, we can conclude that all vectors in V_x that are similar to $\boldsymbol{u}$ must correspond to headlines that are also similar to the ones generated by humans. This assumption is the backbone of our learning algorithm, which will perform error-correction updates on the weight vector for favoring solutions that, in feature space, are closely related to the ones produced by humans. The basis of this learning procedure is depicted in Fig. 2.

For performing the weight updates we followed the proposals made in Refs. 20, 30, and 32, which led to three techniques:

- **Averaged perceptron**
  This method starts with an initial arbitrary weight vector, and makes several iterative scans through the training set. For each case it first computes the top-scoring solution $\hat{\boldsymbol{y}}$, and then updates the weight vector $\boldsymbol{w}$ as:

$$\boldsymbol{w}^* \leftarrow \boldsymbol{w} + \boldsymbol{u} - \hat{\boldsymbol{v}}, \quad \text{where } \hat{\boldsymbol{v}} = \boldsymbol{F(x, \hat{y})}.$$

This update ensures that, if $\boldsymbol{u} \neq \hat{\boldsymbol{v}}$, then the new weight vector will give more score to the desired solution $\boldsymbol{u}$, or will give less score to the predicted $\hat{\boldsymbol{v}}$. Precisely:

$$\boldsymbol{w}^* \cdot \boldsymbol{u} > \boldsymbol{w} \cdot \boldsymbol{u} \quad \text{or} \quad \boldsymbol{w}^* \cdot \hat{\boldsymbol{v}} < \boldsymbol{w} \cdot \hat{\boldsymbol{v}}.$$

This method has the problem of being too sensitive to outliers and biased towards the last update, which can be solved by selecting as final weight the average of the sum of all the vectors that resulted from any update. Furthermore, Ref. 32 shows that this method is guaranteed to converge under a certain margin.

---

[g]If h is the human generated headline, then $\boldsymbol{u} = \boldsymbol{F(a, b)}$, where vectors $\boldsymbol{a}$ and $\boldsymbol{b}$ are built as explained in Section 4.3.1.

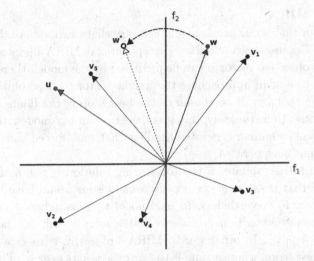

Fig. 2. Graphic representation of the learning procedure. The graphic represents a two-dimensional feature space, where points v_1 through v_5 represent feature vectors of candidate headlines, point u represents the feature vector of the human-generated headline, and point w represents the weight vector. According to this setting, vector v_1 will be selected as the top-scoring proposal, but vector v_5 seems like a more reasonable choice because it is closer to u; if the weight vector is updated to w^*, then the problem would be solved.

- **Margin Infused Relaxed Algorithm (MIRA)**

  Presented in Ref. 33, this algorithm makes a slight change to the perceptron update in order to avoid sensitivity towards outliers and ensure better classifications. The weight update is performed as:

  $$w^* \leftarrow w + \tau \times (u - \hat{v})$$

  where $\tau \in \mathbb{R}$ is the minimal value that satisfies:

  $$w^* \cdot u \geq w^* \cdot \hat{v} + 1$$

  which is equal to:

  $$\tau = max\left(0, \frac{1 - w \cdot (u - \hat{v})}{||u - \hat{v}||^2}\right).$$

  The MIRA update directly ensures that after the weight vector is updated, if the same case is evaluated, the vector that was desired to be obtained (i.e., u) receives a score greater — by a certain margin — than the one that was formerly predicted (i.e., $\hat{v}$).

- **Forced MIRA**

  This algorithm is our proposal and is a very slight variation of the MIRA update. Because both standard perceptron and MIRA updates assume that the objective vector u can be predicted by the model, therefore, the updates consist in approaching the weight vector to this solution while expecting that it will be chosen as the best scoring candidate in future predictions. Unfortunately, this is not the case for our model: the vector u represents a human-generated headline that was "forced" into the text and cannot be generated.

  In the MIRA update, if the top-scoring solution is not u, then it is assumed that $w \cdot u < w \cdot \hat{v}$, because otherwise u would have been preferred over $\hat{v}$. Nevertheless, in our model that assumption cannot be made because even if u receives a better score it will not be chosen, because $u \notin V_x$. In other words, MIRA's objective is to give vector u the highest score, whereas ours is to favor the points near u. The change we propose is to calculate τ as:

  $$\tau = \frac{1 - w \cdot (u - \hat{v})}{||u - \hat{v}||^2}.$$

  The only difference between this update and the standard MIRA is that it allows τ to take negative values, while previously it was set as zero. The variable τ will only be negative when u receives a higher score than $\hat{v}$, and this will force the algorithm to always update the weight vector and leave it at a fixed margin distance from u. What we observed through our experiments is that if this forced update is not performed, the learning algorithm tends to over-exploit features that are highly likely to occur in human-generated titles but difficult to attain with our model's "recycled-words" headlines: if the algorithm manages to build a weight vector that gives the highest scores to human-generated titles, it will obtain a false perception of success and will not update the weight vector because, in principle, the correct solution must have been predicted (i.e., vector u), which will not be the case. Thus, by forcing an update at every step we ensure that the algorithm takes into account that $\hat{v} \neq u$ and perform error corrections at each time.

  These three techniques are basically the same and only differ in the value assigned to the variable τ (where in the standard perceptron it is always equal to 1). The pseudo-code in Fig. 3 is a sketch of the learning algorithm.

```
//Constants
I <- Number of iterations over the data
D <- Number of training samples
A <- Array of D articles
B <- Array of D human-generated headlines

//Variables
w <- weight vector of m floats, initialized randomly
w_avg <- weight vector of m floats, initialized in 0

//Procedure
for k in {1,...,I}:
    for d in {1,...,D}:
        u <- features_of_human_generated_headline(A[d],B[d])
        v_hat <- features_of_best_candidate_headline(A[d],w)
        tau <- compute_tau(u,v_hat)
        w <- w + tau * ( u - v_hat )
        w_avg <- w_avg + w

w <- w_avg / (I*D)
```

Fig. 3. Sketch of the online learning algorithm used for training our model.

5. Implementation

The entire system is summarized as a processing pipeline, as depicted in Fig. 4.

Several frameworks were used for performing different tasks, but most notably the Stanford CoreNLP[h] toolkit was used for NLP-preprocessing tasks, and Apache Hadoop[i] for parallel processing of data.

5.1. *FilterArticles*

The dataset we chose to use for training and testing our model is a subset of news articles published in the Yahoo! News site worldwide,[j] and we only considered articles related to finance, written in English, and targeted to readers in the United States of America. Our interest is to focus our experiments on a single-domain corpus so as to avoid exposing our

---

[h]http://nlp.stanford.edu/software/corenlp.shtml.
[i]http://hadoop.apache.org/.
[j]http://news.yahoo.com/.

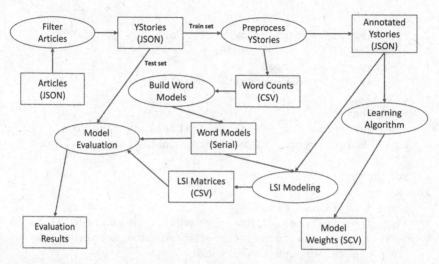

Fig. 4. Processing pipeline of our system for headline generation. Ovals correspond to data processing tasks, and rectangles correspond to data types.

language models to the unnecessary sparseness entailed by multi-domain datasets.

The initial dataset consisted of approximately 11 billion text articles in JSON format, occupying a total of 3 TB of data, and each article contained a headline, a body, and tags for describing its content. The "FilterArticles" process goes through all these data and extracts articles that satisfy our desired conditions, plus some other quality constraints we established, such as not having a one-token headline.

The result of this process was a smaller set of 1.3 million finance articles, which we named "YStories." For data exploration purposes, we took a random sample of about 10% of these YStories and explored the number of tokens in their bodies and headlines. Figure 5 contains the obtained distributions.

5.2. *Preprocess YStories*

This task is in charge of annotating the training dataset. It takes YStories in JSON format as input, and carries a set of operations on each one, as it:

- Tokenizes the text and groups the tokens into sentences
- Obtains the dependency tree of each sentence
- Annotates the tokens with their POS tags and NE tag

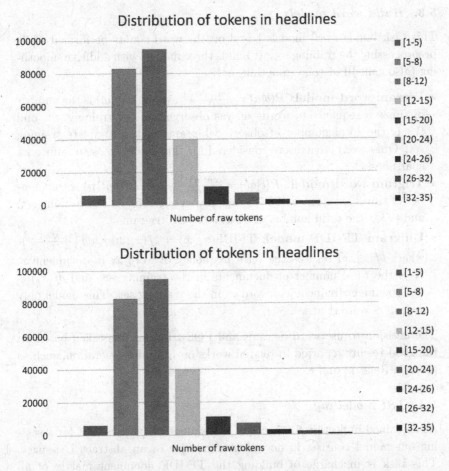

Fig. 5. Distributions of tokens in the bodies and headlines of YStories.

- Removes noisy tokens: those that are too long (more than 20 characters) or those that correspond to UTF-8 special symbols (bullets, check-marks, and similar symbols)
- Counts the word-bigrams and POS trigrams in each sentence, while it also keeps track of all the different unigrams in the text

This process produces two outputs: the set of augmented YStories, called "AnnotatedYStories," and the global counts of all the word-bigrams, POS trigrams, and document frequency of unigrams.

5.3. *Build word models*

This task builds word models based on the word counts performed while preprocessing the training set. It builds three models with additive smoothing (also called Lidstone smoothing):[34]

- **Bigram word-model**: $P(b|a) = \frac{cnt(ab)+1}{cnt(b)+|V|}$, where $cnt(w)$ is the number of times a sequence of words w was observed on the training set, and $|V|$ is the total number of observed bigrams in the complete training set. Only word stems were considered for this model so as to reduce its sparseness.
- **Trigram word-model**: $P(c|ab) = \frac{cnt(abc)+1}{cnt(ab)+|V|}$, where $cnt(p)$ is the number of times a sequence of POS tags p was observed on the training set, and $|V|$ is the total number of observed POS trigrams.
- **Unigram TF-IDF model**: $\text{TFIDF}(x_i, x) = tf(x_i, x) * log\left(\frac{N+1}{df(x_i)+1}\right)$, where $tf(x_i, x)$ returns the term frequency of word x_i in document x, N is the total number of documents in the training set, and $df(x_i)$ is the document frequency of word x_i in the training set. This model only considers word stems.

The decision to use word-bigrams and POS-trigrams was taken based on the good results reported in related works on headline generation, such as those in Refs. 13 and 8.

5.4. *LSI modelling*

As explained in Section 6.1.2, one of the evaluation metrics used for assessing our model consists in document similarity in an abstract LSI-space. This task is in charge of building the TF-IDF document matrix of all the training set and performing singular value decomposition (SVD) on it. Its final objective is to calculate the eigenvalues of the TF-IDF document matrix so as to use them as latent concepts from the training corpus.

5.5. *Learning algorithm*

This process is responsible for executing the learning algorithms described in Section 4.3.2. At this stage we decided to add three important constraints to the learning algorithm which proved to yield positive results with our experiments:

- Our model considers every single token in a news story as a candidate for a headline. Because we are aiming to produce headlines containing around 10 tokens, if an article is too large most of the tokens in it will be irrelevant, redundant, or can be considered as noise. To solve this problem we decided to perform a pre-summarization step on any article whose body contains more than 300 tokens. This number was particularly chosen because it is the average number of tokens in our news stories as illustrated in Fig. 5.

We decided to implement the TextRank summarization technique described in Ref. 35, which identifies the most relevant sentences in the text by using a rather lightweight method that does not require previous training. The result of this summarization step is a subset of the original story's sentences, which in total do not contain more than 300 tokens. In other words, this method reduces the number of sentences in the document by eliminating the most redundant or least informative ones.

- From the results obtained in Fig. 5 it can be concluded that headlines with more than 15 tokens are not common. We therefore decided to constraint the decoding algorithm for not exploring solutions consisting of more than 15 tokens; this was achieved by setting parameter H to equal 15.
- After doing some experimentation, we discovered that our model was placing too many symbols (such as commas, periods, quotation marks, or exclamation sings) on headlines, and it was also generating headlines as inconclusive phrases. To solve these problems we decided to restrain the decoding algorithm from choosing any kind of symbols, but we restrict it to consider as final solutions only headlines that end with a period.

Furthermore, we decided to make the learning algorithms perform five passes over the data (i.e., five iterations). We stopped at the fifth iteration because we observed that after the third, the resulting weight vector from each iteration did not change by a significant amount.

5.6. *Model evaluation*

This task is responsible for going through the test dataset, annotating it in a similar way to the training set, and extracting all the candidate headlines from the implemented baselines and our model. The procedure evaluates the implemented metrics and produces a summary result.

6. Evaluation

This section contains the details concerning the evaluation of our system. It is divided into three parts: Section 6.1 presents the metrics we used for evaluating the system, Section 6.2 explains the baselines we implemented as points of reference to our model's performance, and Section 6.3 presents the results we obtained from our experiments.

6.1. *Metrics*

Automatic evaluation of summaries is a task that has been explored for several decades. In the particular case of headline generation, a candidate headline is commonly assessed with respect to two characteristics: grammaticality (i.e. whether the headline is grammatical), and relevance (i.e. whether the headline reflects the main topic of an article). Building unbiased metrics that manage to make objective evaluations of these properties has proved itself to be a difficult task. Some of the related work, like that of Ref. 8, resort to human-assisted evaluation, which is undoubtedly expensive and not suitable for learning processes.

In the broader task of document summarization, a set of recall-based metrics named ROUGE (an acronym for "Recall-Oriented Understudy for Gisting Evaluation") has been proposed and proven to strongly correlate with human evaluations.[36,37] On that account, the set of metrics has been also broadly used for the evaluation of headlines.[6–8,13,38] The main assumption being that because the metrics work well for standard summaries, the same is applicable to short summaries. Through our experiments, shown in Section 6.3, we obtained statistical evidence that this statement does not necessarily hold.

For evaluating our model we decided to use three of the metrics proposed in the ROUGE package, and we propose two new metrics for experimentation: a variation of a ROUGE metric, and a metric for comparing headlines on a conceptual level. Each of the metrics will be explained in the following subsections. For the rest of this chapter the terms "reference headline" and "candidate headline" will be used to address, respectively, the human-generated title, and the proposed headlines produced by our system or any of the baselines.

6.1.1. *ROUGE metrics*

ROUGE-N

This recall-oriented metric measures the number of N-grams in the reference headline that are also present in a candidate headline. It is defined as:

$$\text{ROUGE-N}(R, C) = \frac{|n\text{-}grams(R) \cap n\text{-}grams(C)|}{|n\text{-}grams(R)|}$$

where R refers to the reference headline, C to the candidate headline, and the function $n\text{-}grams$ returns the set of contiguous N-grams in a text, for instance:

$2\text{-}grams(\text{"This is an example"}) = \{\text{"This-is"}, \text{"is-an"}, \text{"an-example"}\}.$

For this work we decided to use the ROUGE-1 and ROUGE-2 metrics.

ROUGE-SU

One of the problems of using the ROUGE-N metric (with $N > 1$) is that requesting headlines to share contiguous N-grams might be a very strong condition, and difficult to achieve. This is even more problematic when taking into account that headlines are comprised, on average, of 8–10 tokens. This metric combines ROUGE-1 with a relaxed version of ROUGE-2 that takes into account non-contiguous bigrams. Formally:

$$\text{ROUGE-SU}(R, C) = \frac{|su\text{-}grams(R) \cap su\text{-}grams(C)|}{|su\text{-}grams(R)|}$$

$$su\text{-}grams(H) = 1\text{-}grams(H) \ \cup \ s2\text{-}grams(H).$$

Here $1\text{-}grams(H)$ returns the unigrams of a headline, and $s2\text{-}grams(H)$ the skip-bigrams.

By allowing gaps between bigrams this metric detects similarities among phrases that differ by adjectives, or small changes. For instance, take the phrases:

"The president said"

"President Obama said"

ROUGE-2 will not detect any similarity between them, while ROUGE-SU will acknowledge the presence of the skip-bigram "president-said" on both phrases.

ROUGE-WSU

The main problem of ROUGE-SU is that it gives the same importance to all skip-bigrams extracted from a phrase. For instance, suppose that the following phrases were compared:

$$H_1 = \text{"x B C x x"}$$
$$H_2 = \text{"B y y y C"}$$
$$H_3 = \text{"z z B z C"}.$$

The only skip-bigram they all have in common is "B-C" but intuitively the first phrase should be more similar to the third one than the second one; yet ROUGE-SU would give the exact same similarity score between the three of them. Our proposal is to weight the skip-bigrams with respect to their average skip-distance. Formally:

$$\text{ROUGE-WSU}(R,C) = \frac{\displaystyle\sum_{(a,b)\in su(R)\cap su(C)} \frac{2}{dist_R(a,b)+dist_C(a,b)}}{\displaystyle\sum_{(a,b)\in su(R)} \frac{1}{dist_R(a,b)}}$$

$$su(H) = s2\text{-}grams(H) \cup 1\text{-}grams(H)$$

where function $dist_H(a,b)$ returns the skip distance between words "a" and "b" in headline H. For the case of unigrams, the function returns 1. This measure achieves our objective because ROUGE-WSU(H_1, H_3) > ROUGE-WSU(H_1, H_2).

6.1.2. *LSI-DS*

We deem all ROUGE metrics as straightforward measures because they relate two headlines only on the basis of word co-occurrences, i.e., they compare headlines at a syntactic level. It would also be relevant to have a metric that can detect abstract concepts in phrases and compare headlines at a semantic level. For this end, we decided to resort to Latent Semantic Indexing (LSI) to extract latent concepts from our news corpus and represent articles as vectors in this abstract space, so as to compute similarity by means of angular distances. This method is explained in depth in Ref. 39, but in this subsection we will limit ourselves to explain the steps that we performed for achieving the task.

We extract latent semantic concepts by first building a document-TF-IDF matrix M, where each row corresponds to an article in our training set and each column corresponds to a word in the vocabulary. Afterwards, SVD is performed on this matrix resulting in matrices USV^T. The eigenvalues in matrix S were analyzed and we decided to keep 100 of them, which corresponded to about 70% of the total information. Finally, we calculate the transformation matrix VS^{-1}, which enables the translation of TF-IDF document vectors to vectors in latent space.

After performing this technique we assess the similarity of a headline with respect to a news article by computing the latent space vectors of both the headline and the entire document, and then calculating their cosine similarity.

6.2. *Baselines*

In order to have a point of reference for interpreting the performance of our model, we implemented six baseline models which will be briefly explained in this section. Four of them are simple techniques, one is a modern technique for multi-sentence compression, and the last one was designed for obtaining a naive upper-bound of the metrics.

We arbitrarily decide to make all the baselines generate, if possible, nine-token-long headlines, where the last token must always be a period. This follows from the observation that good headlines must contain about eight tokens,[7] plus the constraint we imposed to our model of only selecting headlines that end with a period.

6.2.1. *First sentence baselines*

Many previous studies in headline generation have reported that the first sentence in a news story is most of the time the most informative.[12] For this reason we implemented three baselines that take the first line and, if bigger than eight tokens, perform different compression techniques:

(1) **Chunked first sentence:** this baseline simply takes the first eight tokens of the first sentence and adds a period at the end.
(2) **Dependency tree compression:** this baseline performs a naive compression of the sentence by performing a topological sort of the words in its dependency tree and keeps the first eight when following the topological order. The headline is formed by aligning the selected tokens in the same order as they appear on the sentence, and adds a period at the end.
(3) **Noun and Verb dependency tree compression:** this baseline performs the same compression as dependency tree compression, but only selects words whose POS tag corresponds to nouns or verbs.

6.2.2. *Hidden Markov model*

We implemented a simplified version of the HMM proposed in Ref. 8. It was achieved by changing the local feature function of our model and making it output three features: the two standard word-model features (word-bigram and POS-trigram), which work as the HMM transition probabilities, plus a unigram probability feature that works as an observation probability. For finishing the model the weight vector was set as a vector of ones.

The resulting model selects the eight tokens in the text that, when aligned by preserving their order of appearance in the article, maximize the log probability of the three aforementioned language models.

6.2.3. *Word graphs*

Besides basic baselines, we implemented a modern multi-sentence compression algorithm for comparing its result with our model. The chosen system was the word-graph approach proposed in Ref. 40, which solves the sentence compression task by finding a minimum path in a graph that is constructed based on word relations in the text. We chose this particular model because it is rather simple and does not require previous training.

It is important to highlight that the objective of the original algorithm is to perform multi-sentence compression, not headline generation. For this reason we made a slight change in the original proposal for producing headline-like compressions: instead of searching for the k-shortest paths in the graph and keeping the one with smallest average edge weights, we just keep the shortest path that contains at least eight tokens, and added a period at the end.

6.2.4. *Keywords*

This is not a true baseline because it does not produce proper headlines. We wanted to include a method that tried to obtain the maximum achievable score for our chosen metrics, and came to the conclusion that picking the top-eight keywords in the text, then aligning them in descending order of importance, would be a good naive guess for approximating an upper-bound for the metrics. We ranked keywords through TF-IDF weighting.

It is definitely not certain that this "baseline" would generate unbeatable scores for all the metrics, but our intuition about its behavior is based on the fact that the ROUGE metrics are recall-oriented. Therefore, if we picked the words in the text that are most likely to occur in the human-generated headline, we would arguably be maximizing the achievable value for these metrics. Hence our best estimate would be to select keywords because, intuitively, if a word is very representative of the document's contents, then it is probable that the headline will reference it.

The case is different for the LSI document similarity metric: the metric is totally biased towards TF-IDF weighting of words because the latent topics are extracted from a document-TF-IDF matrix. As a consequence, the most influential words in a document for determining its latent concepts distribution are the words with the highest TF-IDF score, which correspond to the keywords we choose; thus the score of the "keywords-baseline" in this metric will be an actual upper-bound.

6.3. *Results*

Our system was evaluated on a test set consisting of 12,219 previously unseen news articles that were randomly extracted from the initial dataset before training. The evaluation consisted in producing nine candidate headlines — corresponding to six baselines plus three versions of our model, with each version deferring only on the scheme used to learn the weight vector — and then comparing each candidate against the reference headline by means of the five proposed metrics. Additionally, for exploratory purposes the length of each candidate was also noted. Tables 1 and 2 summarize the

Table 1.   Evaluation results: ROUGE metrics.

Method	ROUGE-1	ROUGE-2
Perceptron	0.157±0.145	0.056±0.098
MIRA	0.172±0.147	0.042±0.084
f-MIRA	**0.187±0.153**	0.054±0.098
1stsent: chunk.	0.076±0.119	
1stsent: comp.	0.117±0.123	
1stsent: NV-comp.	0.132±0.126	
HMM	0.090±0.096	0.009±0.037
Word graphs	0.174±0.155	**0.060±0.114**
Keywords	**0.313±0.158**	0.021±0.058
Reference	–	–

Method	ROUGE-SU	ROUGE-WSU
Perceptron	0.053±0.071	0.082±0.095
MIRA	0.057±0.074	0.084±0.091
f-MIRA	**0.065±0.083**	**0.095±0.101**
1stsent: chunk.	0.025±0.061	0.038±0.077
1stsent: comp.	0.036±0.058	0.055±0.075
1stsent: NV-comp.	0.042±0.061	0.063±0.077
HMM	0.023±0.034	0.038±0.049
Word graphs	0.060±0.087	0.084±0.104
Keywords	**0.112±0.093**	**0.148±0.097**
Reference	–	–

Table 2.   Evaluation results: LSI-DS and headline length.

Method	LSI-DS	H. Len.
Perceptron	0.446±0.246	10.096±1.718
MIRA	0.463±0.207	13.045±2.426
f-MIRA	**0.491±0.218**	11.737±2.226
1^{st}sent: chunk.	0.224±0.212	8.932±0.588
1^{st}sent: comp.	0.270±0.210	8.931±0.590
1^{st}sent: NV–comp.	0.338±0.217	8.824±0.877
HMM	0.172±0.165	9.000±0.000
Word graphs	0.480±0.240	10.973±4.391
Keywords	**0.701±0.127**	9.000±0.000
Reference	**0.555±0.222**	11.898±4.226

mean score and standard deviation obtained by each headline generation technique with respect to each metric, and Figs. 6,7, and 8 contain relevant graphical representations.

We use the LSI document similarity (LSI-DS) metric for scoring both reference and candidate headlines: the LSI-DS is our sole metric that compares a candidate headline with the whole document instead of just its title. Therefore, we also use the metric to score reference headlines for comparison purposes.

Tables 1 and 2 show the evaluation results. Rows correspond to our model — with several training schemes — and baselines, where the label "Reference" refers to the scores obtained from human-generated headlines. Columns correspond to metrics, where the label "H. Len." is short for headline length (note that this length counts the imposed period at the end of a produced headline). Each cell shows the obtained average score and standard deviation of a model when measured with the respective metric. The results are very compelling in the sense that our model, when trained with our proposed forced-MIRA update, performs better than all other baselines on all metrics, except for ROUGE-2. Also, as initially thought, the "keywords baseline" produces better scores than all other methods and performs exceptionally well on the LSI-DS metric. As a side comment regarding this last metric (LSI-DS), none of the methods managed to obtain the scores produced by human generated-headlines, which is coherent and gives credence to the metric.

Despite the promising results, there is a rather significant problem we contemplate in the obtained numbers: for all the headline generation techniques the scores obtained for all the implemented ROUGE metrics are

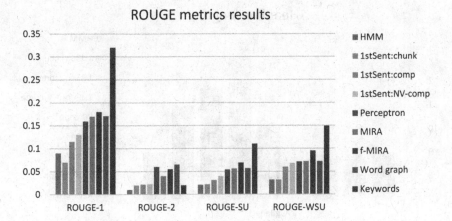

Fig. 6. ROUGE scores.

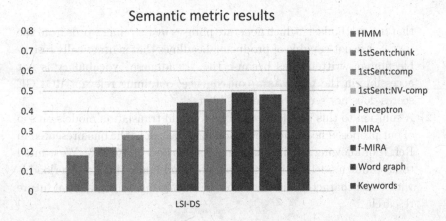

Fig. 7. LSI-DS scores.

not statistically significant because their standard deviation is always as high as their mean, which allows all these outcomes to be interpreted as potential noise. We have two following observations:

(1) The ROUGE metrics are, as exposed in Section 6.1, syntax-level metrics that only evaluate how many word combinations from a reference headline are contained in a candidate headline. Several previous works — such as Ref. 8 — report that humans tend to use a very different vocabulary and writing style on headlines than on articles; the effect of this is

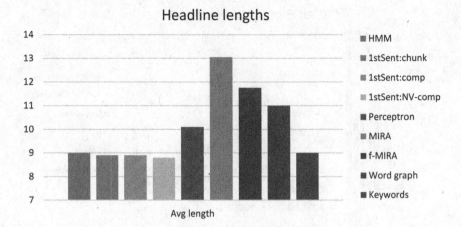

Fig. 8. Mean length of generated headlines.

that our methods — which generate phrases by recycling words from the text — are not capable of producing headlines that syntactically resemble human-written ones because the "Headlinese" vocabulary is not accessible in the text. As a consequence, obtaining relevant ROUGE scores does not seem to be a feasible task.

(2) A solution to this problem would be to build translation models on top of our proposed headline generation model, such as the one presented in Ref. 7, or allowing word transformations, as done in Ref. 13. We wanted to keep our model as simple as possible and hence did not overload it with these characteristics, however they set ground for potential future research.

Figures 6 and 7 demonstrate a graphical summary of the ROUGE and LSI-DS mean scores of all methods with respect to all baselines, respectively. Figure 8 shows the average headline length. Note that the methods in the histograms are sorted — from left to right — in the same order as they appear in the legends when read from top to bottom.

Table 3 contains example groups of headlines generated by our model (trained with the forced-MIRA) and the six implemented baselines. Each example group consists of eight different headlines extracted from the same article. The method labelled as "reference" refers to the actual title of the article (i.e., the human-generated headline).

Table 3.   Example headlines.

Method	Headline
Group #1	
Reference	2 analysts give Chimerix shares highest ratings.
f-MIRA	**The company plans to study as treatment for viruses.**
Keywords	Chimerix CMX001 Nadeau cytomegalovirus virus drug Cowen transplant.
Chunked 1st sent	NEW YORK -LRB- AP -RRB- – Two analysts.
Comp 1st sent	NEW YORK AP Two analysts starting covering Inc.
NVComp 1st sent	NEW YORK AP analysts starting covering Inc. pointing.
Word graphs	Morgan Stanley analyst Phil Nadeau said he thinks CMX001.
HMM	of $million2022of$ 49.6 20.77.
Group #2	
Reference	MCTtest-RI court appoints receiver for 38 Studios.
f-MIRA	**Rhode Island lured 38 Studios from Massachusetts in 2010**.
Keywords	Carlotto Rhode Island Studios court-appointed receiver bankruptcy Delware.
Chunked 1st sent	PROVIDENCE, R.I. -LRB- AP -RRB- – A.
Comp 1st sent	PROVIDENCE R.I. AP A court-appointed receiver take Curt.
NVComp 1st sent	PROVIDENCE R.I. AP receiver take assets Curt failed.
Word graphs	Rhode Island petitioned the state's bankruptcy proceedings.
HMM	$ million In the company in the company.
Group #3	
Reference	REU 1 - UPDATE 2-Libya-Europe gas pipeline repaired - rebels.
f-MIRA	**Rebel fighters are plagued by shortages of water food.**
Keywords	Mellitah rebels Libya pipeline GreenStream Bani Italy gas.
Chunked 1st sent	BENGHAZI, Libya, Aug 28 -LRB- Reuters.
Comp 1st sent	BENGHAZI Libya Aug 28 Reuters paving said on.
NVComp 1st sent	BENGHAZI Libya Aug Reuters supplied paving said Sunday.
Word graphs	gas pipeline system between Mellitah and another refinery.
HMM	of Line February Reuters Europe Europe February National.

7.   Conclusion and discussion

In this study we proposed a CRF model — with state transitions — that
tries to learn how humans title their articles. The learning is performed by

means of a mapping function that, given a document, translates headlines to an abstract feature-rich space, where the characteristics that distinguish human-generated titles can be discriminated. This abstraction allows our model to be trained with any corpus of news articles because it does not impose conditions on the provenance of story headlines i.e., our model maps reference headlines to a feature space and only learns what abstract properties characterize them.

Our system generates headlines based on a news article by taking words from its body and aligning them by preserving their order in the text; this enables us to model the task of finding the best possible producible headline as a discrete optimization problem, where each candidate headline is modeled as a path in a graph of state sequences, thus allowing the best-scoring path to be found in polynomial time by means of dynamic programming.

Because our model uses a rich feature set, its adaptation to other languages requires such advanced preprocessing tools as POS tagger, dependency parser, and NE recognizer. In a case of low resource languages, some features may be omitted from the model. After all necessary features are calculated, training the CRF model is totally language-independent.

We trained our model with a corpus consisting of approximately 1.3 million financial news articles written in English, and used three different online learning algorithms. For evaluating our model we used a test set consisting of roughly 12,000 previously unseen news articles (from the same domain as the training corpus), and compared the performance of our model with respect to six other baselines by using five different metrics — two of which were new metrics proposed by us.

Our obtained results favor our model and corroborate its soundness, but also provide statistical evidence of the lack of suitability of traditional recall-oriented measures for this task. The further work we envisage for augmenting our research can be grouped in three directions:

(1) Our framework depends heavily on the ability of the global feature function to characterize an article's headline; this work can be replicated and tested by using extra features that might improve significantly its performance. For instance, features that exploit advanced discourse-analysis of the text could be implemented, features that use different keyword detection techniques could also be tested and compared, and even features that manage abstract semantic relationships between words could be explored.

(2) Our system could be complemented by a separate translation model: titles tend to be written in a different fashion than articles, and our system can only generate headlines written with the same vocabulary as news' bodies. Therefore, a model that learns correlations between our headlines and their corresponding human-generated titles could be used for translating our system's results to "Headlinese language."

(3) For achieving a more objective evaluation of our generated headlines, some other semantic-level measures could be proposed and tested.

References

1. D. Das and A. F. Martins, A survey on automatic text summarization, *Literature Survey for the Language and Statistics II Course at CMU 4*, pp. 192–195 (2007).

2. A. Nenkova and K. McKeown, A survey of text summarization techniques, *Mining Text Data*, pp. 43–76, Springer (2012).

3. I. Mani and M. T. M. (eds.), *Advances in Automatic Text Summarization*, vol. 293, Cambridge: MIT Press (1999).

4. O. Buyukkokten, H. Garcia-Molina, and A. Paepcke, Seeing the whole in parts: Text summarization for web browsing on handheld devices. In eds. V. Y. Shen, N. Saito, M. R. Lyu, M. E. Zurko, *Proceedings of the 10th International Conference on World Wide Web*, Hong Kong, China, ACM (2001).

5. N. Linke-Ellis, Closed captioning in america: Looking beyond compliance. In *Proceedings of the TAO Workshop on TV Closed Captions for the Hearing Impaired People*, Tokyo, Japan, pp. 43–59 (1999).

6. D. De Kok, *Headline generation for dutch newspaper articles through transformation-based learning.* Master's thesis, University of Groningen (2008).

7. M. Banko, O. Mittal, Vibhu, and J. Witbrock, Michael, Headline generation based on statistical translation. In *Proceedings of the 38th Annual Meeting on Association for Computational Linguistics*, pp. 318–325, ACL (2000).

8. D. Zajic, B. Dorr, and R. Schwartz, Automatic headline generation for newspaper stories. In eds. U. Hahn and D. Harman, *Workshop on Automatic Summarization*, Philadephia, PA, USA (2002).

9. M. Hajime, R. Sasano, H. Takamura, and M. Okumura, Subtree extractive summarization via submodular maximization. In ed. P. Fung, *Proceedings of 51st Annual Meeting of the Association for Computational Linguistics*, Sofia, Bulgaria, ACL (2013).

10. A. F. Martins and N. A. Smith, Summarization with a joint model for sentence extraction and compression. In eds. J. Clarke and S. Riedel, *NAACL-HLT Workshop on Integer Linear Programming for NLP*, Boulder, Colorado, USA, ACL (2009).

11. B. Berger and N. Mittal, Discourse segmentation in aid of document summarization. In ed. R. H. Sprague *Proceedings of the Hawaii International Conference on System Sciences, Minitrack on Digital Documents Understanding*, Maui, Hawaii, USA, IEEE Computer Society (2000).

12. B. Dorr, D. Zajic, and R. Schwartz, Hedge trimmer: A parse-and-trim approach to headline generation. In *Proceedings of the HLT-NAACL 03 on Text Summarization Workshop*, Edmonton, Canada, pp. 1–8 (2003).

13. A. K. Gattani, *Automated natural language headline generation using discriminative machine learning models*, PhD Dissertation, Simon Fraser University (2007).

14. R. Jin and A. G. Hauptmann, Title generation using a training corpus. In *CICLing 2001: Proceedings of the Second International Conference on Computational Linguistics and Intelligent Text Processing*, pp. 208–215 (2001).

15. K. Knight and D. Marcu, Summarization beyond sentence extraction: A probabilistic approach to sentence compression, *Artificial Intelligence*, **139**(1), pp. 91–107 (2001).

16. Y. Unno, T. Ninomiya, Y. Miyao, and J. Tsujii, Trimming CFG parse trees for sentence compression using machine learning approaches. In eds. N. Calzolari, C. Cardie, and P. Isabelle, *Proceedings of the COLING/ACL*, Sydney, Australia, ACL (2006).

17. H. P. Edmundson, New methods in automatic extracting, *Journal of the ACM*, **16**(2), pp. 264–285 (1969).

18. D. Marcu, From discourse structures to text summaries. In eds. P. R. Cohen and W. Wahlster, *Proceedings of the ACL*, Madrid, Spain, Morgan Kaufman (1997).

19. D. Zajic, B. Dorr, and R. Schwartz, BBN/UMD at DUC-2004: Topiary. In eds. R. Florian, H. Hassan, A. Ittycheriah, H. Jing, N. Kambhatla, X. Luo, N. Nicolov, and S. Roukos, *Proceedings of the HLT-NAACL 2004 Document Understanding Workshop*, Boston, MA, USA, ACL (2004).

20. R. T. McDonald, Discriminative sentence compression with soft syntactic evidence. In eds. D. McCarthy and S. Wintner, *European chapter of the Association for Computational Linguistics*, Trento, Italy, ACL (2006).

21. T. Nomoto, Discriminative sentence compression with conditional random fields, *Information Processing and Management*, **43**(6) (2007).

22. National Institute Standards and Technology (NIST). Document Understanding Conferences. Available at: http://duc.nist.gov/.

23. L. Rabiner and B.-H. Juang, An introduction to Hidden Markov Models, *ASSP Magazine*, **3**(1), 4–16 (1986).

24. A. McCallum, D. Freitag, and F. C. Pereira, Maximum entropy markov models for information extraction and segmentation. In ed. P. Langley, *International Conference on Machine Learning*, Stanford, CA, USA, Morgan Kaufman, (2000).

25. J. Lafferty, A. McCallum, and F. C. Pereira, Conditional random fields: Probabilistic models for segmenting and labeling sequence data, ACM New York (2001). Available at: https://repository.upenn.edu/cgi/viewcontent. cgi?article=1162&context=cis_papers.

26. M. Mohri, F. Pereira, and M. Richard, Weighted finite-state transducers in speech recognition, *Computer Speech and Language*, **16**(1) (2002).

27. J. C. Reynar and A. Ratnaparkhi, A maximum entropy approach to identifying sentence boundaries. In eds. P. R. Cohen and W. Wahlster,*Proceedings of the Fifth Conference on Applied Natural Language Processing*, Madrid, Spain, ACL (1997).

28. A. McCallum and W. Li, Early results for named entity recognition with conditional random fields, feature induction and web-enhanced lexicons. In eds. M. A. Hearst and M. Ostendorf, *Proceedings of the Seventh Conference on Natural Language Learning at HLT-NAACL 2003*, Edmonton, Canada, ACL (2003).

29. J. Kupiec, Robust part-of-speech tagging using a hidden markov model, *Computer Speech and Language*, **6**(3) (1992).

30. R. McDonald, K. Crammer, and F. Pereira, Online large-margin training of dependency parsers. In eds. K. Knight, H. T. Ng, and K. Oflazer, *Proceedings of the 43rd Annual Meeting on Association for Computational Linguistics*, University of Michigan, Michigan, MI, USA, pp. 91–98, ACL (2005).

31. D. Shen, J-T. Sun, H. Li, Q. Yang, and Z. Chen, Document summarization using conditional random fields. In *Proceedings of International Joint Conference on Artificial Intelligence (IJCAI)* (2007).

32. M. Collins, Discriminative training methods for hidden markov models: Theory and experiments with perceptron algorithms. In *Proceedings of the Empirical Methods in Natural Language Processing*, Volume 10, pp. 1–8, ACL (2002).

33. K. Crammer and Y. Singer, Ultraconservative online algorithms for multiclass problems, *The Journal of Machine Learning Research*, **3**, 951–991 (2003).

34. G. Lidstone, Note on the general case of the bayes-laplace formula for inductive or a posteriori probabilities, *Transactions of the Faculty of Actuaries*, **8**, 182–192 (1920).

35. R. Mihalcea and P. Tarau, Textrank: Bringing order into texts. In *Proceedings of the Association for Computational Linguistics*, Barcelona, Spain, pp. 404–411, ACL (2004).

36. C.-Y. Lin, Rouge: A package for automatic evaluation of summaries. In *Proceedings of the Text Summarization Branches Out Workshop*, Barcelona, Spain, pp. 74–81, ACL (2004).

37. C. Lin, Cross-domain study of n-gram co-occurrence metrics. In *Proceedings of the Workshop on Machine Translation Evaluation* (2003).

38. S. Wan, M. Dras, C. Paris, and R. Dale, Using thematic information in statistical headline generation. In *Proceedings of the ACL 2003 Workshop on Multilingual Summarization and Question Answering*, Sapporo, Japan, pp. 11–20, ACL (2003). doi: 10.3115/1119312.1119314.

39. S. Deerwester, S. T. Dumais, G. W. Furnas, T. K. Landauer, and R. Harshman, Indexing by latent semantic analysis, *Japan Analytical & Scientific Instruments Show*, **41**(6), 391–407 (1990).

40. K. Filippova, Multi-sentence compression: Finding shortest paths in word graphs. In *Proceedings of the 23rd International Conference on Computational Linguistics*, pp. 322–330. ACL (2010).

Chapter 8

Crowdsourcing in Single-document Summary Evaluation: The Argo Way

Nikiforos Pittaras[*,‡], Stefano Montanelli[†,§], George Giannakopoulos[*,¶], Alfio Ferrara[†,||], and Vangelis Karkaletsis[*,**]

SKEL Lab, IIT, NCSR "Demokritos", Athens, Greece
†*Dept. of Computer Science,*
Università degli Studi di Milano, Milano, Italy
‡*pittarasnikif@iit.demokritos.gr*
§*stefano.montanelli@unimi.it*
¶*ggianna@iit.demokritos.gr*
||*alfio.ferrara@unimi.it*
**vangelis@iit.demokritos.gr*

In this chapter, we present the Argo crowdsourcing system and related functionalities for crowd-based summary evaluation. Then, we evaluate the pros and cons of three different approaches to single-document, multilingual summary evaluation: i) traditional, expert-based; ii) crowdsourcing, majority-based; and iii) crowdsourcing, Argo-based. The evaluation is performed over two languages of the MultiLing-2015 single document summarization (MSS) dataset, examining the result under different aspects.

1. Introduction

Summarization has become a crucial issue in the current society, due to over-information. Thus, summarization systems have been called to compete in a number of settings, covering different aspects of this — highly cognitive — human practice. These settings can be positioned using a number of appropriate factors, such as (for an extensive related discussion, see the Sparck-Jones review paper):[1]

- The number of documents summarized (single-document vs. multi-document);

- The language(s) of input documents (mono-lingual, multi-lingual, cross-lingual);
- The genre of input text (news,[2,3] scientific articles,[4] legal documents,[5] etc.);
- The aim of the summary (informative, comparative, etc.);
- The output type (extracted/abstractive text, answers, keywords, etc.).

Throughout the years, researchers dealt with the challenge of summary evaluation along this wide spectrum of tasks and discussed the possible solutions in a number of scientific events (TIPSTER Text Summarization Evaluation (SUMMAC), the Document Understanding (DUC)/Text Analysis (TAC) conferences,[a] the BioASQ challenge,[6] the MultiLing series[3,7]). Originally, the process was undertaken by humans (e.g. Ref. 8) and the observed high cost for this evaluation highlighted the need of alternative strategies for summary evaluation.

The state-of-the-art of summary evaluation started by building consensus among judges[8] and moves on towards automatic evaluation measures, which still require a number of gold (i.e. human) summaries as input. Solutions of this kind include (among others) ROUGE and its variations,[9] the evaluation aspects of the CLASSY system,[10] and AutoSummENG[11] (and the related n-gram graph based methods). More recently, a certain line of study has been initialized to mitigate the gold-summary requirement, with interesting findings (e.g. Ref. 12).

Despite the above contributions, summary evaluation still remains an actual research topic with a number of open, challenging issues:

- How to judge a single summary versus another, or to consistently compare systems with minor differences.[13]
- How to enforce different types of evaluation on text (e.g. see Ref. 14).
- How to create multilingually applicable automatic measures of evaluation.[3,7]

The cost for the creation of a summarization corpus including evaluation is very high, especially in the multilingual setting. In this respect, crowdsourcing has been recently proposed as a possible solution to limit/reduce the costs of corpus creation. However, issues related to quality assessment of crowd-based evaluation results are still to be addressed.

---

[a]See http://duc.nist.gov/ and http://tac.nist.gov/.

In this chapter, we present the Argo crowdsourcing system[b] and related functionalities for crowd-based summary evaluation. Argo allows to configure the main features of a crowdsourcing execution by focusing on how to assess the quality of task results through a consensus-based mechanism, by also enabling to specify *constraints* about the task-force to be involved and the *worker reputation* required for taking part in the crowdsourcing activities. Furthermore, Argo is characterized by the notion of *worker trustworthiness*, allowing to calculate consensus by properly weighting the worker answer on the basis of his/her reliability/expertise. The ultimate goal of this chapter is to study and compare a traditional, expert-based approach to summary evaluation (called *expert-based approach* in the following) against two different crowd-based approaches: one based on a conventional majority-based mechanism for consensus evaluation (*majority-based approach*); one based on the Argo system (*Argo-based approach*). Through this comparison, we aim at addressing the following research questions:

(1) What is the difference between crowd-based and traditional, expert-based evaluations?
(2) Does the use of trustworthiness increase the quality of the results in a crowdsourcing environment?
(3) How is the quality of the results affected if we rely only on trustworthy workers as experts?

The rest of the chapter is structured as follows. We provide an overview of the related work in Section 2. The Argo system is described in Section 3. We present the experimental setup and related results to our research questions in Section 4. Finally, we discuss findings and conclusions in Section 5.

2. Related work

In this section we provide a brief overview of the related work, which outlines the challenges that the summary evaluation faces. We discuss the main points of automatic and manual evaluation, then we introduce the crowdsourcing approaches in the picture.

---

[b]http://island.ricerca.di.unimi.it/projects/argo/ (website in Italian language).

2.1. *Summarization and summary evaluation*

Summary evaluation has been classified as intrinsic or extrinsic.[15] Intrinsic evaluation relies on the summary content itself to evaluate, which extrinsic aims to judge the appropriateness of the summary as a tool used to reach a specific (external) aim. Sparck-Jones argues[1] that the classification of evaluation methods should be based on the degree to which the evaluation method measures performance, according to the intended purpose of the summary. Therefore, Sparck-Jones classifies evaluation methodologies as:

- **semi-purpose**, e.g., inspection of proper English;
- **quasi-purpose**, based on comparison with models, e.g., n-gram or information nuggets;
- **pseudo-purpose**, based on the simulation of task contexts, e.g., action scenarios;
- **full-purpose**, based on the summary operation in actual context, e.g., report writing.

In this chapter, we focus on a human-based intrinsic/quasi-purpose evaluation of a summary, aiming to judge a specific aspect of the content (namely responsiveness, as discussed in the following sections) given a set of model summaries. However, we describe the problem as a comparison problem between pairs of peer summaries, following the example of Owczarzak *et al.* (2012).[13]

2.1.1. *Manual evaluation methods*

A number of manual evaluation approaches have been introduced in the literature, aiming to provide gold-standard evaluations (see the DUC/TAC conference overviews in Refs. 16 and 17).

Early in this process the subjectivity of the evaluators was identified, while later other challenges were sketched, such as the effect of inconsistent annotators.[18] Methods building on establishing or taking into account consensus among evaluators were created.[19] Of those, the Pyramid[8] method — which allows different levels of consensus — has been widely used in a variety of community tasks, but it has mostly relied on the allocation of expert evaluators to the task. All such approaches imply a significant cost, related to the training of experts — who were commonly expected to be native speakers of the language in which the summaries were written — and the actual evaluation implementation. In order to minimize this cost, automatic methods were undertaken.

2.1.2. *Automatic methods*

As also mentioned in the introduction, from existing automatic methods the most widely used is the ROUGE family[9] of methods, aiming to identify word n-gram content overlap between gold-standard (also called "model") summaries and the evaluated (also called "peer") summary. ROUGE (in its variations) has been applied in a variety of settings, nevertheless holding clearly defined weak spots (e.g. Refs. 3 and 18). Other methods include the evaluation aspect of the CLASSY system,[10] AutoSummENG,[11] as well as the source-document-dependent-only methods of evaluation.[12]

The problems of many automatic methods, as highlighted in the literature, include:

- The need for model summaries.
- Difficulty to correctly (i.e. similarly to humans) and consistently rank summaries and summarization systems in the middle of the performance spectrum (i.e. summaries which are not particularly good or bad).
- The low applicability of the methods on different languages, oftentimes due to language-dependent components, but also due to (morphology) assumptions that may not hold across different languages.

Given those challenges, researchers have studied the application of crowdsourcing approaches to reduce the cost of evaluation, while retaining the consistency of the results as if experts were working on them.

2.2. *Crowdsourcing for summarization*

Crowdsourcing approaches related to text-summarization issues can be distinguished in *crowd-narrative* and *crowd-rating* according to the task typology submitted to crowd workers for execution.

2.2.1. *Crowd-narrative approaches*

In crowd-narrative approaches, the creative role/contribution of workers is emphasized, since they are actually involved in text summarization. In this context, crowdsourcing activities are usually characterized by the execution of *creation tasks*, in which a target text to summarize is given and a crowd worker has to provide her/his own proposed summary as an answer. The focus of crowd-narrative approaches is mostly on how to disciplinate the crowd activities and how to evaluate/compare the quality of summaries crowd-generated by different workers. Examples of crowd-narrative approaches for supporting text-summarization are described in Refs. 20–23.

In Ref. 23, the authors analyze the feasibility to enforce text-summarization by relying on online crowdsourcing services. Popular platforms such as Amazon Mechanical Turk[c] and CrowdFlower[d] are exploited to this end, by surveying the main available features for task design and evaluation that are relevant for text-summarization issues. In Ref. 20, the authors propose a prototype crowdsourcing system called *Storia* in which they exploit the use of narrative theory as a framework for summarizing social-media contents. The designed crowdsourcing tasks ask the crowd to generate summaries of given events based on narrative templates. In particular, the crowd is invoked to contribute by recovering missing contextual information from social media feeds, essentially identifying and filling narrative gaps. Experimental results are provided to show that crowd-generated summaries with support of narrative templates are considered as qualitatively better than those generated exclusively based on crowd contributions without a template.

In Ref. 21, crowdsourcing is employed in summarization of source-code fragments. Workers are invoked to suggest summary lines of source-code with the aim to train and to improve the quality of machine learning algorithms. A similar approach is presented in Ref. 22, where an integrated process for text-summarization is presented, characterized by the seamless combination of tool-created and crowd-generated results. As a general remark on crowd-narrative approaches, we note that the proposed solutions are characterized by the specification of a tailored crowdsourcing process with ad-hoc limitations and requirements on the kind of tasks to execute. The goal is to reduce the complexity of the task evaluation stage. Quality assessment of crowd creation tasks, like those designed for crowd-generating summaries in the above approaches, is still an open issue in the crowdsourcing research field.

2.2.2. *Crowd-rating approaches*

In crowd-rating approaches, the crowd plays an evaluation/validation role on a set of given summaries that is usually generated through some kind of machine learning or extraction/abstraction techniques. In this context, crowdsourcing activities are usually characterized by the execution of *choice tasks*, in which a target text as well as a set of candidate summaries is provided and a crowd worker has to select the preferred one among those

---

[c]http://www.mturk.com.
[d]http://www.crowdflower.com.

available. The focus of crowd-rating approaches is more on the mechanism enforced for selecting the final task result rather than on the kind of task content. In other words, related work on crowd-rating approaches include solutions where workers are asked to choose among alternative options, regardless of whether the options are summaries, or any other kind of enumerable items (e.g., labels, entities, images). Many solutions have been proposed in the literature to address task evaluation in crowd-rating approaches, and reference classifications examples of available techniques can be found in Refs. 24–26.

In Ref. 27, the authors claim that a key problem in quality assessment of crowdsourcing results is how to select the most valuable worker contribution among the set of answers provided by a group of workers rather than to determine an effective combination of them. The use of *trustworthiness* is sometimes exploited to this end, by claiming that the more a worker is trustworthy, the more her/his contributions are valuable. For example, in Ref. 28, the worker task answers are weighted according to the worker reputation which is then used to determine the best task answer. Further solutions for estimation of worker trustworthiness propose the use of *gold-questions* (e.g., Ref. 29) or *peer-review* (e.g., Ref. 30). These solutions are negatively affected by the need to build reliable entry/verification tests and to support extra expenses for review activities, respectively.

In Ref. 31, a framework based on a probabilistic generative model is proposed to estimate the probability of correctness of a task answer. A similar approach is presented in Ref. 30 where the statistical model for estimating the quality of worker answers is defined by analyzing the results of a two-stage procedure in which i) a group of workers is requested to execute a task, and ii) another group of workers is called to review and grade the answers of the first stage (peer-review approach).

The notion of *consensus* is frequently employed for quality assessment in crowd-rating applications, either based on an explicit or implicit notion of worker agreement. Usually, consensus is described as an emerging property that could only be obtained by combining together multiple contributions provided by workers. For instance, in AutoMan,[32] a majority-based approach is presented where each task is initially assigned to a fixed number of workers. When a majority-based consensus (i.e., $q \geq 0.95$) is not reached on any answer, the number of workers involved in the task execution is doubled. This step is repeated until the majority on a task answer is reached. A similar approach based on a cumulative voting mechanism is proposed in Ref. 28. The research activity on this topic is still ongoing. Quality in crowdsourcing systems and marketplaces is periodically exploited for evaluation, with the aim to observe/understand whether the growing variety of task typologies is followed by a corresponding increment in enforced quality assessment mechanisms.[33-36]

2.3. *Original contribution of this chapter*

In this chapter, we rely on the Argo crowdsourcing system for detecting the most appropriate summary among a set of machine-generated candidates (i.e., crowd-rating approach based on choice tasks). With respect to the state-of-the-art solutions described earlier, Argo provides functionalities for task result evaluation where techniques for consensus-based task management and trustworthiness-based worker management are enforced in a seamless and effective way. Such a combined use of different techniques, leveraging multiple aspects, allows to perform quality-oriented task evaluation without requiring a-priori knowledge, supervision, nor training activities, as occurs in most of the literature solutions. Furthermore, Argo provides a flexible configuration environment where the main features of a crowdsourcing execution can be defined by also enabling to specify constraints about the *task-force* to be involved and the worker reputation required for taking part in the crowdsourcing activities.

3. The proposed approach

We recall that the goal of this chapter is to answer the following research questions:

(1) What is the difference between crowd-based and traditional, expert-based evaluations in the summary evaluation setting?
(2) Does the use of trustworthiness increase the quality of the results in a crowdsourcing environment aimed at such an evaluation?
(3) How is the quality of the results affected if we rely only on trustworthy workers as experts?

In the following, we present the Argo system and related functionalities/settings for summary evaluation, then we move on to describe the tasks and experiments carried out to support our study.

3.1. *Overview of the Argo system*

Argo is a web-based crowdsourcing system characterized by the notion of *crowd-consensus*, meaning that a certain task T to execute is assigned to a set of workers $W = \{w_1, \ldots, w_k\}$ and appropriate functionalities are provided to derive the final task result $\bar{A}$ (i.e., a summary) on the basis of the level of agreement among the (possibly different) answers $A = \{a_1, \ldots, a_k\}$ autonomously provided by each worker.[37]

The Argo architecture is articulated in four system components called *task manager*, *consensus manager*, *reward manager*, and *uncommitment manager* (see in Figure 1).[e]

The **task manager** is in charge of dealing with all the aspects related to task execution, and it allows to specify the task-type and the task-force parameters. The task-type is used to define the nature of the request associated with the task T, based on the kind of worker contribution that is required for accomplishing the task. The task types supported in Argo are creation and choice. The creation type denotes a task request where the worker has to formulate an answer from scratch as a result of task execution. On the opposite, the choice type denotes a task request where the worker has to select her/his answer among a set of predefined alternatives.

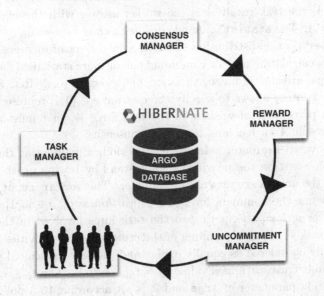

Fig. 1.   The Argo system architecture.

[e]A detailed description of the Argo system and related crowdsourcing framework is provided in Ref. 37.

The `task-force` is used to define the number of workers $|W| = k$ to be involved in the execution of a certain task. In a task force, each worker autonomously executes a received task and independently produces the answer according to her/his personal problem-understanding and expertise. In Argo, a worker $w \in W$ is not aware of other workers being involved in the execution of a certain task, and the composition of the set W changes from one task to another to avoid mutual and history-based influence among workers.

The **consensus manager** has the responsibility to evaluate the level of agreement over the task answers received from the crowd workers. For consensus evaluation, the consensus manager relies on the specification of the `consensus-mode` and the `quorum-majority` parameters. The `consensus-mode` allows to specify the mechanisms used for determining the task result $\bar{A}$ based on the different task answers returned by the involved workers. The consensus modalities supported in `Argo` are `equivalence` and `statistics`. The `equivalence` mode denotes a mechanism based on simply counting the number of "equivalent" worker answers. Given the set of answers A, the task result $\bar{A}$ is the worker answer with the highest frequency in A. The `statistics` mode denotes a consensus-evaluation mechanism based on the distribution of answers in the set of answers A. This is done by calculating and/or combining one or more statistical indicators, for example arithmetic mean, variance, or deviation (e.g., Ref. 38). The `quorum-majority` allows to specify the quorum $q \in [0, 1]$ representing the minimum percentage of workers in the task force W that must agree on the task result $\bar{A}$ for reaching the crowd-consensus.

The **reward manager** is in charge of periodically updating the worker reputation based on the provided task answers by relying on the specification of the `worker-reputation` parameter. The `worker-reputation` is used to define the minimum level of *trustworthiness* $t_{min} \in [0, 1]$ required to a worker w for participating to the task force involved in the execution of a task T. At the beginning of the crowdsourcing activities, workers are initially considered as equally expert and they are associated with the same default trustworthiness value $t_w = t_{init} \in [0, 1]$. The t_{init} value is a configuration parameter of `Argo` and it is set according to a policy-based mechanism depending on the kind of crowdsourcing task to be executed (see Ref. 39). For each worker w, the trustworthiness value t_w is updated during the crowdsourcing activities to capture the capability of w to successfully complete tasks. In particular, the worker trustworthiness t_w increases when the worker w contributes to agreement formation on the result of executed tasks by providing answers that are shared with (the majority of) other workers, and it decreases otherwise. Only workers with a trustworthiness value $t_w \geq t_{min}$ can be involved in the execution of a task, meaning that the worker reputation t_{min} constitutes a lower bound on t_w under which the worker w is banned from the crowdsourcing activities and it is excluded from task assignments.

The **uncommitment manager** has the role to deal with tasks that are *uncommitted*, namely tasks that do not satisfy the consensus constraints specified in the `consensus-mode`. As an option, the uncommitment manager can interact with the task manager to schedule the re-execution of an uncommitted task by specifying new execution constraints, such as for example an increased value of the `worker-reputation` parameter. As an alternative option, the uncommitment manger can decide to terminate an uncommitted task, meaning that the final task result is set to *null* since the crowd did not succeed in reaching the consensus on a shared answer.

3.2. *Argo in summary evaluation*

For crowd-based summary evaluation, each crowdsourcing task asks the worker to consider a reference gold summary and two machine-generated candidates, called candidate A and B, respectively. The worker has to choose the candidate summary that she/he considers to be closer to the given reference/model summary. We note that `Argo` is capable to support tasks where more than a pair of candidate summaries are considered as possible task answers. In the following, we define tasks with exactly a pair of candidate summaries since we aim at comparing machine-generated summaries by two specific systems at a time. The set of tasks to execute as well as the gold summary and the pairs of candidate summaries contained in each task are defined offline and uploaded in the `Argo` system at configuration time, before that crowdsourcing activities are launched. In other words, the task composition and the choice of summary pairs to be inserted in each task for evaluation are not enforced in `Argo`. This means that `Argo` is not responsible for dynamically building the tasks to execute; instead, tasks are given as a predefined set of gold summaries and related pairs of candidates to evaluate. Finally, as a general remark, we stress that `Argo` has been released with English and Italian interfaces, and it is capable to manage and visualize tasks containing summaries in many different languages, including English, Greek, and Italian. The following `Argo` configuration has been enforced for crowd-based summary evaluation.

Task design. An `Argo` task for summary evaluation is based on a *target presentation* followed by a *context description* and a final *answer specification*. The target presentation is a fixed section for illustrating to the worker what is the task goal and the action(s) required for task execution (Fig. 2(a)). The context description is a dynamic section in which the task content to be considered and evaluated is shown. In particular, for summary evaluation, the context contains the gold summary and the two candidates A and B to be considered (Fig. 2(b)). In the task manager of `Argo`, we set the `task-type = choice`, then the answer specification section is populated with a set of alternative options (i.e., `A is better than B, B is better than A, Cannot really say`). The worker is asked to choose the preferred option among the possible task answers (Fig. 2(c)). The worker has also the opportunity to refuse a task execution whether she/he considers to be not sufficiently expert and/or skilled for providing a reliable answer. In case of task refusal, the worker is replaced by another crowd worker in the task force assigned to that task. Moreover, a task has a 15 minutes expiration time for allowing the worker to carefully read both the gold and the candidate summaries before providing her/his own answer. After task expiration without an answer, a task is considered as refused by the worker.

Task setup. For task execution, we rely on a standard `Argo` configuration that we defined for *crowd-rating* tasks, characterized by a set of predefined answer options, as it occurs in the summary evaluation task described above.[39] The `Argo` configuration is defined as follows:

```
task-type          choice
task-force         5
consensus-mode     equivalence
quorum-majority    0.51
worker-reputation  0.1
```

In such a configuration, we expect to collect five different answers for each task T and we rely on a qualified-majority agreement of 51% within the involved workers for successfully committing a task result. The choice of a low-value worker reputation requirement is motivated by the idea to avoid restrictions on worker involvement in crowdsourcing activities, and to rely on a majority-based consensus mechanism to exclude worker contributions that are recognized as inaccurate. We also specify that each worker is

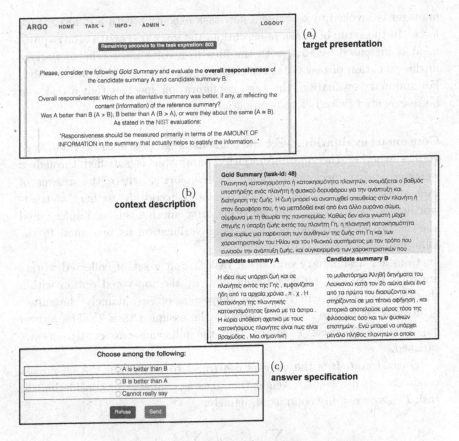

Fig. 2.   Example of `Argo` task for summary evaluation.

associated with a default trustworthiness value $t_{init} = 0.70$. The choice to employ a high value of t_{init} is motivated by the fact that workers received an essential training before being involved in the crowdsourcing activities, thus a sort of basic expertise/reliability can be assumed. A task is queued for scheduling until a task force with appropriate requirements is composed. In `Argo`, a worker is associated with a *status* information with two possible values that are i) *available*, meaning that she/he is ready to be inserted in a task force for executing tasks, and ii) *unavailable*, meaning that she/he cannot be involved in task-forces. The task T is scheduled when a task force with appropriate requirements and available workers is found. A worker is unavailable until she/he has completed an assigned task. In case of unsuccessful task execution (i.e., consensus not reached), the uncommitment manager is invoked to schedule a new task execution with a different task force. In the setup of a task re-execution, the `worker-reputation` requirement is increased by +0.2 with the idea to involve more reliable workers in the execution of tasks that are recognized to be more complex to solve. For summary evaluation, the `Argo` configuration specifies that a task can be re-executed twice before termination.

Consensus evaluation. For the `consensus-mode = equivalence`, `Argo` verifies whether the quorum-majority parameter is satisfied through a weighted-voting mechanism called *supermajority*, where the answer of each worker w in a task force is weighted according to her/his trustworthiness values t_w.[37] The supermajority mechanism is implemented via the q-constraint and bop-constraint verification as presented in the following.

Consider a summary evaluation task T and a set of collected worker answers A. We call *1st-crowd-candidate* ca_1 the top-voted option within those available. We call W_{ca_1} the *supporters* of ca_1, namely the subset of workers that chose ca_1 as answer to the assigned task T. The answer ca_1 becomes the task T result $\bar{A}$ iff the following two constraints are satisfied.

Q-constraint. It is the *quorum constraint* to verify that the 1st-crowd-candidate ca_1 has enough weight (i.e., trustworthiness) for considering the task T as successfully completed, namely:

$$\sum_{w \in W_{ca_1}} t_w \geq q \cdot \sum_{w \in W} t_w$$

where $\sum_{w \in W_{ca_1}} t_w$ is the trustworthiness of the ca_1 supporters, $\sum_{w \in W} t_w$ is the trustworthiness of all the workers that executed the task T, and q is the required quorum majority.

Bop-constraint. It is the *balance-of-power* constraint to verify that a single worker cannot determine the final task result just by her/his own answer, thus limiting the influence of workers with high trustworthiness on the overall consensus evaluation process. The bop-constraint is checked by verifying that it is not possible to satisfy the q-constraint by moving a worker in W_{ca_1} to support another candidate answer, namely:

$$\sum_{w \in W_{ca_2}} t_w + t_w^{max} < q \cdot \sum_{w \in W} t_w$$

Table 1.   Answers to the task of Fig. 2.

Worker w_i	Trustworthiness t_{w_i}	Provided answer a_i
w_1	$t_{w_1} = 0.7$	A is better than B
w_2	$t_{w_2} = 0.4$	Cannot really say
w_3	$t_{w_3} = 0.8$	A is better than B
w_4	$t_{w_4} = 0.8$	A is better than B
w_5	$t_{w_5} = 0.3$	Cannot really say

where ca_2 is the *2nd-crowd-candidate*, that is the 2nd-voted option within those available, and t_w^{max} is the maximum trustworthiness value within the task force W.

Example.   Consider the task answers shown in Table 1. The set of answers A collected from the workers W involved in the execution of the task are the following (each answer is associated with the trustworthiness of the corresponding worker). According to A, the 1st-crowd-candidate is $ca_1 = $ A is better than B. The sum of trustworthiness values for involved workers is $\sum_{w \in W} t_w = 3.0$. Based on a quorum majority $q = 0.51$, the q-constraint is satisfied by ca_1, in that the overall trustworthiness of ca_1 supporters is $t_{w_1} + t_{w_3} + t_{w_4} = 2.3$, which is higher than $(q \cdot \sum_{w \in W} t_w) = (0.51 \cdot 3.0) = 1.53$.

Moreover, we have $t_w^{max} = t_{w_4} = 0.8$. According to the bop-constraint, we evaluate the q-constraint on the 2nd-crowd-candidate $ca_2 = $ Cannot really say to check whether the w_4 worker can determine the final task result just by shifting her/his answer from ca_1 to ca_2. To this end, we include w_4 in the supporters of ca_2, namely $W_{ca_2} = \{w_2, w_4, w_5\}$. The q-constraint is not satisfied by ca_2, in that $t_{w_2} + t_{w_4} + t_{w_5} = 1.5$, which is lower than $(q \cdot \sum_{w \in W} t_w) = (0.51 \cdot 3.0) = 1.53$.

As a result, we obtain that the bop-constraint is satisfied by the 1st-crowd-candidate ca_1. According to the supermajority mechanism, the crowd-consensus is reached and the final task result is $\bar{A} = $ A is better than B.

3.3. *Multilinguality*

The Argo system is inherently multilingual, which is an advantage that stems from its crowdsourcing-based nature. Each task is handled in a language-angostic manner, enabling a straightforward inclusion of new languages in the system without requiring any specific adjustment.

No language-dependent processing is performed and the trustworthiness measure is directly applicable to a worker of any language. As a result, extending the system to further languages mainly involves finding workers to involve in the crowdsourcing activities, with the sole requirement that each worker is proficient enough in the target language. Moreover, the `Argo` system could relax the language proficiency requirement by applying post-evaluation, trustworthiness-based filtering to exclude evaluations of workers which are deemed as unreliable by the system. In our study, we exploited `Argo` on English and Greek summaries, and our preliminary results indicate that most aspects of the evaluation performance remain the same across the two languages.

4. Experimental results

In the following, we describe the experimental setup and related results.

4.1. *Selected setting and dataset*

We evaluate the proposed methods on the MSS challenge of the Multiling 2017 workshop.[7] The objective of the challenge is to construct a single document summary for each document in the provided dataset. The latter consists of a selection of 30 featured Wikipedia articles in 41 languages. Each article represents a topic and fulfills certain criteria with respect to accuracy, neutrality, completeness, and writing style. In the training portion of the dataset, articles are associated with a human-written reference summary and, in both training and validation sets, each document is associated with a summary target length. Participants to the MSS task are asked to generate summaries as close to the target length as possible, the summaries being truncated otherwise, and to submit results for at least one language. In MSS, the evaluation process uses both automatic and manual methods. The automatic evaluation process includes the generation of baseline and oracle summaries for each article. The baseline is the prefix of the article body text equal to the summary target length, while the oracle summary is generated using the combinatorial covering algorithm.[40] These are compared, along with the submitted summaries, to the human reference summary for each article.[3] The evaluation uses the ROUGE-2,-3,-4[9] and MeMoG[11] measures. The manual evaluation process on the other hand, uses human experts, as described in the following section.

4.2. *Expert-based summary evaluation*

4.2.1. *Overview*

In this evaluation, human experts compare and evaluate machine-generated summary pairs. Each evaluator is presented with a triplet consisting of the reference human-written summary and two candidate machine-generated summaries "A" and "B". The evaluator is asked to carefully read the reference summary (i.e. not the original articles) and judge which one of the two candidate summaries is significantly closer to the reference one. Specifically, users are asked to select the best out of the two candidate summaries, with respect to some qualitative measure, i.e., an evaluation axis. The options available are "A is better than B", "B is better than A," and a third "Cannot really say" option, when the candidate summaries are judged to be of a comparable quality. We will often use "A > B", "B > A," and "A ≈ B", or a numeric index to refer to the aforementioned options for the remainder of the chapter (see Table 2). In addition, since the evaluation can be formulated as a classification task of a summary triplet to one of these options, we will use "option" and "class" interchangeably.

4.2.2. *Evaluation axes*

Four (4) qualitative measures were used in the original MMS task evaluation, corresponding to a four-dimensional evaluation of each summary pair. The measures are a subset of the linguistic quality questions, specified by NIST to assess the readability and fluency of a summary[17] and can be evaluated either by comparing each candidate summaries to the reference or by examining a candidate summary by itself. The measures we used are described below.

- **Overall responsiveness**: measures the amount of the information of the reference summary that was reflected in the candidate summary.

Table 2.   Summarization evaluation classes.

Verbose class	Class symbol	Class index
"A is better than B"	A > B	1
"B is better than A"	B > A	2
"Cannot really say"	A ≈ B	3

- **Non-redundancy**: relates to unnecessary repetitions in the summary, in the form of repeated sentences, nouns, noun phrases, or facts.
- **Coherence**: measures the quality of the structure and organization of the summary.
- **Focus**: examines the extent to which the summary sentences only contain information that is related to the rest of the summary.

For all measures, higher values are better. Within the scope of this chapter, we focus on the widely-used "overall responsiveness" for comparisons with majority and Argo-based crowdsourcing evaluations, since this measure is the most intuitive of all measures and mostly uses the reference summary (e.g. versus the non-redundancy).

4.3. *Comparison between expert, majority, and Argo-based summary evaluations*

In order to assess each individual evaluation on a pair of summaries, we compare it to a *consensus evaluation* for that given pair. This consensus evaluation is computed at the level of a summary pair using majority voting. Let p be a summary pair associated with (expert) evaluations $\{3, 2, 1, 1, 3, 1\}$, where we index the classes according to Fig. 2. Here, the consensus is the most frequent class in the evaluations, namely 1, i.e. "A > B" or "A is better than B". It is obvious that for pairs annotated with evaluations such that no single majority class is extractable (e.g. $\{1, 2, 2, 1, 3\}$, $\{3, 2, 1\}$, etc.), consensus is not reached. Such summary pairs are not included in the consensus set. Based on our experience and setting, these cases are mostly the result of subjectivity in the evaluation and not some clearly defined trait of the text. More systematic evaluation may be required to map this subjectivity to specific text attributes (e.g. topic, genre, etc.).

Hence, to examine the performance of a set of individual evaluations E with respect to a consensus evaluation set C, we must restrict E to a subset E_c such that the latter contains only evaluations on pairs that are present in C. This guarantees that $\forall (e, p) \in E_c$ where e is an evaluation on the summary pair p, $\exists (e_c, p_c) \in C$ such that e_c is an evaluation on p_c and $p = p_c$, as mentioned above. We compare each single e to the pair consensus evaluation e_c, which was computed by majority voting as described earlier. To this end, we populate a confusion matrix from these two evaluations. The entry (i, j) in the matrix represents the number of summary pairs that have a ground truth i, but were assigned the class j by the experiment tested. This means that the diagonal represents the retrieved true positives (TP) for the class in that row. Elements not in the diagonal can be seen as false positives (FP) when viewed from the perspective of the column class, or false negatives (FN) when taking point of view of the row class. In the context of this study, we consider the consensus evaluation to be the ground truth. This means that true positives represent individual evaluations that agree with the consensus. On the other hand, an entry on (i, j), $i \neq j$, indicates a summary pair that was classified to i according to the consensus evaluation, but misclassified to j by an individual eval- uation. In Table 3 the confusion matrix on the classes of the evaluation process is presented, with entries with respect to the column (left) and the row (right) classes, representing prediction-wise and ground-truth-wise information respectively.

We extract a set of measures to evaluate class-wise performance of the individual evaluation set over the consensus. Specifically, we use Precision, Recall and F-measure, based on the concept presented by Rankel and Con- roy.[41] Given a binary one-versus-all classification system, precision P_c mea- sures the likelihood that given a classifier prediction over a class c, it will be correct. On the other hand, recall R_c reflects the likelihood that posi- tive examples of c will be detected by the classifier. Both of these measures can be combined in the F-measure F_c, defined as the harmonic mean of the two. To obtain a single measurement for the system, instead of class-specific ones, we use the macro/micro averages of the aforementioned measures. All measures used in our study are defined below.

$$P_c = \frac{\text{TP}_c}{\text{TP}_c + \text{FP}_c} \qquad P_M = \frac{1}{|C|} \sum_{c \in C} P_c \qquad P_m = \frac{\sum_{c \in C} \text{TP}_c}{\sum_{c \in C} [\text{TP}_c + \text{FP}_c]}$$

$$R_c = \frac{\text{TP}_c}{\text{TP}_c + \text{FN}_c} \qquad R_M = \frac{1}{|C|} \sum_{c \in C} R_c \qquad R_m = \frac{\sum_{c \in C} \text{TP}_c}{\sum_{c \in C} [\text{TP}_c + \text{FN}_c]}$$

$$F_c = \frac{2}{\frac{1}{P_c} + \frac{1}{R_c}} \qquad F_M = \frac{2}{\frac{1}{P_M} + \frac{1}{R_M}} \qquad F_m = \frac{2}{\frac{1}{P_m} + \frac{1}{R_m}}$$

where P, R and F represent precision, recall and F-measure, c and C a class and the set of all classes, m and M micro and macro average, respectively.

In the following paragraphs we perform a number of experiments on the Multiling summarization task data for the English and Greek lan- guages, comparing the investigated approaches: the MultiLing manual eval- uation task, where trained experts evaluate summary pairs as described in

Table 3. Confusion matrix on the classes of the evaluation process. "TP" ("FP") stand for true (false) positive, "FN" stands for false negative. In the prediction-wise view (left table), instances in a class column are falsely classified as a positive example for that class (FP) unless they coincide with the same class row, where the classification is correct (TP). In the ground-truth-wise view, elements not in the diagonal are misclassified elements of the ground-truth class represented by their row and are falsely considered negative examples of that class (FN).

Class	$A > B$	$B > A$	$A \approx B$	Class	$A > B$	$B > A$	$A \approx B$
$A > B$	$TP_{A>B}$	$FP_{B>A}$	$FP_{A\approx B}$	$A > B$	$TP_{A>B}$	$FN_{A>B}$	$FN_{A>B}$
$B > A$	$FP_{A>B}$	$TP_{B>A}$	$FP_{A\approx B}$	$B > A$	$FN_{B>A}$	$TP_{B>A}$	$FN_{B>A}$
$A \approx B$	$FP_{A>B}$	$FP_{B>A}$	$TP_{A\approx B}$	$A \approx B$	$FN_{A\approx B}$	$FN_{A\approx B}$	$TP_{A\approx B}$

Section 4.2 (expert-based approach), the Argo-based, crowdsourcing approach, and the crowdsourcing approach using the trustworthiness measure filtering. First, we compare each approach on the consensus reached, i.e. the number of summary pairs and individual evaluations that agree. In addition, we compare individual evaluations for each approach to the consensus, measuring performance with the measures described earlier. Furthermore, we perform participant-wise aggregation, where we compute the consensus with respect to participant summarization system pairs, rather than pairs of individual summaries, to assess the performance of crowd evaluations (with respect to the experts). Finally, we investigate the effect of the trustworthiness measure on the quality of the Argo evaluations. To this end, we filter crowd evaluators with respect to the mean final user trustworthiness per language. We use the evaluations of these "trustworthy" users to compute a consensus and compare it to the consensus reached by both the unfiltered evaluators and the canonical experts of the traditional approach.

4.3.1. *Greek*

The summarization evaluation task for the Greek language consists of 30 topics. A total of three systems participated in the task, resulting in a total of 90 system pairs across all the topics. We will use "A" and "B" to denote each candidate summary in an instance of the evaluation process, along with the class representations described in Section 4.2.

Regarding the expert-based approach, we collected a total of 270 evaluations for all Greek summary pairs, out of which expert agreement (i.e. a consensus evaluation) was reached for 78 pairs out of 234 evaluations, as illustrated in Table 4. The remaining 12 pairs and their 36 evaluations were

Table 4. Consensus results for the expert-based evaluation approach for the Greek language.

	Pairs				Evaluations	
Total	Agreed	A > B	B > A	A ≈ B	Total	Agreed
90	78 (86.7%)	11 (14.10%)	13 (16.66%)	54 (69.23%)	270	234 (86.67%)

Table 5. Performance of 234 individual expert evaluations with respect to the expert consensus on 78 pairs for the Greek language.

Class	A > B	B > A	A ≈ B	Precision	Recall	F-measure
A > B	22	2	9	0.5641	0.6667	0.6111
B > A	2	27	10	0.5400	0.6923	0.6067
A ≈ B	15	21	126	0.8690	0.7778	0.8208
Total (Macro)				0.6577	0.7123	0.6839
Total (Micro)				0.7479	0.7479	0.7479

discarded from the consensus set. The distribution of consensus classes is also displayed.

First, we examine the performance of each individual expert evaluation, with respect to the expert consensus in Table 5. This measurement provides a topline performance, indicative of the expert agreement (one versus consensus). The number of individual evaluations were limited to 234, corresponding to the evaluations associated with pairs that belong to the consensus set. The remaining evaluations were discarded. We present the confusion matrix associated with the available classes, along with precision, recall, and F-measure per class. In addition, macro and micro F-measure scores are computed for the whole dataset.

Moving on to the Argo evaluations, we collected a total of 611 evaluations on all pairs. An agreement was reached over 486 evaluations and 74 pairs, which are presented in Table 6.

Table 7 presents the performance of each evaluation in the Argo-based setting with respect to the consensus of the experts. In this case, the number of assessed evaluations were limited to the 78 pairs for which experts' agreement exists, resulting in 526 crowd evaluations. In Table 8, instead of comparing to the experts' consensus, we examine the individual crowd evaluations with respect to the *crowd* consensus, as an indication of crowd-related agreement level (one versus consensus). This time the evaluations

Table 6. Consensus results on the Argo-based evaluation approach for the Greek language.

Pairs					Evaluations	
Total	Agreed	A > B	B > A	A ≈ B	Total	Agreed
90	74 (82.2%)	18 (24.3%)	22 (29.7%)	34 (45.9%)	611	486 (79.5%)

Table 7. Performance of 586 individual Argo evaluations with respect to the expert consensus on 78 pairs for the Greek language.

Class	A > B	B > A	A ≈ B	Precision	Recall	F-measure
A > B	19	19	34	0.1218	0.2639	0.1667
B > A	38	26	30	0.1711	0.2766	0.2114
A ≈ B	99	107	154	0.7064	0.4278	0.5329
Total (Macro)				0.3331	0.3228	0.3278
Total (Micro)				0.3783	0.3783	0.3783

Table 8. Performance of 486 individual Argo evaluations with respect to the crowd consensus on 74 pairs for the Greek language.

Class	A > B	B > A	A ≈ B	Precision	Recall	F-measure
A > B	57	17	25	0.4130	0.5758	0.4810
B > A	29	78	31	0.5493	0.5652	0.5571
A ≈ B	52	47	150	0.7282	0.6024	0.6593
Total (Macro)				0.5635	0.5811	0.5722
Total (Micro)				0.5864	0.5864	0.5864

are restricted to 486 instances over 74 pairs, for which crowd consensus has been reached.

The above results evaluate *individual user evaluations* with respect to either expert or crowd consensus. To perform *system-level* comparisons, we aggregate all evaluations for each participant system pair and extract a consensus class via majority voting in the same way we aggregated evaluations over individual summary pairs. This aggregation outputs a single evaluation for each of the system pairs, the latter being distinct combinations of the three systems that participated in the summarization task for the Greek language. We apply this method for each evaluation approach and compare the two approaches in Table 9.

Table 9.   Crowd consensus evaluations with respect to expert consensus, both aggregated over system pairs for the Greek language. Note that zero instances for a class yield zero precision and recall values, as is the case for the $A > B$ and $B > A$ classes in the table.

Class	$A > B$	$B > A$	$A \approx B$	Precision	Recall	F-measure
$A > B$	0	0	0	0.0000	0.0000	0.0000
$B > A$	0	0	0	0.0000	0.0000	0.0000
$A \approx B$	0	0	3	1.0000	1.0000	1.0000
Total (Macro)				0.3333	0.3333	0.3333
Total (Micro)				1.0000	1.0000	1.0000

Table 10.   Consensus results on the Argo evaluations from the trustworthiness-filtered users for the Greek language.

		Pairs			Evaluations	
Total	Agreed	$A > B$	$B > A$	$A \approx B$	Total	Agreed
90	69 (76.67%)	9 (13.04%)	17 (24.63%)	43 (62.31%)	465	373 (80.22%)

We continue our investigation by examining the effect of the trustworthiness mechanism adopted in Argo. We compute the mean of the final user trustworthiness to a value of 0.62943 and discard users with a trustworthiness lower than that threshold. This results in 7 "trustworthy" users, out of the 12 Greek language evaluators in total. We end up with 465 evaluations over 90 summary pairs. Consensus is reached on 69 summary pairs, out of 373 evaluations, as displayed in Table 10.

To examine the effect of the trustworthiness filtering on the consensus, we compare the performance of each individual trustworthy evaluation with respect to the trustworthy consensus, in Table 11.

We move on by assessing if the crowdsourcing trustworthy users can act as experts. To this end, we compare the unfiltered crowdsourced evaluations associated with the summary pairs of the trustworthy consensus, to the latter. Restricting the raw crowdsourced evaluations to the ones associated with the summary pairs in the trustworthy consensus results in 484 individual evaluations. The results are presented in Table 12.

Finally, we examine the trustworthy users' evaluations to the expert consensus in Table 13 to see the level of agreement between them. The number of evaluations is limited to 396, corresponding to the 78 pairs in the experts' consensus set.

Table 11. Performance of 373 individual trustworthy evaluations with respect to trustworthy consensus for the Greek language.

Class	A > B	B > A	A ≈ B	Precision	Recall	F-measure
A > B	21	2	10	0.2838	0.6364	0.3925
B > A	10	47	22	0.5000	0.5949	0.5434
A ≈ B	43	45	173	0.8439	0.6628	0.7425
Total (Macro)				0.5426	0.6314	0.5836
Total (Micro)				0.6461	0.6461	0.6461

Table 12. Performance of 484 Argo evaluations with respect to trustworthy crowd consensus for the Greek language.

Class	A > B	B > A	A ≈ B	Precision	Recall	F-measure
A > B	29	6	10	0.2214	0.6444	0.3295
B > A	22	60	22	0.4348	0.5769	0.4959
A ≈ B	80	72	183	0.8512	0.5463	0.6655
Total (Macro)				0.5024	0.5892	0.5424
Total (Micro)				0.5620	0.5620	0.5620

Table 13. Performance of 396 trustworthy evaluations with respect to the expert consensus for the Greek language.

Class	A > B	B > A	A ≈ B	Precision	Recall	F-measure
A > B	11	13	33	0.1222	0.1930	0.1497
B > A	22	22	30	0.2157	0.2973	0.2500
A ≈ B	57	67	141	0.6912	0.5321	0.6013
Total (Macro)				0.3430	0.3408	0.3419
Total (Micro)				0.4394	0.4394	0.4394

As the confusion matrix on the left of Table 13 shows, it is all too common to mix answers that do indicate difference ($A > B$, or $B > A$) with the biggest class ($A \approx B$). This indicates that it is difficult/strongly subjective to say whether two systems are (significantly) different. It is much rarer to provide completely contradicting predictions (e.g. one evaluator says $A > B$ and the other $B > A$). Elaborating, it is twice as common to (wrongly) apply to $A > B$ or $B > A$ instances an $A \approx B$ label ($(33 + 30) = 63$ instances correspondingly), than to mistake an $A > B$ instance for $B > A$, or a $B > A$ instance with an $A > B$ one ($(22+13) = 35$

instances correspondingly). In addition to this, it appears that the experts were much more prone to replying with the majority class $A \approx B$, while the crowd-evaluators showed stronger positioning towards the extreme classes. This led to many $A \approx B$ instances flooding the predictions of extreme classes, which significantly lowers the corresponding precision numbers. Since these classes have much fewer instances than the majority class, the effect of this flooding is very strong.

4.3.2. *English*

The summarization task for the English language consists of 30 topics, same as the Greek language case. A total of four systems participated in the task, resulting in a total of 180 system pairs across all topics. However, we restricted the systems to the three that also participated in the summarization task for the Greek language, in order to be able to evaluate the multilingual aspect of the compared approaches. This results in 90 system pairs and 270 evaluations, similar to the Greek language case.

We collected a total of 270 evaluations for all 90 summary pairs in the expert evaluation process. Agreement was reached for 75 pairs through 225 evaluations, illustrated in Table 14. The remaining 15 pairs and their 45 evaluations were discarded.

Similar to the Greek data, in Table 15 we examine the performance of individual expert evaluations with respect to the expert consensus. The individual evaluations are limited to the 225 individual evaluations on pairs belonging to the consensus set, with the rest of the evaluations being discarded.

Moving on to the Argo evaluations, we collected a total of 377 evaluations on all summary pairs for the English language. An agreement was reached for 77 pairs, using 314 evaluations in total. The consensus results are presented in Table 16.

Table 17 presents the performance of each evaluation in the Argo setting with respect to the consensus of the experts. Similar to the Greek case, we

Table 14. Consensus results for the expert-based evaluation approach for the English language.

Pairs					Evaluations	
Total	Agreed	$A > B$	$B > A$	$A \approx B$	Total	Agreed
90	75 (83.33%)	23 (30.66%)	19 (25.33%)	33 (44.0%)	270	225 (83.33%)

Table 15.   Performance of 225 individual expert evaluations with respect to the expert consensus on 75 pairs for the English language.

Class	A > B	B > A	A ≈ B	Precision	Recall	F-measure
A > B	47	10	12	0.7231	0.6812	0.7015
B > A	7	42	8	0.6885	0.7368	0.7119
A ≈ B	11	9	79	0.7980	0.7980	0.7980
Total (Macro)				0.7365	0.7387	0.7376
Total (Micro)				0.7467	0.7467	0.7467

Table 16.   Consensus results on the Argo-based evaluation approach for the English language.

	Pairs				Evaluations	
Total	Agreed	A > B	B > A	A ≈ B	Total	Agreed
90	77 (85.55%)	26 (33.76%)	21 (27.27%)	30 (38.96%)	377	314 (83.28%)

Table 17.   Performance of 313 individual Argo evaluations with respect to the expert consensus on 75 pairs for the English language.

Class	A > B	B > A	A ≈ B	Precision	Recall	F-measure
A > B	60	20	15	0.6122	0.6316	0.6218
B > A	20	54	17	0.5567	0.5934	0.5745
A ≈ B	18	23	86	0.7288	0.6772	0.7020
Total (Macro)				0.6326	0.6341	0.6333
Total (Micro)				0.6390	0.6390	0.6390

limit the crowdsourced evaluations to those associated with the 75 pairs in the expert consensus set, leading to 313 relevant crowdsourced evaluations. In addition, we compare the crowdsourced evaluations to their consensus in Table 18, restricting the examined evaluations to the 314 for which crowd consensus is reached.

As Table 17 illustrates, when compared to Table 7 (Greek setting), the fact that in the English corpus there is less class imbalance between the three options, reduced the effect of misclassifications from $A \approx B$ to the extreme classes.

We perform a system-level comparison by aggregating all evaluations at the level of each unique system pair in the same way as in the Greek

Table 18. Performance of 314 individual Argo evaluations with respect to the crowd consensus on 77 pairs for the English language.

Class	A > B	B > A	A ≈ B	Precision	Recall	F-measure
A > B	72	19	18	0.6923	0.6606	0.6761
B > A	16	62	20	0.6596	0.6327	0.6458
A ≈ B	16	13	78	0.6724	0.7290	0.6996
Total (Macro)				0.6748	0.6741	0.6744
Total (Micro)				0.6752	0.6752	0.6752

Table 19. Crowd consensus evaluations with respect to expert consensus, both aggregated over system pairs, for the English language. Note that zero-instance classes such as B > A below are scored with a zero value for precision and recall.

Class	A > B	B > A	A ≈ B	Precision	Recall	F-measure
A > B	1	0	0	1.0000	1.0000	1.0000
B > A	0	0	0	0.0000	0.0000	0.0000
A ≈ B	0	0	2	1.0000	1.0000	1.0000
Total (Macro)				0.6667	0.6667	0.6667
Total (Micro)				1.0000	1.0000	1.0000

Table 20. Consensus results on the 202 Argo evaluations from the trustworthiness-filtered users for the English language.

	Pairs				Evaluations	
Total	Agreed	A > B	B > A	A ≈ B	Total	Agreed
90	67 (74.44%)	20 (29.85%)	20 (29.85%)	27 (40.29%)	202	152 (75.25%)

language case. We apply this method for each evaluation approach and compare the two approaches in Table 19.

Regarding the effect on trustworthiness on the English data, the mean final user trustworthiness for English is 0.69322. From a total of 11 evaluators for English, we end up with 5 "trustworthy" users and 202 evaluations after thresholding, for the total 90 summary pairs. Consensus is reached on 67 summary pairs, out of 152 evaluations, as displayed in Table 20.

The performance of the individual trustworthy evaluations with respect to their consensus is examined in Table 21. The number of individual evaluations is limited to the 152 associated with the pairs on which crowd agreement exists.

Table 21. Performance of 152 individual trustworthy evaluations with respect to trustworthy consensus for the English language.

Class	A > B	B > A	A ≈ B	Precision	Recall	F-measure
A > B	39	5	2	0.8125	0.8478	0.8298
B > A	8	45	7	0.8654	0.7500	0.8036
A ≈ B	1	2	43	0.8269	0.9348	0.8776
Total (Macro)				0.8349	0.8442	0.8395
Total (Micro)				0.8355	0.8355	0.8355

Table 22. Performance of 292 crowd evaluations with respect to trustworthy crowd consensus for the English language.

Class	A > B	B > A	A ≈ B	Precision	Recall	F-measure
A > B	58	14	18	0.6304	0.6444	0.6374
B > A	21	61	21	0.6854	0.5922	0.6354
A ≈ B	13	14	72	0.6486	0.7273	0.6857
Total (Macro)				0.6548	0.6547	0.6547
Total (Micro)				0.6541	0.6541	0.6541

Table 23. Performance of 169 crowd evaluations of trustworthy users with respect to the expert consensus for the English language.

Class	A > B	B > A	A ≈ B	Precision	Recall	F-measure
A > B	38	10	1	0.7037	0.7755	0.7379
B > A	10	40	7	0.7018	0.7018	0.7018
A ≈ B	6	7	50	0.8621	0.7937	0.8264
Total (Macro)				0.7558	0.7570	0.7564
Total (Micro)				0.7574	0.7574	0.7574

To examine the suitability of the trustworthy crowdsourcing workers to act as experts, we compare the unfiltered crowdsourcing evaluations to the trustworthy consensus in Table 22. The individual evaluations are limited to the 292 associated with the summary pairs in the trustworthy consensus. We additionally look into the performance of the trustworthy evaluations with respect to the expert consensus. The number of trustworthy crowd evaluations in this case is limited to the 169 associated with the pairs in the experts' consensus set.

5. Conclusion and discussion

According to the experimental results, we discuss some main observations on two levels:(1) the agreement/consensus level; and (2) the performance level with regard to the expert consensus evaluation.

Concerning the agreement:

- For Greek, comparable agreement levels were reached for pairs (Tables 4 and 6), while in individual evaluations experts agreed more often than the crowd-workers. Regarding English, (Tables 14 and 16), the agreement is once again comparable for pairs and individual evaluations — with the interesting finding that crowdsourced agreement is a little higher than the experts' one in the pairs case.
- For Greek, crowdsourcing with mean final trustworthiness filtering (Table 10) leads to about 5–6% lower consensus percentage on the summary-pair level, compared to unfiltered crowdsourcing (Table 6). At the individual evaluation level the agreement is comparable. However, for English (Tables 16 and 20), we observe a drop of about 10% on both the number of pairs and evaluations where consensus was reached, when using trustworthiness-based filtering.

Concerning the evaluation performance:

- Regarding the performance of individual evaluations with respect to the corresponding consensus within each approach, the expert evaluations outperform the crowd-based ones across the investigated languages (Tables 5 and 8 for Greek; Tables 15 and 18 for English), as expected. Employing trustworthiness filtering, performance is on both languages, compared to the unfiltered crowdsourced evaluations, with a more significant increase in the English language (Table 11 for Greek and Table 21 for English).
- When comparing performance (in terms of F-measure) of the crowd-based and expert-based evaluations, each with respect to the expert consensus, the crowdsourced evaluations (Tables 7 and 17) always do worse than the expert evaluations (Tables 5 and 15), with a larger performance gap being observed in the Greek language case (a difference of about 10% for

English versus about 35% for Greek). In the current setting, where the topics are different in each language, we cannot directly analyze whether the gap is expected to be consistent across datasets. Further study is required to understand whether some basic language trait relates to this gap, or it was simply a topic-related effect (which is our intuitive assumption at this moment). This assumption is combined with the explicit finding that the Greek corpus expert evaluations offered imbalanced classes, if compared to the English corpus. This imbalance heavily affects the measured performances in the extreme classes ($A > B$, $B < A$).

- Replacing the expert consensus with the trustworthiness-filtered consensus from the crowdsourced data consistently improves the apparent performance across the investigated languages, when evaluating the crowdsourced evaluations against the new, more lenient, non-expert-based consensus (Tables 12 and 22).
- Using crowd-based evaluations from trustworthiness-filtered workers (Tables 13 and 23) — rather than from all the workers in the Argo approach — improves performance when comparing to unfiltered crowdsourced evaluations (when using experts' consensus as a reference) across the languages we examined (2–5% in Greek and 1–2% in English, in terms of micro-averaged F-measure).
- Performance (micro-averaged F-measure) at the system level is identical across all languages both in the crowdsourced approach and in the expert-based approach.

5.1. *Addressing the research questions*

We now revisit the research questions posed in the problem definition, in an attempt to provide an answer, in light of the experimental results. In the following, when reporting *consensus*, scores refer to the percentage of total number of items that belong in the consensus set (i.e. the set of items where consensus was reached). The items can be either summary pairs or individual evaluations, as described in the following. On the other hand, when discussing *performance* with respect to a consensus set, we use the macro/micro averages of the F-measure. All score comparisons refer to relative differences.

5.1.1. *What is the difference between crowd-based and traditional, expert-based evaluations?*

Regarding the percentage of evaluations reaching consensus, there are no clear advantages between the two approaches from a multilingual perspective. For Greek, using the crowdsourced approach instead of the traditional one results in a deterioration by 5.19% and 8.3% at the summary pair and individual evaluations levels respectively. For English, the crowdsourced approach yields a percentage increase of 2.66% over the traditional one at the summary pair level, with the consensus percentage staying roughly the same at the individual evaluation level.

Regarding performance with respect to the consensus, the experiments show that the expert-based approach greatly outperforms the crowdsourced one. Comparing the performance of individual evaluations with respect to the corresponding consensus, we find that the "traditional" approach outperforms the crowdsourced approach (i.e. experts tend to agree to each other more), with the latter being accompanied by a performance drop of 16.33%/21.59% for Greek and 8.57%/9.58% for English.

Comparison of individual evaluations of both approaches with respect to the expert-based consensus results in the individual expert evaluations outperforming the crowdsourced approach, with the latter lowering performance by 52.07%/49.42% for Greek and 14.14%/14.42% for English, respectively. In other words, experts tend to agree to each other in all the cases investigated.

At the system-level evaluation, there is no clear difference between crowd-sourced and expert-based approaches. However, we need to examine this further taking into account more systems.

5.1.2. *Does the use of trustworthiness increase the quality of the results in a crowdsourcing environment?*

The introduction of trustworthiness filtering reduces the consensus percentage on the *summary pair level* by 6.72% for Greek and 12.98% for English, when measuring the consensus of the evaluations of the trustworthy users. In other words, trustworthy workers are not bound to agree more with each other. The consensus percentage at the *evaluation level* shows a small improvement of 0.9% for Greek, but decreases slightly by 9.64% for the English language.

Using the evaluations from trustworthiness-filtered users rather than the entirety of the collected crowdsourced data with respect to the experts, increases performance across the investigated languages. Specifically, an improvement of 4.30%/16.15% for Greek and 19.44%/18.53% for English is observed. Thus, we can conclude that trustworthiness-based filtering improved quality in our setting.

5.1.3. *How is the quality of the results affected if we rely only on trustworthy workers as experts?*

When using the consensus of the trustworthiness-filtered users instead of the expert consensus, apparent performance of the crowdsourced evaluations versus that consensus consistently improves. Specifically, the improvement observed is 65.47%/48.56% for Greek and 3.38%/2.36% for English. To explain this large difference between the two languages, we examine the comparison of the performance of individual expert evaluations and trustworthy evaluations, both with respect to the expert consensus. Greek evaluations show a significant performance degradation of 50.01%/41.25% when switching from individual expert evaluations to evaluations of trustworthy users. This indicates that the trustworthy crowdsourced evaluation are largely dissimilar to the individual expert evaluations. On the other hand, the same scenario in English results in a slight performance boost of 2.55%/1.43%, indicating that the trustworthy evaluations managed to reflect the expert consensus better than the total individual expert evaluations.

5.2. *Summary of findings and next steps*

Based on all of the above questions and answers, we can conclude that:

- The selection of trustworthy evaluators can be profitable, regarding the expected agreement to experts. However, a small test should be conducted to verify whether the selected trustworthy evaluators appear to agree with the experts in the first place. In other words, we propose that the crowdsourcing process starts to first identify trustworthy evaluators who agree with a small number of experts. As a second step, the evaluation can become fully crowdsourced.
- Consensus between all crowdsourced evaluators appears to be stronger than the case of using trustworthy evaluators only. Thus, the Argo approach of bringing in more people to reach consensus appears to be useful.
- It is not clear whether language affects crowdsourcing performance. However, it is clear that in cases where most summary pairs are of similar quality the evaluation will lead to unsatisfactory results (if compared to expert performance).

In the future, we plan to consider a larger case study for measuring the effects of the trustworthiness mechanism in crowd-based approaches to summary evaluation. This will be examined by including investigation of the trade-off between number of evaluations left and similarity of the trustworthy evaluations to the expert evaluations. In addition, more languages will be considered, so as to discover potential multilingual characteristics of the relationship between the expert-based and the crowd-based approaches, as well as the trustworthiness mechanism. Another aspect we need to examine is whether specific text traits (e.g. genre, topic, language) cause ambiguity/subjectivity in the evaluation. Finally, we will try to integrate evaluations on more systems to better understand what happens at the system level.

References

1. K. Sparck Jones, Automatic summarising: The state of the art, *Information Processing and Management*, **43**(6), 1449–1481 (2007).
2. K. Hong, J. M. Conroy, B. Favre, A. Kulesza, H. Lin, and A. Nenkova, A repository of state of the art and competitive baseline summaries for generic news summarization. In *Language Resources and Evaluation Conference (LREC)*, pp. 1608–1616, LREC (2014).
3. G. Giannakopoulos, J. Kubina, J. M. Conroy, J. Steinberger, B. Favre, M. A. Kabadjov, U. Kruschwitz, and M. Poesio, Multiling 2015: Multilingual summarization of single and multi-documents, on-line fora, and call-center conversations. In *Special Interest Group on Discourse and Dialogue (SIGDIAL) Conference*, pp. 270–274, SIGDIAL (2015).
4. A. Abu-Jbara and D. Radev, Coherent citation-based summarization of scientific papers. In eds. M. Yuji and M. Rada, *Proceedings of the 49th Annual Meeting of the Association for Computational Linguistics: Human Language Technologies-Volume 1*, Portland, Oregon, USA, pp. 500–509, Association for Computational Linguistics (2011). Available at: http://dl.acm.org/citation.cfm?id=2002536.
5. A. Kanapala, S. Pal, and R. Pamula, Text summarization from legal documents: A survey, *Artificial Intelligence Review*, pp. 1–32 (2017).
6. G. Balikas, A. Kosmopoulos, A. Krithara, G. Paliouras, and I. Kakadiaris, Results of the BioASQ tasks of the question answering lab at CLEF 2015. In *CLEF 2015*, Springer (2015).
7. G. Giannakopoulos, J. M. Conroy, J. Kubina, P. A. Rankel, E. Lloret, J. Steinberger, M. Litvak, and B. Favre, Multiling 2017 overview, *MultiLing 2017*, p. 1 (2017).
8. R. J. Passonneau, K. McKeown, S. Sigelman, and A. Goodkind, Applying the pyramid method in the 2006 Document Understanding Conference. In *Proceedings DUC 2006*, Gaithersburg, Maryland, USA, Springer (2006).
9. C.-Y. Lin, Rouge: A package for automatic evaluation of summaries. In *Text Summarization Branches Out: Proceedings of the ACL-04 Workshop*, vol. 8, ACL (2004).

10. J. M. Conroy, J. D. Schlesinger, J. Kubina, P. A. Rankel, and D. P. O'Leary, Classy 2011 at TAC: Guided and multi-lingual summaries and evaluation metrics, *Text Analysis Conference (TAC)*, **11**, 1–8 (2011).

11. G. Giannakopoulos, V. Karkaletsis, G. Vouros, and P. Stamatopoulos, Summarization system evaluation revisited: N-gram graphs, *ACM Transactions on Speech and Language Processing (TSLP)*. **5**(3), 5 (2008).

12. A. Louis and A. Nenkova, Automatically assessing machine summary content without a gold standard, *Computational Linguistics*, **39**(2), 267–300 (Aug., 2012). doi: 10.1162/COLI_a_00123.

13. K. Owczarzak, J. M. Conroy, H. T. Dang, and A. Nenkova, An assessment of the accuracy of automatic evaluation in summarization. In eds. H. Li, C-Y. Lim, M. Osborne, G. G. Lee, and J. C. Park, *Proceedings of Workshop on Evaluation Metrics and System Comparison for Automatic Summarization*, Jeju Island, Korea, pp. 1–9, ACL (2012).

14. S. Ellouze, M. Jaoua, and L. Hadrich Belguith, Mix multiple features to evaluate the content and the linguistic quality of text summaries, *Journal of Computing and Information Technology*, **25**(2), 149–166 (2017).

15. I. Mani and E. Bloedorn, Summarizing similarities and differences among related documents, *Information Retrieval*, **1**(1–2), 35–67 (1999).

16. H. T. Dang, Overview of DUC 2005. In *Proceedings of the Document Understanding Conference*, vol. 2005, pp. 1–12, NIST (2005).

17. P. Over, H. Dang, and D. Harman, DUC in context, *Information Processing & Management*, **43**(6), 1506–1520 (2007).

18. K. Owczarzak, H. T. Dang, P. A. Rankel, and J. M. Conroy, Assessing the effect of inconsistent assessors on summarization evaluation. In eds. H. Li, C-Y. Lim, M. Osborne, G. G. Lee, and J. C. Park, *Proceedings of the 50th Annual Meeting of the Association for Computational Linguistics: Short Papers — Volume 2*, Jeju Island, Korea, pp. 359–362, ACL (2012).

19. C.-Y. Lin, SEE-summary evaluation environment, Information Sciences Institute. Available at: http://www1.cs.columbia.edu/nlp/tides/SEEManual.pdf (2001).

20. J. Kim and A. Monroy-Hernandez, Storia: Summarizing social media content based on narrative theory using crowdsourcing. In ed. D. Gergle, *Proceedings of the 19th ACM Conference on Computer-Supported Cooperative Work & Social Computing (CSCW)*, pp. 1018–1027, ACM (2016).

21. N. Nazar, H. Jiang, G. Gao, T. Zhang, X. Li, and Z. Ren, Source code fragment summarization with small-scale crowdsourcing based features, *Frontiers of Computer Science*, **10**(3), 504–517 (2016).

22. H. Mizuyama, K. Yamashita, K. Hitomi, and M. Anse, A prototype crowdsourcing approach for document summarization service. In eds. V. Prabhu, M. Taisch, and D. Kiritsis, *Proceedings of the International Conference on Advances in Production Management Systems. Sustainable Production and Service Supply Chains — APMS*, State College, PA, USA, pp. 435–442, Springer, Berlin Heidelberg (2013).

23. E. Lloret, L. Plaza, and A. Aker, Analyzing the capabilities of crowdsourcing services for text summarization, *Language Resources and Evaluation*, **47**(2), 337–369 (2013).

24. D. Iren and S. Bilgen, Cost of quality in crowdsourcing, *Human Computation*, **1**(2), 283–314 (2014).

25. T. Hoßfeld, M. Hirth, P. Korshunov, P. Hanhart, B. Gardlo, C. Keimel, and C. Timmerer, Survey of web-based crowdsourcing frameworks for subjective quality assessment. In *Proceedings of the 16th International Workshop on Multimedia Signal Processing (MMSP)*, Jakarta, Indonesia, pp. 1–6, IEEE (2014).

26. L. Yu, P. André, A. Kittur, and R. Kraut, A comparison of social, learning, and financial strategies on crowd engagement and output quality. In eds. S. R. Fussell, W. G. Lutters, M. R. Morris, and M. Reddy, *Proceedings of the 17th ACM Conference on Computer Supported Cooperative Work & Social Computing (CSCW)*, Baltimore, MD, USA, pp. 967–978, ACM (2014).

27. A. Doan, R. Ramakrishnan, and A. Y. Halevy, Crowdsourcing Systems on the World-Wide Web, *Communications of the ACM*, **54**(4), 86–96 (2011).

28. S. Lee, S. Park, and S. Park, A quality enhancement of crowdsourcing based on quality evaluation and user-level task assignment framework. In *Proceedings of the International Conference on Big Data and Smart Computing (BIGCOMP)*, Bangkok, Thailand, pp. 60–65, IEEE (2014).

29. J. S. Downs, M. B. Holbrook, S. Sheng, and L. F. Cranor, Are your participants gaming the system?: screening mechanical turk workers. In eds. E. D. Mynatt, D. Schoner, G. Fitzpatrick, S. E. Hudson, W. K. Edwards, and T. Rodden, *Proceedings of the 28th International Conference on Human Factors in Computing Systems (CHI 2010)*, Atlanta, GA, USA, pp. 2399–2402, ACM (2010).

30. Y. Baba and H. Kashima, Statistical quality estimation for general crowdsourcing tasks. In eds. I. S. Dhillon, Y. Koren, R. Ghani, T. E. Senator, P. Bradley, R. Parekh, J. He, R. L. Grossman, and R. Uthurusamy, *Proceedings of the 19th ACM SIGKDD International Conference on Knowledge Discovery and Data Mining*, Chicago, IL, USA, pp. 554–562, ACM (2013).

31. T. Matsui, Y. Baba, T. Kamishima, and H. Kashima, Crowdordering. In eds. V. S. Tseng, T. B. Ho, Z-H. Zhou, A. L. P. Chen, and H-Y Kao, *Proceedings of the 18th Pacific-Asia Conference on Advances in Knowledge Discovery and Data Mining (PAKDD)*, Tainan, Taiwan, pp. 336–347, Springer International Publishing (2014).

32. D. W. Barowy, C. Curtsinger, E. D. Berger, and A. McGregor, AutoMan: A platform for integrating human-based and digital computation. In eds. G. T. Leavens and M. B. Dwyer, *Proceedings of the 27th Annual ACM SIGPLAN OOPSLA Conference*, Tucson, AZ, USA, pp. 102–109, ACM (2012).

33. P. G. Ipeirotis, F. Provost, and J. Wang, Quality management on amazon mechanical turk. In *Proceedings of the ACM SIGKDD Workshop on Human Computation (HCOMP)*, Washington, DC, USA, pp. 64–67, ACM (2010).

34. M. Lease, On quality control and machine learning in crowdsourcing. In ed. D. Ruths, *Proceedings of the 11th AAAI Conference on Human Computation*, San Francisco, CA, USA, pp. 97–102, ACM (2011).

35. J. Fan, G. Li, B. C. Ooi, K.-l. Tan, and J. Feng, iCrowd: An adaptive crowdsourcing framework. In eds. T. K. Sellis, S. B. Davidson, and Z. G. Ives, *Proceedings of the ACM SIGMOD International Conference on Management of Data*, Melbourne, Australia, pp. 1015–1030, ACM (2015).

36. A. Jain, A. D. Sarma, A. Parameswaran, and J. Widom, Understanding workers, developing effective tasks, and enhancing marketplace dynamics: A study of a large crowdsourcing marketplace, *Proceedings of the VLDB Endowment*, **10**(7), 829–840 (2017).

37. S. Castano, A. Ferrara, L. Genta, and S. Montanelli, Combining crowd consensus and user trustworthiness for managing collective tasks, *Future Generation Computer Systems*, **54** (2016).

38. L. Genta, A. Ferrara, and S. Montanelli, Consensus-based techniques for tange-task resolution in crowdsourcing systems. In eds. Y. E. Ioannidis, J. Stoyanovich, and G. Orsi, *Proceedings of the 7th EDBT International Workshop on Linked Web Data Management (LWDM 2017)*, Venice, Italy, OpenProceedings.org (2017).

39. S. Castano, A. Ferrara, and S. Montanelli, A multi-dimensional approach to crowd-consensus modeling and evaluation. In eds. P. Johannesson, M. L. Lee, S. W. Liddle, A. L. Opdahl, and Ó. P. López, *Proceedings of the 34th International Conference on Conceptual Modeling (ER 2015)*, Stockholm, Sweden, pp. 424–431, Springer (2015).

40. S. T. Davis, J. M. Conroy, and J. D. Schlesinger, Occams — an optimal combinatorial covering algorithm for multi-document summarization. In ed. J. Vreeken, *2012 IEEE 12th International Conference on Data Mining Workshops (ICDMW)*, Berlin, Germany, pp. 454–463, IEEE (2012).

41. P. A. Rankel, J. M. Conroy, H. T. Dang, and A. Nenkova, A decade of automatic content evaluation of news summaries: Reassessing the state of the art. In eds. C. Biemann, S. Handschuh, A. Freitas, F. Meziane, and E. Métais, *Proceedings of the 51st Annual Meeting of the Association for Computational Linguistics*, Solfia, Bulgaria, pp. 131–136, ACL (2013).

Chapter 9

Multilingual Summarization and Evaluation Using Wikipedia Featured Articles

John M. Conroy[*,§], Jeff Kubina[†,¶], Peter A. Rankel[‡,||],
and Julia S. Yang[†]

[*]*IDA/Center for Computing Sciences, Bowie, MD, USA*
[†]*United States Department of Defense, MD, USA*
[‡]*Elder Research, MD, USA*
[§]*conroy@super.org*
[¶]*jmkubin@tycho.ncsc.mil*
[||]*rankel@math.umd.edu*

Multilingual text summarization is a challenging task and an active area of research within the natural language processing community. In this chapter we describe how Wikipedia featured articles are used to create datasets comprising about 40 languages for the training and testing of automatic single document summarization methods, the use of those datasets in the 2015 and 2017 MultiLing Workshop's single document summarization task, the methods used to evaluate the summaries submitted for the tasks, and the overall performance of each participant's system measured using automatic and human evaluations. The results not only suggest which approaches to automatic text summarization generalize across a wide range of languages but also which evaluation metrics are best at predicting human judgments in the multilingual summarization task.

1. Introduction

Automatic document summarization is an active area of research. The ACM Digital Library has 943 reports on the subject published from 1992 to 2016 with about one-quarter of them appearing in the last five years. While the impetus for much of this recent research was the annual Document

Understanding Conference 2001–2007 (DUC) and Text Analysis Conference 2008–2011 (TAC) Workshop on Document Summarization, many conferences now accept reports on document summarization techniques. Since 2011 the biennial MultiLing community driven workshop has been promoting the research and development of *multilingual* text summarization techniques across many domains, such as news articles, online forums, and others. In this chapter we focus on the MultiLing Workshop's single document summarization task (MSS). The objective of the task is to stimulate research by assessing the performance of automatic single-document summarization systems on documents covering a large range of sizes, *languages,* and topics. We start by giving a brief overview of the developments of document summarization research since 2001, then describe the MultiLing Workshop's MSS task, how the datasets for the task were created, the various methods used to evaluate the summaries submitted by the participants, the overall performance of each system, and examine the correlation between human and automatic evaluation systems.

2. Developments in multilingual summarization

Setting the challenge to develop systems to generate text summaries for multiple languages grew out of the international community of researchers that participated at the 2001–2007 DUC and the 2008–2011 TAC conferences. The DUC and TAC evaluations produced the seminal data sets for single document summarization in the early years of 2001 and 2002 and then quickly turned to formulating the problem of multi-document summarization. The conferences largely focused on English news summarization although at the 2004 DUC a parallel corpus of English and Arabic was introduced with the end goal being to produce summaries in English. At the 2004 and 2005 MultiLingual Summarization Evaluation Workshops the parallel English and Arabic task was further developed by Stewart (2009)[1] and Schlesinger *et al.* (2008).[2]

Beyond the evaluations at DUC and TAC, some researchers aimed to develop both summarization and evaluation systems which were language independent. For evaluation, Giannakopoulos *et al.* (2008)[3] tackled the challenging problem of automatic evaluation of multilingual summarization. Their approach was to use character n-gram graphs to compare summarization systems in a language independent way. An alternate approach was proposed by Saggion *et al.* (2010),[4] who presented a language neutral method of summarization evaluation by extending the work of Louis and Nenkova (2009)[5] who used Jensen-Shannon divergence (JSD). Saggion *et al.*, like Louis and Nenkova, demonstrated that JSD between a machine generated summary and a document correlated well with human judgments of the quality of the summary.

One of the earliest efforts to strive for a language independent summarization system was championed by Litvak, Last, and Friedman (2010),[6] who developed MUSE (MUltilingual Sentence Extractor), a system designed to be language independent that initially worked on Arabic, English and Hebrew text.

To help foster research in multilingual summarization, George Giannakopoulos proposed a biennial workshop on multilingual summarization which would include summarization tasks and evaluations in multiple languages. A pilot of this task was held at the 2011 TAC. This pilot workshop became known as MultiLing 2011 and subsequent workshops were held in 2013, 2015, and 2017. The summarization task for 2011 was a multi-document summarization task based on Wikinews articles in eight languages. This task was extended and repeated in 2013 and 2015. In 2013 the single document summarization task was added as a pilot. The task was adapted as a result of the 2013 pilot and was repeated in 2015 and 2017. The following sections give details of the MSS task (see Ref. 29), from how the datasets used were created to the evaluation of the summaries submitted by participants.

3. Datasets of the Multiling MSS tasks

Wikipedia featured articles are model articles that new writers are referred to as exemplars of what a well-written Wikipedia article should be. Specifically,

> Featured articles are considered to be the best articles Wikipedia has to offer, as determined by Wikipedia's editors. They are used by editors as examples for writing other articles. Before being listed ... articles are reviewed as featured article candidates for accuracy, neutrality, completeness, and style according to our featured article criteria.[a]

---

[a]https://en.wikipedia.org/wiki/Wikipedia:Featured_articles.

Not only are Wikipedia featured articles the best written, but their lead section is an excellent summary of the article:

> a lead: a concise lead section that summarizes the topic
> and prepares the reader for the detail in the subsequent
> sections;[b]

There are over 13,000 featured Wikipedia articles covering about 40 languages. So Wikipedia featured articles are an excellent source of data to train and evaluate automatic text summarization systems.

Unfortunately, how a featured article is listed varies from one language to another. So to automatically gather Wikipedia featured articles from all languages Jeff Kubina wrote a set of Perl scripts to extract and reformat them as XML. The code to perform this extraction is available for download.[c]

3.1. *2015 MSS task dataset*

The training and testing datasets for the 2015 MSS task were created from the featured articles of 38 Wikipedias using the same steps as reported in the 2013 MSS Pilot task.[7] Briefly stated, articles that did not have a large enough body size compared to their summary size were discarded and if this filtering resulted in less than 30 articles for a language it was not used. For each language Table 1 contains the mean character size of the summary and body of the articles selected for the test dataset. Within the dataset there is no correlation between the summary and body size of the articles, in fact, the variance in the summary size is small. This is likely because Wikipedia style requirements dictate that a summary be at most four paragraphs,[d] regardless of article size, and paragraphs be reasonably sized.[e]

3.2. *2017 MSS task dataset*

The testing dataset for the 2017 MSS task was created using the same steps as reported in the previous section and excluded the articles in the training dataset (which was the testing dataset for the task in 2015). For each of the 41 languages selected Table 2 contains the mean character size of the summary and body of the articles in the test dataset.

The data from the 2015 and 2017 MSS tasks are available on-line.[f]

---

[b]https://en.wikipedia.org/wiki/Wikipedia:Featured_article_criteria.
[c]http://search.cpan.org/dist/Text-Corpus-Summaries-Wikipedia.
[d]https://en.wikipedia.org/wiki/Wikipedia:LEAD.
[e]https://en.wikipedia.org/wiki/Wikipedia:WBA.
[f]http://multiling.iit.demokritos.gr.

Table 1. The table lists the languages in the 2015 MSS dataset with the first column containing the ISO code for each of the language, the second column the name of the language, and the remaining columns containing the mean size, in characters, and standard deviation, in parentheses, of the summary and body of the article. For example, for English the mean size of the human summaries is 1,857 characters.

ISO	Language	Summary	Body	ISO	Language	Summary	Body
af	Afrikaans	1,199 (218)	26,295 (14335)	ja	Japanese	378 (143)	18,715 (7652)
ar	Arabic	1,877 (141)	44,144 (20993)	ka	Georgian	1,003 (98)	18,076 (10113)
bg	Bulgarian	1,415 (169)	26,582 (7984)	ko	Korean	796 (239)	16,636 (9731)
ca	Catalan	1,531 (86)	26,992 (13635)	ms	Malay	1,309 (644)	19,233 (9047)
cs	Czech	2,003 (160)	34,268 (17078)	nl	Dutch	1,147 (137)	32,450 (15081)
de	German	1,070 (80)	38,200 (20293)	no	Nor.-Bok.	1,581 (143)	35,747 (13497)
el	Greek	1,681 (284)	33,400 (16174)	pl	Polish	1,174 (84)	26,407 (17249)
en	English	1,857 (111)	25,782 (13713)	pt	Portuguese	2,000 (110)	30,793 (11553)
eo	Esperanto	1,172 (134)	24,898 (11884)	ro	Romanian	1,673 (126)	30,540 (12815)
es	Spanish	2,044 (129)	38,368 (21978)	ru	Russian	1,430 (100)	45,118 (24491)
eu	Basque	1,033 (155)	23,893 (16282)	sh	Serbo-Croat.	1,353 (704)	28,302 (13304)
fa	Persian	1,648 (262)	25,781 (9292)	sk	Slovak	1,475 (618)	32,428 (15070)
fi	Finnish	1,176 (95)	30,116 (11169)	sl	Slovenian	1,195 (113)	20,756 (12465)
fr	French	1,792 (95)	55,805 (27157)	sr	Serbian	1,677 (183)	37,107 (12465)
he	Hebrew	908 (75)	21,856 (12509)	sv	Swedish	1,495 (87)	24,509 (9114)
hr	Croatian	1,093 (92)	22,160 (8792)	th	Thai	1,894 (426)	27,409 (6688)
hu	Hungarian	1,450 (81)	30,170 (14321)	tr	Turkish	1,889 (287)	30,871 (14854)
id	Indonesian	1,500 (159)	27,260 (9245)	vi	Vietnamese	2,094 (174)	36,893 (13833)
it	Italian	1,217 (77)	36,173 (18601)	zh	Chinese	636 (55)	14,050 (6269)

Table 2. The table lists the languages in the 2017 MSS dataset with the first column containing the ISO code for each of the language, the second column the name of the language, and the remaining columns containing the mean size, in characters, and standard deviation, in parentheses, of the summary and body of the article. For example, for English the mean size of the human summaries is 1,878 characters.

ISO	Language	Summary	Body	ISO	Language	Summary	Body
af	Afrikaans	1,743 (784)	32,407 (20378)	ka	Georgian	1,114 (682)	23,626 (23018)
ar	Arabic	2,129 (1045)	38,682 (16354)	ko	Korean	905 (491)	15,723 (7098)
az	Azerbaijani	1,375 (937)	48,687 (45855)	li	Limburgish	569 (237)	14,177 (16326)
bg	Bulgarian	1,451 (782)	29,421 (10774)	lv	Latvian	1,334 (514)	25,292 (13464)
bs	Bosnian	1,275 (801)	26,497 (15319)	mr	Marathi	970 (653)	14,727 (8438)
ca	Catalan	1,733 (906)	28,536 (14460)	ms	Malay	1,420 (952)	22,820 (16851)
cs	Czech	1,947 (745)	33,751 (24010)	nl	Dutch	1,316 (562)	36,638 (18062)
de	German	1,122 (470)	42,838 (30382)	nn	Norwegian	965 (493)	17,772 (9073)
el	Greek	1,582 (905)	36,081 (16652)	no	Nor.-Bok.	1,808 (913)	37,128 (22024)
en	English	1,878 (735)	20,683 (9644)	pl	Polish	1,470 (687)	31,460 (16319)
eo	Esperanto	1,286 (875)	22,905 (10279)	pt	Portuguese	2,247 (759)	37,189 (16777)
es	Spanish	2,083 (892)	47,670 (39981)	ro	Romanian	2,204 (710)	38,973 (20349)
eu	Basque	1,105 (742)	23,558 (16672)	ru	Russian	1,855 (915)	59,337 (27360)
fa	Persian	1,850 (581)	29,525 (13172)	simple	Simp. Eng.	973 (351)	9,793 (7027)
fi	Finnish	1,135 (406)	23,971 (10538)	sk	Slovak	1,104 (631)	26,102 (11024)
fr	French	1,924 (884)	65,960 (41289)	th	Thai	1,851 (951)	30,549 (15203)
hr	Croatian	1,398 (1119)	22,430 (13583)	tr	Turkish	2,059 (807)	32,240 (23667)
id	Indonesian	1,813 (964)	26,634 (18564)	tt	Tagalog	1,149 (779)	23,648 (14139)
it	Italian	1,743 (701)	51,461 (20832)	uk	Ukrainian	1,023 (758)	35,552 (32014)
ja	Japanese	383 (275)	21,349 (14694)	zh	Chinese	662 (245)	10,614 (6338)
jv	Javanese	1,118 (855)	14,033 (10810)				

4. Evaluation methods

Each submitted summary was scored both manually and using auto-mated methods. The latter methods were ROUGE-n for $n = 1, 2, 3, 4$, and MeMoG/NPowER.[8] All of these methods compare the candidate summary to the gold-standard summary, which is the lead section at the beginning of the article. ROUGE-n, for example, is a measure of the percentage of phrases of length n that are contained in the gold-standard summary. The formula for ROUGE-n is as follows:

$$\text{ROUGE-}n = \frac{\sum_{S \in \{ReferenceSummaries\}} \sum_{gram_n \in S} Count_{match}(gram_n)}{\sum_{S \in \{ReferenceSummaries\}} \sum_{gram_n \in S} Count(gram_n)}.$$

The comparison is done with each reference summary individually, and the maximum match percentage is reported as the score, which is the standard option used for evaluation of summaries. Note for the MSS task there is only one reference summary for each document. Although ROUGE-n can be calculated for any positive number n, the variants of ROUGE-n used most often are ROUGE-1 and ROUGE-2. We also include ROUGE-3 and ROUGE-4 as Ref. 9 demonstrated for the TAC text summarization eval-uation ROUGE-3 and ROUGE-4 better predict human judgments of a summary's quality.

MeMoG first builds a graph for each summary (candidate summary and gold-standard summary) based on n-gram counts and compares the two using graph similarity metrics. The big difference here is that the n-grams used by MeMoG are character n-grams and those used by ROUGE-n are word n-grams.

NPowER (n-gram graph Powered Evaluation via Regression) is a sum-mary evaluation method based on the linear combination of surface (n-gram graph) methods (AutoSummENG and MeMoG). The linear combination was built from training data with the target being individual summary scores and the objective function being summary-level correlation with human scores (in contrast to many other automatic scoring systems which optimize for system-level correlation such as Ref. 10). NPowER has been shown to be highly competitive when aiming to estimate two different human evaluation measures (responsiveness and Pyramid score) on the summary level.

Since automated evaluation methods are not yet perfect, human evalu-ation is still a necessary part of summarization evaluation. For the human evaluation, pairs of summaries were judged simultaneously according to several different measures of quality and one of three possible decisions resulted for each measure. The human who read the summaries would decide if one summary was significantly better than the other, and if so, which one. The human's decision was essentially one of $\{>, =, <\}$. The four measures decided by the humans were quality, non-redundancy, coherence, and focus. These measures were inspired by the measures used in the past at DUC and TAC and are defined as follows:

- **Quality**: The overall quality of the summary.
- **Non-redundancy**: There should be no unnecessary repetition in the summary. Unnecessary repetition might take the form of whole sentences that are repeated, or repeated facts, or the repeated use of a noun or noun phrase (e.g., "Bill Clinton") when a pronoun ("he") would suffice.
- **Coherence**: The summary should not just be a heap of related information, but should build from sentence to sentence to a coherent body of information about a topic.
- **Focus**: The summary should have a focus; sentences should only contain information that is related to the rest of the summary.

There are several ways to evaluate an automated evaluation method. Since these methods are designed to predict a human score, any measure of success will be based on the level of agreement between the automatic score and the human score. In several DUC and TAC evaluations, Pearson correlation was used to measure success.

In addition, measures are designed to test the directionality of paired comparisons between summaries from two systems, that is which of two summaries is preferred if any? In this realm, both human and automatic scores are used to test the difference between each pair of systems. A significance test is performed separately with the automatic scores and human scores. This series of results is then evaluated using traditional confusion matrix scores such as precision and recall.

When using a significance test of the equality of two systems (or the means or medians), it is best to use a paired test.[9] Paired tests are known to provide the most power when comparing systems in this setting.[9] The human evaluation was done by pairwise comparison of summaries, thus the scores are already in the form of a paired comparison, as such it is then natural to use a paired test. We would have preferred to use a Wilcoxon signed rank test here, but since the scores are directional only and have no actual numerical value, that test cannot be applied. The sign test, however, works directly with directional data. The first step of the sign test is normally to subtract corresponding component scores and record the sign of the difference. Ties are thrown out, and the remaining data is used with the binomial distribution to see if one direction occurs significantly more often than the other.

For the automatic metrics, the scoring process involves a standard application of the Wilcoxon signed rank test.[11] It is designed to test whether the median of a symmetric population is a specific value θ_0. In the case of comparing two summarization systems, X and Y, the first thing we do in this paired context is compute $Z_i = Y_i - X_i$. Then, in order to test whether $P(X > Y) = P(X < Y)$, we use the signed-rank test and test whether the median of $Z_1, \ldots, Z_n$ is 0. One additional assumption for this test is that the input data are continuous, such that $P(Z_i = 0) = 0$. This is usually the case for the automatic metrics we are using, but if a zero does arise, it is dropped from the sample.

The Wilcoxon signed rank test statistic is then defined as:

$$W = \sum_{i=1}^{n} \psi_i R_i$$

where R_i is the rank of $|Z_i|$ among $|Z_1|, \ldots, |Z_n|$, and

$$\psi_i = \begin{cases} 1, & \text{if } Z_i > 0, \\ 0, & \text{if } Z_i < 0. \end{cases}$$

Since $E(W) = \frac{n(n+1)}{4}$, we reject H_0 when W is sufficiently far from this value. For small sample sizes, this can be determined by tabulated values available in statistics textbooks, and for large sample sizes, the normal approximation is used.

5. The 2015 and 2017 MSS tasks and teams

The 2015 and 2017 MSS tasks each consisted of approximately 40 languages. For each language 30 bodies of Wikipedia featured articles were provided as both a flat text file and an XML formatted file. The latter made it easy for systems to identify paragraphs, sections, and sub-sections of the document. For each document a target summary length was specified.

In 2015 a single baseline of the article was created simply by truncating the body of the article to its target summary length, i.e., a lead summary based on the body of the document. In 2017 the *Hierarchical Sentence Interweaving* system, submitted by team CCS in 2015 was used as an additional baseline. (see Section 5.1.5 for a description). In addition to the baselines an oracle summary was included for both years, which approximates the best unigram sentence extract. See Section 5.1.10 for more details.

5.1. *The 2015 MSS task and teams*

5.1.1. *Task description*

Each participating system of the 2015 MSS task was to compute a summary for each document in at least two of the dataset's 38 languages. No restrictions were placed on the languages that could be chosen (though all participants chose English as one of their languages). To remove any potential bias in the evaluation of generated summaries that were too small, a target summary length was specified for each document, which was the human summary length in characters, and generated summaries were expected to be close to it. For evaluation purposes a participant's summary was truncated to the target summary length if necessary.

5.1.2. *Teams*

Seven teams submitted the results for over 23 summarization systems. The teams are denoted by BGU-SCE-M, BGU-SCE-P, CCS, EXB, LCS-IESI, NTNU, and UA-DLSI; for brevity their associated systems are denoted by a number appended to the team name. For example, team BGU-SCE-P submitted three variations, which will be denoted BGU-SCE-P-1, BGU-SCE-P-2, and BGU-SCE-P-3. Table 3 contains the team names, the number of systems submitted, and languages submitted by each team.

Table 3.   Teams, systems, and languages.

Team	Systems	Languages
BGU-SCE-M	5	ar, en, he
BGU-SCE-P	3	ar, en, he
CCS	5	all
EXB	1	all
LCS-IESI	1	all
NTNU	1	all
UA-DLSI	6	de, en, es

We now give a brief summary of the systems that participated in the MSS task of MultiLing 2015. More details on these systems can be found at the MultiLing web site.[g]

5.1.3. *Team BGU-SCE-M*

Team BGU-SCE-M submitted five submissions for each of the languages Arabic (ar), English (en), and Hebrew (he). The system's name is MUSEEC, which is a multilingual text summarization platform built upon the MUSE (MUltilingual Sentence Extractor) algorithm.[6] Leveraging their previous work,[12] where the authors identified 31 language independent statistical features, which fall into three base categories: structure, vector, and graph. The features are employed by a genetic algorithm which was trained and five variations were submitted to MultiLing 2015 as given below:

- BGU-SCE-M-1 MUSE basic (trained on clean files).
- BGU-SCE-M-2 MUSE extended (trained on source files and DUC'02 corpus).
- BGU-SCE-M-3 MUSE basic + AR (trained on source files).
- BGU-SCE-M-4 MUSE basic + AR (trained on clean files).
- BGU-SCE-M-5 MUSE basic (trained on source files).

5.1.4. *Team BGU-SCE-P*

Team BGU-SCE-P submitted three submissions for each of the languages Arabic (ar), English (en), and Hebrew (he).[13] Their approach employs approximating the bounded maximum coverage formulation of text summarization, which can be viewed as an integer programming formulation, as a linear program. As such the method is called a polytope model of text summarization. Three linear objective functions were studied and submitted to MultiLing 2015 maximal sentence relevance (based on a cosine similarity score), a weighted sum of bigrams (inspired by the work of Gillick *et al.* (2008)),[14] and maximal relevance with frequent itemsets. The approach is very efficient and generally performs as well as the integer programming solution, which are more costly to compute.

---

[g]http://multiling.iit.demokritos.gr/pages/view/1573/multiling-2015-proceedings-adden dum.

5.1.5. Team CCS

CCS1: IBNMF A term-weighting method using an interval bounded non-negative matrix factorization (IBNMF).[15] It uses the output of a nonnegative matrix factorization (NNMF) from 20 random starts as initial input to IBNMF. Random starts are beneficial as IBNMF is a non-convex nonlinear optimization problem and more than one start can improve the quality. The sums of the rows of the resulting factorization are used as estimates for the term weights.

CCS2: Nonnegative Matrix Factorization A nonnegative matrix factorization of a term sentence matrix can be used for dimensionality reduction and as such is another alternative to improve over term frequency.[15] NNMF, much like the method of latent semantics analysis, requires a selection of the dimension k for the rank approximation of the term-by-sentence matrix. CCS2 used the method of alternating least squares to compute an approximate factorization $A \approx WH$, where W has k columns and H has k row. The dimension k was chosen based on experiments with the training data. The term-weights are simply the row sums of WH.

CCS3: Personalized Term Rank (PTR) The personalized term rank used in 2013 by Conroy *et al.*,[15] is a variant of TextRank,[16] that uses the high mutual information terms in the computation of the term rank. The personalization vector is simply the normalized term frequency. Thus the resulting stationary vector will reflect not only the frequency of the terms in the document but also the co-occurrence of the terms in the sentences.

CCS4: Term Frequency (TF) Term frequency and its variants are a commonly used term-weight for summarization, information retrieval, and keyword identification tasks. The term frequency f_i of term i, is defined as the count of the number of times i appears in all sentences.

CCS5: Hierarchical Sentence Interweaving To assess how much the structure of a large document alone can contribute to generating a summary, an algorithm that computes a summary of a document using only the hierarchical tree structure of the document's sections, paragraphs, and sentences was developed. The algorithm computes a summary by hierarchically interweaving the sentences of the paragraphs and sections of the document and does not perform any statistical analysis of the document, or the dataset.

The algorithm will be demonstrated using the mock document listed below; within it each line represents a paragraph.

Paragraph 1: Sentence a. Sentence b. Sentence c.
Paragraph 2: Sentence d. Sentence e.

Section 1
Paragraph 3: Sentence f. Sentence g.
Paragraph 4: Sentence h. Sentence i. Sentence j.

Section 1.1
Paragraph 5: Sentence k. Sentence l.
Paragraph 6: Sentence m. Sentence n.

Section 1.2
Paragraph 7: Sentence o. Sentence p.
Paragraph 8: Sentence q.
Paragraph 9: Sentence r.

The algorithm recursively interweaves the sentences of the paragraphs at the greatest depth in the tree representation of the document. For the document above the paragraphs in Sections 1.1 and 1.2 are at the greatest depth so they are individually interweaved forming the new document shown below.

Paragraph 1: Sentence a. Sentence b. Sentence c.
Paragraph 2: Sentence d. Sentence e.

Section 1
Paragraph 3: Sentence f. Sentence g.
Paragraph 4: Sentence h. Sentence i. Sentence j.

Section 1.1
Paragraphs 5,6: Sentence k. Sentence m. Sentence l. Sentence n.

Section 1.2
Paragraphs 7,8,9: Sentence o. Sentence q. Sentence r. Sentence p.

Now the paragraphs at the greatest depth are Paragraphs 3 and 4 at the top of Section 1 and the newly interweaved paragraphs in Sections 1.1 and 1.2. Interveaving those paragraphs yields the new document shown below.

Paragraph 1: Sentence a. Sentence b. Sentence c.
Paragraph 2: Sentence d. Sentence e.

Section 1
Paragraph 3-9: Sentence f. Sentence h. Sentence k. Sentence o. Sentence g. Sentence i. Sentence m. Sentence q. Sentence j. Sentence l. Sentence r. Sentence n. Sentence p.

Finally the two paragraphs at the top of the document and the interweaved paragraphs in Section 1 are interweaved yielding the final ordering of the sentences in the document below.

Paragraphs 1-9: Sentence a. Sentence d. Sentence f. Sentence b. Sentence e. Sentence h. Sentence c. Sentence k. Sentence o. Sentence g. Sentence i. Sentence m. Sentence q. Sentence j. Sentence l. Sentence r. Sentence n. Sentence p.

The summary is obtained from this final document by truncating its character length to the specified length.

5.1.6. *Team EXB*

Team EXB submitted one system, which used their proprietary language pre-processing, which was language dependent in conjunction with TextRank to select a subset of good sentences to form a summary.[17] For each document to be summarized a graph is generated based on sentence similarity. Sentence similarity was computed using a simple bag of words and an edge between sentences exists if the cosine similarity exceeds a threshold of 0.3. This method of similarity was compared with three other approaches; however, the team found this simple method performed best over the set of 38 languages.

5.1.7. *Team LCS-IESI*

Team LSC-IESI submitted one system, AllSummarizer[18] for all of the languages of the task. Their method uses a sentence clustering algorithm to define topics, where each sentence is represented by its unigram and bigram counts. The clustering is a greedy method which clusters sentences based on closeness as measured by cosine similarity. Each sentence is scored on how well it covers the set of topics, employing a naive Bayes classifier trained on the clusters. A subset of the sentence is then selected so as to maximize coverage and minimize redundancy by iteratively selecting sentences in order of score but whose cosine similarity with previously selected sentences is below a specified threshold.

5.1.8. *Team UA-DLSI*

Team UA-DLSI submitted six variations for each of German (de), English (en), and Spanish (es).[19] Their approach is to use principal component analysis (PCA) to determine the most important key terms. This approach uses the Stanford Named Entity Recognizer to extract named entities. These are used to define the terms of a term-sentence matrix upon which PCA is applied. The concepts of the document are defined by the principal components. Two strategies were tried to greedily cover the concepts, one gave preference to the position in the document while the second did not. The six submission submitted by the team were[19]

- UA-DLSI-1: generic language-independent summarizer considering all words in the documents.
- UA-DLSI-2: topic-focused summarizer, including lexical–semantic knowledge into the interpretation stage, but considering only the words included in the headings of the documents.
- UA-DLSI-3: language-independent summarizer considering only the words included in the headings of the documents.
- UA-DLSI-4: generic summarizer, including lexical–semantic knowledge into the interpretation stage, and considering all words in the documents.
- UA-DLSI-4: focused language-independent summarizer considering only the words included in the headings of the documents.
- UA-DLSI-6: topic-focused summarizer, including lexical–semantic knowledge into the interpretation stage, and considering all words in the documents.

5.1.9. *Team NTNU*

Team NTNU submitted one submission for all of the languages of the task.[h] Their approach investigated two word embedding models, a continuous vector space approach. The word embedding considered were continuous bag-of-words (CBOW)[20] and paragraph embedding.[21] Sentences are selected via a greedy algorithm with a threshold to reduce redundancy.

5.1.10. *Preprocessing for evaluation*

For the evaluation the baseline summary for each article in the dataset was the lead portion of article's body text having the target summary length. An oracle summary was also computed for each article using the combinatorial covering algorithm by selecting sentences from its body text

---

[h]This information is a summary of the unpublished paper available at http://multi ling.iit.demokritos.gr/file/view/1591/the-ntnu-summarization-system-at-multiling-2015-hisao-tsung-hung-kai-wun-shih-and-berlin-chen.

to cover the tokens in the human summary using as few sentences as possible until its size exceeded the human summary, upon which it was truncated.[22]

Preprocessing of all the submitted and human summaries was performed, depending on the language, either by the Basis Technology's Rosette software[23] or the Natural Language Toolkit.[24] Stop words were kept, as traditionally done for automatic summarization evaluation. Table 4 lists the software package used for each language and if lemmatization was performed, indicating Basis for Basis Technology's Rosette and NLTK for the Natural Language Toolkit. For each summary the preprocessing steps were: (1) all multiple white-spaces and control characters are converted to a single space (2) any leading space is removed (3) the resulting text string is truncated to the human summary length (4) the text is tokenized and, if possible, lemmatized (5) all tokens without a letter or number are discarded (6) all remaining tokens are lowercased.

5.2. The 2017 MSS task and teams

5.2.1. Task description

Each participating system of the task was to compute a summary for each document in at least three of the datasets from 41 languages. As in Multi-Ling 2015 the human summary length in characters was provided for each test document and generated summaries were trimmed if necessary to the length of the human summary.

5.2.2. Teams

Three teams submitted to MSS 2017 and there was a total of 14 summarization submissions between them. The teams are denoted by CIST, SWAP, and TeamMD; for brevity their associated systems are denoted by a number appended to the team name. Table 5 contains the total systems and languages submitted for each team.

5.2.3. TeamMD: OCCAMS, Doc Sections, and N-Gram LMs

TeamMD had four submissions. Each submission used Optimal Combinatorial Covering Algorithm for Multi-document Summarization (OCCAMS) which selects sentences with an approximate solution to the weighted bounded maximal coverage problem.[22] OCCAMS needs each sentence to be tokenized into terms as well as a global weight for each term. The four submissions used one of four language model term weights either a unigram or bigram language model in conjunction with a document or section language

Table 4. The table lists the software package used to process each language and whether or not lemmatization was performed on the extracted tokens.

ISO	Language	Package	Lemma
af	Afrikaans	Basis	✓
ar	Arabic	Basis	✓
bg	Bulgarian	NLTK	
ca	Catalan	NLTK	
cs	Czech	Basis	✓
de	German	Basis	✓
el	Greek	Basis	✓
en	English	Basis	✓
eo	Esperanto	NLTK	
es	Spanish	Basis	✓
eu	Basque	NLTK	
fa	Persian	NLTK	✓
fi	Finnish	NLTK	✓
fr	French	Basis	·
he	Hebrew	NLTK	
hr	Croatian	NLTK	
hu	Hungarian	Basis	✓
id	Indonesian	NLTK	
it	Italian	Basis	✓
ja	Japanese	Basis	✓
ka	Georgian	Basis	✓
ko	Korean	NLTK	
ms	Malay	NLTK	
nl	Dutch	Basis	✓
no	Norwegian-Bokmal	Basis	✓
pl	Polish	Basis	✓
pt	Portuguese	Basis	✓
ro	Romanian	Basis	✓
ru	Russian	Basis	✓
sh	Serbo-Croatian	NLTK	
sk	Slovak	NLTK	
sl	Slovenian	NLTK	
sr	Serbian	NLTK	
sv	Swedish	Basis	✓
th	Thai	Basis	✓
tr	Turkish	Basis	✓
vi	Vietnamese	NLTK	
zh	Chinese	Basis	✓

Table 5.   The table lists the team names, the total systems submitted, and the languages covered by the systems.

Team	Systems	Languages
CIST	5	all
SWAP	5	de, en, es, fr, it
TeamMD	4	all

model as proposed in Conroy and Davis (2017).[25] The document language model uses the probability a unigram or bigram based on its occurrence in the document, with the weights normalized to be between 0 and 100. The section language model builds a unigram or bigram language model for each section of the Wikipedia feature article and then averages these language models, so attempting to balance the coverage of each section's terms. The four priorities of the submissions for TeamMD were as follows:

- Priority 1: OCCAMS using a bigram Language Model (LM) based on the document sections.
- Priority 2: OCCAMS with a document bigram LM.
- Priority 3: OCCAMS with a unigram Section LM.
- Priority 4: OCCAMS with a unigram LM.

5.2.4.   *CIST: Sampling diverse sentences*

Team CIST uses diverse sentence sampling methods to model the multilingual single document summarization problem. The diversity of sentences is reflected by sentence quality and similarity. The quality of each sentence is estimated using various features, including hierarchical topic model (HTM), sentence position (SP), title similarity (TS), sentence coverage (SC), and sentence length (SL).

Team CIST had five submissions:

- SDS-MSS/HTM: a determinantal point processes (DPPs) model using the HTM score as quality method.
- SDS-MSS/SP: a DPPs model using the SP as quality method.
- SDS-MSS/TS: a DPPs model using the TS as quality method.
- Feature Combination: linear combination of the features HTM, SP, TS, SC, SL, with the parameters learned from the training data.
- Graphical Model: the original LexRank algorithm.[26]

5.2.5. *SWAP: Centroid embeddings*

Team SWAP had five submissions that were linear combinations of derived centroid similarities and sentence length and position.[27] The team made use of word embeddings.

In particular, given a corpus of documents $[D_1, D_2, \ldots]$ and its vocabulary V with $N = |V|$, define the matrix $E \in R^{N,k}$, as a *lookup table*, where $E[w]$ is the word2vec.[20] k dimensional word embedding for a word w in the vocabulary V.

Given a document D to be summarized the following is performed on it:

- Preprocessing: It is split into sentences and stopwords are removed but no stemming is performed.
- Compute the Centroid Embedding: $C = \sum_{w \in D, tfidf(w) > t} E[w]$.
- Compute the Sentence Embedding: $S_j = \sum_{w \in S_j} E[w]$.
- Compute the Sentence Score $sim(C, S_j) = \frac{C^T \cdot S_j}{\|C\| \cdot \|S_j\|}$.

A score for each sentence is computed as follows:

- Always retain the first sentence in the summary.
- Subtract to each word embedding the centroid vector of whole embedding space.
- Combination of four scores:

  (a) sc_1 word2vec centroid similarity
  (b) sc_2 bag-of-words (BOW) centroid similarity
  (c) sc_3 normalized sentence length
  (d) sc_4 normalized sentence position.

- $score(S_j) = \lambda_1 * sc_1 + \lambda_2 * sc_2 + \lambda_3 * sc_3 + \lambda_4 * sc_4$, which for evaluation purposes $\lambda_i = 0$ or 1, generally adding the next strongest score to a running sum of the scores as given in Table 6.

Table 6. The table lists the priority, score function, tf-idf t, and similarity t for the SWAP team submissions where t = threshold.

Priority	Score function	TF-IDF T	Similarity t
1	sc_1	0.3	0.95
2	sc_1	0.2	0.95
3	$sc_1 + sc_2$	0.2	0.95
4	$sc_1 + sc_2 + sc_3$	0.2	0.95
5	$sc_1 + sc_2 + sc_3 + sc_4$	0.2	0.95

5.2.6. *Preprocessing for evaluation*

For the evaluation a baseline summary for each article in the dataset was formed from the lead of the article's body text having the same length as the human summary of the article. A second baseline was the Interweave system submitted by CCS from the 2015 MSS task. (See Section 5.1.5). An oracle summary was also computed for each article using the combinatorial covering algorithm in David *et al.* (2012)[22] by selecting sentences from its body text to cover the tokens in the human summary using as few sentences as possible until its size exceeded the human summary, upon which it was truncated.

6. Results of MSS 2015 and 2017 tasks

For MultiLing 2015 and 2017 both automatic and human evaluation were performed. For automatic evaluation ROUGE-1,2,3,4[28] were performed as well as MeMoG in 2015 and NPowER in 2017.[3] In the 2015 evaluation Basis Technologies tokenization was employed for a number of the languages. For the remaining languages, Python's NLTK tokenizer and stemmer were used to preprocess the submitted summaries prior to their being scored via ROUGE or NPowER. In 2017, we did not have access to Basis Technologies software, so this lack of access gave rise to the opportunity to see what effect preprocessing had on the automatic evaluation method. So, for the 2017 automatic evaluation this preprocessing was not applied. To measure the effect of this change the 2015 data were rescored using the 2017 method which did not have the use of the linguistic preprocessing from Basis Technology's Rosette.

Human evaluation of the summaries was performed for both the 2015 and 2017 data using the same tool to perform pairwise comparison of the submitted summaries relative to the human gold-standard. In the end, the human evaluation is what matters and the automatic methods of evaluation are a stand-in for the human evaluation. In Section 8 a comparison of the 2015 and 2017 methods of automatic evaluation are evaluated based on how well they predict the judgments that the human annotators would make.

6.1. *2015 MSS automatic evaluation*

For the 2015 MSS task summaries were automatically evaluated against the gold-standard summary of each article using ROUGE-1,2,3,4 and MeMoG. For MeMoG the character n-gram size used for each language is the same as in the 2013 pilot task, which are listed in Table 3 of the Pilot Task for the Wikipedia single document summarization.[7] The n-gram size chosen maximizes the standard deviation divided by the mean of the n-gram frequency distribution of the language in the dataset, which maximizes the variability of the distribution n-gram values relative to the mean. A shorter n-gram could inflate the MeMoG scores because of their inherent frequent co-occurrence and a bigger size could penalize MeMoG scores due to their infrequent co-occurrence.

For each language and each metric (ROUGE-1, 2, 3, 4, and MeMoG) we first test if the median score for all the submitted systems and the baseline were the same, i.e., we run a nonparametric analysis of variance test after removing the scores of the oracle system, thus testing if systems without the access of the human summary differed in performance. The last row of Table 7 displays the fraction of times the null hypotheses that the median ROUGE-2, ROUGE-4, and MeMoG scores were equal was rejected, using a rejection threshold of 0.05. Note, in particular for ROUGE-4 there

Table 7. Fraction of times each system significantly out-scored the Lead baseline in ROUGE-2, ROUGE-3, ROUGE-4, and MeMoG.

System	ROUGE-2	ROUGE-3	ROUGE-4	MeMoG
BGU-SCE-M1	2/3	2/3	1/3	1/3
BGU-SCE-M2	1/2	1/2	0/2	1/2
BGU-SCE-M3	1/1	0/1	0/1	1/1
BGU-SCE-M4	1/1	1/1	0/1	1/1
BGU-SCE-M5	1/1	1/1	0/1	1/1
BGU-SCE-P1	0/3	0/3	0/3	0/3
BGU-SCE-P2	2/3	0/3	0/3	1/3
BGU-SCE-P3	2/3	1/3	0/3	0/3
CCS1	20/38	8/38	3/38	19/38
CCS2	21/38	7/38	4/38	19/38
CCS3	21/38	8/38	3/38	19/38
CCS4	20/38	8/38	2/38	20/38
CCS5	23/38	10/38	7/38	20/38
EXB1	15/38	5/38	1/38	11/38
LCS-IESI1	6/38	3/38	2/38	6/38
NTNU1	1/2	0/2	0/2	0/2
UA-DLSI1	2/3	1/3	0/3	2/3
UA-DLSI2	0/3	0/3	0/3	0/3
UA-DLSI3	0/3	0/3	0/3	2/3
UA-DLSI4	1/3	0/3	0/3	2/3
UA-DLSI5	0/3	0/3	0/3	1/3
UA-DLSI6	1/3	0/3	0/3	0/3
ANOVA	25/38	12/38	10/38	21/38

were only 10 out of the 38 languages where the equal median hypothesis was rejected. The remaining rows of the table give the fraction of the time when the null hypothesis was rejected that a given system significantly outperformed the baseline. These tests are performed using a paired Wilcoxon test. We show ROUGE-2 as it is widely reported however we include ROUGE-3 and ROUGE-4 as it has been reported to give more statistical power to discriminant between high performing systems.[9] Based on an analysis of the 2013 multilingual summarization both ROUGE-3 and MeMoG also have good statistical power to predict significant differences in human metrics in the multilingual summarization setting.[i]

Figure 1 gives a scatter plot of ROUGE-3 scores for the oracle, lead, and top scoring system for each team (if applicable) for all languages for which an ANOVA test indicated that there was a significant difference among the submitted systems (i.e., all systems except the oracle). The × symbol gives the scores for the oracle system, which is significantly greater than the

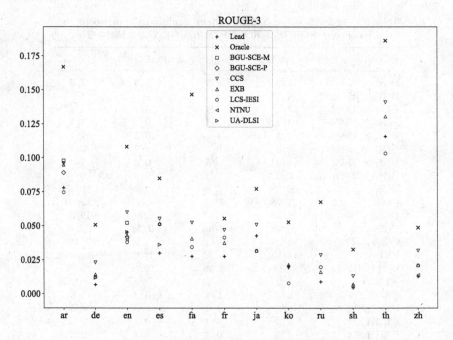

Fig. 1.   ROUGE-3 scores for MSS (2015).

---

[i]ROUGE-4 scores were not available.

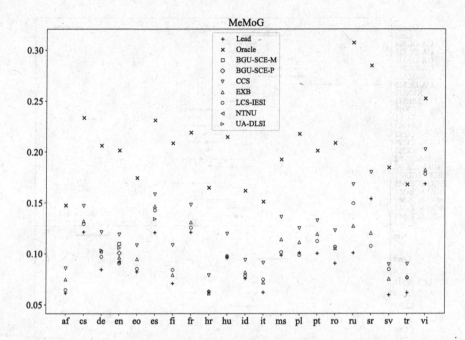

Fig. 2.   MeMoG scores for MSS (2015).

team system scores (for most languages). Figure 2 gives the corresponding scatter plot in the MeMoG metric.

Figure 3 gives an error bar graph of ROUGE-1 scores and 95% confidence intervals for the oracle, lead, and team systems (if applicable) for selected languages. The confidence intervals for the oracle and lead are shown in bold to differentiate those from the team systems. For a given language, the scores for a team are ordered by value; note that the system order for that team can vary based upon the language. Figure 4 gives the corresponding bar graph for ROUGE-2, Figure 5 for ROUGE-3, Figure 6 for ROUGE-4, and Figure 7 for the MeMoG metric.

Note that the ROUGE score is language dependent as the probability distribution of 1, 2, 3, and 4 grams varies across languages. This affect is especially apparent in ideographic languages such as Chinese (zh) and Japanese (ja), which recall were tokenized via Basis Technology's Rosette software. As such, a 1-gram would be one or more ideographic characters.

Although omitted from the plots, the oracle system for Hebrew (he) has a lower ROUGE score than the lead baseline and also in the MeMoG results for Hebrew the oracle and the lead are much closer than expected.

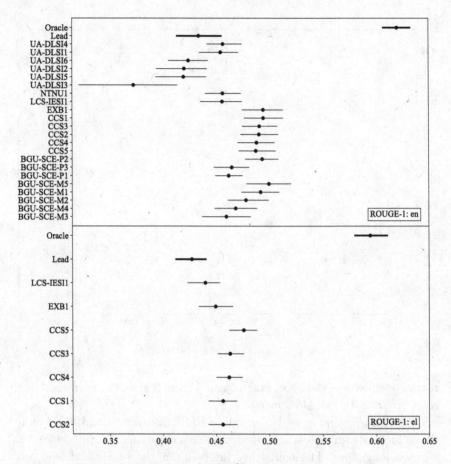

Fig. 3.   ROUGE-1 scores and 95% confidence intervals (2015).

This is believed to be due to a tokenization problem in the application of the Basis tool for this language.

6.2. *2015 MSS human evaluation*

The human evaluation was only performed on the English and Greek languages, as volunteers for the evaluation in 2015 consisted of native speakers in English and Greek. For the evaluation each summary of a document is compared to all the other summaries for responsiveness, non-redundancy, focus, and coherence. For each of these metrics and for the two languages evaluated we compute an aggregate score for each system on each document set summarized. This approach will allow us to perform a non-parametric

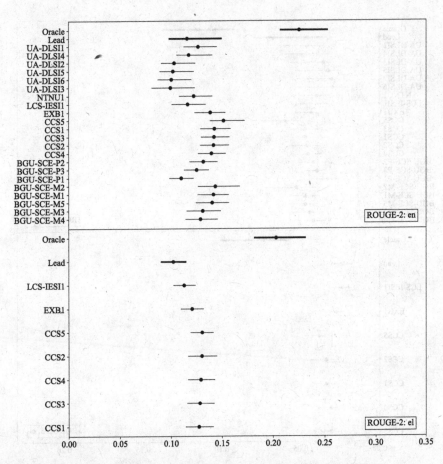

Fig. 4.   ROUGE-2 scores and 95% confidence intervals (2015).

analysis of variance and test the null hypothesis that all systems have the same median performance.[j] In each comparison a system is given a score of 1 if it is chosen to be the preferred summary, a 0 if the other system is preferred and 0.5 if neither system is preferred. To compare two systems we sum all the comparison scores for the system for each language separately. As some documents were judged more than once, the total score is divided by the sum of the number of comparisons made for a system on a document

---

[j]When we reject the null hypothesis the significant differences may be discovered using more powerful paired testing (a sign test for human judgments and Wilcoxon for automatic judgments) as will be done in Section 8.

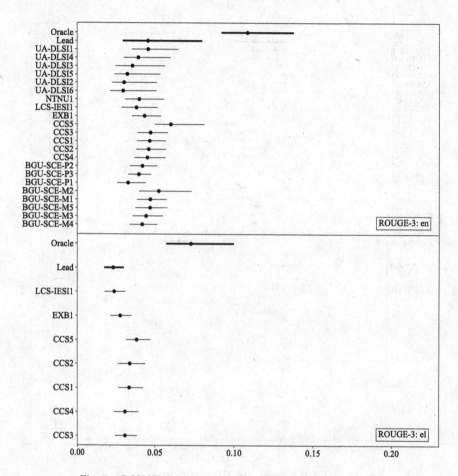

Fig. 5.   ROUGE-3 scores and 95% confidence intervals (2015).

set. Thus, for each document set a system is given a score between 0 and 1. Table 8 gives the mean scores for each metric for both languages evaluated. A non-parametric analysis of variance test was run to test for any significant differences and this test indicates that none of the differences in the mean are significant at the 95% level. Table 9 shows the fraction of times each system significantly out-scored the Weave baseline.

Figures 8 and 9 show how the scores vary in more detail. In these plots the boxes cover the middle 50% of the distribution and the bar in the middle is the median. The notches give the 95% confidence intervals for the median.

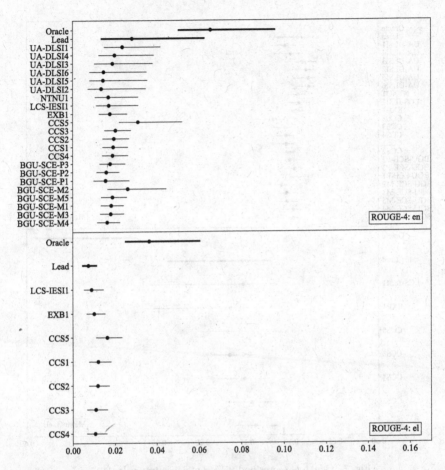

Fig. 6.   ROUGE-4 scores and 95% confidence intervals (2015).

6.3. *2017 MSS automatic evaluation*

Figure 10 gives a scatter plot of the ROUGE-3 scores for the oracle, lead, interweave, and top scoring system for each team (if applicable) for all languages for which an ANOVA test indicated that there was a significant difference among the submitted systems (i.e., all systems except the oracle).[k] The × symbol gives the scores for the oracle system, which is

---

[k]The scores for Thai were divided by two for better visualization as the ROUGE scores are much higher than other languages due to the character based tokenization used for ROUGE scoring. Note there are only 44 characters used in Thai.

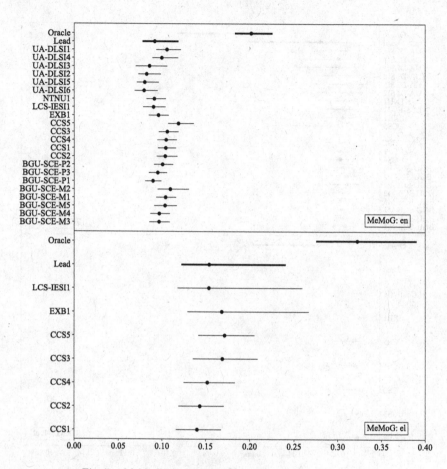

Fig. 7.   MeMoG scores and 95% confidence intervals (2015).

significantly greater than the best team system. Figure 11 gives the corresponding scatter plot in the NPowER metric.

Figure 12 gives a bar graph of ROUGE-1 scores and 95% confidence intervals for the oracle, lead, interweave, and team systems (if applicable) for selected languages. The confidence intervals for the oracle, lead, and interweave are shown in bold to differentiate those systems from the team systems. For a given language, the scores for a team are ordered by value; note that the system order for that team can vary based upon the language. So, we note that a team's best system can vary by language. Figure 13 gives the corresponding bar graph for ROUGE-2, Fig. 14 for ROUGE-3, Fig. 15 for ROUGE-4, and Fig. 16 for the NPowER metric.

Table 8. Human evaluation results for 2015 MSS task.

Lang System	Quality	Non-redundancy	Coherence	Focus
Greek, CCS	0.53	0.40	0.47	0.55
Greek, EXB	0.47	0.57	0.40	0.50
Greek, LCS-IESI	0.50	0.53	0.62	0.45
p-value	9.59e-01	2.68e-01	3.77e-01	7.59e-01
English, BGU-SCE-M	0.48	0.43	0.47	0.43
English, BGU-SCE-P	0.57	0.54	0.63	0.65
English, CCS	0.60	0.47	0.57	0.59
English, EXB	0.49	0.52	0.42	0.49
English, LCS-IESI	0.39	0.49	0.46	0.38
English, NTNU	0.41	0.55	0.38	0.40
English, UA-DLSI	0.55	0.50	0.57	0.56
p-value	5.17e-01	2.35e-01	2.93e-01	2.15e-01

Table 9. Fraction of times each system significantly out-scored the Weave baseline in ROUGE-2, ROUGE-3, ROUGE-4 and NPowER.

System	ROUGE-2	ROUGE-3	ROUGE-4	NPowER
CIST1	3/41	3/41	3/41	7/41
Lead	3/41	3/41	2/41	3/41
Oracle	33/41	24/41	15/41	36/41
SWAP1	0/5	0/5	0/5	1/5
TeamMD1	4/41	3/41	3/41	3/41
ANOVA	34/41	26/41	17/41	37/41

Note that the bar width (confidence interval variance) can change considerably based upon the language, system, and score. Some CIST Priority 4 (CIST4) systems do not have confidence intervals displayed because only one document was summarized (and subsequently scored) for that language.

6.4. *2017 MSS human evaluation*

We now present the results of the human evaluation for 2017 MSS task. In addition, all 30 document summaries for each system's priority 1 submission, the system chosen by the team as their best, were evaluated along with the Interweaving baseline (CCS5 from 2015). To give more confidence of the judgment for English each document set was evaluated by three human judges. Table 10 gives the overall results. We note that almost all the tests

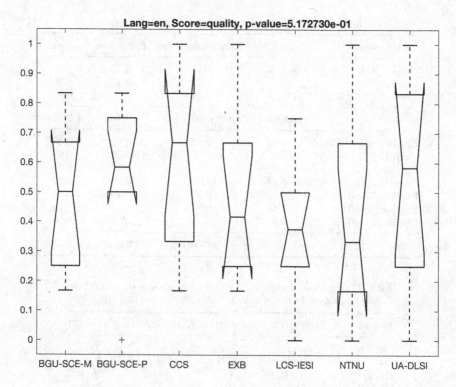

Fig. 8.   Notch box plots for quality of English summaries (2015).

had a significance level of 95% or more and many were extremely significant. As an aside, we note that the single annotator for Italian made the same judgments for quality, non-redundancy, coherence, and focus, i.e. if system A was preferred to system B on quality then the same judgment was made for the other three metrics. For comparison with the 2015 data both notch box plots for English quality and focus are given in Figs. 17 and 18.

7. Scoring 2015 data with 2017 methods

The MSS 2015 data is scored with the 2017 methods to determine if the simplified methods from 2017 provide similar rankings.

Figure 19 gives a scatter plot of the ROUGE-3 scores for the lead and top scoring system for each team (if applicable) from the 2015 MSS task using the 2017 scoring procedure for all languages for which an ANOVA

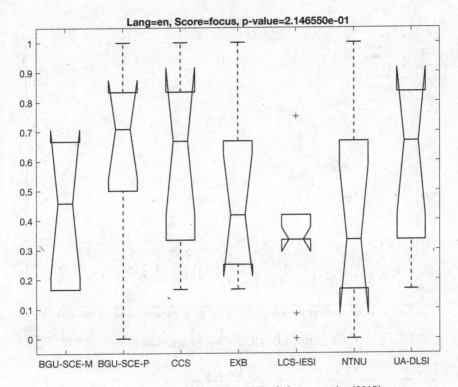

Fig. 9. Notch box plots for focus of English summaries (2015).

test indicated that there was a significant difference among the systems.[1] Figure 20 gives the corresponding scatter plot in the NPowER metric.

Figure 21 gives a bar graph of ROUGE-1 scores and 95% confidence intervals for the lead and team systems (if applicable) for selected languages of the 2015 MSS task submissions using the 2017 scoring. The confidence interval for the lead is shown in bold to differentiate that system from the team systems. Figure 22 gives the corresponding bar graph for ROUGE-2, Fig. 23 for ROUGE-3, Fig. 24 for ROUGE-4, and Fig. 25 for the NPowER metric.

While scoring the MSS 2015 data with the 2015 methods versus the 2017 methods changed some things, the plots were not vastly different. As expected, the oracle continued to significantly out score the systems and is not included in the figures for the 2015 data scored with the 2017

---

[1]The scores for Thai were divided by two for better visualization.

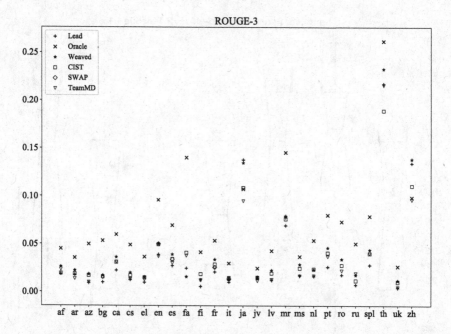

Fig. 10.   ROUGE-3 scores for MSS (2017).

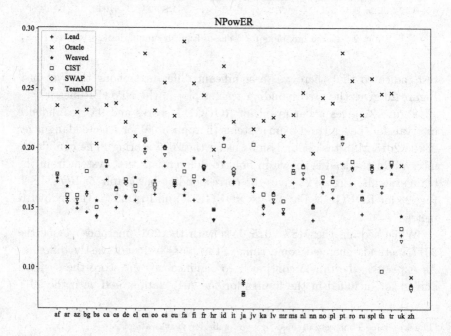

Fig. 11.   NPoWER scores for MSS (2017).

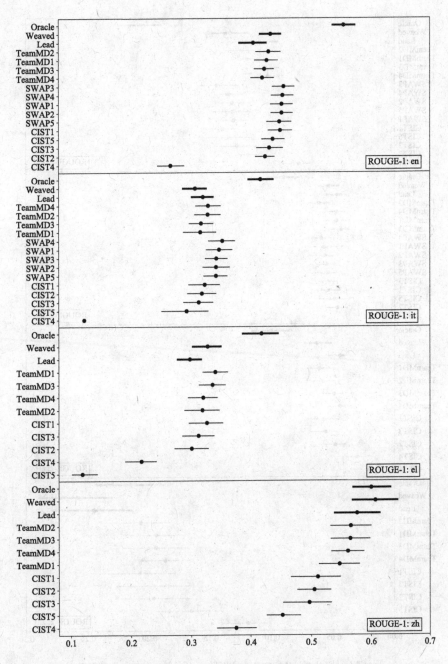

Fig. 12.   ROUGE-1 scores and 95% confidence intervals (2017).

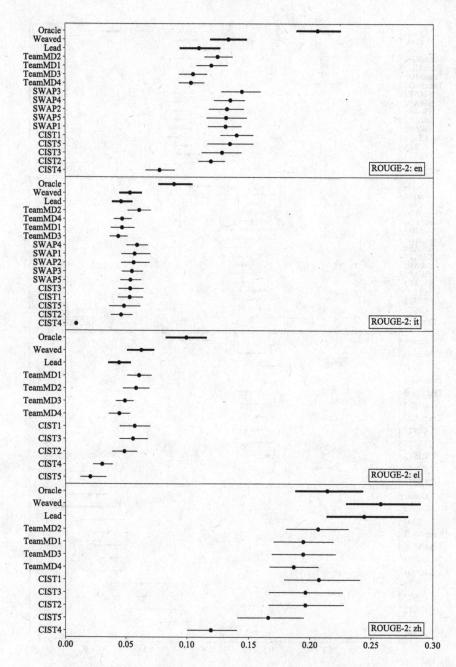

Fig. 13.   ROUGE-2 scores and 95% confidence intervals (2017).

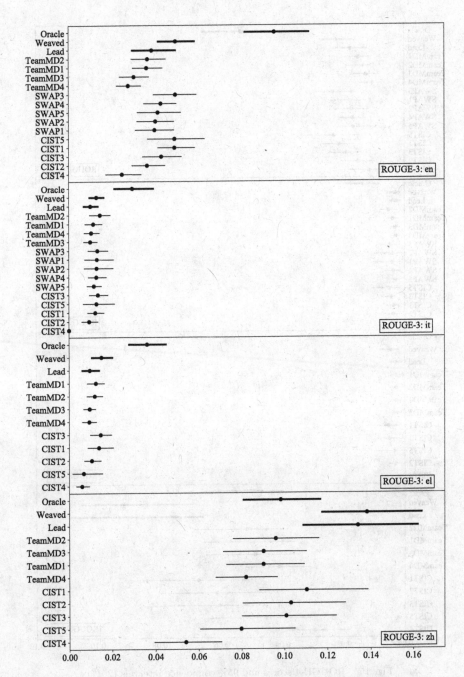

Fig. 14.   ROUGE-3 scores and 95% confidence intervals (2017).

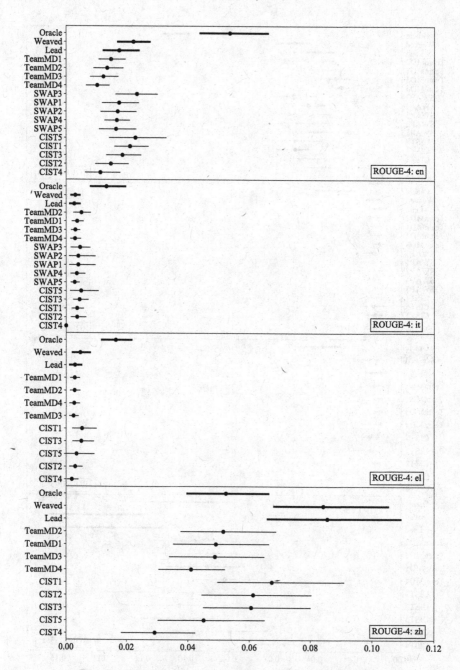

Fig. 15.   ROUGE-4 scores and 95% confidence intervals (2017).

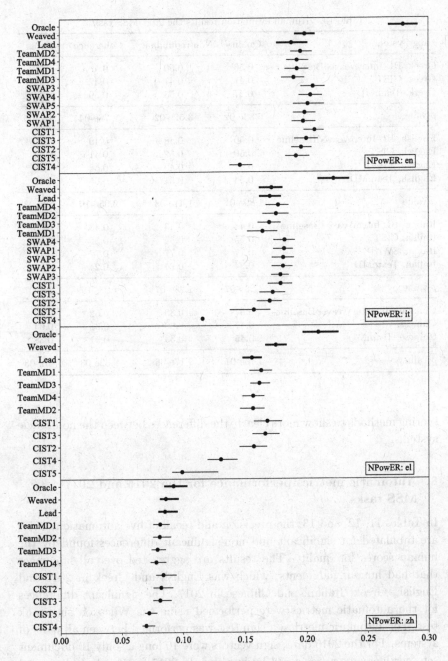

Fig. 16.   NPoWER scores and 95% confidence intervals (2017).

Table 10.   Human evaluation results the 2017 MSS task.

Lang System	Quality	Non-redundancy	Coherence	Focus
Greek, BL-InterWeavedBaseline	0.56	0.50	0.49	0.57
Greek, CIST	0.47	0.47	0.42	0.49
Greek, TeamMD	0.47	0.53	0.59	0.44
p-value	6.83e-02	3.52e-02	2.78e-04	1.43e-03
English, BL-InterWeavedBaseline	0.50	0.48	0.40	0.39
English, CIST	0.50	0.52	0.41	0.44
English, SWAP	0.47	0.49	0.54	0.60
English, TeamMD	0.54	0.51	0.65	0.57
p-value	1.89e-01	1.41e-03	3.05e-10	1.53e-08
Italian, BL-InterWeavedBaseline	0.43	0.43	0.43	0.43
Italian, CIST	0.55	0.55	0.55	0.55
Italian, SWAP	0.77	0.77	0.77	0.77
Italian, TeamMD	0.24	0.24	0.24	0.24
p-value	1.28e-07	1.28e-07	1.28e-07	1.28e-07
Chinese, BL-InterWeavedBaseline	0.57	0.38	0.62	0.47
Chinese, CIST	0.47	0.80	0.38	0.64
Chinese, TeamMD	0.45	0.33	0.51	0.38
p-value	4.16e-01	2.17e-06	2.32e-03	6.47e-03

scoring methods to show more clearly the differences between the non-oracle systems.

8. Automatic metrics performance for the 2015 and 2017 MSS tasks

In Tables 11, 12, and 13, the precision and recall of five automatic metrics are tabulated for significant and non-significant differences found by the human scores for quality. The results are aggregated over all languages that had human judgments, which was English and Greek in 2015 and English, Greek, Italian, and Chinese in 2017. The significant differences for the automatic metrics were performed using the Wilcoxon sign rank test. For automatic metrics, a sign test was performed between all pairs of systems. For the 2015 data, sign vectors were 10 long as only 10 document sets per language were scored by humans. In 2017 for Greek, Italian, and Chinese all 30 document sets were evaluated by at least one human so

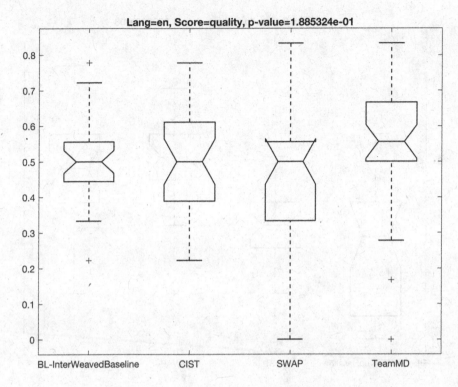

Fig. 17.   Notch box plots for quality of English summaries (2017).

the vectors would be 30 long or more in those cases where more than one judgment was made. For the English data the vectors are all 90 long as each document set and each pair were judged by three human annotators. Note that the 2015 summaries were scored in two different ways, and Tables 11 and 12 illustrate the resulting differences. The scoring changed some things, but the tables are not vastly different.

Table 13 shows how well the automatic metrics match the human annotation in terms of when a significant difference is found between a pair of systems. MeMoG/NPowER seems to perform best at having its conclusions match those of the humans. ROUGE-1 follows closely behind, but the other ROUGEs drop off quickly. ROUGE-2, ROUGE-3, and ROUGE-4, for example, do not find any of the five significant differences found by the humans. As stated earlier, significant differences in human scores are defined to be when a sign test of their pairwise scores gives a p-value less than 0.05. The automatic metrics, on the other hand, conclude a significant

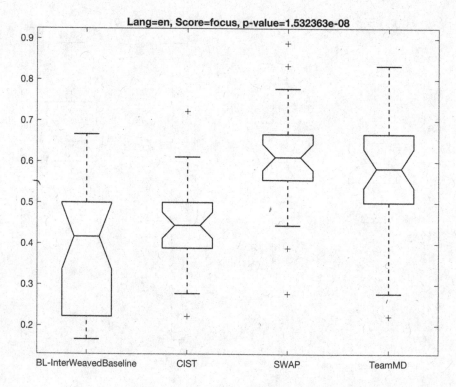

Fig. 18.   Notch box plots for focus of English summaries (2017).

difference has been found if a signed-rank test between each system's scores gives a p-value below the same threshold, 0.05.

8.1. *Tables broken out by language and measure*

In Tables 14–25, the results are separated out by each different language and each different human-scored measure. This has the effect of reducing the amount of comparisons taking place, but now we can see which languages are tougher for which systems. For example, in Table 14, we can see that ROUGE-4 performed better on English than Greek, but every other system performed in the opposite direction. This is true almost throughout Tables 14–21. In Tables 22–25, on the other hand, the results are much more varied. There is a small trend of ROUGE-3 and ROUGE-4 performing better on English than on the other languages, but it does not hold up on every table. These last four tables have such small fractions and so many dimensions, that it is hard to draw any substantial conclusions.

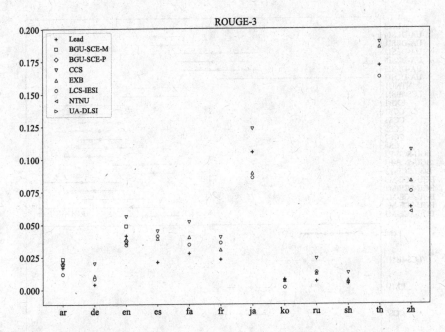

Fig. 19.   ROUGE-3 scores for MSS (2015 with 2017 scoring method).

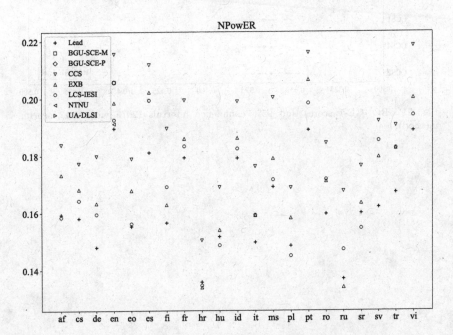

Fig. 20.   NPoWER scores for MSS (2015 with 2017 scoring method).

322 *J. M. Conroy et al.*

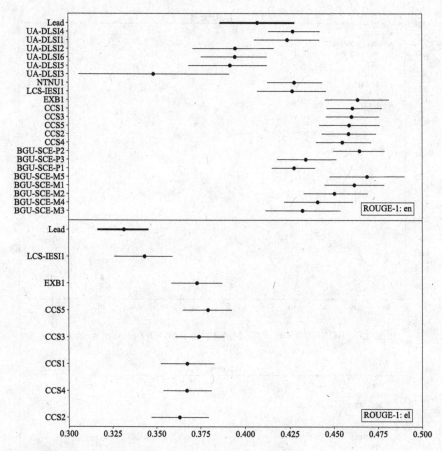

Fig. 21. ROUGE-1 scores and 95% confidence intervals (2015 with 2017 scoring method).

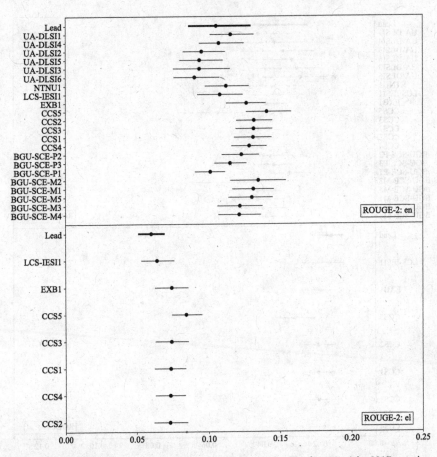

Fig. 22. ROUGE-2 scores and 95% confidence intervals (2015 with 2017 scoring method).

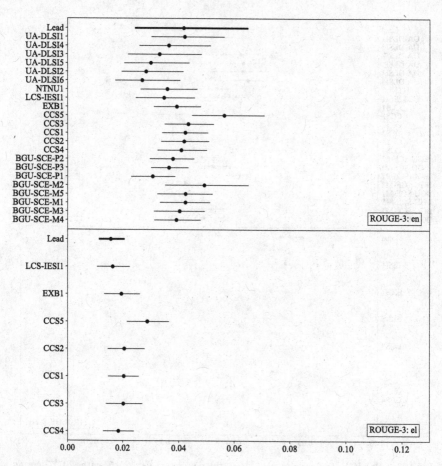

Fig. 23. ROUGE-3 scores and 95% confidence intervals (2015 with 2017 scoring method).

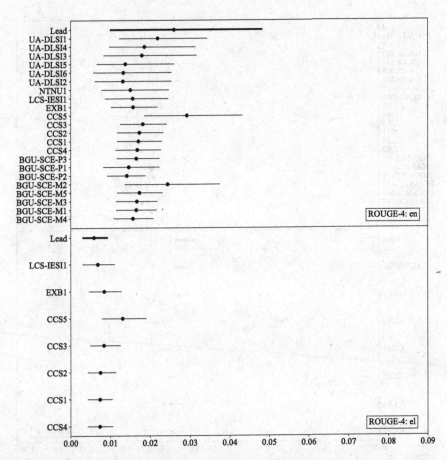

Fig. 24. ROUGE-4 scores and 95% confidence intervals (2015 with 2017 scoring method).

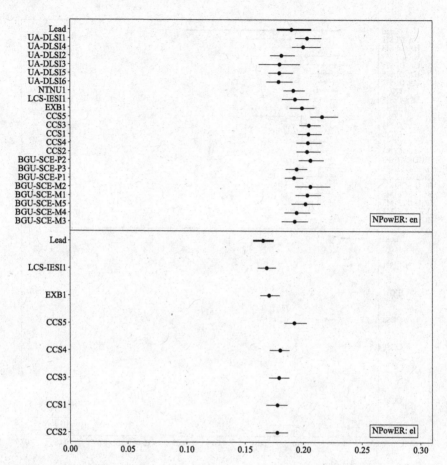

Fig. 25. NPoWER scores and 95% confidence intervals (2015 with 2017 scoring method).

Table 11.   Precision and recall of auto-metrics relative human evaluation: 2015 data scored with 2015 methods.

System	Non-sig prec	Non-sig recall	Sig prec	Sig recall
MeMoG	22/22	22/30	0/8	0/0
ROUGE-1	13/13	13/30	0/17	0/0
ROUGE-2	13/13	13/30	0/17	0/0
ROUGE-3	16/16	16/30	0/14	0/0
ROUGE-4	27/27	27/30	0/3	0/0

Table 12.   Precision and recall of auto-metrics relative human evaluation: 2015 data scored with 2017 methods.

System	Non-sig prec	Non-sig recall	Sig prec	Sig recall
NPowER	19/19	19/30	0/11	0/0
ROUGE-1	11/11	11/30	0/19	0/0
ROUGE-2	15/15	15/30	0/15	0/0
ROUGE-3	21/21	21/30	0/9	0/0
ROUGE-4	29/29	29/30	0/1	0/0

Table 13.   Precision and recall of auto-metrics relative human evaluation: 2017 data scored with 2017 methods.

System	Non-sig prec	Non-sig recall	Sig prec	Sig recall
NPowER	9/11	9/13	3/7	3/5
ROUGE-1	12/15	12/13	2/3	2/5
ROUGE-2	12/17	12/13	0/1	0/5
ROUGE-3	7/12	7/13	0/6	0/5
ROUGE-4	8/13	8/13	0/5	0/5

Table 14.   Precision and recall of auto-metrics relative human evaluation: 2015 data with 2015 scoring for quality.

System	Non-sig prec	Non-sig recall	Sig prec	Sig recall	Language
MeMoG	14/14	14/21	0/7	0/0	en
MeMoG	3/3	3/3	0/0	0/0	el
ROUGE-1	9/9	9/21	0/12	0/0	en
ROUGE-1	2/2	2/3	0/1	0/0	el
ROUGE-2	9/9	9/21	0/12	0/0	en
ROUGE-2	2/2	2/3	0/1	0/0	el
ROUGE-3	13/13	13/21	0/8	0/0	en
ROUGE-3	2/2	2/3	0/1	0/0	el
ROUGE-4	20/20	20/21	0/1	0/0	en
ROUGE-4	2/2	2/3	0/1	0/0	el

Table 15. Precision and recall of auto-metrics relative human evaluation: 2015 data with 2015 scoring for non-redundancy.

System	Non-sig prec	Non-sig recall	Sig prec	Sig recall	Language
MeMoG	14/14	14/21	0/7	0/0	en
MeMoG	3/3	3/3	0/0	0/0	el
ROUGE-1	9/9	9/21	0/12	0/0	en
ROUGE-1	2/2	2/3	0/1	0/0	el
ROUGE-2	9/9	9/21	0/12	0/0	en
ROUGE-2	2/2	2/3	0/1	0/0	el
ROUGE-3	13/13	13/21	0/8	0/0	en
ROUGE-3	2/2	2/3	0/1	0/0	el
ROUGE-4	20/20	20/21	0/1	0/0	en
ROUGE-4	2/2	2/3	0/1	0/0	el

Table 16. Precision and recall of auto-metrics relative human evaluation: 2015 data with 2015 scoring for coherence.

System	Non-sig prec	Non-sig recall	Sig prec	Sig recall	Language
MeMoG	14/14	14/21	0/7	0/0	en
MeMoG	3/3	3/3	0/0	0/0	el
ROUGE-1	9/9	9/21	0/12	0/0	en
ROUGE-1	2/2	2/3	0/1	0/0	el
ROUGE-2	9/9	9/21	0/12	0/0	en
ROUGE-2	2/2	2/3	0/1	0/0	el
ROUGE-3	13/13	13/21	0/8	0/0	en
ROUGE-3	2/2	2/3	0/1	0/0	el
ROUGE-4	20/20	20/21	0/1	0/0	en
ROUGE-4	2/2	2/3	0/1	0/0	el

Table 17. Precision and recall of auto-metrics relative human evaluation: 2015 data with 2015 scoring for focus.

System	Non-sig prec	Non-sig recall	Sig prec	Sig recall	Language
MeMoG	14/14	14/21	0/7	0/0	en
MeMoG	3/3	3/3	0/0	0/0	el
ROUGE-1	9/9	9/21	0/12	0/0	en
ROUGE-1	2/2	2/3	0/1	0/0	el
ROUGE-2	9/9	9/21	0/12	0/0	en
ROUGE-2	2/2	2/3	0/1	0/0	el
ROUGE-3	13/13	13/21	0/8	0/0	en
ROUGE-3	2/2	2/3	0/1	0/0	el
ROUGE-4	20/20	20/21	0/1	0/0	en
ROUGE-4	2/2	2/3	0/1	0/0	el

Table 18. Precision and recall of auto-metrics relative human evaluation: 2015 data with 2017 scoring for quality.

System	Non-sig prec	Non-sig recall	Sig prec	Sig recall	Language
NPowER	15/15	15/21	0/6	0/0	en
NPowER	1/1	1/3	0/2	0/0	el
ROUGE-1	9/9	9/21	0/12	0/0	en
ROUGE-1	1/1	1/3	0/2	0/0	el
ROUGE-2	9/9	9/21	0/12	0/0	en
ROUGE-2	3/3	3/3	0/0	0/0	el
ROUGE-3	15/15	15/21	0/6	0/0	en
ROUGE-3	3/3	3/3	0/0	0/0	el
ROUGE-4	21/21	21/21	0/0	0/0	en
ROUGE-4	3/3	3/3	0/0	0/0	el

Table 19. Precision and recall of auto-metrics relative human evaluation: 2015 data with 2017 scoring for non-redundancy.

System	Non-sig prec	Non-sig recall	Sig prec	Sig recall	Language
NPowER	15/15	15/21	0/6	0/0	en
NPowER	1/1	1/3	0/2	0/0	el
ROUGE-1	9/9	9/21	0/12	0/0	en
ROUGE-1	1/1	1/3	0/2	0/0	el
ROUGE-2	9/9	9/21	0/12	0/0	en
ROUGE-2	3/3	3/3	0/0	0/0	el
ROUGE-3	15/15	15/21	0/6	0/0	en
ROUGE-3	3/3	3/3	0/0	0/0	el
ROUGE-4	21/21	21/21	0/0	0/0	en
ROUGE-4	3/3	3/3	0/0	0/0	el

Table 20. Precision and recall of auto-metrics relative human evaluation: 2015 data with 2017 scoring for coherence.

System	Non-sig prec	Non-sig recall	Sig prec	Sig recall	Language
NPowER	15/15	15/21	0/6	0/0	en
NPowER	1/1	1/3	0/2	0/0	el
ROUGE-1	9/9	9/21	0/12	0/0	en
ROUGE-1	1/1	1/3	0/2	0/0	el
ROUGE-2	9/9	9/21	0/12	0/0	en
ROUGE-2	3/3	3/3	0/0	0/0	el
ROUGE-3	15/15	15/21	0/6	0/0	en
ROUGE-3	3/3	3/3	0/0	0/0	el
ROUGE-4	21/21	21/21	0/0	0/0	en
ROUGE-4	3/3	3/3	0/0	0/0	el

Table 21. Precision and recall of auto-metrics relative human evaluation: 2015 data with 2017 scoring for focus.

System	Non-sig prec	Non-sig recall	Sig prec	Sig recall	Language
NPowER	15/15	15/21	0/6	0/0	en
NPowER	1/1	1/3	0/2	0/0	el
ROUGE-1	9/9	9/21	0/12	0/0	en
ROUGE-1	1/1	1/3	0/2	0/0	el
ROUGE-2	9/9	9/21	0/12	0/0	en
ROUGE-2	3/3	3/3	0/0	0/0	el
ROUGE-3	15/15	15/21	0/6	0/0	en
ROUGE-3	3/3	3/3	0/0	0/0	el
ROUGE-4	21/21	21/21	0/0	0/0	en
ROUGE-4	3/3	3/3	0/0	0/0	el

Table 22. Precision and recall of auto-metrics relative human evaluation: 2017 data with 2017 scoring for quality.

System	Non-sig prec	Non-sig recall	Sig prec	Sig recall	Language
NPowER	1/2	1/2	0/1	0/1	el
NPowER	3/3	3/6	0/3	0/0	en
NPowER	3/3	3/3	0/0	0/0	zh
NPowER	2/3	2/2	3/3	3/4	it
ROUGE-1	2/3	2/2	0/0	0/1	el
ROUGE-1	5/5	5/6	0/1	0/0	en
ROUGE-1	3/3	3/3	0/0	0/0	zh
ROUGE-1	2/4	2/2	2/2	2/4	it
ROUGE-2	2/3	2/2	0/0	0/1	el
ROUGE-2	5/5	5/6	0/1	0/0	en
ROUGE-2	3/3	3/3	0/0	0/0	zh
ROUGE-2	2/6	2/2	0/0	0/4	it
ROUGE-3	2/3	2/2	0/0	0/1	el
ROUGE-3	2/2	2/6	0/4	0/0	en
ROUGE-3	1/1	1/3	0/2	0/0	zh
ROUGE-3	2/6	2/2	0/0	0/4	it
ROUGE-4	2/3	2/2	0/0	0/1	el
ROUGE-4	3/3	3/6	0/3	0/0	en
ROUGE-4	1/1	1/3	0/2	0/0	zh
ROUGE-4	2/6	2/2	0/0	0/4	it

Table 23. Precision and recall of auto-metrics relative human evaluation: 2017 data with 2017 scoring for non-redundancy.

System	Non-sig prec	Non-sig recall	Sig prec	Sig recall	Language
NPowER	2/2	2/3	0/1	0/0	el
NPowER	3/3	3/5	1/3	1/1	en
NPowER	1/3	1/1	0/0	0/2	zh
NPowER	2/3	2/2	3/3	3/4	it
ROUGE-1	3/3	3/3	0/0	0/0	el
ROUGE-1	4/5	4/5	0/1	0/1	en
ROUGE-1	1/3	1/1	0/0	0/2	zh
ROUGE-1	2/4	2/2	2/2	2/4	it
ROUGE-2	3/3	3/3	0/0	0/0	el
ROUGE-2	4/5	4/5	0/1	0/1	en
ROUGE-2	1/3	1/1	0/0	0/2	zh
ROUGE-2	2/6	2/2	0/0	0/4	it
ROUGE-3	3/3	3/3	0/0	0/0	el
ROUGE-3	1/2	1/5	0/4	0/1	en
ROUGE-3	0/1	0/1	1/2	1/2	zh
ROUGE-3	2/6	2/2	0/0	0/4	it
ROUGE-4	3/3	3/3	0/0	0/0	el
ROUGE-4	2/3	2/5	0/3	0/1	en
ROUGE-4	0/1	0/1	1/2	1/2	zh
ROUGE-4	2/6	2/2	0/0	0/4	it

Table 24. Precision and recall of auto-metrics relative human evaluation: 2017 data with 2017 scoring for coherence.

System	Non-sig prec	Non-sig recall	Sig prec	Sig recall	Language
NPowER	0/2	0/0	1/1	1/3	el
NPowER	0/3	0/1	2/3	2/5	en
NPowER	2/3	2/2	0/0	0/1	zh
NPowER	2/3	2/2	3/3	3/4	it
ROUGE-1	0/3	0/0	0/0	0/3	el
ROUGE-1	1/5	1/1	1/1	1/5	en
ROUGE-1	2/3	2/2	0/0	0/1	zh
ROUGE-1	2/4	2/2	2/2	2/4	it
ROUGE-2	0/3	0/0	0/0	0/3	el
ROUGE-2	1/5	1/1	1/1	1/5	en
ROUGE-2	2/3	2/2	0/0	0/1	zh
ROUGE-2	2/6	2/2	0/0	0/4	it
ROUGE-3	0/3	0/0	0/0	0/3	el
ROUGE-3	1/2	1/1	4/4	4/5	en
ROUGE-3	0/1	0/2	0/2	0/1	zh
ROUGE-3	2/6	2/2	0/0	0/4	it
ROUGE-4	0/3	0/0	0/0	0/3	el
ROUGE-4	1/3	1/1	3/3	3/5	en
ROUGE-4	0/1	0/2	0/2	0/1	zh
ROUGE-4	2/6	2/2	0/0	0/4	it

Table 25. Precision and recall of auto-metrics relative human evaluation: 2017 data with 2017 scoring for focus.

System	Non-sig prec	Non-sig recall	Sig prec	Sig recall	Language
NPowER	1/2	1/1	1/1	1/2	el
NPowER	1/3	1/2	2/3	2/4	en
NPowER	3/3	3/3	0/0	0/0	zh
NPowER	2/3	2/2	3/3	3/4	it
ROUGE-1	1/3	1/1	0/0	0/2	el
ROUGE-1	1/5	1/2	0/1	0/4	en
ROUGE-1	3/3	3/3	0/0	0/0	zh
ROUGE-1	2/4	2/2	2/2	2/4	it
ROUGE-2	1/3	1/1	0/0	0/2	el
ROUGE-2	2/5	2/2	1/1	1/4	en
ROUGE-2	3/3	3/3	0/0	0/0	zh
ROUGE-2	2/6	2/2	0/0	0/4	it
ROUGE-3	1/3	1/1	0/0	0/2	el
ROUGE-3	2/2	2/2	4/4	4/4	en
ROUGE-3	1/1	1/3	0/2	0/0	zh
ROUGE-3	2/6	2/2	0/0	0/4	it
ROUGE-4	1/3	1/1	0/0	0/2	el
ROUGE-4	2/3	2/2	3/3	3/4	en
ROUGE-4	1/1	1/3	0/2	0/0	zh
ROUGE-4	2/6	2/2	0/0	0/4	it

9. Conclusion

Researching and developing single document summarization algorithms that perform well across many languages is a challenging task, as the MSS tasks at the biennial MultiLing Workshops have shown. But the tasks enable researchers to see how the algorithms being developed are progressing and it continues to foster improvements in automatic document summarization and evaluation. Many of the systems submitted to the task over the years have used a statistical analysis of the words (or tokens) to score the sentences, along with various methods to remove redundancy, to create a summary. The surprising performance of the interweave baseline summary introduced in 2015 (which uses only the document structure and no statistical analysis) suggests that incorporating document structure into the existing summarization algorithms might yield significant improvement. One team, TeamMD in 2017 did submit entries using document structure and not using it, and overall the structure gave improved system performance.

The use of different systems to sentence split, tokenize, and lemmatize each year for the evaluations precludes us from concluding the significance such parsing has on the automatic evaluations. However, the comparisons of the automatic and human evaluations of the summaries shows significant improvements in systems for automatic evaluation, particularly MeMoG and NPowER. This is very helpful for such research since it is so difficult to get accurate human evaluations of automatic summaries across many languages; of the nearly 40 languages in the datasets only two were human evaluated in 2015 and only four in 2017. For English and Italian in 2017, teams from countries that spoke these languages as their primary language had the highest scores in quality; however for Greek and Chinese the Inter-Weaved baseline scored the best. The Inter-Weaved method scored the highest in Greek and Chinese for most of the linguistic metrics.

Running the MSS task is challenging. Creating the datasets for the tasks involves developing a lot of parsing software since each Wikipedia lists featured articles differently. Plus preprocessing and evaluating all the submissions in a timely manner is always a logistical challenge. But the tasks are worthy of the efforts involved and will continue to be so since they have certainly fostered improvements in the development of summarization algorithms and methods of evaluating them.

Acknowledgments

The authors would like to thank George Giannakopoulos, George Kiomourtzis, and Nikiforos Pittaras for their design and development of the website that supported the human evaluations as well as their tireless efforts in support of document summarization research. We also thank the teams that participated in MultiLing 2013, 2015, and 2017 as the contributions of both their systems and time taken to evaluate human summaries were instrumental for this work.

References

1. J. Stewart, *Genre Oriented Summarization*. Report (Carnegie Mellon University. Language Technologies Institute), Carnegie Mellon University, Language Technologies Institute, School of Computer Science (2009). Available at: https://books.google.com/books?id=krdUewAACAAJ.
2. J. D. Schlesinger, D. P. O'Leary, and J. M. Conroy, *Arabic/English Multi-document Summarization with CLASSY — The Past and the Future*, In ed. A. Gelbukh, *Proceedings of the Computational Linguistics and Intelligent Text Processing 9th International Conference, CICLing 2008*, Haifa, Israel, pp. 568–581. Springer, Berlin, Heidelberg (2008). Available at: http://dx.doi.org/10.1007/978-3-540-78135-6_49.

3. G. Giannakopoulos, V. Karkaletsis, G. Vouros, and P. Stamatopoulos, Summarization system evaluation revisited: N-gram graphs, *ACM Transactions on Speech and Language Processing* **5**(3), 5:1–5:39 (Oct., 2008). ISSN 1550-4875. doi: 10.1145/1410358.1410359.

4. H. Saggion, J.-M. Torres-Moreno, I. d. Cunha, and E. SanJuan, Multilingual summarization evaluation without human models. In eds. C-R. Huang and D. Jurafsky, *Proceedings of the 23rd International Conference on Computational Linguistics: Posters*, COLING '10, Beijing, China, pp. 1059–1067, ACL (2010). Available at: http://dl.acm.org/citation.cfm?id=1944566.1944688.

5. A. Louis and A. Nenkova, Automatically evaluating content selection in summarization without human models. In eds. P. Koehn and R. Mihalcea, *Proceedings of the 2009 Conference on Empirical Methods in Natural Language Processing: Volume 1*, Singapore, pp. 306–314, World Scientific Publishing (2009).

6. M. Litvak, M. Last, and M. Friedman, A new approach to improving multilingual summarization using a genetic algorithm. In eds. J. Hajič, S. Carberry, S. Clark, and J. Nivre, *Proceedings of the 48th Annual Meeting of the Association for Computational Linguistics*, Uppsala, Sweden, pp. 927–936, ACL (2010). Available at: http://dl.acm.org/citation.cfm?id=1858681.1858776.

7. J. Kubina, J. M. Conroy, and J. D. Schlesinger, ACL 2013 MultiLing pilot overview, *MultiLing 2013*, p. 29 (2013).

8. G. Giannakopoulos and V. Karkaletsis, *Summary Evaluation: Together We Stand NPowER-ed*. In ed. A. Gelbukh, *Proceedings of the Computational Linguistics and Intelligent Text Processing 14th International Conference*, Samos, Greece, pp. 436–450. Springer, Berlin, Heidelberg (2013). doi: 10.1007/978-3-642-37256-8_36.

9. P. Rankel, J. Conroy, E. Slud, and D. O'Leary, Ranking human and machine summarization systems. In *Proceedings of the 2011 Conference on Empirical Methods in Natural Language Processing*, Edinburgh, Scotland, UK, pp. 467–473, ACL (2011). Available at: http://www.aclweb.org/anthology/D11-1043.

10. P. A. Rankel, J. M. Conroy, and J. D. Schlesinger, Better metrics to automatically predict the quality of a text summary, *Algorithms*, **5**(4), 398–420 (2012). doi: 10.3390/a5040398.

11. F. Wilcoxon, Individual comparisons by ranking methods, *Biometrics Bulletin*, **1**(6), 80–83 (1945).

12. M. Litvak and M. Last, Cross-lingual training of summarization systems using annotated corpora in a foreign language, *Information Retrieval Journal* **16**(5), 629–656 (2013).

13. N. Vanetik and M. Litvak, Multilingual summarization with polytope model. In *Proceedings of the 16th Annual Meeting of the Special Interest Group on Discourse and Dialogue*, Prague, Czech Republic, pp. 227–231, ACL (2015). Available at: http://aclweb.org/anthology/W15-4632.

14. D. Gillick, B. Favre, and D. Hakkani-Tür, The ICSI summarization system at TAC 2008. Available at: http://www.nist.gov/tac/publications/index.html (2008).

15. J. M. Conroy, S. T. Davis, J. Kubina, Y.-K. Liu, D. P. O'Leary, and J. D. Schlesinger, Multilingual summarization: Dimensionality reduction and a step towards optimal term coverage. In *Proceedings of the MultiLing 2013 Workshop on Multilingual Multi-document Summarization*, Metz, France, pp. 55–63, ACL (2013).

16. R. Mihalcea, Language independent extractive summarization. In eds. K. Knight, H. T. Ng, and K. Oflazer, *Proceedings of ACL 2005*, ACL (2005).

17. S. Thomas, C. Beutenmüller, X. de la Puente, R. Remus, and S. Bordag, Exb text summarizer. In *Proceedings of the SIGDIAL 2015 Conference, The 16th Annual Meeting of the Special Interest Group on Discourse and Dialogue*, Prague, Czech Republic, pp. 260–269, ACL (2015). Available at: https://aclanthology.coli.uni-saarland.de/papers/W15-4637/w15-4637.

18. A. Aries, D. E. Zegour, and K. Hidouci, Allsummarizer system at Multiling 2015: Multilingual single and multi-document summarization. In *Proceedings of the SIGDIAL 2015 Conference, The 16th Annual Meeting of the Special Interest Group on Discourse and Dialogue*, Prague, Czech Republic, pp. 237–244. Available at: http://aclweb.org/anthology/W/W15/W15-4634.pdf.

19. M. E. Vicente, O. Alcón, and E. Lloret, The University of Alicante at Multiling 2015: Approach, results and further insights. In *Proceedings of the SIGDIAL 2015 Conference, The 16th Annual Meeting of the Special Interest Group on Discourse and Dialogue*, Prague, Czech Republic, Ref. 29, pp. 250–259. Available at: http://aclweb.org/anthology/W/W15/W15-4636.pdf.

20. T. Mikolov, I. Sutskever, K. Chen, G. S. Corrado, and J. Dean, Distributed representations of words and phrases and their compositionality. In eds. C. J. C. Burges, L. Bottou, M. Welling, Z. Ghahramani, and K. Q. Weinberger, *Advances in Neural Information Processing Systems 26*, pp. 3111–3119, Curran Associates, Inc. (2013). Available at: http://papers.nips.cc/paper/5021-distributed-representations-of-words-and-phrases-and-their-compositionality.pdf.

21. Q. V. Le and T. Mikolov, Distributed representations of sentences and documents. In *Proceedings of the 31st International Conference on Machine Learning*, Beijing, China, vol. 32, pp. 1188–1196, JMLR.org (2014). Available at: http://jmlr.org/proceedings/papers/v32/le14.html.

22. S. T. Davis, J. M. Conroy, and J. D. Schlesinger, OCCAMS — An optimal combinatorial covering algorithm for multi-document summarization. In eds. J. Vreeken, C. Ling, M. J. Zaki, A. Siebes, J. X. Yu, B. Goethals, G. I. Webb, and X. Wu, *ICDM Workshops*, pp. 454–463, IEEE Computer Society (2012). Available at: http://dblp.uni-trier.de/db/conf/icdm/icdmw2012.html#DavisCS12.

23. Basis Technology, Rosette base linguistics (RBL-GE) version 7.12.0 (2015). Available at: http://www.basistech.com.

24. S. Bird, E. Klein, and E. Loper, *Natural Language Processing with Python*, 1st edition. O'Reilly Media, Inc. (2009).

25. J. M. Conroy and S. T. Davis, Section mixture models for scientific document summarization, *International Journal on Digital Libraries*. pp. 1–18 (2017). doi: 10.1007/s00799-017-0218-6.

26. G. Erkan and D. R. Radev, Lexrank: Graph-based lexical centrality as salience in text summarization, *Journal of Artificial Intelligence Research* **22**(1), 457–479 (2004). Available at: http://dl.acm.org/citation.cfm?id= 1622487.1622501.

27. G. Rossiello, P. Basile, and G. Semeraro, Centroid-based text summarization through compositionality of word embeddings. In *Proceedings of the Multi-Ling 2017 Workshop on Summarization and Summary Evaluation Across Source Types and Genres*, Valencia, Spain, pp. 12–21, ACL (2017) Available at: http://aclanthology.coli.uni-saarland.de/pdf/W/W17/W17-1003.pdf.

28. C.-Y. Lin, ROUGE: A package for automatic evaluation of summaries. In eds. D. Scott, W. Daelemans, and M. A. Walker, *Text Summarization Branches Out: Proceedings of the ACL-04 Workshop*, Barcelona, Spain, pp. 74–81, ACL (2004).

29. *Proceedings of the SIGDIAL 2015 Conference, The 16th Annual Meeting of the Special Interest Group on Discourse and Dialogue*, Prague, Czech Republic, ACL (2015).

Chapter 10

Are Better Summaries Also Easier to Understand? Analyzing Text Complexity in Automatic Summarization

Elena Lloret*, Tatiana Vodolazova[†], Paloma Moreda[‡], Rafael Muñoz[§], and Manuel Palomar[¶]

University of Alicante, Department of Software and Computing Systems, Ctra. San Vicente s/n, San Vicente del Raspeig E-03690, Alicante, Spain
*elloret@dlsi.ua.es
[†] tvodolazova@dlsi.ua.es
[‡] moreda@dlsi.ua.es
[§] rafael@dlsi.ua.es
[¶] mpalomar@dlsi.ua.es

Text summarization and text simplification are research areas in natural language processing that help to analyze information automatically. Text summarization aims to produce a shorter version of a document while preserving its key information and overall meaning. Text simplification aims to adapt the complexity of a text to the reader's level of understanding. Despite being different in their nature and goals, these tasks could be combined, or integrated, not only for reducing a text to its most relevant content, but also for making such content easier to understand, regardless of the type of user that needs to read it.

In this chapter, we conduct an in-depth analysis of how different types of semantic information, when integrated into a summarization process, affect both system performance, in terms of accuracy, as well as the complexity of summaries (i.e., how easy or difficult they can be understood in terms of the way they are written), measured with respect to different standard readability metrics.

From the results obtained, simple techniques that do not involve semantic information (e.g., term-frequency) provide good summaries concerning their content. When more complex semantic information is added (e.g., anaphora resolution), no benefits are obtained regarding the summary's content, but it improves generated summaries in terms of their readability. This indicates the importance of including readability issues in the summarization process, so the generated summaries can be adapted accordingly, making the information they contain accessible to all.

1. Introduction

The digital information society has led to an information overload that requires the use of automatic tools, such as natural language processing tools, to allow feasible management and processing. Despite the wealth of information, not all existing information is accessible to all users, as far as its content is concerned. People with low literacy levels,[1] older users,[2] language learners,[3] non-experts in a field,[4] or people with cognitive disabilities, such as autism,[5] aphasia,[6] or dyslexia,[7] or congenitally deaf people[8] may have difficulties in understanding specific information, thus limiting their access to the information.

Text summarization and text simplification, among others, are two research areas that can help with information processing. On the one hand, text summarization aims to produce a shorter version of a document while preserving its key information and overall meaning.[9] Therefore, a summary can be very useful for saving reading and processing time. On the other hand, text simplification aims to adapt the complexity of a text to the reader's level of understanding.[10] This adaptation may range from word substitution[11] to complex sentence simplification.[12,13] Other approaches address the simplification task as an information reduction problem by compressing or discarding some content or part from sentences.[14,15] The issue of "compressing or discarding information" could be considered to some extent a way to produce a summary. This is not the same as integrating a simplification process (e.g., replacing long or difficult words) when generating a condensed version of the document, with the key information only (i.e., that is the essence of the document).

Nevertheless, despite being different in their nature and goals, these two tasks could be combined or integrated not only for reducing a text to its most relevant content, but also for making such content easier to understand, regardless the type of user that needs to read it. Such a combination would strengthen the joint potential of both tasks, where content reduction would be integrated with simplification techniques.

In this context, a general research question arises as to whether text summarization may lead to easier or more difficult texts than the original ones, because shorter texts do not necessarily mean that they are easier to understand. The state-of-the-art concerning evaluation strategies of text summaries involve quantitative and/or qualitative assessment of extracted sentences in most of the cases. This kind of evaluation normally comes down to a comparison with a gold-standard model (human summary), and a manual assessment of several criteria, such as non-redundancy, grammaticality, focus, responsiveness, or structure and coherence.[a] Although these aspects are important to measure the quality of a summary, the complexity of summaries (either manual or automatically generated) has never been analyzed to the best of our knowledge. This would also be a very interesting criteria to be taken into account in the generation of summaries, so that they can be accessible to anybody or adapted accordingly. In order to take into account the complexity of a text, a study of the readability should be performed. Readability is the ease with which a reader can understand a written text. In natural language, the readability of a text depends on its content (the complexity of its vocabulary and syntax) and its presentation (such as typographic aspects like font size, line height, and line length). In this research work, we only focus on the content aspect.

Therefore, the aim of this chapter is to conduct an exhaustive analysis of the impact of various summarization techniques on the readability of the produced texts. The proposed analysis will cover how different types of semantic information, such as word sense disambiguation (WSD), anaphora resolution (AR), and textual entailment (TE), when integrated into an automatic summarization process, affect both the system performance and the text complexity of generated summaries. Moreover, we would like to study whether the complexity of the summaries increases, decreases, or remains unchanged when more powerful semantic techniques are employed, as well as if there is any correlation with the performance of the summaries (i.e., how good the content of the summary is) using standard quantitative evaluation metrics.

Our experiments confirm that the summarization process can influence the readability of the generated summary with respect to the source document and human summary. For most of the readability metrics, the automatic summaries obtained better results than the source document and human summaries. However, not all the metrics are improved in the same

---

[a]http://www-nlpir.nist.gov/projects/duc/duc2007/quality-questions.txt.

manner for all the semantic information used in the summarization process. In this manner, depending on the specific users' preferences or needs, and the type of complexity they want to reduce, it could be more appropriate to employ different semantic techniques for generating summaries.

The chapter is structured as follows. Section 2 reports on the related work. Section 3 explains our proposed summarization approach, the readability metrics selected, and an illustrative example of how the complexity of a text would vary. Section 4 describes the corpus used for testing our approach, the tools involved in the summarization approach and in the computation of readability metrics, the experiments carried out, and the evaluation environment. Section 5 provides the results obtained, guiding their discussion by a set of defined research questions, and how the experiments could be extended to other languages. Finally, Section 6 briefly summarizes this chapter, draws its main conclusions and outlines some possible further research directions.

2. Related work

Although text summarization and text simplification are two different tasks, previous research works have included one as a preprocessing or intermediate stage to improve the results of the other. For instance, Bothelo-Silveira and Branco (2012)[16] integrate sentence simplification to enhance a multi-document summarization system. The addition of a syntactic simplification module allowed removal of parts without critical information, with respect to the general message of the sentence.

A human evaluation proved that the addition of the text simplification module improved the quality of a summary, obtaining, as expected, better results for the simplified summaries than for the non-simplified ones. Margarido *et al.* (2008)[17] experimented with the *keyword extraction by patterns* technique, as a simplification technique. The authors studied its impact on text readability for a group of people with varied literacy levels. They concluded that text summarization benefits the text simplification task, however, the extent to which it helps depends on the literacy level of the reader. Petersen and Ostendorf (2007)[3] analyzed a corpus of original and manually simplified English news articles with the aim of determining what actions people normally perform when simplifying a text, so that better automatic tools for text simplification could be produced. In their research, they also analyzed an extractive text summarizer[18] that was integrated in the simplification process, obtaining very promising results when the generated summaries were compared to the manually simplified versions of the text using ROUGE.[19] ROUGE is a widespread tool used to automatically evaluate the content of a summary. Specifically, it allows one to compute recall, precision, and F-measure with respect to different metrics, all of them based on the vocabulary overlap between automatic and model summaries. For instance, ROUGE-1 computes the number of common unigrams; ROUGE-2 computes the number of bigrams co-occurrence, and ROUGE-L computes the longest common subsequence (LCS). The results obtained by Petersen and Ostendorf (2007)[3] ranged from 24%–48% and 50%–63% for the recall values of ROUGE-2 and ROUGE-L, respectively.

Different from these previous research works, there are only few studies that explore the effect of text summarization on text complexity.

Among them, one of the earliest studies concerns Web summaries. Web summaries represent a different kind of summaries that are composed of a title, an abstract, and a URL. The abstract itself can be composed of either complete sentences or fragments of sentences. Kanungo and Orr (2009)[20] proposed a machine learning approach to compute the readability of Web summaries based on a model that predicts human judgments. The model was estimated given the features extracted from a corpus composed of random queries and their corresponding search result summaries, which were assessed for their readability by humans. A set of 13 features was selected, including several standard readability metrics, such as Flesch (more details can be found in Section 3.2), average characters or syllables per word, and fraction of capital letters, punctuation marks or stopwords. In addition, novel features, including the number of snippets or the presence of ellipsis in the beginning or end of the abstract were also taken into account. The resulting model showed better correlation with human judgments than common readability models. However, the main drawback of their study was that the methods assumed long, well-written text with complete sentences; this is not the case of Web summaries, so the application of the model in real scenarios is limited.

When it comes to evaluating the readability of the generated summaries, most of the studies focused on a subset of metrics defined in the manual summary assessment of the Text Analysis Conferences (TAC).[b]

---

[b]TAC is a series of evaluation workshops organized to encourage research into different tasks of natural language processing, including text summarization tasks: http://www.nist.gov/tac/.

These metrics included, for instance, grammaticality, coherence, or redundancy. However, these readability metrics were not taken into consideration as part of the summarization process. In this line, Vadlapudi and Katragadda (2010)[21] examined automatic evaluation methods based on N-gram models, lexical chains, and semantic relatedness, in order to account for grammaticality, structure, and coherence aspects of summary evaluation.

Stymne and Smith (2012)[22] studied the impact of extractive text summarization on the readability of summaries and their MTranslatability. MTranslatability refers to how easy a text is for a machine translation system to be translated. In their experiment set-up, a corpus of news stories was summarized using an extractive summarizer; the resulting summaries were then translated to German. The quality of machine translation was shown not to significantly differ between the data sets with various readability degrees. However, the authors reported that the chosen summarizer selected more complex sentences (with the Flesch Reading Ease score[c] of 39.6), while leaving out more readable ones (scoring 47.9).

Research that can be considered as most related to ours was done by Smith and Jönsson (2010).[23] The authors experimented with the extractive summarizer CogSum for Swedish. CogSum uses a random indexing word space model and a modified version of PageRank.[24] The resulting summaries were evaluated against the original text using a set of lightweight linguistic analysis methods that included noun ratio and the use of the Lasbarhetsindex Swedish Readability formula (LIX), syntactic complexity measure for Swedish.[25] The LIX metric takes into account the number of words per sentence and the number of long words (those with more than six characters), with respect to the total number of words in the text. This metric assumes that if the number of words in a sentence increases, so does text complexity. The same assumption is applied if the number of long words increases.

In their results, a significantly lower LIX could be observed across the generated summaries, showing that the complexity of the text was reduced when the text was summarized. The vocabulary load also decreased when articles were summarized, and therefore there were more chances to discard complex words. Furthermore, in Smith *et al.* (2012),[26] the lexical properties of a corpus were analyzed by means of several readability metrics.

---

[c]The higher the values, the better, since they indicate that a text is easier to understand.

The goal was to come up with more efficient text representation using vector spaces for the development of an extractive summarization process. The results obtained showed that text documents with a high word variation index were likely to produce vector spaces that yielded better summaries. The main conclusions in these two research works were that: i) summarization could be used as a means to make a text easier to read, which may work well as a first step in an effort to make texts more accessible; and ii) the integration of readability metrics in the process of summarization could lead to better summaries, although their complexity was not further investigated.

As it can be seen, the issue of analyzing the complexity of summaries has not been studied extensively in previous research. Such analysis would be useful for designing approaches that would be able to generate simplified summaries, thus improving and facilitating information access. As a first step towards this long-term goal, this chapter aims at conducting an in-depth readability analysis (in terms of text complexity) of a wide range of summaries generated using different types of semantic information.

3. Methodology

The methodology proposed in our research is based on a thorough analysis of a wide range of common readability metrics applied to summaries (automatically or manually generated) as well as to the documents from which the summaries were produced. Moreover, the impact of different types of semantic information in the summarization process, and their influence on the summary's complexity, is also investigated. For this reason, we first need to define and explain both the text summarization approach (Section 3.1), the readability measures (Section 3.2) used in the context of our research, and an example of how the complexity of a text would be affected depending on its content (Section 3.3).

3.1. *Our text summarization approach*

The proposed summarization approach is an improved version of the one formerly presented in Vodolazova *et al.* (2012).[27] It comprises a number of text analysis modules that can be combined with each other to produce summaries from a given input under different constraints. Figure 1 depicts an overview of this approach.

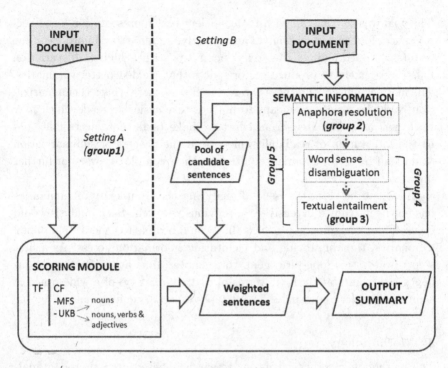

Fig. 1. Overview of our text summarization approach (TF — term frequency; CF — concept frequency; MFS — most frequent sense; UKB — the UKB disambiguation algorithm).

3.1.1. *Basic setting (only scoring)*

The basic setting (setting A in the figure) includes a scoring module only. This scoring module selects relevant sentences to be included into the final summary. This relevance is associated to the weight of each sentence, which is computed based either on the term frequency (TF) of the words that constitute the sentence, or their concept frequency (CF).

On the one hand, TF is a reliable indicator for sentence selection. It has been shown that the likelihood of a word appearing in a final summary depends on its frequency in the original text.[28] On the other hand, TF does not account for semantics of a text, thus not capturing the cases of synonymy. To solve this limitation, CF is used. Concepts are computed by grouping the words according to the WordNet[d] synsets that they belong

---

[d]http://wordnet.princeton.edu/.

to, using one of the following word sense disambiguation algorithms. The most frequent sense (MFS) algorithm, as the name implies, selects the most frequent synset for each word. The UKB[e][29] algorithm is a collection of programs for performing graph-based WSD relying on a pre-existing knowledge base. Once the concepts are identified, their frequencies are adjusted respectively, adding up all those belonging to that concept. In both cases (TF and CF), a standard stopword list[f] was used for ignoring words that are normally very frequent. These words are not relevant for determining the relevance of a sentence. Our stopword list contained 429 words and was extended with the 245 most frequent words of the 2002 corpus of Document Understanding Conferences (DUC).

3.1.2. *Advanced setting (adding complex semantic analysis)*

Additionally, another setting for generating a summary is possible (i.e., setting B in the figure). This setting consists of the use and integration of different types of semantic information previous to the scoring module. This additional semantic information includes anaphora resolution (AR), WSD, and textual entailment (TE). Some of these modules can be run independently (i.e., AR and TE), while WSD always runs together with TE. AR substitutes each pronominal anaphor by its antecedent, and then the term or concept frequencies are adjusted respectively in the scoring module. TE eliminates sentences with redundant information: if this module determines that a sentence can be inferred from the previous sentences, it removes that sentence, so the set of candidate sentences to be passed to the scoring module will be reduced. In other words, if a true entailment is found between a pair of sentences, it means that the meaning of the second one (called the hypothesis) can be deduced from the first one (called the text).To illustrate the idea behind TE, the following example is provided. The hypothesis (H) can be inferred by the text (T).

> **T:** *ASCAP is a membership association of more than 200,000 US composers, songwriters, lyricists and music publishers of every kind of music.*
> **H:** *More than 200,000 US composers, songwriters, lyricists and music publishers are members of ASCAP.*

---

[e]http://ixa2.si.ehu.es/ukb/.
[f]Standard stopword list obtained from: http://www.lextek.com/manuals/onix/stop words1.html.

Lloret *et al.* (2008)[30] reported significant improvement of ROUGE-1 scores when TE was used for semantic redundancy detection. Moreover, TE can be applied after an additional WSD module. This module identifies synonyms using the MFS algorithm in the original document, and substitutes the words by its most frequent synonyms. If this is performed, redundancy detection is carried out on the disambiguated text. Later, the candidate sentences, after performing TE, are weighted in the scoring module, as in the case of setting A.

Finally, the most sophisticated combination of all the modules first passes a text through AR, then it is disambiguated, and finally, TE is applied to detect redundant information. After that, the scoring module evaluates the remaining candidate sentences and, based on the weight assigned by means of its term or concept frequencies, decides which ones to include into the final summary.

Considering the two settings in our text summarization approach, we arrive at five groups with the aim to analyze the influence of the knowledge types we have integrated:

(1) Only the scoring module is applied to the input document.
(2) AR is applied to the input document, and then it is passed through the scoring module.
(3) TE is applied to the input document, and then it is passed through the scoring module.
(4) WSD is applied to the input document, then redundant sentences are discarded using TE, and finally the remaining sentences are passed through the scoring module.
(5) AR is applied to the input document, then WSD is applied to the input document, then redundant sentences are discarded with TE, and finally the remaining sentences are passed through the scoring module.

3.2. *Automatic readability measures*

Readability is a complex notion that refers to the level of ease or difficulty with which a text can be understood by a reader. It depends both upon the text properties and the reader's skills. According to Dubay (2004),[31] there are over 200 readability formulae, and over a thousand studies have been published investigating this matter. More information about readability metrics and methods to compute them can be found in Collins-Thompson (2014).[32]

The readability measures that were considered in this research work are: Flesch reading ease,[33] word variation index,[34] proper noun ratio, unique proper noun ratio, average word length and average sentence length, noun ratio, and pronoun ratio.

We next provide a brief explanation of the readability measures used in our research.

- Flesch reading ease (**FRE**)

$$FRE = 206.825 - 1.015 * \frac{\#words}{\#sentences} - 84.6 * \frac{\#syllables}{\#words} \qquad (1)$$

FRE is a traditional readability metric that depends on the sentence length counted in words and the word length counted in syllables. The formula above returns a number from 1 to 100. Higher FRE scores imply an easy-to-read text.

- Word variation index (**OVIX**)

$$OVIX = \frac{log(\#words)}{log(2 - \frac{log(\#uniquewords)}{log(\#words)})} \qquad (2)$$

OVIX can be used to measure the idea density, because it reflects the ratio of unique words in the text. When measuring inflected forms, their lemmas (instead of the words themselves) should be considered to obtain the correct results. Higher values for OVIX, the better.

- Proper noun ratio (**PNR**)

$$PNR = \frac{\#proper\ nouns}{\#words} \qquad (3)$$

Following Smith *et al.* (2012),[26] we also use PNR index in our analysis. We hypothesize that higher PNR indicate higher readability, because proper nouns refer to unique entities, and thus they can reduce the level of text ambiguity.

- Unique proper noun ratio (**distPNR**)

$$distPNR = \frac{\#unique\ proper\ nouns}{\#words} \qquad (4)$$

The distPNR ratio is a variation of the proper noun ratio metric defined in Eq. (3).

- Average word length (**AWL**)

$$AWL = \frac{\#characters}{\#words} \tag{5}$$

The AWL reflects the amount of long words used. It was decided to include this measure, because it was proven that the use of long words rather than short words makes the understanding of a text more difficult.[35]

- Average sentence length (**ASL**)

$$ASL = \frac{\#words}{\#sentences} \tag{6}$$

Extractive summarization methods tend to favor long sentences.[22,36] However, texts with longer sentences are more difficult to understand, and it is one of the obstacles that text simplification systems often addressed.[37]

- Noun ratio (**NR**)

$$NR = \frac{\#nouns}{\#words} \tag{7}$$

NR can be used to capture the degree of text nominalization, i.e., the proportion of nouns present in the text. Hancke *et al.* (2012)[38] consider texts with fewer nominalizations to be easier to read.

- Pronoun ratio (**PR**)

$$PR = \frac{\#pronouns}{\#words} \tag{8}$$

Pronoun ratio is a lightweight linguistic measure that indicates the level of semantic ambiguity that can arise while searching for the concept the pronoun refers to.[5] In the context of extractive text summarization, a high number of pronouns can cause dangling references. This happens when a sentence containing the noun phrase that a pronoun refers to is removed in the process of sentence selection. Lower values for PR, the better.

In order to conduct the proposed analysis, we focused on a set of commonly used measures that were computed over the entire documents, either the original source documents or the generated manual and automatic summaries.

3.3. *Illustrative examples*

Consider the following original text from the DUC 2002 corpus and two summaries automatically obtained through different configurations (Summary A and Summary B).

Original text from DUC 2002 corpus: *Debi Thomas' dream of Olympic gold turned into disappointment Saturday as East Germany's Katarina Witt won her second straight Olympic championship and Canadian Elizabeth Manley took home the silver before a crowd of cheering countrymen. It's over. Back to school, said Thomas, who won the bronze medal despite three faulty landings. "I'm not going to make any excuses. I was really skating well this week. It wasn't supposed to happen, I guess. But I tried." While the top two skaters in the world staged a shootout to music from Bizet's Carmen, Manley was so sensational in the freestyle that she finished first with seven judges. Combined with a fourth in the compulsory figures and a third-place finish in the short program earlier in the week, the performance put Manley in second place. Witt, a three-time world champion from East Germany, became the first repeat singles champion since Dick Button took Olympic gold in 1948 and '52. Sonja Henie of Norway was the only woman to do it before Witt, winning in 1928, 1932 and 1936. Thomas, of San Jose, Calif., the first black to win a US figure skating crown and the 1986 world champion, skated poorly Saturday after doing well earlier in the Games. By contrast, Manley had the sellout crowd at the Olympic Saddledome enraptured. They cheered, hooted and stamped their feet when she finished hitting every element of her program. Jill Trenary of Minnetonka, Minn., finished fourth. She was fifth heading into the long program, worth 50 percent of the overall score. Thomas' bronze was the third figure skating medal here for the United States. Brian Boitano won the men's crown, and a bronze in pairs went to Jill Watson and Peter Oppegard. In addition to the three figure skating medals, the US team had three speed-skating medals: one each gold, silver and bronze. Speed skater Bonnie Blair, America's only double medalist, tried again Saturday in the 1,500 meters but finished fourth, well off the pace. She won the gold in the 500 and the bronze in the 1,000 meters. As the Olympics winded up its next-to-last day, the Soviet Union had 27 medals, including 11 golds, while East Germany in second place had 22, including nine golds.*

Summary A obtained with anaphora resolution, word sense disambiguation, textual entailment and concept frequency: *Witt, a three-time world champion from East Germany, became the first repeat singles champion since Dick Button took Olympic gold in 1948 and '52. Thomas, of San Jose, Calif., the first black to win a US figure skating crown and the 1986 world champion, skated poorly Saturday after doing well earlier in the Games. Jill Trenary of Minnetonka, Minn., finished fourth. Brian Boitano won the men's crown, and a bronze in pairs went to Jill Watson and Peter Oppegard.*

Summary B obtained with anaphora resolution, word sense disambiguation, and term frequency: *It's over. Back to school, said Thomas, who won the bronze medal despite three faulty landings. I was really skating well this week. They cheered, hooted and stamped their feet when she finished hitting every element of her program. Jill Trenary of Minnetonka, Minn., finished fourth. Thomas bronze was the third figure skating medal here for the United States. In addition to the three figure skating medals, the US team had three speed-skating medals: one each gold, silver and bronze. She won the gold in the 500 and the bronze in the 1,000 meters.*

Computing the Flesh Reading Ease metric as described in Section 3.2, we obtained the values of 68.8 for the original text, 69 for Summary A, and 76.7 for Summary B. According to the scale defined in Flesch (1948),[33] this means that both the original text and Summary A are "standard average", whereas Summary B is "fairly easy" to read. The readability of Summary B is better than the others; therefore this summary is less complex than Summary A, and less complex than the original text. On the other hand, the original text and Summary A have similar readability scores; therefore, the complexity level of both texts remains essentially unchanged. Therefore, both automatic summaries provide a short version of the text without increasing its complexity.

4. Experimental set-up and evaluation environment

This section provides the description of the corpus used as a dataset (Section 4.1), the experiments conducted (Section 4.2), and the evaluation performed (Section 4.3).

4.1. *Corpus and tools*

We used the DUC 2002 corpus as our dataset for the single-document summarization task.[g] It consists of 533 newswire documents covering various topics including sports, medicine, and natural disasters, and being refined, after removing duplicates, to 530 distinct news documents. Each newswire article is accompanied by one or more abstractive model summaries, manually created by human reviewers. These human summaries are approximately 100 words long.

Regarding the tools for obtaining the necessary semantic information in the summarization approach, the BART coreference resolution toolkit[39] was used for detecting and resolving the pronominal anaphoric expressions in the AR module. BART is an open source toolkit that performs around 60% for F-measure, being in line with the state of the art for coreference resolution.[40] For detecting redundant information, the TE module was implemented based on that proposed by the Ferrández (2007, 2009)[41,42] method, which obtains an overall performance of 65% for F-measure. Finally, the Freeling linguistic analyzer[43] was used for the WSD stage, specifically for the implementations of MFS and UKB algorithms. MFS is mainly considered to be a very competitive baseline for the WSD task, which is very difficult to outperform, achieving a performance that ranges between 58.4% and 60% for F-measure.[44,45] The UKB algorithm[29,45] obtains state-of-the-art results close to 60% for F-measure.

The required linguistic properties for computing the readability measures, such as parts of speech, were extracted with the help of NLP tools provided in the Stanford CoreNLP package[h] which has a token accuracy over 97%.[46] Finally, the syllabification for the FRE measure was done with the help of the English syllable counter of the MorphAdorner project.[i]

4.2. *Experiments*

For conducting the experiments, all the documents in the DUC 2002 corpus were automatically processed with respect to the five general groups (groups 1–5) available in our proposed text summarization approach (see Section 3.1).

Moreover, for each of the groups, we have the additional configurations (see Section 3.1.2), depending on the level of abstraction when processing

---

[g]http://duc.nist.gov/.
[h]http://nlp.stanford.edu/software/corenlp.shtml.
[i]http://morphadorner.northwestern.edu/.

the words, the WSD algorithm for computing CF and the type of words that are disambiguated. This gives us the following configurations:

(1) Scoring by TF.
(2) Scoring by CF, using the MFS WSD algorithm, disambiguating nouns, adjectives, and verbs.
(3) Scoring by CF, using the MFS WSD algorithm, disambiguating only nouns.
(4) Scoring by CF, using the UKB WSD algorithm, disambiguating nouns, adjectives, and verbs.
(5) Scoring by CF, using the UKB WSD algorithm, disambiguating only nouns.

Therefore, in the end, a total of 13,250 automatic summaries were generated (530 distinct documents × 5 groups × 5 configurations).

4.3. *Evaluation*

In the research conducted for this book chapter, we want to analyze whether the summaries generated with respect to the previously mentioned configurations exhibit any changes on the level of text complexity. In previous research,[47,48] the techniques proposed for generating the summaries were quantitatively evaluated, obtaining good performance, thus showing that the proposed summarization method was appropriate. Although the evaluation was conducted for all the generated summaries, before assessing the text complexity of the summaries, a preliminary manual verification was carried out in order to check that the generated summaries were meaningful. Because we have more than 13,000 summaries, and due to the difficulty and time-consuming nature of the task that involves manual verification, we did not conduct this type of checking for all the documents and summaries. Instead, we opted for selecting a representative sample of the input documents through a statistical formula called "Representative sample (M)",[49] described in Eq. (9).

$$M = \frac{N * K^2 * P * Q}{E^2 * (N - 1) + K^2 * P * Q} \tag{9}$$

where N is the population size; K represents the value for assigning a confidence level; E is the assumed error rate; P is the probability of success; and Q is the probability of failure. The value for each parameter was set according to the suggestion of Gutiérrez-Vázquez et al. (2011)[50]: $K = 0.95; E = 0.05; P = 0.5; Q = 0.5$.

In this manner, computing M using Eq. (9), we obtained: $M = 77.24$. Based on this, 77 documents were selected; their summaries were manually checked to ensure that they had an acceptable quality before the evaluation of the complexity of all the summaries using the proposed readability metrics. An example of a generated summary of group 5 (AR+WSD+TE, CF_UKB) with an acceptable quality is shown below:

> *Witt, a three-time world champion from East Germany, became the first repeat singles champion since Dick Button took Olympic gold in 1948 and '52. Thomas, of San Jose, Calif., the first black to win a US figure skating crown and the 1986 world champion, skated poorly Saturday after doing well earlier in the Games. Jill Trenary of Minnetonka, Minn., finished fourth. Brian Boitano won the men's crown, and a bronze in pairs went to Jill Watson and Peter Oppegard.*

This verification process determined the appropriate quality of the 77 representative summaries. As a consequence, we extended this sample to include the remaining summaries, and therefore, we conducted the complexity evaluation for all the generated summaries (13,250). After this preliminary verification process and once all the summaries with the different configurations were generated, they were evaluated from two perspectives.

The original DUC documents, together with human and automatic summaries, were assessed for readability using the readability measures selected and explained in Section 3.2. In this manner, we expect to see differences in pronoun ratio between the groups that include AR, when compared to the ones that do not. We also expect to see different noun ratios in the summaries generated using WSD when applied to either nouns, or to the three categories of nouns, verbs, and adjectives.

Additionally, the automatic summaries were evaluated against the human ones using ROUGE metrics,[19] which is a standard measure for the summarization task. With this evaluation, we want to analyze the relationship between the best summaries in terms of their ROUGE performance and their complexity.

As it can be seen from the results obtained in Section 5, we could conclude two main ideas:

(1) Automatic summaries exhibit lower complexity than the gold-standard (human generated summaries). However, not all the summarization techniques imply better results for all readability metrics. This analysis

allows us to determine that depending on the users' needs (e.g., problems with ambiguous words or pronouns, etc.), the use of one specific technique or another would be more appropriate for the summarization process. For instance, if a user had problems with long sentences, it would be better to use anaphora resolution to generate the summary.

(2) The quality of the summaries is appropriate, as far as ROUGE is concerned.

In the next section, the results are reported and discussed in more detail.

5. Results and discussion

The readability results can be found in Table 1. The results were set to four decimal points to better show the differences between them, because most of the readability metrics perform very similarly. The "size" column of the table indicates the average size of the documents measured in words. The best result for each metric is highlighted in boldface, and results improving the gold-standard (human generated summaries) and/or source document are shown in italics.

A two-tailed paired t-test was also performed to account for statistical significance for each readability metric. In this sense, we compared the results obtained from the original document with respect to each configuration in each group. In the same manner, we computed the statistical significance between the automatic and the human-generated summaries for each group as well, so we could also determine whether a human summary was more appropriate in terms of its complexity. For purposes of clarity, we only highlighted the numbers for the "total avg" row, as a representative of the whole group. The average values for each group were computed in order to analyse the overall influence of the main semantic technique employed for generating the summaries, regardless of the specific disambiguation method used at word level (i.e., MFS or UKB).

Taking into consideration the results obtained, it cannot be claimed that a particular semantic technique (e.g., AR,TE, etc.) would help reduce the complexity of the generated summaries in every case. However, these techniques could help to increase the quality content, and therefore, it could be possible to establish some specific preferences depending on the users' needs. For instance, if the user needed an improvement of the general readability of the summary, the use of AR would be appropriate; if she or he would require less variability in the vocabulary, then, word sense disambiguation

Table 1. Evaluation results (TF — term frequency; CF — concept frequency; AR — anaphora resolution; TE — textual entailment; N — disambiguation only for nouns; MFS — most frequent sense; UKB — the UKB disambiguation algorithm. Interpretation of the results: for FRE, OVIX, PNR, and distPNR, the higher values, the better; for AWL, ASL, NR, and PR, the lower values, the better. The best result for each metric is highlighted in boldface, and results improving the gold-standard (human generated summaries) and/or source document are shown in italics. For clarity purposes, we only highlighted the numbers for the "total avg" row, as a representative of the whole group, when this condition is met.

		FRE	OVIX	PNR	distPNR	AWL	ASL	NR	PR	size
	source document	43.3636	58.3624	0.1318	0.0778	4.8872	22.9966	0.3464	0.04269	565.7113
	gold-standard	42.7560	65.1371	0.1436	0.1106	5.0383	19.1479	0.3632	0.0865	102.2382
GROUP 1	TF	42.2916	64.4236	0.1605	0.1176	5.0267	19.0817	0.3842	0.0786	91.5434
	CF_MFS	42.6005	64.4251	0.1598	0.1171	5.017	19.1309	0.3817	0.0793	91.6019
	CF_N_MFS	42.2218	64.4069	0.1632	0.1199	5.0163	19.4732	0.3849	0.0783	91.6642
	CF_UKB	42.6221	64.5689	0.1582	0.1162	5.0167	19.1238	0.3811	0.0806	91.6000
	CF_N_UKB	42.6516	64.4779	0.1614	0.1192	5.0059	19.1701	0.3848	0.0792	91.5943
	Avg CF	42.5240	64.4697	0.1607	0.1181	5.0140	19.2245	0.3831	0.0794	91.6151
	Total avg	42.4775	64.4605	0.1606	0.1180	5.0165	19.1959	0.3833	0.0792	91.6008
GROUP 2 (AR)	TF	46.3372	60.3697	0.1596	0.1093	5.0003	17.0680	0.3721	0.1416	94.6491
	CF_MFS	46.7565	60.5639	0.1583	0.1087	4.9932	17.0494	0.3702	0.143	94.583
	CF_N_MFS	46.8008	60.6988	0.1601	0.1105	4.9898	17.0189	0.3728	0.1408	94.7113
	CF_UKB	46.5961	60.5313	0.1577	0.1088	4.9900	17.1673	0.371	0.1415	94.6170
	CF_N_UKB	47.0653	60.4289	0.1593	0.1096	4.9743	17.1285	0.3741	0.1376	94.5925
	Avg CF	46.8047	60.5557	0.1589	0.1094	4.9868	17.0910	0.3720	0.1407	94.6260
	Total avg	**46.7112**	60.5185	*0.1590*	*0.1094*	**4.9895**	**17.0864**	0.3720	0.1409	94.6306

(Continued)

Table 1. (*Continued*)

		FRE	OVIX	PNR	distPNR	AWL	ASL	NR	PR	size
GROUP 3 (TE)	TF	39.7621	69.5712	0.1582	0.1224	5.0507	20.6433	0.3858	0.0811	90.7623
	CF_MFS	39.8902	69.8737	0.1571	0.1222	5.0514	20.7274	0.3845	0.0812	90.8264
	CF_N_MFS	39.8986	69.8392	0.1605	0.1245	5.0362	20.8273	0.3874	0.0796	90.7226
	CF_UKB	39.9027	69.8304	0.1549	0.1201	5.0506	20.6799	0.383	0.083	90.6226
	CF_N_UKB	40.9117	69.8885	0.1599	0.1247	5.0221	20.5201	0.3869	0.0807	90.6774
	Avg CF	40.1508	69.8580	0.1581	0.1229	5.0401	20.6887	0.3855	0.0811	90.7123
	Total avg	40.0731	*69.8006*	*0.1581*	*0.1228*	5.0422	20.6796	0.3855	0.0811	90.7223
GROUP 4 (WSD+TE)	TF	39.7621	69.5712	0.1582	0.1224	5.0507	20.6433	0.3858	0.0811	90.7623
	CF_MFS	39.9837	69.8598	0.1574	0.1222	5.0486	20.7091	0.3846	0.0817	90.8151
	CF_N_MFS	40.0103	69.7016	0.1604	0.1243	5.0344	20.8109	0.3872	0.0801	90.6566
	CF_UKB	39.7400	70.1320	0.1561	0.1214	5.0438	20.6024	0.3832	0.082	90.4547
	CF_N_UKB	40.6145	69.9413	0.1611	0.1256	5.0178	20.4438	0.3873	0.0793	90.3321
	Avg CF	40.0871	69.9087	0.1588	0.1234	5.0362	20.6416	0.3856	0.0808	90.5646
	Total avg	40.0221	**69.8412**	*0.1586*	*0.1232*	5.0391	20.6419	0.3856	*0.0808*	90.6042
GROUP 5 (AR+WSD+TE)	TF	39.9570	68.3452	0.1706	0.1298	5.1084	19.7559	0.3991	0.0681	94.3113
	CF_MFS	40.1486	68.0112	0.1680	0.1272	5.1002	19.802	0.3960	0.0688	94.3226
	CF_N_MFS	40.2741	67.7710	0.1716	0.1304	5.0869	19.9529	0.4009	0.0669	94.3132
	CF_UKB	39.9267	68.4373	0.1667	0.1265	5.1053	19.9635	0.3967	0.0684	94.2283
	CF_N_UKB	40.6041	67.9702	0.1724	0.1312	5.0773	19.9662	0.4017	0.066	94.1491
	Avg CF	40.2384	68.0474	0.1697	0.1288	5.0924	19.9212	0.3988	0.0675	94.2533
	Total avg	40.1821	*68.1070*	**0.1699**	**0.1290**	5.0956	19.8881	0.3989	**0.0676**	94.2649

together with textual entailment (WSD+TE) would be more suitable than a combination of other techniques.

In order to provide a more detailed analysis of the results, we further analyze and discuss them, taking into account the following research questions:

- *What impact do the summarization techniques have on the complexity of the generated summaries?* The goal of this research question is to determine to what extent the inclusion of specific information within the summarization process (in our case, different types of semantic information) can influence the readability of the resulting summaries, and whether that specific information increases or reduces the complexity of the summaries.
- *Does the complexity of summaries increases, decreases, remains unchanged with respect to their source documents?* With this question, we want to check to what extent the reduction of content made by the summarization process affects the complexity, when compared to the document from which it was obtained.
- *Are the best summaries (evaluated using standard quantitative summarization metrics, such as ROUGE) also the best with respect to their complexity?* The results of this analysis may provide insights about how to design and develop balanced summarization approaches that are capable of achieving an acceptable performance, as well as being easy to understand.

5.1. *Analysis of the impact that summarization techniques have on the complexity of the generated summaries*

This analysis is necessary to determine how the semantic information and the combination of its different types affect the readability indexes. Taking into account the results provided in Table 1, we discuss the most relevant findings below.

Regarding the readability comparison between human and automatic summaries, human summaries only over-performed automatic summaries in the NR, obtaining the best value for this metric (0.3632). For the remaining metrics, the automatic summaries over-performed human summaries. For instance, the FRE metric obtains the best results using AR to generate the summaries (46.7112 vs. 42.7560), and this improvement is statistically significant according to the t-test performed.

Focusing on the automatic summaries and the different configurations for generating them, we first analyzed the impact on readability between term and concept frequency-based scoring methods. We computed TF values with the average CF values for each group. For computing CF, we first need to obtain the synset associated to each word, and group together those that share the same synset. This does not happen with TF, where we consider each word to be independent from the others. It can be concluded that the CF-based scoring strategy generates summaries that are easier to understand. This behavior is reproduced in different metrics (except in PNR) with different configurations, but with some exceptions. In OVIX and distPNR in group 5, and PR in group 3, TF obtains better results than CF.

In addition to the term and concept frequency analysis, we also analyzed the effects of the WSD method itself, MFS vs. UKB. For all the groups, the UKB-based disambiguation method performs better than MFS. Moreover, UKB obtains higher FRE values than their MFS versions. This is explained by the average word length in the UKB-generated summaries, which is lower for all the groups. No other unanimous trends were observed for these disambiguation methods. Within this analysis, we also studied what happened if only nouns were disambiguated. The results show that disambiguating only nouns yields to better performance in most of the metrics (FRE, PR, PNR, distPNR, and AWL) than disambiguating all content words (nouns, verbs, and adjectives). Only for the NR metric does the use of all the grammatical categories improve the readability. For OVIX and ASL there are no concluding results, since depending on the summarization configuration, disambiguating only nouns could not always be the best solution.

Finally, we analyzed whether the integration of different types of semantic information (AR, TE, WSD) positively influenced the complexity of summaries. This analysis is necessary to determine how the semantic information and the combination of its different types affect the readability indexes. Taking into account the results provided in Table 1, we discuss the most relevant findings below comparing the results of automatic summaries with respect to the gold-standard (human generated summaries).

- *Anaphora resolution (AR).* Because pronouns are considered as obstacles for some users, replacing them by their nouns contributes to better readability in general. So, this type of semantic information obtains the best FRE results (46.7112 vs. 42.7560). In addition, the best results for AWL (4.9895 vs. 5.0383), and ASL (17.0864 vs. 19.1479) are also obtained.

This could be due to the fact that AR has a bias for shorter sentences, and a short sentence that contains a topic noun will automatically receive a high score, and would be selected for the summary. Concerning PNR and distPNR, these two metrics are improved when using AR, although AR is not the best technique for obtaining the best values for them.

Therefore, the use of AR could be appropriate when users need either a general readability improvement of the text, or shorter words, or shorter sentences.

- *Textual entailment (TE).* TE tends to discard shorter sentences that are less likely to carry any new information. Moreover, it attempts to retain the sentences with the unique proper nouns and a higher noun ratio. These criteria are good from the point of view of the relevance detection in the summarization process, but it may not be so good from the complexity point of view, where it is normally recommended to write shorter sentences. Therefore, TE achieves a good readability performance for OVIX, PNR, and distPNR, but it would need additional semantic information (e.g., WSD and AR) to obtain the best results, as it will be explained next.

As a consequence, this type of semantic information used independently is not recommended in any case when text complexity wants to be taken into account.

- *Word sense disambiguation + textual entailment (WSD + TE).* Although UKB algorithm is better as a WSD method on its own, when TE is integrated with WSD, MFS algorithm becomes beneficial for the resulting complexity. This disambiguation algorithm increases the number of repeated words, so for TE it is easier to detect redundant sentences and discard them. Once redundant information is removed, the density of unique words should be higher. This is reflected in the results obtained for the OVIX metric, which shows the best value for this group (69.8412 vs. 65.1371). Also, some improvements in PNR and distPNR are observed, although these are not the best results.

Therefore, when users need low levels of redundancy in the text, this combination of semantic information would be the most appropriate.

- *Anaphora Resolution + Word Sense Disambiguation + Textual Entailment (AR + WSD + TE).* The combination of these three types of semantic information performs the best for PNR (0.1699 vs. 0.1436), distPNR (0.1290 vs. 0.1106) and PR (0.0676 vs. 0.0865). Besides the positive influence of WSD + TE discussed in the previous paragraph, the combination of AR and TE increases the possibilities that the TE module finds more overlaps with the other sentences of the document after performing AR, and thus, there are more opportunities to discard the sentence for containing redundant information, reducing the number of pronouns in the text.

Therefore, when users have problems with the use of pronouns and with the high variability in the vocabulary of a text, the combination of AR + WSD + TE would be recommended for generating summaries.

None of the semantic information used in the summarization process was able to improve the NR readability metric. When summarizing, the length of the document is reduced, so the ratio of nouns included in the text would be kept in a similar proportion. Therefore, no improvements were observed in the results obtained.

On the other hand, the results obtained without semantic information (group 1) are improved for all the readability metrics for some of the advanced semantic techniques. Therefore, the use of advanced semantic techniques could be appropriate when dealing with a particular aspect of text simplification, to obtain summaries of better content quality, and less complex summaries with respect to a specific obstacle (e.g., variability of vocabulary or sentence length). In this manner, the generated summaries could be adapted to the users' specific needs.

5.2. *Analysis of the complexity of summaries with respect to their source documents*

The first two rows in Table 1 contain the readability indexes for the original DUC documents and the gold-standard (human generated summaries). Concerning the comparison between original documents and human summaries, the behavior of the different readability metrics varies, and no strong conclusion can be drawn. In human summaries, four of the readability metrics are improved (OVIX, PNR, distPNR, and ASL), whereas four of them are degraded (FRE, AWL, NR, and PR). This means that the users' needs would determine the best criteria to be applied to the summary process (e.g., if the user needs easier vocabulary, OVIX should be used).

When comparing the original source documents with respect to the automatic generated summaries for each readability metric, it can be observed that except for AWL, NR, and PR, the remaining readability metrics are improved. The improvements obtained are significantly better according to the t-test performed.

For the initial research question, *Does the complexity of summaries increase/decrease/remain unchanged with respect to their source documents?*, we can confirm that despite the significant reduction of a document's content as a result simply because it is involved in a summarization process (that is around 80%, keeping only with 20% of the information), in most of the cases, the complexity of the summaries decreases with respect to the complexity of the source documents.

5.3. *Analyze whether the best ROUGE scores correlates with the least complex summaries*

When comparing the readability of human and automatic summaries, the most similar summaries were generated without TE and AR and involve the least sophisticated system setting, based only on frequencies. However, we also saw that the human summaries tend to increase the complexity.

Hence, in order to analyze the relationship between the best summaries according to ROUGE, and the best concerning their complexity (i.e., the easiest ones), we further computed the ROUGE-1 recall metric of the automatic summaries, and tested the correlation with the readability metrics. The ROUGE evaluation results can be found in Table 2.

The best scores were obtained for the setting in group 5 using the TF-based scoring. In contrast, the worst results were obtained for the system settings that involve only AR. Examining the results in Table 2 and Table 1, the summarization approach that yields the best ROUGE values (group 5) fails on the FRE metrics of readability, but scores next to the best after the frequency-based approach on a number of other measures. However, the summaries that were generated using only anaphora resolution (group 2), though belonging to the worst summaries according to the

Table 2. ROUGE-1 recall results for DUC 2002 corpus (boldface indicates that the result is statistically significant (two-tailed paired t-test) with respect to the results obtained for the other groups).

		CF-MFS		CF-UKB	
	TF	NVA	N	NVA	N
Group 1	0.4178	0.4098	0.4147	0.4179	0.4146
Group 2 (AR)	0.3895	0.3887	0.3908	0.3915	0.3899
Group 3 (TE)	0.4181	0.4181	0.4160	0.4190	0.4167
Group 4 (WSD+TE)	0.4181	0.4180	0.4163	0.4189	0.4184
Group 5 (AR+WSD+TE)	**0.4324**	**0.4305**	**0.4296**	**0.4320**	**0.4303**

ROUGE values, performed the best on the FRE, AWL, and ASL readability metrics.

To determine the correlation between the ROUGE metrics and the selected readability measures, we calculated the Pearson's correlation between them. We compared the complete set of ROUGE results with the set of average readability scores, taking into account the meaning behind the results (i.e., for some readability metrics, high results indicate better performance, while for others it was the opposite).

The Pearson's correlation value obtained for ROUGE and readability score was 0.7058, indicating a strong positive correlation. This means that there is a tendency for high readability values to go with high ROUGE scores (and vice versa). However, this trend is not always confirmed, as it can be seen in Fig. 2, where the plot of the data is graphically shown (the X values correspond to the ROUGE scores in percentages, and Y values to the readability results).

As a result of this analysis, we can conclude that better summaries in terms of ROUGE are not always the best in terms of readability, although there may be some correlation between them. This can be shown in the graphic, where we can observe that, for instance, summaries around 39% ROUGE values have better readability than summaries that obtain around 41% ROUGE results.

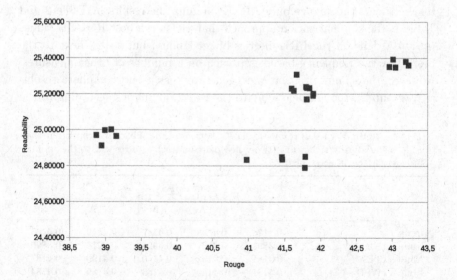

Fig. 2.   Data plot showing ROUGE scores in comparison with readability scores.

5.4. *What would happen with other languages?*

In this research work, different types of semantic information were analyzed to determine their influence in the process of summarization concerning the readability of the generated text. Although our experiments were carried out in English and not in a multilingual environment, the same experiments could be reproduced in other languages, because the semantic information analyzed is common in most of the languages. To do that, specific tools, such as part of speech (POS) taggers, anaphora resolution, and concept identification tools, as well as word sense disambiguation and textual entailment algorithms for those languages would be necessary. This would imply that those tools could also obtain an acceptable performance for that particular language, so the errors introduced by these tools do not affect the overall performance of the approach, in our case, they do not increase the complexity of texts.

In addition, it is important to note that multilinguality could be also approached by using language-independent techniques/tools. In this case, we tested the term frequency for summary generation as a technique that will work in any language, since it simply relies on counting word occurrences. However, given the results obtained, the use of this type of technique is only able to perform a surface analysis of the text. Other semantic techniques, such as word sense disambiguation, anaphora resolution or textual entailment, would provide a better understanding of the text that would result in a better performance.

Regarding the conclusions obtained about the readability metrics, similar results would be obtained in other languages. The metrics analyzed are independent of the specific characteristics of other languages (these metrics depend on the number of words, number of sentences, number of pronouns, etc.). Nevertheless, if we would like to conduct a deeper analysis of a concrete language, particular metrics for that language could also be used. For example, in the case of Spanish, the index of Fernandez-Huerta (1959)[51] could be used.

6. Conclusion and future work

This chapter presented an exhaustive analysis of the influence that the process of summarization based on different types of semantic information has on the complexity of a text. This type of analysis is novel and to the best of our knowledge no previous work on text summarization has paid attention to this issue before. The complexity analysis was performed through different automatic text readability measures: Flesch reading ease, word variation index, proper noun ratio, ratio of distinct proper nouns, average word length, average sentence length, noun ratio, and pronoun ratio. The selected summarization engine included various modules that enable integration of different semantic information (anaphora resolution, word sense disambiguation, and textual entailment). Although the readability measures selected are based on the surface characteristics of a text, the obtained results show that these measures can reflect the changes in the readability of generated summaries across different configurations of the summarizer.

Our experiments confirm that the summarization process, as it is currently conducted, can influence the readability of the generated summary with respect to both the source document and the human summary. For most of the readability metrics used in this research work, the automatic summaries obtained better results than the source document or the human summaries. However, not all the metrics are improved in the same manner for all the semantic information used in the summarization process. Depending on the specific users' preferences or needs, and the type of complexity they want to reduce, it could be more appropriate to employ different semantic techniques for generating the summaries. In this sense, if a user would like to obtain less vocabulary variability in the generated summary, we recommend the use of the combination of word sense disambiguation together with textual entailment; we further recommend avoiding the use of anaphora resolution.

Based on the results obtained when evaluating the content of the summaries with ROUGE, in addition to their readability, we can conclude that term frequency based and concept frequency based extractive summarization are highly competitive baselines, because they provide acceptable ROUGE results and in addition, they can decrease the complexity of the summaries in terms of their readability.

Although in this chapter we analyzed different configurations for the summarization approach, in particular, anaphora resolution, word sense disambiguation, textual entailment, and concept/term frequency, other summarization techniques with additional semantic information could be used for the same purposes. In such case, the influence of the new semantic information should be analyzed and discussed. Our experiments were carried out in English. However, the same experiments could be reproduced in other languages and similar results would be obtained.

For future work, we would like to take into account accessibility issues when generating summaries, so apart from facilitating quick access to the contents of a text, the information contained would be accessible and easily understood, regardless of user type and background. For instance, as part of the relevance detection stage, we could integrate criteria related to complexity of the text, such as the frequency of the words (to know which vocabulary should be easy to use), or the length of the words.

Acknowledgments

This research work has been partially funded by Generalitat Valenciana, and the Spanish Government, through projects, DIIM2.0 (PROMETEOII/ 2014/001), TIN2015-65100-R, and TIN2015-65136-C2-2-R respectively.

References

1. T. C. Davis, M. S. Wolf, P. F. Bass, M. Middlebrooks, E. Kennen, D. W. Baker, C. L. Bennett, R. Durazo-Arvizu, A. Bocchini, S. Savory, and R. M. Parker, Low literacy impairs comprehension of prescription drug warning labels, *Journal of General Internal Medicine*, **21**(8), 847–851 (2006). doi: 10.1111/j.1525-1497.2006.00529.x.
2. P. Vacek and K. Rybenská, The most frequent difficulties encountered by senior citizens while using information and communication technology, *Procedia — Social and Behavioral Sciences*, **217**, 452–458 (2016). doi: http://dx.doi.org/10.1016/j.sbspro.2016.02.013. Available at: http:// www.sciencedirect.com/science/article/pii/S1877042816000380.
3. S. E. Petersen and M. Ostendorf, Text simplification for language learners: A corpus analysis. In *Proceedings of the SLaTE Workshop on Speech and Language Technology for Education*, Farmington, PA, USA, Carnegie Mellon University and ISCA Archive (2007).
4. V. Claveau, T. Hamon, S. L. Maguer, and N. Grabar, Health consumer-oriented information retrieval. In *Digital Healthcare Empowering Europeans — Proceedings of MIE2015*, Madrid Spain, pp. 80–84 (2015). doi: 10.3233/978-1-61499-512-8-80.
5. S. Stajner, R. Evans, C. Orasan, and R. Mitkov, What can readability measures really tell us about text complexity? In eds. L. Rello and H. Saggion, *Proceedings of the LREC'12 Workshop: Natural Language Processing for Improving Textual Accessibility (NLP4ITA)*, European Language Resources Association (ELRA) (2012).
6. J. Carroll, G. Minnen, Y. Canning, S. Devlin, and J. Tait, Practical simplification of english newspaper text to assist aphasic readers. In *Proceedings of the AAAI98 Workshop on Integrating AI and Assistive Technology*, Madison, Wisconsin, USA, pp. 7–10, AAAI (1998).

7. L. Rello, DysWebxia: A model to improve accessibility of the textual web for dyslexic users, *ACM SIGACCESS Accessibility and Computing*, (102), 41–44 (2012).

8. K. Inui, A. Fujita, T. Takahashi, R. Iida, and T. Iwakura, Text simplification for reading assistance: A project note. In eds. M-Y. Kan and S. Bird, *Proceedings of the Second International Workshop on Paraphrasing — Volume 16*, PARAPHRASE '03, Sapporo, Japan, pp. 9–16, ACL (2003). doi: 10.3115/1118984.1118986.

9. K. Spärck Jones, Automatic summarizing: Factors and directions. In eds. Inderjeet Mani and Mark Maybury, *Advances in Automatic Text Summarization*, pp. 1–14, MIT Press (1999).

10. Y. Yano, M. H. Long, and S. Ross, The effects of simplified and elaborated texts on foreign language reading comprehension, *Language Learning*, **44**(2), 189–219 (1994). ISSN 1467-9922. doi: 10.1111/j.1467-1770.1994.tb01100.x.

11. H. Saggion, S. Bott, and L. Rello, Simplifying words in context. Experiments with two lexical resources in Spanish, *Computer Speech & Language*, **35**, 200–218 (2016). doi: 10.1016/j.csl.2015.02.001.

12. K. Woodsend and M. Lapata, Learning to simplify sentences with quasi-synchronous grammar and integer programming. In eds. R. Barzilay and M. Johnson, *Proceedings of the 2011 Conference on Empirical Methods in Natural Language Processing (EMNLP)*, Edinburgh, UK, pp. 409–420, SIGDAT (2011).

13. S. Narayan and C. Gardent, Hybrid simplification using deep semantics and machine translation. In eds. K. Toutanova and H. Wu, *Proceedings of the 52nd Annual Meeting of the Association for Computational Linguistics (Volume 1: Long Papers)*, Baltimore, Maryland, USA, pp. 435–445, ACL (2014). Available at: http://www.aclweb.org/anthology/P14-1041.

14. G. Glavaš and S. Štajner, Event-centered simplification of news stories. In eds. R. Mitkov, G. Angelova and K. Boncheva, *Proceedings of the Student Research Workshop associated with RANLP 2013*, Hissar, Bulgaria, pp. 71–78, INCOMA Ltd. Shoumen (2013). Available at: http://www.aclweb.org/anthology/R13-2011.

15. M. Angrosh, T. Nomoto, and A. Siddharthan, Lexico-syntactic text simplification and compression with typed dependencies. In *Proceedings of COLING 2014, the 25th International Conference on Computational Linguistics: Technical Papers*, pp. 1996–2006, Dublin City University and Association for Computational Linguistics, Dublin, Ireland (2014). Available at: http://www.aclweb.org/anthology/C14-1188.

16. S. Botelho Silveira and A. Branco, Enhancing multi-document summaries with sentence simplification. In eds. H. R. Arabnia, D. de la Fuente, E. B. Kozerenko, P. M. LaMonica, R. A. Liuzzi, J. A. Olivas, A. M. G. Solo, T. Waskiewicz, *Proceedings of ICAI 2012: The 14th International Conference on Artificial Intelligence*, Las Vegas, NV, USA, pp. 742–748, CSREA Press (2012).

17. P. R. A. Margarido, T. A. S. Pardo, G. M. Antonio, V. B. Fuentes, R. Aires, S. M. Aluísio, and R. P. M. Fortes, Automatic summarization for text simplification: Evaluating text understanding by poor readers. In *Companion Proceedings of the XIV Brazilian Symposium on Multimedia and the Web*, WebMedia '08, pp. 310–315, ACM (2008).

18. D. Marcu, Improving summarization through rhetorical parsing tuning. In ed. E. Charniak, *Proceedings of The Sixth Workshop on Very Large Corpora*, Montreal, Canada, pp. 206–215, ACL (1998).

19. C.-Y. Lin, ROUGE: A package for automatic evaluation of summaries. In *Proceedings of the ACL Workshop on Text Summarization Branches Out*, Barcelona, Spain, p. 10, ACL (2004).

20. T. Kanungo and D. Orr, Predicting the readability of short web summaries. In *Proceedings of the Second ACM International Conference on Web Search and Data Mining*, WSDM '09, pp. 202–211, ACM (2009). doi: 10.1145/1498759. 1498827.

21. R. Vadlapudi and R. Katragadda, On automated evaluation of readability of summaries: Capturing grammaticality, focus, structure and coherence. In *Proceedings of the NAACL HLT 2010 Student Research Workshop*, HLT-SRWS '10, pp. 7–12, ACL (2010).

22. S. Stymne and C. Smith, On the interplay between readability, summarization, and MTranslatability. In *Proceedings of the Fourth Swedish Language Technology Conference (SLTC 2012)*, Lund, Sweden, pp. 70–71, ACL (2012).

23. C. Smith and A. Jönsson, Automatic summarization as means of simplifying texts, an evaluation for Swedish. In eds. B. S. Pedersen, G. Nešpore and I. Skadiņa, *Proceedings of the 18th Nordic Conference of Computational Linguistics (NoDaLiDa-2010)*, pp. 198–205, Northern European Association for Language Technology (NEALT) (2010).

24. S. Brin and L. Page, The anatomy of a large-scale hypertextual web search engine, *Computer Networks and ISDN Systems*, **30**(1–7), 107–117 (1998).

25. C. H. Björnsson, *Läsbarhet*. Stockholm, Liber (1968).

26. C. Smith, H. Danielsson, and A. Jönsson, A good space: Lexical predictors in word space evaluation. In eds. N. Calzolari, K. Choukri, T. Declerck, M. U. Doğan, B. Maegaard, J. Mariani, J. Odijk, and S. Piperidis, *Proceedings of the Eighth International Conference on Language Resources and Evaluation (LREC-2012)*, pp. 2530–2535, European Language Resources Association (ELRA) (2012). ACL Anthology Identifier: L12-1159.

27. T. Vodolazova, E. Lloret, R. Muñoz, and M. Palomar, A comparative study of the impact of statistical and semantic features in the framework of extractive text summarization. In eds. P. Sojka, A. Horák, I. Kopecek, and K. Pala, *Proceedings of Text, Speech and Dialogue — 15th International Conference, TSD 2012*, Brno, Czech Republic, vol. 7499, *Lecture Notes in Computer Science*, pp. 306–313, Springer (2012).

28. A. Nenkova, L. Vanderwende, and K. McKeown, A compositional context sensitive multi-document summarizer: Exploring the factors that influence

summarization. In *Proceedings of the 29th Annual International ACM SIGIR Conference on Research and Development in Information Retrieval*, SIGIR '06, pp. 573–580, ACM (2006).

29. E. Agirre and A. Soroa, Personalizing PageRank for word sense disambiguation. In *Proceedings of the 12th Conference of the European Chapter of the Association for Computational Linguistics*, EACL '09, pp. 33–41, ACL (2009).

30. E. Lloret, O. Ferrández, R. Muñoz, and M. Palomar, A text summarization approach under the influence of textual entailment. In *Proceedings of the 5th International Workshop on Natural Language Processing and Cognitive Science (NLPCS 2008) in Conjunction with the 10th International Conference on Enterprise Information Systems (ICEIS 2008)*, Barcelona, Spain, pp. 22–31 (2008).

31. W. H. DuBay, *The Principles of Readability*, Impact Information, Costa Mesa (2004).

32. K. Collins-Thompson, Computational assessment of text readability: A survey of current and future research, *ITL-International Journal of Applied Linguistics*, **165**(2), 97–135 (2014).

33. R. Flesch, A new readability yardstick, *Journal of Applied Psychology*, **32**(3), 221–233 (1948).

34. T. G. Hultman and M. Westman, *Gymnasistsvenska*. Stockholm, Liber (1977).

35. L. Rello, R. Baeza-Yates, L. Dempere-Marco, and H. Saggion, Frequent words improve readability and short words improve understandability for people with dyslexia. In *Proceedings of the 14th IFIP TC13 Conference on Human-Computer Interaction*, Cape Town, South Africa, pp. 203–219. Springer, Berlin, Heidelberg (2013).

36. K. Mckeown, J. Hirschberg, M. Galley, and S. Maskey, From text to speech summarization. In *Proceedings of the International Conference on Acoustics, Speech, and Signal Processing* (Vol. 5), Philadelphia, PA, pp. 997–1000 (2005).

37. B. Arfé, J. Oakhill, and E. Pianta, The text simplification in TERENCE. *Methodologies and Intelligent Systems for Technology Enhanced Learning*, pp. 165–172, Springer International Publishing, Cham (2014).

38. J. Hancke, S. Vajjala, and D. Meurers, Readability classification for German using lexical, syntactic, and morphological features. In eds. K. Martin and B. Christian, *Proceedings of COLING 2012*, pp. 1063–1080, The COLING 2012 Organizing Committee, Mumbai, India (December, 2012).

39. Y. Versley, S. P. Ponzetto, M. Poesio, V. Eidelman, A. Jern, J. Smith, X. Yang, and A. Moschitti, BART: A modular toolkit for coreference resolution. In eds. M. Palmer, G. Boleda and P. Rosso, *Proceedings of the 46th Annual Meeting of the Association for Computational Linguistics on Human Language Technologies: Demo Session*, pp. 9–12, ACL (2008). Available at: http://dl.acm.org/citation.cfm?id=1564144.1564147.

40. O. Uryupina and A. Moschitti, A state-of-the-art mention-pair model for coreference resolution. In eds. M. Palmer, G. Boleda and P. Rosso,

Proceedings of the Fourth Joint Conference on Lexical and Computational Semantics, Denver, CO, USA, pp. 289–298, ACL (2015). Available at: http://www.aclweb.org/anthology/S15-1034.

41. O. Ferrández, D. Micol, R. Muñoz, and M. Palomar, A perspective-based approach for solving textual entailment recognition. In *Proceedings of the ACL-PASCAL Workshop on Textual Entailment and Paraphrasing*, Prague, Czech Republic, pp. 66–71, ACL (June, 2007). Available at: https://aclanthology.coli.uni-saarland.de/papers/S15-1034/s15-1034.

42. O. Ferrández, *Textual Entailment Recognition and its Applicability in NLP Task*. PhD thesis, Universidad de Alicante (2009).

43. L. Padró and E. Stanilovsky, FreeLing 3.0: Towards wider multilinguality. In *Proceedings of the Eight International Conference on Language Resources and Evaluation (LREC'12)*, Istanbul, Turkey, European Language Resources Association (ELRA) (2012).

44. J. Preiss, J. Dehdari, J. King, and D. Mehay, Refining the most frequent sense baseline. In eds. V. Werneck and K. K. Breitman, *Proceedings of the Workshop on Semantic Evaluations: Recent Achievements and Future Directions (SEW-2009)*, Skövde, Sweden, pp. 10–18, ACL (June, 2009). Available at: http://www.aclweb.org/anthology/W09-2403.

45. E. Agirre, O. López de Lacalle, and A. Soroa, Random walks for knowledge-based word sense disambiguation, *Computational Linguistics*, **40**(1), 57–84 (2014). doi: 10.1162/COLI_a_00164.

46. K. Toutanova, D. Klein, C. D. Manning, and Y. Singer, Feature-rich part-of-speech tagging with a cyclic dependency network. In *Proceedings of the 2003 Conference of the North American Chapter of the Association for Computational Linguistics on Human Language Technology — Volume 1*, NAACL '03, Edmonton, Canada, pp. 173–180, ACL (2003). doi: 10.3115/1073445.1073478.

47. T. Vodolazova, E. Lloret, R. Muñoz, and M. Palomar, A comparative study of the impact of statistical and semantic features in the framework of extractive text summarization. In *Text, Speech and Dialogue — Proceedings of the 15th International Conference, TSD 2012*, Brno, Czech Republic, pp. 306–313 (2012). doi: 10.1007/978-3-642-32790-2_37.

48. T. Vodolazova, E. Lloret, R. Muñoz, and M. Palomar, The role of statistical and semantic features in single-document extractive summarization, *Journal of Artificial Intelligence Research*, **2**(3), 35–44 (2013). doi: 10.5430/air.v2n3p35.

49. S. Pita Fernández, Determinación del tamaño muestral, *CAD ATEN PRIMARIA 1996*, **3**, 114–138 (1996).

50. Y. Gutiérrez Vázquez, A. Fernández Orquín, A. Montoyo Guijarro, and S. Vázquez Pérez, Integración de recursos semánticos basados en WordNet, *Procesamiento del Lenguaje Natural*, **47**, 161–168 (2011).

51. J. Fernández Huerta, Medidas sencillas de lecturabilidad, *Consignia*, **214**, 29–32 (1959).

Chapter 11

Twitter Event Detection, Analysis, and Summarization

Natalia Vanetik*, Marina Litvak[†], Efi Levi[‡],
and Andrey Vashchenko[§]

Shamoon College of Engineering,
Software Engineering Department,
Byalik 56, Beer Sheva, Israel, 84100
* *natalyav@sce.ac.il*
[†] *marinal@sce.ac.il*
[‡] *efilvefi@gmail.com*
[§] *andreva.w@gmail.com*

Data analysis in social media is a broad and well-addressed research topic, but the characteristics and sheer volume of Twitter messages with high amounts of noise in them make it a difficult task for Twitter. Tweets reporting real-life events are usually overwhelmed by a flood of meaningless information. This chapter describes the TWItter event Summarizer and Trend detector (TWIST) system that attempts to tackle these challenges by combining *wavelet* and *text* analysis.

The system detects and analyzes real-life events reported in Twitter. For providing high-quality summaries with clean and meaningful content, TWIST analyzes external sources for detected events, which it accomplishes by retrieving links and extracting the main tweets describing those events. Then, all detected events are analyzed by their sentiment distribution over a world map, and visualized in the resolution of countries. This feature enables the TWIST user to see whether, and if so, how the geolocation of Twitter users affects their opinions, and how the sentiments and opinions regarding the same event can be different over different countries. Then, by analyzing wavelet form and user activity, a prediction can be made for an event to be highly active.

In our approach, we utilize unsupervised learning for most stages, except sentiment analysis. Our system does not rely on external ontologies, but incorporates external sources, automatically retrieved, for summarizing events. Also, TWIST uses geolocation of event-related tweets to visualize their sentiments on a map. Finally, we use text and hashtag analysis in order to predict high-activity events before they are fully developed. Because our approach requires basic text preprocessing only, it can therefore be easily adapted to multiple languages.

1. Introduction

One of the most representative examples of microblogging (a form of social media) is Twitter, which gives users the ability to publish short tweets (messages within a 140 character limit) about "what's happening." Alongside of "what's on the user's mind" tweets, real-time events are also reported. For example, the Football World Cup and Israeli-Palestinian conflict were extensively reported by Twitter users. Reporting those events could provide different perspectives to news items than would traditional media; such Twitter reporting can also provide valuable user sentiment about certain events. Twitter users publish short messages, in a faster and summarized way, which makes Twitter the preferred tool for the quick dissemination of information over the web. Tweets may relate to anything that came to the user's mind; some relate to real-life events.

Twitter grows rapidly. Every second, on average, around 6000 tweets reporting about real-life events are published on Twitter.[1] To analyze the Twitter information flow efficiently, event detection is needed. A Twitter event is a collection of tweets and re-tweets that discuss the same subject in a relatively short (minutes, hours or days) time period. Existing algorithms typically detect events by clustering together words with similar burst patterns. Moreover, it is usually necessary to set the number of events that would be detected, which is difficult to obtain in Twitter due to its real-time nature. The study in Ref. 2 conducted by Pear Analytics states about 40% of all tweets are pointless "bubbles" and an additional 37% are conversational. Although such tweets are popular among users, they interfere with performance of event detection algorithms and should be treated as noise.

Event detection in traditional media has been broadly divided into retrospective event detection and new event detection,[3-5] where the former requires the data to be pre-collected and the latter addresses the news stream as it arrives in real-time. Two main Twitter event detection categories are *unspecified event detection*, where an event is not identified beforehand, and *specified event detection*,[3-5] where an event is known or planned. Our method is directed to retrospective unspecified event detection.

Event detection in Twitter employs techniques from different fields of computer science. New events emerge fast and typically attract the attention of a large number of users. If no prior information is available, the classic approach to unspecified detection of such events exploits temporal bursts of Twitter stream features such as *hashtags* and specific words. A hashtag is an unspaced phrase prefixed with # to form a type of label that specifies a main theme of a tweet. Users can start a new theme by initiating their own hashtags, and other users can use these hashtags in their own tweets in order to incorporate them into one of the existing themes. Hashtags make it easier for users to find messages with a specific theme or content.

In this chapter we present TWItter event Summarizer and Trend detector (TWIST) — a system that detects, summarizes, analyzes sentiment for, and predicts real-world events in Twitter.

This chapter is organized as follows. Section 2 describes prior works related to event detection in Twitter. Section 3 describes our methodology for event detection, summarization, sentiment analysis, and prediction. Section 4 describes the TWIST architecture and implementation of its main modules. Section 5 summarizes the pilot study that was performed on two datasets of collected tweets. The last section concludes our approach and the performed study.

2. Related work

In general, events can be defined as real-world occurrences that unfold over space and time.[4–7] Event detection from traditional media sources has been addressed in the Topic Detection and Tracking research program, which mainly aims at finding events in a stream of news stories.[4,5]

Twitter contents are dynamically changing and increasing by the minute. According to the website Twee Speed,[a] on average there are more than 15,000 tweets per minute published in Twitter. Therefore, event detection in Twitter streams is more challenging and difficult than similar tasks in traditional media. News articles are usually well-written, structured, and edited, while Twitter messages are restricted in length and written by users who are not professional writers. Tweets include large amounts of informal and irregular words and abbreviations, and contain large numbers of spelling and grammatical errors. Twitter messages often have improper

---

[a]http://tweespeed.com.

sentence syntactic structure and mix different languages. When tweets report big real-life events, they are usually mixed with a large amount of meaningless messages. Twitter streams contain large amounts of garbage, polluted content, and rumors.[8] Therefore, not every word or hashtag in tweets that show burst behavior is related to a real-life event. A good example is the popular hashtag "#musicmonday". It shows some bursts every Monday because it is commonly used to suggest music on Mondays. However, such bursts obviously do not correspond to an event that a majority of the users would pay attention to. Event detection in Twitter is expected to differentiate the big events from the trivial ones.

There are a multitude of methods for event detection from Twitter that are based on techniques from different fields, such as machine learning, data mining, natural language processing, information extraction, text mining, and information retrieval. When no prior information is available about a Twitter event, *unspecified event detection* relies on the temporal signal of Twitter streams to detect the occurrence of a real-world event. These techniques typically require monitoring for bursts or trends in Twitter streams, grouping features with similar trends into events, and then classifying the events into different categories. On the other hand, *specified event detection* relies on specific information and features that are known about the event, such as geo-location, time, type, and description, which are provided by the user or are derived from the event context. These features can be exploited by adapting traditional information retrieval and extraction techniques such as filtering, query generation and expansion, clustering, and information aggregation, to the unique characteristics of tweets.

2.1. *Unspecified event detection in Twitter*

The nature of Twitter posts reflect events as they unfold; hence, these tweets are particularly useful for unknown event detection. Unknown events of interest are typically driven by things such as

- emerging events
- breaking news
- general topics that attract the attention of a large number of Twitter users.

Because no event information is available ahead of time, unknown events are typically detected by exploiting the temporal patterns or signals of

Twitter streams. New events of general interest exhibit a burst of features in Twitter streams yielding, for instance, a sudden increased use of specific keywords. Bursty features that occur frequently together in tweets can then be grouped into trends. In addition to trending events, endogenous or non-event trends are also abundant on Twitter. Techniques for unspecified event detection in Twitter must discriminate trending events of general interest from trivial or nonevent trends.

2.1.1. *Textual features-based systems*

The TwitterStand system[9] is a news processing system that captures tweets corresponding breaking news. The system uses a naive Bayes classifier to separate news from irrelevant information and an online clustering algorithm, based on a weighted term vector according to *tf-idf* and cosine similarity, to form clusters of news.

The authors of Ref. 10 present a method for collecting, grouping, ranking, and tracking news in Twitter. Their approach groups together similar messages in order to form a news story. Similarity between messages is computed using *tf-idf*, with an increased weight for proper noun terms, hashtags, and usernames.

The authors of Ref. 11 adapt the traditional media news event detection approach of Ref. 12 to Twitter. Here, cosine similarity between news documents is used in order to discover new events.

The authors of Ref. 13 use an online clustering technique to identify real-world event content and its associated Twitter messages. Similar tweets are clustered in a continuous manner and then classified into events and non-events (trending activities in Twitter that do not reflect any real-world occurrences). Messages are represented by their *tf-idf* weight vectors, and cluster distance is computed using cosine similarity. A cluster is classified as an event or a non-event with the help of a support vector machine (SVM) trained on a labeled cluster features.

The authors of Ref. 14 integrate topical-word microblog features into a traditional clustering approach. These features are based on topical words that are extracted from daily messages on the basis of word frequency, word occurrence in hashtag, and word entropy. Event tracking is performed with the help of maximum-weighted bipartite graph matching, where a Jaccard coefficient is used as a cluster similarity measure; cosine similarity is used to measure the distance between messages.

2.1.2. *Wavelet-based systems*

The authors of Ref. 15 propose event detection that is based on clustering of discrete wavelet signals built from individual hashtags. Unlike Fourier transforms that are used for event detection in traditional media, wavelet transformations are localized in both time and frequency domain and are therefore able to identify the time and the duration of an event within the signal. Wavelets are used to convert the signals from the time domain to a time-scale domain, where the scale is the inverse of hashtag frequency. Signal construction is performed using *df-idf* (document frequency–inverse document frequency), where df counts the number of tweets (i.e., documents) containing a specific hashtag. Trivial words are filtered out on the basis of signals' cross-correlation, which measure similarity between two signals as function of a time lag. The remaining words are then clustered to form events with a modularity-based graph partitioning technique, which splits the graph into subgraphs, each corresponding to an event. Finally, significant events are detected on the basis of cross-correlation among the hashtags.

Similarly, Ref. 16 proposes a continuous wavelet transformation based on hashtag occurrences combined with a topic model inference using latent Dirichlet allocation (LDA).[17] An abrupt increase in the number of a given hashtag is considered a good indicator of an event that is happening at a given time. When an event is detected within a given time interval, LDA is applied to all tweets related to the hashtag in each corresponding time series, in order to extract a set of latent topics, which provides a summary of event description.

2.2. *Sentiment analysis of tweets*

Sentiment analysis[18] is a process that automates mining of attitudes, opinions, views, and emotions from text, speech, tweets, and database sources. Through natural language processing (NLP), it involves classifying opinions in text into categories like *positive* or *negative* or *neutral*.

Several works examined supervised learning that used the Naive Bayes classification model. Pak and Paroubek (2010), in Ref. 19, proposed a model to classify tweets. They used Twitter API to create a twitter corpus, enabling their model to automatically use emoticons to annotate the tweets. Using that corpus, they developed a sentiment classifier based on the multinomial Naive Bayes method, which uses features like N-gram and POS-tags. Parikh and Movassate (2009), in Ref. 20, used a Naive Bayes bigram model and a maximum entropy model to classify tweets; they found that the Naive Bayes classifiers worked much better than a maximum entropy model. Go *et al.* (2009), in Ref. 21, proposed a solution for sentiment analysis for Twitter data by using distant supervision, in which their training data consisted of tweets with emoticons that served as noisy labels, using Naive Bayes, maximum entropy, and SVM. Liang and Dai (2013), in Ref. 22, used training data of three different categories (camera, movie, mobile), which were labeled as positive, negative and non-opinions. A unigram Naive Bayes model was implemented and the Naive Bayes simplifying independence assumption was employed. Pablo *et al.* (2014), in Ref. 23, presented variations of a Naive Bayes classifier for detecting polarity of English tweets. Xia *et al.* (2011), in Ref. 24, used an ensemble framework for sentiment classification that is obtained by combining various feature sets and classification techniques. In their work, they used two types of feature sets (POS information and word-relations) and three base classifiers (Naive Bayes, maximum entropy, and SVM) in ensemble approaches.

Another group of works relied heavily on statistical properties of tweet word and hashtag usage. Barbosa *et al.* (2010), in Ref. 25, designed a two phase automatic sentiment analysis method for classifying tweets; the feature space they used included retweets, hashtags, link, punctuation, and exclamation marks. Bifet and Frank (2010), in Ref. 26, used Twitter streaming data provided by the Firehouse API and multinomial Naive Bayes, stochastic gradient descent (SGD), and the Hoeffding tree. Agarwal *et al.* (2011), in Ref. 27, developed a model for classifying sentiment into positive, negative, and neutral classes, with the help of unigram model, a feature based model, and a tree kernel-based model. Davidov *et al.* (2010), in Ref. 28, proposed an approach to utilize Twitter user-defined hashtags in tweets as a classification of sentiment type. Turney *et al.* (2002), in Ref. 29, used the bag-of-words method for sentiment analysis; in this method the relationships between words is not considered at all, and a document is represented as just a collection of words.

Deep linguistic features and advanced mining techniques were also studied in this field. Kamps *et al.* (2004), in Ref. 30, used the WordNet lexical database to determine the emotional content of a word along different dimensions. They developed a distance metric on WordNet and determined the semantic polarity of adjectives. Luo *et al.* (2015), in Ref. 31, used efficient mining techniques to retrieve opinions from Twitter tweets, which is a challenging task due to spam and wildly varying language.

2.3. *Event prediction for Twitter*

Empirical analysis of social networks data shows that real-world news events produce collective patterns of bursty behavior, in combination with long periods of inactivity. Events for which most of their activity is concentrated into very high-activity periods can be identified in the analysis as high-activity events. These high-activity events have unique characteristics, and these characteristics can be predicted very early in their lifecycle.

Kalyanam and Quezada (2016), in Ref. 32, suggested a VQ-event model, designed to filter events based on the distribution of the arrival times between consecutive messages. The method learns a set of the most representative arrival times from a large training corpus of events and then, using features like retweets and sentiment of the posts about the event, it can predict high-activity events using only the earliest 5% of the data of each event.

Kallus (2014), in Ref. 33, offered a statistic method of prediction based on the number of event mentions in mainstream media and Twitter posts, comparing that to the number of data during the past few months. Analysis of entities and time statements mentioned in related data, as well as publication dates, are used for modeling the future significant event.

Gruhl *et al.* (2005), in Ref. 34, using a cross-correlation between a time series of blog mentions of books, and Amazon sales rank data, found that a sudden increase in blog mentions is a potential strong predictor of a spike in a sales rank. Model-based prediction methods where a mathematical model of an object must be tailored to the task, are also used for this purpose.[35,36] A Bayes classifier was used in Ref. 37, where the prediction result must be discretized first. A comprehensive survey of Twitter event prediction methods can be found in Ref. 38.

3. Methodology

This section contains the detailed description of methods that we used in TWIST for event detection, text ranking, text clustering, summarization, sentiment analysis, and prediction, respectively.

3.1. *Capabilities*

Our method aims at unspecified event detection and analysis in Twitter. Our system performs the following tasks:

(1) Employs wavelet and text features to detect unspecified events in the Twitter data stream. It combines the wavelet-based method suggested

in Ref. 15 with textual features, thereby enabling better separation between events with similar burst patterns. Wavelet approach, in turn, is responsible for the separation and elimination of non-events from important real-world events.

(2) **Event filtering** by country or event size. If a user is interested in events reported in a certain country or in big- or small-scale events, she can target event detection to these event types.

(3) Twitter **event summarization** using internal and external data sources. TWIST retrieves the most important tweets, hashtags, and keywords for every detected event and builds event summaries from most salient tweets (*internal event summary*) and from the relevant external sources (*external event summary*).

(4) **Sentiment analysis** for detected events. All detected events are analyzed by their sentiment distribution over a world map, and visualized in the resolution of countries. This feature enables the TWIST user to see whether and how the geolocation of Twitter users affects their opinions, and how the sentiments and opinions regarding the same political or other event can be different over different countries.

(5) High-activity **event prediction**. We use the method described in Ref. 32 in order to detect and report events with potentially strong impact early on, using event characteristics that are distinguishable at the beginning stages of event.

3.2. *Text preprocessing*

TWIST analyzes the textual content of tweets by performing preprocessing on all collected tweets, before they are stored in a database and then analyzed. We perform the following preprocessing steps for each collected tweet:

(1) tokenization (hashtags are retrieved and stored separately from regular tokens);
(2) POS tagging and filtering;
(3) stop-words removal; and
(4) stemming for remaining words.[39]

The result of preprocessing is a collection of normalized terms (stems) and hashtags, linked to their tweets. Then the frequency-based statistics are calculated and also stored in our database. Namely, for each normalized term (or hashtag) t_i in a tweet T_j we calculate:

$$tf_{ij} = \frac{\text{number of } t_i \text{ occurrences in } T_j}{|T_j|}.$$
(1)

$$idf_i = \frac{\log\left(\text{number of tweets}\right)}{|\{T_j|t_i \in T_j\}|}.$$
(2)

$$tf\text{-}idf_{ij} = tf_{ij} * idf_i.$$
(3)

All tweets are linked to their hashtags, which enables us to later use these statistics for operating hashtag signals and detected events, formed by signals.

3.3. *Event detection*

3.3.1. *EDCoW algorithm*

The EDCoW algorithm was first introduced in Ref. 15. Its main idea is to build wavelet signals for individual words or hashtags that appear in tweets and then use these signals to capture the bursts in their appearances. The signals can be computed quickly using wavelet analysis, and their representation requires much less storage than do the original tweets. The algorithm filters away the trivial hashtags (their triviality is determined by measuring auto-correlation of their signals) and then detects the events by clustering hashtag signals together using a graph partitioning approach. EDCoW differentiates real and trivial events by computing the significance of an event by using the number of hashtags and the connections among the hashtags related to the event. This algorithm has four components:

(1) hashtag signal construction,
(2) hashtag filtering,
(3) cross-correlation computation, and
(4) graph partitioning.

These components are described in detail in the following.

Component (1): hashtag signal construction. This component uses wavelets to construct a signal for each individual hashtag that appears in tweets. A *wavelet* is a wave-like oscillation with an amplitude that begins at zero, increases, and then decreases back to zero. Figure 1 illustrates the notion of a wavelet.

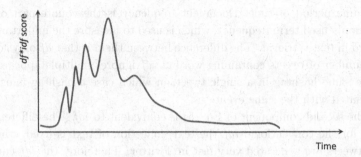

Fig. 1.   Wavelet example.

Generally, wavelets are purposefully crafted to have specific properties that make them useful for signal processing. Wavelet analysis is applied to build signals for individual hashtags. The wavelet analysis provides precise measurements regarding when and how the frequency of the signal changes over time; wavelets are relatively localized in both time and frequency.

The core of wavelet analysis is wavelet transformation. It converts a signal from the time domain to the time-scale domain (using a scale that can be considered as the inverse of frequency). In general, *wavelet transformation* can be either continuous (CWT) or discrete (DWT). CWT provides a redundant representation of the signal under analysis. Unfortunately, it is also time-consuming to compute directly. In contrast, DWT provides a non-redundant, highly efficient wavelet representation of the signal; therefore, DWT is used by the algorithm.

The signal for each individual hashtag is built in two stages. In the **first stage**, the signal for a hashtag ω, at the current time T_c is written as a sequence

$$S_\omega = [s_\omega(1), s_\omega(2), \ldots, s_\omega(T_c)] \tag{4}$$

where $s_\omega(t)$ at each sample point, t, is the *df-idf*-alike score of ω. This score is defined as

$$s_\omega(t) = \frac{N_\omega(t)}{N(t)} \times \log \frac{\sum_{i=1}^{T_c} N(i)}{\sum_{i=1}^{T_c} N_\omega(i)}. \tag{5}$$

The first component of Eq. (5) is *df* (document frequency), where $N_\omega(t)$ is the number of tweets that contain hashtag ω and that appear after sample point $t-1$ but before t, and where $N(t)$ is the number of all tweets in the same period of time. Document frequency is the counterpart of the commonly used term frequency, which is used to measure the importance of a word in text retrieval. The difference between them is that df only counts the number of tweets containing word ω. df ignores multiple appearances of the same hashtag in a single tweet, in which case a hashtag is usually associated with the same event.

The second component of Eq. (5) is equivalent to idf. The difference is that, for the conventional idf the text/collection of text is fixed, whereas new tweets are generated very fast in Twitter. Therefore, the idf component in the formula makes it possible to accommodate new hashtags. The value of $s_\omega(t)$ is high if hashtag ω is used more often than others from time $t - 1$ to time t, while it is rarely used before the current time T_c.

The **second stage** builds the smooth signal with the help of a sliding window that covers a number of first-stage sample points; sliding window size is denoted by Δ.

In the sliding window, each second-stage sample point captures the magnitute of the change in $s_\omega(t)$, if there is any. In this stage, the signal for word ω at current time T'_c is again represented as a sequence:

$$S'_\omega = [s'_\omega(1), s'_\omega(2), \ldots, s'_\omega(T_c)]. \tag{6}$$

Note that time units t in the first stage and t' in the second stage are not necessarily the same. For example, the interval between two consecutive time points in the first stage could be 10 minutes, while that in the second stage could be one hour. In this case $\Delta = 6$.

To compute the value of $s'_\omega(t')$ at each sample point, the EDCoW algorithm first moves the sliding window to cover first-stage sample points from $s_\omega((t' - 1) * \Delta)$. Denote that signal fragment by $D_{t'}$. The algorithm then derives the H-measure of the signal in $D_{t'-1}$ and denotes it by $H_{t'-1}$. Next, EDCoW shifts the sliding window to cover first-stage sample points from $s_\omega((t' - 1) * \Delta + 1)$ to $s_\omega(t' * \Delta)$. This new fragment is denoted by $D_{t'}$. Then, EDCoW concatenates segments $D_{t'-1}$ and $D_{t'}$ sequentially to form a larger segment D_{t^*}, whose H-measure H_{t^*} is also computed. Subsequently, the value of $s'_\omega(t' - 1)$ is computed as:

$$s'_\omega(t') = \begin{cases} \dfrac{H_{t^*} - H_{t'-1}}{H_{t'-1}} & \text{if } H_{t^*} > H_{t'-1} \\ 0, & \text{otherwise.} \end{cases} \tag{7}$$

If there is no change in $s_\omega(t)$ within interval D_{t^*}, there will be no significant difference between $s'_\omega(t')$ and $s'_\omega(t' - 1)$. On the other hand, an increase or decrease in the usage of hashtag ω would cause $s_\omega(t)$ in interval D_{t^*} to appear in more or fewer scales.

Component (2): discarding weak signals. In signal processing, cross-correlation is a common measure to determine similarity between two signals, measured as a function of a time-lag applied to one of them. The EDCoW algorithm applies cross-correlation twice, once to compute auto-correlation between every signal and itself, and the second time to find correlation between every pair of hashtag signals.

The second component of EDCoW receives as input a segment of signals; the length of the segment varies depending on the application scenario. This segment is denoted by S^I, and an individual signal in this segment is denoted by S_i^I.

For two signal functions $f(t)$ and $g(t)$, their *cross correlation* is defined as:

$$(f * g)(t) = \sum f^*(\tau)g(t + \tau) \tag{8}$$

where f^* is the complex conjugate of f. Computation of cross correlation basically shifts one signal (in Eq. (8) it is g) and calculates the dot product between the two signals.

Cross-correlation applied on the signal itself is called *auto-correlation*, which always shows a peak at a lag of zero, unless the signal is a zero signal. Therefore, auto-correlation can be used to evaluate the importance of a hashtag. Auto-correlation of signal S_i^I is denoted by A_i^I.

EDCoW discards all signals with $A_i^I < \theta_1$, where the bound θ_1 is set as follows. First, the median absolute deviation (MAD) of all auto-correlation values A_i^I within segment S_i^I is computed as

$$\text{MAD} = \text{median}(|A_i^I - \text{median}(A_i^I)|). \tag{9}$$

MAD is a statistically robust measure of the variability of a sample data in the presence of "outliers." Then the θ_1 boundary is set as

$$\theta_1 = \text{median}(A_i^I) + \gamma * \text{MAD}(S^I). \tag{10}$$

Empirically, the value of γ is set to be no less than 10, which is due to the high skewness of the A_i^I distribution.

Component (3): computing cross-correlation. EDCoW performs this computation only for pairs of non-trivial signals; all trivial hashtag signals were filtered out in the previous phase. Let the number of the remaining signals be $\mathcal{K}$. Cross-correlation between a pair S_i^I, S_j^I of the remaining signals is denoted by X_{ij}. Because the distribution of X_{ij} exhibits a skewness, EDCoW applies another threshold θ_2 to X_{ij} as follows:

$$\theta_2 = \text{median}_{S_i^I \in S^I}(X_{ij}) + \gamma * \text{MAD}_{S_i^I \in S^I}(X_{ij}), \qquad (11)$$

where γ is the same as in Eq. (10). Then the value of X_{ij} is set to zero if $X_{ij} < \theta_2$. The remaining non-zero X_{ij} instances are arranged in a square matrix to form *correlation matrix* M; diagonal values of M are set to be zero. The matrix M is very sparse because threshold θ_2 was applied.

Component (4): grouping signals to events. This component views event detection as a graph partitioning problem for a weighted graph whose adjacency matrix is the cross-correlation matrix M, which was constructed during the second stage of the algorithm. Figure 2 illustrates the notation of graph partitioning for a hashtag similarity graph.

The purpose is to divide a graph into closely-connected subgraphs, where each subgraph stands for an event and contains a set of hashtags with high cross-correlation. The cross-correlation between hashtags in different subgraphs is expected to be low.

Matrix M is a symmetric sparse matrix and thus it can be viewed as the adjacency matrix of a sparse undirected weighted graph $G = (V, E, W)$.

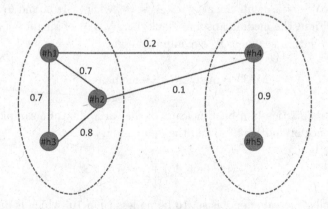

Fig. 2.   Weighted graph partitioning example.

Here, the vertex set V contains all the $\mathcal{K}$ signals after filtering with auto-correlation, while the edge set $E = V \times V$. An edge between two vertices $v_i, v_j \in V$ exists if $X_{ij} \geq \theta_2$, and its weight is $w_{ij} = X_{ij}$. Then the event detection problem can be re-formulated as a graph partitioning problem of separating the graph into closely-connected subgraphs. Each subgraph corresponds to an event, that contains a set of hashtags with high cross-correlation.

Newman (2006), in Ref. 40, proposes a metric called *modularity*, to measure the quality of such partitioning. The modularity of a graph is defined as the sum of weights of all the edges that fall within subgraphs (after partitioning), subtracted by the expected edge weight sum if edges were placed at random. A positive modularity indicates the possible presence of partitioning.

Denote the weighted degree of node v_i by $d_i = \sum_j w_{ji}$. The sum of all the edge weights in graph G is defined as $m = \sum_i \frac{d_i}{2}$. The modularity of the partitioning is defined as:

$$Q = \frac{1}{2m} \sum_{i,j} \left(w_{i,j} - \frac{d_i d_j}{2m} \right) \delta_{c_i, c_j}, \tag{12}$$

where c_i and c_j are the index of the subgraph that nodes v_i and v_j belong to respectively, and $\delta_{c_i, c_j} = \begin{cases} 1, & c_i = c_j \\ 0, & c_i \neq c_j \end{cases}$.

The goal is to partition G such that Q is maximized. Newman has proposed a very intuitive and efficient spectral graph theory-based approach to solve this problem. First, a modularity matrix B of graph G is built as:

$$B_{ij} = w_{ij} - \frac{d_i d_j}{2m}. \tag{13}$$

Then, the eigenvalue vector of the symmetric matrix B is computed. Finally, G is split into two subgraphs based on the signs of the elements in the eigenvalue vector. The spectral method is recursively applied to each of the two pieces to further divide them into smaller subgraphs.

The modularity-based graph partitioning lets the EDCoW detect events without knowing their number in advance. Graph partitioning stops automatically when no more subgraphs can be constructed (i.e. $Q < 0$). The main computation task in this component is finding the largest eigenvalue (and the corresponding eigenvector) of the sparse symmetric modularity matrix B, which can be done efficiently by using the power iteration method.

3.3.2. *Text similarity analysis for better event detection*

TWIST adapts the EDCoW algorithm for wavelet-based analysis. We use a wavelet correlation, calculated according to the EDCoW methodology, as one of two features for hashtag clustering into events. TWIST combines wavelet analysis with text analysis for better event recognition. Our choice of this particular algorithm is motivated by its robustness, accuracy, and efficiency.

Our system extends the third stage of the EDCoW algorithm by integrating a text similarity knowledge between tweets into a graph representation. The motivation behind this idea was dictated by a possible situation where two or more unrelated events evolve at the same time, following the same pattern of burst. In such a case, a wavelet analysis will not distinguish between these events; only analyzing the *content* of tweets may point to the differences between them. In TWIST, the weights on graph edges are calculated as a weighted linear combination of cross-correlation values that are computed during the second stage, together with *textual similarity* scores for every pair of signals. Every signal is represented by its textual "profile," which is compiled from the texts of all tweets belonging to it. Because all tweets are preprocessed in advance, we only need to integrate the preprocessed data of all tweets belonging to the signal's hashtag. Given a cross-correlation score cc_{ij} and a similarity score sim_{ij} between signals i and j, the weight on the edge between signal nodes is computed as

$$w_{ij} = \alpha \times cc_{ij} + (1 - \alpha) \times sim_{ij}, \tag{14}$$

where $0 \leq \alpha \leq 1$ is a system parameter.

3.4. *Event filtering*

TWIST enables the user to focus on events of certain sizes or events reported in certain countries. Filtering by country is based on location tags contained in tweets. Events are roughly divided to *big*, *small*, and *regular-sized* events. This type of filtering is applied to hashtag wavelets before the cross-correlation matrix is computed. It is based on distribution of wavelet auto-correlation values — immediately after all wavelets with auto-correlation below the median are removed as noise. The range of auto-correlation is divided to thirds, where the upper third represents big wavelets, the middle third represents regular-sized wavelets, and the lower third represents small wavelets. Note that grouping wavelets and assigning them to actual events happens at the next stage of event detection. The intuition behind this part of TWIST is that in many cases, smaller country-oriented events are swallowed by bigger ones, but they still carry information considered important by many users. Our approach enables us to focus on hashtags of prescribed importance, before grouping them to events.

3.5. *Event summarization*

After detecting events, TWIST performs an additional (fourth) step — describing the detected events by generating their summaries. We create two different types of summaries: *internal* and *external*. An *internal summary* (or *"Twitter profile"*) uses strictly internal Twitter sources such as hashtags, keywords, and tweets, while an *external summary* is built from external sources such as news articles. The summarization approach in both cases follows a strictly extractive principle, as most appropriate for the Twitter domain, both in terms of accuracy and efficiency. We used two state-of-the-art algorithms in the summarization process — TextRank[41] and Lingo[42] — for text ranking and clustering, respectively. The following subsections describe summary types supported in the system, summarization algorithms, and their adaptation and usage in our system.

3.5.1. *Internal summary*

The internal summary is built from the most salient *hashtags*, *keywords*, and *tweets*. It is retrieved by taking tweets with the highest PageRank score obtained from a weighted tweets graph, with nodes standing for tweets, according to the TextRank method.[41] A tweets graph is built on the tweets that are filtered by length and keywords coverage ratio in order to reduce the size and TextRank processing time for a graph. Hashtags are considered as extremely important keywords and give a higher weight to a coverage score. A similarity between tweets for weighting the graph's edges can be calculated by either Jaccard similarity between sets of tweets' terms, or by cosine similarity (according to user's choice) between their *tf-idf* vectors. The keywords and hashtags are ranked by their *tf-idf* score and the top-ranked ones are extracted.

3.5.2. *External summary*

The external summary of the detected event is compiled by extracted parts from the relevant external sources. The summary is created in the following phases:

(1) Retrieving the relevant sources, including their collection and filtering;
(2) Preprocessing and ranking relevant sources; and
(3) Summarizing the top-ranked ones.

The relevant sources for each detected event are retrieved by collecting, analyzing, and filtering links appearing in tweets. For each link, the number of its appearances in tweets is counted and stored. We used a classic vector-space model to represent the text; namely, each source is represented by a vector of *tf-idf* values for its terms. For ranking relevant external sources we applied eigenvector centrality in the document graph. We can then build a graph with nodes standing for documents (each document is retrieved from a link) and edges — standing for similarity relationship — are weighted by the similarity score. The PageRank score (as a variant of the eigenvector centrality) is measured, and the top-ranked sources are selected for summarization, following the TextRank approach. We used the text selected for summarization by performing steps described in two following paragraphs.

Extracting theme sentences. Every real-world event may be described by several related themes. For example, an event of earthquake may involve such characteristics as the geo-location of the earthquake, its power, victims, other countries' involvement in humanitarian help, and more. Because we summarize many event-related documents, it is quite natural to suppose that reports about the same themes contain lexically similar sentences. We consider theme as a group of lexically similar sentences, and retrieve all event-related themes by a clustering of theme sentences collected from relevant sources. We use the Lingo clustering algorithm of Ref. 42 that, in addition to finding clusters, also provides a label and a score for each cluster.

Ranking and selecting sentences. Given clusters, we select theme sentences as representatives of their clusters. Lingo forms clusters by assigning documents to the cluster labels using vector space model (VSM) and a distance-based approach. Because of this, we look for the sentences that are close to the centroids of the clusters. First, a centroid, as an average of the vectors representing the cluster documents, is calculated for each cluster. Then, the distance between a centroid and its cluster sentences is calculated, with the closest sentence being selected from each cluster. After this procedure, we have one sentence for each theme describing the detected event.

A summary that describes the detected event must cover all (or at least most) of its important themes. Given theme sentences, we rank them using the TextRank approach and compile a summary from those that are top-ranked. An undirected graph of sentences with lexical similarity relationships is built from event theme sentences, and the PageRank is applied for scoring sentences.

TextRank algorithm. TextRank is a graph-based ranking model for text processing, which was applied as an unsupervised method for keyword and sentence extraction by Mihalcea and Tarau (2004) in Ref. 41. The summarized text is represented by a graph so that the basic idea of "voting" or "recommendation" implemented by a graph-based ranking model can be applied. Namely, TextRank operates eigenvector centrality of nodes standing for text units (sentences or words) that need to be ranked. The PageRank algorithm[43] is used for calculating eigenvector centrality.

Formally, let $G = (V, E)$ be a directed graph with a set of vertices V and a set of edges E, where E is a subset of $V \times V$. For a given vertex $v_i \in V$, let $In(v_i)$ be the set of vertices that points to it (predecessors), and let $Out(v_i)$ be the set of vertices that vertex v_i points to (successors). The score of a vertex v_i is defined as follows, in Ref. 43:

$$S(v_i) = (1 - d) + d * \sum_{j \in In(v_i)} \frac{1}{|Out(v_j)|} S(v_j), \tag{15}$$

where $0 \leq d \leq 1$ is a damping factor, which has the role of integrating into the model the probability of jumping from a given vertex to another random vertex in the graph, according to the "random surfer model." Factor d is usually set to 0.85 (this selection is justified in Ref. 43), defining a 15% probability for jumping to a completely new page. We use the same value in our implementation of TextRank.

To enable the application of graph-based ranking algorithms to natural language texts, one must build a graph that represents the text. That graph interconnects text entities with meaningful relations; for example, TextRank uses words and sentences as text entities. However, depending on the application at hand, text units of various sizes and characteristics can be added as vertices in the graph, such as collocations, entire paragraphs, or short documents. Similarly, the application should dictate the type of relations that are used to draw connections between any two such vertices, like lexical or semantic relations or contextual overlap. Regardless of the type and characteristics of the elements added to the graph, TextRank consists of the following main steps:

(1) Identify text units that best define the task at hand, and add them as vertices in the graph.
(2) Identify relations that connect such text units, and use these relations to draw edges between vertices in the graph. Edges can be directed or undirected, weighted or unweighted.
(3) Iterate the graph-based ranking algorithm until convergence.
(4) Sort vertices based on their final score. Use the values attached to each vertex for ranking and selection decisions.

Usage of TextRank in TWIST. We apply TextRank three times, for the following purposes:

(1) extracting the most important external sources for summarization,
(2) ranking and extracting clusters (themes) of sentences, and, finally,
(3) ranking and extracting sentences covering the most important themes into a summary.

According to the main steps of TextRank, we identify the text units and relations between them that best fit the task at each stage. Our choice of TextRank is very natural and motivated by the following requirements. Due to the real-time nature of Twitter and the event detection approach (we recognize unknown and unspecified events), we need an *unsupervised* summarization methodology. Also, because of the enormous amount of retrieved data, we need an efficient algorithm, both in terms of space and run-time. TextRank fills both requirements. Due to the high popularity of Twitter across the international community there is an additional characteristic that we would like to have in our summarizer — an ability to process texts in multiple languages. Because TextRank is known for its *language-independent extractive* approach, it can be easily applied to different languages. The minimal effort required for its adaptation to a different language is sentence splitting and tokenization. Also, the texts must be written in UTF-8 encoding.

Lingo clustering algorithm. Lingo was designed as a web search clustering algorithm, with special attention given to ensuring that both content and description (labels) of the resulting groups are meaningful to humans. Lingo first attempts to ensure that a human-perceivable cluster label can be created, and only then assigns documents to it. Specifically, it extracts frequent phrases — as the most informative source of human-readable topic descriptions — from the input documents. Next, by performing reduction of the original term-document matrix using singular value decomposition (SVD), Lingo discovers any existing latent structure of diverse topics in the input documents. Finally, it matches group descriptions with the extracted topics and assigns relevant documents to them. Formally, Lingo contains five specific steps, described as follows.

During preprocessing, three steps are performed: text filtering removes entities and non-letter characters except for sentence boundaries. Next, the language of each snippet is identified, and finally, appropriate stemming and stop words removal end the preprocessing phase.

For frequent phrase extraction, these phrases are defined as recurring ordered sequences of terms appearing in the input documents. To be a candidate for a cluster label, a frequent phrase or a single term must:

(1) appear in the input documents at least a certain number of times (specified by a *term frequency threshold*),
(2) not cross sentence boundaries,
(3) be a *complete phrase*,
(4) not begin or end with a stop word.

A *complete phrase* is a complete subsequence of the collated text of the input documents, considered as a sequence of terms. The authors of Ref. 42 define complete subsequence as a sequence that cannot be "extended" by adding preceding or trailing terms. In other words, a complete phrase cannot be a part of another, bigger complete phrase.

Once frequent phrases — including single terms — are known, they are used for cluster label induction. This is done in four steps:

(1) term-document matrix building,
(2) abstract concept discovery,
(3) phrase matching, and
(4) label pruning.

The term-document matrix is constructed of single frequent terms, using their *tf-idf* weights.

In abstract concept discovery, the SVD method is applied to the term-document matrix to find its orthogonal basis (SVDś U matrix), which vectors represent the abstract concepts appearing in the input documents. Only the first k vectors of matrix U are used in the further phases of the algorithm. The value of k is estimated by selecting the Frobenius norms of the term-document matrix A and its k-rank approximation, A_k. Let threshold q be a percentage-expressed value that determines the extent to which the k-rank approximation should retain the original information in matrix A. k is hence defined as the minimum value that satisfies the following condition: $||A_k||_F/||A_k|| \geq q$, where the $||X||_F$ symbol denotes the Frobenius norm of matrix X. The larger value of q induces more cluster candidates. The choice of the optimal value for this parameter ultimately depends on user preferences, and is expressed by the Candidate Label Threshold parameter. In TWIST, we use a default value for this threshold.

Phrase matching, where group descriptions are discovered, relies on an important observation that both abstract concepts and frequent phrases are expressed in the same vector space — the column space of the original term-document matrix A. Thus, the classic cosine similarity can be used to calculate how "close" a phrase or a single term is to an abstract concept. The matrix P of size $t \times (p + t)$, where t is the number of frequent terms and p is the number of frequent phrases, is built by treating phrases and keywords as pseudo-documents and using one of the term weighting schemes. Having the P matrix and the i-th column vector of the SVD's U matrix, a vector m_i of cosines of the angles between the i-th abstract concept vector and the phrase vectors is calculated as $m_i = U_i^T P$. The phrase that corresponds to the maximum component of the m_i vector is selected as the human-readable description of i-th abstract concept. Additionally, the value of the cosine becomes the score of the cluster label candidate. A single matrix multiplication $M = U_k^T P$ yields the result for all pairs of abstract concepts and frequent phrases.

The final step of label induction is to prune overlapping label descriptions. For doing that, the similarity between cluster labels is calculated and similar labels are pruned. Let V be a vector of cluster label candidates and their scores. A term-document matrix Z, where cluster label candidates from V serve as documents, is calculated. After column length is normalized, a matrix of similarities between cluster labels is calculated as

$Z^T Z$. For each row the columns that exceed the Label Similarity Threshold (another Lingo parameter) are picked and all but the single cluster label with the maximum score are discarded. As with other Lingo parameters, the default value for the Label Similarity Threshold was used in our system.

In the cluster content discovery phase, the input documents are re-queried with all induced cluster labels. The documents are assigned to labels based on VSM. Let $C = Q^T A$, where Q is a matrix in which each cluster label is represented as a column vector, and A is the original term-document matrix for input documents. This way, element c_{ij} of matrix C indicates the strength of membership of the j-th document in the i-th cluster. A document is added to a cluster if c_{ij} exceeds the Snippet Assignment Threshold, yet another control parameter of the Lingo algorithm. Documents not assigned to any cluster are ultimately located in an artificial cluster called Others.

Finally, clusters are ranked by a score, calculated as follows: $C_{score} = label\ score \times ||C||$, where $||C||$ is the number of documents assigned to cluster C. The scoring function prefers well-described and relatively large groups over smaller, possibly noisy ones. For the time being, no cluster merging strategy or hierarchy induction is proposed for Lingo.

Usage of Lingo in TWIST. We apply the Lingo algorithm for clustering sentences into themes as one of the steps of our summarization approach requirements. In addition to its availability, Lingo provides such nice "extensions" as cluster labels and weights that supply important additional information to our summarization process.

Suffix Tree Clustering Algorithm. Suffix tree clustering (STC)[44] is a linear time clustering algorithm (linear in the size of the document set) that is based on identifying phrases that are common to groups of documents. A phrase in its context is an ordered sequence of one or more words. STC defines a base cluster to be the set of documents that share a common phrase. The STC algorithm creates overlapping clusters, i.e., a document can appear in more than one cluster. STC has three logical steps:

(1) document "cleaning",
(2) identifying base clusters using a suffix tree, and
(3) merging these base clusters into clusters.

In the document "cleaning" step, the string of text representing each document is transformed using a light stemming algorithm. Sentence boundaries are marked and non-word tokens (such as numbers, HTML tags, and most punctuation) are stripped.

The second step — the identification of base clusters — can be viewed as the creation of an inverted index of phrases for the document set. This is done efficiently using a data structure called a suffix tree.[45] This data structure can be constructed in linear time in the size of the document set, and can be constructed incrementally as the documents are being read. Each base cluster is assigned a score that is a function of the number of documents it contains, and the number of words that make up its phrase. Stopwords — which can be identified by either using a predefined list or by their *tf-idf* weight — are not considered as contributing to the score of a base cluster.

The final step of the STC algorithm merges base clusters with a high degree of overlap in their document sets. This creates clusters that are more coherent semantically enabling documents to be in the same cluster even if they do not share a common phrase, but instead share phrases with other documents of the cluster. This step also reduces the fragmentation of the produced clusters. The STC algorithm creates overlapping clusters, i.e., a document can appear in more than one cluster.

STC usage in TWIST.   As required by one of the steps of our summarization approach, we apply the STC algorithm for clustering sentences into themes. We used the Carrot2 implementation[46] of the STC algorithm, as described in Ref. 47. STC also provides cluster labels and weights that we use as additional information for our summarization process. Because we use full phrases that are derived from the suffix-tree, the cluster labels are very informative and can represent the main themes describing the detected events. The shared phrases of a cluster provide an informative way of summarizing its contents to the user. Also, using those phrases for identifying similarities between documents, instead of a bag-of-words, and the consequent cluster construction derived therefrom, improves the clustering quality. Most other clustering algorithms treat a document as a bag of words and disregard the additional information that is present in the ordering of the words. The STC algorithm is particularly well suited for Twitter data, as it is fast, incremental, and has been shown to be robust in a noisy domain. STC does not require a predefined number of clusters, thus letting the documents themselves determine the number of clusters generated.

3.6. *Geo-sentiment analyzer*

The geo-sentiment analyzer is the only module of TWIST that needs annotated data for supervised learning. It uses the Naive Bayes algorithm, as
one of the most simple and reliable classification methods for textual data.
The textual data is preprocessed and represented in a bag-of-words format,
per tweet. Each bag is labeled by a particular detected event (event detector output) and country (we filter out tweets that lack geolocation data).
Then a model trained on the Sentiment140 dataset[48] of Naive Bayes is
used for a sentiment classification of tweets, and the resulting statistics are
displayed on the world map. A user can choose to see majority sentiment,
with corresponding color, and full distribution statistics for the event of
interest. We use the Google GeoChart API for a map visualization.

3.7. *Event prediction*

We use a methodology introduced in Ref. 32 for modeling and classifying
Twitter events, based on the intensity of the activity they produce. The
method does not depend on event size and scope, and it provides an indicator of the event impact on the social network. This approach is based on
the fact (verified empirically in Ref. 32) that real-world news events produce
collective patterns of bursty behavior combined with long periods of inactivity. Events with most of their activity concentrated into high-activity
periods, are called *high-activity events*. Such events can be predicted very
early in their life cycle.

Several parameters of an event are used for prediction of its activity:

(1) the number of tweets decays rapidly over time,
(2) high-activity events have a higher fraction of retweets (or shares) relative to their overall message volume,
(3) high-activity events tend to spark more conversations between users
than other events,
(4) the number of different users that engage with high-activity events is
much higher than in events that are not high-activity, and
(5) posts about high-activity events are much more topic-focused than in
other events. The vocabulary of unique words as well as hashtags used
in high-activity events is much more narrow than for other events.

We compute the median value for every one of the above parameters.
A high-activity event is expected to be placed well above median in all

these parameters; this value is a user-defined parameter. By default, we are interested in the top third of the median range. If an event passes the threshold (measured by taking an average over all parameters), it is marked as a high-activity event.

Event decay is measured as an exponential decay

$$N(t) = N_0 e^{-\lambda t} \tag{16}$$

and we are interested in computing λ, with larger values implicating faster decay. The retweet fraction is measured as

$$Rf = \frac{|retweets \in event|}{|tweets \in event|}. \tag{17}$$

To measure conversation activity, we simply compute the ratio of conversation messages to the number of tweets in an event.

Finally, the event activity parameter is defined as:

$$EventActivity = \alpha\lambda + (1 - \alpha)Rf. \tag{18}$$

A high-activity event is a binary function defined as follows:

$$HAE(EventActivity) \begin{cases} 1, & EventActivity \geq \beta \\ 0, & EventActivity < \beta \end{cases} \tag{19}$$

where β is a user-defined threshold that is usually set to be above the median.

4. System architecture of TWIST

TWIST is written in C# and it uses a MySQL database. The general architecture of our system is shown in Fig.3.

4.1. *The Twitter stream*

The dataset object of analysis is retrieved using the twitter streaming API that, using the default access level, returns a random sample of all public tweets. This access level provides a small proportion of all public tweets (1%). The data are returned as a set of documents, one per tweet, in JavaScript Object Notation. These documents also contain additional user- and tweet-related data. Given the average number of 140 million tweets sent per day in Twitter, the size of the data retrieved by the streaming API (1%) in a 24 hour time span is roughly 1.4 million tweets.

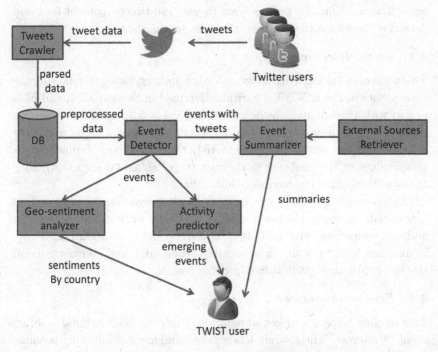

Fig. 3. Data flow of TWIST.

The 140 character limit of tweets gives an expected 196 MBytes per day or a 2269 bytes per second data stream.

4.2. *Tweets crawler*

Tweets Crawler uses Tweetinvi to retrieve tweets data and store them in a database. All the tweets are stored with their additional features provided by the Twitter streaming API. Tag IDs, text, creation time, and location, whether it was retweeted (and retweets count), whether the tweet was shortened (that is, user has originally entered more than 140 symbols), whether it was a response to a different tweet, the user ID and more. User information is also collected, including ID, username, location, and other users mentioned in one's tweets. Users do not always disclose their true location, therefore we are only interested in the user's time-zone (reading the time-zone gives us a general idea of the user and tweet locations). If the user has geo-enabled points, the system, using the Google Maps API, can find geographic coordinates. We are mainly interested in hashtags, as an explicit annotation of a tweet's main theme, and tweets' content for event detection, and links they contain for event summarization.

4.3. *Event detector*

This component detects events by operating hashtag wavelets, following the three stages of the EDCoW algorithm described in Section 3.3.1, and integrated with text analysis, as described in Section 3.3.2. Before requesting event detection, user can filter future events by country of origin and event relative size (big, small, or regular). After the wavelets are formed by the *tf-idf* values of the hashtags in the first stage (signal construction), they are smoothed using the Savitzky-Golay filter.[49]

The user can compute events from hashtag wavelets by selecting an appropriate method: (1) using wavelet similarity only; (2) using wavelet and text cosine similarity; and (3) using wavelet and text Jaccard similarity. In all cases, a hashtag similarity matrix is computed, and events are found by the partitioning graph defined by this matrix.

4.4. *Event summarizer*

This module helps a user get summaries — internal and external — of an event of interest. The module lets a user configure the following parameters for the internal summary: the impact factor of hashtags (by default, TWIST multiplies their *tf-idf* scores by 3), the similarity metric for weighting edges in a sentence graph (by default, the system will use Jaccard similarity), and the size of a sentence graph (by default, a graph can contain a maximum of 2000 nodes). For summarizing the external sources, the user can set the following parameters: clustering algorithm (Lingo or STC) and maximal number of selected sentences.

4.5. *External sources retriever*

For building a readable and informative summary (external profile) for each detected event, TWIST retrieves the external sources — such as news articles — that describe the real-world event. TWIST collects the links appearing in the event's tweets, retrieves their content using the alchemyAPI,[50] and provides that content to the summarizer module. No user-specified parameters exist in this module.

4.6. *Geo-sentiment analyzer*

After events are detected, TWIST can show a distribution of sentiments over different countries on the map (see Fig. 4). All tweets in every country

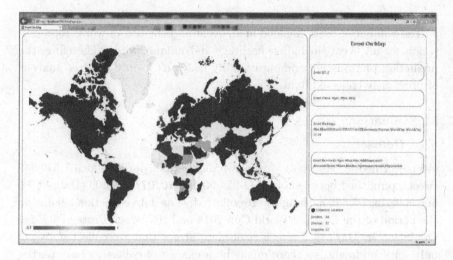

Fig. 4.   Map of event sentiments.

Fig. 5.   Detailed sentiment information.

(if these tweets exist and they are written in English) are classified into positive, negative, and neutral. A country receives its color (red, yellow, or green) depending on what sentiment prevails in tweets originating it that country. For every country, a detailed sentiment count is shown if the user points to it on the map (see Fig. 5).

4.7. *High-activity event predictor*

During wavelet construction, wavelets with a potential to be a part of high-activity events are selected according to wavelet form and retweet ratio. The TWIST Event Predictor analyzes all wavelets according to Eqs. (18)–(19), with $\alpha = 0.7$ and β set to median value. Note that all of the data required for computing these parameters is already stored in the TWIST database before event detection and analysis takes place, such as, the number of users engaged in an event and the bag-of-words representation for an event, including hashtags and unique words. Therefore, the prediction phase is not computationally heavy as it only requires analysis of previously collected data.

5. Evaluation

5.1. *Datasets*

We performed a pilot study over a two day period, during which 7,549,339 tweets, published between 08/07/14 24:00 and 10/07/14 24:00 (Dataset 1), and covering 95,889 hashtags, were collected. The data collection fell during the period of the Football World Cup 2014 and the Israeli Protective Edge Operation in Gaza.[51] There is a need to stress that we collected tweets only until midnight, so there might be a chance of collecting only partial events (for instance, the football game between Argentina and Holland took place in the late hours of the evening, and, therefore, only some of the tweets about the game were collected). Dataset 2 contains 567,799 tweets and covers 218,952 hashtags. This dataset was collected between the dates 10/09/2017 24:00 to 12/09/2017 24:00, at the dates where hurricane Irma[52] hit the Caribbean islands and the US coast.

5.2. *Event detection results*

Using pure wavelet similarity on Dataset 1 resulted in inaccurate event detection, when different unrelated events mistakenly fell into the same category. As an example, signals related to the football game between Holland and Argentina fell in the same cluster with signals hashtagged by Gaza. Figure 6 shows the clusters, representing events, that were found by using hashtag wavelets only, without taking tweet text into account. The system detected one event perfectly — the World Cup 2014. The clique contains BRA, GER, WorldCup2014, Brazil, and similar hashtags. However, the Protective Edge Operation event was not detected.

Figure 7 shows events detected by TWIST with the text analysis component activated. The edge weights for a partitioned graph were calculated as an average (with $\alpha = 0.5$) of correlation and similarity scores. There was no significant difference between results of event clustering using either cosine or Jaccard similarity metrics. Figure 7 shows the results using cosine similarity. As can be seen, Gaza and World Cup 2014 were detected as separate unrelated events. The Protective Edge Operation event is detected

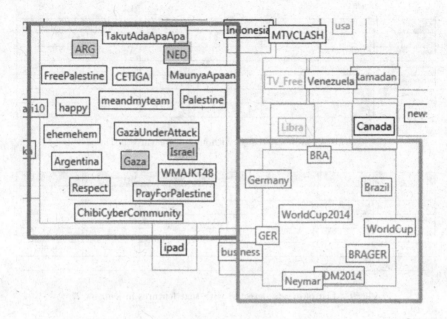

Fig. 6.   Events detected without text features in Dataset 1.

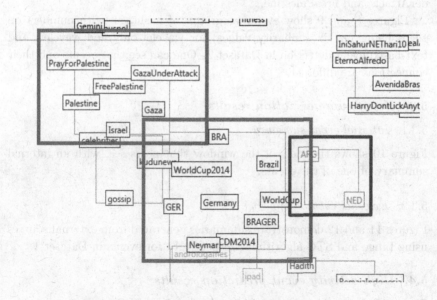

Fig. 7.   Events detected with text features in Dataset 1.

A	Irma	MPN	PushAwardsMayAwards	kcargentina	KCAColombia	EXO
Irma	1	0.181433711440745	0	0	0	0
MPN	0.181433711440745	1	0	0	0.127539349649209	0
PushAwardsMayAwards	0	0	1	0	0	0
kcargentina	0	0	0	1	0	0
KCAColombia	0	0.127539349649209	0	0	1	0.446560331865479
EXO	0	0	0	0	0.446560331865479	1

Fig. 8.   List of events detected without text features in Dataset 2.

A	Irma	MPN	PushAwardsMayAwards	kcargentina	KCAColombia	EXO
Irma	1	0	0	0	0	0
MPN	0	1	0	0	0	0
PushAwardsMayAwards	0	0	1	0	0	0
kcargentina	0	0	0	1	0	0
KCAColombia	0	0	0	0	1	0.2271423328776
EXO	0	0	0	0	0.2271423328776	1

Fig. 9.   List of events detected with text features in Dataset 2.

properly. The event contains hashtags such as PrayForPalestine, GazaUnderAttack, and FreePalestine.

Figures 8 and 9 show events as groups of hashtags (with numbers on edges being matrix similarity values) for wavelet-only and wavelet- and text-based event detection in Dataset 2. One can see that events and their connections are different.

5.3. *Event summarization results*

5.3.1. *Internal event summary*

Figure 10 shows the view of the window that users see, with an internal summary of one of the events.

5.3.2. *External event summary*

Figures 11 and 12 demonstrate summaries generated from external sources using Lingo and STC algorithms, respectively, for events in Dataset 1.

5.4. *High-activity event prediction results*

Figure 13 shows that a wavelet of hashtag $\#Irma$ in Dataset 2, representing hurricane Irma, was indeed detected as a high-activity event, which is denoted by the bold line of that wavelet.

RT @HarryMexOficial'. Encuentra las diferencias...

#MPN #HarryStyles httpsJ/tso/OTCthETSrRT @BieberSNoticias: Tire 26 segundos do seu dia para ver Justin Bieber treinando a sua v02.

#MPN #JustinBieberShow hnpszfluoflkoNWmQJAYRT @BrasilBigTime'. Quando voc fde Big Time Rush e algum vem dizer que a banda fake porque s conhece a srie #MPN #BigTimeRush http@Rose5_TimeSM |#ArianaGrandeInstagram #M PN httpsfltxojARF3XthQS©LightsDn_TimeSM furaco #MPN #ShawnMendes #TheresNothing #TheresNethingClipe@portaltattinhos Estados unidos #M PN #BibiTatto #BibiTattoGe 'Deixo Barbara

|#MPN #JustinBieber@p0rTaltattinhos Hot dog #M PN #BIBITAITOGAMES #BIBITATID #REZEN DEEVILGATORT @ChaoMendesPage: Me chamou pra ver fiime fl vimos o filme mesmo.

#MPN #ShawnMendes #TheresNothing #TheresNothingClipe http5:f/t.co/JJnRT @dedicoIr: Luan me ilude em todas as redes sociais sobre o topete, comeou pelo twitter, agr no app #MPN #LuanSantanaRT @COI #JustI'nBieber #MPN httpst/p'trochpyGPZTrqPor favor recuerden NO hacer spam, hagan tweets entre 8—10 minuto 5r cambia palabras 0 agregar emojis

#CamilaCabello #HeyMaFeat #MPN@P0rtaIDaNoob @LoiraNoob Tern corao pra mimmmmmm

TEAM MALENA

#MPN #MalenaGamesRT @nahcardosompn: Cada rt um vote. #MPN #NahCardoso https://t.cof3€fi2an6dRT @TeamHelp1D: SE VOCS QUEREM REALM ENTE GANHAR ENTD VAMDS VOTAR SEM PARAR!

|ALL THE LOVE ONED

'Irma' event internal summary

Fig. 10. Event summarizer. Internal event profile.

However most of the rockets from Gaza targeted southern Israel, with more than 100 projectiles fired.

As the Israeli army launched a massive search campaign in the West Bank [for three Israeli youths who went missing while hitchhiking], arresting hundreds of Palestinians and killing at least six, militant factions in Gaza increased rocket fire on Israel.

Israel confirmed that a rocket hit the city of Hadera, which is some 62 miles (100 kilometers) from Gaza.

Rocket attacks on Israel's southern communities increased in frequency, as did Israeli air strikes on Gaza.

After the Palestinian president Mahmoud Abbas declared his willingness to travel to Gaza and sign an agreement, the IDF killed two Hamas activists in Gaza; the IDF stated the killings were in response to the launching of a single Qassam rocket, which hit no one, but Yedioth Ahronoth's Alex Fishman argued they were a "premeditated escalation" by Israel.

"We strongly condemn the continuing rocket fire inside of Israel and the deliberate targeting of civilians by terrorist organizations in Gaza," White House spokesman Josh Earnest said at a news briefing.

While there has been intermittent rocket fire from Gaza since the cease-fire that ended the November 2012 Pillar of Defense conflict, Israel has credited Hamas with largely doing its best to keep the various militant factions in line.

According to one report, "nearly all the 2,500–3,000 rockets and mortars Hamas has fired at Israel since the start of the war seem to have been aimed at towns", including an attack on "a kibbutz collective farm close to the Gaza border", in which an Israeli child was killed. The prime minister will stress that Israel had tried to bring about calm in Gaza but Hamas has escalated the situation and increased the rocket fire on Israel.

On July 6 the Israeli army tweeted, "Over 150 Gaza rockets have hit Israel in less than a month."

Summary using Lingo clustering

Fig. 11.   External summary generated with Lingo algorithm in Dataset 1.

"Palestinian [Authority] President Mahmoud Abbas demanded Israel immediately stop its escalation and the raids on Gaza," the Palestinian Ma'an news agency quotes a statement from Abbas's office as saying.

Conflicting figures are coming out of Gaza as to the death toll, with figures ranging from one to five dead.

Hamas has denied involvement in their abductions.

Sometimes Israel has formally done so, while quickly violating it.

Voices are growing on the right to retake the Gaza Strip.

The number would put the Gazan death toll at 11, several hours into Operation Protective Edge.

The Palestinian people have the right to face the Israeli occupation with all their power and tools.

"The continued attacks on Palestinian civilians by Israel is a flagrant violation of international humanitarian law, the Geneva Convention and international resolutions on occupied Palestine," said the Arab League chief.

Summary using the STC clustering algorithm

Fig. 12.   External summary generated with STC algorithm in Dataset 1.

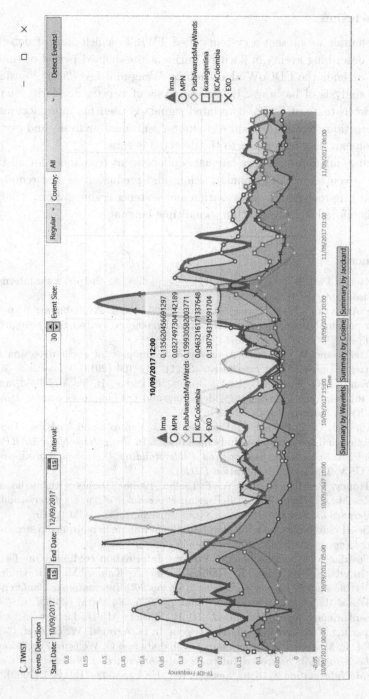

Fig. 13. High-activity event detected in Dataset 2.

6. Conclusion

In this chapter we present a system called TWIST, which aims at detecting and describing events in Twitter during a pre-defined period of time. TWIST extends the EDCoW algorithm by Weng and Lee (2011),[15] using wavelet analysis of hashtags, by text analysis of tweets. Similarity analysis between texts of highly correlated signals is used for more accurate event detection. Summarization techniques, sentiment analysis, and event prediction can then be applied to the detected events.

Because our approach uses language-independent techniques for all its stages — event detection, summarization, and prediction — and requires basic text preprocessing — tokenization and sentence segmentation — only, it can therefore be easily adapted to multiple languages.

References

1. Twitter, Twitter statistics (2017). Available at: http://www.internet livestats.com/twitter-statistics/.
2. Pear Analytics, *Twitter Study - August 2009* (2009). Available at: http://www.pearanalytics.com/wp-content/uploads/2009/08/Twitter-Study-August-2009.pdf.
3. F. Atefeh and W. Khreich, A survey of techniques for event detection in Twitter, *Computational Intelligence*, **31**(1), 132–164 (2013).
4. Y. Yang, J. G. Carbonell, R. D. Brown, T. Pierce, B. T. Archibald, and X. Liu, Learning approaches for detecting and tracking news events, *IEEE Intelligent Systems*, **14**(4), 32–43 (1999).
5. J. Allan, J. G. Carbonell, G. Doddington, J. Yamron, and Y. Yang, Topic detection and tracking pilot study final report. In *Proceedings of the DARPA: Broadcast News Transcription and Understanding Workshop*, Lansdowne, VA, USA, The BDM Corporation (1998).
6. R. Troncy, B. Malocha, and A. T. Fialho, Linking events with media. In A. Paschke, N. Henze and T. Pellegrini, *Proceedings of the 6th International Conference on Semantic Systems*, Graz, Austria, p. 42, ACM (2010).
7. L. Xie, H. Sundaram, and M. Campbell, Event mining in multimedia streams, *Proceedings of the IEEE*, **96**(4), 623–647 (2008).
8. C. Castillo, M. Mendoza, and B. Poblete, Information credibility on Twitter. In eds. S. Srinivasan, K. Ramamritham, A. Kumar, M. P. Ravindra, E. Bertino and R. Kumar, *Proceedings of the 20th International Conference on World Wide Web*, Hyderabad, India, pp. 675–684, ACM (2011).
9. J. Sankaranarayanan, H. Samet, B. E. Teitler, M. D. Lieberman, and J. Sperling, Twitterstand: news in tweets. In D. Agrawal, W. G. Aref, C-T. Lu, M. F. Mokbel, P. Scheuermann, C. Shahabi and O. Wolfson, *Proceedings of the 17th ACM Sigspatial International Conference on Advances in Geographic Information Systems*, Seattle, WA, USA, pp. 42–51, ACM (2009).

10. S. Phuvipadawat and T. Murata, Breaking news detection and tracking in Twitter. In eds. R. Kaplan, J. Burstein, M. Harper and G. Penn, *2000 IEEE/WIC/ACM International Conference on Web Intelligence and Intelligent Agent Technology (WI-IAT)*, vol. 3, pp. 120–123, IEEE (2010).
11. S. Petrović, M. Osborne, and V. Lavrenko, Streaming first story detection with application to Twitter. In *Human Language Technologies: The 2010 Annual Conference of the North American Chapter of the Association for Computational Linguistics*, Los Angeles, CA, USA, pp. 181–189, ACL (2010).
12. J. Allan, V. Lavrenko, and H. Jin, First story detection in TDT is hard. In *Proceedings of the 9th International Conference on Information and Knowledge Management*, Washington, DC, USA, pp. 374–381, ACM (2000).
13. H. Becker, M. Naaman, and L. Gravano, Beyond trending topics: Real-world event identification on Twitter. *International Conference on Weblogs and Social Media (ICWSM)*. **11**, 438–441 (2011).
14. R. Long, H. Wang, Y. Chen, O. Jin, and Y. Yu, Towards effective event detection, tracking and summarization on microblog data. In *Web-Age Information Management*, pp. 652–663. Springer (2011).
15. J. Weng and B.-S. Lee, Event detection in Twitter, *International Conference on Weblogs and Social Media (ICWSM)*, **11**, 401–408 (2011).
16. M. Cordeiro, Twitter event detection: Combining wavelet analysis and topic inference summarization. In *Doctoral Symposium on Informatics Engineering, DSIE*, Faculdade de Engenharia da Universidade do Porto (2012).
17. D. M. Blei, A. Y. Ng, and M. I. Jordan, Latent dirichlet allocation, *Journal of Machine Learning Research*, **3**, 993–1022 (2003).
18. V. Kharde and P. Sonawane, Sentiment analysis of Twitter data: A survey of techniques, *arXiv preprint arXiv:1601.06971* (2016).
19. A. Pak and P. Paroubek, Twitter as a corpus for sentiment analysis and opinion mining. In *LREC*, vol. 10, Association for Computational Linguistics (2010).
20. R. Parikh and M. Movassate, Sentiment analysis of user-generated Twitter updates using various classification techniques, *CS224N Final Report*, **118** (2009).
21. A. Go, R. Bhayani, and L. Huang, Twitter sentiment classification using distant supervision, *CS224N Project Report, Stanford*, **1**(2009), 12 (2009).
22. P.-W. Liang and B.-R. Dai, Opinion mining on social media data. In *2013 IEEE 11th International Conference on Mobile Data Management (MDM)*, Milan, Italy, vol. 2, pp. 91–96, IEEE (2013).
23. P. Gamallo and M. Garcia, Citius: A naive-bayes strategy for sentiment analysis on english tweets. In eds. P. Nakov and T. Zesch, *SemEval COL-ING*, Dublin, Ireland, pp. 171–175, Association for Computational Linguistics (2014).
24. R. Xia, C. Zong, and S. Li, Ensemble of feature sets and classification algorithms for sentiment classification, *Information Sciences*, **181**(6), 1138–1152 (2011).
25. L. Barbosa and J. Feng, Robust sentiment detection on Twitter from biased and noisy data. In eds. J. Hajič, S. Carberry, S. Clark and J. Nivre,

Proceedings of the 23rd International Conference on Computational Linguistics: Posters, Uppsala, Sweden, pp. 36–44, Association for Computational Linguistics (2010).

26. A. Bifet and E. Frank, Sentiment knowledge discovery in Twitter streaming data. In eds. B. Pfahringer, G. Holmes and A. Hoffmann, *International Conference on Discovery Science*, Canberra, Australia, pp. 1–15, Springer (2010).

27. A. Agarwal, B. Xie, I. Vovsha, O. Rambow, and R. Passonneau, Sentiment analysis of Twitter data. In eds. M. Nagarajan and M. Gamon, *Proceedings of the Workshop on Languages in Social Media*, Portland, OR, USA, pp. 30–38, Association for Computational Linguistics (2011).

28. D. Davidov, O. Tsur, and A. Rappoport, Enhanced sentiment learning using Twitter hashtags and smileys. In eds. J. Hajič, S. Carberry, S. Clark and J. Nivre, *Proceedings of the 23rd International Conference on Computational Linguistics: Posters*, Uppsala, Sweden, pp. 241–249, Association for Computational Linguistics (2010).

29. P. D. Turney, Thumbs up or thumbs down?: Semantic orientation applied to unsupervised classification of reviews. In *Proceedings of the 40th Annual Meeting on Association for Computational Linguistics*, Philadelphia, PA, USA, pp. 417–424, Association for Computational Linguistics (2002).

30. J. Kamps, M. Marx, R. J. Mokken, and M. De Rijke, Using wordnet to measure semantic orientations of adjectives. In *LREC*, vol. 4, pp. 1115–1118, Association for Computational Linguistics (2004).

31. Z. Luo, M. Osborne, and T. Wang, An effective approach to tweets opinion retrieval, *World Wide Web*, **18**(3), 545–566 (2015).

32. J. Kalyanam, M. Quezada, B. Poblete, and G. Lanckriet, Prediction and characterization of high-activity events in social media triggered by real-world news, *PloS one*, **11**(12), e0166694 (2016).

33. N. Kallus, Predicting crowd behavior with big public data. In C-W. Chung, A. Z. Broder, K. Shim and T. Suel, *Proceedings of the 23rd International Conference on World Wide Web*, Seoul, Korea, pp. 625–630, ACM (2014).

34. D. Gruhl, R. Guha, R. Kumar, J. Novak, and A. Tomkins, The predictive power of online chatter. In eds. Y. Guo and F. Farooq, *Proceedings of the 11th ACM SIGKDD International Conference on Knowledge Discovery in Data Mining*, Sydney, Australia, pp. 78–87, ACM (2005).

35. D. M. Romero, W. Galuba, S. Asur, and B. A. Huberman, Influence and passivity in social media. In eds. S. Srinivasan, K. Ramamritham, A. Kumar, M. P. Ravindra, E. Bertino and R. Kumar, *Proceedings of the 20th International Conference Companion on World Wide Web*, Hyderabad, India, pp. 113–114, ACM (2011).

36. K. Lerman and T. Hogg, Using a model of social dynamics to predict popularity of news. In M. Rappa, P. Jones, J. Freire and S. Chakrabarti, *Proceedings of the 19th International Conference on World Wide Web*, Raleigh, NC, USA, pp. 621–630, ACM (2010).

37. R. Sharda and D. Delen, Predicting box-office success of motion pictures with neural networks, *Expert Systems with Applications*, **30**(2), 243–254 (2006).

38. S. Yu and S. Kak, A survey of prediction using social media, *arXiv preprint arXiv:1203.1647* (2012).
39. M. Porter, An algorithm for suffix stripping, *Program*, **14**(3), 130–137 (1980).
40. M. E. Newman, Modularity and community structure in networks, In *Proceedings of the National Academy of Sciences*, **103**(23), 8577–8582 (2006).
41. R. Mihalcea and P. Tarau, Textrank: Bringing order into texts. In *Proceedings of the Conference on Empirical Methods in Natural Language Processing (EMNLP)*, Barcelona, Spain, ACL (2004).
42. S. Osiński, J. Stefanowski, and D. Weiss, Lingo: Search results clustering algorithm based on singular value decomposition. In eds. M. A. Klopotek, S. T. Wierzchon and K. Trojanowski, *Advances in Soft Computing, Intelligent Information Processing and Web Mining, Proceedings of the International IIS: IIPWM'04 Conference*, Beijing, China, p. 359–368, Springer (2004).
43. S. Brin and L. Page, The anatomy of a large-scale hypertextual web search engine, *Computer Networks and ISDN Systems*, **30**, 1–7 (1998).
44. O. Zamir and O. Etzioni, Web document clustering: A feasibility demonstration. In eds. W. B. Croft, A. Moffat, C. J. van Rijsbergen, R. Wilkinson and J. Zobel, *Proceedings of the 19th International ACM SIGIR Conference on Research and Development in Information Retrieval (SIGIR'98)*, Melbourne, Australia, pp. 46–54, ACM (1998).
45. D. Gusfield, *Algorithms on Strings, Trees and Sequences: Computer Science and Computational Biology.* Cambridge University Press (1997).
46. D. Weiss and S. Osinski, Open source search results clustering engine (2016). Available at: http://www.carrot2.org.
47. O. Zamir and O. Etzioni, Grouper: A dynamic clustering interface to web search results, *Computer Networks*, **31**(11–16), 1361–1374 (1999).
48. Twitter, Twitter sentiments (2017). Available at: http://www.sentiment140.com.
49. W. H. Press and S. A. Teukolsky, Savitzky-golay smoothing filters, *Computers in Physics*, **4**(6), 669–672 (1990).
50. IBM, Alchemylanguage service (2016). Available at: https://www.ibm.com/watson/developercloud/alchemy-language.html.
51. C. News, Hurricane Irma (2017). Available at: https://www.cbsnews.com/news/irma-live-updates-florida-power-outages-09-11-2017/.
52. Wikipedia, Protective edge operation (2014). Available at: http://en.wikipedia.org/wiki/2014_IsraelGaza_conflict.

Chapter 12

Linguistic Bias in Crowdsourced Biographies: A Cross-lingual Examination

Jahna Otterbacher[*,‡], Ioannis Katakis[†,§], and Pantelis Agathangelou[†,¶]

*Faculty of Pure and Applied Sciences,
Open University of Cyprus, Nicosia, Cyprus
† Computer Science Department, University of Nicosia,
Nicosia, Cyprus
‡ jahna.otterbacher@ouc.ac.cy
§ katakis.i@unic.ac.cy
¶ pandelisagathangelou@gmail.com

Biographies make up a significant portion of Wikipedia entries and are a source of information and inspiration for the public. We examine a threat to their objectivity, *linguistic biases*, which are pervasive in human communication. Linguistic bias, the systematic asymmetry in the language used to describe people as a function of their social groups, plays a role in the perpetuation of stereotypes. Theory predicts that we describe people who are expected — because they are members of our own in-groups or are stereotype-congruent — with more abstract, subjective language, as compared to others. Abstract language has the power to sway our impressions of others as it implies stability over time. Extending our monolingual work, we consider biographies of intellectuals at the English- and Greek-language Wikipedia. We use our recently introduced sentiment analysis tool, DidaxTo, which extracts domain-specific opinion words to build lexicons of subjective words in each language and for each gender, and compare the extent to which abstract language is used. Contrary to expectation, we find evidence of gender-based linguistic bias, with women being described more abstractly as compared to men. However, this is limited to English-language biographies. We discuss the implications of using DidaxTo to monitor linguistic bias in texts produced via crowdsourcing.

1. Introduction

Wikipedia continues to be one of the world's most popular websites, and is often described as being the largest collaboratively-edited source of free information. In addition to providing a platform for both informal[1] and formal[2] learning amongst citizens, Wikipedia has become a rich data source for researchers. For instance, corpora built from Wikipedia entries are often used by natural language processing[3,4] and machine learning[5] researchers. In addition, Wikipedia is often considered a prime case study for those researching information diffusion[6] and the growth of social networks.[7] Given Wikipedia's influence across a number of domains, it is not surprising that many have raised concerns as to its quality and reliability.

A number of researchers has attempted to develop generalized automated methods for detecting articles of high and low quality. Some of these methods rely on article metadata, including the edit history and profiles of contributing editors[8] or the patterns over time in article activity and overall lifecycles.[9] Others have attempted to exploit the textual characteristics of articles, such as linguistic and stylistic features[10] or even simple wordcounts.[11] Nonetheless, Wikipedia itself does not provide users with any such metrics, maintaining that quality is ensured by its unique collaborative editorial control processes. Indeed, it has been reported that given a critical mass of contributors to a given article, high levels of accuracy, completeness, and clarity are reached.[12]

The current work concerns a specific type of Wikipedia entry that is particularly sensitive to issues of information quality — biographies of persons, living or deceased. Pentzold (2009), in characterizing Wikipedia as a place where collective memories are negotiated and archived, notes that Wikipedia biographies detail the public view of a person's character and lifetime accomplishments.[13] Not surprisingly, Wikipedia maintains a page on "Biographies of living persons," in which it emphasizes the sensitive nature of such entries, as well as the need for participants to adhere to its three core policies of conveying a neutral point of view (NPOV), verifiability of all information, and no original research.[a] These guidelines are necessary not only because of the sensitive nature of biographies, but also because they are a very common type of entry at Wikipedia.

In fact, Flekova *et al.* (2014) found that over one-fifth of all Wikipedia articles describes persons. Therefore, they argued for the development of

---

[a] https://en.wikipedia.org/wiki/Wikipedia:Biographies_of_living_persons.

automated methods for ensuring the quality of biographies. To this end, they developed a means for scoring a given article with respect to four dimensions of quality: completeness, writing style, trustworthiness and, closely related to our work, objectivity. In gauging the extent to which a given biography reflects the subjectivity/objectivity of its authors, they used both textual features (e.g., words expressing sentiment) and Wikipedia features (i.e., article metadata). Given the importance of the textual features in their predictive model, their results demonstrated that the manner in which Wikipedia participants describe others not only conveys information about the target persons, but also about the authors as information sources. In contrast to this approach, we focus on a particular phenomenon that might negatively impact the objectivity of Wikipedia biographies, *linguistic biases*, which are known to be not only persistent in human communication, but also very subtle. As will be explained in detail, we shall study how famous scientists and intellectuals, both women and men, are described in their Wikipedia biographies in two language editions, English and Greek. In particular, we shall examine which types of linguistic biases are likely to pose a threat to objectivity in biographies.

1.1. *Linguistic bias and social stereotypes*

Social psychologists have long been convinced that the stylistic features of language play a key role in the transmission and maintainance of social stereotypes.[15,16] In other words, when we are describing others, it is not only what we say about them (i.e., the content of our message) but also how we say what we say, which reveals the stereotypes that influence our perceptions of others. Beukeboom (2013) defines the term *linguistic bias* as:

> A systematic asymmetry in the way that one uses language, as a function of the social group of the person(s) being described.

Given Wikipedia's NPOV policy, and its extensive editorial control processes, it is not likely that we would find explicit indicators of bias, such as the use of racial slurs or sexist language being used in biographies. However, we may find that there are systematic asymmetries in the manner in which social groups (e.g., gender- or ethnicity-based) are described. Consider the following three statements:

(1) Thomas Edison invented several devices.
(2) Thomas Edison was an American inventor and businessman.
(3) Thomas Edison was America's greatest inventor.

The first of the three descriptions is the most concrete and objective; it contains no subjective words and details a specific action. In contrast, the second description is a bit more abstract, since it describes an enduring characteristic of the target person. Finally, the third description is the most abstract, as it makes a general statement about Edison using a subjective adjective ("greatest"). The question of interest is whether such subtle differences in biographies are systematic, with respect to three characteristics: (1) the gender of the target person (i.e., men vs. women intellectuals), (2) the ethnic background of the target person (i.e., individuals hailing from the English-speaking world vs. others), and (3) the language in which the biography is written (i.e., Greek vs. English). Theory holds that such systematic differences are likely to reinforce social stereotypes. For instance, if men intellectuals were consistently described more abstractly and positively, as compared to women, this would reinforce the notion that men are expected to be successful and famous, while women are not.

A growing number of social media platforms allows participants to collaboratively produce biographies. Given their potential influence, both in terms of a source of information for readers as well as a source of data for researchers, it is of growing importance to consider their quality and objectivity. In previous work, we analyzed English-language biographies of actors and actresses produced at the Internet Movie Database (IMDb).[18] Specifically, we considered gender- and race-based linguistic biases, and found that Caucasian men actors were more likely than other social groups to be described in an abstract, positive manner. The current work extends our research in a number of ways. First, we analyze biographies from Wikipedia, which as mentioned, is one of the most popular sites worldwide. In addition, we study biographies not only from the largest of the Wikipedias, English, but also from a smaller community, the Greek-language Wikipedia, in order to examine whether linguistic biases occur across languages, as predicted by theory.[19] To this end, we utilize a recently introduced tool, DidaxTo[20] that extracts opinion words that the authors use in a collection of documents. It operates in both languages: English and Greek.

As we will show, there are interesting cross-lingual differences in terms of the linguistic biases that manifest in biographies of famous intellectuals that are produced collaboratively at Wikipedia. In addition, our results suggest that it is not always the case that theories of linguistic bias, which have been developed by social psychologists in offline, experimental settings, can predict the types of biases observed in online, crowdsourced biographical texts. As will be explained, our findings underscore the need to continue to explore the phenomenon of linguistic bias in social media spaces where social actors (i.e., writers) are often anonymous. In the next section, we provide the theoretical background that underlies our work, before detailing our methodology.

2. Background

Our work is inspired by social psychology theories surrounding two types of linguistic biases: the Linguistic Expectancy Bias (LEB) and the Linguistic Intergroup Bias (LIB). Both are manifested through two stylistic characteristics of the language that a communicator uses to describe someone: the specificity of the description, as well as the use of subjective words (i.e., words that reveal sentiment). In order to provide adequate background on the LEB and the LIB, we must first start with an overview of the Linguistic Category Model (LCM).[21]

2.1. *Linguistic Category Model*

Semin and Fiedler's Linguistic Category Model is a tool for understanding language as a social behavior. More specifically, it proposes a shift in the methodological approach to analyzing language, from the individual to the social perceptive. According to a manual for analysts applying LCM, "to understand social behavior, one has to develop a handle on language as a tool that carries communication and makes social interaction possible."[22]

As shown in Fig. 1, the LCM consists of four categories of predicates, which relate to the level of abstraction in a person description. The most concrete category comprises predicates involving a descriptive action verb, which describes an observed event with no additional interpretation of that event. At the other extreme, the most abstract predicates involve an adjective. Here, the respective description is general; it applies across events and scenarios. In between these two categories, we have the use of a state verb or the use of an interpretive action verb. A state verb describes an ongoing state of affairs, and is thus relatively abstract. An interpretive action verb denotes a description that can be attributed only to a specific event or action, and is thus, relatively less abstract.

The two types of biases, the LEB and the LIB, can be detected based on the extent to which a person description uses abstract language. There

		Description	**Example**
	Adjectives	Describes a characteristic or feature of a person.	Albert Einstein was an amazing mind.
	State verb	Describes an enduring cognitive or emotional state with no clear beginning or end.	Albert Einstein still amazes students today.
	Interpretive action verb	Refers to various actions with clear beginning and end.	Albert Einstein was amazing as a professor at the Swiss Federal Polytechnic.
	Descriptive action verb	Refers to a single, specific action with a clear beginning and end.	Albert Einstein was a professor of theoretical physics at the Swiss Federal Polytechnic.

Fig. 1.   The Linguistic Category Model.

are cognitive underpinnings to both, as familiar or expected (i.e., stereo-typical) scenes are more easily processed.[23] But while their underpinnings are cognitive, the consequences of these biases are social in nature. As they are known to be pervasive in face-to-face interpersonal communication, it is important to understand the extent to which they are also pervasive in technology-mediated contexts, and especially in crowdsourcing platforms such as Wikipedia.

Abstract descriptions are more powerful than concrete ones. This is because they imply stability over time as well as generalizability. It has been confirmed that message recipients are impacted by the level of abstraction in the language used in person descriptions, with more abstract descriptions being interpreted as enduring characteristics of the target person, in contract to concrete descriptions, which are seen as being transient.[24] In this way, linguistic biases can contribute significantly to the maintenance and transmission of social stereotypes, as information encoded abstractly is more resistant to disconfirmation, as compared to very concrete information.

2.2. Linguistic Expectancy Bias

While known to be pervasive in interpersonal communication, the Linguistic Expectancy Bias (LEB) has only been studied in laboratory settings, with few exceptions.[25] The LEB reflects the fact that it is easier for us to process information that is expected (e.g., persons who are stereotype-confirming). We tend to describe other people and situations that are consistent with expectations in a more interpretive and abstract manner. In turn, more abstract descriptions of the target person contain more information about their characteristics and traits, and less about a particular action taken by the person. Laboratory studies have demonstrated that when participants are asked to describe someone who violates their expectations, they are likely to focus on particular details, providing tangible and concrete information.[19,24] On the other hand, when describing stereotype-congruent (i.e., expectation confirming) individuals, participants are more likely to provide abstract details, using language that references the perceived disposition and traits of the target person.

2.3. *Linguistic Intergroup Bias*

The Linguistic Intergroup Bias (LIB) builds on the LEB; we expect our in-group members to have positive qualities and behaviors, while we may not hold such expectations for out-group members. The LIB predicts that we use language in such a way that it is difficult to disconfirm our pre-existing ideas about social groups.[15] Therefore, we are more likely to describe the positive actions and attributes of fellow in-group members with abstract language, whereas any negative traits and actions are more likely described concretely. The converse is predicted for descriptions of out-group members.

2.4. *Detecting linguistic bias in crowdsourced texts*

Having reviewed the key theories of linguistic biases, we shall now propose a method for their detection in the collaboratively-produced Wikipedia biographies. Figure 2 summarizes the linguistic characteristics of our textual biographies, based on the relationship between Wikipedia authors and the target individuals being described.

It is important to note that previous research on linguistic biases has involved manual annotation; in other words, researchers analyze texts with respect to the LCM guidelines. As mentioned in our previous work,[18] while the LCM is a rather precise and complicated model, it is possible to conduct an automated analysis, inspired by key elements of the LCM, such that one can analyze a large corpus of texts. Proponents of the LCM emphasize that the textual segments that one should annotate, and the particular manner in which we apply the LCM depend on the researcher's particular

	Expectancy-congruent (LEB) In-group (LIB)	Expectancy-incongruent (LEB) Out-group (LIB)
Familiar/ Desirable Actions and Traits	More abstract	More concrete
	More adjectives More subjective words	Fewer adjectives Fewer subjective words
Unfamiliar/ Undesirable Actions and Traits	More concrete	More abstract
	Fewer adjectives Fewer subjective words	More adjectives More subjective words

Fig. 2.   Linguistic features predicted by theory.

questions. As in previous work, we can note that adjectives play a key role in conveying abstract information about a target person. Furthermore, we can accurately distinguish between adjectives and other parts of speech.[26] Therefore, a person description in which there is a preference for more adjectives, is indicative of a relatively more abstract description.

Secondly, subjective words also play a key role in the construction of more abstract descriptions. Such words inject authors' sentiment into the description, as well as their inferences about the target person. In fact, in psychological studies of social stereotypes, which involved the "trait adjective method," researchers often ask participants to associate subjective adjectives with target social groups.[27]

Given the above observations, we consider four linguistic characteristics of the biographies in our corpus:

(1) The extent to which the text comprises adjectives.
(2) The extent to which the text comprises subjective, positive words.
(3) The extent to which the text comprises subjective, negative words.
(4) The ratio of subjective positive to negative words in a text.

2.5. Domain-independent sentiment analysis

For the extraction of subjective words we utilize our recently introduced unsupervised tool for domain-specific opinion word discovery, DidaxTo.[28,29] The novelty of the tool is that it enables the extraction of subjective terms that are used in each domain independently. Therefore our analysis does not rely on a pre-defined list of opinion words like the one offered in Hu and Liu (2004). This is an important feature for several reasons. For instance, some opinion words might be used only in a sub-set of circumstances while others might change meaning and even polarity depending on the respective domain. In order to achieve this goal, DidaxTo utilizes opinion modifiers, sentiment consistency theories, polarity assignment graphs, and pattern similarity metrics.

In previous work, DidaxTo was used to learn subjective lexicons in a number of different domains and the resulting lexicons were compared against those obtained via other state-of-the-art approaches. In an explicit evaluation (i.e., where human judges evaluated the accuracy of the learned lexicons), DidaxTo outperformed other sentiment classifiers. Likewise, in the implicit evaluation, where human judgments were available only for the overall sentiment of a text and not individual words, DidaxTo outperformed other methods in the majority of domains tested. Details of the algorithm, as well as the evaluations, can be found in Agathangelou *et al.* (2017).

3. Data and method

In this section, we first lay out three specific research questions motivated by the theory presented in Section 2, which extends our previous research on linguistic biases in crowdsourced biographies.[18] We then detail the construction of our corpus as well as the processing of the English- and Greek-language biographies.

3.1. *Research questions*

The present study will examine the following three research questions:

- RQ1: Is there evidence of linguistic biases based on the gender of the target person?
- RQ2: Is there evidence of linguistic biases based on the ethnicity of the target person?
- RQ3: Do we observe linguistic biases more frequently in one language as compared to the other?

We shall answer questions one and two within each language edition of Wikipedia, before then comparing the linguistic style used in biographies between the two languages.

3.2. *Corpus*

We built a corpus of biographies of famous intellectuals, including scientists and engineers, inventors and writers. To be included, the target individual must have a biography entry in both the English- and Greek-language Wikipedias. This criterion significantly limited the number of biographies available for inclusion in our corpus; the Greek Wikipedia is a small resource with just over 133,000 entries at the time of writing, compared to the nearly 5.5 million entries at the English-language site.[b] In the end, we have collected and processed 197 biographies of men and 187 biographies of women, in both the Greek and English languages. In other words, the corpus consists of 768 carefully chosen biographies.

Next, biographies were coded for ethnicity of the target persons. To have an objective means to do this, we used citizenship. We distinguished individuals whose Wikipedia biography indicates that they are/were a citizen of an anglophone country (the United States, Canada, England, Ireland, Australia, and New Zealand citizens appeared in our corpus) from those who were/are a citizen of other countries. It should be noted that in classifying immigrants and dual citizens (e.g., Albert Einstein, Zaha Hadid) we based the classification on the country in which they died or currently reside. The corpus contains biographies of 154 anglophone intellectuals (61 men, 93 women) and 230 intellectuals from other regions (136 men, 94 women). Given the small size of the Greek Wikipedia, it was not feasible to create groups based on more specific ethnic background criteria.

Table 1 provides summary statistics concerning the length of biographies (number of words). Since the distributions are skewed to the right, we used non-parametric tests to compare lengths across languages and gender. The non-parametric Wilcoxon Signed-Ranked Test[31] (an alternative to the paired t-test) revealed that English-language biographies tend to

Table 1.   Median/mean length of biographies.

	Men	Women
English	4798/3070	3557/2515
Greek	1313/601	900/543

---

[b]https://en.wikipedia.org/wiki/List_of_Wikipedias.

be longer than Greek-language biographies of both women ($V = 17,080$, $p < .001$) and men ($V = 19,124$, $p < .001$). The two-group Mann-Whitney U test was used to compare across genders within a given language. Results indicated that at the English-language Wikipedia, men's biographies tend to be longer than those of women ($W = 20,592$, $p < .05$). However, there was no significant gender-based difference for the Greek-language biographies.

Below, we provide two example biographies of famous men, which appear in our corpus. Below each Greek-language entry, we have provided an English translation. In particular, we provide the opening sentence for each biography, which sets the tone for the text and is likely read by anyone visiting the entry at Wikipedia. Likewise, the first few sentences of a biography are important as they appear in the snippet provided by a search engine in response to a query on the respective person's name. As can be seen, there are some subtle differences between these opening sentences. In the García Márquez biographies, while slightly different information is detailed in the English vs. Greek entries, both contain a bit of subjectivity, with the use of the words "affectionately" in the English entry and "important" in the Greek entry. In contrast, in the opening sentences describing Thomas Edison, the Greek entry is notably more objective, as compared to English entry, which refers to Edison as the country's "greatest inventor."

Gabriel José de la Concordia García Márquez
English
Gabriel José de la Concordia García Márquez (6 March 1927 – 17 April 2014) was a Colombian novelist, short-story writer, screenwriter and journalist, known affectionately as Gabo or Gabito throughout Latin America.

Greek
Ο Γκαμπριέλ Γκαρσία Μάρκες (ισπ. Gabriel José García Márquez, 6 Μαρτίου 1927 – 17 Απριλίου 2014) ήταν σπουδαίος Κολομβιανός συγγραφέας, βραβευμένος με Βραβείο Νόμπελ Λογοτεχνίας.
Gabriel García Márquez (Spanish: Gabriel José García Márquez, 6 March 1927 – 17 April 2014) was an important Colombian author, awarded with the Nobel Prize in literature.

(*Continued*)

(*Continued*)

Thomas Alva Edison
English
Thomas Alva Edison (February 11, 1847 – October 18, 1931) was an American inventor and businessman, who has been described as America's greatest inventor.

Greek
Ο Τόμας Έντισον (Thomas Alva Edison, 11 Φεβρουαρίου 1847 – 18 Οκτωβρίου 1931) ήταν Αμερικανός εφευρέτης και επιχειρηματίας.
Thomas Edison (Thomas Alva Edison, 11 February 1847 – 18 October 1931) was an American inventor and businessman.

In addition, we provide examples of the opening sentences of two famous women. Between languages, we can again observe some differences. For both women, the Greek biographies open with more subjective sentences. Austen is described as "popular" and "widely-read", while Yourcenar is a "top literary figure."

Jane Austen
English
Jane Austen (16 December 1775 – 18 July 1817) was an English novelist known primarily for her six major novels, which interpret, critique and comment upon the British landed gentry at the end of the 18th century.

Greek
Η Τζέιν Όστεν (Jane Austen, 16 Δεκεμβρίου 1775 - 18 Ιουλίου 1817) είναι μία από τις πιο δημοφιλείς και πολυδιαβασμένες μυθιστοριογράφους της αγγλικής λογοτεχνίας.
Jane Austen (16 December 1775 – 18 July 1817) is one of the most popular and widely-read novelists of English literature.

Marguerite Yourcenar
English
Marguerite Yourcenar (8 June 1903 – 17 December 1987) was a French novelist and essayist born in Brussels, Belgium, who became a US citizen in 1947.

(*Continued*)

(*Continued*)

Greek

Η Μαργκερίτ Γιουρσενάρ (γαλλ. Marguerite Yourcenar) (8 Ιουνίου 1903
– 17 Δεκεμβρίου 1987) ήταν Γαλλίδα συγγραφέας και ποιήτρια, μια από
τις κορυφαίες λογοτεχνικές μορφές της Γαλλίας του εικοστού αιώνα.
Marguerite Yourcenar (8 June 1903 – 17 December 1987) was a French
author and poet, one of France's top literary figures of the twentieth
century.

3.3. *Text processing*

DidaxTo was used to learn a lexicon of subjective words of each polarity
(negative and positive) for each domain (i.e., by language in which the biography was written and gender of the target individual). Using the extracted
lexicon, we obtained the number of positive and negative domain words used
in each textual biography, as well as the number of adjectives used. For the
part of speech (POS) tagging process we used the implementation of the
Stanford parser included in the NLTK Python library.[c]

3.3.1. *Learned dictionaries*

Table 2 details the sizes of the eight dictionaries that were learned using
DidaxTo. One can immediately note a striking difference across genders
in the sizes of the dictionaries learned from the English-language entries.
In other words, Wikipedians appear to have a much larger vocabulary of
subjective words for describing women vs. men. It remains to be seen if
these words are used at a greater frequency overall (i.e., if, in general,
subjective words are used more often in biographies of women vs. men),
or if more unique words are used in women's biographies (i.e., while the
dictionaries of subjective positive and negative words are larger, the words
are not necessarily used more often in the entries). It can also be seen that
across languages but within a given gender, the dictionary sizes differ. This
can be partially explained by the fact that, as examined in Table 1, Greek
biographies are significantly shorter than the respective English versions.
However, it again remains to be seen from the analysis if the frequency of
use of subjective words exhibits a systematic difference between languages.

---

[c]http://www.nltk.org/.

Table 2.   Sizes of dictionaries.

| | Positive | | Negative | |
	Men	Women	Men	Women
GR	553	424	260	185
EN	887	2,175	979	2,086

In order to explore how the learned sentiment dictionaries vary by the target persons' gender, we first translated the Greek-language dictionary entries to English, so that we could make comparisons. Specifically, the extracted Greek words were submitted to Google Translate[d] and then manually corrected where necessary by a native speaker. Next, the words in all four dictionaries were stemmed via Porter's stemming algorithm,[32] such that we could find all unique lemmas.

For each gender and polarity (i.e., negative and positive), we found the intersection of the Greek- and English-language dictionaries. We then identified which words were uniquely used to describe one gender but not the other. Table 3 summarizes this analysis and provides example words that are used to describe persons of each gender. For instance, there are 111 negative words that are used to describe men at both the Greek and English Wikipedias, and 52 of these are used to describe men and not women.

A qualitative observation one can make from Table 3 is that the dictionaries learned by DidaxTo largely reflect prevalent gender-based stereotypes. Researchers of person perception have found that there are two universal dimensions upon which we judge other people — how *warm* (i.e., non-threatening) someone is and how *competent* or *agentic* she is.[33] Traditional gender stereotypes include expectations that men are (and should be) high in competence/low in warmth, and vice versa for women.[34] Similarly, in the dictionaries, we find that many positive sentiment-bearing words used to describe women refer to warmth (e.g., affection, cheer, family, nice) while those used to describe men are more often related to competence (e.g., best, glory, inspire, rich). While a critique of the social and ethical implications of the dictionaries is beyond the scope of the current work, we can conclude that DidaxTo's results are quite logical, given the documented underlying gender biases in Wikipedia biographical texts[35,36] as well as the nature of prevalent gender stereotypes.

---

[d]https://translate.google.com/.

Table 3. Subjective words by polarity and associated gender.

		Common words in both GR/EN	Unique for gender	Example words unique for gender
Negative	M	111	52	awkward, barbarian, careless, cheap, foolish, poorly, stuck, stupid, weak, wrong
Negative	W	107	48	fail, greed, guilt, miser, nightmare, sad, shock spoil, weird, wreck
Positive	M	212	86	affirm, best, charm, competitive, convince, fair, glory, inspire, passion, rich
Positive	W	222	96	affection, cheer, clever, creation, colleague, family, friend, host, nice, pioneer sexual, stylish, young

4. Analysis

We analyze the extent to which the target person's gender and ethnicity, as well as the interaction between them, explain the variance in four independent variables, all of which correlate to an increased level of abstraction in the language used, per the LCM. In particular, we examine the variables described in Table 4.

We examine the four variables in each of the three textual segments of interest: the full-text biography, the first five sentences (i.e., textual "snippet") and the opening or first sentence of the biography. For the full-text biographies and snippets we examine the continuous variables. In contrast, for opening sentences, we examine the binary variables, as the length of opening sentences can often be brief. As we used Analysis of Variance

Table 4. Linguistic characteristics analyzed.

Characteristic	Continuous variable	Binary variable
Adjectives	$\frac{Adjectives}{Total\_words}$	$\geq$ one adjective used
Positive words	$\frac{Positive\_words}{Total\_words}$	$\geq$ one positive word used
Negative words	$\frac{Negative\_words}{Total\_words}$	$\geq$ one negative word used
Ratio of positive-to-negative	$\frac{Positive\_words+1}{Negative\_words+1}$	Ratio $\geq$ 1

Table 5.   Variable transformations used.

Characteristic	Full-text	Snippet
Adjectives	GR: N/A	N/A
	EN: N/A	N/A
Positive words	GR: N/A	sqrt
	EN: N/A	N/A
Negative words	GR: log	GR: log
	EN: N/A	EN: log
Ratio of positive-to-negative	GR: log	log
	EN: log	log

(ANOVA) to analyze the continuous variables, we transformed those that did not meet the normality assumption as described in Table 5. Entries of "N/A" in the table indicate cases where the variables met the normality assumption.

For each of the four independent variables, we fit models to examine the extent to which the target person's gender and ethnicity, and their interaction, explain a significant portion of variance in the variable, and in each case (full-text biography, snippet of five sentences, opening sentence of the biography). In other words, all models test main effects for gender and ethnicity, and an interaction term. In the case of continuous variables, we fit a two-way ANOVA. In the event of statistically significant effects, we report effect sizes using partial η^2 and use Cohen's conventions for interpreting their magnitude.[37]

Briefly, partial η^2 aids in the interpretation of effect sizes between studies. It expresses the ratio of the sum of squares of the effect in question (e.g., gender) to the sum of squares of the effect and the sum of squares of the error associated with the effect. An η^2 ranging from 0.01 to 0.05 is interpreted as indicating a small effect size, while an η^2 ranging from 0.06 to 0.13 indicates a medium effect size. In addition, we follow up with Tukey's Honestly Significant Differences (HSD) test,[38] which compares all possible pairs of means, in order to determine which pairwise differences are meaningful.

For the binary variables, we fit a logit regression model in which we predict the likelihood of a text exhibiting the respective linguistic characteristic. In the event of statistically significant effects, we report the odds ratios as a measure of effect size following Hilbe (2011). As the odds ratio indicates how many times bigger the odds of one outcome is for a given value of the independent variable as compared to the other (e.g., for women intellectuals versus men, or for anglophone intellectuals versus others), it can be interpreted as an unstandardized effect size.

4.1. *Full-text biographies*

Table 6 details the ANOVA results with respect to the use of adjectives in the biographies, in each language. The right-most column provides the pairwise differences that are significant, per the HSD test, where the p-value is less than 0.05. As can be seen, in both the Greek- and English-language biographies, there is a tendency for Wikipedians to use more adjectives when describing men as compared to women (i.e., there is a significant main effect on gender, albeit with a small effect size, in both models). In addition, target persons from non-anglophone countries tend to be described with significantly more adjectives as compared to citizens of anglophone countries (i.e., main effect on ethnicity).

The ANOVAs on the proportion of words that are positive and negative in full-text biographies of both languages are detailed in Tables 7 and 8, respectively. In addition, Table 9 details the ANOVA on the ratio of positive to negative words. From Tables 7 and 8, we observe that in Greek biographies, positive words are used more often when describing men as compared to women although negative words are used just as often to describe both genders; however, there are no ethnicity-based differences. In contrast, in English-language biographies, women are more often described with subjective words of both polarities (positive and negative) as compared to men. In addition, famous persons from anglophone countries are more likely to be described with positive words than are other individuals. When it comes to the ratio of positive to negative words used in biographies, there are no significant effects on either gender or ethnicity, for either language version, in Table 9.

Table 6. ANOVA on proportion of words that are adjectives (full-text): F-statistic[a] and effect size (η^2).

	Gender	Ethnicity	Gender*Ethnicity	Sig. Diff.
GR	13.8***	5.30*	2.49	M > W
	(.03)	(.01)	n.s.	Other > Ang
EN	17.3***	6.50*	0.48	M > W
	(.03)	(.02)	n.s.	Other > Ang

[a]***$p < .001$, **$p < .01$, *$p < .05$

Table 7. ANOVA on proportion of words that are subjective and positive (full-text): F-statistic[a] and effect size (η^2).

	Gender	Ethnicity	Gender*Ethnicity	Sig. Diff.
GR	6.65*	0.000	0.168	M > W
	(.02)	n.s.	n.s.	
EN	41.0***	19.7***	1.31	W > M
	(.07)	(.04)	n.s.	Ang > Other

[a]***$p < .001$, **$p < .01$, *$p < .05$

Table 8. ANOVA on proportion of words that are subjective and negative (full-text): F-statistic[a] and effect size (η^2).

	Gender	Ethnicity	Gender*Ethnicity	Sig. Diff.
GR	2.23	0.408	0.539	n.s.
	n.s.	n.s.	n.s.	
EN	10.4**	0.639	3.40	W > M
	(.02)	n.s.	n.s.	

[a]***$p < .001$, **$p < .01$, *$p < .05$

Table 9. ANOVA on ratio of positive to negative words (full-text): F-statistic[a] and effect size (η^2).

	Gender	Ethnicity	Gender*Ethnicity	Sig. Diff.
GR	0.526	0.728	0.094	n.s.
	n.s.	n.s.	n.s.	
EN	0.043	1.646	3.407	n.s.
	n.s.	n.s.	n.s.	

[a]***$p < .001$, **$p < .01$, *$p < .05$

4.2. First paragraph

As previously explained, we also analyzed the first five sentences of biographies. This is meant to approximate the textual "snippet" of a Wikipedia entry that appears in search engine results.

As shown in Table 10, in the first five sentences, just as in the full-text English-language texts, there is a tendency for Wikipedians to use more adjectives when describing men vs. women. However, there is also a significant interaction between gender and ethnicity, such that women

Table 10. ANOVA on proportion of words that are adjectives (snippet): F-statistic[a] and effect size (η^2).

	Gender	Ethnicity	Gender*Ethnicity	Sig. Diff.
GR	0.192	0.759	1.443	n.s.
	n.s.	n.s.	n.s.	
EN	4.74*	.542	6.02*	M > W
	(.01)	n.s.	(.01)	Other-W > Ang-W

[a]***$p < .001$, **$p < .01$, *$p < .05$

Table 11. ANOVA on proportion of words that are subjective and positive (snippet): F-statistic[a] and effect size (η^2).

	Gender	Ethnicity	Gender*Ethnicity	Sig. Diff.
GR	3.218	1.372	0.015	n.s.
	n.s.	n.s.	n.s.	
EN	17.5***	11.1***	0.971	W > M
	(.05)	(:03)	n.s.	Ang > Other

[a]***$p < .001$, **$p < .01$, *$p < .05$

Table 12. ANOVA on proportion of words that are subjective and negative (snippet): F-statistic[a] and effect size (η^2).

	Gender	Ethnicity	Gender*Ethnicity	Sig. Diff.
GR	5.129*	4.134*	0.169	M > W
	(.01)	(.01)	n.s.	Other > Ang
EN	13.04***	5.306*	0.708	W > M
	(.02)	(.01)	n.s.	Ang > Other

[a]***$p < .001$, **$p < .01$,* $p < .05$

from anglophone regions are described with fewer adjectives as compared to other women.

Tables 11 and 12 detail the analysis of the use of positive and negative words in the first five sentences (i.e., the "snippet") of a biography, respectively. Table 13 analyzes the ratio of positive to negative words used. As can be seen, the trends across language diverge. In the Greek-language biographies, more abstract language (negative words) is used in biographies of men and individuals from non-anglophone countries. In English-language biographies, more abstract language (positive and negative words) is observed in biographies of women and those from anglophone countries.

Table 13. ANOVA on ratio of positive to negative words (snippet): F-statistic[a] and effect size (η^2).

	Gender	Ethnicity	Gender*Ethnicity	Sig. Diff.
GR	0.031	8.552**	0.026	Ang > Other
	n.s.	(.02)	n.s.	
EN	0.411	0.065	0.171	n.s.
	n.s.	n.s.	n.s.	

[a]***$p < .001$, **$p < .01$, *$p < .05$

Table 14. Logit regression to predict the use of $\geq$ one adjective in opening sentences: coefficients[a] and odds ratios.

	Intercept	Gender	Ethnicity	Gender*Ethnicity
GR	2.088***	−0.2582	−0.5736	0.7529
	(8.07)	n.s.	n.s.	n.s.
EN	0.7376***	1.948***	0.3830	−0.9523
	(2.09)	(7.01)	n.s.	n.s.

[a]***$p < .001$, **$p < .01$, *$p < .05$

4.3. *Opening sentence*

Finally, we analyzed the opening sentences of biographies, as they are arguably the most-read unit of text in a biography. In addition, the first sentence (i.e., the topic sentence) sets the overall tone of the text and are often used as a summary, which indicates the article's content and tone.[40]

In Table 14, it can be seen that in the English-language biographies, there is evidence that women of any ethnicity tend to be described with more abstract language (i.e., more adjectives) as compared to men. This is an interesting finding as it is the opposite of what the LEB would predict.

Tables 15 and 16 present the logit regression models for the prediction of there being at least one positive and negative word in the opening sentence of a given biography. Similarly, Table 17 presents the model for predicting the event that, in the first sentence, there are more positive than negative words (i.e., the ratio of positive to negative words is greater than one). We observe no gender- or ethnicity-based differences in the use of abstract language in Greek-language biographies. However, in the English-language texts, women are described with more abstract language (i.e., using words of both positive and negative polarity) as compared to men. It is also interesting to note that women's biographies appear to be more positive than

Table 15. Logit regression to predict the use of ≥ one positive word in opening sentences: coefficients[a] and odds ratios.

	Intercept	Gender	Ethnicity	Gender*Ethnicity
GR	−0.9474***	−0.2382	0.07656	0.3175
	(0.39)	n.s.	n.s.	n.s.
EN	0.3264	1.047***	0.5444	−1.0237*
	n.s.	(2.85)	n.s.	(0.36)

[a]***$p < .001$, **$p < .01$, *$p < .05$

Table 16. Logit regression to predict the use of ≥ one negative word in opening sentences: coefficients[a] and odds ratios.

	Intercept	Gender	Ethnicity	Gender*Ethnicity
GR	−3.076***	0.3902	0.1139	−0.5307
	(0.05)	n.s.	n.s.	n.s.
EN	−1.540***	0.6316*	0.9679**	−0.5186
	(0.21)	(1.88)	(2.63)	n.s.

[a]***$p < .001$, **$p < .01$, *$p < .05$

Table 17. Logit regression to predict the ratio of positive to negative words being ≥ one in opening sentences: coefficients[a] and odds ratios.

	Intercept	Gender	Ethnicity	Gender*Ethnicity
GR	−1.021***	−0.4187	0.0707	0.5781
	(0.36)	n.s.	n.s.	n.s.
EN	0.02941	0.9858***	0.4035	−0.8208
	n.s.	(2.68)	n.s.	n.s.

[a]***$p < .001$, **$p < .01$, *$p < .05$

those of men (i.e., there is a significant effect on gender in predicting the ratio of positive to negative words).

5. Discussion

We now interpret our results, answering each of the three research questions put forward. As previously explained, two theories, Linguistic Expectancy Bias and Linguistic Intergroup Bias, have been developed in the context of "offline," laboratory experiments. These theories make particular predictions regarding the characteristics of language that we can expect to find in

Table 18. Summary of observations (Full-text and Snippet).

		Full-text		Snippet	
		GR	EN	GR	EN
ADJ	Gender	M > W	M > W	n.s.	M > W
	Ethnicity	Other > Ang	Other > Ang	n.s.	Other > Ang
Positive	Gender	M > W	W > M	n.s.	W > M
	Ethnicity	n.s.	Ang > Other	n.s.	Ang > Other
Negative	Gender	n.s.	W > M	M > W	W > M
	Ethnicity	n.s.	n.s.	Other > Ang	Ang > Other
Pos/neg	Gender	n.s.	n.s.	n.s.	n.s.
	Ethnicity	n.s.	n.s.	Ang > Other	n.s.

Table 19. Summary of observations (Opening sentence).

		Opening sentence	
		GR	EN
ADJ	Gender	n.s.	W > M
	Ethnicity	n.s.	n.s.
Positive	Gender	n.s.	W > M
	Ethnicity	n.s.	Other-W > Ang-W
Negative	Gender	n.s.	W > M
	Ethnicity	n.s.	Ang > Other
Pos/neg	Gender	n.s.	W > M
	Ethnicity	n.s.	n.s.

descriptions of people. Figure 2 details the features that we would expect to find in Wikipedia biographies of famous intellectuals, under the LEB and LIB, as relates to the use of abstract, subjective language. Tables 18 and 19 provide a summary of the observations from our analyses presented in Section 4, to aid interpretation.

5.1. *Gender-based differences*

Our first research question (RQ1) asked whether there are systematic differences in terms of the frequency of markers of abstract language in the biographies of women vs. men intellectuals. Both the LEB and the LIB predict that we should observe more abstract language in the biographies of men as compared to women. As mentioned, the prevailing gender stereotypes in Western societies tend to cast women as less agentic or competent as compared to men.[34] Therefore, men can be said to be more stereotype-congruent, and therefore more expected, as famous intellectuals. In addition, it is well-known that there is a substantial gender gap at Wikipedia, with men participants greatly outnumbering women.[41,42] While the gender distribution of participants who collaborate in the writing of a given entry certainly varies, the LIB predicts that men will describe other men using more abstract language, and men are the majority in general.

In the Greek-language Wikipedia, we observe several cases where men are indeed described more frequently using markers of abstract, subjective language, as compared to women. Specifically, in full-text biographies, men are described using more adjectives and positive words than women. In snippets, men are described with more negative words than are women. However, in English-language Wikipedia biographies, the results are less consistent. That said, one salient finding concerns the opening sentences of English-language biographies, in which women's biographies contain significantly more markers of abstract language (adjectives, positive and negative words) as compared to men.

Previous studies have revealed that while famous women and men are covered in Wikipedia equally well (i.e., there is little to no gender-based coverage bias),[35] the topics covered in men and women's biographies vary. Specifically, women's biographies are more likely to emphasize her family and social relationships while men's biographies do not.[43] As mentioned in Section 3, our lexicons of subjective words certainly reflect this difference and this explains why, in the English data, women are systematically described more positively and abstractly than are men. Still another possible explanation is that women who make it into Wikipedia are systematically more notable than men[43] and thus, may be more familiar figures to Wikipedians as compared to men in our corpus.

5.2. *Ethnicity-based differences*

RQ2 asked whether there are significant differences in the use of abstract, subjective language, in the biographies of famous intellectuals from anglophone countries vs. others. Even though Wikipedia is open to participants worldwide and enjoys an international user base, the fact remains that the project is based in North America and that the English-language version draws the most participation. It is also well-known that a good deal of translation from one version to another takes place.[44] Therefore, in light of the LEB, anglophone individuals might be seen as more "expected" at

Wikipedia and therefore, more likely to be described in a more abstract manner. Likewise, the LIB would predict that Wikipedians describe intellectuals from their own ethnic in-group in a more positive, abstract manner. Therefore, we might expect that at the English-language site, that intellectuals hailing from anglophone countries would be described in a more abstract manner as compared to those from other regions.

In the Greek-language biographies, there are only three cases where we observe ethnicity-based differences, and these do not reveal a consistent trend, as shown in Table 18. In the English-language texts, while there are more cases where there are significant differences in the use of abstract, subjective language, again the findings are rather inconsistent. It should be noted that since we studied only biographies of people that appeared at both the Greek and English Wikipedias, the individuals described are internationally revered. Perhaps this explains why we do not observe a salient ethnicity-based linguistic bias (i.e., Wikipedians may not differentiate between "ours" and "theirs" when describing individuals that are internationally famous and thus, familiar to all).

It also may be the case that, because our corpus has a large number of individuals who have immigrated to anglophone countries, our classification technique did not capture ethnic in- and out-groups precisely enough. Another reason for a lack of ethnicity-based linguistic bias is that participation at the largest of the Wikipedias, the English-language community, is international. For instance, our own previous research found that Greek Wikipedians very often contribute to the English-language site in addition to (or even instead of) the Greek-language site.[45]

5.3. *Between-language differences*

Our third research question asked whether linguistic biases are more likely to occur in one language over the other. As illustrated in Tables 18 and 19, there were many more significant differences in the use of markers of abstract language discovered in the English-language biographies as compared to the Greek-language texts. In addition, as mentioned above, there were also more consistent differences in the English-language texts.

It is believed that linguistic biases occur regardless of the language in which the target person(s) are described, as some of the key studies that developed the LEB and LIB were conducted in non-English, European languages.[19] However, we are not aware of previous work that makes cross-lingual comparisons of the extent to which linguistic biases occur.

As mentioned, the cross-lingual study of linguistic biases is challenged by the need for appropriate sentiment or subjectivity lexicons for each domain/language. Ours is the first study to attempt such a cross-lingual comparison and the results suggest intriguing differences in the types of linguistic biases that occur.

There are reasons to expect varying degrees of linguistic bias across language editions of Wikipedia. For example, in their comparison of six Wikipedia language communities, Wagner *et al.* (2015) analyzed gender biases with respect to structural features (i.e., to which other pages a biography links) and the use of gender-related words. They found significant differences between English- and Russian-language biographies, with more gender-based biases in the Russian-language data. They suggested that there may be a correlation between offline measures of gender equality (e.g., the Gender Inequality Index of the World Economic Forum) and inequality at Wikipedia. Similarly, it is likely the case that different content about a given individual is covered at different versions of Wikipedia. For instance, in their bilingual analysis of Polish- and English-language biographies, Callahan and Herring (2011) noted a tendency for the English-language edition to highlight a target person's social life and personal preferences as compared to the Polish edition. Therefore, future work on cross-linguistic comparisons of linguistic bias should take into account these factors.

6. Conclusion

Linguistic biases are known to be extremely common in interpersonal communication, and are believed to be an important means by which social stereotypes are maintained in society.[15] Increasingly, scholars are noting the need to examine the presence of linguistic biases in media, including social media. Collaborative knowledge sources such as Wikipedia are of particular interest in this respect, not only because of their popularity with the public but also because of their open, participatory nature.

Our previous monolingual work motivated the need to develop methods to detect linguistic biases in crowdsourced descriptions of people.[26] Specifically, we relied on the Subjectivity Lexicon[46] to assess the extent to which English-language biographies of Hollywood actors used abstract, subjective language in describing various social groups. In order to extend our work to a more general, cross-lingual case of Greek- and English-language biographies of intellectuals from various backgrounds, we used DidaxTo, a novel unsupervised method, to train sentiment lexicons on biographies for each language (Greek and English) and gender.

As previously explained, DidaxTo offers a significant advantage over lexicon-based approaches, in that we can discover words that are used in a particular domain to convey sentiment. For instance, in the Subjectivity Lexicon, words are labeled as being either strongly subjective (i.e., always sentiment-bearing, regardless of context of use) and weakly subjective (i.e., could be sentiment-bearing, depending on the specific context of use). Indeed, as discussed in Section 3, even the extracted lexicons reveal differences in terms of how Wikipedians describe women versus men, and which aspects of famous women and men are seen as positive and negative.

Our chapter describes the application of the DidaxTo method to the study of the phenomenon of linguistic biases in Wikipedia biographies of famous persons. DidaxTo is an unsupervised sentiment analysis tool for discovering opinion words from text. Currently it can be applied to any domain and across two languages: Greek and English. DidaxTo can be extended to cover other similar-in-structure languages. In the current work, we demonstrate its utility by learning sentiment lexicons from Wikipedia entries across two languages — English and Greek.

In future work, we plan to continue to explore cross-lingual differences in linguistic biases exhibited in crowdsourced descriptions of people, using DidaxTo, as well as comparing to other approaches. One direction will be the study of other types of documents like historical events (e.g. wars, inventions, empires, important constructions or art) or research papers. In addition, we plan to conduct longitudinal studies of how linguistic biases evolve over time as a function of the pool of participants collaborating on a given article, taking into consideration their demographic and behavioral characteristics exhibited through their digital traces at Wikipedia. In conclusion, this work will help to ensure that Wikipedia serves as an objective knowledge source for the public. In addition, it will also allow us to learn more about the linguistic behaviors that correlate to the maintenance of social stereotypes, by enabling new methodological approaches beyond laboratory experiments.

Acknowledgements

This work is partially funded by the European Union's Horizon 2020 Research and Innovation Programme under grant agreement No. 739578.

References

1. S. Downes, New technology supporting informal learning, *Journal of Emerging Technologies in Web Intelligence*, **2**(1), 27–33 (2010).
2. A. Forte and A. Bruckman, From Wikipedia to the classroom: Exploring online publication and learning. In eds. S. Barab, K. Hay and D. Hickey, *Proceedings of the 7th International Conference on Learning Sciences*, pp. 182–188 (2006).
3. M. Strube and S. P. Ponzetto, Wikirelate! computing semantic relatedness using wikipedia. In eds. Y. Gil and R. J. Mooney, *Proceedings of the 21st AAAI Conference on Artificial Intelligence*, pp. 1419–1424 (2006).
4. G. Giannakopoulos, M. El-Haj, B. Favre, M. Litvak, J. Steinberger, and V. Varma, TAC 2011 multiling pilot overview. In *Text Analysis Conference (TAC) 2011* (2011).
5. H.-F. Yu, P. Jain, P. Kar, and I. Dhillon, Large-scale multi-label learning with missing labels. In eds. E. P. Xing and T. Jebara, *International Conference on Machine Learning*, pp. 593–601 (2014).
6. M. Kimura, K. Saito, and R. Nakano, Extracting influential nodes for information diffusion on a social network. In eds. R.C. Holt and A. Howe, *Proceedings of the 22nd AAAI Conference on Artificial Intelligence*, pp. 1371–1376 (2007).
7. A. Capocci, V. D. Servedio, F. Colaiori, L. S. Buriol, D. Donato, S. Leonardi, and G. Caldarelli, Preferential attachment in the growth of social networks: The internet encyclopedia wikipedia, *Physical Review E*, **74**(3), 036116 (2006).
8. M. Hu, E.-P. Lim, A. Sun, H. W. Lauw, and B.-Q. Vuong, Measuring article quality in Wikipedia: Models and evaluation. In eds. M. J. Silva, A. H. F. Laender, R. A. Baeza-Yates, D. L. McGuinness, D. Olstad, O. H. Olsen and A. O. Falcão, *Proceedings of the Sixteenth ACM Conference on Information and Knowledge Management*, pp. 243–252 (2007).
9. T. Wöhner and R. Peters, Assessing the quality of Wikipedia articles with lifecycle based metrics. In eds. D. Riehle and A. Bruckman, *Proceedings of the 5th International Symposium on Wikis and Open Collaboration*, p. 16 (2009).
10. D. Hasan Dalip, M. André Gonçalves, M. Cristo, and P. Calado, Automatic quality assessment of content created collaboratively by web communities: A case study of wikipedia. In eds. F. Heath, M. L. Rice-Lively and R. Furuta, *Proceedings of the 9th ACM/IEEE-CS Joint Conference on Digital Libraries*, pp. 295–304 (2009).
11. J. E. Blumenstock, Size matters: word count as a measure of quality on Wikipedia. In J. Huai, R. Chen, H-W. Hon, Y. Liu, W-Y. Ma, A. Tomkins and X. Zhang, *Proceedings of the 17th International Conference on World Wide Web*, pp. 1095–1096 (2008).
12. A. Kittur and R. E. Kraut, Harnessing the wisdom of crowds in Wikipedia: Quality through coordination. In *Proceedings of the 2008 ACM Conference on Computer Supported Cooperative Work*, CSCW '08, pp. 37–46, ACM

(2008). doi: 10.1145/1460563.1460572. Available at: http://doi.acm.org/10.1145/1460563.1460572.

13. C. Pentzold, Fixing the Floating Gap: The online encyclopedia wikipedia as a global memory place, *Memory Studies*, **2**(2), 255–272 (2009).

14. L. Flekova, O. Ferschke, and I. Gurevych, What makes a good biography?: Multidimensional quality analysis based on wikipedia article feedback data. In eds. C-W. Chung, A. Z. Broder, K. Shim and T. Suel, *Proceedings of the 23rd International Conference on World Wide Web*, WWW '14, pp. 855–866, ACM (2014). doi: 10.1145/2566486.2567972.

15. A. Maass, Linguistic intergroup bias: Stereotype perpetuation through language. In ed. M. Zanna, *Advanced in Experimental Social Psychology*, pp. 79–121. Academic Press, San Diego, CA (1999).

16. W. von Hippel, D. Sekaquaptewa, and P. Vargas, The linguistic intergroup bias as an implicit indicator of prejudice, *Journal of Experimental Social Psychology*, **33**, 490–509 (1997).

17. C. Beukeboom, Mechanisms of linguistic bias: How words reflect and maintain stereotypic expectations. In eds. J. Laszlo, J. Forgas, and O. Vincze, *Social Cognition and Communication*, pp. 313–330. Psychology Press, New York, NY (2013).

18. J. Otterbacher, Linguistic bias in collaboratively produced biographies: crowdsourcing social stereotypes? In *Proceedings of the AAAI International Conference on Web and Social Media (ICWSM)*, pp. 298–307 (2015).

19. A. Maass, D. Salvi, L. Arcuri, and G. Semin, Language use in intergroup context: The linguistic intergroup bias, *Journal of Personality and Social Psychology*, **57**(6), 981–993 (1989).

20. P. Agathangelou, I. Katakis, I. Koutoulakis, F. Kokkoras, and D. Gunopulos, Learning patterns for discovering domain-oriented opinion words, *Knowledge and Information Systems*, pp. 1–33 (2017).

21. G. Semin and K. Fiedler, The cognitive functions of linguistic categories in describing persons: Social cognition and language, *Journal of Personality and Social Psychology*, **54**, 558–568 (1988).

22. L. Coenen, L. Hedebouw, and G. Semin, Measuring language abstraction: The linguistic category model manual. Technical report, Free University Amsterdam, Amsterdam, The Netherlands (June, 2006). Available at: http://www.cratylus.org/resources/uploadedFiles/1151434261594-8567.pdf.

23. P. Winkielman, J. Halberstadt, T. Fazendeiro, and S. Catty, Prototypes are attractive because they are easy on the mind, *Psychological Science*, **17**(9), 799–806 (2006).

24. D. Wigboldus, R. Spears, and G. Semin, When do we communicate stereotypes? Influence of the social context on the linguistic expectancy bias, *Group Processes & Intergroup Relations*, **8**(3), 215–230 (2005).

25. A. Hunt, *The linguistic expectancy bias and the american mass media*. PhD thesis, Temple University, Philadelphia, PA (2011).

26. J. Otterbacher, Crowdsourcing stereotypes: Linguistic bias in metadata generated via gwap. In eds. B. Begole, J. Kim, K. Inkpen and W. Woo, *Proceedings of the 33rd Annual ACM Conference on Human Factors in Computing Systems*, pp. 1955–1964, ACM (2015).

27. P. Devine and A. Elliot, Are racial stereotypes really fading? The princeton trilogy revisited, *Personality and Social Psychology Bulletin*, **21**(11), 1139–1150 (1995).

28. P. Agathangelou, I. Katakis, I. Koutoulakis, F. Kokkoras, and D. Gunopulos, Learning patterns for discovering domain oriented opinion words, *Knowledge and Information Systems* (2017).

29. P. Agathangelou, I. Katakis, F. Kokkoras, and K. Ntonas, *Mining domain-specific dictionaries of opinion words*, In eds. B. Benatallah, A. Bestavros, Y. Manolopoulos, A. Vakali, and Y. Zhang, *Proceedings of the 15th International Conference on Web Information Systems Engineering — WISE 2014*, Thessaloniki, Greece, Part I, pp. 47–62. Springer International Publishing (2014).

30. M. Hu and B. Liu, Mining and summarizing customer reviews. In eds. W. Kim, R. Kohavi, J. Gehrke and W. DuMouchel, *Proceedings of the Tenth ACM SIGKDD International Conference on Knowledge Discovery and Data Mining*, KDD '04, Seattle, WA, USA, pp. 168–177, ACM (2004). doi: 10.1145/1014052.1014073.

31. J. D. Gibbons and S. Chakraborti, Nonparametric statistical inference. In *International Encyclopedia of Statistical Science*, pp. 977–979. Springer (2011).

32. P. Willett, The porter stemming algorithm: then and now, *Program*, **40**(3), 219–223 (2006).

33. S. T. Fiske, A. J. Cuddy, and P. Glick, Universal dimensions of social cognition: Warmth and competence, *Trends in Cognitive Sciences*, **11**(2), 77–83 (2007).

34. S. T. Fiske, A. J. Cuddy, P. Glick, and J. Xu, A model of (often mixed) stereotype content: competence and warmth respectively follow from perceived status and competition, *Journal of Personality and Social Psychology*, **82**(6), 878 (2002).

35. C. Wagner, D. Garcia, M. Jadidi, and M. Strohmaier, It's a man's Wikipedia? Assessing gender inequality in an online encyclopedia. In eds. M. Cha, C. Mascolo and C. Sandvig, *Proceedings of the AAAI International Conference on Web and Social Media (ICWSM)*, Oxford, United Kingdom, pp. 454–463 (2015).

36. E. Graells-Garrido, M. Lalmas, and F. Menczer. First women, second sex: gender bias in wikipedia. In eds. Y. Yesilada, R. Farzan and G-J Houben, *Proceedings of the 26th ACM Conference on Hypertext & Social Media*, Guzelyurt, TRNC, Cyprus, pp. 165–174 (2015).

37. J. Cohen, P. Cohen, S. G. West, and L. S. Aiken, *Applied Multiple Regression/Correlation Analysis for the Behavioral Sciences*. Routledge (2013).

38. H. Abdi and L. J. Williams, Tukey's honestly significant difference (HSD) test, *Encyclopedia of Research Design*, Sage, Thousand Oaks, CA, pp. 1–5 (2010).

39. J. M. Hilbe, Logistic regression. In ed. M. Lovric, *International Encyclopedia of Statistical Science*, pp. 755–758. Springer (2011).

40. D. Radev, J. Otterbacher, A. Winkel, and S. Blair-Goldensohn, Newsinessence: summarizing online news topics, *Communications of the ACM*, **48**(10), 95–98 (2005).

41. J. Antin, R. Yee, C. Cheshire, and O. Nov, Gender differences in Wikipedia editing. In eds. F. Ortega and A. Forte, *Proceedings of the 7th International Symposium on Wikis and Open Collaboration*, pp. 11–14, ACM (2011).

42. B. Collier and J. Bear, Conflict, criticism, or confidence: An empirical examination of the gender gap in wikipedia contributions. In eds. F. Ortega and A. Forte, *Proceedings of the ACM 2012 Conference on Computer Supported Cooperative Work*, Mountain View, CA, USA, pp. 383–392, ACM (2012).

43. C. Wagner, E. Graells-Garrido, D. Garcia, and F. Menczer, Women through the glass ceiling: gender asymmetries in wikipedia, *EPJ Data Science*, **5**(1), 5 (2016).

44. E. S. Callahan and S. C. Herring, Cultural bias in wikipedia content on famous persons, *Journal of the Association for Information Science and Technology*, **62**(10), 1899–1915 (2011).

45. I. Protonotarios, V. Sarimpei, and J. Otterbacher, Similar gaps, different origins? Women readers and editors at greek Wikipedia. In *Wiki@ ICWSM, The Workshops of the 10th International AAAI Conference on Web and Social Media Wiki: Technical Report WS-16-17*, pp. 80–87, AAAI (2016).

46. T. Wilson, J. Wiebe, and P. Hoffman, Recognizing contextual polarity in phrase-level sentiment analysis. In eds. R. Mooney, C. Brew, L-F. Chien and K. Kirchhoff, *Proceedings of the Association for Computational Linguistics (ACL) Human Language Technology Conference and Conference on Empirical Methods in Natural Language Processing (HLT/EMNLP)*, Vancouver, Canada, pp. 347–354, ACL (2005).

Chapter 13

Multilingual Financial Narrative Processing: Analyzing Annual Reports in English, Spanish, and Portuguese

Mahmoud El-Haj*, Paul Rayson*, Paulo Alves†,
Carlos Herrero-Zorita‡, and Steven Young§

*School of Computing and Communications,
Lancaster University, UK
† Universidade Católica Portuguesa, Portugal
‡Department of Linguistics,
Universidad Autónoma de Madrid, Spain
§ Management School, Lancaster University, UK

This chapter describes and evaluates the use of information extraction (IE) and natural language processing (NLP) methods for extraction and analysis of financial annual reports in three languages: English, Spanish, and Portuguese. The work described retains information on document structure which is needed to enable a clear distinction between narrative and financial statement components of annual reports and between individual sections within the narratives component. Extraction accuracy varies between languages with English exceeding 95%. We apply the extraction methods on a comprehensive sample of annual reports published by UK, Spanish, and Portuguese non-financial firms between 2003 and 2014.

1. Introduction

Companies use a number of different methods to communicate with their shareholders and investors and to report to the financial markets. These include annual financial reports, quarterly reports, preliminary earnings announcements, conference calls, and press releases. Much previous research has focused on the quantitative numerical elements of these reports. In addition, researchers in accounting and finance have been able to carry out small scale manual analysis of the narrative textual elements of these reports for many years, but recently a trend has emerged of applying automatic NLP techniques to enable replication of these earlier studies on a much larger scale, as well as to improve the accuracy and depth of the metrics that are studied. Much of the previous text mining work has been performed in the US context where annual 10-K filings are required to follow a rigid structure with a standard set of headings, and are written in plain text. This enables more straightforward selection of relevant sections for further analysis. In contrast, in the UK and elsewhere, annual report structure is much less rigid and companies produce glossy brochures with a much looser structure, and this has prevented large-scale long-term narrative research until recently. In this paper, we describe not only the structure detection and extraction process that we have designed and implemented for English annual reports, but also our initial work to extend this research to other national contexts, in this case to Spain and Portugal. We report on our experiments to port the system from UK annual report analyzes to those published in Spanish and Portuguese, and describe the adaptations made to the system to enable this. Our resulting software is made freely available for academic research.

2. Related work

Previous related work on financial narrative analysis has taken place in a number of areas including accounting and finance research, NLP, and corpus linguistics. Some early approaches in the accounting and finance literature employed painstaking manual approaches and were therefore limited in scale due to time constraints. Further studies have become larger scale but are still using manually constructed word lists for detecting features without considering local context for disambiguation purposes or more advanced machine learning methods. Well-known studies include one by Feng Li in 2010[1] which considered forward-looking statements in 10-K (annual) and 10-Q (quarterly) filings in the US and found a link between positive statements and better current performance and other indicators. Li also found that general content analysis dictionaries such as Diction, General Inquirer, and LIWC are not helpful in predicting future performance. Loughran and McDonald (2011)[2] also found that negative words in the general purpose

Harvard Dictionary were not typically considered as negative in financial contexts, and so were less appropriate than domain specific versions. They also considered US 10-K reports for their study. Schleicher and Walker (2010)[3] found that companies with impending performance downturns bias the tone in outlook sections of the financial narrative. A good survey of text analysis methods in accounting and finance research was recently published by Loughran and McDonald (2016).[4]

In the NLP research area, previous research has been carried out to extract document structure mainly from scientific articles and books.[5-7] Other than this, there has been much recent work in using text mining and sentiment analysis, in particular to Twitter, with the goal of predicting stock market performance[8-12] although presumably any really successful methods would not be published.

From the other end of the language analysis spectrum, in linguistics, there has been a large amount of research on the language of business communication. Merkl-Davies and Koller (2012)[13] introduced the critical discourse analysis (CDA) approach to the accounting community and showed how it can be used to systematically analyze corporate narrative documents to explore how grammatical devices can be used to obfuscate and guide interpretations. Brennan and Merkl-Davies (2013)[14] considered communication choices and devices which contribute to the phenomena of impression management, where individuals or companies use language to present themselves favourably to others.

In terms of the context for financial narrative analysis in other countries, as some authors explain,[15-19] apart from the economic data, information explaining the intellectual capital, organisation, human activities, and resources is key for a company's visibility on the market and transparency of information with shareholders. This has driven Spanish entities in recent years to voluntarily include them in annual reports and especially sustainability reports.[19] Oliveras *et al.* (2008)[20] show that among the 12 most important Spanish companies this type of information has increased significantly between 2000 and 2002, particularly intellectual, human, and structural capital; a claim also supported by Villacorta (2006).[21] Tejero Romero (2014)[18] analyzes annual reports between 2004 and 2008 located in companies' websites and also claims there has been an increase, more especifically concerning management control and network systems followed by research. This has been more significant in entities related to technology, communications, and construction.

3. Dataset

We collected annual reports from UK, Spanish, and Portuguese large firms. For UK annual reports, we gathered more than 10,000 annual reports for non-financial firms listed on the London Stock Exchange for the years in the range 2003 and 2014. The extraction methods have been tested and evaluated on English annual reports and were later adapted to work with other languages. For Spanish, we gathered 100 annual reports from the biggest companies of the country from the year 2015. The selection criteria was made using the Orbis international Database, focusing only on the very large businesses and excluding those with no recent financial data as well as banks and public authorities/governments. The query returned a list of 9,126 companies. The next step was to manually retrieve the annual reports of the top 100 companies from their public web pages. Our Portuguese annual report sample consists of 576 reports, issued by 77 firms, for the period 2006–2015. All firms are listed on the Portuguese Stock Exchange. The annual reports were collected automatically from Perfect Information.[a]

3.1. *Description of dataset*

Before describing the dataset it is worth explaining what is an annual report. An annual report is a comprehensive report on a company's activities throughout the preceding year. Annual reports are intended to give shareholders and other interested people information about the company's activities and financial performance. They may be considered as grey literature.

It was not until legislation was enacted after the stock market crash in 1929 that the annual report became a regular component of corporate financial reporting. Typically, an annual report will contain the following sections:

- Financial Highlights
- Letter to the Shareholders
- Narrative Text, Graphics, and Photos
- Management's Discussion and Analysis
- Financial Statements
- Notes to Financial Statements
- Auditor's Report

---

[a]www.perfectinfo.com.

Table 1.   Dataset size.

Language	Reports	Words
English (UK)	11,009	300M
Portuguese	396	7.50M
Spanish	100	2.40M

- Summary Financial Data
- Corporate Information

The annual reports dataset files are all in PDF format, and variation in formatting makes it a challenge for automatically extracting and detecting structure. The annual reports vary in respect to their style and number of pages. In contrast to the US, stock exchange-listed firms in UK, Spain, and Portugal do not present their financial information and accompanying narratives in a standardized format when creating annual reports. Firms in the aforementioned countries have much more discretion regarding the structure and content of the annual report. Added to this is the problem of nomenclature: no standardized naming convention exists for different sections in UK annual reports so that even firms adopting the same underlying structure and content may use different terminology to describe the same section(s).

Table 1 shows the dataset size in words in addition to the number of reports for each language.

4. Extraction methods

We used IE and NLP methods to detect the structure of the annual reports and extract sections and their narratives. The methods automatically detect the annual report's table of contents, synchronize page numbers in the native report with page numbers in the corresponding PDF file, and then use the synchronized page numbers to retrieve the textual content (narratives) for each header (hereinafter section) listed in the table of contents. Section headings presented in the table of contents are used to partition retrieved content into the audited financial statements component of the report and the "front-end" narratives component, with the latter subclassified further into a set of generic report elements including the letter to shareholders, management commentary, the governance statement, the remuneration report, and residual content.

4.1. *Structure extraction process*

In this section, we discuss in detail the process of detecting the structure for UK, Spanish, and Portuguese annual reports. As mentioned in Section 3 we processed more than 10,000 UK annual reports in PDF file format and used the same methods at a later stage to analyze a smaller sample of Spanish and Portuguese annual reports.

Unlike the US Stock Exchange, firms in the UK do not follow a standard reporting template when writing annual reports. Firms and management in the UK have more discretion regarding the format, structure, and contents of the annual reports. On the other hand the US Securities and Exchange Commission forces firms to follow a standard format and a pre-labeled annual reports template which they publish in HTML file format. This has helped in creating a reporting standard making it easy for investors, firms, and analysts to access and acquire information automatically from a bulk of annual reports. This is different in the UK where firms tend to publish their annual reports in PDF file format. Despite being cross-platform and a portable file format it is deemed a difficult task to automatically extract information from PDF annual reports since companies' reports vary significantly especially when it comes to the contents and the section headers. In order to automatically analyze a large dataset of UK annual reports we first needed to automatically detect the structure of the PDF annual reports so we can extract the information needed.

To detect and extract the structure of the annual reports each PDF file goes through the following five steps: (1) detecting the contents page, (2) parsing the detected contents page and extracting the sections, (3) detecting page numbering, (4) adding the extracted sections to the annual report PDFs as bookmarks, and (5) using the added bookmarks to extract the narrative sections under each heading.

4.1.1. *Detecting the contents page*

An annual report contents page includes information about the main sections of the report and its associated page numbers. Information in the contents page helped us detect the structure of the annual reports. However, detecting the contents page was not a straightforward task. We created a list of gold-standard section names extracted manually from the contents page of a random sample of 50 annual reports. We filtered the gold-standard keywords by removing duplicates and preserving the structure of how they appeared in the annual reports. We matched each page in the annual report against the list of section names in gold-standard, then we selected the page with the highest matching score as the *potential* contents page. The score was calculated by an increment of 1 for each match. To improve the matching process and avoid false positives, we match the gold-standard keywords against lines of text that follow a contents-page-like style (e.g. a section name followed by a page number, such as "Chairman's Statement 13").

4.1.2. *Parsing the contents page*

In order to get the structure of the annual report we automatically parse the selected contents page by extracting the name of each section and its associated page number. To do this we matched each line of text in the selected contents page against a regular expression commands that will extract any line starting or ending with a number between 1 and the number of pages of the annual report.

We built a simple filtering tool that filters out any block of text that matches our regular expression commands. This is done by removing text containing addresses, dates, and postal codes. The filtering tool can also detect email addresses, websites, references to branches, and locations using regular expression commands and a gazetteer.

We differentiate between dates and actual page numbers to avoid extracting incorrect section headers. However, lines containing text such as an address (e.g., 77 Bothwell Road) might still be confusing for the tool. We tackled this problem by matching the list of extracted sections against a list of gold-standard section synonyms which we explain in more details in Section 4.1.5.

The structure of the PDF files makes it difficult to extract text in its actual format. Extracting plain text from PDFs results in many line breaks being added in between the text. This makes extracting a section name that is split into two lines a difficult task. To tackle the problem of broken sections (i.e., appearing on two lines or more), we implemented an algorithm to detect broken section headers and fix them by concatenating lines that end or begin with prepositions such as "of", "in" ... etc. The algorithm also concatenates sentences ending with singular or plural possessives, symbolic, and textual connectors (e.g. "and", "or", "&"... etc.), and sentences ending with hyphenations. This method was also adapted to Spanish and Portuguese prepositions and other stop-words needed to concatenate lines of text by forming a list of most common stop-words for each language.

4.1.3. *Detecting page numbering*

The page numbers appearing on the contents page do not usually match with the actual page numbers in the PDF files. For example, page 4 in the annual report could refer to page 6 in the PDF file, which may lead to incorrect extraction.[b] We address this problem by creating a page detection tool that crawls through annual report pages taking three consecutive pages in each iteration. The tool aims to extract a pattern of sequential numbers with an increment of 1 (e.g. 31, 32, 33) but with the complex structure of the PDF files this has been proven to be a difficult task. The tool starts by reading the contents three pages at a time starting from the report's number of pages minus one. For example, assume we are trying to detect the page numbering pattern for a report of 51 pages. The tool starts by extracting text from pages 48, 49, and 50. A regular expression command is then used to extract all the numbers in each page contents that is made up of maximum three digits creating a vector of numbers for each page. Figure 1 shows a sample of three vectors for the pages 48, 49, and 50. As shown in Fig. 1 the algorithm will only keep numbers that are within a range of 10 pages those linked with small double arrows. The algorithm will then try to form a pattern of sequential numbers with an increment of 1. Figure 1 shows that the pattern 49, 50, and 51 (dark circles) has been found which is equivalent to a one page difference (*page-increment*) between the reports page numbering and those found in the PDF file. The tool will repeat the same process for all the pages in the annual report until it reaches pages 1, 2, and 3 where it stops.

As shown in Fig. 2 for each of the three vectors the tool will store the page-increment in an array of numbers and at the end of the process the most popular (most frequent) page-increment will be selected as the difference between the annual report and the PDF numbering.

This process on the sample yielded an accuracy rate of more than 95%. Manual examination of the remaining less than 5% revealed the following reasons for non-detection: (1) encoding, (2) formatting, and (3) design.

4.1.4. *Adding section headers as bookmarks*

Using the sections and their correct page numbers from Sections 4.1.1 and 4.1.3 we implemented a tool to insert the extracted contents page

---

[b]The algorithm responsible for extraction of sections uses start and end page numbers to locate the text and therefore accurate page numbers are required.

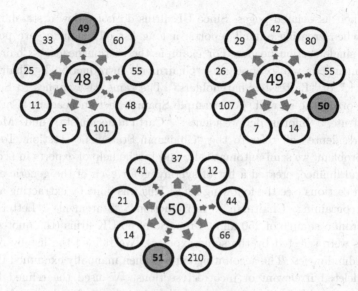

Fig. 1.   Detecting page numbering.

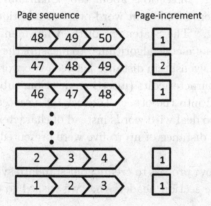

Fig. 2.   Popular page increment.

sections as bookmarks (hyperlinks) to sample PDFs. This process helped in extracting narratives associated with each section for further processing (see Section 4.1.5 below).

4.1.5. *Extracting sections' narratives*

We implemented an automatic extraction algorithm to crawl through the data collection and, for each PDF file, extract all inserted bookmarks

and their associated pages. Since UK firms do not follow a standard format when creating annual reports, a long list of synonyms are possible
for a single section header. For example the section header "Chairman's
Statement" may also appear as "Chairman's Introduction," "Chairman's
Report," or "Letter to Shareholders." The same case applies to Spanish
and Portuguese as well. For example Spanish section headers "Carta del
presidente," "Informe del presidente," "Carta al accionista," and "Mensaje
del presidente" all refer to the "Chairman Statement" section. To solve
this problem, we semi-automatically and by the help of experts in accounting and finance, created a list of synonyms for each of the generic annual
report sections (see the following list). This was done by extracting all sections containing "Chairman," "Introduction," "Statement," "Letter to"...
etc. from a sample of 250 annual reports of 50 UK firms (the quoted unigrams were selected by the same experts). We refined the list by removing redundancies. The accounting experts then manually examined the list
and deleted irrelevant or incorrect sections. We used the refined list as
gold-standard synonyms to extract all the sections related to each of our
generic sections (e.g. all sections about the "Chairman's Statement"). To
overcome the problem of different word-order or additional words included
in the headline (e.g. "The Statement of the Chairman"), we used *Levenshtein Distance* string metric algorithm[22] to measure the difference between
two sections. The Levenshtein distance between two words is the minimum
number of single-character edits (insertion, deletion, substitution) required
to change one word into the other. To work on a sentence level we modified the algorithm to deal with words instead of characters. All the sections
with a Levenshtein distance of up to five were presented to the accounting
expert.

We used the above process to create gold-standard synonym lists for the
following 11 generic section headers that we wished to extract for further
analysis:

(1) Chairman Statement
(2) CEO Review
(3) Corporate Government Report
(4) Directors Remuneration Report
(5) Business Review
(6) Financial Review
(7) Operating Review
(8) Highlights

Having detected and extracted section headers (or their gold-standard synonyms) and their sections, we then extract the sections' narratives using iText,[c] an open source library to manipulate and create PDF documents,[23] to apply our text analysis metrics, which include readability measurement and counting word frequencies using financial domain hand-crafted word lists.

5. Extraction tools

We used the extraction methods described in Section 4 to create publicly available web and desktop tools for users to automatically and freely analyze annual reports in different languages. The tools deal with multilingual annual reports of firms within the UK, Spain, or Portugal written in either English, Spanish, or Portuguese and distributed in PDF file format.[d]

The tool is called CFIE-FRSE standing for Corporate Financial Information Environment (CFIE) -Final Report Structure Extractor (FRSE). The tool is available as a web application[e] or as desktop application, which is freely available on GitHub.[f] The tools detect the structure of annual reports by detecting the key sections, their start and end pages in addition to the narrative contents. This works for all three languages. The tools provide further analysis for reports written in English such as readability metrics, section classification, and tone scores. This is because the tool was built to analyze UK annual reports where we have a large dataset to train the system to provide an extra level of analysis.

The extra level of analysis will be made available for Spanish and Portuguese at a later stage. For now we do not have enough reports for both languages to be able to train the system. As explained earlier the aim of this chapter is to show that our extraction methods can be applied to Spanish and Portuguese, a vital step towards fully analyzing reports in these two languages and other languages later in the future.

6. Multilingual extraction

In this section we explain the process we followed to extracting sections from annual reports in each of the three languages: English, Spanish, and Portuguese.

---

[c]http://itextpdf.com/api.
[d]For now only the Desktop version of the tool can work with multilingual annual reports.
[e]https://cfie.lancaster.ac.uk:8443.
[f]https://github.com/drelhaj/CFIE-FRSE.

6.1. *English*

As mentioned earlier the work was first designed to analyze UK English annual reports.[24] We automatically harvested more than 10,000 annual reports for firms listed on the London Stock Exchange (LSE). Prior to analyzing the annual reports we first worked on sorting them by firm and we created our own unique report identifier which we called "LANCS_ID." Sorting annual reports was done semi-automatically where we used a Java tool to match firm names and extract the reports' years. This was followed by manual post editing to make sure the matching was correct. Firms without a match could be firms that do not exist anymore or firms with a new name due to merging with another firm, those had to be manually matched. PDF filenames do not contain a unique firm identifier. For example, reports collected from Perfect Information use a standard naming convention comprising firm name and publication year. We use filenames as the basis for a fuzzy matching algorithm that pairs firm names extracted from the PDF filename with firm names provided by Thomson Datastream. Matching on name is problematic because firms can change their name over the sample period. The matching procedure must therefore track name changes. To address this problem, we combine firm registration numbers and archived names from the London Share Price Database with Datastream's firm name archive in our fuzzy matching algorithm. For those cases where our algorithm fails to find a sufficiently reliable match, we perform a second round of matching by hand.[g] Licensing restrictions prevent direct publication of proprietary identifiers.

Annual report structures vary significantly across reporting regimes and therefore to make the initial development task feasible we focus on reports for a single reporting regime. We select the UK due to the LSE's position as largest equity market by capitalization outside the US. The extraction process is nevertheless generic insofar as reports published in other reporting regimes and languages can be analyzed by modifying the language- and regime-dependent aspects of our tool without editing the underlying java source code. Further guidance will be provided in an online appendix, together with full technical details of our method, in due course.

---

[g]Further details of the matching procedure, including a copy of the algorithm and a step-by-step guide to implementing the matching procedure in Statistical Analysis System (SAS) are available at cfie.lancaster.ac.uk:8443.

Table 2.   UK annual reports analysis.

Number of downloaded annual reports	11,009
Number of reports analyzed	10,820
Percentage of correctly retrieved table of contents	98.28%
Percentage of correctly retrieved pages	95.00%
Percentage of correctly retrieved text from sections	95.00%

Table 2 shows the structure detection and extraction accuracy for UK annual reports.

As shown in the table the tool analyzed more than 98% of the downloaded annual reports. Firms management in the UK have more discretion over what, where, and how much information on topics such as risk, strategy, performance, etc. is reported, which leads to reports varying significantly in terms of structure and design. Despite the dissimilarity between the structure of the downloaded annual report, our methods were able to accurately analyze the majority of the reports. Those failing the analysis process were due to one of the following reasons:

(1) The file does not allow the text to be extracted (image-based documents). This problem is more common in the early years of our sample (i.e. 2000–2005), as some of the annual reports were poor quality scanned files. Reports from the more recent years tend not to be of this type.
(2) Reports with a table of contents that could not be read due to the limitation imposed by how the table was designed. For example where a table of contents is designed with numbers and text in two different columns, or where the table of contents is split into two pages which causes problems for the PDF library.
(3) Absence of page numbers.

6.2. *Spanish*

The analysis of the Spanish reports will deal mainly with four challenges: (1) the difficulty of retrieving the documents from the companies; (2) the lack of a standard and common structure; (3) the high amount of variation in the headers of the tables of contents, due to the previous point as well as linguistic reasons; and (4), the amount of noise in the PDFs.

We manually collected 100 annual reports from the biggest firms in Spain for the year 2015. The selection criteria was made using the Orbis

International Database,[h] focusing only on the very large businesses and excluding those with no recent financial data as well as banks and public authorities/governments. The query returned a list of 9126 firms. The next step was to manually retrieve the annual reports of the top 100 firms from their public web pages.

This initial step proved problematic since not every company made available the annual reports on their websites. Spanish legislation obliges firms to display their financial statements[i] and corporate governance reports, but not the annual reports.[j] Therefore, the decision to provide a report relies entirely on the company, which will either present it freely at their website along with the financial statements, display it in a restricted section only available to shareholders, or not show it at all. This issue becomes more frequent among subsidiaries or branch companies that belong to a bigger group, which, if international, may only present its annual report in English. Overall, reports were found in nearly 1 of each 7 companies from the Orbis Database. In order to obtain 100 documents, 638 web pages were accessed.

Following this, we manually extracted all the sections from the tables of contents of the reports, creating a keyword list of 1503 tokens. This will be fed to the CFIE-FRSE program later on in order to extract and process the text.

The second challenge brought by Spanish reports that will undoubtedly influence their automatic processing has to do with their lack of standardized structure. In other words, Spanish legislation does not provide guidelines for the development of these documents, leaving each company to design them as they see fit. The structure of today's reports are the result of an evolution over the years, adapted to the shareholders' demands and information the companies have considered relevant to the public, some of them based on overseas countries.[k]

There are, nevertheless, some common points regarding their composition. The typical sections include a letter from the CEO, lineup of the owners of the company, a business review of the last year, and an analysis of

---

[h]https://www.bvdinfo.com/en-gb/our-products/company-information/international-products/orbis.

[i]According to Title 7 of Corporation Law.

[j]Arts. 538 and 540 of Corporation Law, available at: https://www.companyformationspain.com/company-act-spain.

[k]https://www.icsa.org.uk/knowledge/resources/contents-list-annual-report-uk-company.

Table 3. Most frequent sections in Spanish annual reports.

Section (Spanish)	Section (English translation)	Frequency
Carta del Presidente	Letter from the Chairman	58
Gobierno Corporativo	Corporate Governance	26
Anexos	Appendix	19
Consejo de Administración	Board of Directors	14
Sociedad	Society	12
Principales Magnitudes	Main Events	12
Modelo de Negocio	Business Model	12
Estrategia	Strategy	12
Responsabilidad Social Corporativa	Corporate Responsibility	11
Recursos Humanos	Human Resources	11
Medio Ambiente	Environment	11
Informe de Gestión	Financial Statement	11
Órganos de Gobierno	Board of Directors	10
Informe de Auditoría	Auditor's Report	10
Clientes	Clients	10
Acerca de este Informe	About this Report	10

the future including global reporting initiative (GRI) parameters. Table 3 shows the 50 most frequent items from our table of contents keyword list.

The most frequent items seem to show these aspects. *Carta del Presidente*, the "Letter from the Chairman", appears in 58 documents. In second place, in 29 documents, is the "Board of Directors" (*Gobierno Corporativo*) followed by the annexes (which seldom contain the GRI indicators) and the main events (*"Principales Magnitudes"*).

The frequencies, however, lead us to the third problem of Spanish reports: a great variation in the sections. For example, the letter from the chairman, "Carta del Presidente," appears in 58 documents. This does not mean that 42 reports lack this section, but that the sections are written differently. For example, in the complete frequency list (Table 4), the letter from the chairman/CEO appears as a number of different variants. Instead of "letter" we may find "message," "report," or "greetings," or sometimes including the name of the company CEO. We can also find the variation of "chairman" in its female inflection, *presidenta*. The same happens in the rest of the sections which may oblige us in the future to lemmatize and unify the sections in order to make the tool quicker and more efficient.

The following step was to prepare the tool to perform the analysis or, in other words, to adapt the English algorithms to work for Spanish. The most important feature was to include alphabetic characters missing in English. Spanish uses the standard Latin writing system but with a series

Table 4.   Synonyms of Chairman and CEO letters.

Section (Spanish)	Section (English translation)	Frequency
Carta del presidente	Letter from the Chairman	58
Carta del consejero delegado	Letter from the CEO	9
Mensaje del presidente	Message from the Chairman	3
Mensaje del consejero delegado	Message from the CEO	3
Informe del presidente	Report from the Chairman	3
Carta del presidente a los accionistas	Letter from the Chairman to the shareholders	3
Carta de la presidenta	Letter from the Chairman (female)	3
Carta al accionista	Letter to the shareholder	3
Cartas	Letters	2
Carta de Xabier Etxeberria, director general ejecutivo	Letter from Xabier Etxeberria, CEO	2
Carta del presidente y consejero delegado	Letter from the Chairman and CEO	2
Carta del CEO	Letter from the CEO	2
Carta de Ignacio Martín, presidente ejecutivo	Letter from Ignacio Martín, CEO	2

Table 5.   Spanish annual reports analysis.

Number of downloaded annual reports	100
Number of reports analyzed	73
Percentage of reports completely analyzed	46.60%
Percentage of correctly retrieved table of contents	91.70%
Percentage of correctly retrieved pages	53.40%
Percentage of correctly retrieved text from sections	58.90%

of additional characters such as the stressed vowels with the diacritic acute and umlaut over the letter *u*, the *ñ* (*eñe*) letter and the cedilla letter *ç*. The second was to include a Spanish list of stop-words to deal with line breaking.

Lastly, we performed the analysis of the reports with the CFIE-FRSE program and observed the results, summarised in Table 5.

The program successfully processes the documents and Spanish characters, albeit having some problems that are caused, mainly, by the composition of the table of contents page, the fourth and final challenge encountered in this language. Firstly, it analyzed only 65 documents, skipping the remaining 35. This appears to be caused by a series of reasons: the nature of the generation of the PDF that does not allow the text to be accessed (e.g. it is locked or protected); the table of contents page is not in a good format (e.g. one report featured the pages and the sections in different lines); or it is divided into several pages.

Secondly, almost 70% of the table of contents page was retrieved properly, but only around 34% of the documents were analyzed completely (good retrieval of pages and text per section). No analysis that failed the table of contents retrieval was correctly analyzed afterwards, which indicates the key importance of this first step. These failures occurred in reports that contained a lot of noise or a complex array of the text: pages and sections in different lines, table of contents spanning several pages, sections scattered among the page joined with images, etc. Automatically extracting the raw text from these cases fails and therefore the program cannot proceed. Finally, some PDF documents contain double paging or blank pages that affect the automatic retrieval of the pages.

Overall, the CFIE-FRSE program appears to work well for Spanish. However the irregularity of the composition of the annual reports makes it difficult to succeed in every document. In addition to this, the keyword list of sections should be updated and improved in order to deal with the high amount of variation in the sections and make the analysis faster.

6.3. *Portuguese*

Firms listed in the Portuguese Stock Exchange[l] are required to submit an annual report in Portuguese[m] and, as in most countries, Portuguese market regulations and the. Companies Act impose very few requirements concerning the contents of the annual reports and there is no mandatory or recommended structure for the Portuguese annual reports.[n] In addition, firms can voluntarily disclose other information, such as sustainability

---

[l]The Portuguese Stock Exchange is a relatively small stock exchange currently listing 52 firms totalling a market value of 60,763 million Euros (53,352 million Sterling Pounds), as of June 30, 2017. Research on the Portuguese market is scarce and tends to focus on disclosures on specific aspects of the annual report such as CEO letters,[25] governance,[26] or intangibles.[27]

[m]We found that approximately two thirds of the firms opt to disclose both a Portuguese and an English version of their annual reports. When considering the historical time series of the firms currently included in the main index — PSI-20 — the percentage of firms reporting in both languages increases to 93%..

[n]The Companies Act requires the annual report to include, amongst other items, a review of the firm's activities, performance and financial position, a description of the main risks and uncertainties, a description of subsequent events, the expected evolution of the firm, and a proposed net income allocation and dividends.

Table 6. Number of reports per year.

Year	2005	2006	2007	2008	2009	2010
Downloaded	51	52	60	61	61	62
Processed	23	26	38	37	38	40
	(45%)	(50%)	(63%)	(61%)	(62%)	(65%)

Year	2011	2012	2013	2014	2015	Total
Downloaded	64	62	58	59	37	627
Processed	44	43	42	36	29	396
	(69%)	(69%)	(72%)	(61%)	(78%)	(63%)

related information, however firms tend to disclose this type of information via their websites.

Our sample includes 627 reports, issued by 77 firms, for the period 2005–2015. All reports were submitted in an unstructured PDF format (Table 6).°

The tool was able to process 396 (63%) of the annual reports. An analysis of some of the non-processed reports seems to indicate that the most common problems are related to the same issues as for the English data.

The process of adapting the CFIE-FRSE Desktop tool to the Portuguese language was divided into several steps:

- The detection and extraction of the table of contents
- Aggregate sections into a standard set of pre-defined sections (Chairman's Statement, Performance Review, etc.)

The detection and extraction of the table of contents was based on a specific algorithm that looks for expressions that commonly appear as headings in an annual report. For this purpose, we created a list of gold-standards by collecting 67 reports in Portuguese from different firms and listing all sections in those reports. The initial list contained 2053 section headers. We then cleaned the list for firm-specific sections and duplicates. The final list had 694 entries, including a considerable number of variations for the same section. For the second step, we analyzed the final list and assigned each entry to a pre-defined section: Chairman, CEO, Performance, Auditor, Financial Statements, and Other. This standardization is

---

°The Portuguese Stock Exchange Website has a repository of filings where all annual reports are available. However, the interface is not designed to download batches of reports and, therefore, we retrieved all available in Perfect Information in October 2016.

necessary to deal with the lack of structure in the report and the numerous alternative names for a given section. The Portuguese reports presented some additional challenges, some of which we would like to highlight in this section.

Firstly and as with Spanish, the Portuguese alphabet includes additional characters in comparison to the English language. These additional characters are phonetic modifications of common characters, such as "À", "Á", "Ã", "Â", and "Ç".

Secondly, we had to develop a list of stop-words to deal with the line breaking. In addition to the common problems, we had to deal with the specificity of the Portuguese language that includes different variations for masculine and feminine and singular and plural words. One such example is the proposition "of", which can be translated as "de", "do", "da", "dos", and "das".

Thirdly, in 2008 the Portuguese Language Orthographic Agreement was signed into law with a transition period, ending on December 31, 2015. During the transition period, different firms used different spelling variations for some words and, therefore, the algorithm has to recognize all spelling variations. For instance the Portuguese word for shareholders changed from "Accionistas" to "Acionistas." On the other hand, the double spelling of some words was kept, such as the word "Sector," which can also be spelled "Setor." This imposes an additional layer of difficulty when analyzing narratives.

Fourthly, virtually all reports include an Auditor's Report. However, the Portuguese Companies Act imposed additional monitoring mechanisms. Firms have to have a Fiscal Committee and an Audit Committee.[p] Some firms, have separate headings for each report, others have a section for the Auditor's Report and one for the remaining reports. Other firms have one single section for all these reports. For this reason, we subdivided the Auditor section into three subsections: External Auditor, Audit Commission, and Fiscal Committee. In the absence of any indication, we assume that it is the External Auditor's report.

Finally, the Portuguese Companies Act allows different governance structures to have different names, which correspond to the Chairman and CEO roles. This in turn involves aligning the different names to the role.

---

[p]The Companies Act allows for some variation in this requirement, which are not relevant for this discussion.

Table 7.   Summary of Portuguese reports analysis.

Reports	Count	Percentage
Correctly processed	71	71%
Errors		
TOC with more than 1 page	9	9%
TOC without page numbers	8	8%
No TOC	1	1%
More than one TOC	1	1%
Incorrectly processed	10	10%
Total	100	100%

As an overall view of the whole process, the software is capable of processing the annual reports well in Portuguese and we believe that the adaptation process will be similar for other languages. Out of the 396 reports processed, we analyzed a random sample of 100 reports and based on these analyzes (Table 7), we conclude that the software was able to correctly process 71 of these reports. The main problems arise from: (i) table of contents (TOC) split into more than one page; (ii) TOC without page numbers; (iii) reports without a TOC; or (iv) reports with more than one TOC.

6.4. *Multilinguality*

The methods reported in this chapter demonstrate adaptability of our extraction and classification procedures to non-English annual reports published in regulatory settings other than the UK. This was achieved by developing methods that are language independent where the extraction process relies on the structure of the annual reports rather than the deep language characteristics. The methods will still require dictionaries and word-lists to be in the same language as the annual reports but the extraction process remains the same across languages. The reported work paves the way for investors, firms, and analysts to access and acquire information automatically from a large volume of annual reports in languages other than English.

7. Conclusion

The work reported in this chapter demonstrates the adaptability of our extraction and classification procedures to non-English annual reports published in regulatory settings other than the UK. This work develops, describes, and evaluates the first procedure for automatically extracting and analyzing qualitative information in digital PDF annual reports in three languages showing that our extraction methods could be expanded to be applied to other languages with minor tweaks to regular expressions and through providing a hand crafted gold-standard for each language. The results show that our extraction methods were able to process more than 98% of UK annual reports despite the non-standard format and layout. Running the same methods over Spanish and Portuguese annual reports shows that the methods are capable of processing more than 63% of the tested annual reports. The program successfully processes the documents and Spanish characters, albeit having some problems that are caused, mainly, by the composition of the table of contents page, the fourth and final challenge encountered in this language. The reported work makes it easier for investors, firms, and analysts to access and acquire information automatically from a large volume of annual reports. Around 70% of the table of contents page was retrieved properly, but only around 34% of the documents were analyzed completely. Overall, the CFIE-FRSE program appears to work well for Spanish. However the irregularity of the composition of the annual reports makes it difficult to succeed in every document. For Portuguese annual reports the tool was able to process 396 (63%) of the annual reports.

Acknowledgements

The work described in this paper has been undertaken as part of three projects. We acknowledge the support of the Economic and Social Research Council (ESRC) (grant references ES/J012394/1 and ES/K002155/1), the Institute of Chartered Accountants in England and Wales (ICAEW) and the International Centre for Research in Accounting (ICRA) at Lancaster University. We would also like to thank Professor Ana Gisbert, Universidad Autónoma de Madrid, for her help with the Spanish annual reports.

References

1. F. Li, The information content of forward-looking statements in corporate filings — a naïve bayesian machine learning approach, *Journal of Accounting Research*, **48**(5), 1049–1102 (2010). doi: 10.1111/j.1475-679X.2010.00382.x.
2. T. Loughran and B. McDonald, When is a liability not a liability? Textual analysis, dictionaries, and 10-ks, *The Journal of Finance*, **66**(1), 35–65 (2011). doi: 10.1111/j.1540-6261.2010.01625.x.

3. T. Schleicher and M. Walker, Bias in the tone of forward-looking narratives, *Accounting and Business Research*, **40**(4), 371–390 (2010). doi: 10.1080/00014788.2010.9995318.
4. T. Loughran and B. Mcdonald, Textual analysis in accounting and finance: A survey, *Journal of Accounting Research*, **54**(4), 1187–1230 (2016). doi: 10.1111/1475-679X.12123.
5. A. Doucet, G. Kazai, B. Dresevic, A. Uzelac, B. Radakovic, and N. Todic, ICDAR 2009 book structure extraction competition. In *Proceedings of the Tenth International Conference on Document Analysis and Recognition (ICDAR'2009)*, Barcelona, Spain, pp. 1408–1412, IEEE Computer Society (2009).
6. S. Teufel, *The structure of scientific articles: Applications to Citation Indexing and Summarization*. CSLI Studies in Computational Linguistics, Center for the Study of Language and Information, Stanford, California (2010).
7. L. McConnaughey, J. Dai, and D. Bamman, The labeled segmentation of printed books. In eds. M. Palmer, R. Hwa and S. Riedel, *Proceedings of the 2017 Conference on Empirical Methods in Natural Language Processing (EMNLP 2017)*, Copenhagen, Denmark, pp. 737–747, ACL (2017).
8. A. Devitt and K. Ahmad, Sentiment polarity identification in financial news: A cohesion-based approach. In K-Y. Su, J. Su and J. Wiebe, *Proceedings of the 45th Annual Meeting of the Association of Computational Linguistics*, pp. 984–991, ACL (2007).
9. R. P. Schumaker, An analysis of verbs in financial news articles and their impact on stock price. In eds. B. Hachey and M. Osborne, *Proceedings of the NAACL HLT 2010 Workshop on Computational Linguistics in a World of Social Media*, WSA '10, Los Angeles, CA, USA, pp. 3–4, ACL (2010).
10. T. L. Im, P. W. San, C. K. On, R. Alfred, and P. Anthony, Analysing market sentiment in financial news using lexical approach. In *2013 IEEE Conference on Open Systems (ICOS)*, pp. 145–149, IEEE (2013).
11. J. Z. Ferreira, J. Rodrigues, M. Cristo, and D. F. de Oliveira, Multi-entity polarity analysis in financial documents. In eds. R. Kulesza and T. A. Tavares, *Proceedings of the 20th Brazilian Symposium on Multimedia and the Web*, WebMedia '14, pp. 115–122, ACM (2014). doi: 10.1145/2664551.2664574.
12. B. Neuenschwander, A. C. Pereira, W. Meira, and D. Barbosa, Sentiment analysis for streams of web data: A case study of brazilian financial markets. In eds. R. Kulesza and T. A. Tavares, *Proceedings of the 20th Brazilian Symposium on Multimedia and the Web*, WebMedia '14, João Pessoa, Brazil, pp. 167–170, ACM (2014).
13. D. Merkl-Davies and V. Koller, 'Metaphoring' people out of this world: A critical discourse analysis of a chairman's statement of a uk defence firm, *Accounting Forum*, **36**(3), 178–193 (2012). doi: 10.1016/j.accfor.2012.02.005.
14. N. M. Brennan and D. M. Merkl-Davies, Accounting narratives and impression management. In *The Routledge Companion to Communication in Accounting* (2013). Available at: https://ssrn.com/abstract=1873188.
15. A. Brooking, *El Capital Intelectual: El Principal Activo De Las Empresas del Tercer Milenio*. Paidós Empresa, Barcelona (1997).

16. L. Edvinsson and M. Malone, *El Capital Intelectual: Cómo Identificar y Calcular El Valor de Los Recursos Intangibles de Su Empresa*. Gestión, Barcelona (1999).

17. E. García-Meca, I. Parra, M. Larrán, and I. Martínez, The explanatory factors of intellectual capital disclosure to financial analysts, *European Accounting Review*, **14**(1), 63–94 (2005).

18. F. Tejedo Romero, Información del conocimiento organizacional a través de los informes anuales publicados en las páginas web de las empresas, *Revista Española de Documentación Científica*, **37**(1) (2014). doi: http://dx.doi.org/10.3989/redc.2014.1.1068.

19. F. Tejedo Romero, Información de los recursos intangibles ocultos: ¿memorias de sostenibilidad o informe anual?, *European Research on Management and Business Economics*, **22**(2), 101–109 (2016).

20. E. Oliveras, C. Gowthorpe, Y. Kasperskaya, and J. Perramon, Reporting intellectual capital in Spain, *Corporate Communications: An International Journal*, **13**(2), 168–181 (2008). doi: http://dx.doi.org/10.1108/.

21. M. A. Villacorta, Revelation of the voluntary information about Human Capital in the Annual Reports, *Intangible Capital*, **2**(1) (2006). doi: http://dx.doi.org/10.3926/ic.43.

22. V. I. Levenshtein, Binary codes capable of correcting deletions, insertions, and reversals, *Soviet Physics Doklady*, **10**(8), 707–710 (1966).

23. B. Lowagie, *iText in Action*. Covers iText 5, Manning Publications Company (2010).

24. M. El-Haj, P. Rayson, S. Young, and M. Walker, Detecting document structure in a very large corpus of UK financial reports. In *Proceedings of the Ninth International Conference on Language Resources and Evaluation (LREC)*, Reykjavik, Iceland, pp. 1335–1338 (2014). Available at: http://www.lrec-conf.org/proceedings/lrec2014/summaries/402.html.

25. L. Costa, L. Rodrigues, and R. Craig, Factors associated with the publication of a CEO letter, *Corporate Communications: An International Journal*, **18**(4), 432–450 (2013).

26. R. L. F. Romero, and R. Craig, Corporate governance and intellectual capital reporting in a period of financial crisis: Evidence from portugal, *International Journal of Disclosure and Governance*, **14**(1), 1–29 (2017).

27. M. Marques, Os activos intangíveis nas contas das empresas do PSI 20: uma evidência empírica, *Pecvnia: Revista de la Facultad de Ciencias Económicas y Empresariales*, **8**, 183–201 (2009).

List of Abbreviations

A

ABS A neural attention model for sentence summarization. 190–192, 195
AIC Akaike information criterion. 147
ANOVA analysis of variance. 142, 426–430
AR anaphora resolution. 339, 345, 346, 351, 353–355, 357–361
ASL average sentence length. 348, 355, 358, 360, 362
ATB attention-based encoder. 187
AWL average word length. 348, 355, 358, 360, 362

B

BiRNN bidirectional recurrent neural network. 180, 181
BLEU Bilingual Evaluation Understudy. 135, 136
BOW bag-of-words. 299

C

CART classification and regression trees. 120, 128, 138, 144, 150
CBOW continuous bag-of-words. 178, 295
CDA critical discourse analysis. 443
CE convolutional encoder. 187
CF concept frequency. 344, 345, 352, 355, 358
CRF conditional random fields. 209–212, 215, 219–221, 239
CRP Chinese restaurant process. 158, 159
CWT continuous wavelet transformation. 381

D

distPNR unique proper noun ratio. 347, 355, 358–360
DPP determinantal point process. 298
DUC Document Understanding Conference. 3, 53, 61–65, 72, 74, 75, 104, 107, 109, 112, 113, 120, 130, 137, 138, 140, 143, 144, 146, 147, 149,

151, 183, 184, 187, 190, 191, 205, 246, 248, 282, 288, 345, 349, 351, 353, 360, 361

DWT discrete wavelet transformation. 381

E

EDU elementary discourse unit. 60

ESRC Economic and Social Research Council. 461

F

FN false negative. 263

FP false positive. 263

FRE Flesch reading ease. 347, 351, 355, 357, 358, 360–362

G

GA genetic algorithm. 119, 122, 129, 144, 147

GloVe global vector model. 177–179

GPU graphics processing unit. 176, 188, 193

GRI global reporting initiative. 455

GRU gated recurrent unit. 179

H

hLDA hierarchical latent Dirichlet allocation. 82, 93–96, 155, 156, 158–169, 171

HMM hidden Markov model. 122, 127, 204, 206–208, 233, 234

HSD honestly significant differences. 426, 427

HTM hierarchical topic model. 298

I

IBNMF bounded nonnegative matrix factorization. 292

ICAEW Institute of Chartered Accountants in England and Wales. 461

ICRA International Center for Research in Accounting. 461

IE information extraction. 5, 441, 445

ILP integer linear programming. 33, 71, 72, 74, 121

IM information measure. 111

IMDb Internet movie Database. 414

IR information retrieval. 2, 4, 19

J

JSD Jensen-Shannon divergence. 283

L

LCM linguistic category model. 415, 417, 425

LDA latent Dirichlet allocation. 52, 53, 55, 82, 123, 124, 129, 130, 138, 156, 164, 376

LDC Linguistic Data Consortium. 183

LEB Linguistic Expectancy Bias. 415–417, 430, 432–434

LIB Linguistic Intergroup Bias. 415, 417, 432–434

LIX Lasbarhetsindex Swedish Readability formula. 342

LM language model. 120, 144, 146, 147, 149, 298

LP linear programming. 31, 32, 43, 55, 59, 107

LSE London Stock Exchange. 452

LSI latent semantic indexing. 156, 228, 235, 236

LSI-DS latent semantic indexing document similarity. 236, 238

LSTM long short term memory networks. 179, 186, 195

LVT large vocabulary trick. 188–192

M

MDL minimum description length. 21, 81, 82, 84, 86–89, 92, 93, 95, 98, 100, 103, 106–108, 112

MDS multi-document summarization. 160

MEMM maximum entropy Markov model. 207–209

MFS most frequent sense. 344–346, 351, 352, 354, 355, 358, 359

ML machine learning. 121, 122, 126

MLP multi-layer perceptron. 178

MSE mean square error. 129

MSS multilingual single-document summarization. 156, 245, 260, 282–286, 289–291, 296, 300, 302–304, 307, 309–312, 318, 321, 332, 333

MWE multi-word expression identification. 125, 131, 132, 140, 141, 150

N

nCRP nested Chinese restaurant process. 158

NE named entity. 126, 132, 133, 140, 141, 150, 151, 210, 214

NER named entity recognition. 2, 11, 17, 125, 126, 138

NIST National Institute of Standards and Technology. 3

NLP natural language processing. 1, 7, 20, 119, 125, 126, 155, 176, 210, 376, 441–443, 445

NNMF nonnegative matrix factorization. 292

NPOV neutral point of view. 412, 413

NR noun ratio. 348, 355, 357, 358, 360

O

OCCAMS Optimal Combinatorial Covering Algorithm for Multi-document Summarization. 296, 298

OLS Ordinary Least Squares. 127, 128

OVIX word variation index. 347, 355, 358–360

P

PCA principal component analysis. 294, 295

PenPr penalized precision. 151

PLSI probabilistic latent semantic indexing. 123, 156

PM polytope model. 32, 34, 42, 50, 60, 76

PNR proper noun ratio. 347, 355, 358–360

POS part of speech tagging. 2, 11, 17, 119, 120, 125–127, 133, 134, 138, 143, 144, 149, 150, 179, 180, 210, 363, 376, 423

PR pronoun ratio. 348, 355, 358–360

PTR personalize term rank. 292

Q

QA question answering. 18

QP quadratic programming. 43

QS query-based summarization. 81, 83, 98, 100

R

RL reinforcement learning. 193–195

RNN recurrent neural network. 178–181, 186–188, 195

RQ research question. 419, 432, 433

S

SAS Statistical Analysis System. 452

SBD sentence boundaries detection. 6, 15

SC sentence coverage. 298

SDPP structured determinantal point process. 163

seq2seq sequence-to-sequence. 180, 182, 186, 189, 194

SGD stochastic gradient descent. 220, 377

SL sentence length. 298

SP sentence position. 298

SSE sum of the squared errors. 127, 128

STC suffix tree clustering. 393, 394, 398, 402, 404

SUMMAC TIPSTER Text Summarization Evaluation. 246

SVD singular value decomposition. 143, 228, 232, 391, 392
SVM support vector machine. 126, 178, 375, 377
SVR support vector regression. 121

T
TA text analytics. 2–5, 9, 13, 15, 18, 19
TAC Text Analysis Conference. 3, 183, 184, 246, 248, 282, 288, 341
TE textual entailment. 339, 345, 346, 351, 354, 355, 358, 359, 361
TF term frequency. 292, 344, 345, 352, 355, 358, 361
TM topic modeling. 4, 19, 32, 33, 52, 53, 56, 71, 73, 82, 83, 93–95, 97, 98, 107, 119, 130
TOC table of contents. 460
TP true positive. 263
TREC Text Retrieval Conference. 3
TS title similarity. 298

V
VSM vector space model. 32, 388, 393

W
WLCS weighted longest common subsequence. 105
WSD word sense disambiguation. 339, 345, 346, 351–353, 358, 359

List of Contributors

Natalia Vanetik is currently a faculty member at the Department of Software Engineering of Shamoon Academic College of Engineering in Beer Sheva, Israel. Her main field of interest is Text Analysis, focusing on multilingual Text Summarization, and unsupervised optimization methods. She is the author of multiple scientific publications in international peer-reviewed conferences and refereed journals. She has served on the program committee for several international conferences. She obtained her Ph.D. in Computer Science from Ben-Gurion University of the Negev in 2009 in the field of Graph Mining and Combinatorial Optimization. Since 2010, she has been involved in teaching activities at Shamoon Academic College of Engineering, more specifically she teaches multiple courses at the undergraduate degree in Software Engineering and the master's degree in Software Engineering, with focus on courses in fields of Databases, Algorithms, and Data Mining.

Marina Litvak obtained a Ph.D. in Information Systems Engineering from Ben-Gurion University of the Negev, Israel. She is currently a faculty member at Department of Software Engineering of Shamoon College of Engineering in Beer Sheba, Israel. Her research interests include information retrieval, text mining, automated summarization, and social media analysis. She is a member of the Association for Computational Linguistics. Marina is a co-designer of the MUSE summarizer and the MUSEEC system, which are known summarization systems in multilingual text summarization. She serves as a program committee member and a reviewer in the summarization and multilinguality tracks in the ACL sponsored conferences. Marina is a co-organizer of the MultiLing contest since 2011.

Alex Dlikman is a senior algorithm developer at Cortica, an international start-up company specializing in recognition digital images and videos. He holds a M.Sc. degree in Information Systems Engineering and B.Sc. in Industrial Engineering from Ben-Gurion University of the Negev, Israel. His main research interests include Text Mining, Image Recognition, Deep Learning, and Autonomous Vehicles.

Mark Last is a full Professor at the Department of Software and Information Systems Engineering, Ben-Gurion University of the Negev, Israel and the Head of the Data Science and Text Mining Group. Professor Last obtained his Ph.D. degree from Tel Aviv University, Israel in 2000. Between the years 2009–2012, Prof. Last has served as the Head of the Software Engineering Program at Ben-Gurion University. He has published over 190 peer-reviewed papers and 11 books on data mining, text mining, and cyber security. Professor Last is a Senior Member of the IEEE Computer Society and a Professional Member of the Association for Computing Machinery (ACM). He currently serves as an Associate Editor of *IEEE Transactions on Cybernetics* and an Editorial Board Member of *Data Mining and Knowledge Discovery*. From 2007 to 2016, he has served as an Associate Editor of *Pattern Analysis and Applications*. His main research interests are focused on data mining, cross-lingual text mining, cyber intelligence, and medical informatics.

Lei Li is an Associate professor with the School of Computer, Beijing University of Posts and Telecommunications (BUPT). Her current research interests include text summarization, natural language processing, social network analysis, and machine learning.

Yazhao Zhang received an M.Sc. degree from BUPT, Beijing, China in March, 2018. His research focuses on Machine Learning, Document Summarization (especially multi-lingual multi-document summarization), and Text Analysis of Social Networks.

Tal is a Ph.D. student in Ben-Gurion University of the Negev, Israel under the supervision of Professor Michael Elhadad. He is interested in query focused summarization and sequence-to-sequence models. He also worked on applying such models for public healthcare and music generation.

Michael Elhadad is a Professor at the Department of Computer Science, Ben-Gurion University of the Negev, Israel. His research interests are in Computational Linguistics, Natural Language Generation, and Intelligent User Interfaces. He is specifically working on Hebrew Computational Linguistics.

Carlos A. Colmenares is a software engineer working for Google. He specializes in Natural Language Processing, and currently focuses on query understanding for sponsored search.

Amin Mantrach is currently Research Scientist with Criteo where he works on improving the performance of online advertising campaigns guided by machine learning techniques.

Prior to Criteo, Amin worked on relevance for Yahoo Sponsored Search, and worked on improving video recommendation for the users of the Yahoo Screen platform. Amin did postdoctoral research in the Xerox Research Center Europe where he worked on various matrix factorization techniques. Amin holds a Ph.D. from the Free University of Brussels in Belgium.

Fabrizio is currently a software engineer at Facebook working in the search team on various topics related to science and technology of query recommendation and query analysis in general. Prior to joining Facebook, Fabrizio was a principal scientist at Yahoo where he has worked on sponsored search and native ads within the Gemini project. Fabrizio holds a Ph.D. in Computer Science from the University of Pisa, Italy where he studied problems related to Web Information Retrieval with particular focus on efficiency related problems like Caching, Collection Partitioning, and Distributed IR in general. He has been the recipient (together with Ranieri Baraglia) of the best Web Intelligence 2004 paper award, and the recipient of the European Conference on Information Retrieval (ECIR) 2006 best paper award. In 2014 he was a recipient of the best paper award at the internal Yahoo conference: Tech Pulse. He is the author of more than 130 papers and has patents filed in the area of web advertising. In 2018 he was the recipient of the Test of Time Award for the paper "Sorting Out the Document Identifier Assignment Problem."

Horacio Rodríguez Hontoria is an Associate Professor at the Department of Computer Science in Technical University of Catalunya (UPC) in Spain and a researcher at The Center for Language and Speech Technologies and Applications (TALP). He served as a main researcher in such projects as SKATER, Arabic WordNet, and EuroWordNet. His areas of expertise are Information Extraction and Information Retrieval, Speech and Language Resources, Natural Language Analysis tools, and Natural Language User Interfaces.

Nikiforos Pittaras received his B.Sc. in Computer Science from the University of Ioannina in Greece. He worked as a Research Associate of IIT-NCSR and ITI-CERTH in Greece where he participated in many EU research projects, most notably Big-DataEurope, ForgetIT and LinkedTV. His research focuses on machine learning methods in text and multimedia, specifically event and concept detection and retrieval, neural networks and deep learning architectures. He is currently a M.Sc. senior student in Signal and Information Processing and Learning and a Ph.D. candidate in Machine Learning, at Department of Informatics and Telecommunications, National and Kapodistrian University of Athens (NKUA) in Greece.

Stefano Montanelli is Assistant Professor in Informatics at the University of Milano (UNIMI) in Italy, where he received his Ph.D. in Informatics in 2007. His main research interests include Semantic Web, ontology matching and evolution, and web data classification. Recent research activities are focused on visual exploration of web data, smart-city data management, and crowd phenomena.

Dr. George Giannakopoulos is a Research Fellow of National Center for Scientific Research (NCSR) "Demokritos" in Greece, as well as a co-founder of SciFY, an open innovation, not-for-profit company. He also acts as Chief Technology Officer of the WinningMinds technology company, working on Artificial Intelligence (AI) methods for business meeting analysis. He has 20 years of experience in Information Technologies, at least 10 of which in the research domains of Data Analysis and Mining, AI, and Natural Language Processing. He also works as a Professor of Intelligent Systems for the Congitive Science M.Sc. program of the NKUA. During the last 10 years he has worked on a number of EU and national research projects related to Big Data Analysis, Summarization, the Semantic Web, Data Journalism and Bioinformatics. He is a reviewer for major events and journals on Natural Language Processing and Computational Linguistics and acts as the organizer of the MultiLing community on multilingual summarization.

Alfio Ferrara is Associate Professor of Computer Science at the University of Milano, Italy, where he received his Ph.D. in Computer Science in 2005. His research interests include Database, Semantic Web, and Information Analysis and Retrieval. On these topics, he worked in national and international research projects, has been author of more than 80 contributions as papers in international conferences and journals, and chapters in international books.

He served as program committee member of various international conferences and he is a founder and part of the board of the instance matching track at the Ontology Alignment Evaluation Initiative (OAEI).

 Dr. Vangelis Karkaletsis is the head of the Software and Knowledge Engineering Laboratory (SKEL) of the Institute of Informatics and Telecommunications at NCSR "Demokritos", and responsible for the Institute's educational activities. His research interests are in the areas of Language and Knowledge Engineering, as applied to content analysis, natural language interfaces, and ontology engineering. He has extensive experience in the coordination and technical management of European and national projects. He has organized international workshops, conferences, and summer schools. He teaches for many years at post-graduate courses on language and knowledge technologies. He is co-founder of the spin-off company "i-sieve Technologies" that exploited SKEL research work on online content analysis. He is currently involved in the founding of a new spin-off company that exploits SKEL technology on multilingual and multi-document summarization.

 John M. Conroy is a graduate of Central High School of Philadelphia with a B.A. and St. Joseph's University of Philadelphia, USA where he received a B.Sc. in Mathematics. Conroy then studied Applied Mathematics with a concentration in Computer Science at the University of Maryland, USA where he received an M.Sc. and Ph.D. in Mathematics. He has been a research staff member at the IDA Center for Computing Sciences for over 30 years. Conroy is the co-developer of the CLASSY and the OCCAMS text summarization systems. He has published widely in text summarization and evaluation and serves on numerous program committees for summarization. He is also a co-inventor of patented summarization methods. Other publications by Conroy include high performance matrix computations, graph matching and anomaly detection, with application to neural science and network security. He is a member of

the Association for Computational Linguistics, a life member of the Society for Industrial and Applied Mathematics, and a member of the Institute for Electronics and Electrical Engineers.

 Jeff Kubina is an applied mathematician for the United States Department of Defense who currently directs and conducts the design and implementation of heterogeneous cloud architectures; the research and development in statistical methods for the automatic prediction, detection, and correction of system faults in cloud systems; and research in automatic document summarization algorithms. In 2011 he co-created the Multilingual Single Document summarization task, a component of the biennial MultiLing Workshop, to advance the research and development of multilingual single document summarization algorithms and has co-authored reports about the task and automatic document summarization algorithms. He is also an avid photographer with many of his photographs published on thousands of websites.

 Peter Rankel researches and applies statistical techniques to create advanced analytics for information security clients. He has worked in the defense industry for over a decade as a Data Scientist and Software Engineer, and elsewhere as an independent statistical consultant. His interests include applications of Statistics and Machine Learning to areas such as Natural Language Processing. One of his main areas of research has been the evaluation of automatic summarization systems. Peter earned a Ph.D. in Statistics from the University of Maryland, USA and a B.A. in Mathematics from Boston College, USA.

Julia Yang is an applied mathematician for the United States Department of Defense. Her research interests include Algorithms, Machine Learning, Computer Security, and Visualization. She has a S.B. in Mathematics and a Ph.D. in applied mathematics from the Massachusetts Institute of Technology, USA.

Dr. Elena Lloret is a Ph.D. Assistant Professor at the University of Alicante in Spain. There, she obtained her Ph.D. on Text Summarization in 2011. Her main field of interest is Natural Language Processing (more specifically Text Summarization) and Natural Language Generation. She is the author of over 60 scientific publications in international peer-reviewed conferences and refereed journals. She has served on the program committee for several international conferences, such as ACL, EACL, RANLP, and COLING. She is a member of the Spanish Society for Natural Language Processing (SEPLN), and she has participated in a number of national and EU-funded projects, among which the current and latest are: Canonical Representation and transformations of texts applied to the Human Language Technologies (TIN2015-65100-R) and SAM - Dynamic Social & Media Content Syndication for 2nd Screen (Grant No. 611312). She has also been collaborating with international groups at the University of Wolverhampton (UK), the University of Sheffield (UK), the University of Edinburgh (UK), and the Lorraine Research Laboratory in Computer Science and its Applications in France. Since 2009, she has been involved in teaching activities at the University of Alicante. More specifically she teaches 200 hours per year at the undergraduate degree in Computer Engineering and the degree in Multimedia Engineering, as well as at the Master's degree in Information & Communication Technologies for Education and the Master's degree in English and Spanish for Specific Purposes.

Tatiana Vodolazova is currently working as a product manager and E-Commerce Assistant at Tempe, a company that belongs to the INDITEX group. In particular, she is the product Manager for STRADI-VARIUS brand, being responsible for footwear in the countries of Eastern Europe. Her tasks include daily sales monitoring and analysis, annual budget planning and stock forecasting, market research and consumer behavior analysis, development and implementation of in-store marketing and visual merchandising strategies, and management of over 100 stores in Eastern Europe, and maintaining communication with country directors, regular store visits, among others. Concerning her background and research, she obtained her Masters in Computational Linguistics at the University of Tuebinguen, Germany in 2011 and was a visiting researcher at the University Alicante in Spain from October 2011 until August 2014. Her main research fields include Natural Language Processing (NLP), Computational Linguistics, Text Summarization, Natural Language Generation, Machine Learning for NLP, Pattern Recognition for NLP, Information Retrieval, Text Categorization, and Named Entity Recognition.

Dr. Paloma Moreda is an Associate Professor of the University of Alicante in the Department of Software and Computing Systems in which she is currently the Head. She obtained her Ph.D. in Computer Science at the University of Alicante in 2008. As a member of the Natural Language Processing and Information System Research Group (GPLSI) her main research areas of interest focus on Computational Linguistics and Human Language Technologies, in particular semantic analysis, informality and text normalization, and simplification of texts. She has participated in a number of national and EU-funded projects, being the PI for the Flexible Interactive Reading Support Tool (FP7-287607 FIRST) European project at the University of Alicante and the PI for Canonical Representation and transformations of texts applied to the Human Language Technologies (TIN2015-65100-R RESCATA) Spanish project. She has collaborated in the organization of several conferences and workshops related with her research areas and contributed with more than 50 scientific publications in international relevant journals, conferences, and workshops.

Prof. Dr. Rafael Muñoz (1967) has been a researcher and lecturer in the Department of Software and Computing Systems of the University of Alicante since 1996. Moreover, he is Vice-president of Campus and Technology and previously, the Head of Technology Transfer Office at the University of Alicante in Spain. His research areas are: Computer Linguistics and Natural Language Processing and more specifically, text summarization, opinion mining, information extraction and retrieval, and named entity recognition. He has been the main conference chair in several conferences, especially in NLDB. He is a member of the Research Group on Language Processing and Information Systems at the University of Alicante since 1996 and member of Natural Language Processing Spanish Society. He is the author of two books, has edited three books and published more than 150 papers in prestigious journals and conferences, including Computational Linguistics, Information Sciences, and DKE journal and international conferences like ACL, COLING, to mention the most relevant ones.

Prof. Dr. Manuel Palomar is the University President of the University of Alicante in Spain and Head of the Natural Language Processing and Information Systems Research Group of the same university. He has been a full Professor of this University since 1991 and his main teaching area focuses on the analysis, design and management of databases, data warehouses, and information systems. He received his Master's degree and Ph.D. in Computer Science at the Polytechnic University of Valencia, Spain. His research interests are Human Language Technologies (HLT) and Natural Language Processing (NLP), in particular Text Summarization, Semantic Roles, Textual Entailment, Information Extraction and Anaphora Resolution. He has supervised more than 12 theses and is the author of more than 70 scientific publications on international journals and conferences on different topics related to HLT and NLP. Furthermore, he has coordinated and been involved in a number of regional, national, and international research projects funded by the Generalitat Valenciana (Valencian Government), the Ministry of Science and Innovation (Spanish Government) and the European Council.

Efi Levi is a graduate of the Israel Defense Force's Mamram Unit. He holds a B.Sc. in Software Engineering from Shamon College of Engineering in Israel. He is a fullstack developer with knowledge in a variety of technologies. Efi works as a senior software engineer at Dell EMC.

Andrey Vashchenko is currently a graduate M.Sc. student at the faculty of Software Engineering in Shamoon College of Engineering in Israel, where he also obtained his B.Sc. His research interests lie in the world of Big Data and Machine Learning, with an emphasis on Natural Language Processing. Starting his career in the gaming development sphere as end-to-end developer led him to specialize in modern web technologies, and nowadays he is working as senior server-side developer.

Jahna Otterbacher received her doctorate from the School of Information, University of Michigan (Ann Arbor, USA), where she was a member of the Computational Linguistics and Information Retrieval (CLAIR) research group. She is a faculty member at the Open University of Cyprus, where she coordinates the M.Sc. in Social Information Systems. She is also a team leader and Principal Investigator at RISE (Research Center on Interactive media, Smart systems and Emerging technologies), a new center of excellence in Nicosia, Cyprus funded by the H2020 Widespread Teaming program.

Dr. Ioannis Katakis is an Associate Professor and co-Director of the Artificial Intelligence Lab at the University of Nicosia, Cyprus. Born and raised in Thessaloniki, Greece, he studied Computer Science and holds a Ph.D. in Machine Learning for Text Classification. After his post-graduate studies, he served at various universities as a lecturer and a senior researcher. His research interests include Mining Social, Web and Urban Data, Sentiment Analysis and Opinion Mining, Deep Learning, Data Streams, and Multi-label Learning. He has extensive experience in European Projects where he participated as Quality Assurance Coordinator and Senior Researcher. He published papers in International Conferences and Scientific Journals related to his areas of expertise, organized three workshops and is an Editor at the journal *Information Systems*. His research has been cited more than 4,500 times in the literature.

Pantelis Agathangelou holds an M.Sc. in Information Systems from the Faculty of Pure and Applied Sciences, Open University of Cyprus. His research interests include Data Mining, Pattern Classification, Sentiment Analysis, Mining Social Networks, and Artificial intelligence. He has co-developed DidaxTo (http://deixto.com/didaxto/) a tool that implements an unsupervised approach for discovering patterns that will extract a domain-specific dictionary from product reviews. He is currently a Ph.D. candidate at the University of Nicosia Department of Computer Science.

Mahmoud El-Haj is a Senior Research Associate at the School of Computing and Communications at Lancaster University. Mahmoud received his Ph.D. in Computer Science from The University of Essex working on Arabic Multi-document Summarization. His research interests include Arabic and Multilingual NLP, Machine Learning, Information Extraction, Financial Narratives Processing, and Corpus and Computational Linguistics. Mahmoud worked on multidisciplinary research projects at Lancaster University, UK collaborating with big financial firms in London and has previously worked as a Data Mining developer and researcher at the UK Data Archive.

Paul Rayson is the director of the UCREL research center and a Reader in the School of Computing and Communications, in Infolab21 at Lancaster University, UK. A long term focus of his work is the application of semantic-based NLP in extreme circumstances where language is noisy e.g. in historical, learner, speech, email, txt and other CMC varieties. His applied research is in the areas of dementia detection, online child protection, cyber security, learner dictionaries, and text mining of historical corpora and annual financial reports.

Paulo Alves is an Assistant Professor at Católica Porto Business School, Universidade Católica Portuguesa in Portugal and a Researcher at the International Centre for Research in Accounting at Lancaster University, UK. Paulo holds a Ph.D. in Accounting and Finance awarded by Lancaster University. His main areas of research are the impact of information on capital markets and financial narratives.

Carlos Herrero-Zorita studied English Studies and East Asian Studies at the Autonomous University of Madrid, Spain where he has also developed his Ph.D. on the automatic annotation of Spanish and Japanese modality. His main interest in recent years has been the study of specialised terminology, morphology and syntax in Spanish, English, and Japanese corpora. At the moment he is working as a linguist at a language engineering company in Madrid.

Steven Young is Professor of Accounting and Head of the Department of Accounting and Finance at Lancaster University Management School in UK. His research interests cover topics at the interface between accounting and corporate finance including executive remuneration, narrative reporting, and financial reporting quality. His research has been published in leading academic journals including *The Accounting Review*, *Review of Accounting Studies*, and *Accounting, Organisations and Society*. He is Associate Editor and an Editorial Board member for several leading journals and he is also a member of the Research Advisor Board for the Institute of Chartered Accountants in England and Wales.

Index

algorithm
    Apriori, 50, 85, 86, 113
    Apriori-TID, 85, 86, 91, 98
    EDCoW, 380, 382–386, 398, 406
    FreeSpan, 50
    Gibbs sampling, 159
    GSP, 50
    Hoeffding tree, 377
    K-means, 82
    Krimp, 81, 84, 86–91, 93, 96
    LexRank, 298
        Biased, 84
    Lingo, 387, 388, 391, 393, 398, 402, 404
    MIRA, 223, 224
        forced, 224, 236, 238
    Naive Bayes, 376, 377, 395
        bigram, 376
        multinomial, 377
        unigram, 377
    PageRank, 143, 342, 387–389
    PathSum, 161
    STC, 393, 394, 398, 402, 404
    sumHLDA, 160
    TextRank, 229, 292, 294, 387–390
ANOVA test, 302, 307, 311
auto-correlation, 380, 383, 385–387
AutoMan, 251
AutoSummENG system, 246, 249, 287

BART toolkit, 351
BioASQ challenge, 246
BLEU, 195

Carrot2 package, 394
CLASSY system, 246, 249
convex polyhedron, 40
corpus
    AQUAINT, 183
    Brown, 126
    CNN/Daily Mail, 183, 188, 191–193
    DT, 183
    Gigaword, 183, 184, 187, 188, 190
    North American News text, 183
    Wikipedia PWKP, 183, 184
coverage
    information, 31, 32, 34, 41, 52, 139
    lexicon, 54, 139
    maximum, 32, 33
    topic, 53, 55, 56, 71, 72, 74, 139
cross-correlation, 376, 378, 380, 383–386
CrowdFlower, 250
Cubist model, 119, 120, 128, 129, 138, 144, 147, 150, 151

dictionary
    Diction, 442
    General Inquirer, 442

Harvard, 443
LIWC(2011), 442
distance
    Euclidean, 44, 46
    Manhattan, 43–46

frequent itemset, 33, 42, 50, 70,
    86–88, 96, 100–102, 112, 113
function
    SARI, 195

Google GeoChart, 395
Google Maps, 397
graph partitioning, 384, 385

HAL feature, 110, 111
Hanzi script, 93
hashtag, 372–377, 379–387, 395, 397,
    398, 400, 402, 406

ICTCLAS tool, 93, 165

jMWE library, 138

linear constraint, 36, 37

MAD measure, 383
MALLET software, 138
Mann-Whitney test, 421
maximum entropy, 377
Mechanical Turk, 250
MeMoG, 287, 300–303, 308, 319, 333
MeMOG measure, 260
MMS task, 71
model
    Baysean
        non-parametric, 156
MSS task, 70, 71
MTranslatability, 342
MultiLing, 4, 22, 61, 246, 263, 282,
    291
    2011, 4, 283
    2013, 61–63, 120, 137, 138, 143,
        144, 147–149, 164, 169, 283,
        333

2015, 22, 61, 62, 70, 94, 156, 245,
    281, 283, 291, 296, 300, 333
2017, 260, 281, 283, 300, 333
MySQL, 396

N-gram, 32, 33, 48, 62, 105, 125, 134,
    342, 376
    bigram, 42, 48, 49, 62, 63, 72,
        121, 125, 127, 227, 228, 231,
        234, 291, 294, 296, 298
    graph, 282, 287
    trigram, 127, 227, 228, 234
    unigram, 48, 63, 72, 105, 121,
        227, 228, 231, 232, 234, 294,
        296, 298, 341
naive Bayes classifier, 122, 294
NLPCC 2015 competition, 104–107,
    112
NLTK, 296, 423
NP-hard, 32, 33, 88
NPowER, 287, 300, 308, 309, 311,
    312, 317, 319, 321, 333

objective function, 31–34, 41–51, 56,
    57, 59–63, 70–72, 74, 76, 77
Orbis database, 454
order
    candidate
        standard, 88, 91, 97, 101
        TM, 97
    cover
        query, 101
        standard, 88, 91, 92, 96
        TM, 97
    summary, 91, 92, 98, 102
        updated, 97

parameter
    ETA, 167
    GEM, 167
    SCALING, 167
Pearson correlation, 288
Penn Treebank, 127
Pspace-complete problem, 113
Pyramid score, 287

ROUGE, 61, 63, 75, 76, 105, 106,
121, 135, 136, 140, 142, 150, 151,
169, 175, 184, 187, 190, 193, 230,
232, 234, 236–238, 246, 249, 287,
300, 303, 307, 319, 341, 353, 354,
357, 361, 362, 364

Savitzky-Golay filter, 398
sentence-term matrix, 34, 36–39, 42,
47, 56, 76
similarity
cosine, 42, 51, 54, 58, 70, 291,
294, 375, 387, 392, 398, 400
Jaccard, 42, 387, 398, 400
SPLITTA tool, 165
Stanford NLP tool, 138, 168, 225
system
ABS, 190
CIST, 164, 165, 169, 296, 298,
309

term frequency, 33, 42, 44–46, 48, 62
normalized, 48
TF-IDF, 213, 228, 232–235, 375, 387,
388, 392, 394, 398

Thomson Datastream, 452
transactional dataset, 81, 84, 87
Tweetinvi, 397
Twitter event detection, 372–374,
376, 378–380, 384–387, 390, 398,
400, 402, 406
new, 372
retrospective, 372
specified, 372, 374
unspecified, 372, 374, 375

wavelet, 371, 376, 378–381
Weibo, 93, 104
Wikipedia, 281, 283, 284, 298,
411–414, 416, 417, 419–421, 424,
428, 432–436
Wikipedians, 423, 427, 428, 433,
434, 436
Wilcoxon test, 107, 288, 289, 302,
318, 420
word embeddings, 176, 177
word2vec, 177–179, 299
WordNet, 8, 9, 155, 377

Yahoo search engine, 110